China Integrated City Index
Megalopolis Development Strategy
Development Strategy of Core City

Department of Development Planning
National Development and Reform Institute
Cloud River Urban Research Institute

Zhou Muzhi, Chen Yajun, Xu Lin
Chief Editors

CNPIEC
Pace University Press

Contents

Foreword

Characteristics and Significance of the China Integrated City Index

Zhou Muzhi

President of Cloud River Urban Research Institute,
Professor of Tokyo Keizai University, Ph.D. in Economics

Four decades of reform and opening-up have enabled China's leap to the second largest economy in the world. However, the general competition that encourages the pursuit of GDP indicators by individual cities, which are the most important factor in China's development, has triggered serious urban issues such as environmental pollution, the widening gap between the rich and the poor, the frequent occurrence of social problems, traffic congestion, and inconvenient living, to name but a few.

In response, the Department of Development Planning in the National Development and Reform Commission (NDRC), the able authority in charge of China's urbanization policies, has worked with the Cloud River Urban Research Institute to develop the *China Integrated City Index*, providing a comprehen-sive assessment of China's major cities in environmental, social, and economic dimensions. The *Index* attempts to guide cities toward more harmonious and sustainable development by changing the way cities are evaluated in China, moving from a traditional, purely GDP-based approach to an integrated one.

As the subject matter of our study, Chinese cities are very difficult to observe. After an extended period of research and development, the *Index* now covers 297 cities across China, including all the cities of prefecture level and above, providing a multi-angle and three-dimensional comprehensive analysis and evaluation for each. At the same time, by taking into account data from these cities, the whole country has been successfully analyzed by a range of indicators. The *Index* presents this vast amount of information by way of visualization. What is more important, China under the socialist market economy works with a unique logic, a considerable part of which may remain opaque to the outside world. The *Index* measures Chinese cities by using globally accepted standards, presenting to the world a China and her cities that are understandable and real.

The *Index* has been released once a year since 2016, for publication in China and Japan, having significant impact both at home and abroad. With the release of this English version, researchers from all over the world are welcome to use the *Index* as a primary source of information on China.

As the major theme of modernization, urbanization is not only the engine that drives China's economic growth, but is also the prime power behind the transformation of its economic and social structures. It can be said that urbanization has opened up intense, rapid, and inevitable economic and social changes that are unprecedented to the Chinese society.

Urbanization as a process of change requires forward-looking, high-level considerations and designs, and it involves the re-examination and reform of institutional mechanisms such as the fiscal and taxation system, the household registration system, and the social security system. Compared to the aggressive wave of urbanization in China, however, research and discussions on the best practices in urban planning has proceeded relatively slowly.

Problems in urban planning and construction mechanisms can also have a negative impact on urban development. Planning is very important to a city. Unplanned urban space would end up a nightmare, so would poor urban planning. A city needs good rules of planning and design to regulate the flow of various forms of social capital. Only by adding and aggregating planned and regulated investments can we develop pleasing urban spaces and nurture urban competitiveness, whereby the best of urban living can be realized.

Urban planning should involve long-term strategies for the integration of resources in an area, but China's current planning mechanisms do not support such positioning. Due to the fragmentation of efforts in urban development, there are different authorities to manage development planning, urban planning, land use planning, transportation planning, environmental planning, and industrial planning. Preventing the coordination of these authorities are their respective stakes in political and fiscal processes. This disorganization is responsible for the issues common to Chinese cities, including the unreasonable utilization of space, disjointed transportation networks, inconvenience to urban residents, and the deterioration of environmental conditions.

This last round of urbanization, whether viewed from a macro or micro perspective, benefited from much less brainstorming on mechanisms, systems, and planning as compared to many other practices. One of the key reasons is the inability to analyze and manage data. Advanced ideas and frameworks have been successively introduced into recent policies covering principal functional zones and new directions in urbanization. The next steps will be to embody these policies and to evaluate and supervise their planning, implementation, and execution.

To that end, the Department of Development Planning of NDRC has worked with the Cloud River Urban Research Institute to compile and publish the *Index*, a quantifiable and visualized system for the evaluation of urbanization indicators, setting up a suite of digital benchmarks and frames of reference for the urbanization of China.

The *Index* is designed to assist with policy-making and planning by means of advanced concepts and visualized data indicators in order to guide the relevant investments that promote urban development. It is intended to work as a policy instrument for urbanization at the macro level, and it can also be relied upon in urban planning at the micro level, while providing the criteria through which policies and plans will be evaluated. The *Index* is characterized by the following:

As an extension of the *Index*, the *China Integrated City Development Report* brings a focus to particular cities, and it includes analysis of rankings, indicators, surroundings, advantages, problems, and strategies, among other elements. The *Index* and *Report* are the work of a group of established Chinese and global experts who have applied the latest concepts in urban development and data collection to this comprehensive and detailed analysis of the environmental, social, and economic dimensions of urban areas. These experts have provided new perspectives and ideas for the formulation of an integrated development strategy reflecting "multiple planning integration" based on the advantages and issues confronting a particular city.

The *Index* jointly prepared by the Department of Development Planning of NDRC and the Cloud River Urban Research Institute is an exploration and development of a quantifiable and visualized system for the evaluation of urbanization indicators. By bringing together understandings of China's urbanization issues as well as incorporating domestic and foreign experiences and leading philosophy, the *Index* has set up a suite of "digital benchmarks and frames of reference" for the urbanization and urban development of China.

The *Index* may work as a policy instrument for urbanization at the macro level and can be relied upon for urban development strategies and planning at the micro level. Also capable of being used as the criteria by which policies and plans will be evaluated, the *Index* is featured by three characteristics:

1. A Three-dimensional View of "Green"

It is clearly indicated in the *National New Style Urbanization Plan,* that to integrate ecological principles fully into the urbanization process, the concept of "green" has to become the key. As a result of this heightened attention to ecology, countless competitions or ratings of the greenest towns and "most beautiful villages" have taken place, but most of them are focused on natural ecology, and the awards these small cities and towns receive are mostly environmental ones. However, any analysis or evaluation of green urbanization, whether from a national perspective or as a part of China's modernization plan, should not be confined to a narrow conception of the environment.

Consisting of the environmental, social, and economic dimensions, the *Index* seeks to explain what "green" means from a broader perspective and to provide a full-scale evaluation of a city from those three dimensions. In other words, the *Index* aims to evaluate a city in a organic manner and from a green perspective, which means focusing on all the green indicators of environment, economy, and society.

As such, unlike the indicators that encourage "physical" results (i.e., GDP, and railway, highway, or building construction, etc.), the indicators of green urbanization of China advocate for the quality of development. "Green" is not a narrow environmental element, but a broad concept that promotes or gives prominence to green development. Integrated into this concept are economic performance, spatial structure or design, and the quality of life, culture, and the society. Every index at each level of the indicator system has a strong "green" orientation.

2. A Concise Structure to Quantify Cities

The digitization and indexing of the issues, tasks, and ambitions coming before China in her urbanization, as well as information on domestic and foreign best practices and most updated philosophies, has been arduous in itself. After enormous rounds of discussions between Chinese and global experts over the past four years, the *Index* has finally been shaped in a unique and concise 3×3×3 structure: each one of the environmental, economic, and social dimensions is composed of three sub-dimensional indicators, and each of the sub-dimensional indicators is supported by three indicator groups, and further, each of the indicator groups is supported by one or more sets of data.

Each of the 27 indicator groups represents a criterion or a value pursuit, a major feature of the *Index*. The indicator system needs data support, but finding and organizing such data in China is a vast and difficult task. Its first challenge is the fragmentation of data, where the data between departments, levels and years are inconsistent, unregulated, and discontinuous. Second is the issue of distortion with some of the data. International data on some of the indicators used to evaluate other cities are also not available in China.

Besides the availability of data, the authenticity and real value of data should also be taken into consideration when selecting indicators and data for the *Index*. Thus, as the working team, The Cloud River Urban Research Institute opts for generated data when possible and then applies big data techniques to turn the huge amount of generated data into usable ones. At the same time, in addition to the full utilization of satellite data and spatial geographic data for the calculation of missing data, efforts are made to apply the data economics techniques in order to combine some relevant data into a specific value-oriented index. After four years of hard work, a variety of public and socially available data have been "sewn" into a comprehensive indicator system covering all the 297 cities of prefecture level and above in China.

3. A Value-oriented Guide in Cognitive Development

The *Index* is intended to build up a framework for any three-dimensional analysis of the structures and contents of a city. It aims to provide scientific, policy-oriented planning for the "green" or mobile, and resident-based aspects of China's urbanization. Therefore, the *Index* serves as a conceptual guide to green development.

With a focus on cultural heritage and the quality of life. It is strongly concerned with the issue of low-density development amidst Chinese urbanization, and it calls attention to the question of taking the "density" of Chinese cities as an indicator.

It should be noted that China today erroneously attributes many urban problems to the high density of her cities. In fact, the problem that plagues Chinese cities is not the density being too high, but the contrary. Through increasing urban density, improving management capabilities, and enriching the contents of the city, Chinese cities can better develop their economy and society, and thus the next step of urbanization in China actually lies in "the densification of cities." The *Index* will call for efforts to stay focused on the "urban densification" process that encourages and promotes the development of compact urban areas, the enrichment of urban connotations, and an improvement in urban quality of life.

Project Members

Zhou Muzhi
President, Cloud River Urban Research Institute

Professor, Tokyo Keizai University

Chen Yajun
Director, Department of Development Planning, NDRC

Xu Lin
Chairman, U.S.-China Green Fund

Former Director, Department of Development Planning, NDRC

Chief Expert

Yang Weimin
Deputy Director, Subcommittee of Economy of National Committee of the Chinese People's Political Consultative Conference

Former Deputy Director, Office of the Central Leading Group for Financial and Economic Affairs, PRC

Expert Team Members (by Last Name in Alphabetical Order)

Du Ping
Secretary-General, 13th Five-Year National Development Planning Expert Committee, PRC

Former Executive Vice Director, State Information Center, PRC

Hu Cunzhi
Former Vice Minister, Ministry of Land and Resources, PRC

Minamikawa Hideki
President, Japan Environmental Sanitation Center

Former Vice Minister of the Environment, Japan

Li Xin
Professor, Chinese Academy of Sciences

Deputy Secretary-General , Beijing Municipal Political Consultative Conference

Ming Xiaodong
Inspector, Department of Development Planning, NDRC

Former Minister-counsellor, Embassy of the People's Republic of China in Japan

Mu Rongping
Director, Center for Innovation and Development, Chinese Academy of Sciences

Onishi Takashi
President, Toyohashi University of Technology

Former President, Science Council of Japan

Professor Emeritus, University of Tokyo

Takeuchi Kazuhiko
Project Professor, The University of Tokyo

Chair, Central Environment Council, Government of Japan

Former Vice Rector, United Nations University

Yamamoto Kazuhiko	*Former President and CEO, MORI Urban Planning Corporation*
Yokoyama Yoshinori	*Director of EMP (Executive Management Program) of the University of Tokyo*
	Dean of HBMS (Hiroshima Business and Management)
	Former head of Tokyo office, McKinsey & Company
Yue Xiuhu	*Director, Department of Price, NDRC*
Zhang Zhongliang	*Former Director, Department of Social, Science and Technology and Culture Industryof*
	National Bureau of Statistics, PRC
Zhou Qiren	***Langrun Chair Professor, National School of Development at Peking University***

Cloud River Urban Research Institute CICI & CCCI Study Team Members

Sugita Masaaki	*Research Director, Cloud River Urban Research Institute*
Zhen Xuehua	*Senior Researcher, Cloud River Urban Research Institute*
Kurimoto Kenichi	*Senior Researcher, Cloud River Urban Research Institute*
Kazuno Junya	*Senior Researcher, Cloud River Urban Research Institute*
Zhao Jian	*Senior Researcher, Cloud River Urban Research Institute*

Acknowledgments

In the development of the *China Integrated City Index*, we hereby would like to extend our sincere thanks to Xu Lin (Director) and Nakai Tokutaro (Director-General for Environmental Policy, Ministry of the Environment, Japan) for the strong support from the *Sino-Japan Cooperation Mechanism on Urbanization and Environmental Issues* signed between the Department of Development Planning of NDRC and the Ministry of the Environment Minister's Secretariat. At the same time, we would like to thank the following experts and scholars inside and outside China for their guidance and assistance in the development of this book:

Anzai Takashi (Chairman, Seven Bank, Ltd., Former Bank-of-Japan Executive Director), Andoh Haruhiko (Deputy Director-General for International Projects Promotion, Trade and Economic Cooperation Bureau, Ministry of Economy, Trade and Industry), Fujino Junichi (Senior Researcher, National Institute for Environmental Studies), Fujita Tsuyoshi (Director, National Institute for Environmental Studies, Center for Social and Environmental Systems Research), Ico Migliore (Migliore+Servetto Architects CEO), Ide Takatoshi (Senior Adviser, Cherry Terrace, Inc.), Ishii Kisaburo (Ambassador of Japan to Romania, Former Vice-Minister for Land, Infrastructure, Transport and Tourism, Japan), Kishimoto Yoshio (Vice Chairman, Research Institute of Economy, Trade and Industry), Komuro Yukino (Senior Researcher, International Development Center of Japan), Kotegawa Daisuke (Research Director, The Canon Institute for Global Studies, Former Executive Director for Japan, IMF), Mario Bellini (CEO, Mario Bellini Architects), Miwa Yasuyuki (Chief Researcher, Institute for Urban Strategies, The Mori Memorial Foundation), Morimoto Akinori (Professor, Waseda University), Okabe Akiko (Professor, The University of Tokyo), Okazaki Yuta (Associate Professor, GENV, Sophia University), Ohta Katsutoshi (Director, Toyota Transportation Research Institute, Professor Emeritus, The University of Tokyo), Sako Keiichiro (CEO, SAKO Architects), Seta Fumihiko (Associate Professor, The University of Tokyo), Shimada Akira (Executive Vice President, Nippon Telegraph and Telephone Public Corporation), Shiraishi Katsutaka (Professor, Ryukoku University), Someno Kenji (Long-term Specialist, Japan International Cooperation Agency), Suzuki Masatoshi (President and Chief Executive Officer, MIRAIT Holdings Corporation), Takase Masanao (Representative Director, ZUNO Co., Ltd.), Takeda Shinji (President, TBS Holdings, Inc.), Takeoka Rinji (Senior Managing Executive Officer, Nikkei Inc.), Takeuchi Masaoki (President, International Development Center of Japan), Toda Eisaku (Principal Researcher, Institute for Global Environmental Strategies), Tsuchiya Ryosuke (Former Kanagawa Prefectural Hospital Organization Chief Director), Victor Fung Shuen Sit (Visiting Professor, Beijing University, Honorary Professor, University of Hong Kong), Yahagi Hiroshi (Professor, Ryukoku University), Yuan Xilu (Director, the General Administration of the State Administration for Industry & Commerce of the People's Republic of China), Zhu Xiaoming (Director, Jiangsu Development & Reform Commission). (Courtesy titles omitted and listed in alphabetical order)

The *Index* encompasses the essence of the bilateral policy exchanges, studies, and surveys between China and Japan for more than 20 years. We feel so grateful for the great support from the following experts and scholars in this process:

Abe Kazuhiko (Executive Director, Research Institute for Urban & Environmental Development, Japan), Arai Ryosuke (Chairman and CEO, LUMINE Co., Ltd.), Aruga Yuji ((President, Katsunuma Winery Co., Ltd.), Chen Haosu (Former Vice Mayor, Beijing Municipal People's Government, Former President, the Chinese People's Association for Friendship with Foreign Countries), Ezra Vogel (Professor Emeritus, Harvard University), Fukukawa Shinji (Chairmans, Toyo University, Former Vice-Minister of International Trade and Industry), Funabashi Yoichi (Chairman, Asia Pacific Initiative, Former Managing Editor,The Asahi Shimbun Company), Goto Kenichi (Director, Snow Peak Inc.), Hatanaka Ryutaro (Former Ambassador of Japan to Colombia, Former Commissioner, Financial Services Agency), Hayashi Masakazu (Former Chairperson of the Board, Japan Exchange Group, Inc., Former Vice-Minister of Finance), Hoshino Shinyasu (Former Vice-Minister of Economic Planning Agency, Former Chairmans, Nippon Institute for Research Advancement [deceased]), Ito Makoto (Professor Emeritus, The University of Tokyo), Kamatani Naoyuki (Chairman, StaGen Co., Ltd., Chairman, Gout Research Foundation), Kato Koichi (Former Secretary-General, The Liberal Democratic Party of Japan [deceased]), Kawai Yoshinari (Former Vice-Minister of Administrative Management Agency, Former Chairperson, International Development Center of Japan [deceased]), Kitano Naohiro (Former Director, Japan International Cooperation Agency Research Institute), Kiyonari Tadao (Adviser, The Graduate School of Project Design, Former President, Hosei University), Konno Syuhei (Former Professor, Osaka Sangyo University), Li Zhaoxing (Former Minister, Foreign Affairs of the People's Republic of China, Former Chairman, Foreign Affairs Committee of National People's Congress), Liu Jinqing (Honorary Professor, Tokyo Keizai University [deceased]), Maeta Toshihiro (President and CEO, MTI Ltd.), Masuda Yuji (Former Professor, The University of Tokyo, Former Executive Vice President, The University of Shimane [deceased]), Morimoto Hideka (Vice Minister of the Environment), Nomura Akio (Professor Emeritus, Tokyo Keizai University [deceased]), Ren Zhongyi (Former Secretary, Guangdong Province Committee of the CPC [deceased]), Sakurada Yukihisa (Former Managing Director, Japan International Cooperation System, Former Director, JICA China Office), Samejima Keiji (Former Senior Managing Director, Nikkei Inc., Former Chairman, Japan National Press Club [deceased]), Shioya Takafusa (Former Vice-Minister of Economic Planning Agency, Former Chairman, Nippon Institute for Research Advancement), Shirai Mamoru (Director, PIA Corporation), Sugimoto Kazuyuki (Chairman, Japan Fair Trade Commission, Former Vice Minister of Finance), Sumiya Mikio (Professor Emeritus, The University of Tokyo [deceased]), Takagi Yuki (President, Japan Professional-Agriculture Total Support Organization, Former Vice Minister of Agriculture, Forestry and Fisheries), Tanaka Naoki (President, Center for International Public Policy

Studies), Tanaka Osamu (Faculty, The University of Tokyo Executive Management Program, Former Executive Vice President, Policy Research Institute, Former President, National Tax College), Tanaka Takuji (Deputy Vice Minister of Finance for International Affairs), Tang Wensheng (Former Vice Editor, *China Daily*, Former Vice President , China Soong Ching Ling Foundation), Tao Siliang (Former Vice President , China Association of Mayors), Uryu Kentaro (Managing Partner, URYU & ITOGA, Lawyer), Yabuta Jinichiro (Former President, International Development Center of Japan), Yanagisawa Kae (Ambassador of Japan to Malawi, Former President, Japan International Cooperation Agency), Yasuda Hiroshi (Representative Director, National Congress of Industrial Heritage, Former Vice Minister of Finance), Yatsu Ryutaro (President & Representative Director, Japan Environmental Storage & Safety Corporation, Former Vice Minister of the Environment), Yoshizawa Yasuyuki (Honorary Director, Basyobunka Forum), Yu Guangyuan (Former Vice President , Chinese Academy of Social Sciences, Former Vice Director, State Scientific and Technological Commission [deceased]), Zhao Qizheng (Former Minister , the State Council Information Office of the People's Republic of China, Former Minister, Foreign Affairs Committee of the Chinese People's Political Consultative Conference), Zhu Yinghuang (Vice President , China National Committee for Pacific Economic Cooperation, Former Chief Editor , *China Daily*)

(Courtesy titles omitted and listed in alphabetical order)

Our heartfelt thanks will be given to Li Chunsheng (Vice President), Zheng Haiyan (Director of Economic Editorial Department) and Meng Xue (Editor) under the People's Publishing House for their support in the publication of the Chinese Version of the *Index*, as well as to Hasebe Toshiharu (President), Yokoyama Hideyuki (Managing Director), Saito Kimitaka (Deputy Director), Kauchi Mayuko (Editor) and Matuda Nanae (Production Manager) under NTT Publishing Co., Ltd. for the same in the publication of the Japanese Version.

Supervisor of translation: Feng Wen , District Assistant, Chaoyang District, Beijing

Planned by: Tokyo Keizai University Zhou Muzhi Laboratory, and ZUNO Co., Ltd.
Charts designed by: hclab
Book designed by: Hayashi Yuya

(Courtesy titles omitted and latest posts at the publication of this book)

Preface

Using Comprehensive Evaluation to Identify the Direction of Development for Chinese Cities

Yang Weimin

Deputy Director, Subcommittee of Economy of National Committee of the Chinese People's Political Consultative Conference
Former Deputy Director, Office of the Central Leading Group for Financial and Economic Affairs, PRC

As a report jointly prepared by the Department of Development Planning, NDRC and Cloud River Urban Research Institute, the *China Integrated City Index 2016* provides an evaluation for the status of urban development in China from a brand-new perspective. It is a truly comprehensive and genuine evaluation of development. Any judgment of a city's development merely based on her economic achievements is lacking. No evaluation would be complete without the social and environmental indicators, regardless of how many economic indicators were used.

The philosophy and principles of spatial balance should be established for development. The purpose of spatial balance is to achieve the harmony among population (society), economy, resources and environment within a certain space. The establishment of such philosophy and principles is of great significance to the correct understanding and sound enhancement of coordinated regional development, as well as to the promotion of green urbanization and the harmonious development between human and nature. For example, spatial imbalance will take place when the ecological environment in some areas deteriorates as a result of the local resources and environment being overloaded with the size of the local population and the economic developments for raising living standards. If we only pursue the realization of a well-off and modernized society, we will be unable to stop the economic development of such areas under the "right to development" and hence will be unable to reverse the deterioration of the ecological environment from its source. When the ecological environment is destroyed, a large amount of funds will have to be spent in implementing "ecological Construction" projects, such as returning farmland to forests, returning grazing land to grassland, soil erosion control, sand source control, and rocky desertification control, among others. Another example is that some areas are already under excessively intense development, which has weakened the bearing capacity of their resources and environment. If no adjustments are made to any industrial structures that have gone beyond the bearing capacity of the resources and environment of these areas, nothing can stop any further consumption of energy and water resources, which will make it difficult to maintain control over the discharge of pollutants from the source. When water shortage and environmental deterioration affect people's lives, one after another water delivery project and pollution control project will have to be implemented. In addition, some cities are already suffering from "urban diseases" due to the

2

conditions of the city, such as an overcrowded central urban area and unbalanced spatial structure. If we do not properly relieve these central urban areas from some urban functions, but indulge their ongoing development into and reinforcement as economic centers, industrial bases, trade logistics centers, transportation hubs, shipping centers, education centers, research and development bases, and medical centers, etc., we will be unable to stop people from swarming in and unable to stop the property price from rising every day, and will inevitably come across traffic congestion and frequent smog.

The *China Integrated City Index 2016* provides an evaluation of urban development from the environmental, social and economic perspectives, and embodies the idea of spatial balance. That is why I say it is a truly comprehensive and genuine evaluation of development. Only in this way will the evaluation of urban development be scientific and conducive to guiding the development of cities in a more comprehensive, coordinated and sustainable manner.

Cities are the main carriers of economic development and social progress. The first 30 years have witnessed the influx of hundreds of millions of people into cities in China, and the same will happen again in the future. The biggest pressure the cities confront and their weakest point, both at present and in the future, should be the ecological environment. In urban development, the pursuit of bigger economic scale, more mileage of roads, taller buildings and more spacious homes should not come at the cost of the shining stars, clear rivers and lakes, and the singing birds.

The urban development of China must adhere to the philosophy of ecological living, promote the green development, cyclic development and low-carbon development, and minimize the interference and damage to nature through the economical and intensive utilization of resources including land, water and energy. A high level of attention should be paid to eco-safety and the ratio of green and ecological spaces such as forests, lakes and wetlands should be increased, while the water conservation capacity and environmental capacity are enhanced. the quality of environment should be improved, with reduction in the total discharge of major pollutants, control over the intensity of development, and enhancement of the capability to withstand and mitigate natural disasters. The *China Integrated City Index 2016* provides a number of implementable green indicators. All cities should measure their gaps from the indicators and seek out the areas to work on for urban development. In this regard, the *China Integrated City Index 2016* is not only an evaluation, but also points out the direction to move forward.

Profile

Yang Weimin

Born in 1956, Mr. Yang served as the Director of the Department of Development Planning, NDRC and the Deputy Secretary-General and Secretary-General of the NDRC. He has been in service since 2011.

Mr. Yang has long been engaged in the research and development of China's macro policies and medium-to-long-term plans. He participated in and organized the preparation for the outlines of the "9th Five-year Plan" "10th Five-year Plan" "11th Five-year Plan" and the "12th Five-year Plan" for China, took part in the report drafted for the CPC's 18th National Congress and the Third, Fourth and Fifth Plenary Sessions of the 18th National Congress of CPC, and provided part of the advice for the "11th Five-year Plan" "12th Five-year Plan" and "13th Five-year Plan" of the Central Government. He is a member and liaison officer of the Special Panel for Central Economic System and Ecological Civilization System Reform, and has participated in the coordination of a number of major reforms.

Editor-in-Chief for: *China 30 Years from Now* (2011, Joint Publishing HK, co-edited by Zhou Muzhi), *The Third Thirty Years: A New Direction for China* (2010, People's Publishing House, co-edited by Zhou Muzhi), *Studies on Industrial Policies for Sustainable Development in China* (2004, China Market Press), *Theoretical Exploration for the Planning System Reform* (2003, China Price Press).

Continually Developing Cities and Continuously Improving Indicators

Chen Yajun

Director, Department of Development Planning, NDRC
Ph.D. in Management

The three revolutions of science and technology and the three waves of urbanization have changed the global economic system, with an emerging viewpoint that "the world is not flat." Developed countries represented by the U.S, the European Union and Japan dominate the world economy, while a large number of developing countries are in an affiliated position. Such "unflatness" is even more obvious within the country. The *World Development Report 2009* by the World Bank describes the transformation of economic space using three characteristics, namely, density, distance and segmentation, and illustrates the development gap between city-based regions. The gap is shocking. The Tokyo Metropolitan Area is one of the areas covering the world's largest "cities" with a population of 38 million, creating 32.3% of Japan's GDP with 3.6% of the country's land area. It accommodates 58.2% of the listed companies in Japan, 68.7% of her researchers and 60.6% of her patents. Large cities attract talent, technology and funds from all around the world, and expand rapidly, while small and medium cities and regions are relatively underdeveloped, resulting in the gap between cities even greater than that between countries.

Viewed from this perspective, China is not flat either. On the southeast side of the "Hu Line (or Heihe-Tengchong Line)" 43% of the country's land holds 94% of her population, while on the northwest side, 57% of the country's land holds only 6% of her population. This is the most basic feature of economic geography of China. Even in the southeast, the internal difference is significant and the levels of economic development, construction and modernization between urban and rural areas and between cities differ largely. In 2016, Shanghai had a permanent resident population of 24.19 million, with per capita GDP of about 113,600 CNY; Hefei, 7.86 million, with per capita GDP of about 80,100 CNY; and Guiyang, 4.69 million, with per capita GDP of about 67,700 CNY. This is only a comparison between provincial capital cities and beyond. The difference in the level of development between prefecture-level cities and county-level cities in the eastern and western regions is even more disparate. Of course, characterization by such a single indicator is not always convincing. The more reliable approach is to design a set of indicators that reflect the strength of urban development, integrating differences in multiple areas to more comprehensively reflect the gap. This also a scientific basis for appropriate interventions in the "unflatness" of economic geographical space, which can inspire people to explore the best combination of existing laws, current development status, public policies, and future visions.

Doing this research, the Department of Development Planning, NDRC and Cloud River Urban Research Institute have been committed to establishing a scientific and reasonable indicator system by drawing upon international experience in urban development in three major sectors, i.e., environment, society and economy, for the purpose of exploring and constructing a comprehensive indicator system for Chinese cities that are environment-friendly, create better social life with culture and support sustainable industrial innovation. We use indicators to evaluate the level of urban development and use data to identify the path of urban development. Urban development is a dynamic and evolving process with complex contributing factors. The evaluation of such development involves complicated types and categories of indicators. Some indicators inter-relate and interplay, and some individual ones are difficult to quantify. There are many ways to address them, and our research takes only one of the approaches.

In the future, such "unflatness" will become more complicated. Modern technologies such as informatization, big data, and artificial intelligence will have a deeper impact on the pattern of urban development. Central cities enjoy first-mover advantages and scale effects in the generation and application of modern technologies, in an increasingly polarized way. However, benefiting from the low space cost of information technology and the connectivity of modern infrastructure, small and medium cities find their development advantages growing and disadvantages diminishing, in particular through emerging ways of space organizing. As "anchor points" in the global production network, and the towns that were studied in China's Zhejiang Province brought new opportunities to their underdeveloped or depressed areas, and some regions and cities have even surpassed their original developed areas by taking other paths. It is both important and exciting to have real-time tracking and accurate descriptions to reflect the dynamism of these changes. This is also a new space for urban index research.

Moreover, in the future, the development of individual cities will gradually give way to metropolitan areas, where information networks and transportation infrastructure will be interconnected, public services will be co-built and shared, development will be integrated between cities, and "depressions" surrounding central cities will gradually be filled up and made even. The metropolitan areas will develop increasingly as a whole, integrating a group of cities into one city, and the subject of evaluation will change from city to metropolitan area. In any case, these changes will bring new issues to research, because theory is gray, and only the tree of life is evergreen.

High-quality Development Requires High-Quality Urbanization Support

Xu Lin

Chairman, U.S.-China Green Fund
Former Director, Department of Development Planning, NDRC
M.S. in Economics, M.S. in Public Administration

Urbanization is one of the driving forces behind the rapid development of the economy and society in China over the past 40 years. Essentially a structural reform issue, urbanization promotes the free flow and efficient allocation of elements by lifting restrictions on the movement of such elements between urban-rural areas and regions. It will remain an important driving force for the high-quality development of China in the future, since high-quality urbanization is conducive to further improving the efficiency of resource allocation. There is still a need in China for the unfinished reform of urbanization and for improved efficiency in resource allocation, and we need to continue our hard work on the exploration of all aspects.

It was proposed in the 19th National Congress of the Communist Party of China held in 2017 that China has entered a stage of transition from high-speed growth to high-quality development. The realization of high-quality development requires the support from all aspects of development. Considering the allocation of various resources and elements is concentrated in the urbanized areas of China, improving the quality of urbanization and urban development is thus undoubtedly the most important area to support the high-quality development.

The reform and opening-up policy has brought China into the rapidest urbanization and development process in world history. In just 40 years, the permanent residents of urban areas in China have reached 790 million, representing an urbanization rate of 57.4%, with an average annual increase of more than one percentage. Relevant research even presents that China's urbanization rate may have exceeded 60%, with ever expanding urban built-up areas reaching 100,000 square kilometers, with cities constituting about 50,000 square kilometers of this urban development.

1. Problems and Challenges

Urbanization's rapid progress has generated many issues that cannot be ignored. These issues, the existence of which has lowered the quality of urbanization and urban development in China, require a high-level attention and shall be tackled in a serious manner.

(1) A city's failure to grant a residency permit to a large number of its permanent residents has

resulted in a dual structure within the city. The current migration of the rural population in China has relocated about 270 million people, and there are an additional 80 million-plus permanent urban residents moving between cities for employment purposes. These people, economically exploited as part of the labor force but in a discriminated position, unfairly regarded for welfare benefits in our society, are not being treated as urban citizens. Their sacrifice and contributions have virtually pushed down the cost of urbanization and urban development in China. Their sufferings, sacrifice, and helplessness is behind our glamorous and bright cities. These new migrants barely have any sense of belonging or ownership in the cities they reside in. They lead a wandering life for an extended period of time and find it too difficult to have long-term and stable expectations and plans for their own lives and careers, and even more difficult to become a defender and builder of urban social order.

(2) There has been a disorderly expansion and an inefficient use of urban spaces. In the process of urban development, an excessive number of oversized new towns and new districts and a variety of industrial parks are set up as part of the urban planning for many cities. Some of these cities, whose existing new districts and parks have yet to be fully developed, are keen to move on to build up new and larger urban areas or parks, eventually making it difficult to improve the efficiency of utilizing urban land and spaces. Also as a product of such development, a good number of ghost cities and empty towns appear, piling up sizeable real estate inventories. The fact that "the urbanization of land outpaces that of the population" has for past decades not only prevented China from improving, but has led to a continuous decline in her efficiency or intensity of urban land utilization. This trend is clearly adverse to the effective protection of farmland. Land ownership and land finance, among other aspects, should be factored into any discussions and improvements.

(3) The problematic or "rotten" legacy from the construction of infrastructure networks is too extensive and is the outcome of unplanned or unreasonable layout. Due to the oversized areas under urban planning, many cities have accordingly expanded their infrastructure network coverage, increasing the scale of infrastructure investment and burden of government debt. The construction and operation of infrastructure can be financially unsustainable, with hidden risks of both debts and finance. The problem of the unreasonable layout of infrastructure networks is common, since urban infrastructure networks can fail to keep up with population density. Due to the difficulty and cost of infrastructure construction, central urban areas with high population density may end up having lower density of infrastructure; however, in areas with lower population density, the network density is instead higher due to the relative ease of construction. Therefore, the underutilization and supply shortage of infrastructure networks may exist at the same time, and a spatial mismatch can exist between the supply and demand of infrastructure.

(4) The cities are not open or inclusive enough. Due to the difficulty of urban management and concerns about urban order as cities continue to expand in size, there is a trend among Chinese cities that the larger the city, the less in openness and inclusivity. Such practice of sacrificing urban openness and

inclusivity in exchange for convenience in management and stability will in fact restrict the positive effects of urban economies of scale, the scope of economic growth, and the efficiency of a division of labor, diminishing the city's innovative ability and entrepreneurial space, and weakening the vitality and creativity of the city as an organic entity of various aggregated elements. The governance philosophy of co-building, sharing, and co-governance has not been fully implemented in urban social governance.

(5) There is a lack of scientificity and forward-looking in urban planning. The defects in the philosophy, methodology, and system of urban planning have resulted in China's failure to provide scientific and reasonable guidance and standardization on urban construction and development via urban planning. Some urban plans cover oversized areas and populations, but fall short of expectation at the end of the planning period; others seek to manage undersized areas and population, and end up failing to accommodate the actual development before the close of the planning period. Difficulties lie in the alignment and coordination between the rigid constraints of planning and the flexibility of market-based economic development. Different plans related to urban development are not managed in a coordinated manner. Conflicts and even fights between plans are also common, affecting the authority of planning and the effectiveness of their implementation.

(6) The urban industrial structure is aging, and the transformation or upgrading of this structure is rather slow. Some cities, as traditional industrial bases and resource-based cities, are under the pressure of transformation and upgrading, as well as the challenge of weakening the momentum of their traditional industries. The industrial support for urban development is weakened with the loss of job opportunities, resulting in an outflow of the urban population. Some cities, especially old industry-based cities in the northern region, are thus facing the risk and pressure of recession.

2. Directions and Measures

For the purpose of improving the quality of urbanization and urban development in China, we must take numerous measures from the perspective of system, policy, and technology to fully address the above problems and challenges on a continuous basis.

(1) Accelerating the Urbanization of Rural Migrants. This is a further explicit requirement from the 19th National Congress of the CPC. All kinds of cities, whether they are megacities, large cities, megalopolises, or small and medium cities, should take measures to provide those rural migrants who have already maintained stable employment in the city and are willing to transfer their household registration to the city, with an option to do so; and provide the same public services for those rural migrants who have been employed locally and those permanent residents employed in the city but without urban household registration, as to local residents. This group of people who have already been employed locally make equal contributions to the local economy and taxation base, and some at even higher rates than the local residents. From the perspective of public finance, fairness, and justice, there is no reason to implement discriminatory

welfare policies on them. In addition, since population migration mainly starts from economically under-developed areas to economically developed areas, accelerating the urbanization of urban permanent residents will better coordinate the spatial distribution of China's economy and population. This will help promote the coordinated development of regional and urban-rural areas in China, and it will facilitate and support the implementation of the coordinated regional development strategy and the rural revitalization strategy proposed in the 19th National Congress of the CPC. When more rural residents move into urban areas, they will be more immersed in the modern life of the cities and improve the conditions for their children's education, which is conducive to the improvement of population quality and the modernization of the people.

(2) Strengthening Industrial Support for Cities. A city will inevitably opt for the ongoing strengthening of industrial support for urban development through industrial upgrade, which is a perennial topic for sustainable urban development. This does not mean, however, that the city government will have to invest more public resources to provide direct support for industrial development. The government is mainly required to provide good basic conditions, including infrastructural conditions and human capital conditions, to foster a more open, inclusive, and transparent business environment and industrial eco-environment that is conducive to industrial innovation and development, to maintain a reasonable cost setting for industrial development, and to facilitate independent investment and attract all kinds of talent for market entities. China's urban leaders and planners generally have the will and power to choose the leading industries for their city, but they need to take into account their respective city's own advantages and location characteristics, as well as the functional positioning of the megalopolis or metropolitan area where their city is located, to plan for their own industrial development options by industrial clustering or the division of labor and collaboration, or by applying such philosophies as urban entanglement and industrial entangle-ment in order to give better play to the effects of clustering and division of labor.

(3) Improving Urban Governance and Urban Management. An urban society can be better character-ized as a civil society. This means that urban governance should call for broader resident involvement. To do so, the openness and inclusivity of urban governance should be maintained, which is also the core spirit of a modern city that fundamentally ensures the city is attractive. The most dynamic and innovative cities in the world are the most open and inclusive ones. China is no exception. One of the important reasons why all kinds of innovative elements tend to cluster in Shenzhen is that Shenzhen is an immigrant city, more open and inclusive than other cities in China. If urban governance is open and inclusive enough to attract more members of the public, it can enhance the urban residents' sense of ownership of the city so that they will truly call it home, and participate in her construction and maintenance and the protection of her wellbe-ing in a constructive manner. China's urban management requires more human care, rather than the author-ity and coldness of the government. By advancing the in-depth integration of technology such as the Internet, big data, and artificial intelligence into urban management, we will find more opportunities to improve our urban governance and management,

improve the efficiency of urban public services, and make our urban management and services smarter, more convenient, and closer to the people. The construction of a smart city is also an important way to improve urban governance and management.

(4) Applying Science to the Spatial Arrangements of Urbanization. In accordance with the requirements of the urban pattern whereby the coordinated development of large, medium, and small cities and small towns is centered around the metropolitan area, the reform of the philosophy, system, and methodology of urban spatial planning should be accelerated. Any planning philosophy and methodology continued from the original planning system should be changed in order to provide sound guidance for the economic and industrial layout, transportation network layout, eco-space protection, social and cultural protection, and military readiness, among other planning efforts, required for coordinated development of metropolitan areas, cities, and small towns. Moving forward, multiple areas of planning should be coordinated in order to support the mutual development of industrial clusters, infrastructure networks, and the city-town division of labor, so that the spatial layout and functional integration of urban industries, transportation networks, environmental protections, and public life, among other concerns, is reasonably arranged. To promote above-ground-and-underground integrated planning, manage from an executive level the utilization and coordination of above-ground and underground spaces. Make better use of urban underground spaces to pave the way for the development of a compact city, reduce the waste of space resources, promote the improvement of the urban eco-environment, and facilitate sustainable development.

(5) Innovating Financing Mechanisms for Urban Infrastructure. Urban infrastructure, especially urban rail transit networks, can involve large, one-time investments in long-serving structures and requires moderately advanced planning and construction. Debt financing is used to resolve funding issues for urban infrastructure, and it can be secured by intergenerational sharing, or the sharing of the construction cost of urban infrastructure across generations. This method reflects equity between generations and is a reasonable financing arrangement. At present, many cities in China are faced with financing problems and debt servicing risks for urban infrastructure construction, mainly for two reasons. First, the excessive scale of infrastructure construction, which is a problematic or rotten legacy, results in an excessive scale of investment and debt. Second is the lack of effective institutional security for finance, where fiscal expenditures from the government are relatively insufficient. To solve this problem, in addition to solving existing urban infrastructure problems through scientific and reasonable planning, it is also necessary to innovate the investment and financing mechanisms for urban infrastructure. This innovation will provide better support for government assets and liabilities, revitalize government assets and income, and more closely align the relationship between the cost and term of debt financing and the cash flows and income period of the project. It is also necessary to increase the supply of long-term financing instruments, and to provide financing services as security for urban infrastructure at a reasonable cost and for a matching term.

(6) Paying More Attention to Improvement of Urban Construction Quality. In less than 40 years,

China has increased her urbanization rate by 40%, with all kinds of buildings erected in her cities like spring bamboo shoots after a spring rain. Such scale and experience of construction is unprecedented to any country in the world. It is conceivable that due to various factors such as technology, labor, funds, and design ideas, a variety of existing problems in urban buildings will become increasingly obvious over time. Today, it is necessary for us to pay more attention to improving the quality of urban construction. Building design and construction standards must be revised and improved as soon as possible, and benchmarks should include such criteria as extended building life and improved low-carbon, energy-efficient standards. The current cost with an additional 1,000 CNY per square meter would be acceptable for the market and consumers in many middle- and high-income areas. The multiple benefits generated would last decades or even a century. It is absolutely worth the investment and the price.

3. The Significance of the Integrated City Index

In summary, the quality of urbanization and urban development needs to be considered and evaluated from many angles. It is precisely for this reason that we have worked with the Cloud River Urban Research Institute headed by Professor Zhou Muzhi of Tokyo Keizai University to conduct research for the *China Integrated City Index*, which applies a consistent system of indicators for the evaluation of 297 Chinese cities at the prefecture level or above in order to observe the overall and specific differences in the quality of urban development.

Of course, no evaluation method using an indicator system is perfect. Even if the selection of the indicator system is flawless, the authenticity of the statistical data may not stand the test, and there are points of controversy and needed improvements. Fortunately, this type of evaluation is for research purposes rather than serving as an assessment standard, with no potential impact on merit reviews, bonus payments, or job promotions, for instance, and it allows us to improve while reviewing and discussing its findings. We may wish to continue such evaluation as research and make gradual improvements. This is conducive to the systematic observation and evaluation of the quality of urban development, and it enables us to obtain a complete set of historical records on urban development.

Chapter I
China Integrated City Index and City Rankings

1. Target Cities

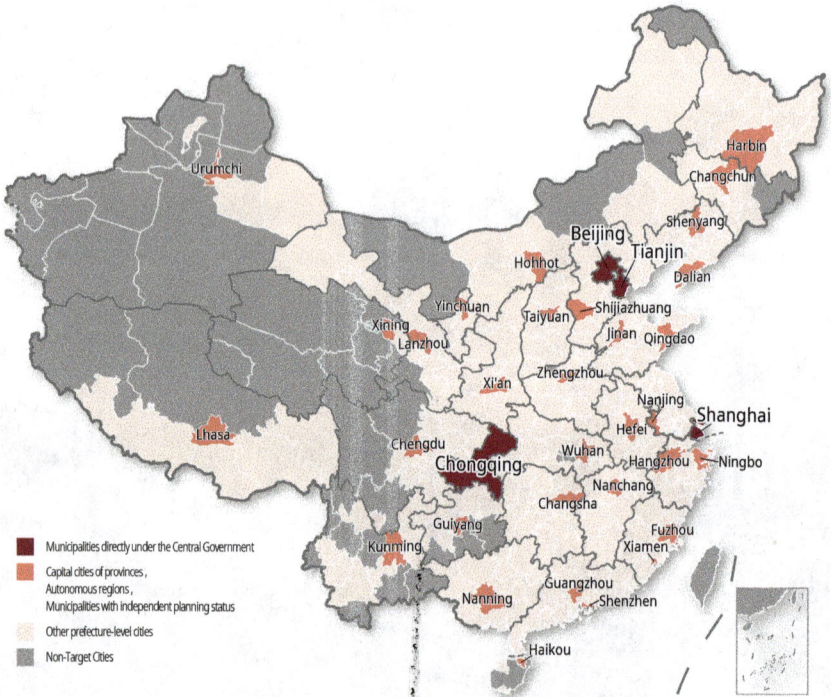

Figure 1-1 Target Cities of the Index

Target Cities of the Index

On the basis of the 2016 edition, *China Integrated City Index 2017* includes two more cities, Shannan and Hami, now covering all 297 cities at the prefecture level or above in China:

· Municipalities directly under the Central Government (4: Beijing, Tianjin, Shanghai and Chongqing)

· Capital cities of provinces and autonomous regions (27: Shijiazhuang, Taiyuan, Hohhot, Shenyang, Changchun, Harbin, Nanjing, Hangzhou, Hefei, Fuzhou, Nanchang, Jinan, Zhengzhou, Wuhan, Changsha, Guangzhou, Nanning, Haikou, Chengdu, Guiyang, Kunming, Lhasa, Xi'an, Lanzhou, Xining, Yinchuan and Urumqi)

· Cities specifically designated in the state plan (5: Dalian, Qingdao, Ningbo, Xiamen and Shenzhen)

· Other prefecture-level cities (261)

Note: Figure 1-1 is made according to the data from *China Integrated City Index 2017*. In the book, we will no longer cite sources for any charts based on the data from *China Integrated City Index 2017* hereafter. All the "maps" that appear in this book are simply "schematics" to visually convey the meaning of indicators, not actually the real maps.

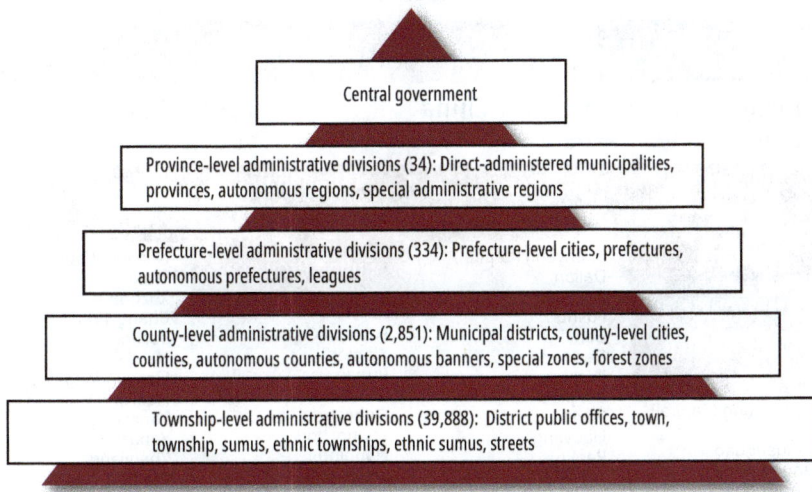

Figure 1-2 The diagram of the administrative divisions in China

Source: According to *China Statistical Yearbook* compiled by the National Bureau of Statistics and the statistics of administrative divisions from the Ministry of Civil Affairs.

The Administrative Divisions of China

China's administrative divisions are mainly defined as four levels: province-level administrative divisions, prefecture-level administrative divisions, county-level administrative divisions, and township-level administrative divisions.

According to the statistics of administrative divisions from the Ministry of Civil Affairs, as of December 31, 2017, China's administrative divisions are:

First-level administrative divisions (province-level administrative divisions): 34 in total, including 4 direct-administered municipalities, 23 provinces, 5 autonomous regions, and 2 special administrative regions.

Second-level administrative divisions (prefecture-level administrative divisions): 334 in total, including 294 prefecture-level cities, 7 prefectures, 30 autonomous prefectures, and 3 leagues.

Third-level administrative divisions (county-level administrative divisions): 2,851 in total, including 962 municipal districts, 363 county-level cities, 1,355 counties and 117 autonomous counties, 49 banners, 3 autonomous banners, 1 special zone, and 1 forest zone.

Fourth-level administrative divisions (township-level administrative divisions): 39,888 in total, including 2 district public offices, 21,116 towns, 9,392 townships, 152 sumus, 984 ethnic townships, 1 ethnic sumu, and 8,241 streets.

Table 1-1 List of Target Cities

Prefecture Level			
North China 33 cities	**Northeast China** 34 cities	**East China** 78 cities	
Beijing (Municipalities directly under the Central Government)	**Liaoning Province** 14 cities	**Shanghai** (Municipalities directly under the Central Government)	**Jiangsu Province** 13 cities
Tianjin (Municipalities directly under the Central Government)	Shenyang (Capital) Dalian Anshan Fushun	**Fujian Province** 9 cities	Nanjing (Capital) Wuxi Xuzhou Changzhou
Hebei Province 11 cities	Benxi Dandong Jinzhou Yingkou	Fuzhou (Capital) Xiamen Putian Sanming	Suzhou Nantong Lianyungang Huai'an
Shijiazhuang (Capital) Tangshan Qinhuangdao Handan Xingtai Baoding Zhangjiakou Chengde Cangzhou Langfang Hengshui	Fuxin Liaoyang Panjin Tiding Chaoyang Huludao	Quanzhou Zhangzhou Nanping Longyan Ningde	Yancheng Yangzhou Zhenjiang Taizhou Suqian
		Jiangxi Province 11 cities	**Zhejiang Province** 11 cities
Shanxi Province 11 cities	**Jilin Province** 8 cities	Nanchang (Capital) Jingdezhen Pingxiang Jiujiang Xinyu Yingtan	Hangzhou (Capital) Ningbo Wenzhou Jiaxing Huzhou Shaoxing
Taiyuan (Capital) Datong Yangquan Changzhi Jincheng Shuozhou Jinzhong Xinzhou Linfen Yuncheng Lvliang	Changchun (Capital) Jilin Siping Liaoyuan Tonghua Baishan Baicheng Songyuan	Ganzhou Shangrao Fuzhou Ji'an Yichun	Jinhua Quzhou Zhoushan Taizhou Lishui
		Shandong Province 17 cities	**Anhui Province** 16 cities
Inner Mongolia Autonomous Region 9 cities	**Heilongjiang Province** 12 cities	Jinan (Capital) Qingdao Zibo	Hefei (Capital) Wuhu Bengbu
Hohhot (Capital) Baotou Wuhai Chifeng Tongliao Hulunbuir Ordos Ulanqab Bayannur	Harbin (Capital) Qiqihar Jixi Hegang Shuangyashan Daqing Yichun Jiamusi Qitaihe Mudanjiang Heihe Suihua	Zaozhuang Dongying Yantai Weifang Jining Tai'an Dezhou Weihai Liaocheng Linyi Laiwu Rizhao Heze Binzhou	Huainan Ma'anshan Huaibei Tongling Anqing Huangshan Fuyang Bozhou Suzhou Chuzhou Lu'an Chizhou Xuancheng

(297 cities)

Central China	South China	Southwest China	Northwest China
42 cities	39 cities	38 cities	33 cities

Central China — 42 cities

Henan Province
17 cities

Zhengzhou (Capital)
Kaifeng
Luoyang
Pingdingshan
Anyang
Hebi
Xinxiang
Jiaozuo
Puyang
Xuchang
Luohe
Sanmenxia
Shangqiu
Nanyang
Xinyang
Zhoukou
Zhumadian

Hubei Province
12 cities

Wuhan (Capital)
Huangshi
Shiyan
Jingzhou
Yichang
Xiangyang
Ezhou
Jingmen
Xiaogan
Huanggang
Xianning
Suizhou

Hunan Province
13 cities

Changsha (Capital)
Zhuzhou
Xiangtan
Hengyang
Shaoyang
Yueyang
Yiyang
Changde
Chenzhou
Yongzhou
Huaihua
Zhangjiajie
Loudi

South China — 39 cities

Guangdong Province
21 cities

Guangzhou (Capital)
Shaoguan
Shenzhen
Zhuhai
Shantou
Foshan
Jiangmen
Zhanjiang
Huizhou
Maoming
Zhaoqing
Chaozhou
Meizhou
Zhongshan
Dongguan
Shanwei
Heyuan
Yangjiang
Qingyuan
Jieyang
Yunfu

Guangxi Zhuang Autonomous Region
14 cities

Nanning (Capital)
Liuzhou
Guilin
Wuzhou
Beihai
Fangchenggang
Qinzhou
Yulin
Guigang
Baise
Laibin
Chongzuo
Hezhou
Hechi

Hainan Province
4 cities

Haikou (Capital)
Sanya
Sansha
Danzhou

Southwest China — 38 cities

Chongqing
(Municipalities directly under the Central Government)

Sichuan Province
18 cities

Chengdu (Capital)
Zigong
Panzhihua
Luzhou
Deyang
Mianyang
Guangyuan
Suining
Neijiang
Ziyang
Leshan
Yibin
Nanchong
Dazhou
Guang'an
Ya'an
Meishan
Bazhong

Guizhou Province
6 cities

Guiyang (Capital)
Liupanshui
Zunyi
Anshun
Tongren
Bijie

Yunnan Province
8 cities

Kunming (Capital)
Yuxi
Qujing
Zhaotong
Lijiang
Baoshan
Pu'er
Lincang

Tibet Autonomous Region
5 cities

Lhasa (Capital)
Shigatse
Chamdo
Nyingchi
Shannan

Northwest China — 33 cities

Shaanxi Province
10 cities

Xi'an (Capital)
Tongchuan
Baoji
Xianyang
Yan'an
Hanzhong
Weinan
Yulin
Shangluo
Ankang

Gansu Province
12 cities

Lanzhou (Capital)
Jiayuguan
Jinchang
Baiyin
Tianshui
Wuwei
Zhangye
Pingliang
Jiuquan
Qingyang
Dingxi
Longnan

Qinghai Province
2 cities

Xining (Capital)
Haidong

Ningxia Hui Autonomous Region
5 cities

Yinchuan (XXXX)
Shuizuishan
Wuzhong
Guyuan
Zhongwei

Xinjiang Uyghur Autonomous Region
4 cities

Urumchi (Capital)
Karamay
Turpan
Hami

2. Index Structure

Triple Bottom Line

China Integrated City Index 2017 follows the idea of Triple Bottom Line in the 2016 edition to provide an evaluation and analysis of sustainable urban development from the environmental, social, and economic dimensions.

The so-called Triple Bottom Line (TBL) is a representative approach for the evaluation of sustainability, which evaluates human activities from three dimensions, namely, "environment," "society," and "economy." Led by the sustainability evaluation indicators from the Secretariat of the United Nations Commission on Sustainable Development (UNCSD), a number of international surveys and studies related to sustainability evaluation have been conducted with the TBL approach. However, *China Integrated City Index* is indeed a pioneering undertaking by providing a three-dimensional evaluation for all the major cities of a big country.

3×3×3 Structure

China Integrated City Index 2017 follows the 3×3×3 structure of the 2016 edition. The indicator system consists of three major dimensions: environment, society, and economy. Further, each dimension comprises three sub-dimensions, and each sub-dimension includes three indicator groups. All of the three levels (i.e., dimension, sub-dimension, and indicator group) add up to 39 categories (i.e., 3 + 9 + 27) in total, forming a simple and clear 3×3×3 pyramid structure. Such an indicator system thus provides a comprehensive analysis to quantify and visualize the complex urban conditions in a simple and clear structure.

Dimension

China Integrated City Index

Environment

Society

Economy

Sub-Dimension	Indicator Group
Natural Ecology	Soil and Water Condition
	Climate Condition
	Natural Disaster
Environmental Quality	Pollution Load
	Environmental Protection Effort
	Resource Efficiency
Spatial Structure	Compact City
	Transportation Network
	Urban Facilities
Status and Governance	City Status
	Quality of Population
	Social Management
Inheritance and Exchange	Historical Relics
	Cultural and Entertainment
	Personal Exchange
Quality of Life	Residential Environment
	Level of Consumption
	Life Services
Quality of Economic Development	Economic Scale
	Economic Structure
	Economic Efficiency
Dynamic Development	Business Environment
	Openness
	Innovation and Entrepreneurship
Urban Influence	Urban and Rural Integration
	Wide-area Hab
	Core Influence

Figure 1-3 Index Structure Diagram

Data Support

China Integrated City Index 2017 is a relative enhancement of the data for the 133 indicators in the 2016 edition, and it further strengthens the use of satellite remote sensing data, as well as big data from the Internet. Presently, 175 indicators are chosen to support the 3×3×3 structure, establishing an indicator system for more perspectives with greater accuracy. These indicators consist of 56 categories in the environmental dimension, 55 categories in the social dimension, and 64 categories in the economic dimension, respectively.

Taking the environmental dimension as an example, the newly added satellite remote sensing data cover more thorough and more accurate information on ecological resources. While the 2016 edition tends to focus on the per-capita evaluation of ecological resources, the 2017 edition places a stronger emphasis on the evaluation of the total volume. At the same time, the weight of data for air pollution indicators has been adjusted to some extent in the 2017 edition, given the mitigated air pollution. These improvements and changes have had an impacts on the ranking of cities within the environmental dimension.

Nevertheless, through a comparative analysis using the Spearman's rank correlation coefficient, it shows that the correlation coefficients for the comprehensive ranking, environmental ranking, social rank-ing, and economic ranking in the 2016 and 2017 editions are as high as 0.94, 0.87, 0.90, and 0.88, respectively. Based on this observation, we conclude that the comprehensive ranking as well as the environmental, social and economic rankings have remained fairly stable, despite the addition and removal of indicator data and the adjustment to their weights.

3. Ranking Method

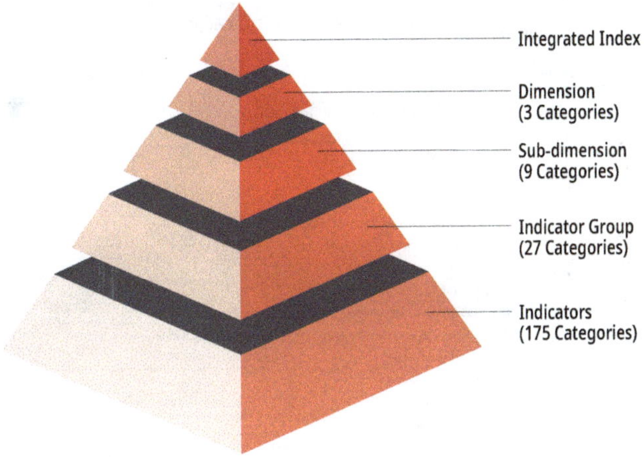
Integrated Index
Dimension
(3 Categories)
Sub-dimension
(9 Categories)
Indicator Group
(27 Categories)
Indicators
(175 Categories)

Figure 1-4 Index Structure Concept Diagram

Data Collection and Indexation

Data for the *China Integrated City Index* mainly came from three types of sources: 1. statistics released by governments at all levels (2015); 2. data collected from the Internet (2016); 3. satellite remote sensing data (2015).

The concept of deviation value is applied in the *China Integrated City Index* to convert a large amount of complicated data collected from different sources into comparable indicator data, by setting the maximum and minimum values of the deviation to 100 and 0 respectively.

Evaluation Method

The *China Integrated City Index* provides an evaluation using deviation values. Every indicator is calculated by combining the deviation values of its component data, that is: every indicator group is calculated by combining the deviation values of its indicators; every sub-dimension indicator is calculated by combining the deviation values of its indicator groups; every dimension indicator is calculated by combining the deviation values of its sub-dimension indicators; and finally, the integrated index is calculated by combining the deviation values of three dimension indicators.

Thus an important feature of the *China Integrated City Index* is that the evaluation can be decomposed into different levels to analyze the development of different cities in a detailed and three-dimensional way.

4. List of Indicators

Table 1-2 List of Indicators: Environment

Dimension	Sub-dimension	Indicator Group	ID	Indicators
Environment	Natural Ecology	Soil and Water Condition	1	Available Land Area Per Ten Thousand People
			2	Forest Area
			3	Farmland Area
			4	Pasture Area
			5	Water Area
			6	Water Resources Per Ten Thousand People
			7	National Park · Conservation Area · Scenic Area Index
		Climate Condition	8	Climate Comfort Index
			9	Rainfall
		Natural Disaster	10	Natural Disaster-caused Direct Economic Loss Index
			11	Geological Disaster-caused Direct Economic Loss Index
			12	Disaster Warning
	Environmental Quality	Pollution Load	13	Air Quality Index (AQI)
			14	PM$_{2.5}$ Index
			15	CO_2 Emissions Per Unit of GDP
			16	Volume of Sulphur Dioxide Emission
			17	Volume of Industrial Soot(dust) Emission
			18	Proportion of National and Provincial Water Sections in Category III and Above Meeting the Quality Standard
			19	Areas Environmental Average Noise Value
			20	Radiation Environmental Air Absorption Dose Rate
		Environmental Protection Efforts	21	Environmental Effort Index
			22	Water-saving Effort Index
			23	Social Organizations for Ecological Environment
			24	National Environmental Protection City Index
			25	National Ecological Environment Evaluation Index
		Resource Efficiency	26	Land Productivity in Built District
			27	Land Productivity in Agriculture, Forestry, Animal Husbandry and Fisheries
			28	Energy Consumption Per Unit of GDP
			29	Projects Labeled with Green Building Design and Evaluation
			30	Comprehensive Utilization Rate of Industrial Solid Waste
			31	Circular Economical City Index
	Spatial Structure	Compact City	32	Population of Densely Inhabited Districts (DIDs)
			33	Area of Densely Inhabited Districts (DIDs)
			34	Proportion of the Population of Densely Inhabited Districts (DIDs)
			35	Proportion of Densely Inhabited Districts (DIDs) in Built District
			36	Population of Super Densely Inhabited Districts (DIDs)
			37	Area of Super Densely Inhabited Districts (DIDs)
			38	Proportion of the Population of Super Densely Inhabited Districts (DIDs)
			39	Proportion of Densely Super Densely Inhabited Districts (DIDs) in Built District
		Transportation Network	40	Urban Rail Transit Density Index
			41	Urban Arterial Road Density Index
			42	Urban Life Road Density Index
			43	Urban Sidewalk · Bicycle Lane Density Index
			44	Urban Rail Transit Distance
			45	Public Bus Passenger Volume Per Ten Thousand People
			46	Public Bus Ownership Per Ten Thousand People
			47	Private Vehicle Ownership Per Ten Thousand People
			48	Taxis Ownership Per Ten Thousand People
			49	Rush Hour Traffic Jam Delay Index
		Urban Facilities	50	Fixed Assets Investment Scale Index
			51	Area of Park Green Land
			52	Green Coverage Rate in Built District
			53	Density of Water Supply Pipelines in Built District
			54	Density of Sewers in Built District
			55	Gas Coverage Rate
			56	Urban Underground Facilities Index

Table 1-3 List of Indicators: Society

Dimension	Sub-dimension	Indicator Group	ID	Indicators
Society	Status and Governance	City Status	57	Administrative Levels
			58	Megalopolis Levels
			59	Core City Levels
			60	Embassies · Consulates
			61	International Organizations
			62	Belt and Road Index
		Quality of Residents	63	Population Natural Growth Rate Index
			64	Population Social Growth Rate Index
			65	Population Structure Index
			66	Population Education Structure Index
			67	Higher Education Index
			68	Outstanding Talent Cultivation Index
			69	Public Finance Expenditure for Education Index
		Social Management	70	Social Services Index
			71	Safe and Reliable City Index
			72	Traffic Safety Index
			73	Social Security Index
			74	Social Organizations
			75	Health and Civilized City Index
			76	Government Website Performance
	Inheritance and Exchange	Historical Relics	77	Historical Status
			78	World Heritage
			79	Famous Historical and Cultural Cities
			80	Intangible Cultural Heritage
			81	Key Cultural Relics Sites Under the Protection
		Culture and Entertainment	82	Theater Consumer Index
			83	Museums · Art Galleries
			84	Sports Venues Index
			85	Zoos · Botanical Gardens · Aquariums
			86	Public Library Collection
			87	Cultural Master Index
			88	Olympic Champion Index
			89	National Culturally Advanced Unit Index
		Personal Exchange	90	Inbound Tourists
			91	Domestic Tourists
			92	Foreign Exchange Earnings from International Tourism
			93	Earnings from Domestic Tourism
			94	International Conferences
			95	Exhibition Industry Development Index
			96	World Tourism City Index
	Quality of Life	Residential Environment	97	Average Life Expectancy
			98	Medicare · Endowment Insurance Coverage Index
			99	Ratio of Average House Prices to Income
			100	Habitat City Index
			101	China's Happiness City Index
		Level of Consumption	102	Retail Sales of Consumer Goods Per Ten Thousand People
			103	Revenue of Hotels and Catering Services Per Ten Thousand People
			104	Telecom Consumption Per Ten Thousand People
			105	Water Consumption for Residential Use Per Ten Thousand People
			106	Top International Brand Index
		Life Service	107	Number of Children in Kindergartens Per Ten Thousand People
			108	Year-end Number of Beds in Nursing Homes
			109	Number of Practicing (Assistant) Physicians
			110	Number of Beds in Health Institutions
			111	First-class Hospitals

Table 1-4 List of Indicators: Economy

Dimension	Sub-dimension	Indicator Group	ID	Indicators
Economy	Quality of Economic Development	Economic Scale	112	Size of GDP
			113	Population Size of Permanent Residents
			114	Scale of Tax Collection
			115	Electricity Consumption
		Economic Structure	116	Industrial Structure Index
			117	Mainboard Listed Enterprises
			118	Top 500 Chinese Enterprises in the World
			119	China's Top 500 Enterprises
			120	China's Top 500 Private-owned Enterprises
			121	Gross Industrial Output Value Above Designated Size
		Economic Efficiency	122	GDP Growth Index
			123	GDP Per Ten Thousand People
			124	Fiscal Revenue Per Ten Thousand People
			125	Dependent Population Index
			126	Size and Debt Rate of Bonds Issued by the City Investment Enterprises
			127	Number of Registered Unemployed Persons Per Ten Thousand People
	Dynamic Development	Business Environment	128	Employee Average Salary
			129	Number of Employees of Enterprise Services
			130	Star Hotel Index
			131	Top International Restaurant Index
			132	National Industrial Park Index
		Openness	133	Population Migration
			134	Export of Goods · Import of Goods
			135	Foreign Investment Utilized
			136	Outward Foreign Direct Investment
			137	The Output Value of Foreign-invested Enterprises Above Designated Size
			138	International Schools
			139	Free Trade Area Index
		Innovation and Entrepreneurship	140	The World's Top University Index
			141	R&D Expenditure Index
			142	R&D Human Resources
			143	GEM,New Third Board Listed Enterprise Index
			144	The Amount of Patent Authorization Index
			145	Trademark Registration Index
			146	Academicians Index
			147	National Reform Experiment
			148	National Innovative Model City Index
			149	Information · Knowledge Industry City Index
			150	National Key Laboratory · Engineering Research Center Index
	Urban Influence	Urban and Rural Integration	151	Urban-rural Income Ratio Index
			152	Primary School Education Level Population Ratio
			153	Illiteracy Rate
			154	Balanced Development of Compulsory Education Index
		Wide-area Hub	155	Airport Convenient
			156	Air Traffic Volume Index
			157	Container Port Convenient
			158	Port Container Throughput
			159	Water Transport Volume Index
			160	Railway Convenient
			161	Railway Traffic Volume Index
			162	Railway Density
			163	Road Traffic Volume Index
			164	Expressway Density
			165	National Road · Provincial Road Density
			166	Circulation City Index
		Core Influence	167	Higher Education Radiation
			168	Science and Technology Radiation
			169	IT Industry Radiation
			170	Culture and Sports and Entertainment Radiation
			171	Financial Radiation
			172	Manufacturing Radiation
			173	Medical Radiation
			174	Wholesale and Retail Radiation
			175	Catering and Hotel Radiation

Chapter II
China Integrated City Index 2017 Ranking Top 150 Cities

1. Comprehensive Ranking

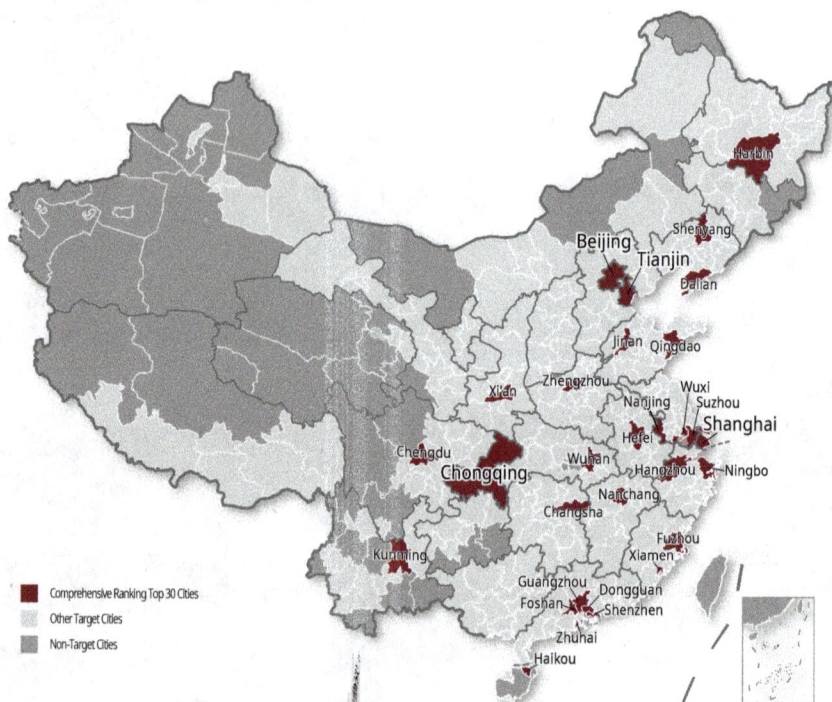

Figure 2-1 Comprehensive Ranking Top 30 Cities

The Comprehensive Ranking: Beijing, Shanghai, and Shenzhen Respectively Winning the 1st, 2nd, and 3rd Places Again

In addition, Beijing, Shanghai, and Shenzhen each won the 1st place in the social, economic, and environmental rankings, again.

Specifically, within the social dimension, Beijing ranked first in the country with her prevailing advantages in all the three sub-dimension indicators of quality of life, inheritance, and exchange, as well as status and governance. Shanghai won the national 1st place in two sub-dimension indicators (i.e., quality of economic development and urban influence) within the economic dimension and in one sub-dimension indicator (i.e., spatial structure) within the environmental dimension. Shenzhen was ranked relatively even across the environmental, economic, and social dimensions, taking the 1st, 3rd, and 7th places respectively. From the rankings of different indicators, however, it is also observed Beijing and Shanghai still have many problems within the environmental dimension to be solved in a timely manner.

Figure 2-2 Comprehensive Ranking 1-30

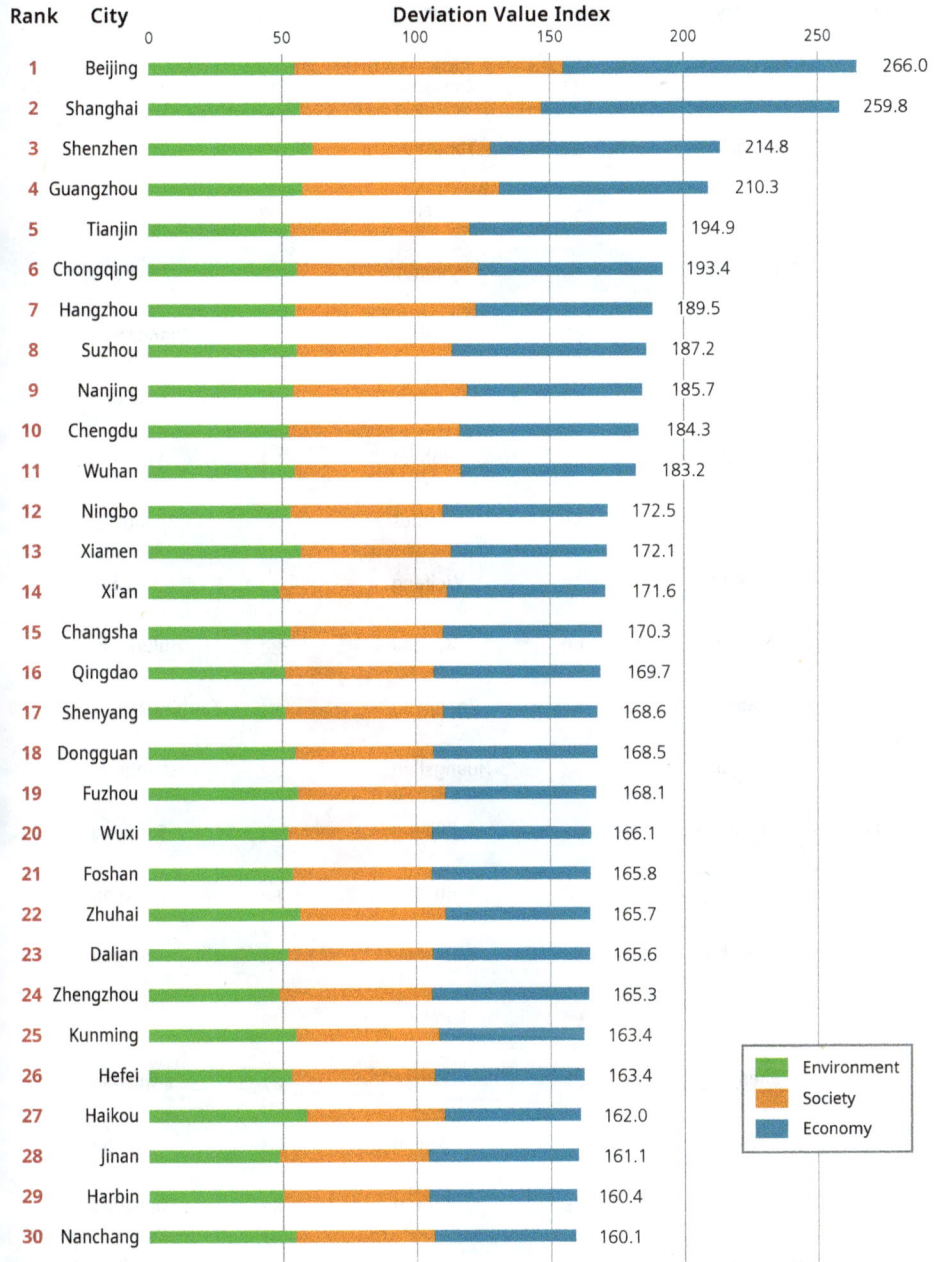

Rank	City	Deviation Value Index
1	Beijing	266.0
2	Shanghai	259.8
3	Shenzhen	214.8
4	Guangzhou	210.3
5	Tianjin	194.9
6	Chongqing	193.4
7	Hangzhou	189.5
8	Suzhou	187.2
9	Nanjing	185.7
10	Chengdu	184.3
11	Wuhan	183.2
12	Ningbo	172.5
13	Xiamen	172.1
14	Xi'an	171.6
15	Changsha	170.3
16	Qingdao	169.7
17	Shenyang	168.6
18	Dongguan	168.5
19	Fuzhou	168.1
20	Wuxi	166.1
21	Foshan	165.8
22	Zhuhai	165.7
23	Dalian	165.6
24	Zhengzhou	165.3
25	Kunming	163.4
26	Hefei	163.4
27	Haikou	162.0
28	Jinan	161.1
29	Harbin	160.4
30	Nanchang	160.1

Legend:
- Environment
- Society
- Economy

Figure 2-3 Comprehensive Ranking 31-90

Rank	City	Rank	City	Rank	City
31	Sanya	51	Zhoushan	71	Yencheng
32	Changchun	52	Yangzhou	72	Longyan
33	Zhongshan	53	Weihai	73	Nanping
34	Changzhou	54	Shantou	74	Yichang
35	Guiyang	55	Lanzhou	75	Zhangzhou
36	Nanning	56	Jiangmen	76	Yinchuan
37	Quanzhou	57	Hohhot	77	Yueyang
38	Wenzhou	58	Ordos	78	Zhaoqing
39	Yantai	59	Weifang	79	Zibo
40	Nantong	60	Xuzhou	80	Hulunbuir
41	Shaoxing	61	Zhanjiang	81	Taizhou (Jiangsu)
42	Taiyuan	62	Huangshan	82	Shangrao
43	Lhasa	63	Jiujiang	83	Sanming
44	Shijiazhuang	64	Huzhou	84	Zhuzhou
45	Huizhou	65	Tangshan	85	Ningde
46	Jiaxing	66	Luoyang	86	Jining
47	Zhenjiang	67	Putian	87	Quzhou
48	Jinhua	68	Guilin	88	Lishui
49	Urumqi	69	Baotou	89	Ganzhou
50	Taizhou (Zhejiang)	70	Wuhu	90	Huai'an

Figure 2-4 Comprehensive Ranking 91-150

Rank	City	Rank	City	Rank	City
91	Chenzhou	111	Meizhou	131	Pingxiang
92	Yangjiang	112	Changde	132	Qinhuangdao
93	Jilin	113	Tai'an	133	Baoding
94	Maoming	114	Panzhihua	134	Fangchenggang
95	Jingdezhen	115	Pu'er	135	Linyi
96	Heihe	116	Ji'an	136	Xinyu
97	Lijiang	117	Ma'anshan	137	Mudanjiang
98	Xiangtan	118	Dandong	138	Ezhou
99	Zunyi	119	Karamay	139	Nanyang
100	Beihai	120	Qingyuan	140	Yiyang
101	Shanwei	121	Dongying	141	Heyuan
102	Yuxi	122	Yingtan	142	Qiqihar
103	Liuzhou	123	Hengyang	143	Huangshi
104	Jieyang	124	Anqing	144	Keifeng
105	Lianyungang	125	Yichun (Jiangxi)	145	Yulin (Guangxi)
106	Xining	126	Shaoguan	146	Xianyang
107	Tongling	127	Bijie	147	Huainan
108	Anshan	128	Mianyang	148	Shiyan
109	Chaozhou	129	Leshan	149	Anshun
110	Xiangyang	130	Daqing	150	Fushun

2. Environmental Ranking

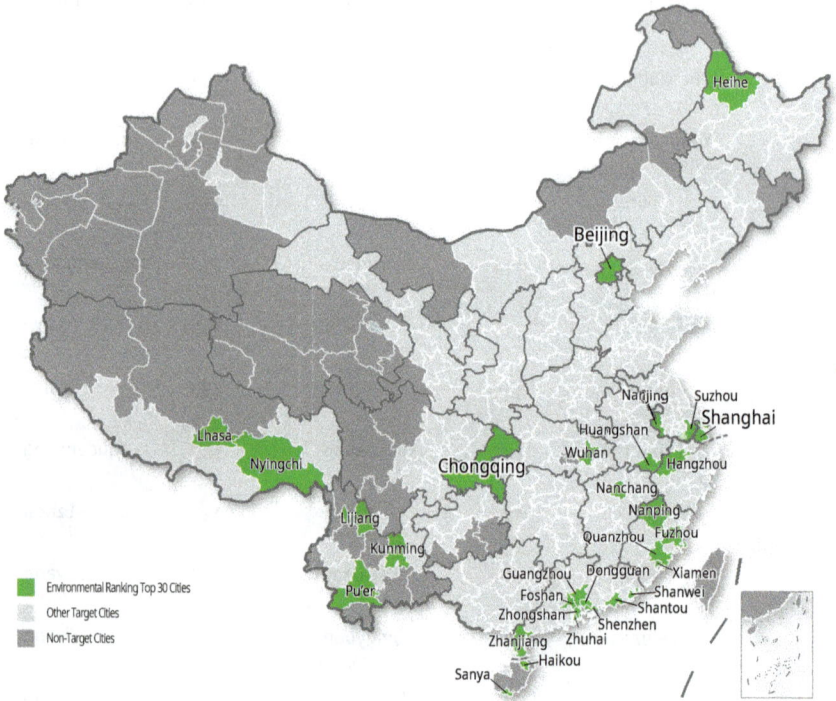

Figure 2-5 Environmental Ranking Top 30 Cities

Shenzhen Continued to Be the Champion in the Environmental Ranking while Sanya and Haikou Ranked 2nd and 3rd Respectively

Shenzhen's success in the environmental ranking mainly relied on her high standards of urbanization, con-venient urban transportation, high population density, and compact spatial structure. As an emerging coastal megacity, Shenzhen has achieved a relatively balanced development in environmental, social, and economic dimensions.

From 2nd to 10th in the environmental ranking are respectively Sanya, Haikou, Guangzhou, Shanghai, Xiamen, Zhuhai, Fuzhou, Chongqing and Suzhou.

Among the top 10 cities in the environmental dimension, Chongqing and Suzhou are located along the Yangtze River, and the other eight cities sit on the coastline. Coastal and riverside cities have not only achieved a rapid economic development in the era of big exchanges and big transactions but have enjoyed natural advantages in ecological resources. These cities, pioneering in China's opening to the outside world, have also excelled in spatial structure and environmental quality.

Figure 2-6 Environmental Ranking 1-30

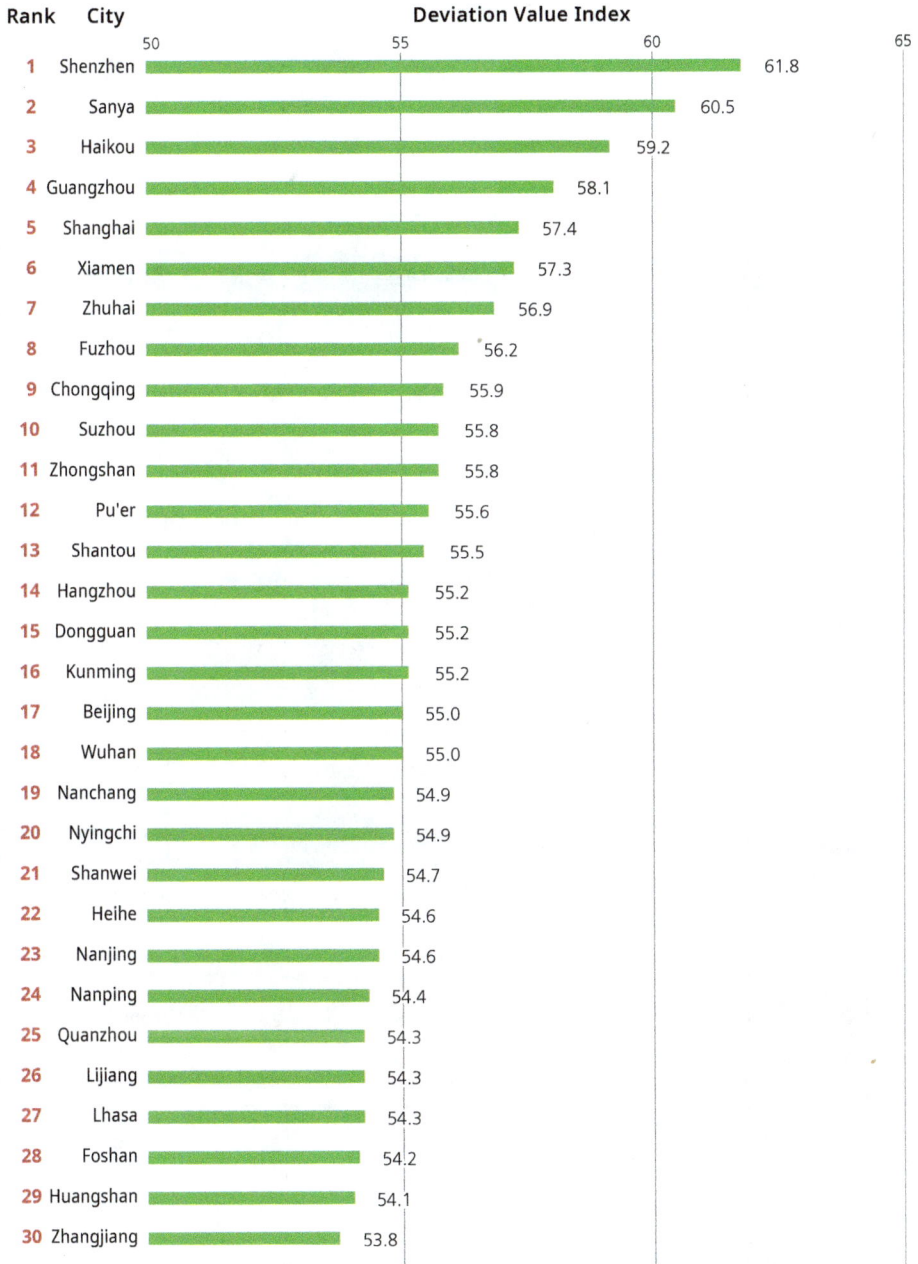

Rank	City	Deviation Value Index
1	Shenzhen	61.8
2	Sanya	60.5
3	Haikou	59.2
4	Guangzhou	58.1
5	Shanghai	57.4
6	Xiamen	57.3
7	Zhuhai	56.9
8	Fuzhou	56.2
9	Chongqing	55.9
10	Suzhou	55.8
11	Zhongshan	55.8
12	Pu'er	55.6
13	Shantou	55.5
14	Hangzhou	55.2
15	Dongguan	55.2
16	Kunming	55.2
17	Beijing	55.0
18	Wuhan	55.0
19	Nanchang	54.9
20	Nyingchi	54.9
21	Shanwei	54.7
22	Heihe	54.6
23	Nanjing	54.6
24	Nanping	54.4
25	Quanzhou	54.3
26	Lijiang	54.3
27	Lhasa	54.3
28	Foshan	54.2
29	Huangshan	54.1
30	Zhangjiang	53.8

Figure 2-7 Environmental Ranking 31-90

Rank	City	Rank	City	Rank	City
31	Zhoushan	51	Bijie	71	Yueyang
32	Putian	52	Lincang	72	Chamdo
33	Hefei	53	Taizhou (Zhejiang)	73	Guilin
34	Ningbo	54	Maoming	74	Tongren
35	Ningde	55	Wuxi	75	Zhenjiang
36	Wenzhou	56	Zhangzhou	76	Shenyang
37	Yuxi	57	Dalian	77	Qingdao
38	Tianjin	58	Chaozhou	78	Changzhou
39	Changsha	59	Jiangmen	79	Anshun
40	Nanning	60	Jieyang	80	Qujing
41	Baoshan	61	Jingdezhen	81	Yingtan
42	Longyan	62	Yichun (Heilongjiang)	82	Wuhu
43	Huizhou	63	Beihai	83	Yangzhou
44	Yangjiang	64	Ganzhou	84	Yulin (Guangxi)
45	Shangrao	65	Ordos	85	Ji'an
46	Guiyang	66	Chenzhou	86	Zhaoqing
47	Chengdu	67	Meizhou	87	Qingyuan
48	Hulunbuir	68	Fangchenggang	88	Bazhong
49	Jiujiang	69	Lishui	89	Shaoxing
50	Sanming	70	Heyuan	90	Weihai

Figure 2-8 Environmental Ranking 91-150

Rank	City	Rank	City	Rank	City
91	Daqing	111	Karamay	131	Baoji
92	Ma'anshan	112	Rizhao	132	Jiaozuo
93	Leshan	113	Puyang	133	Changzhi
94	Nanyang	114	Yiyang	134	Xiaogan
95	Guilin	115	Xingtai	135	ZaoZhuang
96	Binzhou	116	Ganzhou	136	Wuhai
97	Qinhuangdao	117	Changde	137	Qingyuan
98	Zhanjiang	118	Quzhou	138	Hulunbuir
99	Liuzhou	119	Suqian	139	Sanming
100	Jiujiang	120	Xuchang	140	Shuozhou
101	Songyuan	121	Deyang	141	Weinan
102	Hengyang	122	Lhasa	142	Chenzhou
103	Yueyang	123	Huainan	143	Datong
104	Jilin	124	Pingxiang	144	Mudanjiang
105	Mianyang	125	Xinxiang	145	Ningde
106	Yingkou	126	Bengbu	146	Longyan
107	Anshan	127	Jieyang	147	Jinzhou
108	Yulin	128	Yichun (Jiangxi)	148	Jinzhong
109	Liaocheng	129	Heze	149	Lishui
110	Xining	130	Zunyi	150	Shangrao

3. Social Ranking

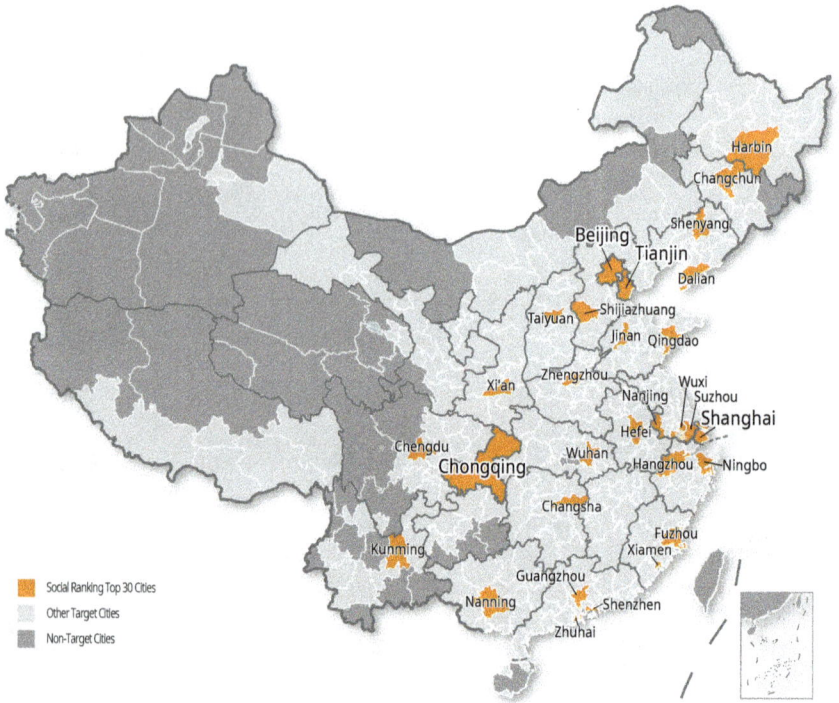

Figure 2-9 Social Ranking Top 30 Cities

Beijing Continued to Be the Champion in the Social Ranking, with Shanghai and Guangzhou in 2nd and 3rd Places

As the capital of China, Beijing has unparalleled advantages in the social dimension. Shanghai ranked 2nd for each of the three sub-dimension indicators, namely, quality of life, inheritance and exchange, as well as status and governance. In addition to the 3rd place in quality of life, Guangzhou ranked 4th for other two sub-dimension indicators.

Chongqing, Hangzhou, Tianjin, Shenzhen, Nanjing, Chengdu, and Xi'an ranked from 4th to 10th respectively within the social dimension.

The top 10 cities within the social dimension are predominately municipalities directly under the Central Government, capital cities of provinces, and cities specifically designated in the state plan. Except for Shenzhen, which is a new city emerging as a special economic zone under the reform and opening-up policy, all other nine cities have a long history, wherein Beijing, Hangzhou, Nanjing and Xi'an were capitals of ancient empires.

Figure 2-10 Social Ranking 1-30

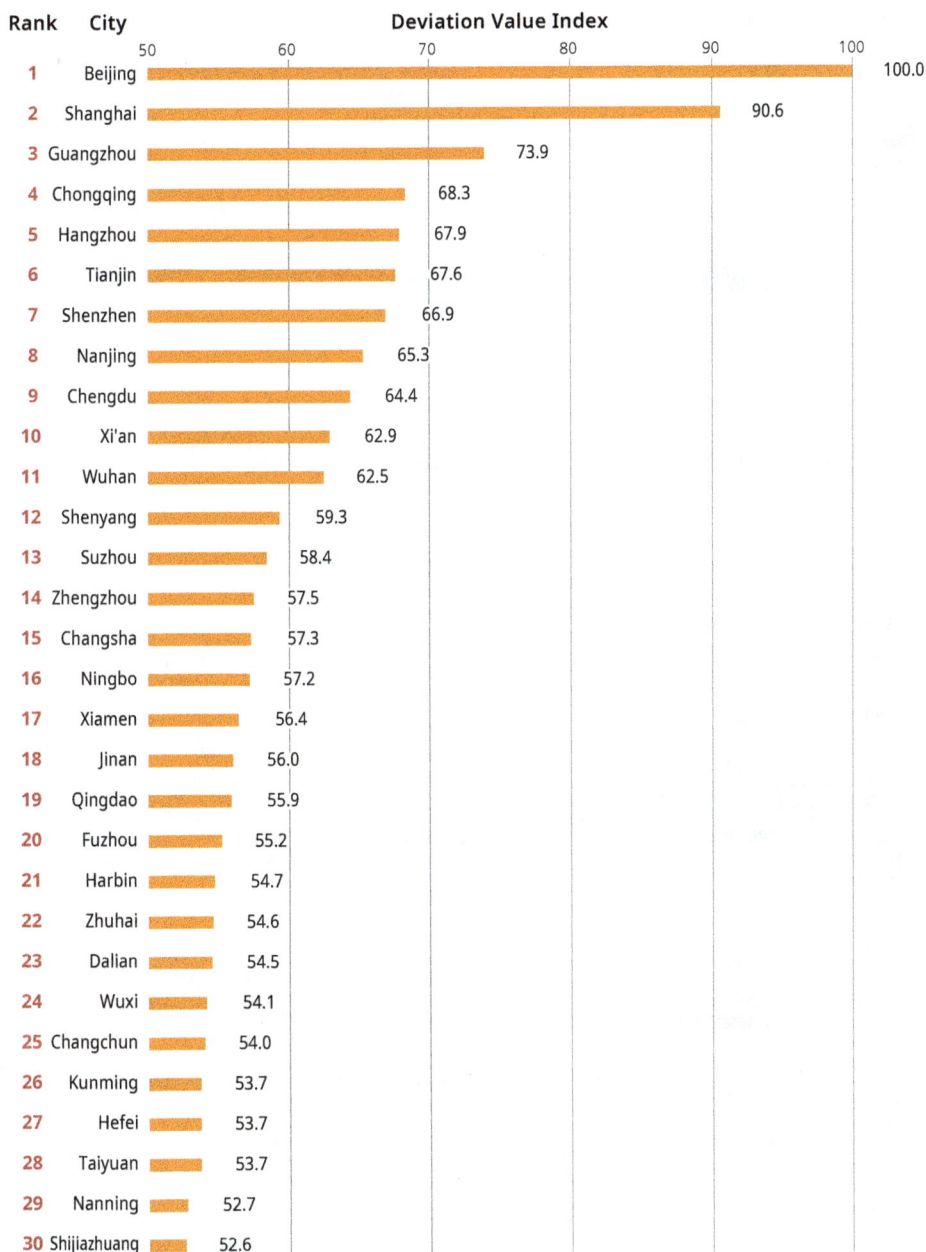

Rank	City	Deviation Value Index
1	Beijing	100.0
2	Shanghai	90.6
3	Guangzhou	73.9
4	Chongqing	68.3
5	Hangzhou	67.9
6	Tianjin	67.6
7	Shenzhen	66.9
8	Nanjing	65.3
9	Chengdu	64.4
10	Xi'an	62.9
11	Wuhan	62.5
12	Shenyang	59.3
13	Suzhou	58.4
14	Zhengzhou	57.5
15	Changsha	57.3
16	Ningbo	57.2
17	Xiamen	56.4
18	Jinan	56.0
19	Qingdao	55.9
20	Fuzhou	55.2
21	Harbin	54.7
22	Zhuhai	54.6
23	Dalian	54.5
24	Wuxi	54.1
25	Changchun	54.0
26	Kunming	53.7
27	Hefei	53.7
28	Taiyuan	53.7
29	Nanning	52.7
30	Shijiazhuang	52.6

Figure 2-11 Social Ranking 31-90

Rank	City	Rank	City	Rank	City
31	Foshan	51	Weifang	71	Quzhou
32	Nanchang	52	Xining	72	Huangshan
33	Dongguan	53	Weihai	73	Tai'an
34	Haikou	54	Quanzhou	74	Jilin
35	Urumqi	55	Yangzhou	75	Ordos
36	Guiyang	56	Huzhou	76	Jiujiang
37	Lhasa	57	Zhenjiang	77	Anshan
38	Huhhot	58	Huizhou	78	Qinhuangdao
39	Yantai	59	Taizhou (Zhejiang)	79	Longyan
40	Lanzhou	60	Jiangmen	80	Taizhou (Jiangsu)
41	Changzhou	61	Zibo	81	Dongying
42	Luoyang	62	Tangshan	82	Linyi
43	Wenzhou	63	Jining	83	Wuhu
44	Jinhua	64	Zhoushan	84	Xiangyang
45	Jiaxing	65	Yichang	85	Baoji
46	Zhongshan	66	Baotou	86	Jiayuguan
47	Sanya	67	Xuzhou	87	Zhaoqing
48	Shaoxing	68	Guilin	88	Zhuzhou
49	Yinchuan	69	Baoding	89	Lishui
50	Nantong	70	Yencheng	90	Zhanjiang

Figure 2-12 Social Ranking 91-150

Rank	City	Rank	City	Rank	City
91	Daqing	111	Nanping	131	Benxi
92	Liuzhou	112	Qiqihar	132	Dandong
93	Kaifeng	113	Shangrao	133	Hengyang
94	Shantou	114	Panzhihua	134	Jincheng
95	Yueyang	115	Hulunbuir	135	Anqing
96	Huai'an	116	ZaoZhuang	136	Rizhao
97	Xianyang	117	Chenzhou	137	Ganzhou
98	Karamay	118	Sanming	138	Changde
99	Mianyang	119	Handan	139	Yan'an
100	Jingdezhen	120	Langfang	140	Lianyungang
101	Xiangtan	121	Panjin	141	Leshan
102	Jinzhong	122	Mudanjiang	142	Luzhou
103	Xinyu	123	Dezhou	143	Anyang
104	Ma'anshan	124	Jiaozuo	144	Xian'ning
105	Weinan	125	Cangzhou	145	Shaoguan
106	Chengde	126	Yingkou	146	Liaocheng
107	Changzhi	127	Nanyang	147	Jingzhou
108	Fushun	128	Beihai	148	Datong
109	Zunyi	129	Jingmen	149	Xinxiang
110	Shiyan	130	Huangshi	150	Yangjiang

4. Economic Ranking

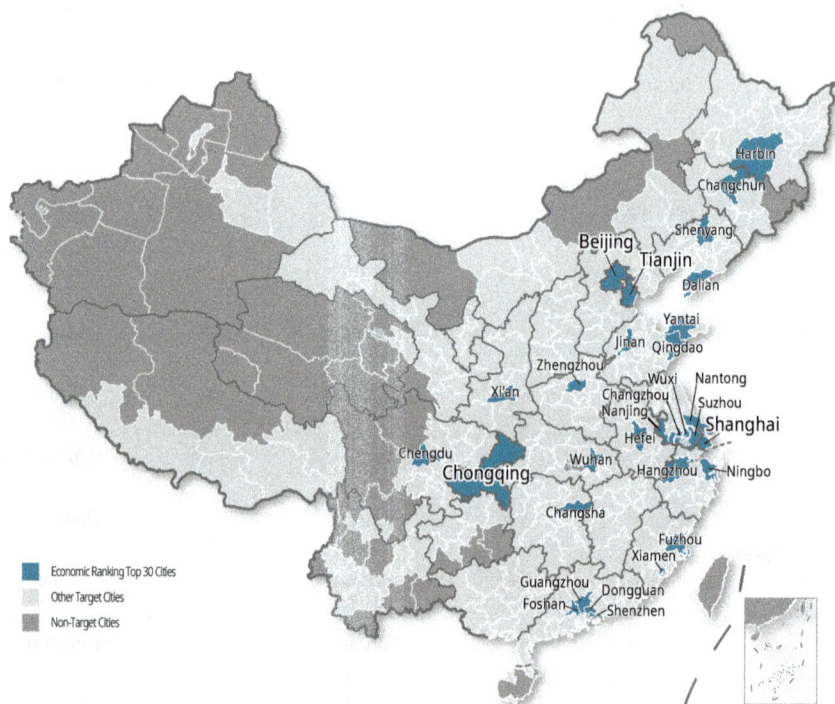

Figure 2-13 Economic Ranking Top 30 Cities

Shanghai, Beijing, and Shenzhen Continued to Hold Their Places as Top Three in the Economic Ranking

As the leader in the development of the Yangtze River Delta Megalopolis and the Yangtze River Economic Zone, Shanghai continued to be the champion in the economic ranking. Although Beijing slightly lagged behind Shanghai in terms of quality of economic development and urban influence, she ranked 1st in dynamic development nationwide. Shenzhen, which ranked 3rd within the economic dimension, also ranked 3rd for all three sub-dimension indicators, namely, quality of economic development, dynamic development, and urban influence.

Guangzhou, Tianjin, Suzhou, Chongqing, Chengdu, Hangzhou and Nanjing ranked from 4th to 10th within the economic dimension, respectively.

Figure 2-14 Economic Ranking 1-30

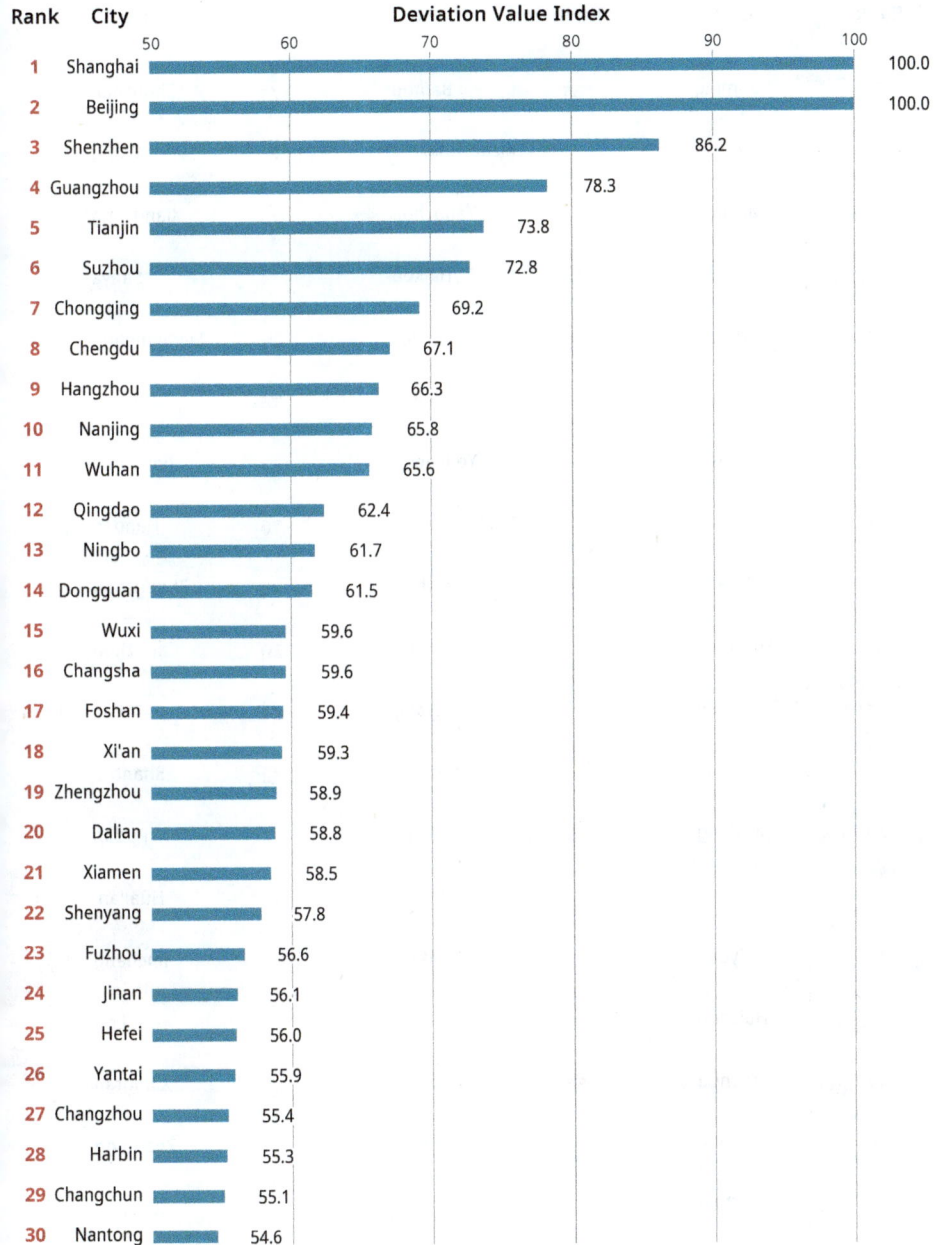

Rank	City	Deviation Value Index
1	Shanghai	100.0
2	Beijing	100.0
3	Shenzhen	86.2
4	Guangzhou	78.3
5	Tianjin	73.8
6	Suzhou	72.8
7	Chongqing	69.2
8	Chengdu	67.1
9	Hangzhou	66.3
10	Nanjing	65.8
11	Wuhan	65.6
12	Qingdao	62.4
13	Ningbo	61.7
14	Dongguan	61.5
15	Wuxi	59.6
16	Changsha	59.6
17	Foshan	59.4
18	Xi'an	59.3
19	Zhengzhou	58.9
20	Dalian	58.8
21	Xiamen	58.5
22	Shenyang	57.8
23	Fuzhou	56.6
24	Jinan	56.1
25	Hefei	56.0
26	Yantai	55.9
27	Changzhou	55.4
28	Harbin	55.3
29	Changchun	55.1
30	Nantong	54.6

Figure 2-15 Economic Ranking 31-90

Rank	City	Rank	City	Rank	City
31	Kunming	51	Baotou	71	Zhoushan
32	Zhuhai	52	Taizhou (Zhejiang)	72	Wuhu
33	Quanzhou	53	Yangzhou	73	Xiangyang
34	Shaoxing	54	Haikou	74	Sanya
35	Zhongshan	55	Ordos	75	Lianyungang
36	Jiaxing	56	Weihai	76	Zhuzhou
37	Guiyang	57	Yencheng	77	Jiangmen
38	Wenzhou	58	Taizhou (Jiangsu)	78	Handan
39	Shijiazhuang	59	Lanzhou	79	Zhangzhou
40	Nanchang	60	Langfang	80	Cangzhou
41	Tangshan	61	Xianyang	81	Tai'an
42	Urumqi	62	Dongying	82	Shantou
43	Weifang	63	Linyi	83	Putian
44	Zhenjiang	64	Yichang	84	Huai'an
45	Taiyuan	65	Baoding	85	Jincheng
46	Huizhou	66	Hohhot	86	Tongling
47	Xuzhou	67	Huzhou	87	Xiangtan
48	Jinhua	68	Jining	88	Zhaoqing
49	Zibo	69	Luoyang	89	Dezhou
50	Nanning	70	Yinchuan	90	Liaoyang

Figure 2-16 Economic Ranking 91-150

Rank	City	Rank	City	Rank	City
91	Daqing	111	Karamay	131	Baoji
92	Ma'anshan	112	Rizhao	132	Jiaozuo
93	Leshan	113	Puyang	133	Changzhi
94	Nanyang	114	Yiyang	134	Xiaogan
95	Guilin	115	Xingtai	135	ZaoZhuang
96	Binzhou	116	Ganzhou	136	Wuhai
97	Qinhuangdao	117	Changde	137	Qingyuan
98	Zhanjiang	118	Quzhou	138	Hulunbuir
99	Liuzhou	119	Suqian	139	Sanming
100	Jiujiang	120	Xuchang	140	Shuozhou
101	Songyuan	121	Deyang	141	Weinan
102	Hengyang	122	Lhasa	142	Chenzhou
103	Yueyang	123	Huainan	143	Datong
104	Jilin	124	Pingxiang	144	Mudanjiang
105	Mianyang	125	Xinxiang	145	Ningde
106	Yingkou	126	Bengbu	146	Longyan
107	Anshan	127	Jieyang	147	Jinzhou
108	Yulin	128	Yichun (Jiangxi)	148	Jinzhong
109	Liaocheng	129	Heze	149	Lishui
110	Xining	130	Zunyi	150	Shangrao

Chapter III

Analysis of Top 10 Cities in the Comprehensive Ranking of China Integrated City Index 2017

1st Beijing

Beijing defended her championship in the comprehensive ranking of 2017.

As the capital city, Beijing has far outperformed other cities in social dimension and ranks first in the country. As the political and cultural center, a historic city and an international metropolis, Beijing's traditional culture and modern society enhance the other's brilliance, promoting diversity and inclusivity. Her international influence on urban living and consumption standards is unique among cities. and thus Beijing ranked 1st nationwide for all the three sub-dimension indicators: quality of life, inheritance and exchange, as well as status and governance.

Within the economic dimension, Beijing's performance remained the same as in 2016, ranking No. 2 and slightly behind Shanghai. Since the founding of the People's Republic of China, Beijing has managed to turn from a heavy industry developer to a modern international metropolis, showing tremendous development vitality for transformation and innovation. Therefore, in terms of three sub-dimension indicators of the economic dimension, Beijing had the best dynamic development, ranking 1st in this respect and 2nd in both quality of economic development and urban influence.

Compared to 2016, Beijing's ranking within the environmental dimension improved by taking the 17th place. Specifically, among the three sub-dimension indicators, Beijing had the best spatial structure and ranked 3rd, which mainly attributes to the large population in her densely inhabited districts (DID), highly dense transportation networks, and investment in urban facilities. However, due to water shortage, air pollution, and serious traffic congestion, among other issues, her performance for other two sub-dimension indicators (i.e., natural ecology and environmental quality) was not satisfactory, ranking 237th and 48th respectively.

Table 3-1 Key Index

Environment

Number of permanent residents:	21,710,000
Land area of administrative region:	16,411 km²
Ranking of available land area per capita:	278
Ranking of forest coverage:	78
Ranking of water resources per capita:	276
Ranking of climate comfort index:	272
Ranking of PM$_{2.5}$ Index:	265
Ranking of densely inhabited district (DID) population :	2
Ranking of rail transit route mileage :	1

Society

Ranking of average house prices :	1
Ranking of cinemas and theater numbers :	1
Ranking of museum and art gallery numbers :	1
Number of domestic tourists:	268,590,000
Number of inbound tourists:	4,200,000
Ranking of world heritage number :	1
Ranking of international conference number :	2

Economy

Size of GDP:	RMB 2301.5 billion
Per-capita GDP:	RMB 106,034 / person
GDP growth rate:	7.3 %
Ranking of per capita revenue in :	4
Ranking of average salaries :	1
Ranking of mainboard listed enterprises :	2
Ranking of goods export in China:	9
Ranking of airport convenience in China:	2
Ranking of container port convenience :	62
Ranking of financial radiation :	2
Ranking of manufacturing radiation :	19
Ranking of IT industry radiation :	1
Ranking of higher education radiation :	1
Ranking of science and technology radiation :	1
Ranking of medical radiation :	1
Ranking of culture and sports and entertainment radiation :	1
Ranking of catering and hotel radiation :	2
Ranking of wholesale and retail radiation :	2

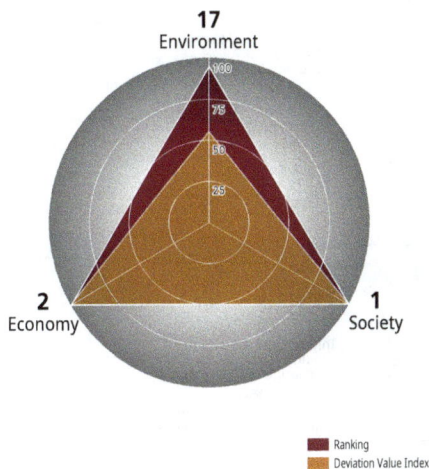

Figure 3-1 Scores of Dimension

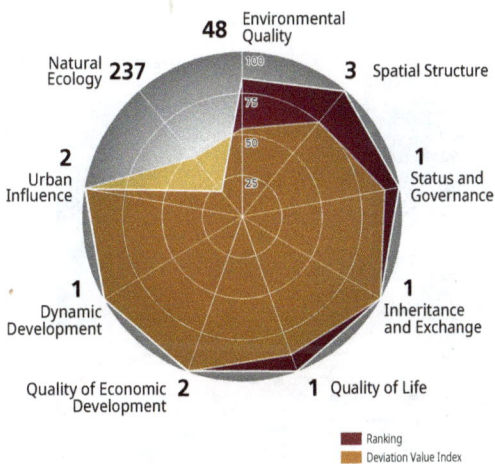

Figure 3-2 Scores of Sub-Dimension

Beijing

Dimension	Sub-Dimension	Indicator Group	Deviation Value Index
Environment	Natural Ecology	Soil and Water Condition	49.3
		Climate Condition	40.1
		Natural Disaster	48.7
	Environmental Quality	Pollution Load	47.6
		Environmental Protection Efforts	76.1
		Resource Efficiency	61.3
	Spatial Structure	Compact City	77.8
		Transportation Network	72.9
		Urban Facilities	75.8
Society	Status and Governance	City Status	97.0
		Quality of Residents	95.3
		Social Management	73.7
	Inheritance and Exchange	Historical Relics	100.0
		Culture & Entertainment	100.0
		Exchange	100.0
	Quality of Life	Residential Environment	65.4
		Level of Consumption	94.1
		Life Service	100.0
Economy	Quality of Economic Development	Economic Aggregate	100.0
		Economic Structure	99.9
		Economic Efficiency	64.5
	Dynamic Development	Business Environment	100.0
		Openness	100.0
		Innovation and Entrepreneurship	100.0
	Urban Influence	Urban and Rural Integration	75.8
		Wide-area Hub	86.4
		Core Influence	100.0

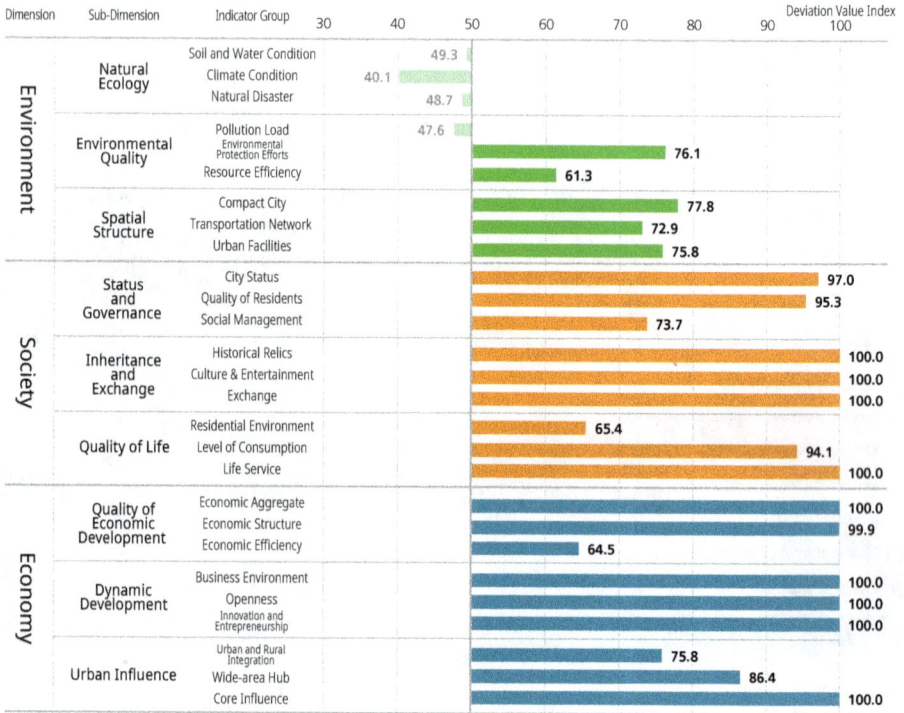

Figure 3-3 Deviation Value of Indicator Group

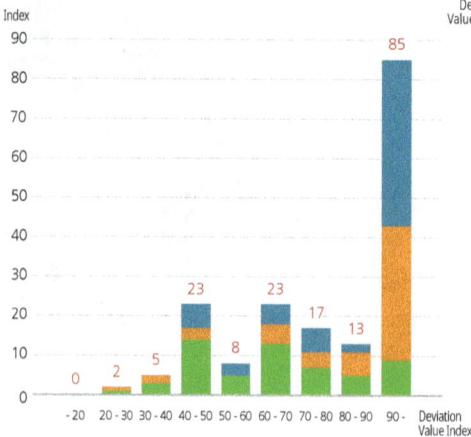

Figure 3-4 Deviation Value Distribution of Indicators

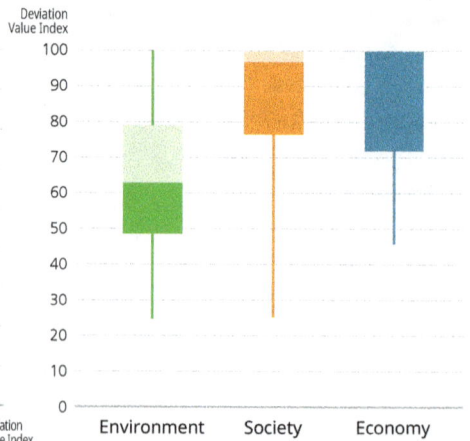

Figure 3-5 Box Plot Distribution of Indicators

46

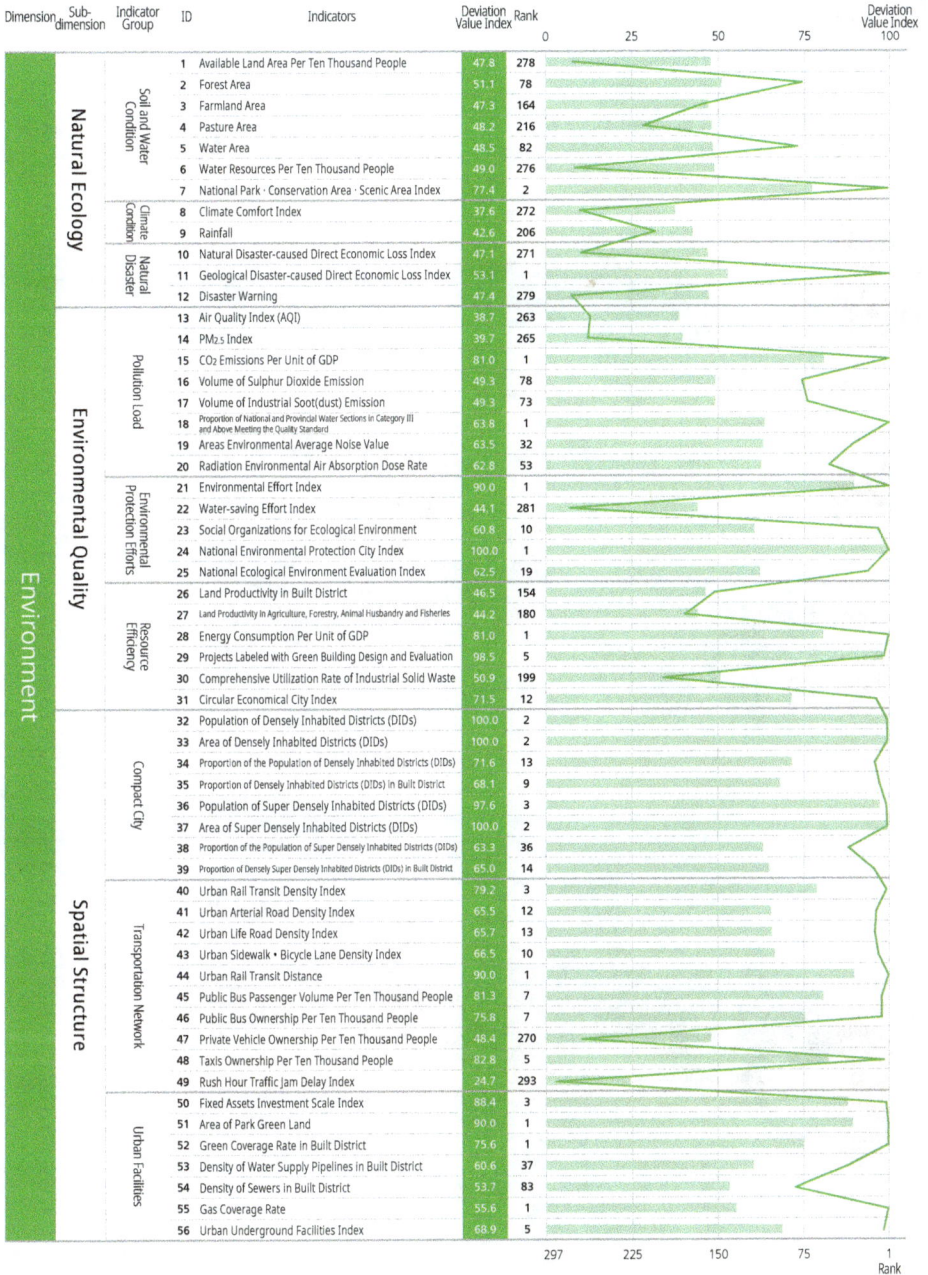

Dimension	Sub-dimension	Indicator Group	ID	Indicators	Deviation Value Index	Rank
Environment	Natural Ecology	Soil and Water Condition	1	Available Land Area Per Ten Thousand People	47.8	278
			2	Forest Area	51.1	78
			3	Farmland Area	47.3	164
			4	Pasture Area	48.2	216
			5	Water Area	48.5	82
			6	Water Resources Per Ten Thousand People	49.0	276
			7	National Park · Conservation Area · Scenic Area Index	77.4	2
		Climate Condition	8	Climate Comfort Index	37.6	272
			9	Rainfall	42.6	206
		Natural Disaster	10	Natural Disaster-caused Direct Economic Loss Index	47.1	271
			11	Geological Disaster-caused Direct Economic Loss Index	53.1	1
			12	Disaster Warning	47.4	279
	Environmental Quality	Pollution Load	13	Air Quality Index (AQI)	38.7	263
			14	PM2.5 Index	39.7	265
			15	CO₂ Emissions Per Unit of GDP	81.0	1
			16	Volume of Sulphur Dioxide Emission	49.3	78
			17	Volume of Industrial Soot(dust) Emission	49.3	73
			18	Proportion of National and Provincial Water Sections in Category III and Above Meeting the Quality Standard	63.8	1
			19	Areas Environmental Average Noise Value	63.5	32
			20	Radiation Environmental Air Absorption Dose Rate	62.8	53
		Environmental Protection Efforts	21	Environmental Effort Index	90.0	1
			22	Water-saving Effort Index	44.1	281
			23	Social Organizations for Ecological Environment	60.8	10
			24	National Environmental Protection City Index	100.0	1
			25	National Ecological Environment Evaluation Index	62.5	19
		Resource Efficiency	26	Land Productivity in Built District	46.5	154
			27	Land Productivity in Agriculture, Forestry, Animal Husbandry and Fisheries	44.2	180
			28	Energy Consumption Per Unit of GDP	81.0	1
			29	Projects Labeled with Green Building Design and Evaluation	98.5	5
			30	Comprehensive Utilization Rate of Industrial Solid Waste	50.9	199
			31	Circular Economical City Index	71.5	12
	Spatial Structure	Compact City	32	Population of Densely Inhabited Districts (DIDs)	100.0	2
			33	Area of Densely Inhabited Districts (DIDs)	100.0	2
			34	Proportion of the Population of Densely Inhabited Districts (DIDs)	71.6	13
			35	Proportion of Densely Inhabited Districts (DIDs) in Built District	68.1	9
			36	Population of Super Densely Inhabited Districts (DIDs)	97.6	3
			37	Area of Super Densely Inhabited Districts (DIDs)	100.0	2
			38	Proportion of the Population of Super Densely Inhabited Districts (DIDs)	63.3	36
			39	Proportion of Densely Super Densely Inhabited Districts (DIDs) in Built District	65.0	14
		Transportation Network	40	Urban Rail Transit Density Index	79.2	3
			41	Urban Arterial Road Density Index	65.5	12
			42	Urban Life Road Density Index	65.7	13
			43	Urban Sidewalk · Bicycle Lane Density Index	66.5	10
			44	Urban Rail Transit Distance	90.0	1
			45	Public Bus Passenger Volume Per Ten Thousand People	81.3	7
			46	Public Bus Ownership Per Ten Thousand People	75.8	7
			47	Private Vehicle Ownership Per Ten Thousand People	48.4	270
			48	Taxis Ownership Per Ten Thousand People	82.8	5
			49	Rush Hour Traffic Jam Delay Index	24.7	293
		Urban Facilities	50	Fixed Assets Investment Scale Index	88.4	3
			51	Area of Park Green Land	90.0	1
			52	Green Coverage Rate in Built District	75.6	1
			53	Density of Water Supply Pipelines in Built District	60.6	37
			54	Density of Sewers in Built District	53.7	83
			55	Gas Coverage Rate	55.6	1
			56	Urban Underground Facilities Index	68.9	5

Figure 3-6 Index Ranking: Environment

Beijing

Dimension	Sub-dimension	Indicator Group	ID	Indicators	Deviation Value Index	Rank	Chart
Society	Status and Governance	City Status	57	Administrative Levels	85.5	1	
			58	Megalopolis Levels	68.8	1	
			59	Core City Levels	74.6	1	
			60	Embassies · Consulates	100.0	1	
			61	International Organizations	100.0	1	
			62	Belt and Road Index	92.2	1	
		Quality of Residents	63	Population Natural Growth Rate Index	47.6	169	
			64	Population Social Growth Rate Index	100.0	2	
			65	Population Structure Index	60.2	9	
			66	Population Education Structure Index	85.2	1	
			67	Higher Education Index	92.1	4	
			68	Outstanding Talent Cultivation Index	100.0	1	
			69	Public Finance Expenditure for Education Index	100.0	1	
		Social Management	70	Social Services Index	70.4	5	
			71	Safe and Reliable City Index	90.3	2	
			72	Traffic Safety Index	41.9	294	
			73	Social Security Index	33.9	293	
			74	Social Organizations	87.0	5	
			75	Health and Civilized City Index	100.0	1	
			76	Government Website Performance	68.5	1	
	Inheritance and Exchange	Historical Relics	77	Historical Status	100.0	1	
			78	World Heritage	100.0	1	
			79	Famous Historical and Cultural Cities	61.7	7	
			80	Intangible Cultural Heritage	100.0	1	
			81	Key Cultural Relics Sites Under the Protection	100.0	1	
		Culture and Entertainment	82	Theater Consumer Index	100.0	1	
			83	Museums · Art Galleries	100.0	1	
			84	Sports Venues Index	100.0	1	
			85	Zoos · Botanical Gardens · Aquariums	94.2	1	
			86	Public Library Collection	100.0	2	
			87	Cultural Master Index	100.0	1	
			88	Olympic Champion Index	100.0	1	
			89	National Culturally Advanced Unit Index	100.0	1	
		Personal Exchange	90	Inbound Tourists	84.3	4	
			91	Domestic Tourists	100.0	3	
			92	Foreign Exchange Earnings from International Tourism	100.0	4	
			93	Earnings from Domestic Tourism	100.0	1	
			94	International Conferences	100.0	2	
			95	Exhibition Industry Development Index	100.0	3	
			96	World Tourism City Index	96.9	2	
	Quality of Life	Residential Environment	97	Average Life Expectancy	69.5	2	
			98	Medicare · Endowment Insurance Coverage Index	85.4	3	
			99	Ratio of Average House Prices to Income	25.3	290	
			100	Habitat City Index	46.9	36	
			101	China's Happiness City Index	87.1	6	
		Level of Consumption	102	Retail Sales of Consumer Goods Per Ten Thousand People	75.8	8	
			103	Revenue of Hotels and Catering Services Per Ten Thousand People	96.7	3	
			104	Telecom Consumption Per Ten Thousand People	100.0	1	
			105	Water Consumption for Residential Use Per Ten Thousand People	66.6	18	
			106	Top International Brand Index	100.0	1	
		Life Service	107	Number of Children in Kindergartens Per Ten Thousand People	37.5	266	
			108	Year-end Number of Beds in Nursing Homes	100.0	1	
			109	Number of Practicing (Assistant) Physicians	100.0	1	
			110	Number of Beds in Health Institutions	95.6	4	
			111	First-class Hospitals	100.0	1	

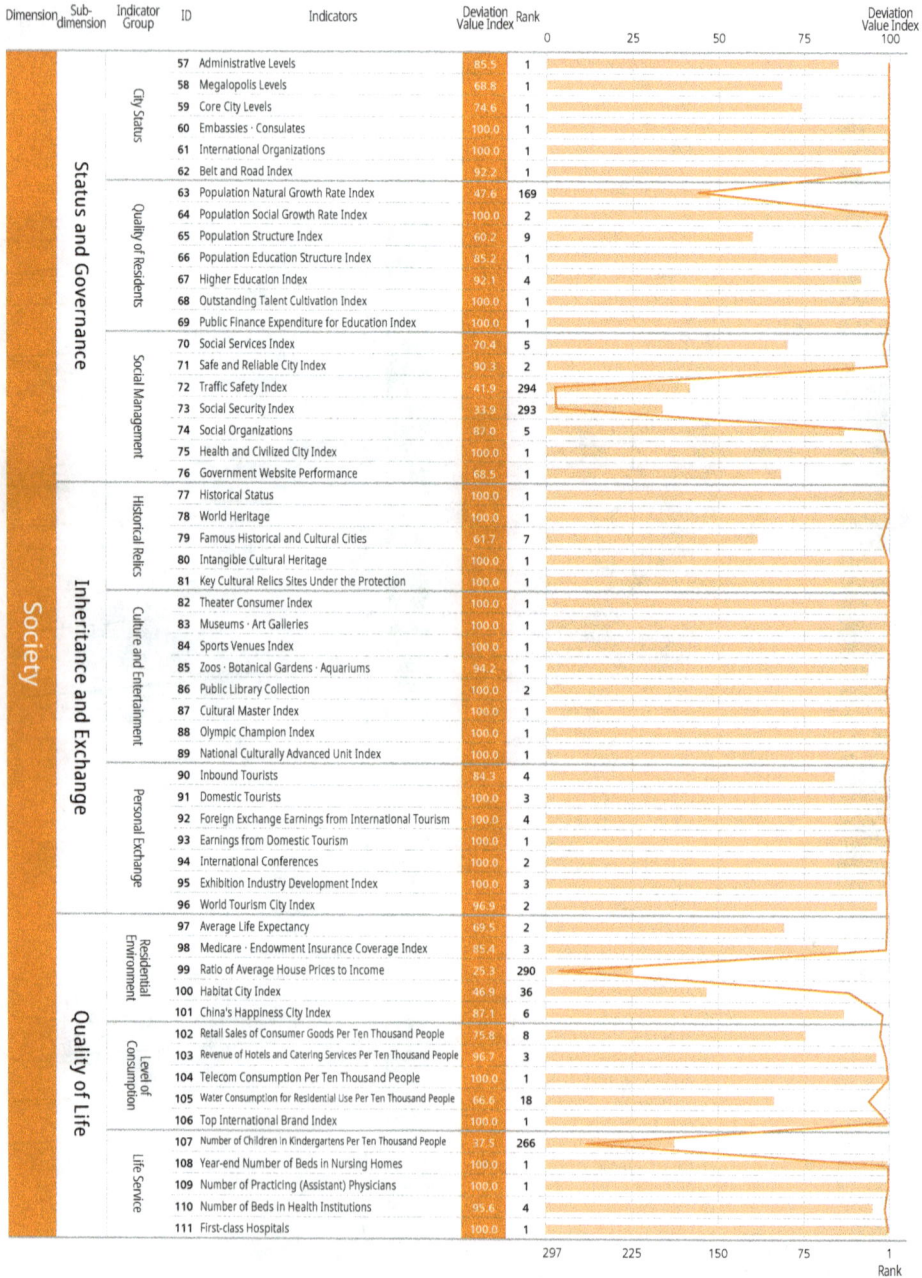

Figure 3-7 Index Ranking: Society

Dimension	Sub-dimension	Indicator Group	ID	Indicators	Deviation Value Index	Rank
Economy / Quality of Economic Development	Quality of Economic Development	Economic Scale	112	Size of GDP	100.0	2
			113	Population Size of Permanent Residents	100.0	3
			114	Scale of Tax Collection	100.0	2
			115	Electricity Consumption	100.0	2
		Economic Structure	116	Industrial Structure Index	100.0	2
			117	Mainboard Listed Enterprises	100.0	2
			118	Top 500 Chinese Enterprises in the World	100.0	1
			119	China's Top 500 Enterprises	100.0	1
			120	China's Top 500 Private-owned Enterprises	63.7	18
			121	Gross Industrial Output Value Above Designated Size	78.4	8
		Economic Efficiency	122	GDP Growth Index	53.2	135
			123	GDP Per Ten Thousand People	68.9	19
			124	Fiscal Revenue Per Ten Thousand People	95.0	4
			125	Dependent Population Index	72.5	5
			126	Size and Debt Rate of Bonds Issued by the City Investment Enterprises	46.5	194
			127	Number of Registered Unemployed Persons Per Ten Thousand People	50.9	113
	Dynamic Development	Business Environment	128	Employee Average Salary	99.1	1
			129	Number of Employees of Enterprise Services	100.0	1
			130	Star Hotel Index	100.0	2
			131	Top International Restaurant Index	100.0	3
			132	National Industrial Park Index	50.1	56
		Openness	133	Population Migration	100.0	2
			134	Export of Goods · Import of Goods	100.0	3
			135	Foreign Investment Utilized	98.7	3
			136	Outward Foreign Direct Investment	100.0	2
			137	The Output Value of Foreign-invested Enterprises Above Designated Size	80.7	5
			138	International Schools	100.0	2
			139	Free Trade Area Index	55.0	32
		Innovation and Entrepreneurship	140	The World's Top University Index	100.0	1
			141	R&D Expenditure Index	100.0	1
			142	R&D Human Resources	100.0	1
			143	GEM,New Third Board Listed Enterprise Index	100.0	1
			144	The Amount of Patent Authorization Index	100.0	1
			145	Trademark Registration Index	100.0	1
			146	Academicians Index	100.0	1
			147	National Reform Experiment	70.3	12
			148	National Innovative Model City Index	73.6	12
			149	Information · Knowledge Industry City Index	100.0	1
			150	National Key Laboratory · Engineering Research Center Index	100.0	1
	Urban Influence	Urban and Rural Integration	151	Urban-rural Income Ratio Index	63.9	16
			152	Primary School Education Level Population Ratio	100.0	2
			153	Illiteracy Rate	58.9	34
			154	Balanced Development of Compulsory Education Index	100.0	1
		Wide-area Hub	155	Airport Convenient	100.0	2
			156	Air Traffic Volume Index	100.0	2
			157	Container Port Convenient	49.7	62
			158	Port Container Throughput	48.0	24
			159	Water Transport Volume Index	46.0	201
			160	Railway Convenient	95.2	4
			161	Railway Traffic Volume Index	100.0	3
			162	Railway Density	74.8	13
			163	Road Traffic Volume Index	99.3	4
			164	Expressway Density	64.8	20
			165	National Road · Provincial Road Density	70.2	17
			166	Circulation City Index	82.3	5
		Core Influence	167	Higher Education Radiation	100.0	1
			168	Science and Technology Radiation	100.0	1
			169	IT Industry Radiation	100.0	1
			170	Culture and Sports and Entertainment Radiation	100.0	1
			171	Financial Radiation	100.0	1
			172	Manufacturing Radiation	61.0	19
			173	Medical Radiation	100.0	1
			174	Wholesale and Retail Radiation	100.0	2
			175	Catering and Hotel Radiation	100.0	2

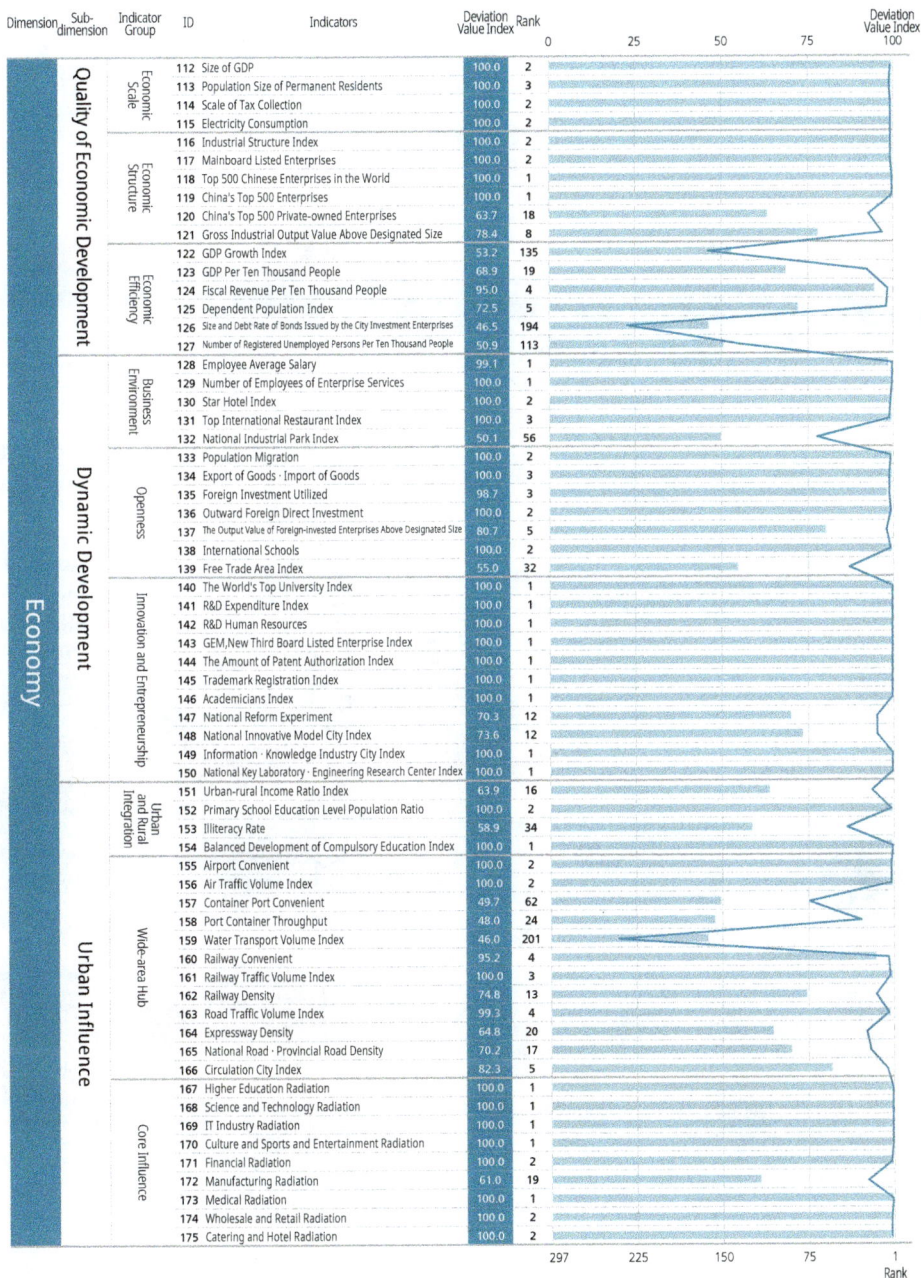

Figure 3-8 Index Ranking: Economy

Beijing

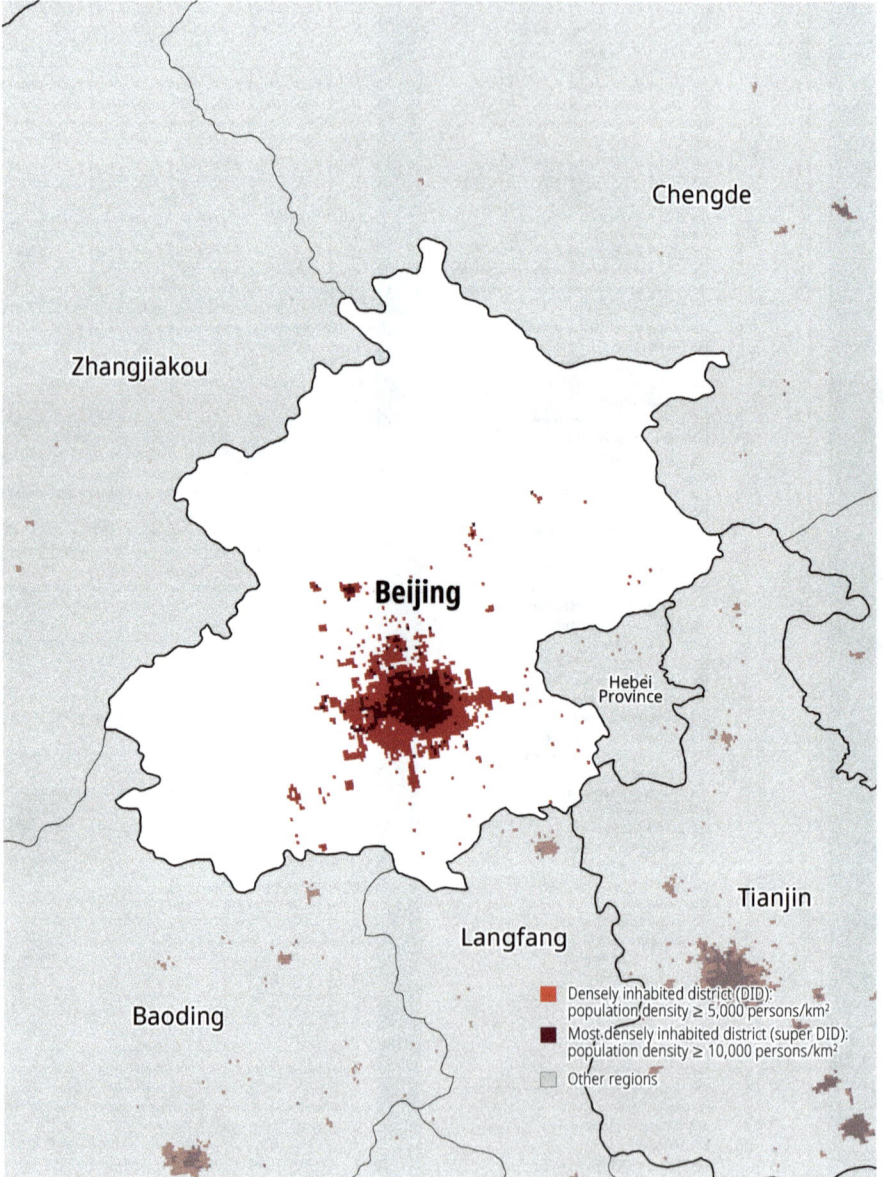

Figure 3-9 DID Analysis

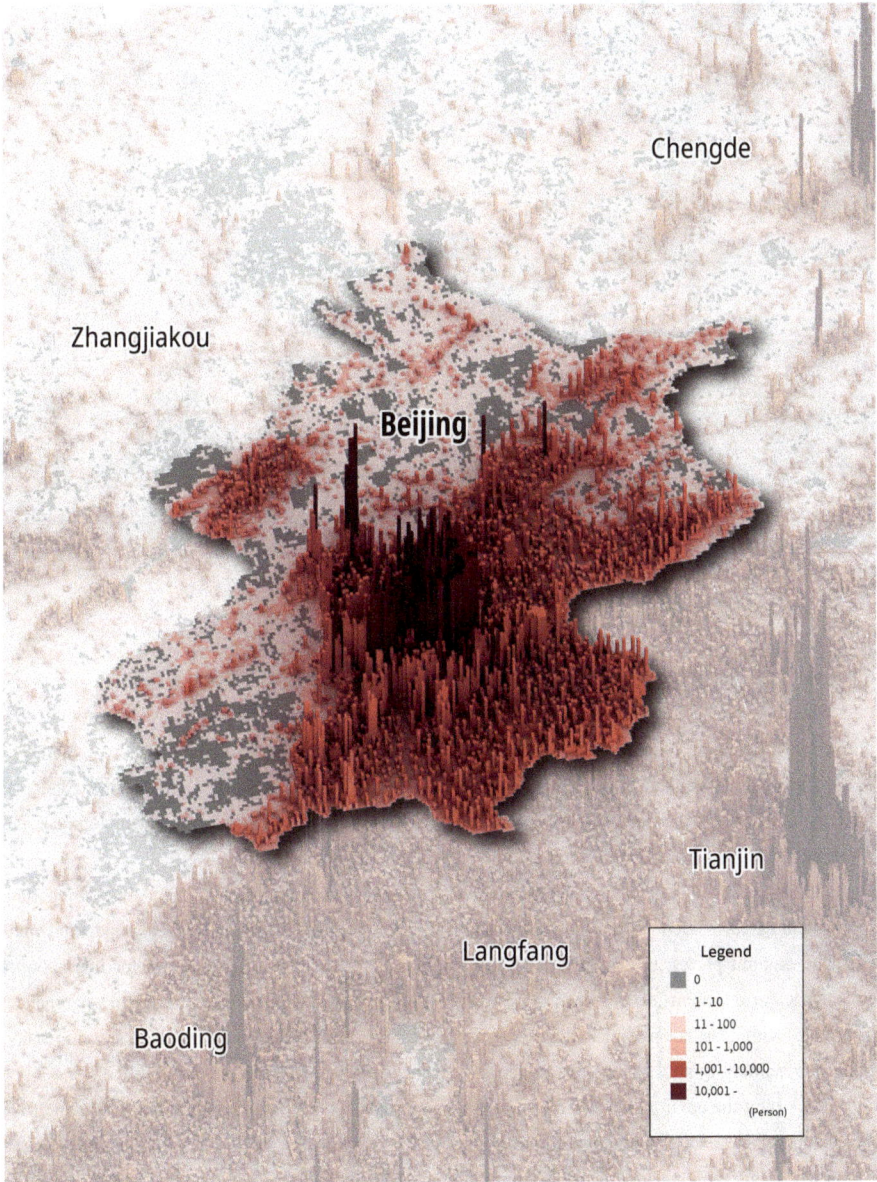

Figure 3-10 Population Size and Density Analysis

2nd Shanghai

Shanghai has won the 2nd place in the comprehensive ranking for two years in a row.

Shanghai managed to defend her championship within the economic dimension. As the national economic center, shipping center, and a radiant point of foreign interest into China (and vice versa), Shanghai is the leader of the Yangtze River Delta Megalopolis and the Yangtze River Economic Zone. Shanghai ranked 1st for two of the three sub-dimension indicators, namely, quality of economic development and urban influence. Her dynamic development ranked 2nd, slightly behind Beijing.

Within the social dimension, Shanghai ranked No. 2, which is the same as in 2016. As a cosmopolitan city with the greatest modern look in China, Shanghai is not only outstanding in terms of residential environment, cultural places, life services, and consumption standards, but a big platform for international exchanges. An excellent job has been done with respect to quality of residents and urban governance. Therefore, within the social dimension, Shanghai has won the 2nd place for all the three sub-dimension indicators, namely, quality of life, inheritance and exchange, as well as status and governance.

Regarding the environmental dimension, Shanghai remained the same ranking of No. 6 as in 2016. Thanks to her large DID population and dense networks for intra-city transportation, Shanghai was the most outstanding city by taking the first place for the sub-dimension indicator of spatial structure, but she also had many problems that require urgent attention in natural ecology and environmental quality, ranking 117th and 52nd respectively.

Table 3-2 Key Index

Environment

Number of permanent residents:	24,150,000
Land area of administrative region:	6,341 km²
Ranking of available land area per capita:	293
Ranking of forest coverage:	250
Ranking of water resources per capita:	258
Ranking of climate comfort index:	29
Ranking of PM$_{2.5}$ Index:	148
Ranking of densely inhabited district (DID) population :	1
Ranking of rail transit route mileage :	2

Society

Ranking of average house prices :	3
Ranking of cinemas and theater numbers :	5
Ranking of museum and art gallery numbers :	2
Number of domestic tourists:	275,690,000
Number of inbound tourists:	8,000,000
Ranking of world heritage number :	64
Ranking of international conference number :	1

Economy

Size of GDP:	RMB 2512.3 billion
Per-capita GDP:	RMB 104,019 / person
GDP growth rate:	6.2 %
Ranking of per capita revenue in :	2
Ranking of average salaries :	2
Ranking of mainboard listed enterprises :	1
Ranking of goods export in China:	2
Ranking of airport convenience in China:	1
Ranking of container port convenience :	1
Ranking of financial radiation :	1
Ranking of manufacturing radiation :	3
Ranking of IT industry radiation :	2
Ranking of higher education radiation :	2
Ranking of science and technology radiation :	2
Ranking of medical radiation :	2
Ranking of culture and sports and entertainment radiation :	2
Ranking of catering and hotel radiation :	1
Ranking of wholesale and retail radiation :	1

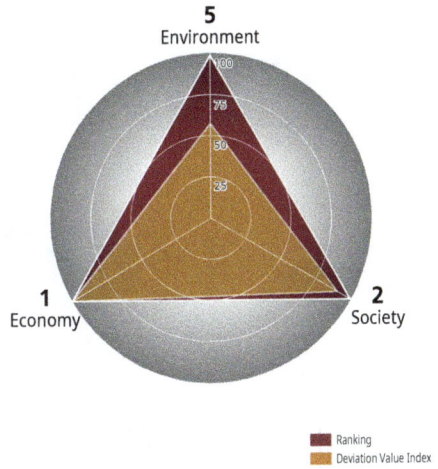

Figure 3-11 Scores of Dimension

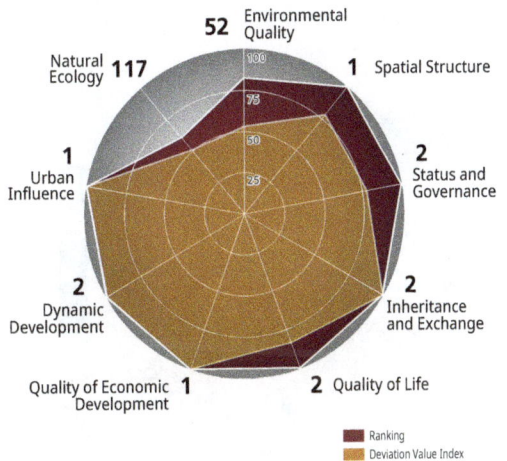

Figure 3-12 Scores of Sub-Dimension

Shanghai

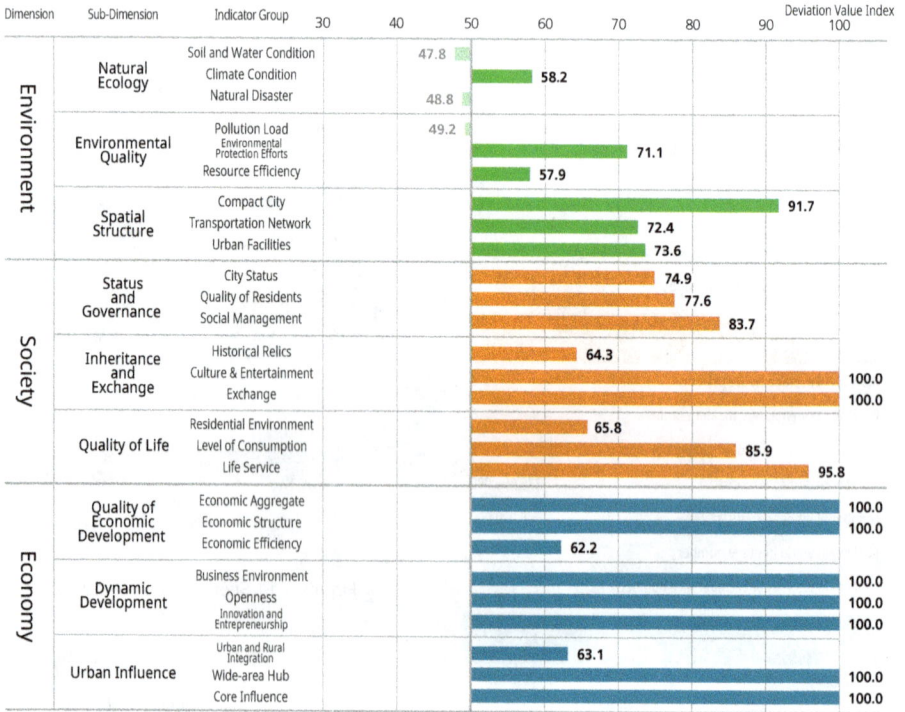

Dimension	Sub-Dimension	Indicator Group	Deviation Value Index
Environment	Natural Ecology	Soil and Water Condition	47.8
		Climate Condition	58.2
		Natural Disaster	48.8
	Environmental Quality	Pollution Load	49.2
		Environmental Protection Efforts	71.1
		Resource Efficiency	57.9
	Spatial Structure	Compact City	91.7
		Transportation Network	72.4
		Urban Facilities	73.6
Society	Status and Governance	City Status	74.9
		Quality of Residents	77.6
		Social Management	83.7
	Inheritance and Exchange	Historical Relics	64.3
		Culture & Entertainment	100.0
		Exchange	100.0
	Quality of Life	Residential Environment	65.8
		Level of Consumption	85.9
		Life Service	95.8
Economy	Quality of Economic Development	Economic Aggregate	100.0
		Economic Structure	100.0
		Economic Efficiency	62.2
	Dynamic Development	Business Environment	100.0
		Openness	100.0
		Innovation and Entrepreneurship	100.0
	Urban Influence	Urban and Rural Integration	63.1
		Wide-area Hub	100.0
		Core Influence	100.0

Figure 3-13 Deviation Value of Indicator Group

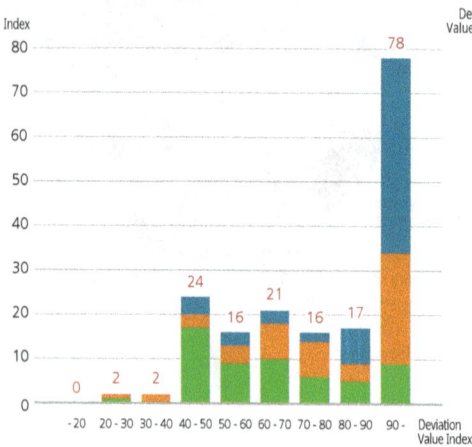

Figure 3-14 Deviation Value Distribution of Indicators

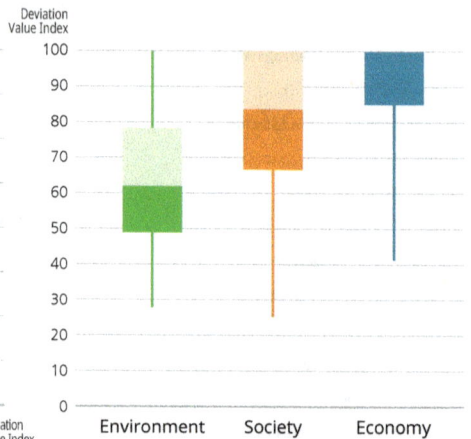

Figure 3-15 Box Plot Distribution of Indicators

Dimension	Sub-dimension	Indicator Group	ID	Indicators	Deviation Value Index	Rank	Chart
Environment	Natural Ecology	Soil and Water Condition	1	Available Land Area Per Ten Thousand People	47.6	293	
			2	Forest Area	44.7	250	
			3	Farmland Area	46.2	177	
			4	Pasture Area	48.3	83	
			5	Water Area	49.1	73	
			6	Water Resources Per Ten Thousand People	49.0	258	
			7	National Park · Conservation Area · Scenic Area Index	62.5	13	
		Climate Condition	8	Climate Comfort Index	61.9	29	
			9	Rainfall	54.5	95	
		Natural Disaster	10	Natural Disaster-caused Direct Economic Loss Index	47.3	100	
			11	Geological Disaster-caused Direct Economic Loss Index	53.1	1	
			12	Disaster Warning	47.5	263	
	Environmental Quality	Pollution Load	13	Air Quality Index (AQI)	49.5	124	
			14	PM2.5 Index	48.0	148	
			15	CO2 Emissions Per Unit of GDP	66.0	25	
			16	Volume of Sulphur Dioxide Emission	48.1	269	
			17	Volume of Industrial Soot(dust) Emission	45.4	280	
			18	Proportion of National and Provincial Water Sections in Category III and Above Meeting the Quality Standard	44.1	209	
			19	Areas Environmental Average Noise Value	41.3	279	
			20	Radiation Environmental Air Absorption Dose Rate	62.2	57	
		Environmental Protection Efforts	21	Environmental Effort Index	86.9	4	
			22	Water-saving Effort Index	54.3	50	
			23	Social Organizations for Ecological Environment	57.1	16	
			24	National Environmental Protection City Index	82.2	5	
			25	National Ecological Environment Evaluation Index	59.2	33	
		Resource Efficiency	26	Land Productivity in Built District	47.1	139	
			27	Land Productivity in Agriculture, Forestry, Animal Husbandry and Fisheries	51.8	99	
			28	Energy Consumption Per Unit of GDP	66.0	25	
			29	Projects Labeled with Green Building Design and Evaluation	100.0	1	
			30	Comprehensive Utilization Rate of Industrial Solid Waste	56.2	91	
			31	Circular Economical City Index	44.6	98	
	Spatial Structure	Compact City	32	Population of Densely Inhabited Districts (DIDs)	100.0	1	
			33	Area of Densely Inhabited Districts (DIDs)	100.0	1	
			34	Proportion of the Population of Densely Inhabited Districts (DIDs)	78.6	3	
			35	Proportion of Densely Inhabited Districts (DIDs) in Built District	100.0	1	
			36	Population of Super Densely Inhabited Districts (DIDs)	100.0	1	
			37	Area of Super Densely Inhabited Districts (DIDs)	100.0	1	
			38	Proportion of the Population of Super Densely Inhabited Districts (DIDs)	71.5	15	
			39	Proportion of Densely Super Densely Inhabited Districts (DIDs) in Built District	100.0	2	
		Transportation Network	40	Urban Rail Transit Density Index	80.1	1	
			41	Urban Arterial Road Density Index	70.7	2	
			42	Urban Life Road Density Index	70.8	2	
			43	Urban Sidewalk • Bicycle Lane Density Index	71.4	2	
			44	Urban Rail Transit Distance	90.0	2	
			45	Public Bus Passenger Volume Per Ten Thousand People	63.6	31	
			46	Public Bus Ownership Per Ten Thousand People	62.9	31	
			47	Private Vehicle Ownership Per Ten Thousand People	49.2	147	
			48	Taxis Ownership Per Ten Thousand People	67.9	20	
			49	Rush Hour Traffic Jam Delay Index	27.8	285	
		Urban Facilities	50	Fixed Assets Investment Scale Index	80.1	6	
			51	Area of Park Green Land	82.0	1	
			52	Green Coverage Rate in Built District	50.2	196	
			53	Density of Water Supply Pipelines in Built District	85.1	4	
			54	Density of Sewers in Built District	65.9	21	
			55	Gas Coverage Rate	55.6	1	
			56	Urban Underground Facilities Index	68.9	5	

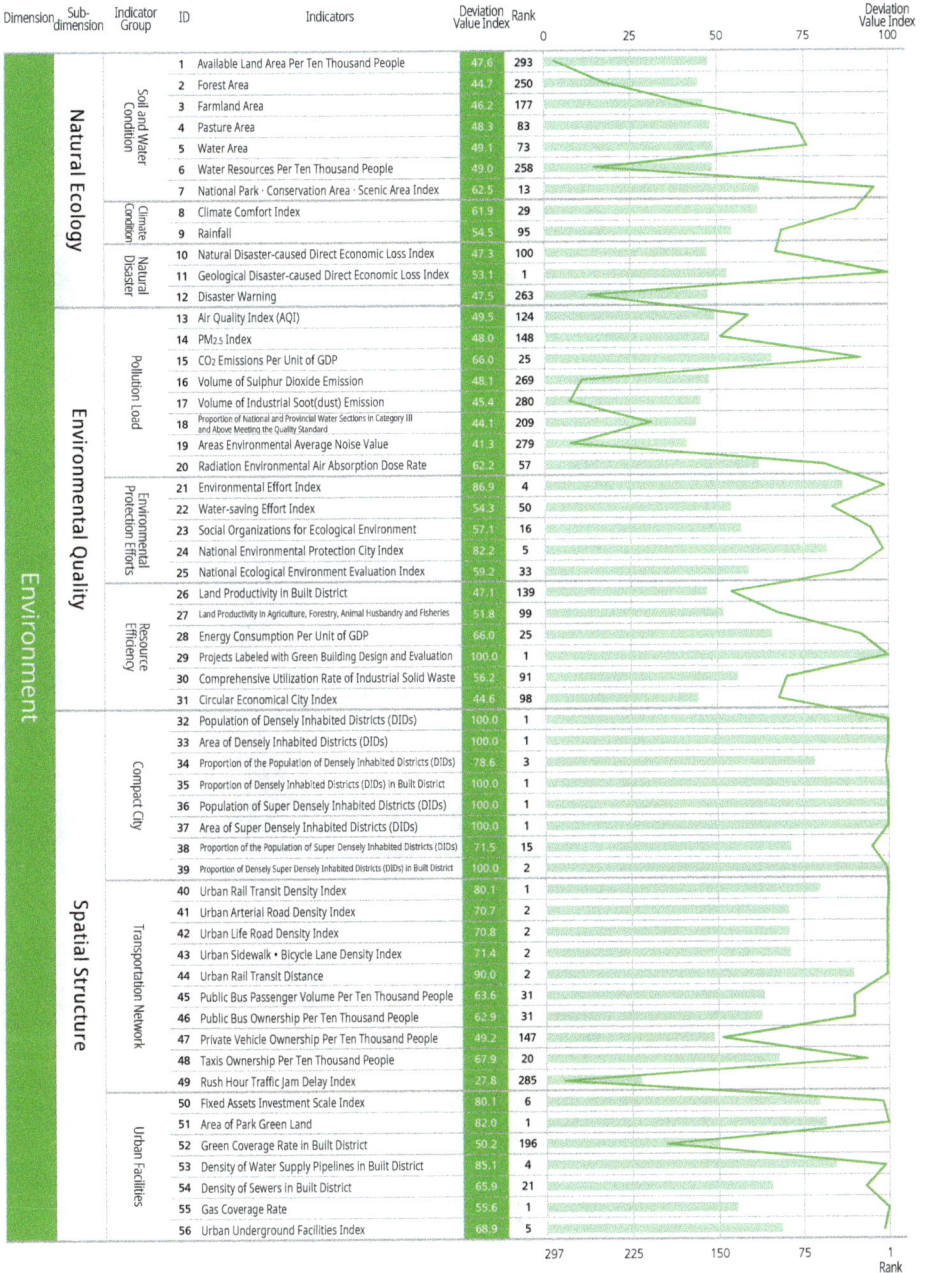

Figure 3-16 Index Ranking: Environment

Shanghai

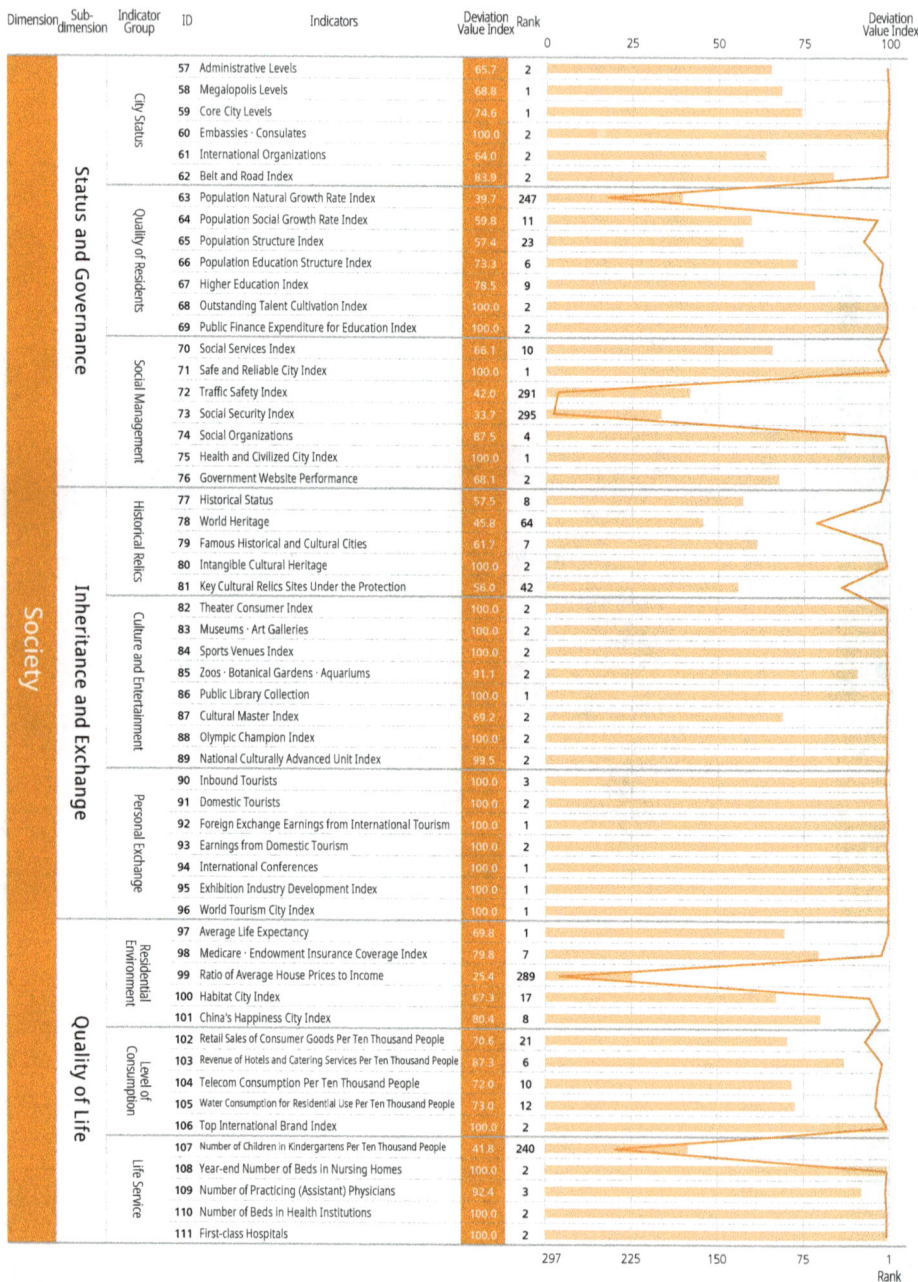

Dimension	Sub-dimension	Indicator Group	ID	Indicators	Deviation Value Index	Rank
Society	Status and Governance	City Status	57	Administrative Levels	65.7	2
			58	Megalopolis Levels	68.8	1
			59	Core City Levels	74.6	1
			60	Embassies · Consulates	100.0	2
			61	International Organizations	64.0	2
			62	Belt and Road Index	83.9	2
		Quality of Residents	63	Population Natural Growth Rate Index	39.7	247
			64	Population Social Growth Rate Index	59.8	11
			65	Population Structure Index	57.4	23
			66	Population Education Structure Index	73.3	6
			67	Higher Education Index	78.5	9
			68	Outstanding Talent Cultivation Index	100.0	2
			69	Public Finance Expenditure for Education Index	100.0	2
		Social Management	70	Social Services Index	66.1	10
			71	Safe and Reliable City Index	100.0	1
			72	Traffic Safety Index	42.0	291
			73	Social Security Index	33.7	295
			74	Social Organizations	87.5	4
			75	Health and Civilized City Index	100.0	1
			76	Government Website Performance	68.1	2
	Inheritance and Exchange	Historical Relics	77	Historical Status	57.5	8
			78	World Heritage	45.8	64
			79	Famous Historical and Cultural Cities	61.7	7
			80	Intangible Cultural Heritage	100.0	2
			81	Key Cultural Relics Sites Under the Protection	56.0	42
		Culture and Entertainment	82	Theater Consumer Index	100.0	2
			83	Museums · Art Galleries	100.0	2
			84	Sports Venues Index	100.0	2
			85	Zoos · Botanical Gardens · Aquariums	91.1	2
			86	Public Library Collection	100.0	1
			87	Cultural Master Index	69.2	2
			88	Olympic Champion Index	100.0	2
			89	National Culturally Advanced Unit Index	99.5	2
		Personal Exchange	90	Inbound Tourists	100.0	3
			91	Domestic Tourists	100.0	2
			92	Foreign Exchange Earnings from International Tourism	100.0	1
			93	Earnings from Domestic Tourism	100.0	2
			94	International Conferences	100.0	1
			95	Exhibition Industry Development Index	100.0	1
			96	World Tourism City Index	100.0	1
	Quality of Life	Residential Environment	97	Average Life Expectancy	69.8	1
			98	Medicare · Endowment Insurance Coverage Index	79.8	7
			99	Ratio of Average House Prices to Income	25.4	289
			100	Habitat City Index	67.3	17
			101	China's Happiness City Index	80.4	8
		Level of Consumption	102	Retail Sales of Consumer Goods Per Ten Thousand People	70.6	21
			103	Revenue of Hotels and Catering Services Per Ten Thousand People	87.3	6
			104	Telecom Consumption Per Ten Thousand People	72.0	10
			105	Water Consumption for Residential Use Per Ten Thousand People	73.0	12
			106	Top International Brand Index	100.0	2
		Life Service	107	Number of Children in Kindergartens Per Ten Thousand People	41.8	240
			108	Year-end Number of Beds in Nursing Homes	100.0	2
			109	Number of Practicing (Assistant) Physicians	92.4	3
			110	Number of Beds in Health Institutions	100.0	2
			111	First-class Hospitals	100.0	2

Figure 3-17 Index Ranking: Society

Dimension	Sub-dimension	Indicator Group	ID	Indicators	Deviation Value Index	Rank
Economy	Quality of Economic Development	Economic Scale	112	Size of GDP	100.0	1
			113	Population Size of Permanent Residents	100.0	2
			114	Scale of Tax Collection	100.0	1
			115	Electricity Consumption	100.0	1
		Economic Structure	116	Industrial Structure Index	100.0	1
			117	Mainboard Listed Enterprises	100.0	1
			118	Top 500 Chinese Enterprises in the World	75.3	2
			119	China's Top 500 Enterprises	100.0	2
			120	China's Top 500 Private-owned Enterprises	80.9	6
			121	Gross Industrial Output Value Above Designated Size	100.0	1
		Economic Efficiency	122	GDP Growth Index	49.4	198
			123	GDP Per Ten Thousand People	68.2	20
			124	Fiscal Revenue Per Ten Thousand People	97.8	2
			125	Dependent Population Index	66.8	13
			126	Size and Debt Rate of Bonds Issued by the City Investment Enterprises	49.4	78
			127	Number of Registered Unemployed Persons Per Ten Thousand People	41.4	252
	Dynamic Development	Business Environment	128	Employee Average Salary	92.1	2
			129	Number of Employees of Enterprise Services	100.0	2
			130	Star Hotel Index	100.0	1
			131	Top International Restaurant Index	100.0	1
			132	National Industrial Park Index	86.7	6
		Openness	133	Population Migration	100.0	1
			134	Export of Goods · Import of Goods	100.0	1
			135	Foreign Investment Utilized	100.0	2
			136	Outward Foreign Direct Investment	100.0	1
			137	The Output Value of Foreign-invested Enterprises Above Designated Size	100.0	1
			138	International Schools	100.0	1
			139	Free Trade Area Index	99.3	1
		Innovation and Entrepreneurship	140	The World's Top University Index	100.0	2
			141	R&D Expenditure Index	100.0	2
			142	R&D Human Resources	100.0	2
			143	GEM,New Third Board Listed Enterprise Index	100.0	3
			144	The Amount of Patent Authorization Index	85.2	3
			145	Trademark Registration Index	100.0	2
			146	Academicians Index	100.0	2
			147	National Reform Experiment	100.0	1
			148	National Innovative Model City Index	100.0	1
			149	Information · Knowledge Industry City Index	97.9	2
			150	National Key Laboratory · Engineering Research Center Index	100.0	2
	Urban Influence	Urban and Rural Integration	151	Urban-rural Income Ratio Index	64.4	15
			152	Primary School Education Level Population Ratio	80.9	5
			153	Illiteracy Rate	50.5	106
			154	Balanced Development of Compulsory Education Index	54.1	57
		Wide-area Hub	155	Airport Convenient	100.0	1
			156	Air Traffic Volume Index	100.0	1
			157	Container Port Convenient	100.0	1
			158	Port Container Throughput	100.0	1
			159	Water Transport Volume Index	86.2	2
			160	Railway Convenient	98.5	2
			161	Railway Traffic Volume Index	89.7	6
			162	Railway Density	85.2	5
			163	Road Traffic Volume Index	50.3	96
			164	Expressway Density	97.0	2
			165	National Road · Provincial Road Density	90.9	3
			166	Circulation City Index	84.4	4
		Core Influence	167	Higher Education Radiation	100.0	2
			168	Science and Technology Radiation	99.6	2
			169	IT Industry Radiation	100.0	2
			170	Culture and Sports and Entertainment Radiation	88.9	2
			171	Financial Radiation	100.0	1
			172	Manufacturing Radiation	100.0	3
			173	Medical Radiation	100.0	2
			174	Wholesale and Retail Radiation	100.0	1
			175	Catering and Hotel Radiation	100.0	1

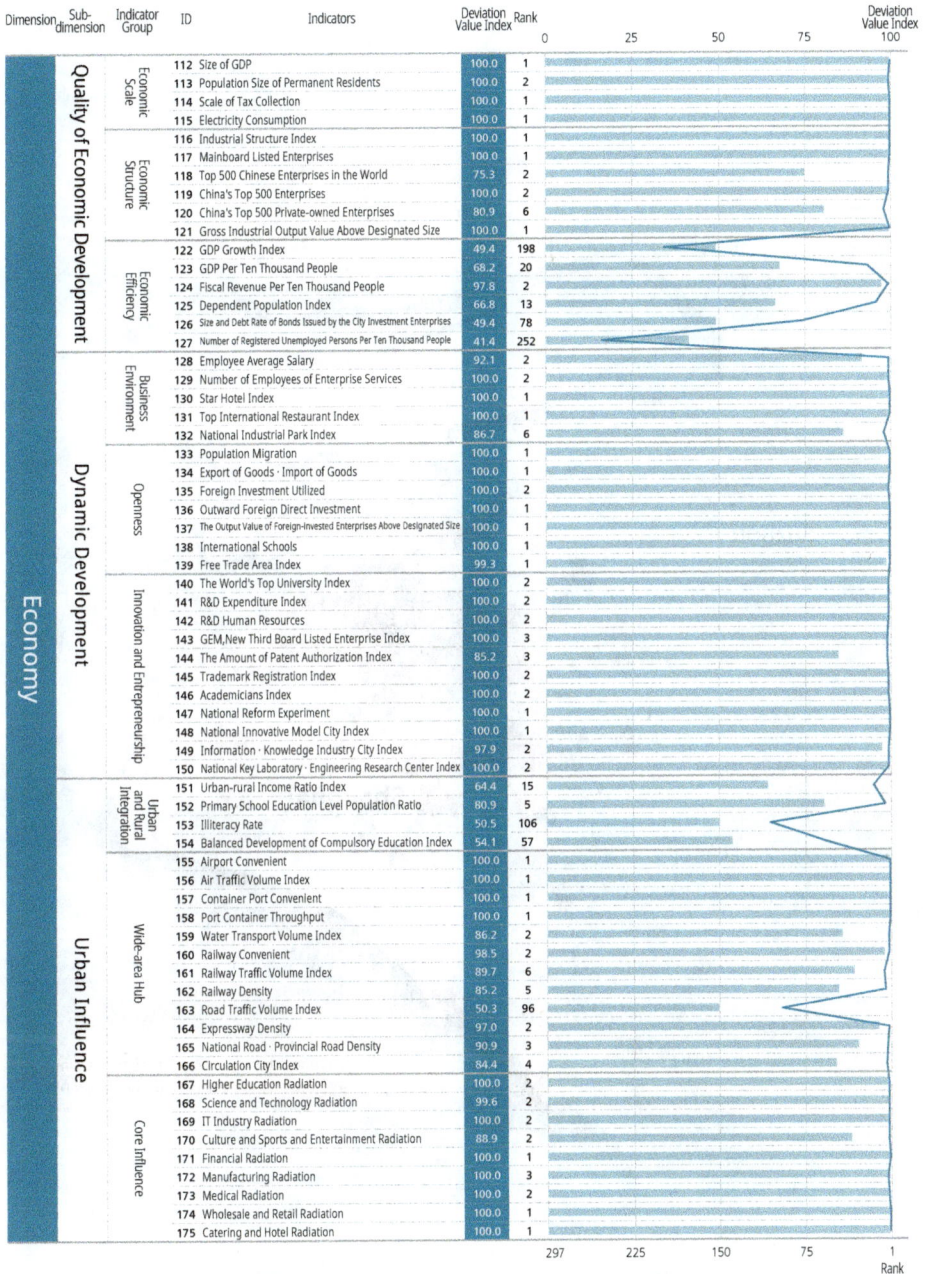

Figure 3-18 Index Ranking: Economy

Shanghai

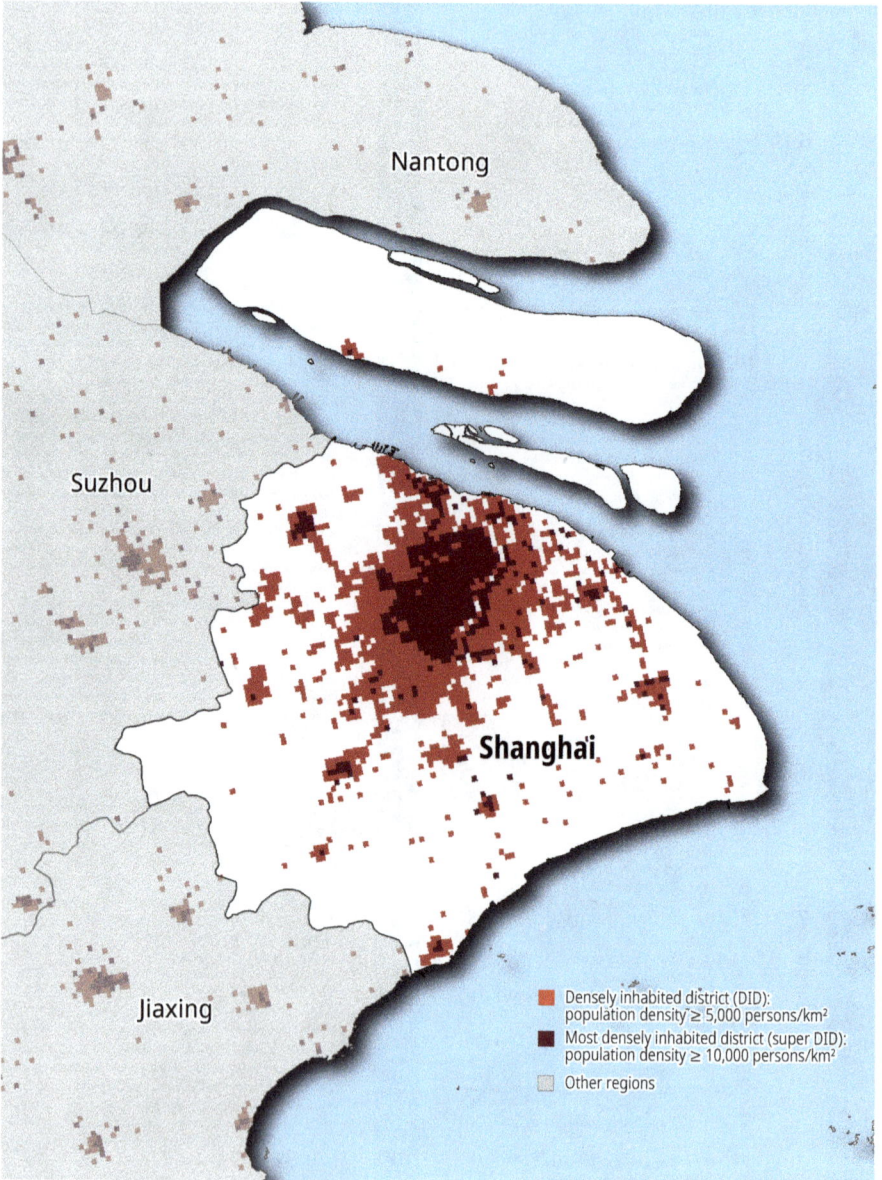

Densely inhabited district (DID):
population density ≥ 5,000 persons/km²

Most densely inhabited district (super DID):
population density ≥ 10,000 persons/km²

Other regions

Figure 3-19 DID Analysis

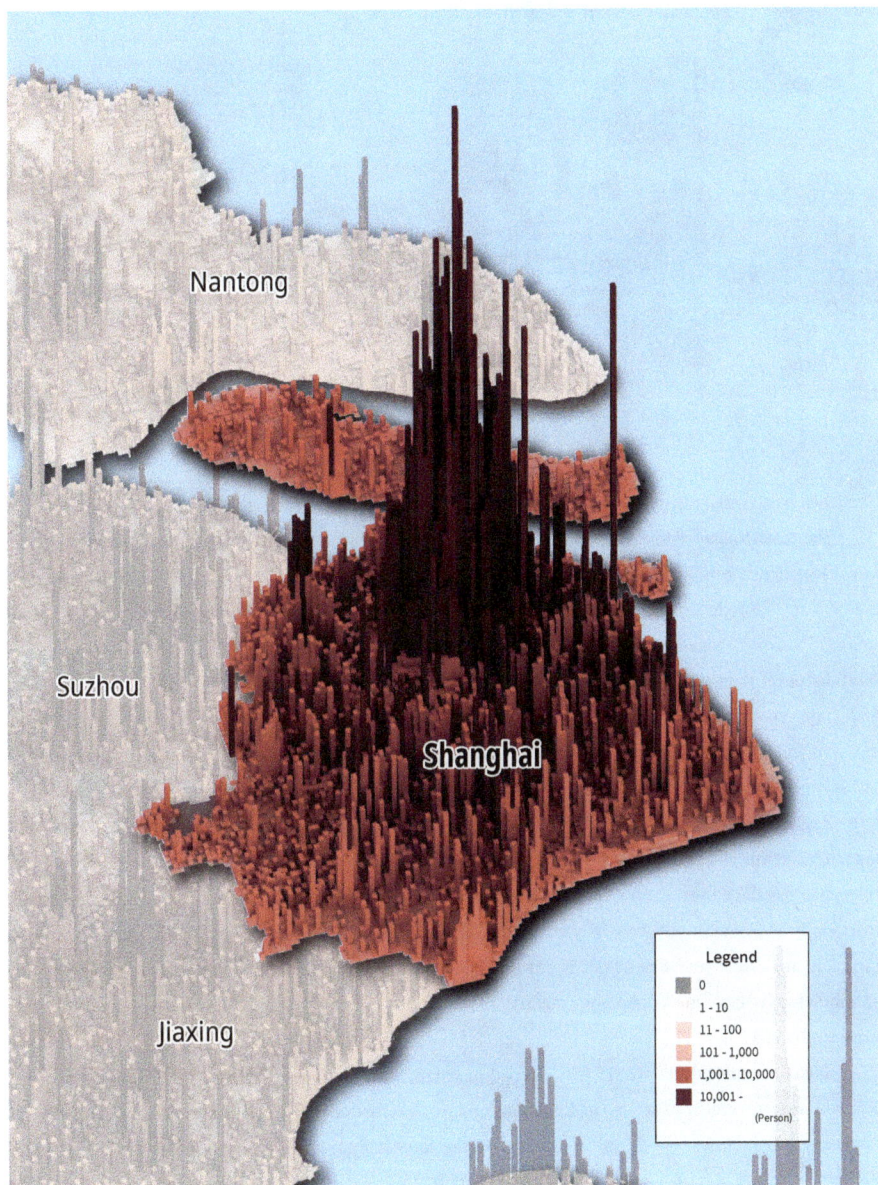

Figure 3-20 Population Size and Density Analysis

3rd Shenzhen

Shenzhen has consecutively taken the 3rd place in the comprehensive ranking since 2016.

Shenzhen managed to defend her championship in the environmental ranking. As an emerging coastal city, Shenzhen is a waterfront city with a beautiful environment. She has successively won the titles and honors of "Excellent Tourism City," "National Garden City," and "China Habitat Environment Prize." Shenzhen ranked 1st nationwide in her proportion of the population of DIDs, proportion of DIDs in built district, urban life road, and area of park green land, emphasizing her high level of urbanization and high standards of urban spatial structure. In terms of three sub-dimension indicators of the environmental dimension, Shenzhen ranked 2nd for spatial structure and 3rd for environmental quality, but relatively lagged for natural ecology with a ranking of 92nd.

Regarding the economic ranking, Shenzhen remained the 3rd place as in 2016. By taking full advantage of her status as a special economic zone and her special geographical location adjacent to Hong Kong, Shenzhen has developed from a fishing village into the most innovative and entrepreneurial international metropolis of China in just over 30 years, creating a miracle that has caught worldwide attention. Within the economic dimension, Shenzhen, as a rising star, achieved excellent results and ranked 3rd for all three sub-dimension indicators, namely, quality of economic development, dynamic development, and urban influence.

Shenzhen ranked 7th within the social dimension, which is better than the 2016 ranking. Having evolved from a window of reform and opening-up to an international metropolis, Shenzhen is a city full of openness and inclusivity—she not only claims the largest immigrant city in China, but also attracts the largest population of inbound or domestic visitors. In terms of three sub-dimension indicators of the social dimension, Shenzhen ranked 5th for both quality of life and inheritance and exchange, and ranked 11th for status and governance.

Table 3-3 Key Index

Environment

Number of permanent residents:	11,380,000
Land area of administrative region:	1,997 km²
Ranking of available land area per capita:	295
Ranking of forest coverage:	203
Ranking of water resources per capita:	270
Ranking of climate comfort index:	16
Ranking of PM$_{2.5}$ Index:	26
Ranking of densely inhabited district (DID) population :	4
Ranking of rail transit route mileage :	5

Society

Ranking of average house prices :	2
Ranking of cinemas and theater numbers :	4
Ranking of museum and art gallery numbers :	18
Number of domestic tourists:	41,570,000
Number of inbound tourists:	12,190,000
Ranking of world heritage number :	64
Ranking of international conference number :	3

Economy

Size of GDP:	RMB 1750.3 billion
Per-capita GDP:	RMB 153,821 / person
GDP growth rate:	8.6 %
Ranking of per capita revenue in :	1
Ranking of average salaries :	6
Ranking of mainboard listed enterprises :	3
Ranking of goods export in China:	1
Ranking of airport convenience in China:	4
Ranking of container port convenience :	2
Ranking of financial radiation :	3
Ranking of manufacturing radiation :	1
Ranking of IT industry radiation :	3
Ranking of higher education radiation :	294
Ranking of science and technology radiation :	3
Ranking of medical radiation :	74
Ranking of culture and sports and entertainment radiation :	6
Ranking of catering and hotel radiation :	6
Ranking of wholesale and retail radiation :	8

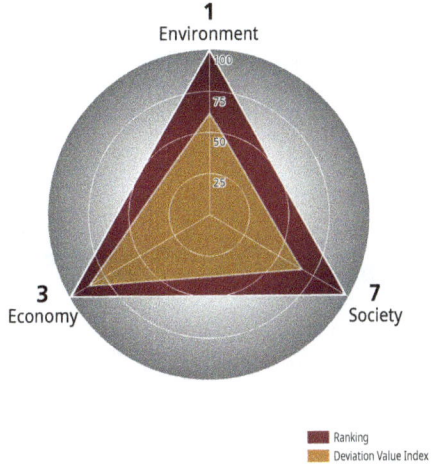

Figure 3-21 Scores of Dimension

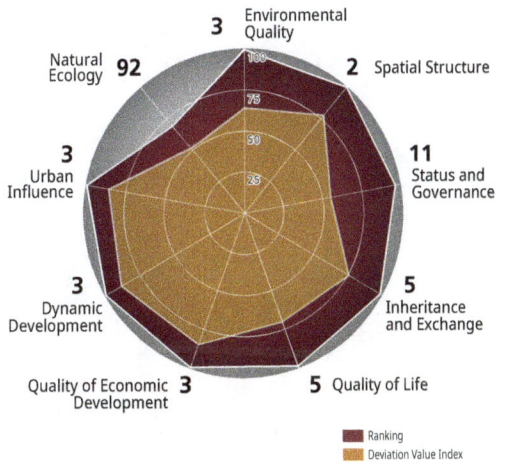

Figure 3-22 Scores of Sub-Dimension

Shenzhen

Dimension	Sub-Dimension	Indicator Group	Deviation Value Index
Environment	Natural Ecology	Soil and Water Condition	45.9
		Climate Condition	64.4
		Natural Disaster	49.2
	Environmental Quality	Pollution Load	64.7
		Environmental Protection Efforts	72.4
		Resource Efficiency	60.5
	Spatial Structure	Compact City	91.4
		Transportation Network	74.4
		Urban Facilities	62.6
Society	Status and Governance	City Status	50.0
		Quality of Residents	63.9
		Social Management	56.1
	Inheritance and Exchange	Historical Relics	46.5
		Culture & Entertainment	71.7
		Exchange	91.9
	Quality of Life	Residential Environment	61.2
		Level of Consumption	81.5
		Life Service	57.0
Economy	Quality of Economic Development	Economic Aggregate	88.1
		Economic Structure	85.1
		Economic Efficiency	77.1
	Dynamic Development	Business Environment	77.6
		Openness	92.8
		Innovation and Entrepreneurship	89.2
	Urban Influence	Urban and Rural Integration	90.7
		Wide-area Hub	91.2
		Core Influence	79.1

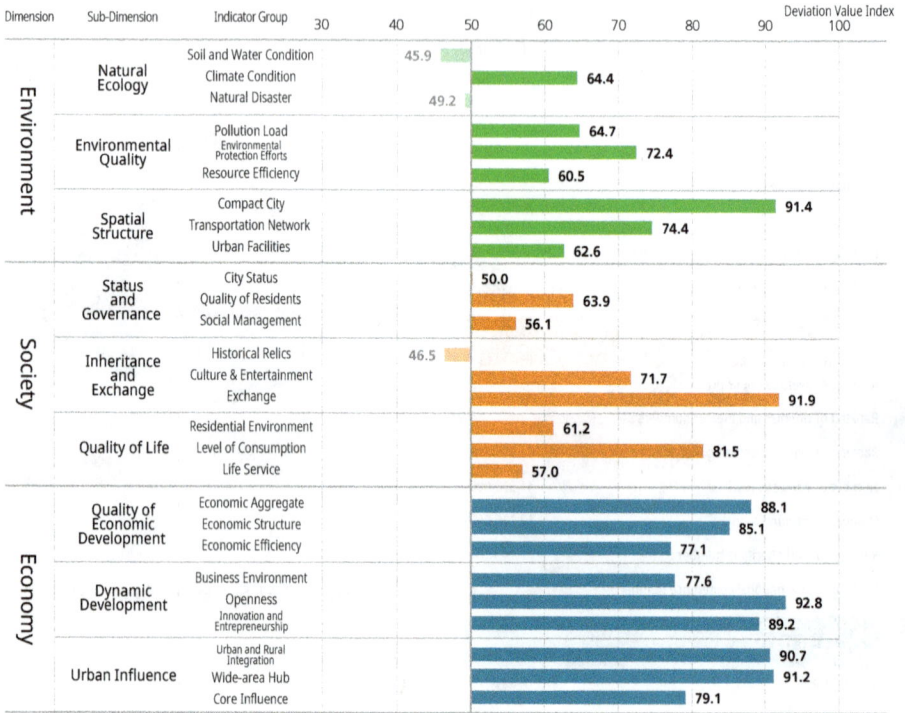

Figure 3-23 Deviation Value of Indicator Group

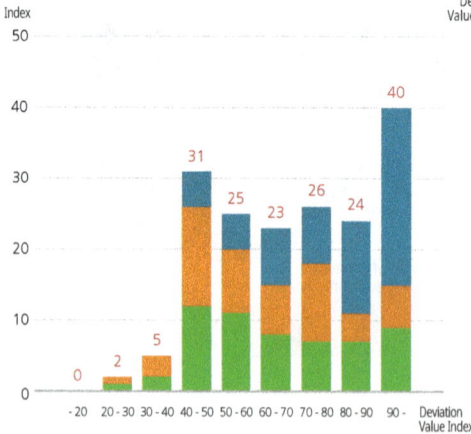

Figure 3-24 Deviation Value Distribution of Indicators

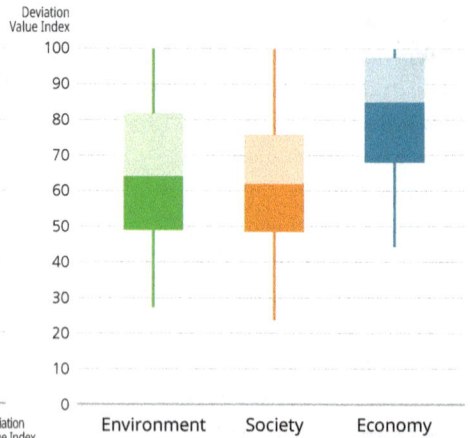

Figure 3-25 Box Plot Distribution of Indicators

62

Dimension	Sub-dimension	Indicator Group	ID	Indicators	Deviation Value Index	Rank
Environment	Natural Ecology	Soil and Water Condition	1	Available Land Area Per Ten Thousand People	47.5	295
			2	Forest Area	45.1	203
			3	Farmland Area	39.5	292
			4	Pasture Area	48.2	201
			5	Water Area	46.2	189
			6	Water Resources Per Ten Thousand People	49.0	270
			7	National Park · Conservation Area · Scenic Area Index	47.1	190
		Climate Condition	8	Climate Comfort Index	64.5	16
			9	Rainfall	64.3	32
		Natural Disaster	10	Natural Disaster-caused Direct Economic Loss Index	49.2	48
			11	Geological Disaster-caused Direct Economic Loss Index	53.1	1
			12	Disaster Warning	47.4	285
	Environmental Quality	Pollution Load	13	Air Quality Index (AQI)	69.4	11
			14	PM$_{2.5}$ Index	63.6	26
			15	CO$_2$ Emissions Per Unit of GDP	72.8	7
			16	Volume of Sulphur Dioxide Emission	55.9	8
			17	Volume of Industrial Soot(dust) Emission	98.1	8
			18	Proportion of National and Provincial Water Sections in Category III and Above Meeting the Quality Standard	43.2	211
			19	Areas Environmental Average Noise Value	37.0	286
			20	Radiation Environmental Air Absorption Dose Rate	44.4	79
		Environmental Protection Efforts	21	Environmental Effort Index	88.8	3
			22	Water-saving Effort Index	50.8	109
			23	Social Organizations for Ecological Environment	51.9	41
			24	National Environmental Protection City Index	85.3	4
			25	National Ecological Environment Evaluation Index	69.0	13
		Resource Efficiency	26	Land Productivity in Built District	52.5	71
			27	Land Productivity in Agriculture, Forestry, Animal Husbandry and Fisheries	42.3	222
			28	Energy Consumption Per Unit of GDP	72.8	7
			29	Projects Labeled with Green Building Design and Evaluation	100.0	2
			30	Comprehensive Utilization Rate of Industrial Solid Waste	57.7	17
			31	Circular Economical City Index	65.5	17
	Spatial Structure	Compact City	32	Population of Densely Inhabited Districts (DIDs)	90.2	4
			33	Area of Densely Inhabited Districts (DIDs)	88.8	3
			34	Proportion of the Population of Densely Inhabited Districts (DIDs)	83.9	1
			35	Proportion of Densely Inhabited Districts (DIDs) in Built District	100.0	1
			36	Population of Super Densely Inhabited Districts (DIDs)	93.0	4
			37	Area of Super Densely Inhabited Districts (DIDs)	92.9	4
			38	Proportion of the Population of Super Densely Inhabited Districts (DIDs)	81.9	4
			39	Proportion of Densely Super Densely Inhabited Districts (DIDs) in Built District	100.0	1
		Transportation Network	40	Urban Rail Transit Density Index	80.0	2
			41	Urban Arterial Road Density Index	74.6	1
			42	Urban Life Road Density Index	74.6	1
			43	Urban Sidewalk • Bicycle Lane Density Index	75.5	1
			44	Urban Rail Transit Distance	75.3	5
			45	Public Bus Passenger Volume Per Ten Thousand People	87.6	4
			46	Public Bus Ownership Per Ten Thousand People	100.0	1
			47	Private Vehicle Ownership Per Ten Thousand People	48.3	288
			48	Taxis Ownership Per Ten Thousand People	57.9	50
			49	Rush Hour Traffic Jam Delay Index	27.3	290
		Urban Facilities	50	Fixed Assets Investment Scale Index	58.6	36
			51	Area of Park Green Land	84.0	4
			52	Green Coverage Rate in Built District	58.0	27
			53	Density of Water Supply Pipelines in Built District	58.6	44
			54	Density of Sewers in Built District	60.8	38
			55	Gas Coverage Rate	55.6	52
			56	Urban Underground Facilities Index	68.9	5

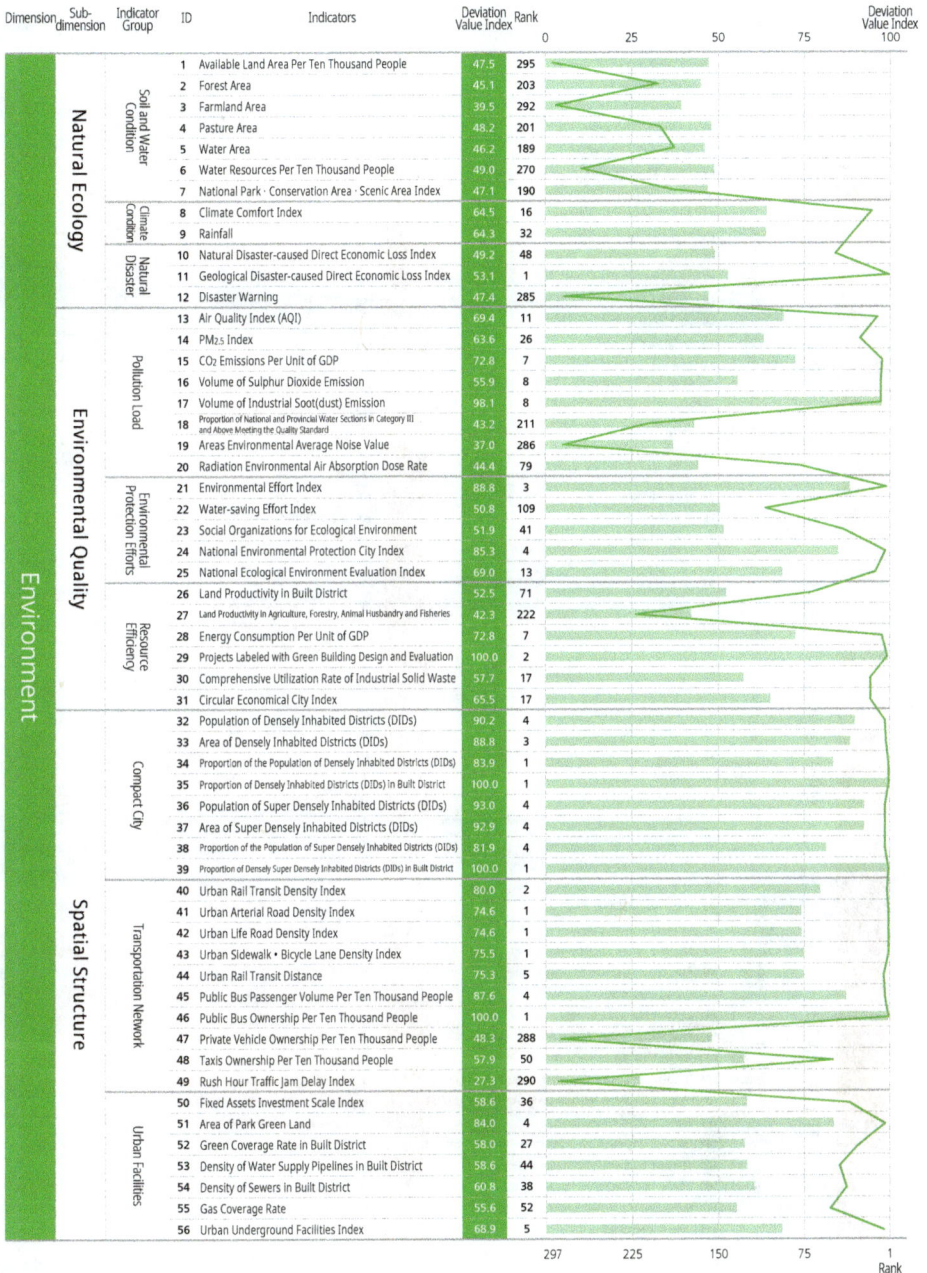

Figure 3-26 Index Ranking: Environment

Shenzhen

Dimension	Sub-dimension	Indicator Group	ID	Indicators	Deviation Value Index	Rank
Society	Status and Governance	City Status	57	Administrative Levels	36.0	32
			58	Megalopolis Levels	68.8	1
			59	Core City Levels	59.3	4
			60	Embassies · Consulates	48.9	17
			61	International Organizations	49.4	3
			62	Belt and Road Index	79.7	3
		Quality of Residents	63	Population Natural Growth Rate Index	74.5	6
			64	Population Social Growth Rate Index	31.2	292
			65	Population Structure Index	77.3	2
			66	Population Education Structure Index	70.5	12
			67	Higher Education Index	45.5	76
			68	Outstanding Talent Cultivation Index	47.6	156
			69	Public Finance Expenditure for Education Index	70.3	7
		Social Management	70	Social Services Index	50.0	131
			71	Safe and Reliable City Index	65.3	25
			72	Traffic Safety Index	42.6	278
			73	Social Security Index	37.1	262
			74	Social Organizations	78.6	7
			75	Health and Civilized City Index	50.0	91
			76	Government Website Performance	67.4	3
	Inheritance and Exchange	Historical Relics	77	Historical Status	47.9	64
			78	World Heritage	45.8	64
			79	Famous Historical and Cultural Cities	42.7	108
			80	Intangible Cultural Heritage	48.1	122
			81	Key Cultural Relics Sites Under the Protection	43.7	249
		Culture and Entertainment	82	Theater Consumer Index	93.9	3
			83	Museums · Art Galleries	69.2	18
			84	Sports Venues Index	45.9	109
			85	Zoos · Botanical Gardens · Aquariums	62.1	36
			86	Public Library Collection	95.5	3
			87	Cultural Master Index	50.5	21
			88	Olympic Champion Index	46.7	105
			89	National Culturally Advanced Unit Index	65.1	14
		Personal Exchange	90	Inbound Tourists	100.0	1
			91	Domestic Tourists	52.0	68
			92	Foreign Exchange Earnings from International Tourism	100.0	3
			93	Earnings from Domestic Tourism	62.8	20
			94	International Conferences	81.6	3
			95	Exhibition Industry Development Index	78.5	5
			96	World Tourism City Index	70.8	8
	Quality of Life	Residential Environment	97	Average Life Expectancy	55.9	6
			98	Medicare · Endowment Insurance Coverage Index	100.0	1
			99	Ratio of Average House Prices to Income	23.8	292
			100	Habitat City Index	80.5	4
			101	China's Happiness City Index	46.9	52
		Level of Consumption	102	Retail Sales of Consumer Goods Per Ten Thousand People	72.9	15
			103	Revenue of Hotels and Catering Services Per Ten Thousand People	92.0	4
			104	Telecom Consumption Per Ten Thousand People	84.3	5
			105	Water Consumption for Residential Use Per Ten Thousand People	85.0	6
			106	Top International Brand Index	72.4	7
		Life Service	107	Number of Children in Kindergartens Per Ten Thousand People	59.2	53
			108	Year-end Number of Beds in Nursing Homes	45.9	177
			109	Number of Practicing (Assistant) Physicians	70.0	11
			110	Number of Beds in Health Institutions	55.7	50
			111	First-class Hospitals	56.1	30

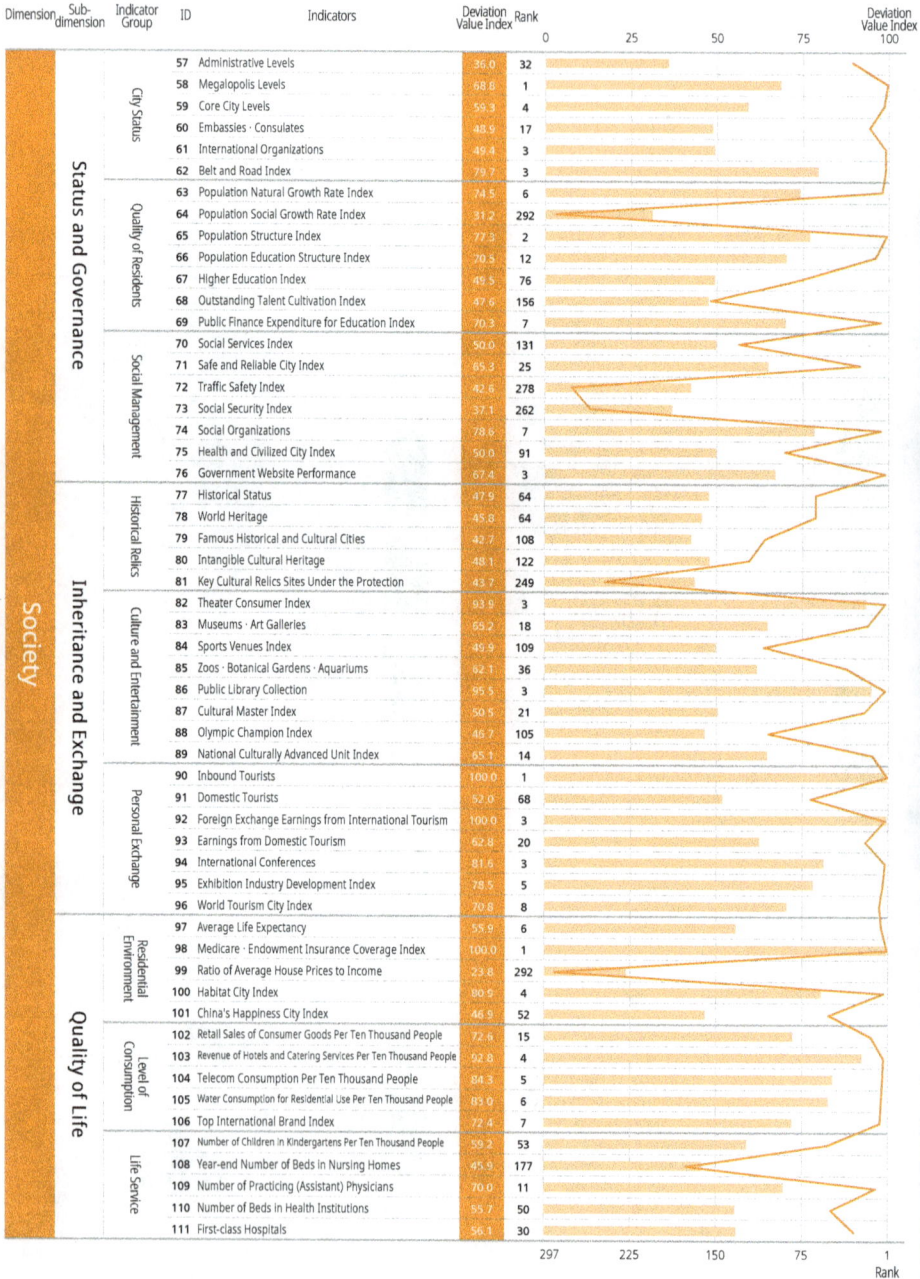

Figure 3-27 Index Ranking: Society

Figure header columns: Dimension | Sub-dimension | Indicator Group | ID | Indicators | Deviation Value Index | Rank | (bar chart, Deviation Value Index 0–100 / Rank)

Dimension	Sub-dimension	Indicator Group	ID	Indicators	Deviation Value Index	Rank
Economy	Quality of Economic Development	Economic Scale	112	Size of GDP	96.5	4
			113	Population Size of Permanent Residents	70.6	8
			114	Scale of Tax Collection	97.1	3
			115	Electricity Consumption	97.1	3
		Economic Structure	116	Industrial Structure Index	86.2	5
			117	Mainboard Listed Enterprises	100.0	3
			118	Top 500 Chinese Enterprises in the World	63.6	3
			119	China's Top 500 Enterprises	95.3	3
			120	China's Top 500 Private-owned Enterprises	63.7	18
			121	Gross Industrial Output Value Above Designated Size	95.2	4
		Economic Efficiency	122	GDP Growth Index	56.8	44
			123	GDP Per Ten Thousand People	85.0	4
			124	Fiscal Revenue Per Ten Thousand People	100.0	1
			125	Dependent Population Index	100.0	1
			126	Size and Debt Rate of Bonds Issued by the City Investment Enterprises	65.2	8
			127	Number of Registered Unemployed Persons Per Ten Thousand People	54.9	65
	Dynamic Development	Business Environment	128	Employee Average Salary	74.0	6
			129	Number of Employees of Enterprise Services	83.5	4
			130	Star Hotel Index	75.4	8
			131	Top International Restaurant Index	68.3	5
			132	National Industrial Park Index	88.6	3
		Openness	133	Population Migration	100.0	3
			134	Export of Goods · Import of Goods	100.0	2
			135	Foreign Investment Utilized	74.8	10
			136	Outward Foreign Direct Investment	87.7	3
			137	The Output Value of Foreign-Invested Enterprises Above Designated Size	74.0	8
			138	International Schools	89.9	3
			139	Free Trade Area Index	93.1	4
		Innovation and Entrepreneurship	140	The World's Top University Index	47.9	45
			141	R&D Expenditure Index	100.0	3
			142	R&D Human Resources	100.0	3
			143	GEM,New Third Board Listed Enterprise Index	100.0	2
			144	The Amount of Patent Authorization Index	95.4	3
			145	Trademark Registration Index	100.0	3
			146	Academicians Index	49.0	41
			147	National Reform Experiment	84.7	4
			148	National Innovative Model City Index	61.3	4
			149	Information · Knowledge Industry City Index	89.9	4
			150	National Key Laboratory · Engineering Research Center Index	52.5	25
	Urban Influence	Urban and Rural Integration	151	Urban-rural Income Ratio Index	94.7	1
			152	Primary School Education Level Population Ratio	100.0	1
			153	Illiteracy Rate	100.0	1
			154	Balanced Development of Compulsory Education Index	44.5	179
		Wide-area Hub	155	Airport Convenient	87.3	4
			156	Air Traffic Volume Index	85.3	4
			157	Container Port Convenient	100.0	2
			158	Port Container Throughput	100.0	2
			159	Water Transport Volume Index	66.3	18
			160	Railway Convenient	89.9	5
			161	Railway Traffic Volume Index	68.1	9
			162	Railway Density	85.2	3
			163	Road Traffic Volume Index	52.0	70
			164	Expressway Density	100.0	1
			165	National Road · Provincial Road Density	100.0	1
			166	Circulation City Index	79.9	7
		Core Influence	167	Higher Education Radiation	45.8	294
			168	Science and Technology Radiation	87.0	3
			169	IT Industry Radiation	82.1	3
			170	Culture and Sports and Entertainment Radiation	66.4	6
			171	Financial Radiation	91.1	3
			172	Manufacturing Radiation	100.0	1
			173	Medical Radiation	50.0	74
			174	Wholesale and Retail Radiation	73.3	8
			175	Catering and Hotel Radiation	70.7	6

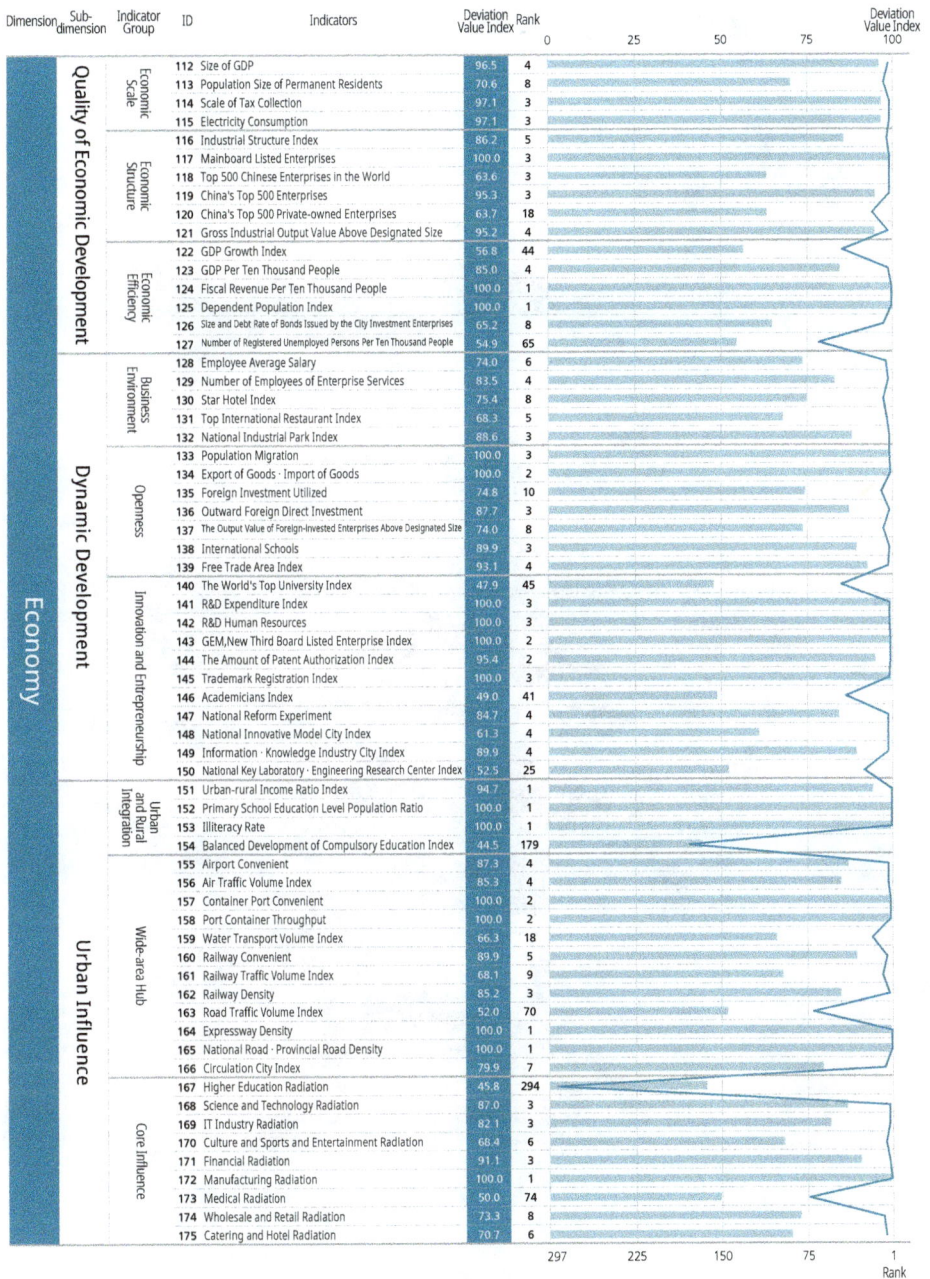

Figure 3-28 Index Ranking: Economy

Shenzhen

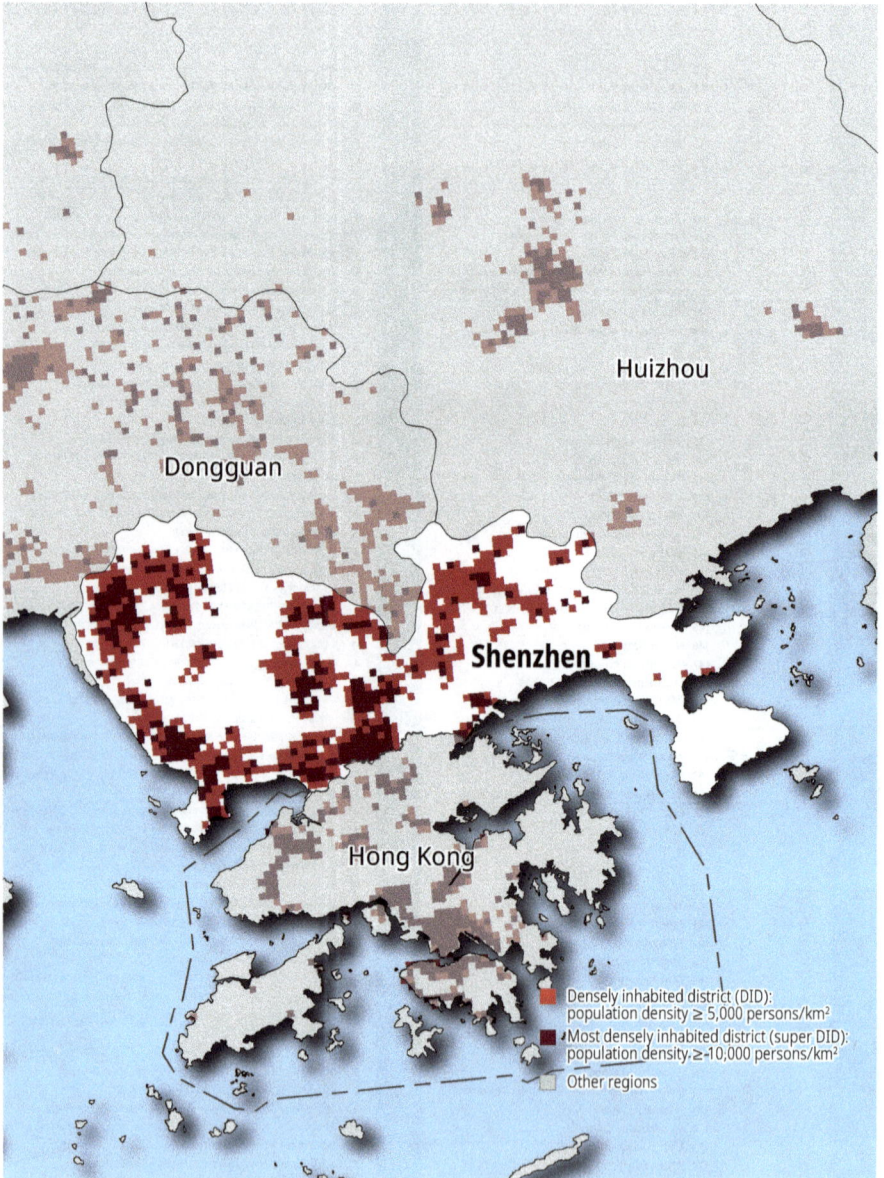

Figure 3-29 DID Analysis

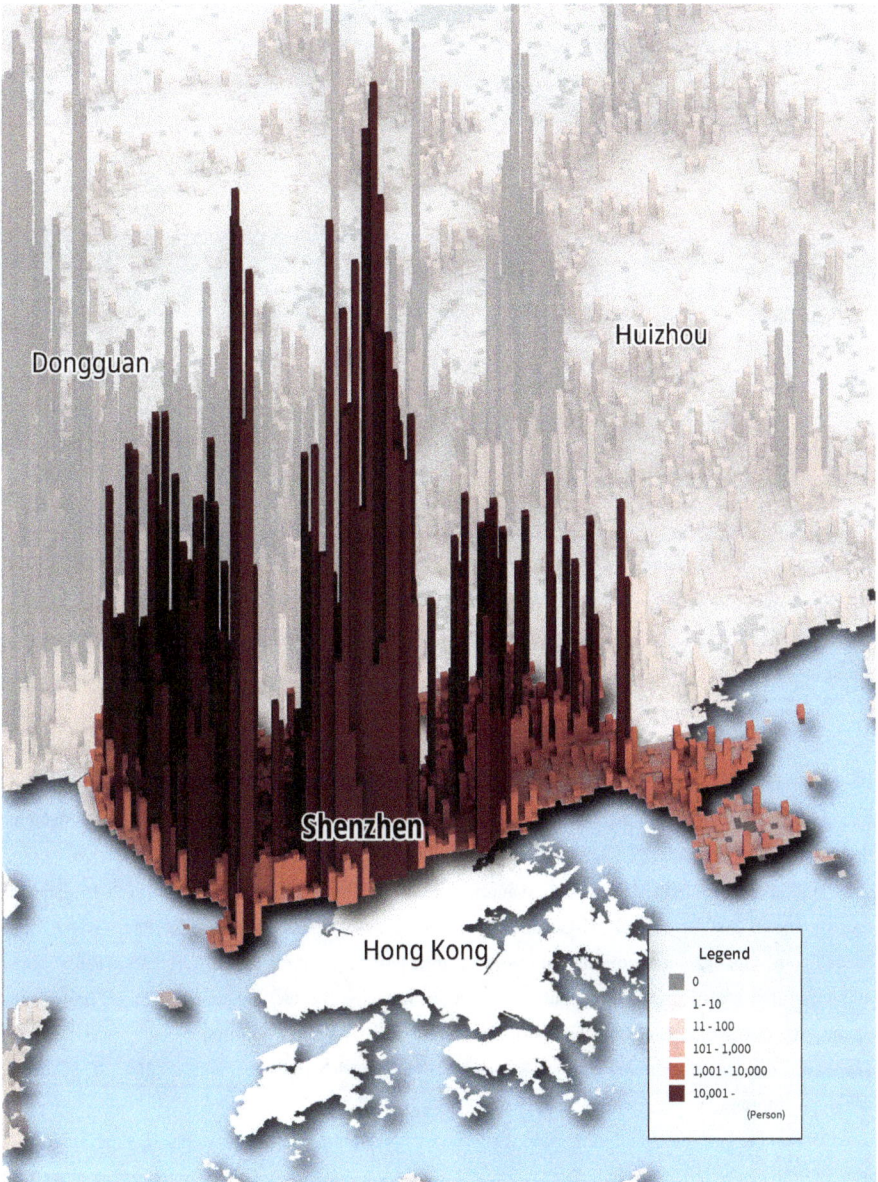

Figure 3-30 Population Size and Density Analysis

4th Guangzhou

Guangzhou remained No. 4 in the comprehensive ranking, the same place as in 2016.

Within the social dimension, Guangzhou moved up two ladders to 3rd. As the center of politics, economy, and culture in South China, Guangzhou is also one of the first Famous Historical and Cultural Cities. Guangzhou was the main port of the ancient Maritime Silk Road and became the largest port of China during the Tang and Song Dynasties. She was the only port for foreign trade in China during the Qianlong [reign name of the 4th emperor of the Qing (Manchu) Dynasty] period of the Qing Dynasty, and thus enjoys an important historical position with a strong tradition of foreign exchange. In terms of three sub-dimension indicators of the social dimension, Guangzhou ranked 4th for inheritance and exchange and for status and governance, as well as 3rd for quality of life (next to Beijing and Shanghai only).

Within the economic dimension, Guangzhou maintained her good performance in 2016 and took the 4th place. As the capital of Guangdong Province and the core city of the Pearl River Delta Megalopolis, Guangzhou is not only an important international business center, foreign exchange center and integrated transportation hub, but is also a banner city for the implementation of reform and opening-up in China. Guangzhou has performed very well with three sub-dimension indicators of the economic dimension, namely, urban influence, dynamic development, and quality of economic development, ranking 4th, 5th, and 6th respectively.

Within the environmental dimension, Guangzhou ranked No. 4, higher than her ranking in 2016. In terms of three sub-dimension indicators of the environmental dimension, Guangzhou performed well for spatial structure and ranked 4th, and she also ranked 51st and 25th respectively for natural ecology and environmental quality.

Table 3-4 Key Index

Environment

Number of permanent residents:	13,500,000
Land area of administrative region:	7,434 km²
Ranking of available land area per capita:	286
Ranking of forest coverage:	136
Ranking of water resources per capita:	176
Ranking of climate comfort index:	58
Ranking of PM$_{2.5}$ Index:	70
Ranking of densely inhabited district (DID) population :	3
Ranking of rail transit route mileage :	3

Society

Ranking of average house prices :	6
Ranking of cinemas and theater numbers :	11
Ranking of museum and art gallery numbers :	8
Number of domestic tourists:	48,540,000
Number of inbound tourists:	8,040,000
Ranking of world heritage number :	64
Ranking of international conference number :	10

Economy

Size of GDP:	RMB 1810.0 billion
Per-capita GDP:	RMB 134,066 / person
GDP growth rate:	7.7 %
Ranking of per capita revenue in :	21
Ranking of average salaries :	5
Ranking of mainboard listed enterprises :	6
Ranking of goods export in China:	5
Ranking of airport convenience in China:	3
Ranking of container port convenience :	3
Ranking of financial radiation :	4
Ranking of manufacturing radiation :	7
Ranking of IT industry radiation :	7
Ranking of higher education radiation :	6
Ranking of science and technology radiation :	4
Ranking of medical radiation :	3
Ranking of culture and sports and entertainment radiation :	3
Ranking of catering and hotel radiation :	5
Ranking of wholesale and retail radiation :	5

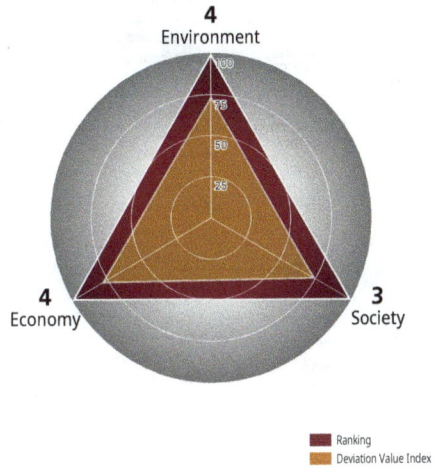

Figure 3-31 Scores of Dimension

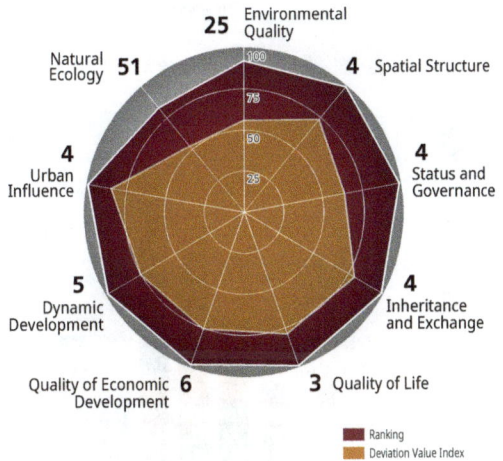

Figure 3-32 Scores of Sub-Dimension

Guangzhou

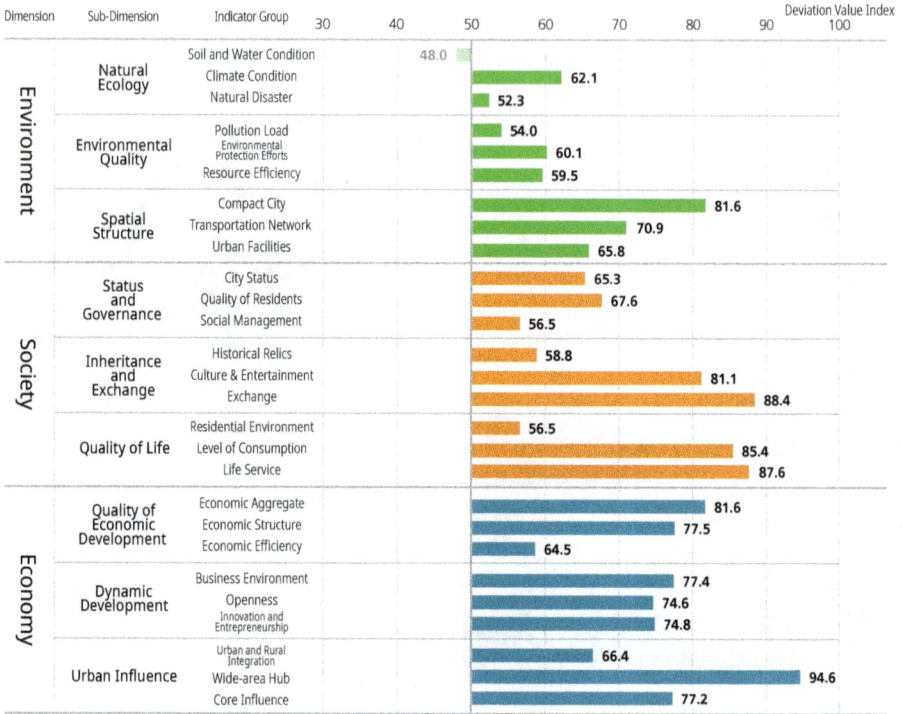

Figure 3-33 Deviation Value of Indicator Group

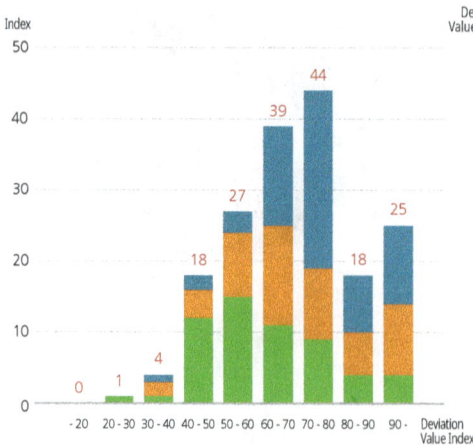

Figure 3-34 Deviation Value Distribution of Indicators

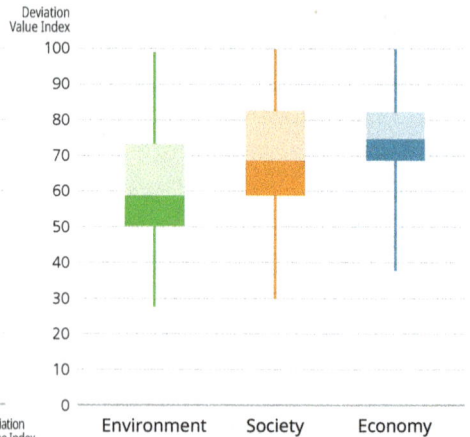

Figure 3-35 Box Plot Distribution of Indicators

Figure with table and line chart.

Dimension	Sub-dimension	Indicator Group	ID	Indicators	Deviation Value Index	Rank
Environment	Natural Ecology	Soil and Water Condition	1	Available Land Area Per Ten Thousand People	47.7	286
			2	Forest Area	47.3	136
			3	Farmland Area	43.7	224
			4	Pasture Area	48.2	112
			5	Water Area	51.3	53
			6	Water Resources Per Ten Thousand People	49.1	176
			7	National Park · Conservation Area · Scenic Area Index	50.7	100
		Climate Condition	8	Climate Comfort Index	58.0	58
			9	Rainfall	66.2	21
		Natural Disaster	10	Natural Disaster-caused Direct Economic Loss Index	61.2	42
			11	Geological Disaster-caused Direct Economic Loss Index	53.1	1
			12	Disaster Warning	47.6	217
	Environmental Quality	Pollution Load	13	Air Quality Index (AQI)	59.1	52
			14	PM$_{2.5}$ Index	54.8	70
			15	CO$_2$ Emissions Per Unit of GDP	67.9	15
			16	Volume of Sulphur Dioxide Emission	48.5	181
			17	Volume of Industrial Soot(dust) Emission	51.1	50
			18	Proportion of National and Provincial Water Sections in Category III and Above Meeting the Quality Standard	33.9	275
			19	Areas Environmental Average Noise Value	48.7	83
			20	Radiation Environmental Air Absorption Dose Rate	59.1	63
		Environmental Protection Efforts	21	Environmental Effort Index	69.6	6
			22	Water-saving Effort Index	43.8	285
			23	Social Organizations for Ecological Environment	51.2	51
			24	National Environmental Protection City Index	80.3	6
			25	National Ecological Environment Evaluation Index	46.2	170
		Resource Efficiency	26	Land Productivity in Built District	50.5	91
			27	Land Productivity in Agriculture, Forestry, Animal Husbandry and Fisheries	55.8	70
			28	Energy Consumption Per Unit of GDP	67.9	15
			29	Projects Labeled with Green Building Design and Evaluation	73.6	8
			30	Comprehensive Utilization Rate of Industrial Solid Waste	55.7	114
			31	Circular Economical City Index	62.3	32
	Spatial Structure	Compact City	32	Population of Densely Inhabited Districts (DIDs)	92.4	3
			33	Area of Densely Inhabited Districts (DIDs)	86.9	4
			34	Proportion of the Population of Densely Inhabited Districts (DIDs)	75.8	7
			35	Proportion of Densely Inhabited Districts (DIDs) in Built District	73.3	7
			36	Population of Super Densely Inhabited Districts (DIDs)	99.1	2
			37	Area of Super Densely Inhabited Districts (DIDs)	92.9	3
			38	Proportion of the Population of Super Densely Inhabited Districts (DIDs)	77.6	6
			39	Proportion of Densely Super Densely Inhabited Districts (DIDs) in Built District	77.5	6
		Transportation Network	40	Urban Rail Transit Density Index	76.0	5
			41	Urban Arterial Road Density Index	68.6	6
			42	Urban Life Road Density Index	68.8	5
			43	Urban Sidewalk · Bicycle Lane Density Index	69.4	5
			44	Urban Rail Transit Distance	84.7	3
			45	Public Bus Passenger Volume Per Ten Thousand People	81.6	6
			46	Public Bus Ownership Per Ten Thousand People	74.5	9
			47	Private Vehicle Ownership Per Ten Thousand People	48.5	245
			48	Taxis Ownership Per Ten Thousand People	62.2	33
			49	Rush Hour Traffic Jam Delay Index	27.8	286
		Urban Facilities	50	Fixed Assets Investment Scale Index	71.0	16
			51	Area of Park Green Land	88.0	2
			52	Green Coverage Rate in Built District	54.0	109
			53	Density of Water Supply Pipelines in Built District	57.7	50
			54	Density of Sewers in Built District	47.8	150
			55	Gas Coverage Rate	55.4	68
			56	Urban Underground Facilities Index	68.9	5

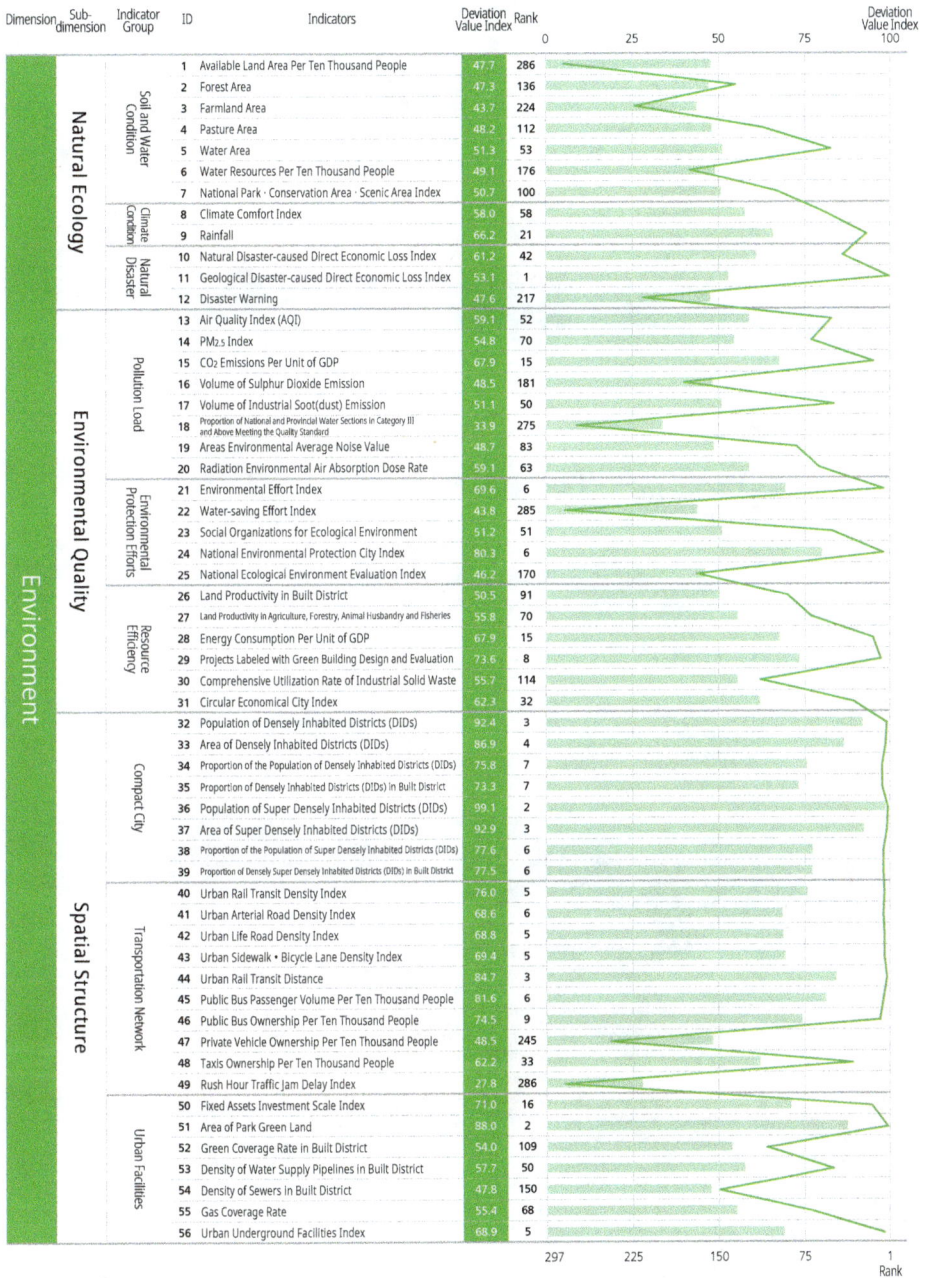

Figure 3-36 Index Ranking: Environment

Guangzhou

Dimension	Sub-dimension	Indicator Group	ID	Indicators	Deviation Value Index	Rank
Society	Status and Governance	City Status	57	Administrative Levels	55.9	5
			58	Megalopolis Levels	68.8	1
			59	Core City Levels	74.6	1
			60	Embassies · Consulates	100.0	3
			61	International Organizations	49.4	3
			62	Belt and Road Index	71.1	4
		Quality of Residents	63	Population Natural Growth Rate Index	53.8	105
			64	Population Social Growth Rate Index	51.8	77
			65	Population Structure Index	61.1	8
			66	Population Education Structure Index	71.4	10
			67	Higher Education Index	100.0	1
			68	Outstanding Talent Cultivation Index	68.8	7
			69	Public Finance Expenditure for Education Index	67.3	9
		Social Management	70	Social Services Index	58.3	30
			71	Safe and Reliable City Index	69.7	16
			72	Traffic Safety Index	42.0	292
			73	Social Security Index	34.5	289
			74	Social Organizations	68.0	20
			75	Health and Civilized City Index	61.9	14
			76	Government Website Performance	66.0	8
	Inheritance and Exchange	Historical Relics	77	Historical Status	55.7	7
			78	World Heritage	45.8	64
			79	Famous Historical and Cultural Cities	61.7	7
			80	Intangible Cultural Heritage	62.6	15
			81	Key Cultural Relics Sites Under the Protection	59.4	29
		Culture and Entertainment	82	Theater Consumer Index	89.4	5
			83	Museums · Art Galleries	76.8	4
			84	Sports Venues Index	91.5	5
			85	Zoos · Botanical Gardens · Aquariums	81.7	4
			86	Public Library Collection	78.4	5
			87	Cultural Master Index	64.4	3
			88	Olympic Champion Index	84.8	4
			89	National Culturally Advanced Unit Index	65.1	14
		Personal Exchange	90	Inbound Tourists	100.0	2
			91	Domestic Tourists	53.8	54
			92	Foreign Exchange Earnings from International Tourism	100.0	2
			93	Earnings from Domestic Tourism	96.3	4
			94	International Conferences	56.7	10
			95	Exhibition Industry Development Index	100.0	2
			96	World Tourism City Index	70.8	8
	Quality of Life	Residential Environment	97	Average Life Expectancy	55.9	6
			98	Medicare · Endowment Insurance Coverage Index	80.2	5
			99	Ratio of Average House Prices to Income	30.1	284
			100	Habitat City Index	46.9	36
			101	China's Happiness City Index	67.0	14
		Level of Consumption	102	Retail Sales of Consumer Goods Per Ten Thousand People	86.3	1
			103	Revenue of Hotels and Catering Services Per Ten Thousand People	90.7	5
			104	Telecom Consumption Per Ten Thousand People	74.5	8
			105	Water Consumption for Residential Use Per Ten Thousand People	97.0	1
			106	Top International Brand Index	72.4	7
		Life Service	107	Number of Children in Kindergartens Per Ten Thousand People	53.3	114
			108	Year-end Number of Beds in Nursing Homes	75.7	6
			109	Number of Practicing (Assistant) Physicians	84.0	5
			110	Number of Beds In Health Institutions	79.5	5
			111	First-class Hospitals	100.0	3

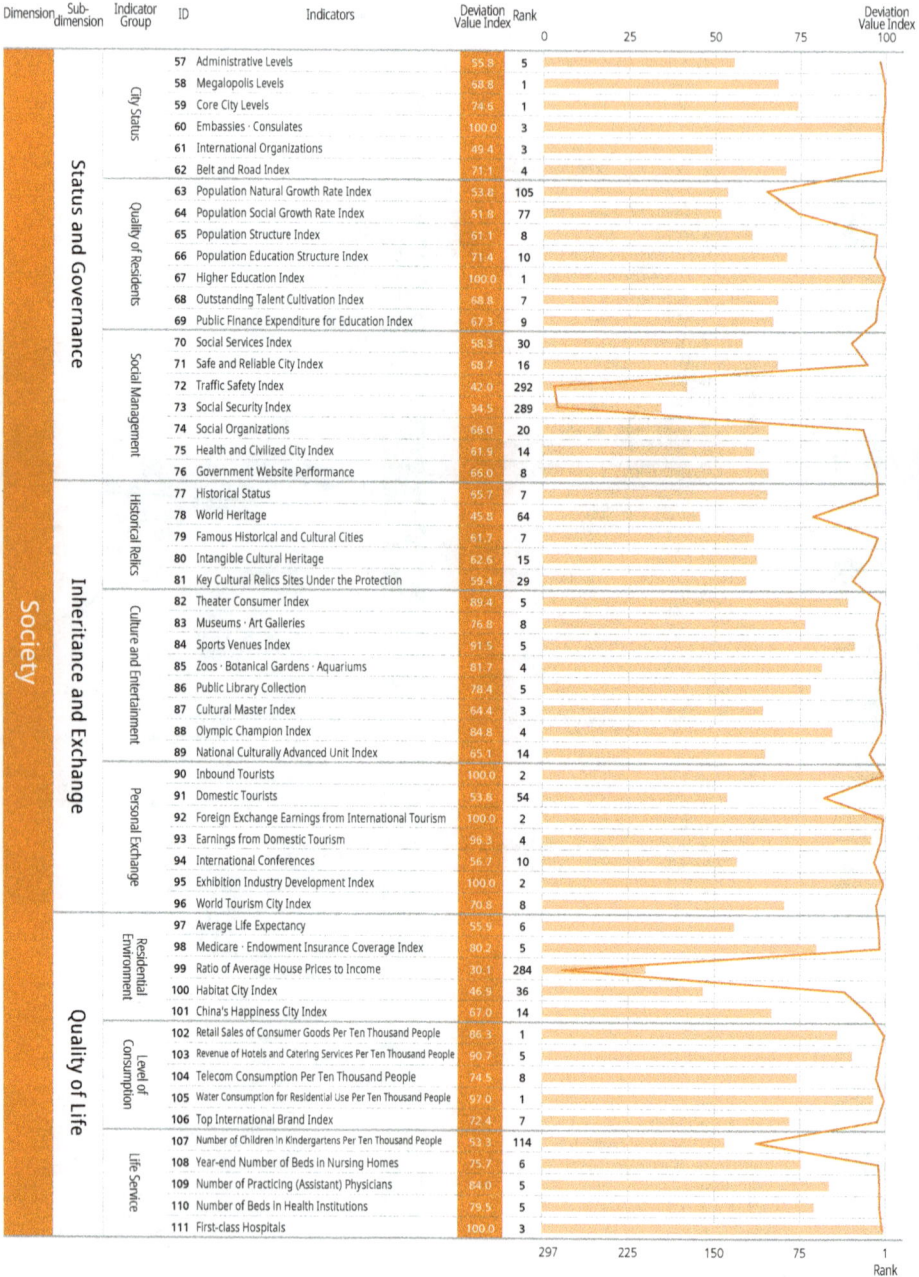

Figure 3-37 Index Ranking: Society

Dimension	Sub-dimension	Indicator Group	ID	Indicators	Deviation Value Index	Rank
Economy	Quality of Economic Development	Economic Scale	112	Size of GDP	98.3	3
			113	Population Size of Permanent Residents	76.8	6
			114	Scale of Tax Collection	69.7	8
			115	Electricity Consumption	69.7	8
		Economic Structure	116	Industrial Structure Index	89.7	3
			117	Mainboard Listed Enterprises	66.8	6
			118	Top 500 Chinese Enterprises in the World	57.8	4
			119	China's Top 500 Enterprises	71.6	4
			120	China's Top 500 Private-owned Enterprises	61.5	21
			121	Gross Industrial Output Value Above Designated Size	81.0	7
		Economic Efficiency	122	GDP Growth Index	54.3	100
			123	GDP Per Ten Thousand People	78.3	6
			124	Fiscal Revenue Per Ten Thousand People	64.3	21
			125	Dependent Population Index	69.3	8
			126	Size and Debt Rate of Bonds Issued by the City Investment Enterprises	47.3	151
			127	Number of Registered Unemployed Persons Per Ten Thousand People	38.0	289
	Dynamic Development	Business Environment	128	Employee Average Salary	75.0	5
			129	Number of Employees of Enterprise Services	82.1	6
			130	Star Hotel Index	78.1	5
			131	Top International Restaurant Index	77.0	4
			132	National Industrial Park Index	74.8	13
		Openness	133	Population Migration	87.1	6
			134	Export of Goods · Import of Goods	73.9	6
			135	Foreign Investment Utilized	70.7	12
			136	Outward Foreign Direct Investment	63.2	8
			137	The Output Value of Foreign-invested Enterprises Above Designated Size	99.5	3
			138	International Schools	82.6	4
			139	Free Trade Area Index	94.2	3
		Innovation and Entrepreneurship	140	The World's Top University Index	78.1	5
			141	R&D Expenditure Index	77.3	6
			142	R&D Human Resources	74.9	9
			143	GEM,New Third Board Listed Enterprise Index	78.2	6
			144	The Amount of Patent Authorization Index	74.0	4
			145	Trademark Registration Index	100.0	4
			146	Academicians Index	53.2	14
			147	National Reform Experiment	67.7	15
			148	National Innovative Model City Index	72.0	15
			149	Information · Knowledge Industry City Index	78.6	8
			150	National Key Laboratory · Engineering Research Center Index	74.9	62
	Urban Influence	Urban and Rural Integration	151	Urban-rural Income Ratio Index	61.7	21
			152	Primary School Education Level Population Ratio	71.7	10
			153	Illiteracy Rate	76.3	7
			154	Balanced Development of Compulsory Education Index	65.3	22
		Wide-area Hub	155	Airport Convenient	99.6	3
			156	Air Traffic Volume Index	100.0	3
			157	Container Port Convenient	78.7	3
			158	Port Container Throughput	100.0	4
			159	Water Transport Volume Index	68.1	12
			160	Railway Convenient	100.0	1
			161	Railway Traffic Volume Index	100.0	4
			162	Railway Density	66.3	17
			163	Road Traffic Volume Index	100.0	1
			164	Expressway Density	92.0	4
			165	National Road · Provincial Road Density	70.6	15
			166	Circulation City Index	94.6	2
		Core Influence	167	Higher Education Radiation	78.5	6
			168	Science and Technology Radiation	83.4	4
			169	IT Industry Radiation	66.7	7
			170	Culture and Sports and Entertainment Radiation	76.5	3
			171	Financial Radiation	70.8	4
			172	Manufacturing Radiation	71.5	7
			173	Medical Radiation	93.7	3
			174	Wholesale and Retail Radiation	80.0	5
			175	Catering and Hotel Radiation	73.7	5

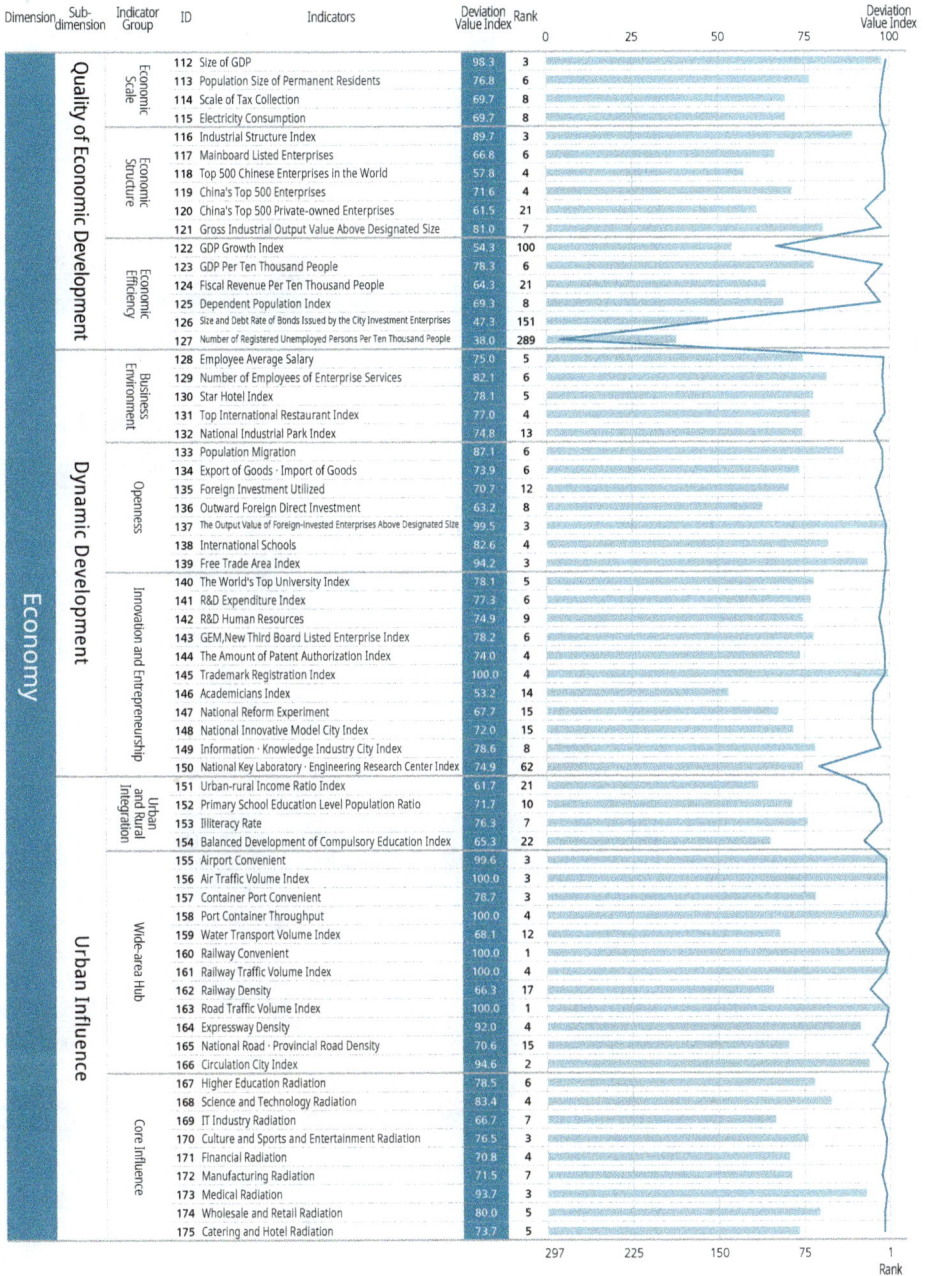

Figure 3-38 Index Ranking: Economy

Guangzhou

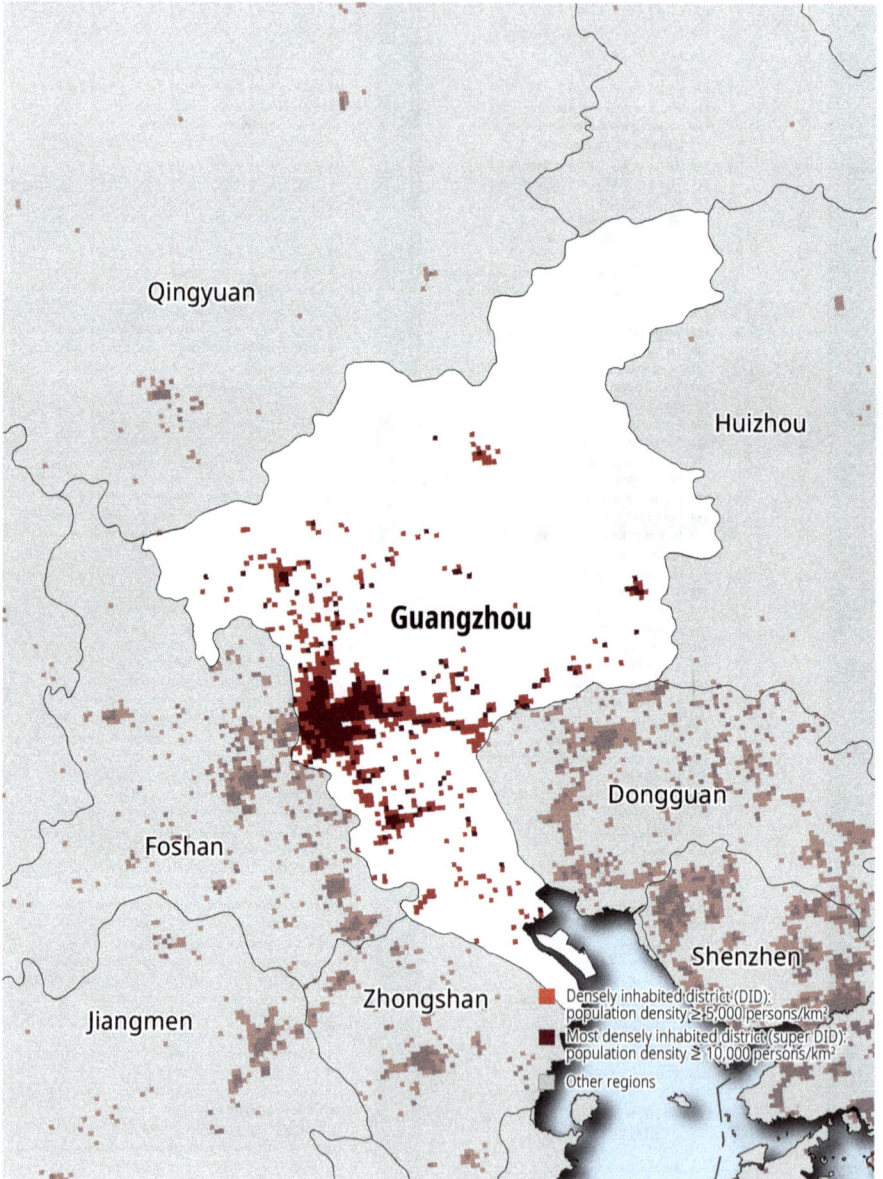

Figure 3-39 DID Analysis

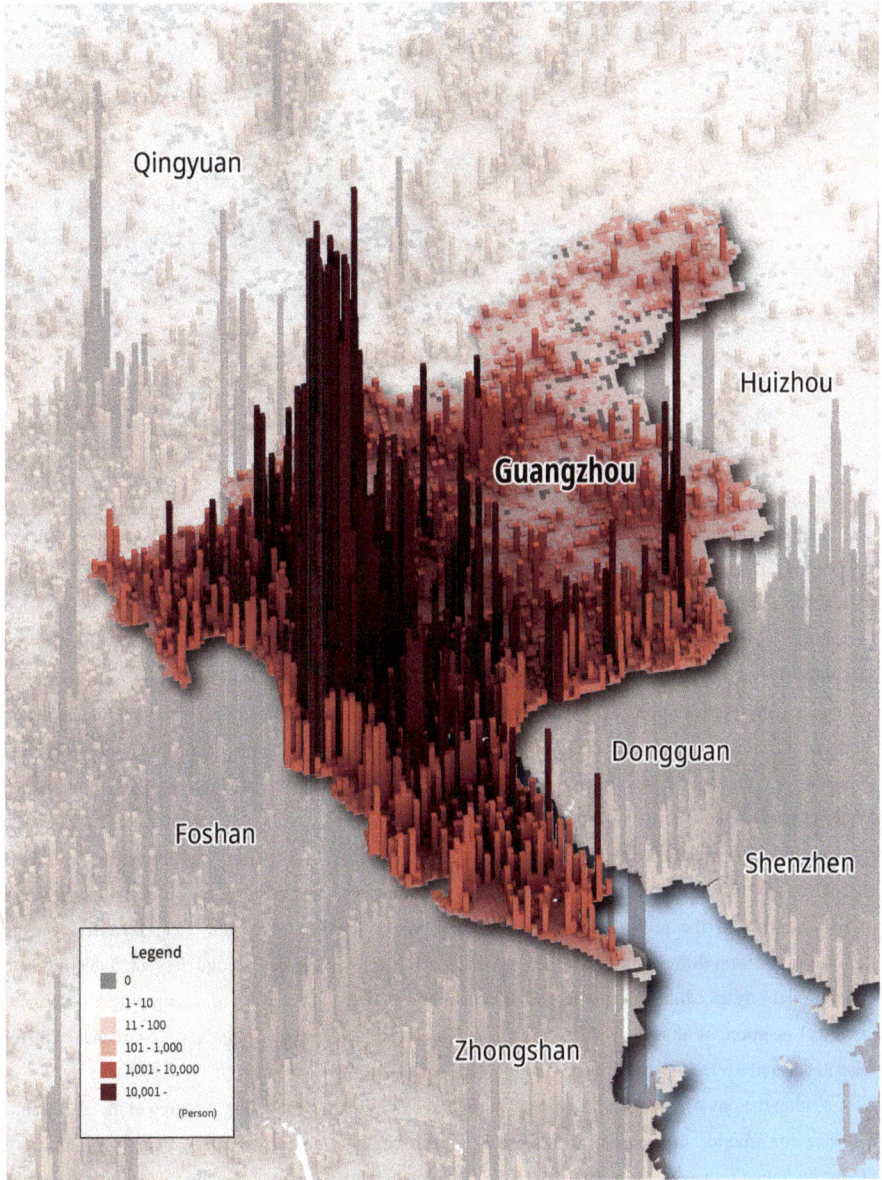

Figure 3-40 Population Size and Density Analysis

5th Tianjin

Tianjin continued to rank 5th in the comprehensive ranking.

Tianjin remained 5th within the economic dimension, as in 2016. As a municipality directly under the Central Government and the second largest city in the Beijing-Tianjin-Hebei Megalopolis, Tianjin not only has a large population and economy, but also enjoys natural advantages on the coastline given her location as a hub for water and land transportation. Tianjin is the core area for northern international shipping. By way of such initiatives as the construction of Binhai New District, Tianjin has become an advanced manu-facture and R&D base nationwide, a finance innovation and operation demo zone, and a pioneering zone of reform and opening-up. Tianjin performed well in terms of all three sub-dimension indicators of the economic dimension, ranking 5th for both quality of economic development and dynamic development, as well as 6th for urban influence.

Within the social dimension, Tianjin ranked 6th. During the Sui Dynasty, Tianjin was the water and land wharf for the northward transport of southern grain products, and as the gateway to Beijing, it was a garrison town and the pivotal point of grain transport to Beijing since the Yuan Dynasty. During the Westernization Movement (A.D.1861~A.D.1894), Tianjin was the second largest industrial and commer-cial city in China and the largest financial and trade center in the north, enjoying a prominent historical position. Within the social dimension, Tianjin ranked 3rd for status and governance, 7th for inheritance and exchange, and 9th for quality of life.

Within the environmental dimension, Tianjin moved up to 38th place as compared to the 2016 rank-ing. The construction of urban infrastructure in Tianjin began at an earlier date with a high ranking of urban rail transit mileage nationwide, and thus Tianjin ranked 6th for spatial structure. However, restricted by a shortage of natural ecological resources and also by her air pollution, Tianjin ranked 217th and 68th respectively for natural ecology and environmental quality.

Table 3-5 Key Index

Environment

Number of permanent residents:	15,470,000
Land area of administrative region:	11,917 km²
Ranking of available land area per capita:	280
Ranking of forest coverage:	191
Ranking of water resources per capita:	287
Ranking of climate comfort index:	229
Ranking of $PM_{2.5}$ Index:	261
Ranking of densely inhabited district (DID) population :	5
Ranking of rail transit route mileage :	8

Society

Ranking of average house prices :	68
Ranking of cinemas and theater numbers :	36
Ranking of museum and art gallery numbers :	11
Number of domestic tourists:	170,590,000
Number of inbound tourists:	3,260,000
Ranking of world heritage number :	14
Ranking of international conference number :	46

Economy

Size of GDP:	RMB 1653.8 billion
Per-capita GDP:	RMB 106,908 / person
GDP growth rate:	4.9 %
Ranking of per capita revenue in :	6
Ranking of average salaries :	3
Ranking of mainboard listed enterprises :	8
Ranking of goods export in China:	11
Ranking of airport convenience in China:	13
Ranking of container port convenience :	6
Ranking of financial radiation :	8
Ranking of manufacturing radiation :	9
Ranking of IT industry radiation :	41
Ranking of higher education radiation :	9
Ranking of science and technology radiation :	8
Ranking of medical radiation :	7
Ranking of culture and sports and entertainment radiation :	12
Ranking of catering and hotel radiation :	15
Ranking of wholesale and retail radiation :	7

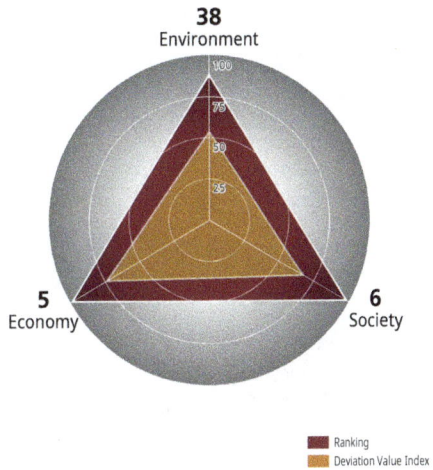

Figure 3-41 Scores of Dimension

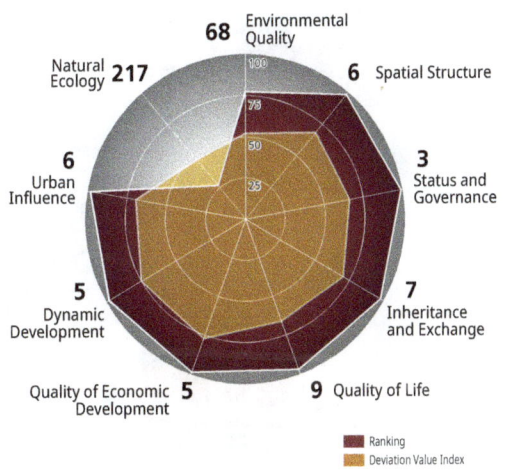

Figure 3-42 Scores of Sub-Dimension

Tianjin

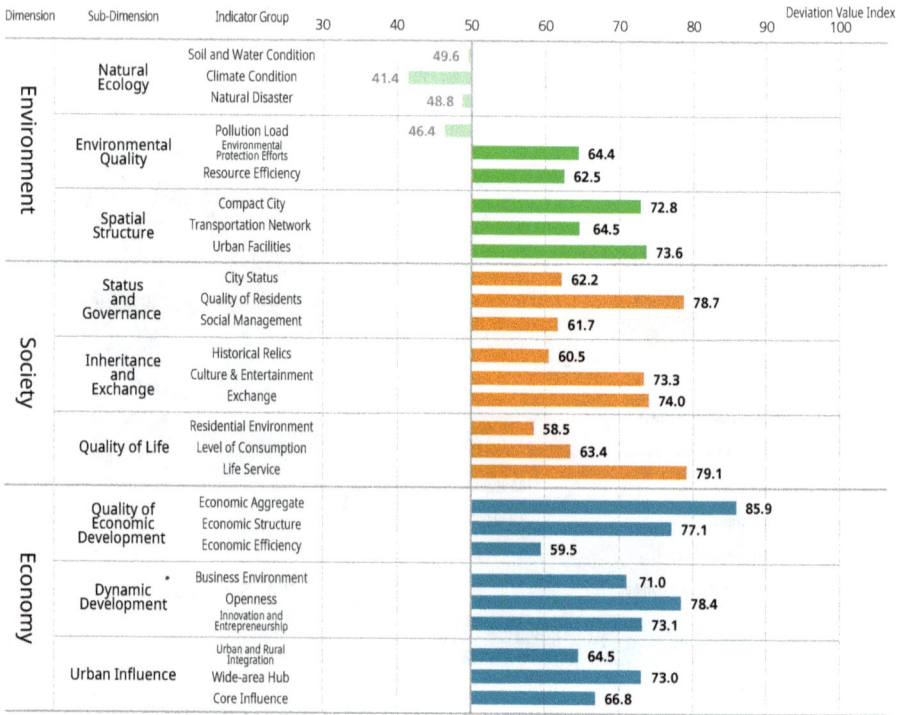

Dimension	Sub-Dimension	Indicator Group	Deviation Value Index
Environment	Natural Ecology	Soil and Water Condition	49.6
		Climate Condition	41.4
		Natural Disaster	48.8
	Environmental Quality	Pollution Load	46.4
		Environmental Protection Efforts	64.4
		Resource Efficiency	62.5
	Spatial Structure	Compact City	72.8
		Transportation Network	64.5
		Urban Facilities	73.6
Society	Status and Governance	City Status	62.2
		Quality of Residents	78.7
		Social Management	61.7
	Inheritance and Exchange	Historical Relics	60.5
		Culture & Entertainment	73.3
		Exchange	74.0
	Quality of Life	Residential Environment	58.5
		Level of Consumption	63.4
		Life Service	79.1
Economy	Quality of Economic Development	Economic Aggregate	85.9
		Economic Structure	77.1
		Economic Efficiency	59.5
	Dynamic Development	Business Environment	71.0
		Openness	78.4
		Innovation and Entrepreneurship	73.1
	Urban Influence	Urban and Rural Integration	64.5
		Wide-area Hub	73.0
		Core Influence	66.8

Figure 3-43 Deviation Value of Indicator Group

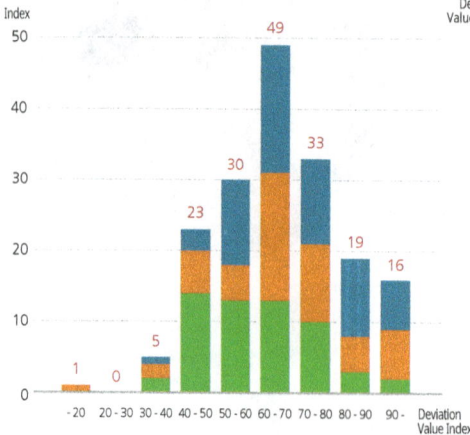

Figure 3-44 Deviation Value Distribution of Indicators

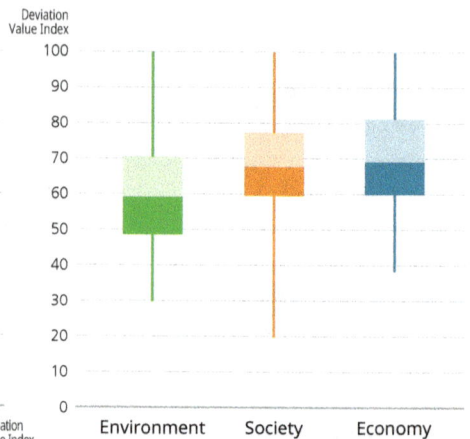

Figure 3-45 Box Plot Distribution of Indicators

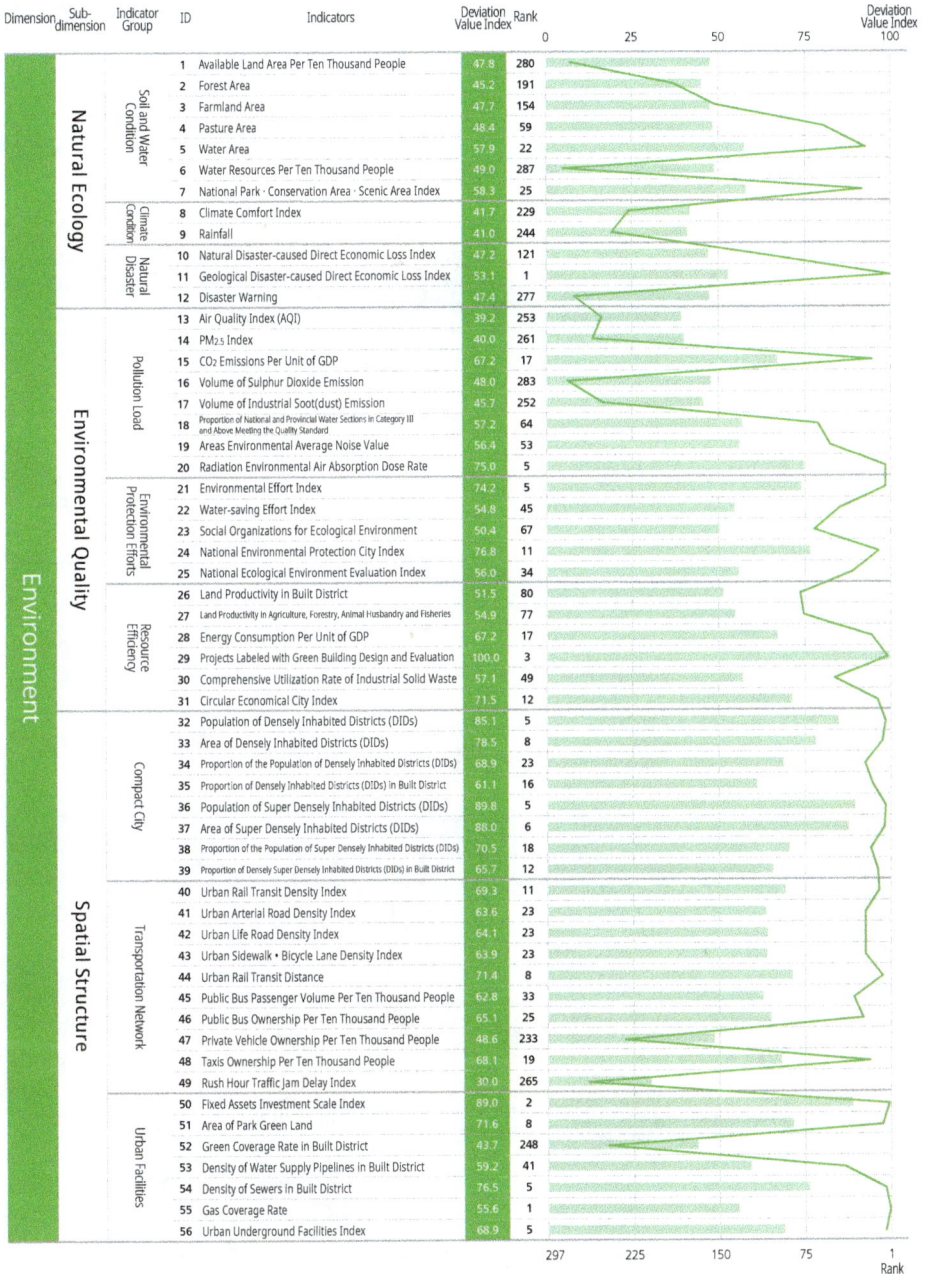

Dimension	Sub-dimension	Indicator Group	ID	Indicators	Deviation Value Index	Rank
Environment	Natural Ecology	Soil and Water Condition	1	Available Land Area Per Ten Thousand People	47.8	280
			2	Forest Area	45.2	191
			3	Farmland Area	47.7	154
			4	Pasture Area	48.4	59
			5	Water Area	57.9	22
			6	Water Resources Per Ten Thousand People	49.0	287
			7	National Park · Conservation Area · Scenic Area Index	58.3	25
		Climate Condition	8	Climate Comfort Index	41.7	229
			9	Rainfall	41.0	244
		Natural Disaster	10	Natural Disaster-caused Direct Economic Loss Index	47.2	121
			11	Geological Disaster-caused Direct Economic Loss Index	53.1	1
			12	Disaster Warning	47.4	277
	Environmental Quality	Pollution Load	13	Air Quality Index (AQI)	39.2	253
			14	PM2.5 Index	40.0	261
			15	CO2 Emissions Per Unit of GDP	67.2	17
			16	Volume of Sulphur Dioxide Emission	48.0	283
			17	Volume of Industrial Soot(dust) Emission	45.7	252
			18	Proportion of National and Provincial Water Sections in Category III and Above Meeting the Quality Standard	57.2	64
			19	Areas Environmental Average Noise Value	56.4	53
			20	Radiation Environmental Air Absorption Dose Rate	75.0	5
		Environmental Protection Efforts	21	Environmental Effort Index	74.2	5
			22	Water-saving Effort Index	54.8	45
			23	Social Organizations for Ecological Environment	50.4	67
			24	National Environmental Protection City Index	76.8	11
			25	National Ecological Environment Evaluation Index	56.0	34
		Resource Efficiency	26	Land Productivity in Built District	51.5	80
			27	Land Productivity in Agriculture, Forestry, Animal Husbandry and Fisheries	54.9	77
			28	Energy Consumption Per Unit of GDP	67.2	17
			29	Projects Labeled with Green Building Design and Evaluation	100.0	3
			30	Comprehensive Utilization Rate of Industrial Solid Waste	57.1	49
			31	Circular Economical City Index	71.5	12
	Spatial Structure	Compact City	32	Population of Densely Inhabited Districts (DIDs)	85.1	5
			33	Area of Densely Inhabited Districts (DIDs)	78.5	8
			34	Proportion of the Population of Densely Inhabited Districts (DIDs)	68.9	23
			35	Proportion of Densely Inhabited Districts (DIDs) in Built District	61.1	16
			36	Population of Super Densely Inhabited Districts (DIDs)	89.8	5
			37	Area of Super Densely Inhabited Districts (DIDs)	88.0	6
			38	Proportion of the Population of Super Densely Inhabited Districts (DIDs)	70.5	18
			39	Proportion of Densely Super Densely Inhabited Districts (DIDs) in Built District	65.7	12
		Transportation Network	40	Urban Rail Transit Density Index	69.3	11
			41	Urban Arterial Road Density Index	63.6	23
			42	Urban Life Road Density Index	64.1	23
			43	Urban Sidewalk • Bicycle Lane Density Index	63.9	23
			44	Urban Rail Transit Distance	71.4	8
			45	Public Bus Passenger Volume Per Ten Thousand People	62.8	33
			46	Public Bus Ownership Per Ten Thousand People	65.1	25
			47	Private Vehicle Ownership Per Ten Thousand People	48.6	233
			48	Taxis Ownership Per Ten Thousand People	68.1	19
			49	Rush Hour Traffic jam Delay Index	30.0	265
		Urban Facilities	50	Fixed Assets Investment Scale Index	89.0	2
			51	Area of Park Green Land	71.6	8
			52	Green Coverage Rate in Built District	43.7	248
			53	Density of Water Supply Pipelines in Built District	59.2	41
			54	Density of Sewers in Built District	76.5	5
			55	Gas Coverage Rate	55.6	1
			56	Urban Underground Facilities Index	68.9	5

Figure 3-46 Index Ranking: Environment

Tianjin

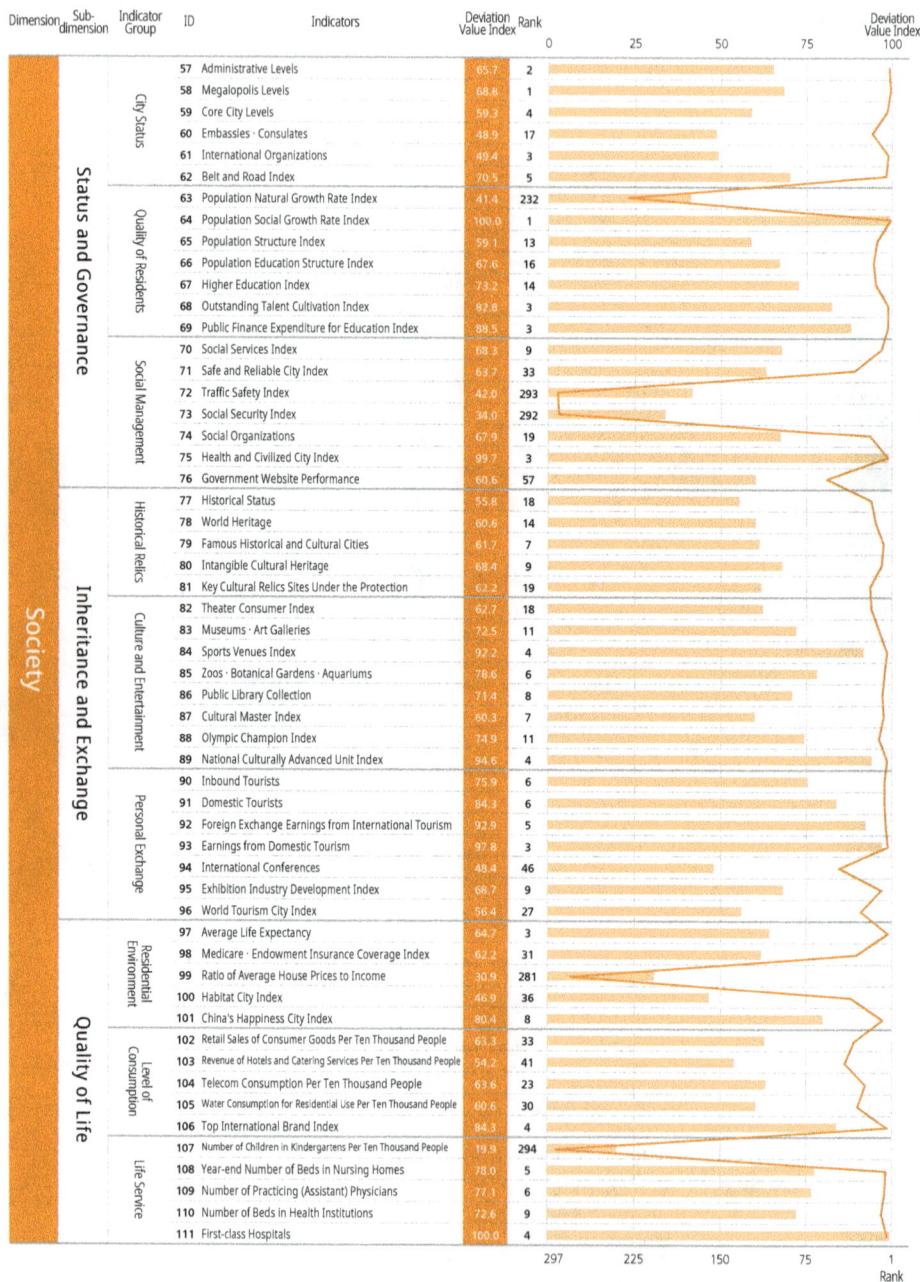

Dimension	Sub-dimension	Indicator Group	ID	Indicators	Deviation Value Index	Rank
Society	Status and Governance	City Status	57	Administrative Levels	65.7	2
			58	Megalopolis Levels	68.8	1
			59	Core City Levels	59.3	4
			60	Embassies · Consulates	48.9	17
			61	International Organizations	49.4	3
			62	Belt and Road Index	70.5	5
		Quality of Residents	63	Population Natural Growth Rate Index	41.4	232
			64	Population Social Growth Rate Index	100.0	1
			65	Population Structure Index	59.1	13
			66	Population Education Structure Index	67.6	16
			67	Higher Education Index	73.2	14
			68	Outstanding Talent Cultivation Index	82.8	3
			69	Public Finance Expenditure for Education Index	88.5	3
		Social Management	70	Social Services Index	68.3	9
			71	Safe and Reliable City Index	63.7	33
			72	Traffic Safety Index	42.0	293
			73	Social Security Index	34.0	292
			74	Social Organizations	67.9	19
			75	Health and Civilized City Index	99.7	3
			76	Government Website Performance	60.6	57
	Inheritance and Exchange	Historical Relics	77	Historical Status	55.8	18
			78	World Heritage	60.6	14
			79	Famous Historical and Cultural Cities	61.7	7
			80	Intangible Cultural Heritage	68.4	9
			81	Key Cultural Relics Sites Under the Protection	62.2	19
		Culture and Entertainment	82	Theater Consumer Index	62.7	18
			83	Museums · Art Galleries	72.5	11
			84	Sports Venues Index	92.2	4
			85	Zoos · Botanical Gardens · Aquariums	78.6	6
			86	Public Library Collection	71.4	8
			87	Cultural Master Index	60.3	7
			88	Olympic Champion Index	74.9	11
			89	National Culturally Advanced Unit Index	94.6	4
		Personal Exchange	90	Inbound Tourists	75.9	6
			91	Domestic Tourists	84.3	6
			92	Foreign Exchange Earnings from International Tourism	92.9	5
			93	Earnings from Domestic Tourism	97.8	3
			94	International Conferences	48.4	46
			95	Exhibition Industry Development Index	68.7	9
			96	World Tourism City Index	56.4	27
	Quality of Life	Residential Environment	97	Average Life Expectancy	64.7	3
			98	Medicare · Endowment Insurance Coverage Index	62.2	31
			99	Ratio of Average House Prices to Income	30.9	281
			100	Habitat City Index	46.9	36
			101	China's Happiness City Index	80.4	8
		Level of Consumption	102	Retail Sales of Consumer Goods Per Ten Thousand People	63.3	33
			103	Revenue of Hotels and Catering Services Per Ten Thousand People	54.2	41
			104	Telecom Consumption Per Ten Thousand People	63.6	23
			105	Water Consumption for Residential Use Per Ten Thousand People	60.6	30
			106	Top International Brand Index	84.3	4
		Life Service	107	Number of Children in Kindergartens Per Ten Thousand People	19.9	294
			108	Year-end Number of Beds in Nursing Homes	78.0	5
			109	Number of Practicing (Assistant) Physicians	77.1	6
			110	Number of Beds in Health Institutions	72.6	9
			111	First-class Hospitals	100.0	4

Figure 3-47 Index Ranking: Society

Figure header columns: Dimension | Sub-dimension | Indicator Group | ID | Indicators | Deviation Value Index | Rank | (chart 0–100) | Deviation Value Index 100

Dimension	Sub-dimension	Indicator Group	ID	Indicators	Deviation Value Index	Rank
Economy	Quality of Economic Development	Economic Scale	112	Size of GDP	93.5	5
			113	Population Size of Permanent Residents	82.6	4
			114	Scale of Tax Collection	81.4	4
			115	Electricity Consumption	81.4	4
		Economic Structure	116	Industrial Structure Index	85.9	6
			117	Mainboard Listed Enterprises	64.7	8
			118	Top 500 Chinese Enterprises in the World	52.0	7
			119	China's Top 500 Enterprises	60.5	7
			120	China's Top 500 Private-owned Enterprises	72.3	11
			121	Gross Industrial Output Value Above Designated Size	100.0	3
		Economic Efficiency	122	GDP Growth Index	52.6	142
			123	GDP Per Ten Thousand People	69.2	18
			124	Fiscal Revenue Per Ten Thousand People	83.2	6
			125	Dependent Population Index	68.5	10
			126	Size and Debt Rate of Bonds Issued by the City Investment Enterprises	45.4	268
			127	Number of Registered Unemployed Persons Per Ten Thousand People	38.4	284
	Dynamic Development	Business Environment	128	Employee Average Salary	76.5	3
			129	Number of Employees of Enterprise Services	67.9	8
			130	Star Hotel Index	65.0	17
			131	Top International Restaurant Index	55.1	10
			132	National Industrial Park Index	82.1	9
		Openness	133	Population Migration	88.9	5
			134	Export of Goods · Import of Goods	69.9	7
			135	Foreign Investment Utilized	100.0	1
			136	Outward Foreign Direct Investment	63.4	6
			137	The Output Value of Foreign-invested Enterprises Above Designated Size	93.6	4
			138	International Schools	64.2	10
			139	Free Trade Area Index	92.9	5
		Innovation and Entrepreneurship	140	The World's Top University Index	75.4	7
			141	R&D Expenditure Index	88.0	4
			142	R&D Human Resources	93.5	4
			143	GEM,New Third Board Listed Enterprise Index	58.8	19
			144	The Amount of Patent Authorization Index	60.1	11
			145	Trademark Registration Index	57.9	20
			146	Academicians Index	58.1	6
			147	National Reform Experiment	92.4	2
			148	National Innovative Model City Index	79.1	2
			149	Information · Knowledge Industry City Index	74.7	10
			150	National Key Laboratory · Engineering Research Center Index	71.0	6
	Urban Influence	Urban and Rural Integration	151	Urban-rural Income Ratio Index	58.7	27
			152	Primary School Education Level Population Ratio	67.3	16
			153	Illiteracy Rate	54.7	58
			154	Balanced Development of Compulsory Education Index	88.6	3
		Wide-area Hub	155	Airport Convenient	65.5	13
			156	Air Traffic Volume Index	59.7	19
			157	Container Port Convenient	68.8	6
			158	Port Container Throughput	90.5	6
			159	Water Transport Volume Index	51.3	66
			160	Railway Convenient	83.1	10
			161	Railway Traffic Volume Index	65.5	13
			162	Railway Density	85.2	4
			163	Road Traffic Volume Index	61.2	17
			164	Expressway Density	81.6	6
			165	National Road · Provincial Road Density	68.6	18
			166	Circulation City Index	78.0	10
		Core Influence	167	Higher Education Radiation	72.4	9
			168	Science and Technology Radiation	73.4	8
			169	IT Industry Radiation	49.9	41
			170	Culture and Sports and Entertainment Radiation	59.0	12
			171	Financial Radiation	68.7	8
			172	Manufacturing Radiation	69.2	9
			173	Medical Radiation	77.7	7
			174	Wholesale and Retail Radiation	73.6	7
			175	Catering and Hotel Radiation	57.3	15

Chart bottom axis (Rank): 297 225 150 75 1

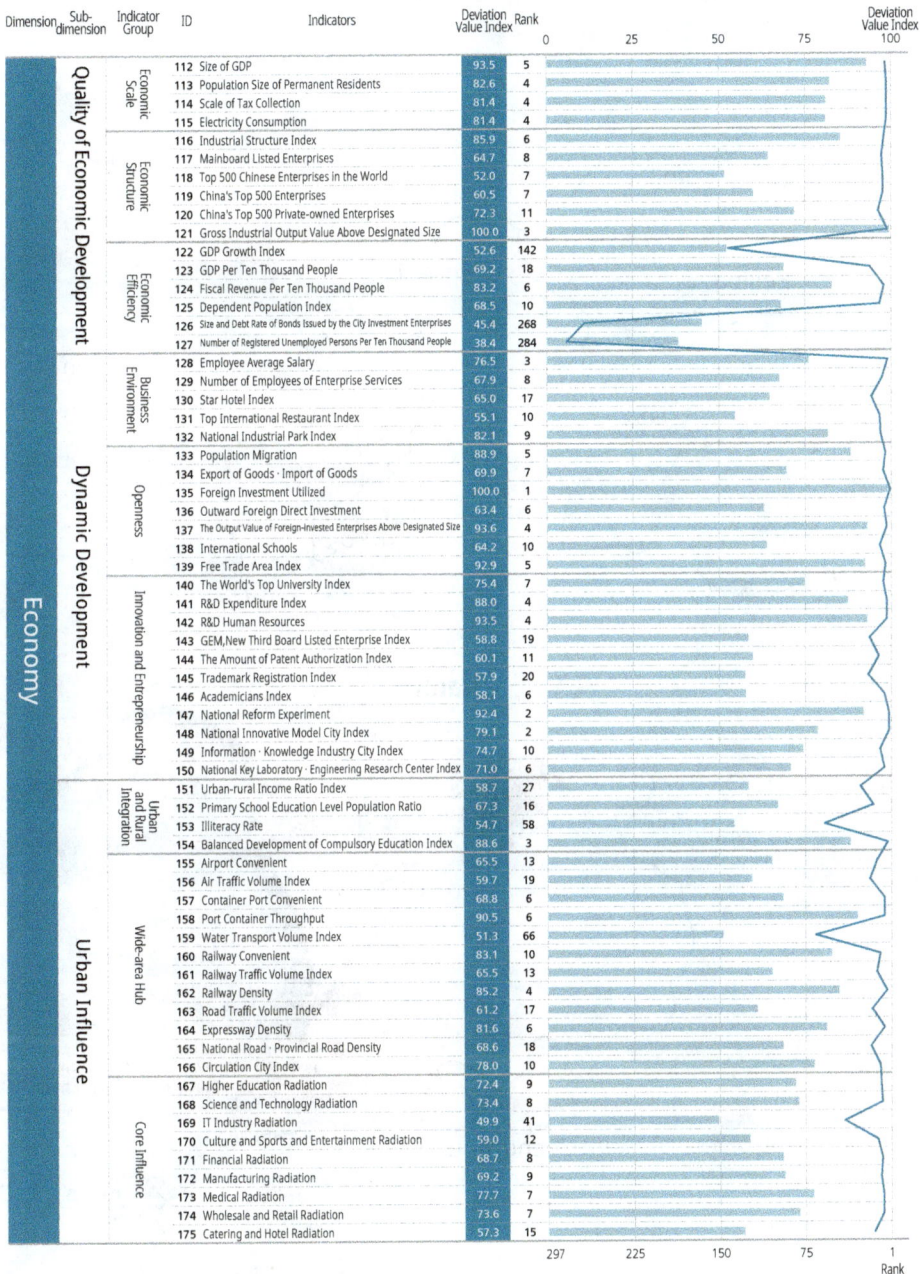

Figure 3-48 Index Ranking: Economy

Tianjin

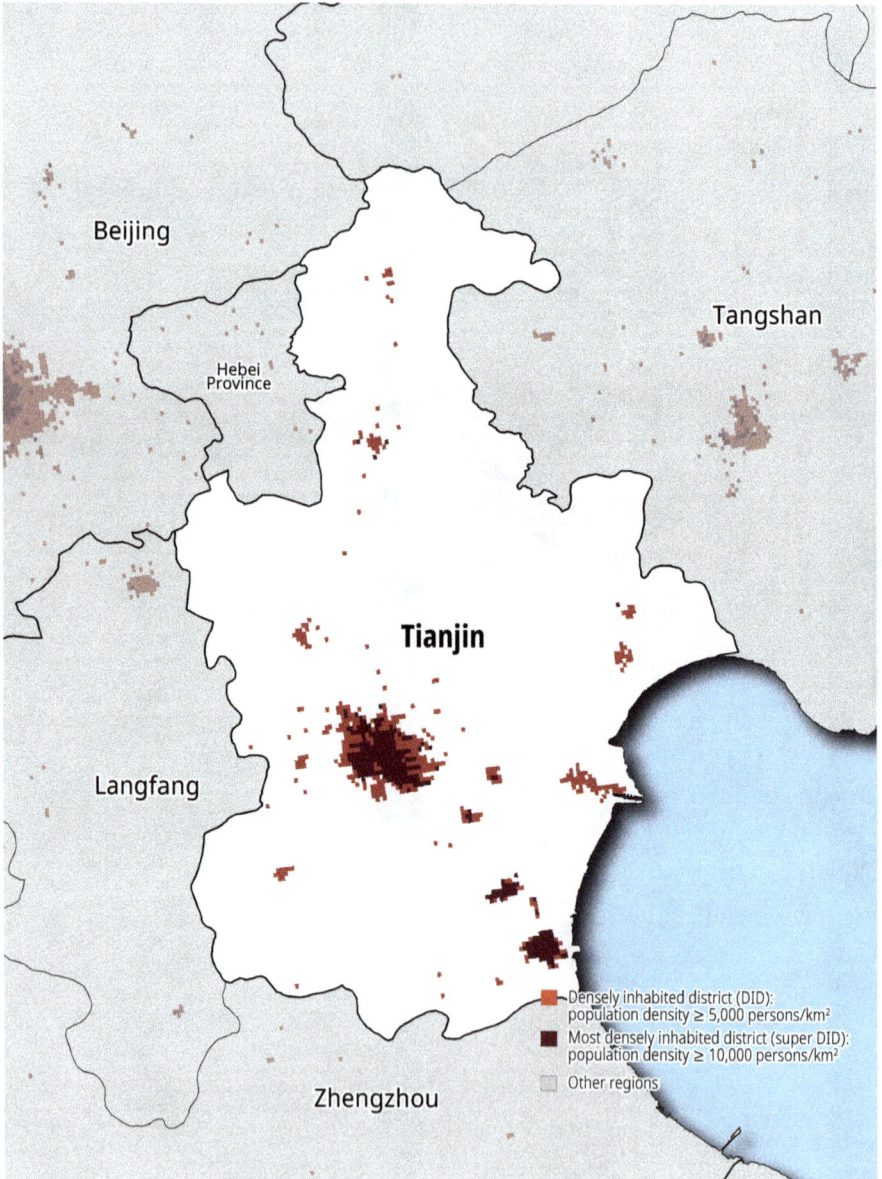

Figure 3-49 DID Analysis

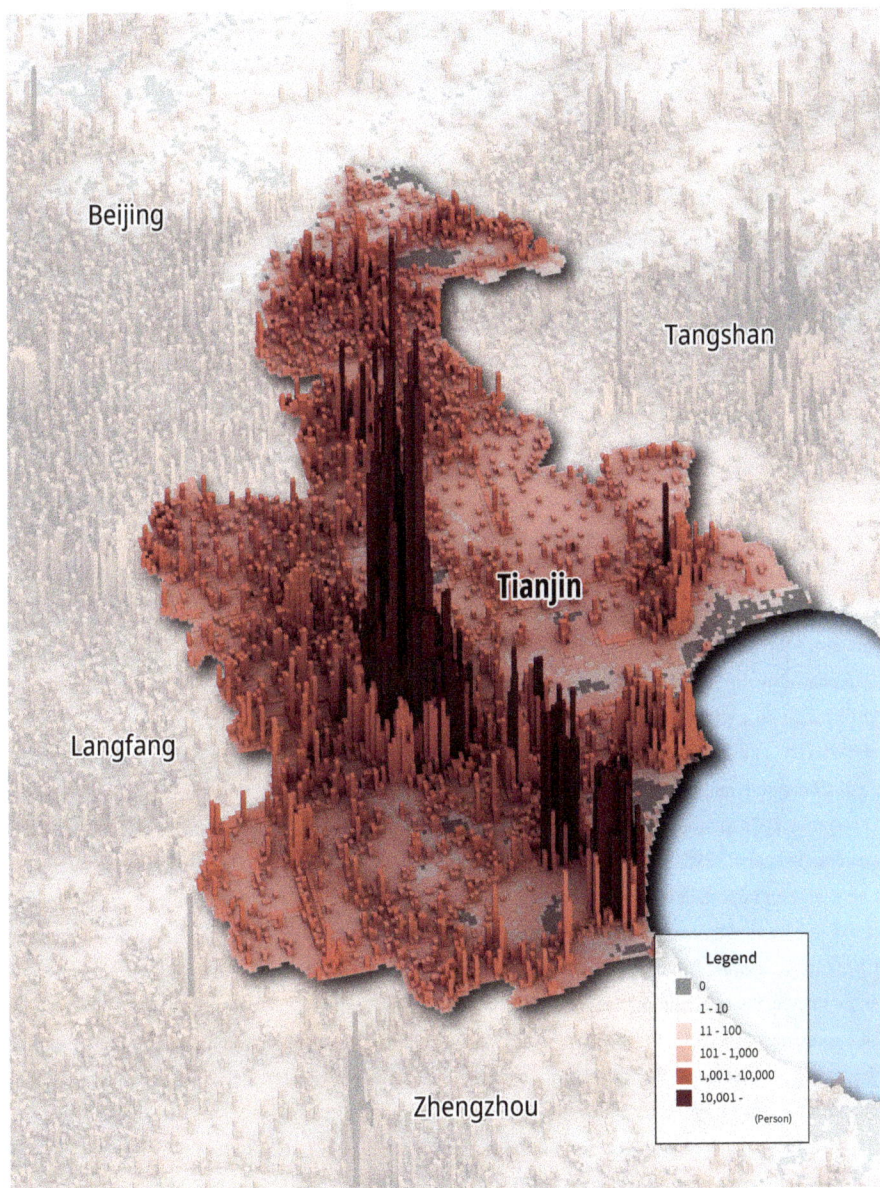

Figure 3-50 Population Size and Density Analysis

6th Chongqing

Chongqing moved up to No. 6 in the comprehensive ranking.

Within the social dimension, Chongqing ranked 4th. As the birthplace of Bayu culture (culture origi-nating from the areas of Chengdu and Chongqing) and a famous historical and cultural city, Chongqing offers pleasant natural sceneries and strong human culture. She was the earliest foreign trade port in China's hinterland and the wartime second capital during the Second World War. Chongqing integrated the func-tions of a regional political, economic, and cultural center with a city that combined the elements of liveliness, calm, excitement, and leisure. Chongqing had excellent performance for status and governance as well as for inheritance and exchange within the social dimension, ranking 5th and 3rd respectively, and she also ranked 17th for quality of life.

Chongqing ranked 7th within the economic dimension. As a municipality directly under the Central Government, Chongqing not only has a large population and economic volume, but is also an economic center in the upper reach of the Yangtze River and an integrated transportation hub in the southwest region. She is also an important modern manufacturing base of the country. In particular, the electronics industry is developing rapidly here, becoming a major industrial cluster for electronics. As the leading city of the Chengdu-Chongqing Urban Agglomeration, Chongqing has a strong capability of radiation into such fields as commerce, finance, culture, science and technology, and education and medical care, thus functioning as an important central point for the development of the region. In terms of three sub-dimension indicators of the economic dimension, Chongqing was excellent for quality of economic development, dynamic devel-opment and urban influence, ranking 4th, 14th and 8th respectively.

Ranking 11th within the environmental dimension, mountain town Chongqing is restricted by her geographical environment, but enjoys the advantage of having a natural eco-environment. In terms of three sub-dimension indicators of the environmental dimension, Chongqing ranked 39th for spatial structure, 5th for the natural ecology, and 56th for environmental quality.

Table 3-6 Key Index

Environment

Number of permanent residents:	30,170,000
Land area of administrative region:	82,374 km²
Ranking of available land area per capita:	149
Ranking of forest coverage:	3
Ranking of water resources per capita:	119
Ranking of climate comfort index:	19
Ranking of PM$_{2.5}$ Index:	201
Ranking of densely inhabited district (DID) population :	6
Ranking of rail transit route mileage :	11

Society

Ranking of average house prices :	56
Ranking of cinemas and theater numbers :	111
Ranking of museum and art gallery numbers :	6
Number of domestic tourists:	388,850,000
Number of inbound tourists:	2,830,000
Ranking of world heritage number :	2
Ranking of international conference number :	4

Economy

Size of GDP:	RMB 1571.7 billion
Per-capita GDP:	RMB 52,103 / person
GDP growth rate:	9.3 %
Ranking of per capita revenue in :	58
Ranking of average salaries :	53
Ranking of mainboard listed enterprises :	5
Ranking of goods export in China:	8
Ranking of airport convenience in China:	7
Ranking of container port convenience :	225
Ranking of financial radiation :	10
Ranking of manufacturing radiation :	6
Ranking of IT industry radiation :	8
Ranking of higher education radiation :	16
Ranking of science and technology radiation :	12
Ranking of medical radiation :	10
Ranking of culture and sports and entertainment radiation :	10
Ranking of catering and hotel radiation :	3
Ranking of wholesale and retail radiation :	4

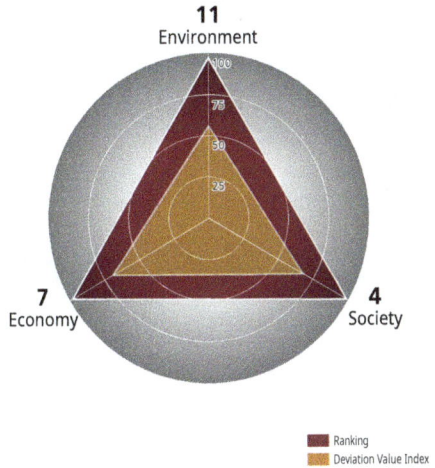

Figure 3-51 Scores of Dimension

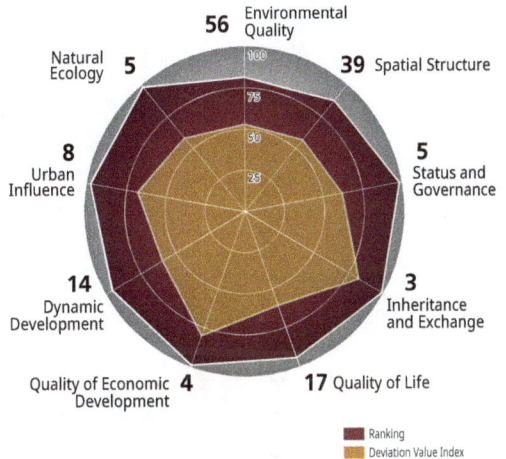

Figure 3-52 Scores of Sub-Dimension

Chongqing

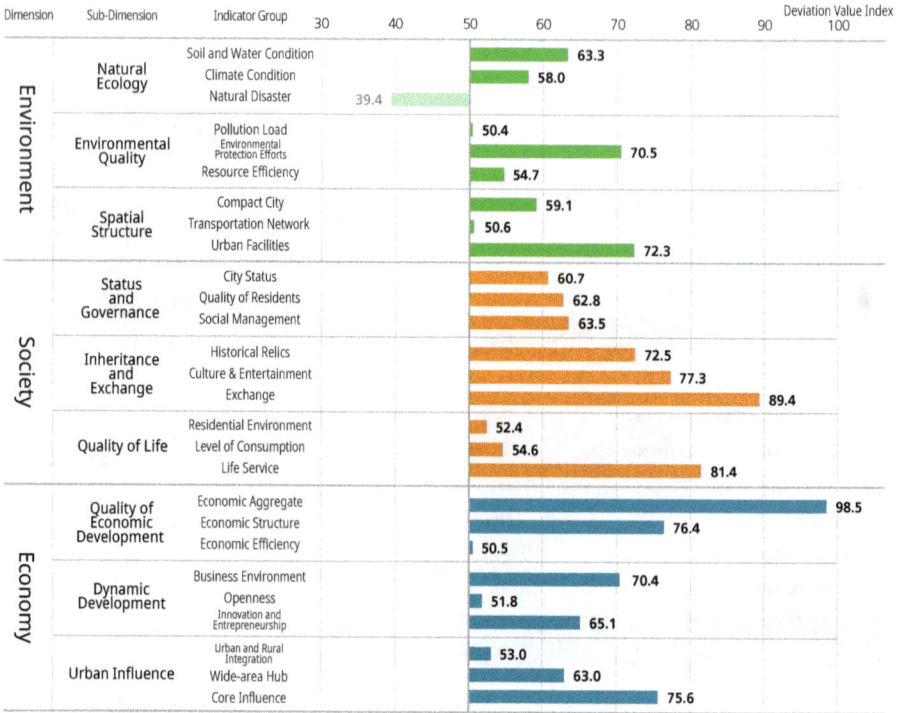

Figure 3-53 Deviation Value of Indicator Group

Dimension	Sub-Dimension	Indicator Group	Deviation Value Index
Environment	Natural Ecology	Soil and Water Condition	63.3
		Climate Condition	58.0
		Natural Disaster	39.4
	Environmental Quality	Pollution Load	50.4
		Environmental Protection Efforts	70.5
		Resource Efficiency	54.7
	Spatial Structure	Compact City	59.1
		Transportation Network	50.6
		Urban Facilities	72.3
Society	Status and Governance	City Status	60.7
		Quality of Residents	62.8
		Social Management	63.5
	Inheritance and Exchange	Historical Relics	72.5
		Culture & Entertainment	77.3
		Exchange	89.4
	Quality of Life	Residential Environment	52.4
		Level of Consumption	54.6
		Life Service	81.4
Economy	Quality of Economic Development	Economic Aggregate	98.5
		Economic Structure	76.4
		Economic Efficiency	50.5
	Dynamic Development	Business Environment	70.4
		Openness	51.8
		Innovation and Entrepreneurship	65.1
	Urban Influence	Urban and Rural Integration	53.0
		Wide-area Hub	63.0
		Core Influence	75.6

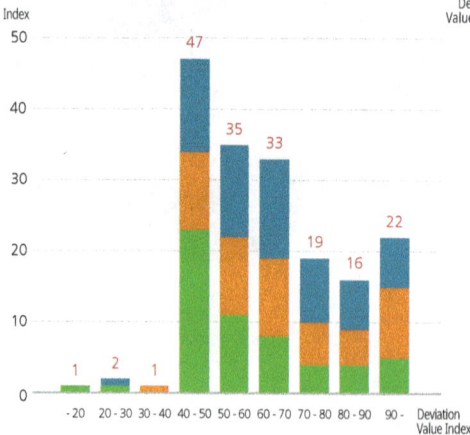

Figure 3-54 Deviation Value Distribution of Indicators

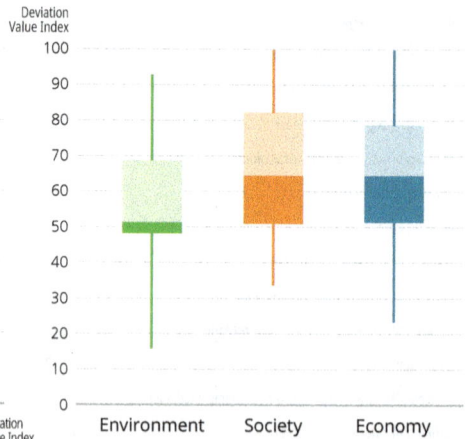

Figure 3-55 Box Plot Distribution of Indicators

86

Dimension	Sub-dimension	Indicator Group	ID	Indicators	Deviation Value Index	Rank
Environment	Natural Ecology	Soil and Water Condition	1	Available Land Area Per Ten Thousand People	48.7	149
			2	Forest Area	84.1	3
			3	Farmland Area	93.0	1
			4	Pasture Area	48.4	60
			5	Water Area	50.3	61
			6	Water Resources Per Ten Thousand People	49.3	119
			7	National Park · Conservation Area · Scenic Area Index	90.8	1
		Climate Condition	8	Climate Comfort Index	63.7	19
			9	Rainfall	52.4	113
		Natural Disaster	10	Natural Disaster-caused Direct Economic Loss Index	47.1	294
			11	Geological Disaster-caused Direct Economic Loss Index	15.9	291
			12	Disaster Warning	47.3	288
	Environmental Quality	Pollution Load	13	Air Quality Index (AQI)	47.6	156
			14	PM₂.₅ Index	44.7	201
			15	CO₂ Emissions Per Unit of GDP	55.9	79
			16	Volume of Sulphur Dioxide Emission	47.9	290
			17	Volume of Industrial Soot(dust) Emission	45.2	287
			18	Proportion of National and Provincial Water Sections in Category III and Above Meeting the Quality Standard	63.8	1
			19	Areas Environmental Average Noise Value	61.1	37
			20	Radiation Environmental Air Absorption Dose Rate	68.2	31
		Environmental Protection Efforts	21	Environmental Effort Index	90.0	2
			22	Water-saving Effort Index	45.2	239
			23	Social Organizations for Ecological Environment	69.7	5
			24	National Environmental Protection City Index	78.8	7
			25	National Ecological Environment Evaluation Index	49.4	51
		Resource Efficiency	26	Land Productivity in Built District	51.6	79
			27	Land Productivity in Agriculture, Forestry, Animal Husbandry and Fisheries	45.1	168
			28	Energy Consumption Per Unit of GDP	55.9	79
			29	Projects Labeled with Green Building Design and Evaluation	62.0	14
			30	Comprehensive Utilization Rate of Industrial Solid Waste	51.4	195
			31	Circular Economical City Index	85.0	1
	Spatial Structure	Compact City	32	Population of Densely Inhabited Districts (DIDs)	82.0	6
			33	Area of Densely Inhabited Districts (DIDs)	84.7	5
			34	Proportion of the Population of Densely Inhabited Districts (DIDs)	48.4	137
			35	Proportion of Densely Inhabited Districts (DIDs) in Built District	47.7	135
			36	Population of Super Densely Inhabited Districts (DIDs)	77.5	9
			37	Area of Super Densely Inhabited Districts (DIDs)	78.7	8
			38	Proportion of the Population of Super Densely Inhabited Districts (DIDs)	49.5	114
			39	Proportion of Densely Super Densely Inhabited Districts (DIDs) in Built District	47.8	116
		Transportation Network	40	Urban Rail Transit Density Index	51.7	51
			41	Urban Arterial Road Density Index	48.3	141
			42	Urban Life Road Density Index	48.0	153
			43	Urban Sidewalk • Bicycle Lane Density Index	48.5	133
			44	Urban Rail Transit Distance	65.2	11
			45	Public Bus Passenger Volume Per Ten Thousand People	54.6	60
			46	Public Bus Ownership Per Ten Thousand People	49.7	106
			47	Private Vehicle Ownership Per Ten Thousand People	49.3	126
			48	Taxis Ownership Per Ten Thousand People	46.7	137
			49	Rush Hour Traffic Jam Delay Index	25.3	292
		Urban Facilities	50	Fixed Assets Investment Scale Index	90.0	1
			51	Area of Park Green Land	86.0	3
			52	Green Coverage Rate in Built District	52.5	143
			53	Density of Water Supply Pipelines in Built District	48.3	134
			54	Density of Sewers in Built District	50.9	112
			55	Gas Coverage Rate	52.4	182
			56	Urban Underground Facilities Index	68.9	5

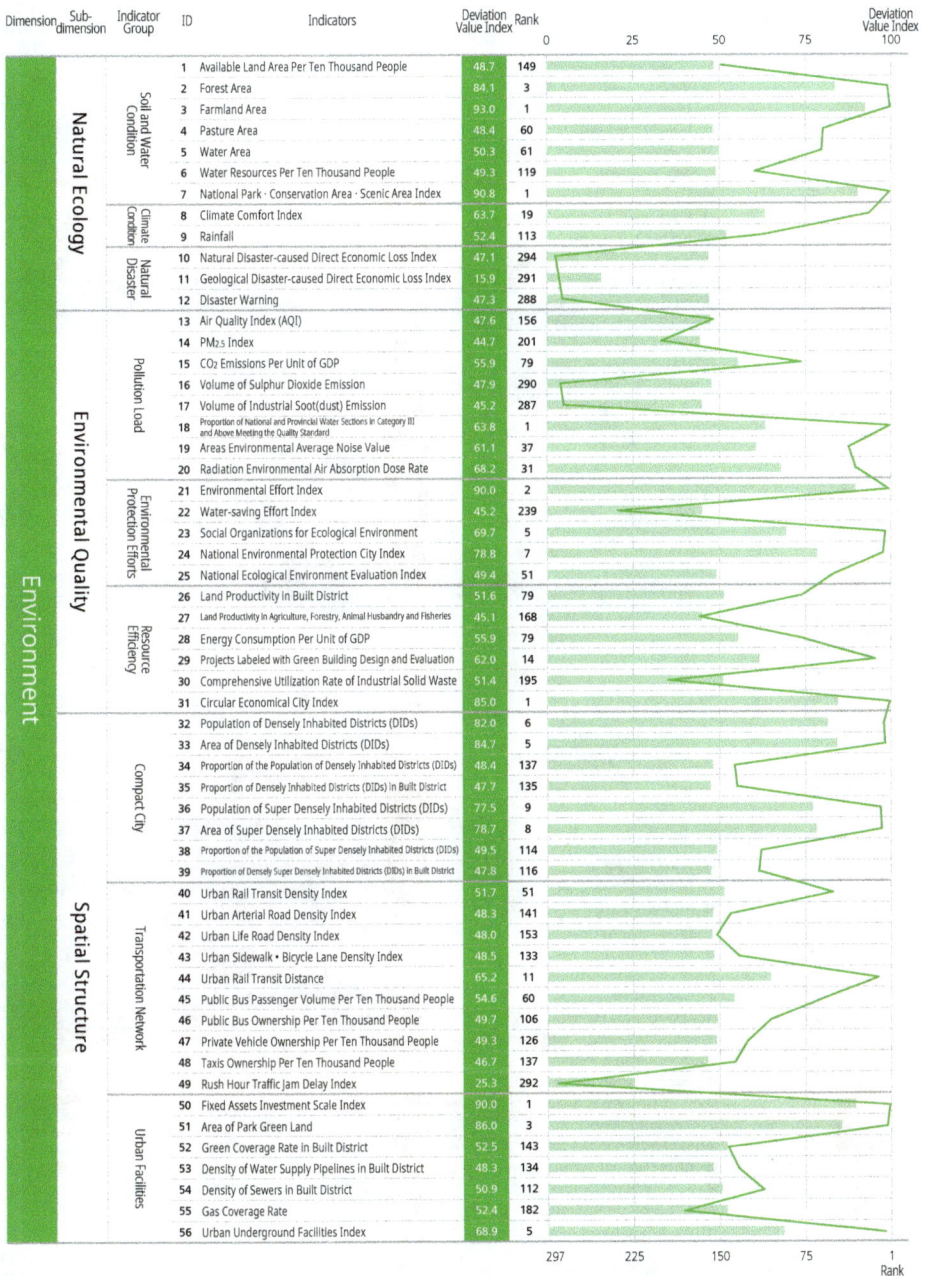

Figure 3-56 Index Ranking: Environment

Chongqing

Dimension	Sub-dimension	Indicator Group	ID	Indicators	Deviation Value Index	Rank
Society	Status and Governance	City Status	57	Administrative Levels	65.7	2
			58	Megalopolis Levels	49.8	46
			59	Core City Levels	59.3	4
			60	Embassies · Consulates	58.3	5
			61	International Organizations	49.4	3
			62	Belt and Road Index	67.2	6
		Quality of Residents	63	Population Natural Growth Rate Index	48.0	163
			64	Population Social Growth Rate Index	79.9	4
			65	Population Structure Index	44.5	245
			66	Population Education Structure Index	49.6	128
			67	Higher Education Index	88.5	7
			68	Outstanding Talent Cultivation Index	64.1	11
			69	Public Finance Expenditure for Education Index	79.4	4
		Social Management	70	Social Services Index	50.6	115
			71	Safe and Reliable City Index	65.2	26
			72	Traffic Safety Index	41.9	295
			73	Social Security Index	33.8	294
			74	Social Organizations	100.0	1
			75	Health and Civilized City Index	94.8	4
			76	Government Website Performance	41.1	134
	Inheritance and Exchange	Historical Relics	77	Historical Status	54.2	25
			78	World Heritage	90.3	2
			79	Famous Historical and Cultural Cities	61.7	7
			80	Intangible Cultural Heritage	83.9	4
			81	Key Cultural Relics Sites Under the Protection	80.7	8
		Culture and Entertainment	82	Theater Consumer Index	73.5	8
			83	Museums · Art Galleries	78.7	6
			84	Sports Venues Index	100.0	3
			85	Zoos · Botanical Gardens · Aquariums	86.9	3
			86	Public Library Collection	65.4	12
			87	Cultural Master Index	49.3	40
			88	Olympic Champion Index	64.7	15
			89	National Culturally Advanced Unit Index	99.5	2
		Personal Exchange	90	Inbound Tourists	72.0	8
			91	Domestic Tourists	100.0	1
			92	Foreign Exchange Earnings from International Tourism	67.3	10
			93	Earnings from Domestic Tourism	88.5	6
			94	International Conferences	62.9	4
			95	Exhibition Industry Development Index	96.1	4
			96	World Tourism City Index	56.4	27
	Quality of Life	Residential Environment	97	Average Life Expectancy	53.9	113
			98	Medicare · Endowment Insurance Coverage Index	53.7	67
			99	Ratio of Average House Prices to Income	44.3	224
			100	Habitat City Index	46.9	36
			101	China's Happiness City Index	67.0	14
		Level of Consumption	102	Retail Sales of Consumer Goods Per Ten Thousand People	51.8	92
			103	Revenue of Hotels and Catering Services Per Ten Thousand People	55.8	29
			104	Telecom Consumption Per Ten Thousand People	47.7	129
			105	Water Consumption for Residential Use Per Ten Thousand People	58.2	47
			106	Top International Brand Index	63.4	17
		Life Service	107	Number of Children in Kindergartens Per Ten Thousand People	50.5	141
			108	Year-end Number of Beds in Nursing Homes	100.0	3
			109	Number of Practicing (Assistant) Physicians	100.0	2
			110	Number of Beds in Health Institutions	100.0	1
			111	First-class Hospitals	73.1	9

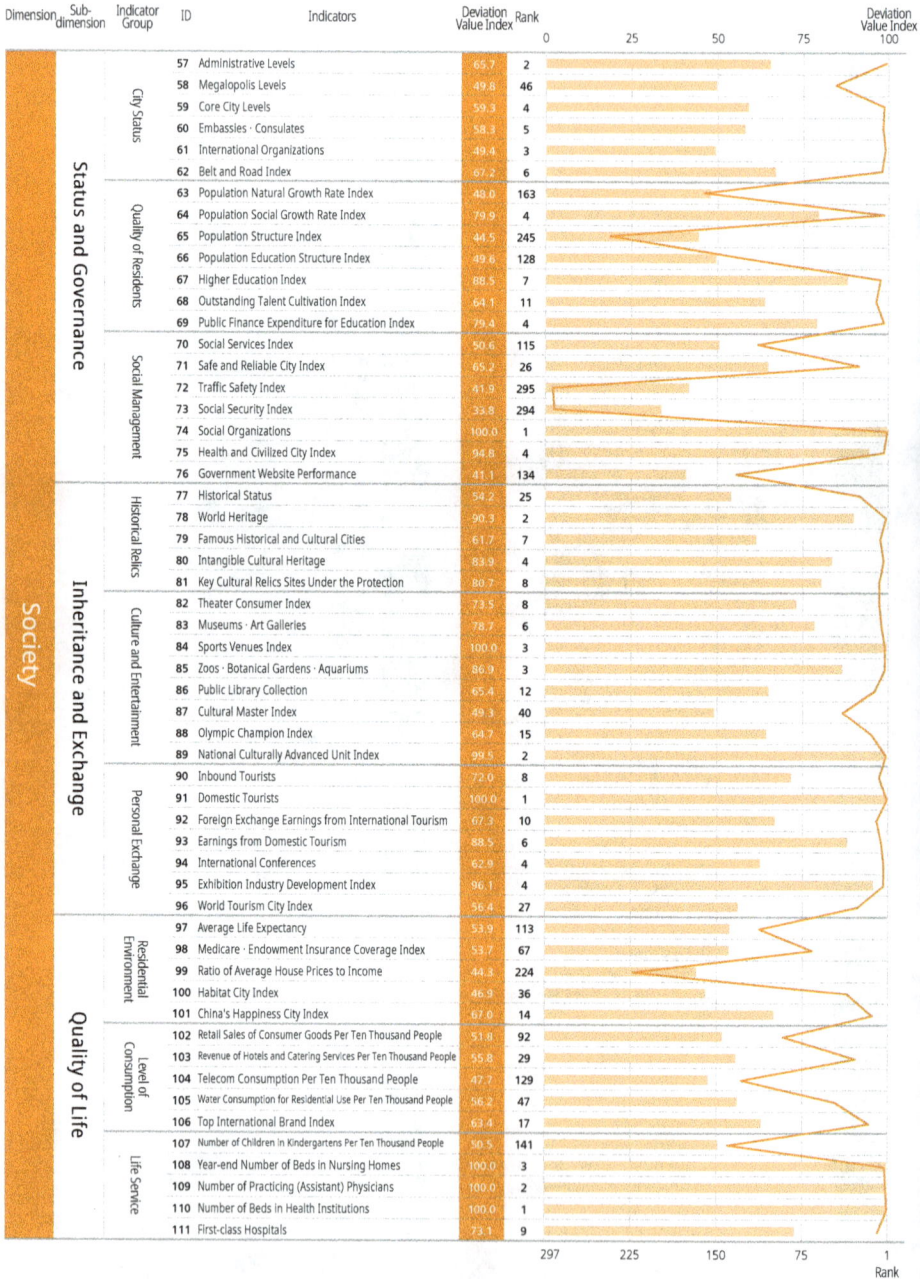

Figure 3-57 Index Ranking: Society

Dimension	Sub-dimension	Indicator Group	ID	Indicators	Deviation Value Index	Rank
Economy	Quality of Economic Development	Economic Scale	112	Size of GDP	91.0	6
			113	Population Size of Permanent Residents	100.0	1
			114	Scale of Tax Collection	78.6	5
			115	Electricity Consumption	78.6	5
		Economic Structure	116	Industrial Structure Index	89.5	4
			117	Mainboard Listed Enterprises	68.4	5
			118	Top 500 Chinese Enterprises in the World	49.0	25
			119	China's Top 500 Enterprises	55.7	12
			120	China's Top 500 Private-owned Enterprises	70.2	12
			121	Gross Industrial Output Value Above Designated Size	86.6	5
		Economic Efficiency	122	GDP Growth Index	58.7	22
			123	GDP Per Ten Thousand People	50.6	110
			124	Fiscal Revenue Per Ten Thousand People	56.9	58
			125	Dependent Population Index	43.3	217
			126	Size and Debt Rate of Bonds Issued by the City Investment Enterprises	45.6	263
			127	Number of Registered Unemployed Persons Per Ten Thousand People	47.8	159
	Dynamic Development	Business Environment	128	Employee Average Salary	57.2	53
			129	Number of Employees of Enterprise Services	88.9	3
			130	Star Hotel Index	84.1	3
			131	Top International Restaurant Index	50.2	20
			132	National Industrial Park Index	79.3	10
		Openness	133	Population Migration	23.5	294
			134	Export of Goods · Import of Goods	62.2	11
			135	Foreign Investment Utilized	96.8	4
			136	Outward Foreign Direct Investment	57.1	12
			137	The Output Value of Foreign-Invested Enterprises Above Designated Size	68.2	10
			138	International Schools	58.6	16
			139	Free Trade Area Index	85.2	10
		Innovation and Entrepreneurship	140	The World's Top University Index	54.9	19
			141	R&D Expenditure Index	64.3	10
			142	R&D Human Resources	72.7	10
			143	GEM,New Third Board Listed Enterprise Index	55.0	31
			144	The Amount of Patent Authorization Index	59.7	13
			145	Trademark Registration Index	69.7	7
			146	Academicians Index	51.6	16
			147	National Reform Experiment	88.9	3
			148	National Innovative Model City Index	85.9	3
			149	Information · Knowledge Industry City Index	83.6	6
			150	National Key Laboratory · Engineering Research Center Index	62.3	11
	Urban Influence	Urban and Rural Integration	151	Urban-rural Income Ratio Index	46.5	212
			152	Primary School Education Level Population Ratio	41.4	246
			153	Illiteracy Rate	45.5	188
			154	Balanced Development of Compulsory Education Index	91.8	2
		Wide-area Hub	155	Airport Convenient	75.5	7
			156	Air Traffic Volume Index	74.2	7
			157	Container Port Convenient	46.9	225
			158	Port Container Throughput	48.0	24
			159	Water Transport Volume Index	79.6	4
			160	Railway Convenient	61.1	29
			161	Railway Traffic Volume Index	65.3	16
			162	Railway Density	46.8	157
			163	Road Traffic Volume Index	100.0	3
			164	Expressway Density	49.0	124
			165	National Road · Provincial Road Density	46.6	144
			166	Circulation City Index	69.5	25
		Core Influence	167	Higher Education Radiation	60.8	16
			168	Science and Technology Radiation	67.5	12
			169	IT Industry Radiation	59.6	8
			170	Culture and Sports and Entertainment Radiation	64.7	10
			171	Financial Radiation	65.1	10
			172	Manufacturing Radiation	79.2	6
			173	Medical Radiation	74.4	10
			174	Wholesale and Retail Radiation	99.7	4
			175	Catering and Hotel Radiation	100.0	3

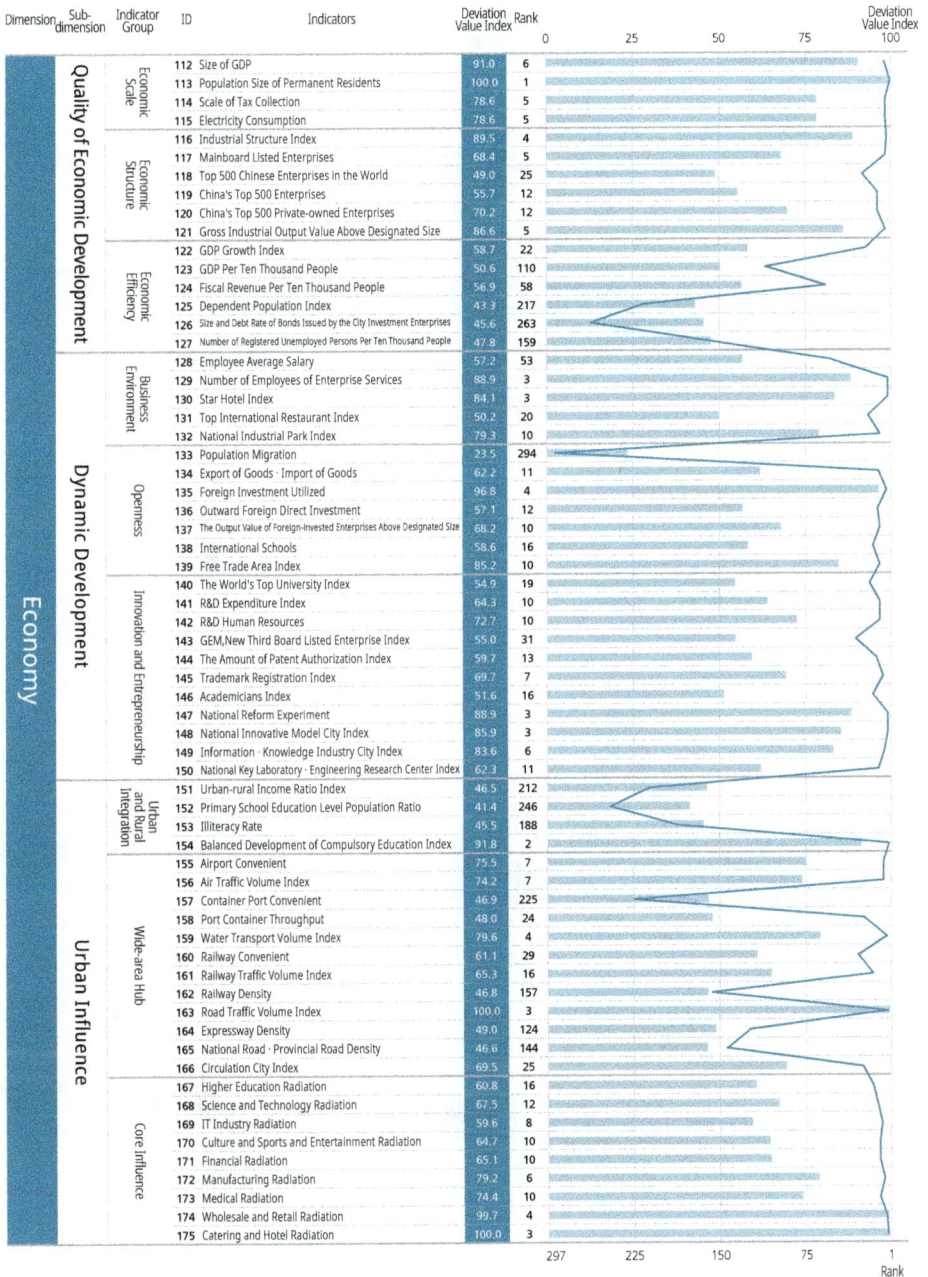

Figure 3-58 Index Ranking: Economy

Chongqing

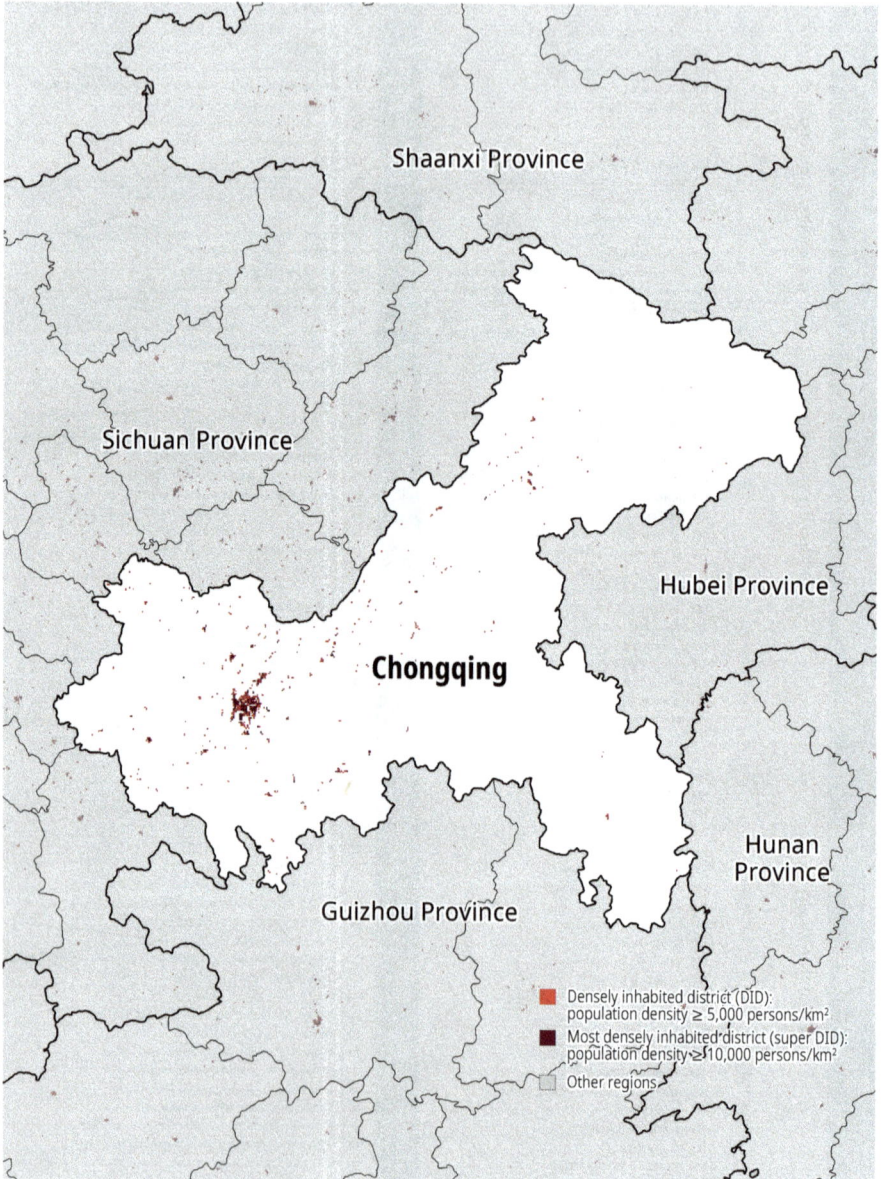

Figure 3-59 DID Analysis

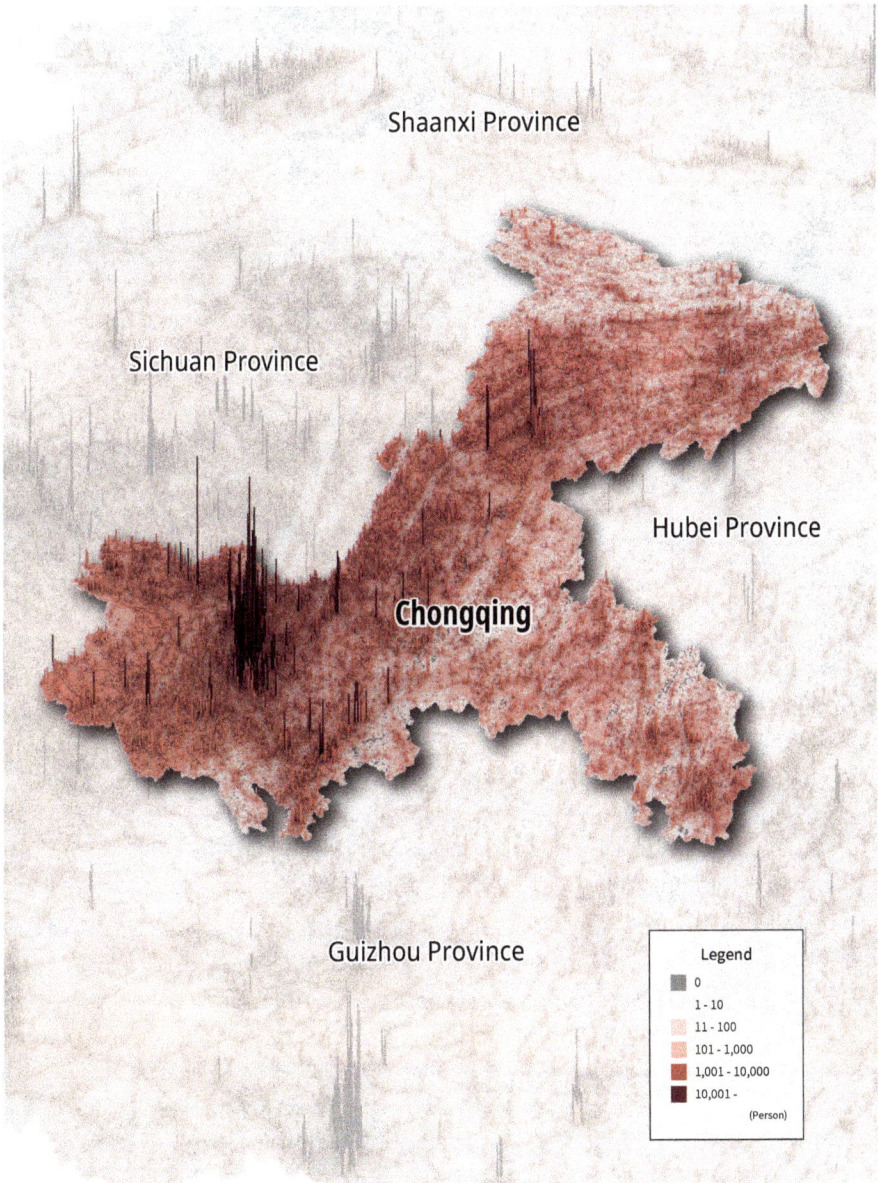

Figure 3-60 Population Size and Density Analysis

7th Hangzhou

Hangzhou kept her satisfactory scores by holding the 7th place in the comprehensive ranking.

Hangzhou ranked 5th within the social dimension. Once the capital of the State of Wuyue (A.D.907~A.D.978) and the Southern Song Dynasty (A.D.1127~A.D.1279), Hangzhou—one of the eight ancient capitals of China—is a famous historical and cultural city and also an important city for scenic tourism. She is well known as the "Paradise on Earth" and carries such titles as the "Happiest City in China," "National Civilized City," and "National Ecological Garden City." In terms of three sub-dimension indicators of the social dimension, Hangzhou ranked 8th, 6th, and 4th respectively for status and governance, inheritance and exchange, and quality of life, showing a competitive strength.

Hangzhou ranked 9th within the economic dimension. Thanks to the convenience of the Beijing-Hangzhou Grand Canal, Hangzhou has been an important commercial distribution center in history. Today, as the capital city of Zhejiang Province and one of the central cities of the Yangtze River Delta Megalopolis, Hangzhou has also leaped forward and become one of China's important e-commerce centers and a city with both heritage and vitality. Hangzhou had excellent performance in terms of all three sub-dimension indica-tors of the economic dimension, ranking 8th for both quality of economic development and dynamic devel-opment as well as 11th for urban influence.

Within the environmental dimension, Hangzhou ranked 14th. Troubled by the issue of air pollution, Hangzhou ranked 58th for environmental quality, but did a better job for spatial structure and natural ecol-ogy, ranking 15th and 20th, respectively.

Table 3-7 Key Index

Environment

Number of permanent residents:	9,020,000
Land area of administrative region:	16,596 km²
Ranking of available land area per capita:	196
Ranking of forest coverage:	41
Ranking of water resources per capita:	68
Ranking of climate comfort index:	59
Ranking of $PM_{2.5}$ Index:	165
Ranking of densely inhabited district (DID) population :	14
Ranking of rail transit route mileage :	18

Society

Ranking of average house prices :	7
Ranking of cinemas and theater numbers :	7
Ranking of museum and art gallery numbers :	9
Number of domestic tourists:	120,000,000
Number of inbound tourists:	3,420,000
Ranking of world heritage number :	4
Ranking of international conference number :	21

Economy

Size of GDP:	RMB 1005.0 billion
Per-capita GDP:	RMB 111,446 / person
GDP growth rate:	8.4 %
Ranking of per capita revenue in :	12
Ranking of average salaries :	9
Ranking of mainboard listed enterprises :	7
Ranking of goods export in China:	12
Ranking of airport convenience in China:	8
Ranking of container port convenience :	30
Ranking of financial radiation :	7
Ranking of manufacturing radiation :	12
Ranking of IT industry radiation :	4
Ranking of higher education radiation :	13
Ranking of science and technology radiation :	6
Ranking of medical radiation :	5
Ranking of culture and sports and entertainment radiation :	8
Ranking of catering and hotel radiation :	8
Ranking of wholesale and retail radiation :	6

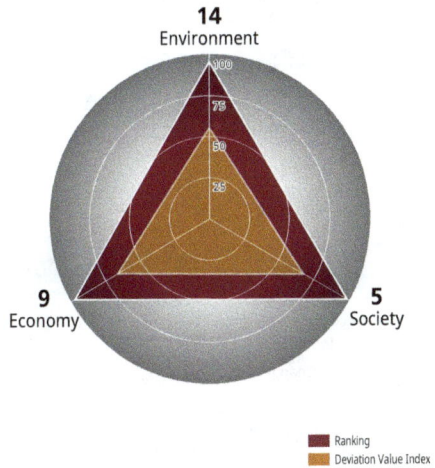

Figure 3-61 Scores of Dimension

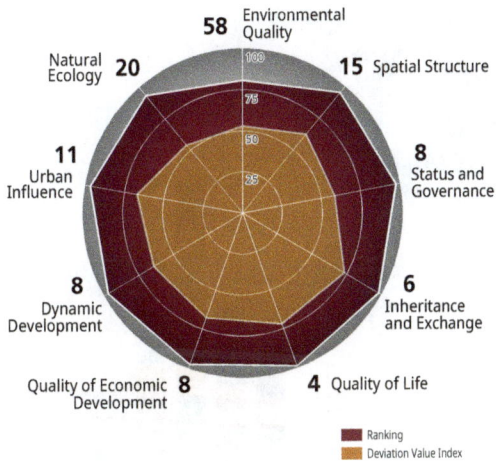

Figure 3-62 Scores of Sub-Dimension

Hangzhou

Dimension	Sub-Dimension	Indicator Group		Deviation Value Index

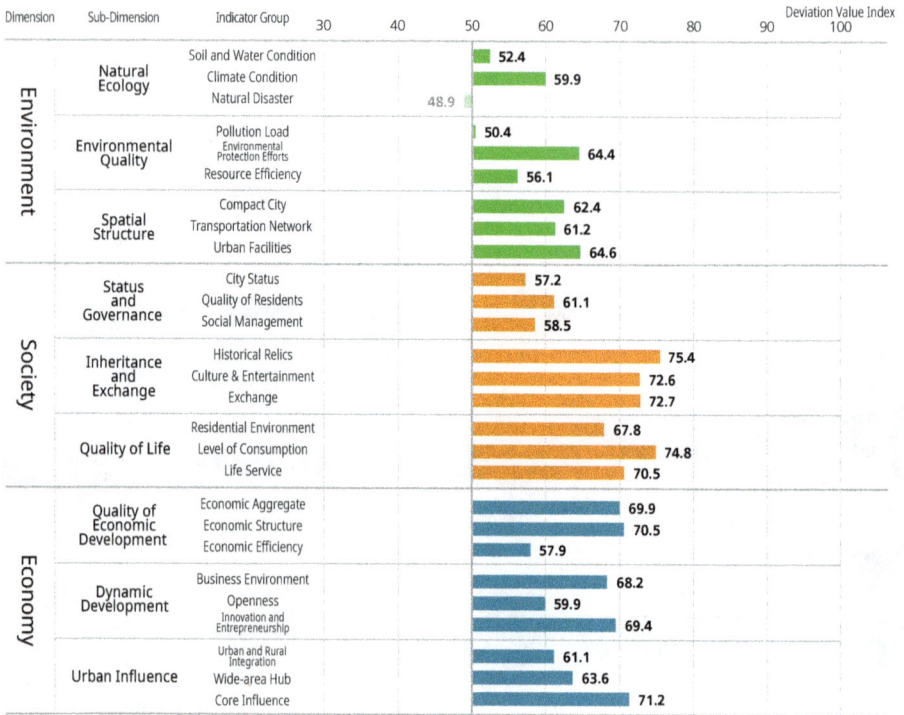

Figure 3-63 Deviation Value of Indicator Group

The chart shows the following Deviation Value Index values:

Environment

Natural Ecology:
- Soil and Water Condition: 52.4
- Climate Condition: 59.9
- Natural Disaster: 48.9

Environmental Quality:
- Pollution Load: 50.4
- Environmental Protection Efforts: 64.4
- Resource Efficiency: 56.1

Spatial Structure:
- Compact City: 62.4
- Transportation Network: 61.2
- Urban Facilities: 64.6

Society

Status and Governance:
- City Status: 57.2
- Quality of Residents: 61.1
- Social Management: 58.5

Inheritance and Exchange:
- Historical Relics: 75.4
- Culture & Entertainment: 72.6
- Exchange: 72.7

Quality of Life:
- Residential Environment: 67.8
- Level of Consumption: 74.8
- Life Service: 70.5

Economy

Quality of Economic Development:
- Economic Aggregate: 69.9
- Economic Structure: 70.5
- Economic Efficiency: 57.9

Dynamic Development:
- Business Environment: 68.2
- Openness: 59.9
- Innovation and Entrepreneurship: 69.4

Urban Influence:
- Urban and Rural Integration: 61.1
- Wide-area Hub: 63.6
- Core Influence: 71.2

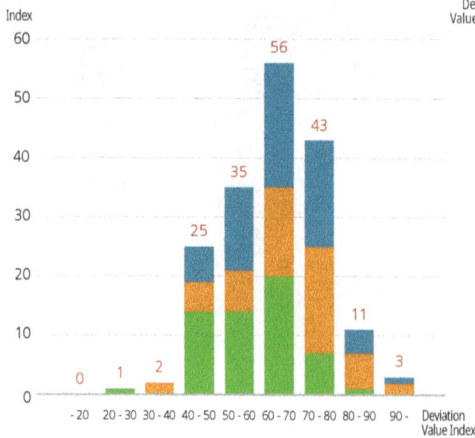

Figure 3-64 Deviation Value Distribution of Indicators

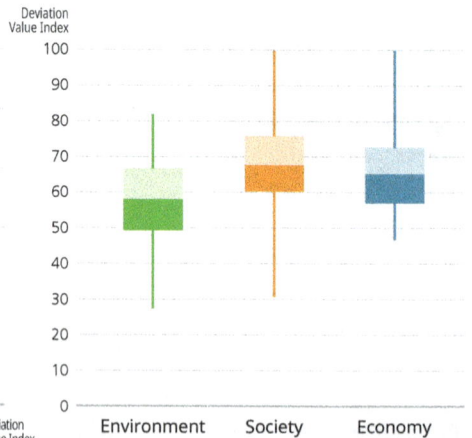

Figure 3-65 Box Plot Distribution of Indicators

94

Dimension	Sub-dimension	Indicator Group	ID	Indicators	Deviation Value Index	Rank	Graph	Deviation Value Index 100
Environment	Natural Ecology	Soil and Water Condition	1	Available Land Area Per Ten Thousand People	48.2	196		
			2	Forest Area	55.7	41		
			3	Farmland Area	45.4	196		
			4	Pasture Area	48.3	76		
			5	Water Area	65.5	18		
			6	Water Resources Per Ten Thousand People	49.5	68		
			7	National Park · Conservation Area · Scenic Area Index	61.5	15		
		Climate Condition	8	Climate Comfort Index	57.6	59		
			9	Rainfall	62.1	51		
		Natural Disaster	10	Natural Disaster-caused Direct Economic Loss Index	47.1	275		
			11	Geological Disaster-caused Direct Economic Loss Index	53.1	1		
			12	Disaster Warning	47.8	118		
	Environmental Quality	Pollution Load	13	Air Quality Index (AQI)	48.9	134		
			14	PM2.5 Index	47.2	165		
			15	CO2 Emissions Per Unit of GDP	64.5	33		
			16	Volume of Sulphur Dioxide Emission	48.3	213		
			17	Volume of Industrial Soot(dust) Emission	46.1	220		
			18	Proportion of National and Provincial Water Sections in Category III and Above Meeting the Quality Standard	62.9	42		
			19	Areas Environmental Average Noise Value	41.3	279		
			20	Radiation Environmental Air Absorption Dose Rate	58.3	67		
		Environmental Protection Efforts	21	Environmental Effort Index	57.1	15		
			22	Water-saving Effort Index	51.6	82		
			23	Social Organizations for Ecological Environment	60.4	12		
			24	National Environmental Protection City Index	78.1	9		
			25	National Ecological Environment Evaluation Index	82.1	8		
		Resource Efficiency	26	Land Productivity in Built District	49.3	107		
			27	Land Productivity in Agriculture, Forestry, Animal Husbandry and Fisheries	46.0	160		
			28	Energy Consumption Per Unit of GDP	64.5	33		
			29	Projects Labeled with Green Building Design and Evaluation	74.8	7		
			30	Comprehensive Utilization Rate of Industrial Solid Waste	53.1	178		
			31	Circular Economical City Index	65.5	17		
	Spatial Structure	Compact City	32	Population of Densely Inhabited Districts (DIDs)	69.3	14		
			33	Area of Densely Inhabited Districts (DIDs)	70.2	12		
			34	Proportion of the Population of Densely Inhabited Districts (DIDs)	66.6	27		
			35	Proportion of Densely Inhabited Districts (DIDs) in Built District	53.1	40		
			36	Population of Super Densely Inhabited Districts (DIDs)	67.6	17		
			37	Area of Super Densely Inhabited Districts (DIDs)	69.6	16		
			38	Proportion of the Population of Super Densely Inhabited Districts (DIDs)	63.3	37		
			39	Proportion of Densely Super Densely Inhabited Districts (DIDs) in Built District	53.2	44		
		Transportation Network	40	Urban Rail Transit Density Index	64.7	20		
			41	Urban Arterial Road Density Index	61.8	27		
			42	Urban Life Road Density Index	61.7	30		
			43	Urban Sidewalk • Bicycle Lane Density Index	62.5	26		
			44	Urban Rail Transit Distance	57.2	18		
			45	Public Bus Passenger Volume Per Ten Thousand People	74.9	9		
			46	Public Bus Ownership Per Ten Thousand People	71.7	12		
			47	Private Vehicle Ownership Per Ten Thousand People	48.4	273		
			48	Taxis Ownership Per Ten Thousand People	58.0	49		
			49	Rush Hour Traffic Jam Delay Index	27.4	288		
		Urban Facilities	50	Fixed Assets Investment Scale Index	70.4	18		
			51	Area of Park Green Land	67.9	10		
			52	Green Coverage Rate in Built District	52.6	138		
			53	Density of Water Supply Pipelines in Built District	66.7	18		
			54	Density of Sewers in Built District	52.7	97		
			55	Gas Coverage Rate	55.6	1		
			56	Urban Underground Facilities Index	68.9	5		

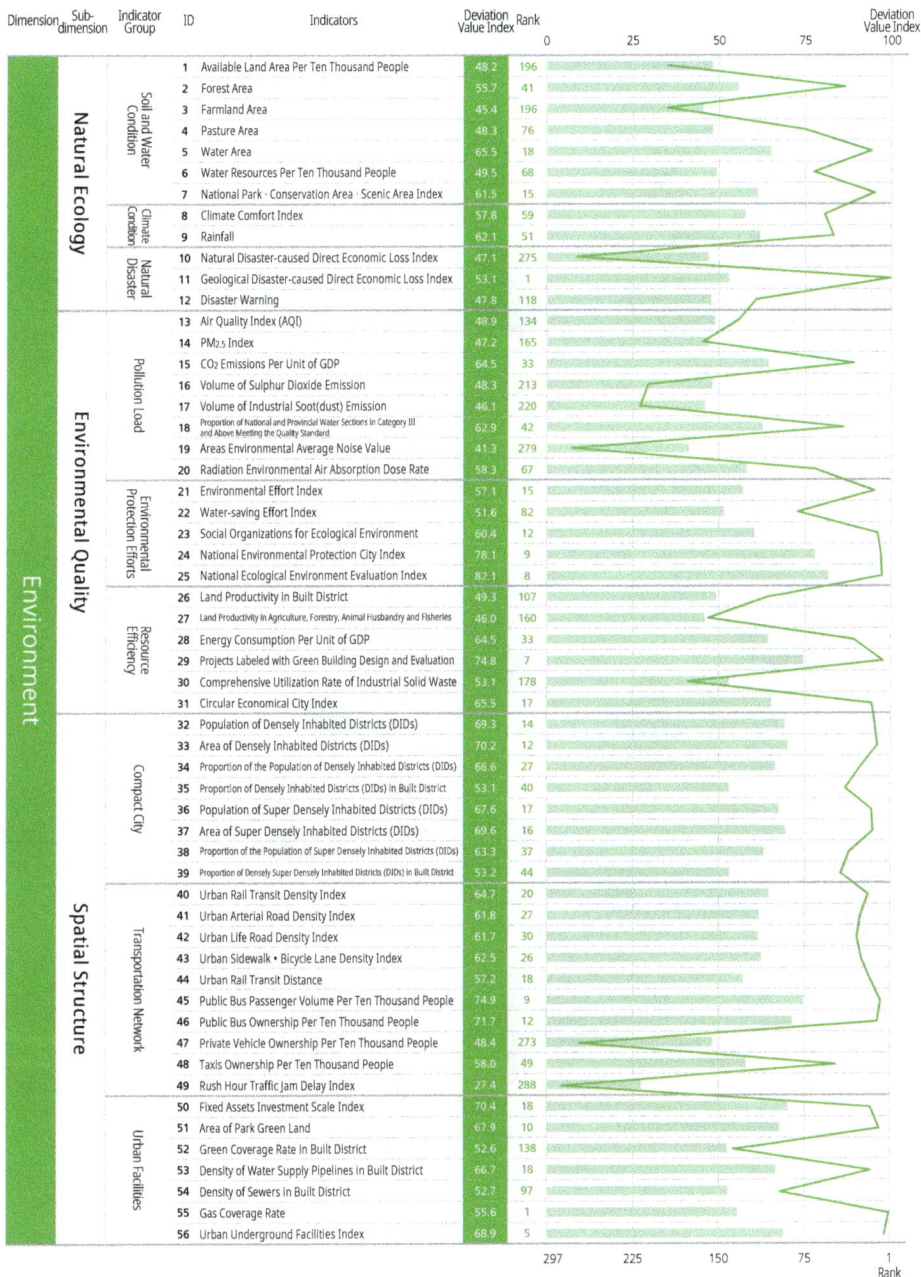

Figure 3-66 Index Ranking: Environment

Hangzhou

Dimension	Sub-dimension	Indicator Group	ID	Indicators	Deviation Value Index	Rank
Society	Status and Governance	City Status	57	Administrative Levels	55.8	5
			58	Megalopolis Levels	68.8	1
			59	Core City Levels	59.3	4
			60	Embassies · Consulates	48.9	17
			61	International Organizations	49.4	3
			62	Belt and Road Index	65.2	7
		Quality of Residents	63	Population Natural Growth Rate Index	46.7	181
			64	Population Social Growth Rate Index	55.9	21
			65	Population Structure Index	48.0	181
			66	Population Education Structure Index	66.2	21
			67	Higher Education Index	71.2	16
			68	Outstanding Talent Cultivation Index	77.1	5
			69	Public Finance Expenditure for Education Index	66.1	10
		Social Management	70	Social Services Index	54.9	47
			71	Safe and Reliable City Index	65.5	23
			72	Traffic Safety Index	42.3	288
			73	Social Security Index	35.6	277
			74	Social Organizations	72.0	13
			75	Health and Civilized City Index	74.3	5
			76	Government Website Performance	62.7	39
	Inheritance and Exchange	Historical Relics	77	Historical Status	71.1	5
			78	World Heritage	75.5	4
			79	Famous Historical and Cultural Cities	61.7	7
			80	Intangible Cultural Heritage	94.5	3
			81	Key Cultural Relics Sites Under the Protection	67.7	14
		Culture and Entertainment	82	Theater Consumer Index	78.8	6
			83	Museums · Art Galleries	76.0	9
			84	Sports Venues Index	64.0	17
			85	Zoos · Botanical Gardens · Aquariums	67.2	23
			86	Public Library Collection	75.8	6
			87	Cultural Master Index	56.7	11
			88	Olympic Champion Index	84.5	5
			89	National Culturally Advanced Unit Index	65.1	14
		Personal Exchange	90	Inbound Tourists	77.3	5
			91	Domestic Tourists	71.6	7
			92	Foreign Exchange Earnings from International Tourism	87.8	6
			93	Earnings from Domestic Tourism	85.6	7
			94	International Conferences	52.5	21
			95	Exhibition Industry Development Index	65.7	12
			96	World Tourism City Index	88.3	4
	Quality of Life	Residential Environment	97	Average Life Expectancy	60.4	4
			98	Medicare · Endowment Insurance Coverage Index	79.9	6
			99	Ratio of Average House Prices to Income	30.8	282
			100	Habitat City Index	80.9	4
			101	China's Happiness City Index	100.0	2
		Level of Consumption	102	Retail Sales of Consumer Goods Per Ten Thousand People	79.9	4
			103	Revenue of Hotels and Catering Services Per Ten Thousand People	75.5	7
			104	Telecom Consumption Per Ten Thousand People	67.4	14
			105	Water Consumption for Residential Use Per Ten Thousand People	64.1	22
			106	Top International Brand Index	81.3	6
		Life Service	107	Number of Children in Kindergartens Per Ten Thousand People	55.2	96
			108	Year-end Number of Beds in Nursing Homes	71.9	7
			109	Number of Practicing (Assistant) Physicians	76.0	7
			110	Number of Beds in Health Institutions	70.7	11
			111	First-class Hospitals	73.1	9

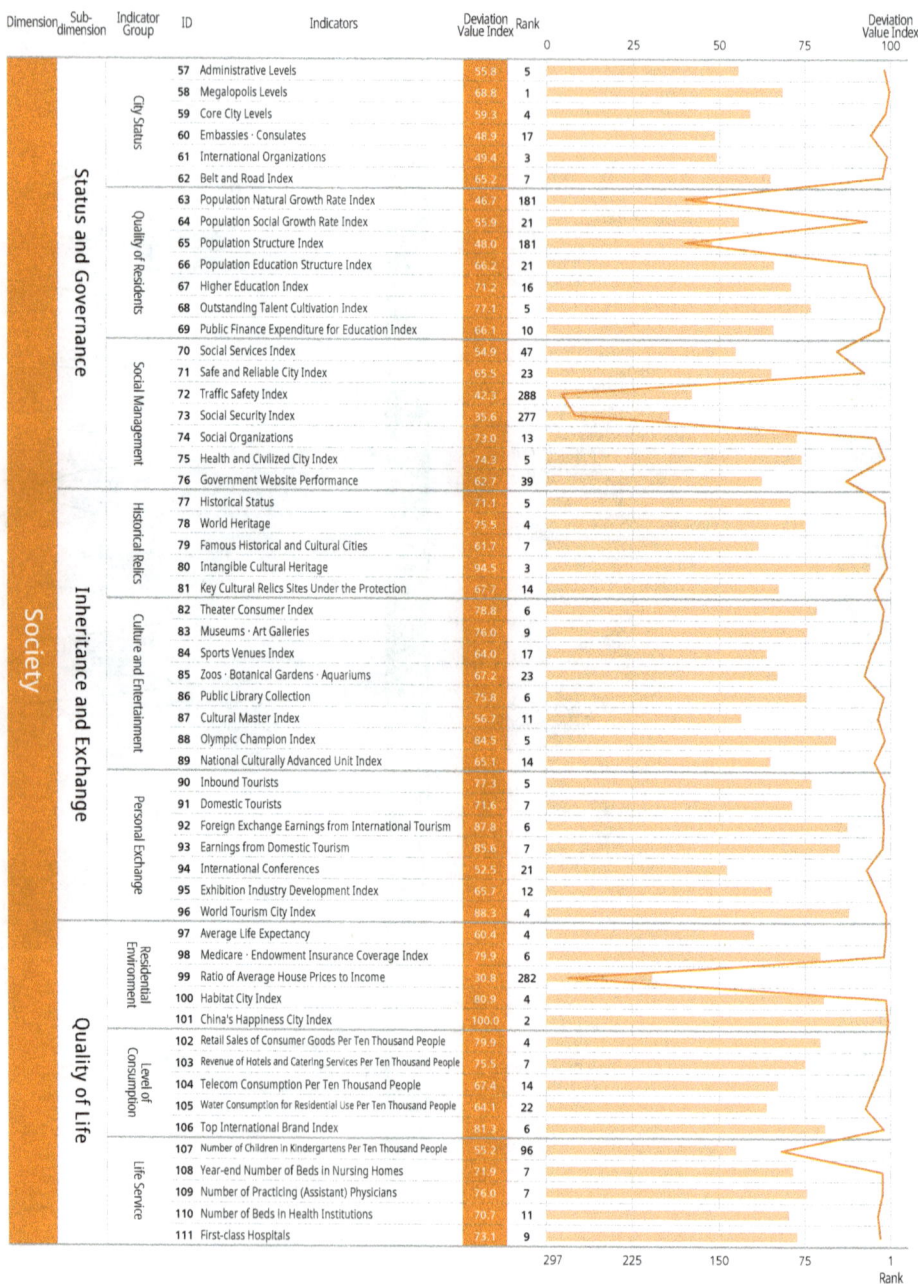

Figure 3-67 Index Ranking: Society

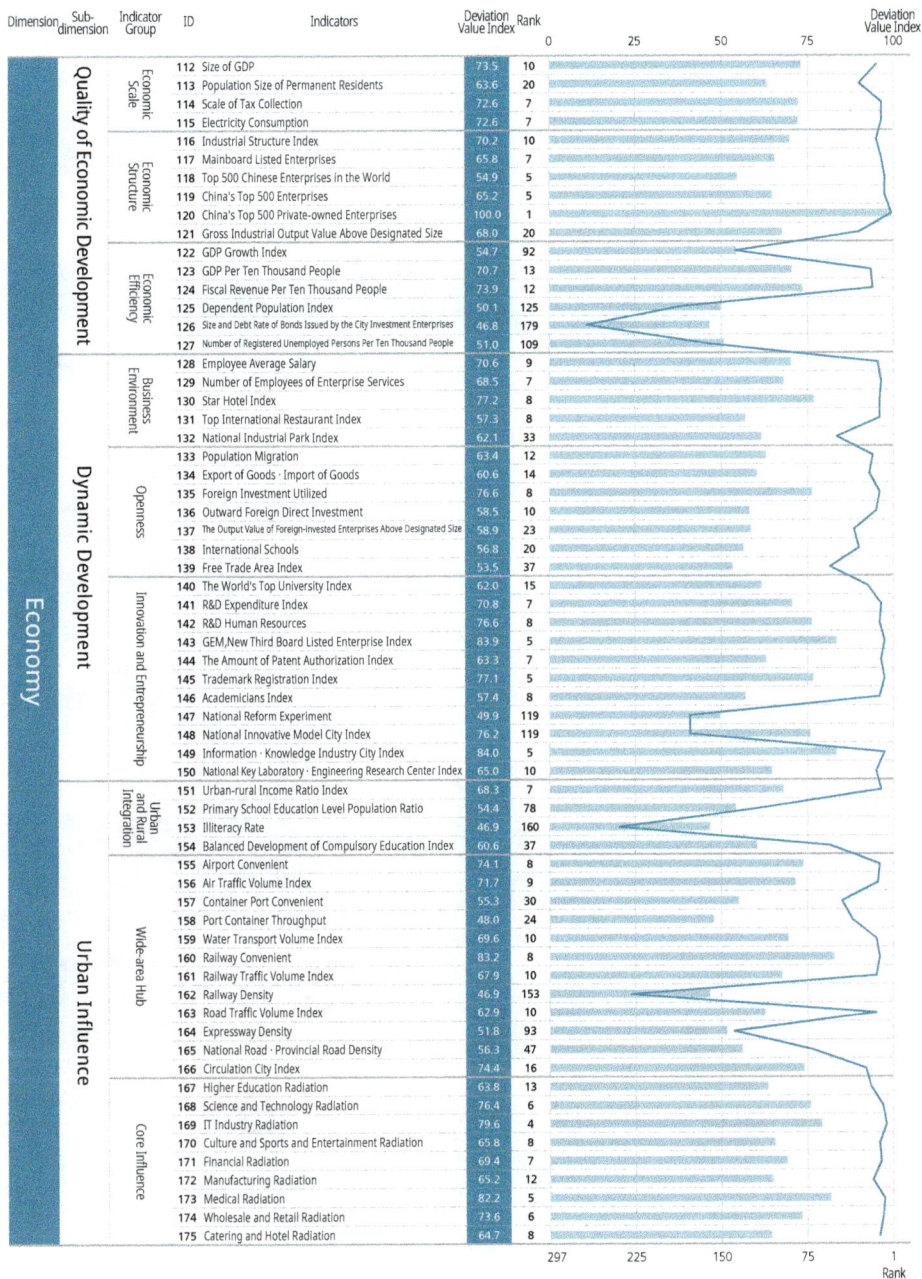

Dimension	Sub-dimension	Indicator Group	ID	Indicators	Deviation Value Index	Rank
Economy	Quality of Economic Development	Economic Scale	112	Size of GDP	73.5	10
			113	Population Size of Permanent Residents	63.6	20
			114	Scale of Tax Collection	72.6	7
			115	Electricity Consumption	72.6	7
		Economic Structure	116	Industrial Structure Index	70.2	10
			117	Mainboard Listed Enterprises	65.8	7
			118	Top 500 Chinese Enterprises in the World	54.9	5
			119	China's Top 500 Enterprises	65.2	5
			120	China's Top 500 Private-owned Enterprises	100.0	1
			121	Gross Industrial Output Value Above Designated Size	68.0	20
		Economic Efficiency	122	GDP Growth Index	54.7	92
			123	GDP Per Ten Thousand People	70.7	13
			124	Fiscal Revenue Per Ten Thousand People	73.9	12
			125	Dependent Population Index	50.1	125
			126	Size and Debt Rate of Bonds Issued by the City Investment Enterprises	46.8	179
			127	Number of Registered Unemployed Persons Per Ten Thousand People	51.0	109
	Dynamic Development	Business Environment	128	Employee Average Salary	70.6	9
			129	Number of Employees of Enterprise Services	68.5	7
			130	Star Hotel Index	77.2	8
			131	Top International Restaurant Index	57.3	8
			132	National Industrial Park Index	62.1	33
		Openness	133	Population Migration	63.4	12
			134	Export of Goods · Import of Goods	60.6	14
			135	Foreign Investment Utilized	76.6	8
			136	Outward Foreign Direct Investment	58.5	10
			137	The Output Value of Foreign-invested Enterprises Above Designated Size	58.9	23
			138	International Schools	56.8	20
			139	Free Trade Area Index	53.5	37
		Innovation and Entrepreneurship	140	The World's Top University Index	62.0	15
			141	R&D Expenditure Index	70.8	7
			142	R&D Human Resources	76.6	8
			143	GEM,New Third Board Listed Enterprise Index	83.9	5
			144	The Amount of Patent Authorization Index	63.3	7
			145	Trademark Registration Index	77.1	5
			146	Academicians Index	57.4	8
			147	National Reform Experiment	49.9	119
			148	National Innovative Model City Index	76.2	119
			149	Information · Knowledge Industry City Index	84.0	5
			150	National Key Laboratory · Engineering Research Center Index	65.0	10
	Urban Influence	Urban and Rural Integration	151	Urban-rural Income Ratio Index	68.3	7
			152	Primary School Education Level Population Ratio	54.4	78
			153	Illiteracy Rate	46.9	160
			154	Balanced Development of Compulsory Education Index	60.6	37
		Wide-area Hub	155	Airport Convenient	74.1	8
			156	Air Traffic Volume Index	71.7	9
			157	Container Port Convenient	55.3	30
			158	Port Container Throughput	48.0	24
			159	Water Transport Volume Index	69.6	10
			160	Railway Convenient	83.2	8
			161	Railway Traffic Volume Index	67.9	10
			162	Railway Density	46.9	153
			163	Road Traffic Volume Index	62.9	10
			164	Expressway Density	51.8	93
			165	National Road · Provincial Road Density	56.3	47
			166	Circulation City Index	74.4	16
		Core Influence	167	Higher Education Radiation	63.8	13
			168	Science and Technology Radiation	76.4	6
			169	IT Industry Radiation	79.6	4
			170	Culture and Sports and Entertainment Radiation	65.8	8
			171	Financial Radiation	69.4	7
			172	Manufacturing Radiation	65.2	12
			173	Medical Radiation	82.2	5
			174	Wholesale and Retail Radiation	73.6	6
			175	Catering and Hotel Radiation	64.7	8

Figure 3-68 Index Ranking: Economy

Hangzhou

Figure 3-69 DID Analysis

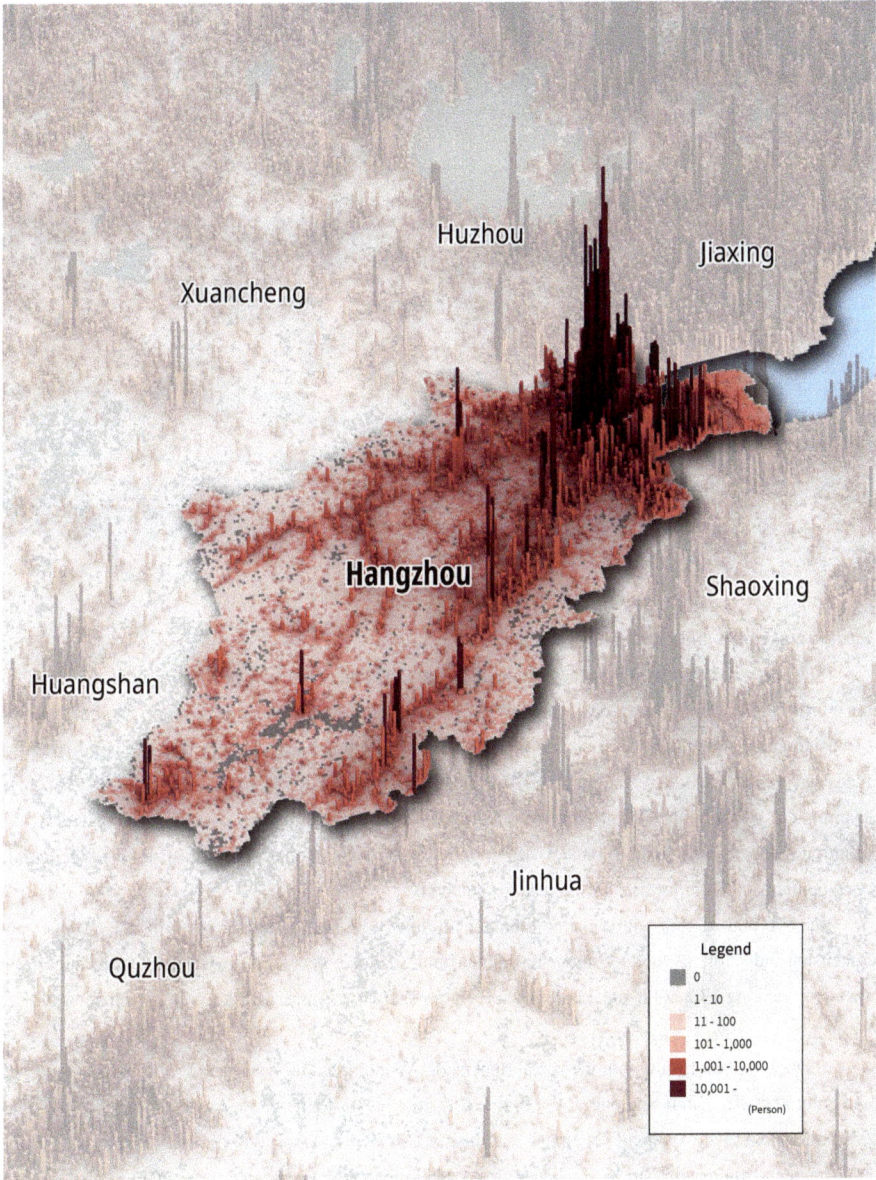

Figure 3-70 Population Size and Density Analysis

8th Suzhou

Suzhou ranked 8th in the comprehensive ranking.

Suzhou ranked 6th within the economic dimension. As one of the best performing cities in China for the construction of park zones (designated by the government for specific purposes) and for the attraction of business investments, Suzhou ranked No. 3 nationwide in goods export performance with her strong industrial export capacity. Suzhou's GDP is only next to Beijing, Shanghai, Guangzhou, Shenzhen, Tianjin, and Chongqing, ranking 7th in the country. In terms of three sub-dimension indicators of the economic dimension, Suzhou ranked 4th for dynamic development, 7th for quality of economic development, and 10th for urban influence, respectively.

Suzhou ranked 10th within the environmental dimension. Regarding her performance in three sub-dimension indicators of the environmental dimension, Suzhou's development is relatively balanced and excellent, ranking 17th, 28th and 32nd respectively for spatial structure, natural ecology, and environmental quality.

Suzhou ranked 13th within the social dimension. With a long history, Suzhou is a famous historical and cultural city in China and one of the first excellent cities for tourism. She has been awarded the titles of "National Garden City" and "National Health City." In terms of three sub-dimension indicators of the environmental dimension, Suzhou ranked 37th for status and governance as restricted by her administrative level (not being either a provincial capital or a city specifically designated in the state plan), and she ranked 12th and 13th for inheritance and exchange and for quality of life, respectively.

Table 3-8 Key Index

Environment

Number of permanent residents:	10,620,000
Land area of administrative region:	8,657 km^2
Ranking of available land area per capita:	285
Ranking of forest coverage:	229
Ranking of water resources per capita:	182
Ranking of climate comfort index:	152
Ranking of PM$_{2.5}$ Index:	156
Ranking of densely inhabited district (DID) population :	11
Ranking of rail transit route mileage :	12

Society

Ranking of average house prices :	13
Ranking of cinemas and theater numbers :	47
Ranking of museum and art gallery numbers :	16
Number of domestic tourists:	106,050,000
Number of inbound tourists:	1,510,000
Ranking of world heritage number :	4
Ranking of international conference number :	10

Economy

Size of GDP:	RMB 1450.4 billion
Per-capita GDP:	RMB 136,625 / person
GDP growth rate:	5.1 %
Ranking of per capita revenue in :	9
Ranking of average salaries :	14
Ranking of mainboard listed enterprises :	27
Ranking of goods export in China:	3
Ranking of airport convenience in China:	166
Ranking of container port convenience :	9
Ranking of financial radiation :	11
Ranking of manufacturing radiation :	2
Ranking of IT industry radiation :	17
Ranking of higher education radiation :	29
Ranking of science and technology radiation :	7
Ranking of medical radiation :	62
Ranking of culture and sports and entertainment radiation :	23
Ranking of catering and hotel radiation :	4
Ranking of wholesale and retail radiation :	12

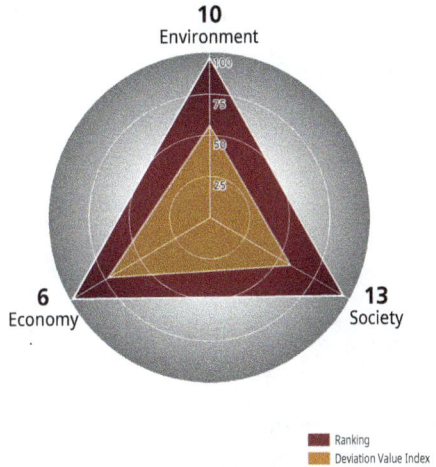

Figure 3-71 Scores of Dimension

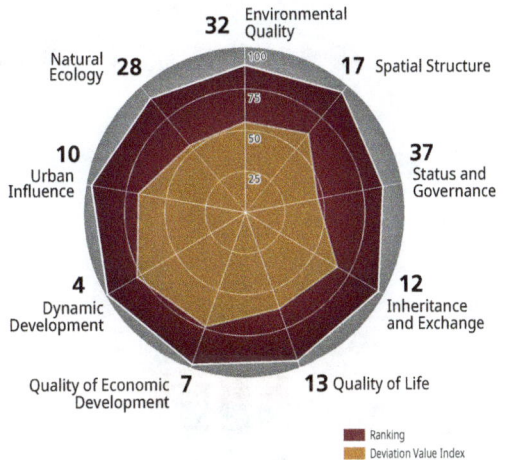

Figure 3-72 Scores of Sub-Dimension

Suzhou

Dimension	Sub-Dimension	Indicator Group	Deviation Value Index
Environment	Natural Ecology	Soil and Water Condition	54.8
		Climate Condition	51.7
		Natural Disaster	52.6
	Environmental Quality	Pollution Load	51.2
		Environmental Protection Efforts	74.9
		Resource Efficiency	58.9
	Spatial Structure	Compact City	65.7
		Transportation Network	58.3
		Urban Facilities	67.6
Society	Status and Governance	City Status	31.8
		Quality of Residents	58.7
		Social Management	63.0
	Inheritance and Exchange	Historical Relics	68.9
		Culture & Entertainment	66.9
		Exchange	65.3
	Quality of Life	Residential Environment	62.6
		Level of Consumption	64.1
		Life Service	58.5
Economy	Quality of Economic Development	Economic Aggregate	77.2
		Economic Structure	75.4
		Economic Efficiency	62.9
	Dynamic Development	Business Environment	76.6
		Openness	84.0
		Innovation and Entrepreneurship	68.0
	Urban Influence	Urban and Rural Integration	61.4
		Wide-area Hub	66.5
		Core Influence	69.0

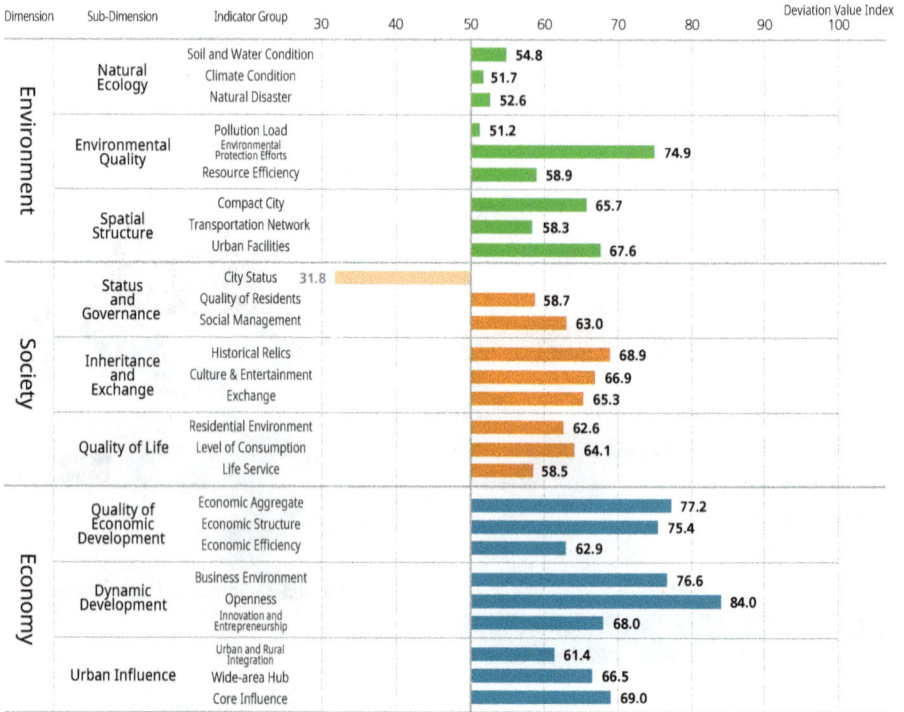

Figure 3-73 Deviation Value of Indicator Group

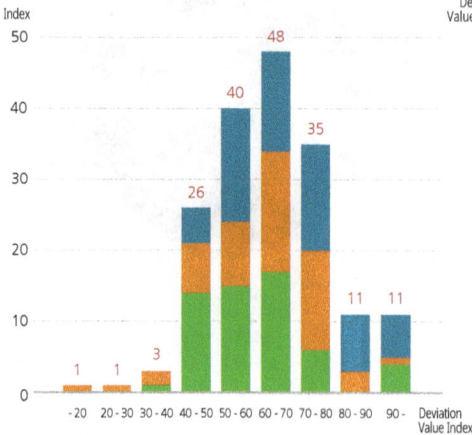

Figure 3-74 Deviation Value Distribution of Indicators

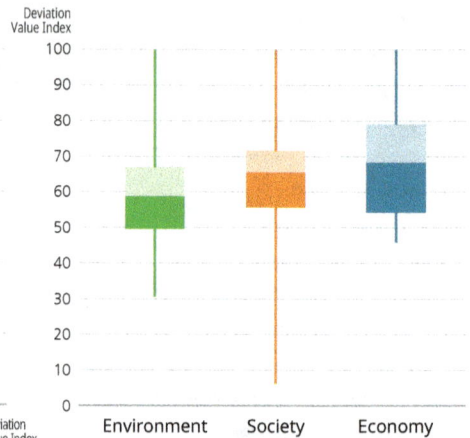

Figure 3-75 Box Plot Distribution of Indicators

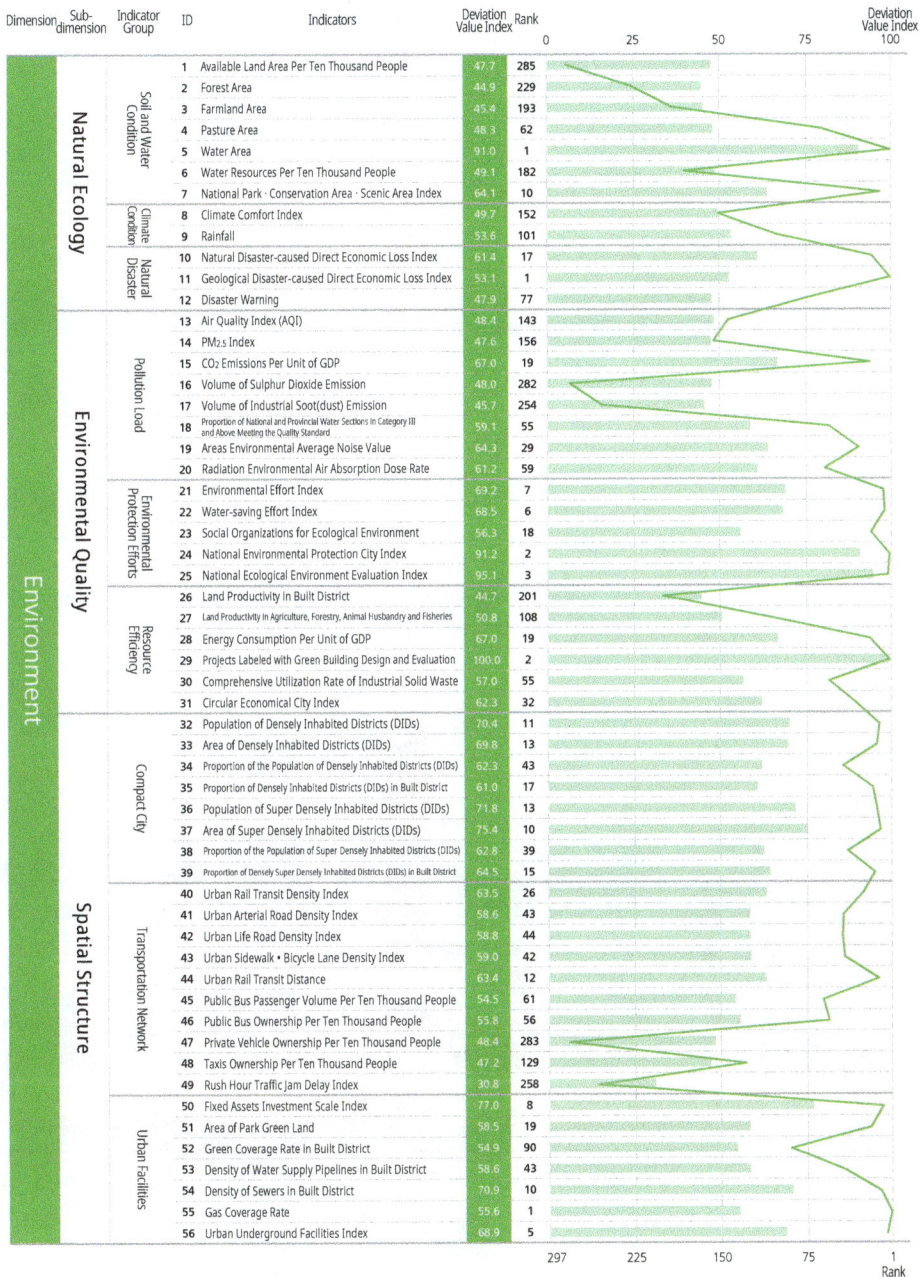

Figure 3-76 Index Ranking: Environment

Dimension	Sub-dimension	Indicator Group	ID	Indicators	Deviation Value Index	Rank
Environment	Natural Ecology	Soil and Water Condition	1	Available Land Area Per Ten Thousand People	47.7	285
			2	Forest Area	44.9	229
			3	Farmland Area	45.4	193
			4	Pasture Area	48.3	62
			5	Water Area	91.0	1
			6	Water Resources Per Ten Thousand People	49.1	182
			7	National Park · Conservation Area · Scenic Area Index	64.1	10
		Climate Condition	8	Climate Comfort Index	49.7	152
			9	Rainfall	53.6	101
		Natural Disaster	10	Natural Disaster-caused Direct Economic Loss Index	61.4	17
			11	Geological Disaster-caused Direct Economic Loss Index	53.1	1
			12	Disaster Warning	47.9	77
	Environmental Quality	Pollution Load	13	Air Quality Index (AQI)	48.4	143
			14	PM$_{2.5}$ Index	47.6	156
			15	CO$_2$ Emissions Per Unit of GDP	67.0	19
			16	Volume of Sulphur Dioxide Emission	48.0	282
			17	Volume of Industrial Soot(dust) Emission	45.7	254
			18	Proportion of National and Provincial Water Sections in Category III and Above Meeting the Quality Standard	59.1	55
			19	Areas Environmental Average Noise Value	64.3	29
			20	Radiation Environmental Air Absorption Dose Rate	61.2	59
		Environmental Protection Efforts	21	Environmental Effort Index	69.2	7
			22	Water-saving Effort Index	68.5	6
			23	Social Organizations for Ecological Environment	56.3	18
			24	National Environmental Protection City Index	91.2	2
			25	National Ecological Environment Evaluation Index	95.1	3
		Resource Efficiency	26	Land Productivity in Built District	44.7	201
			27	Land Productivity in Agriculture, Forestry, Animal Husbandry and Fisheries	50.8	108
			28	Energy Consumption Per Unit of GDP	67.0	19
			29	Projects Labeled with Green Building Design and Evaluation	100.0	2
			30	Comprehensive Utilization Rate of Industrial Solid Waste	57.0	55
			31	Circular Economical City Index	62.3	32
	Spatial Structure	Compact City	32	Population of Densely Inhabited Districts (DIDs)	70.4	11
			33	Area of Densely Inhabited Districts (DIDs)	69.8	13
			34	Proportion of the Population of Densely Inhabited Districts (DIDs)	62.3	43
			35	Proportion of Densely Inhabited Districts (DIDs) in Built District	61.0	17
			36	Population of Super Densely Inhabited Districts (DIDs)	71.8	13
			37	Area of Super Densely Inhabited Districts (DIDs)	75.4	10
			38	Proportion of the Population of Super Densely Inhabited Districts (DIDs)	62.8	39
			39	Proportion of Densely Super Densely Inhabited Districts (DIDs) in Built District	64.5	15
		Transportation Network	40	Urban Rail Transit Density Index	63.5	26
			41	Urban Arterial Road Density Index	58.6	43
			42	Urban Life Road Density Index	58.8	44
			43	Urban Sidewalk • Bicycle Lane Density Index	59.0	42
			44	Urban Rail Transit Distance	63.4	12
			45	Public Bus Passenger Volume Per Ten Thousand People	54.5	54
			46	Public Bus Ownership Per Ten Thousand People	55.8	56
			47	Private Vehicle Ownership Per Ten Thousand People	48.4	283
			48	Taxis Ownership Per Ten Thousand People	47.2	129
			49	Rush Hour Traffic Jam Delay Index	30.8	258
		Urban Facilities	50	Fixed Assets Investment Scale Index	77.0	8
			51	Area of Park Green Land	58.5	19
			52	Green Coverage Rate in Built District	54.9	90
			53	Density of Water Supply Pipelines in Built District	58.6	43
			54	Density of Sewers in Built District	70.9	10
			55	Gas Coverage Rate	55.6	1
			56	Urban Underground Facilities Index	68.9	5

Figure 3-76 Index Ranking: Environment

Suzhou

Dimension	Sub-dimension	Indicator Group	ID	Indicators	Deviation Value Index	Rank
Society	Status and Governance	City Status	57	Administrative Levels	6.3	37
			58	Megalopolis Levels	68.8	1
			59	Core City Levels	28.9	32
			60	Embassies · Consulates	48.9	17
			61	International Organizations	49.4	3
			62	Belt and Road Index	64.7	8
		Quality of Residents	63	Population Natural Growth Rate Index	43.9	211
			64	Population Social Growth Rate Index	49.5	172
			65	Population Structure Index	59.8	10
			66	Population Education Structure Index	61.8	28
			67	Higher Education Index	55.9	31
			68	Outstanding Talent Cultivation Index	65.8	10
			69	Public Finance Expenditure for Education Index	64.3	11
		Social Management	70	Social Services Index	62.1	15
			71	Safe and Reliable City Index	71.3	13
			72	Traffic Safety Index	42.6	281
			73	Social Security Index	35.2	284
			74	Social Organizations	76.3	10
			75	Health and Civilized City Index	70.6	7
			76	Government Website Performance	65.8	10
	Inheritance and Exchange	Historical Relics	77	Historical Status	52.5	31
			78	World Heritage	75.5	4
			79	Famous Historical and Cultural Cities	80.7	1
			80	Intangible Cultural Heritage	78.1	6
			81	Key Cultural Relics Sites Under the Protection	84.1	7
		Culture and Entertainment	82	Theater Consumer Index	67.1	12
			83	Museums · Art Galleries	66.4	16
			84	Sports Venues Index	61.6	24
			85	Zoos · Botanical Gardens · Aquariums	74.5	10
			86	Public Library Collection	72.1	7
			87	Cultural Master Index	49.8	26
			88	Olympic Champion Index	61.8	17
			89	National Culturally Advanced Unit Index	79.9	5
		Personal Exchange	90	Inbound Tourists	60.1	20
			91	Domestic Tourists	68.7	9
			92	Foreign Exchange Earnings from International Tourism	74.8	8
			93	Earnings from Domestic Tourism	79.6	8
			94	International Conferences	56.7	10
			95	Exhibition Industry Development Index	55.3	24
			96	World Tourism City Index	85.6	5
	Quality of Life	Residential Environment	97	Average Life Expectancy	56.4	5
			98	Medicare · Endowment Insurance Coverage Index	72.7	11
			99	Ratio of Average House Prices to Income	34.1	276
			100	Habitat City Index	100.0	1
			101	China's Happiness City Index	73.7	11
		Level of Consumption	102	Retail Sales of Consumer Goods Per Ten Thousand People	70.7	19
			103	Revenue of Hotels and Catering Services Per Ten Thousand People	57.2	20
			104	Telecom Consumption Per Ten Thousand People	65.7	19
			105	Water Consumption for Residential Use Per Ten Thousand People	59.0	36
			106	Top International Brand Index	67.9	11
		Life Service	107	Number of Children in Kindergartens Per Ten Thousand People	48.4	162
			108	Year-end Number of Beds in Nursing Homes	70.9	9
			109	Number of Practicing (Assistant) Physicians	67.1	14
			110	Number of Beds in Health Institutions	69.6	13
			111	First-class Hospitals	51.1	54

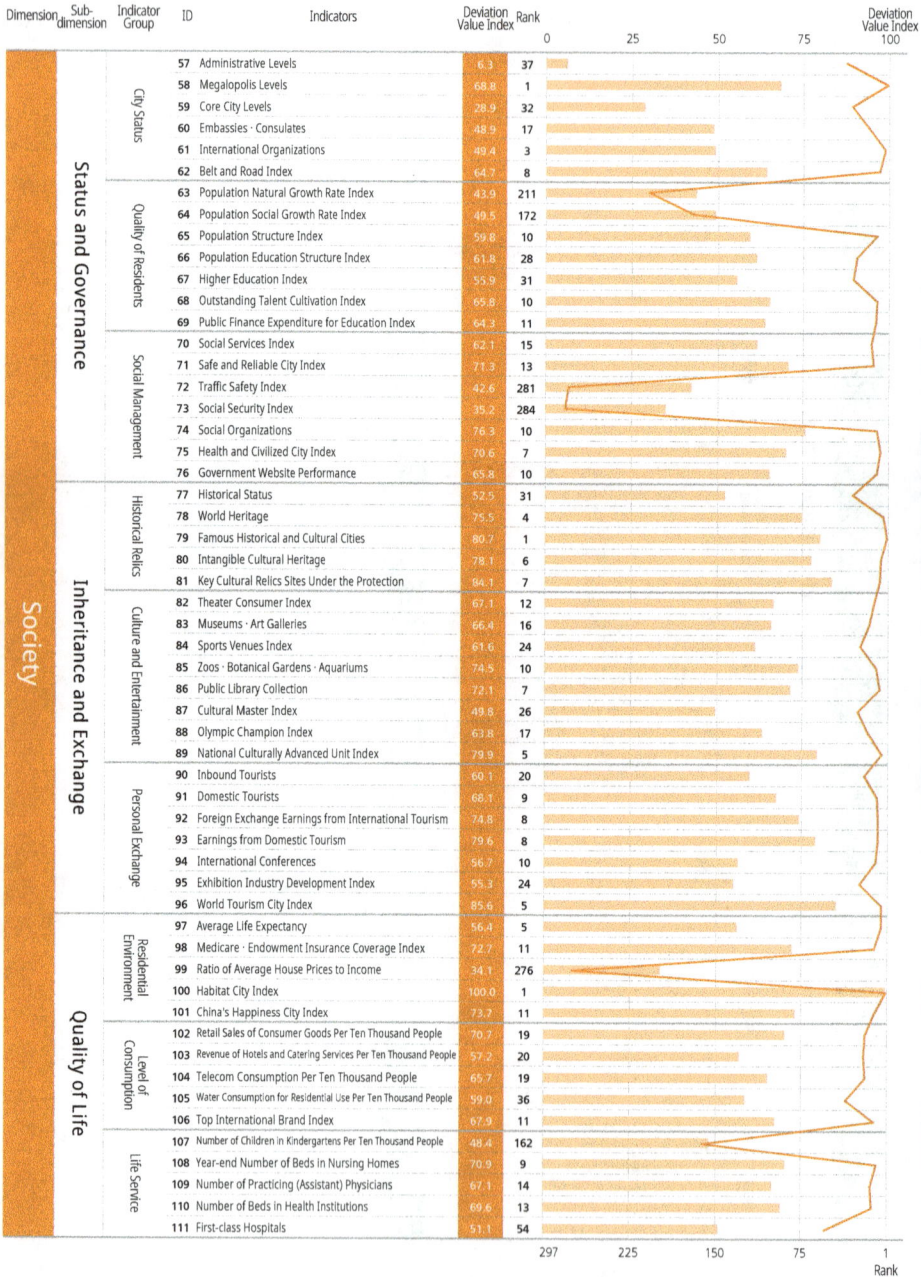

Figure 3-77 Index Ranking: Society

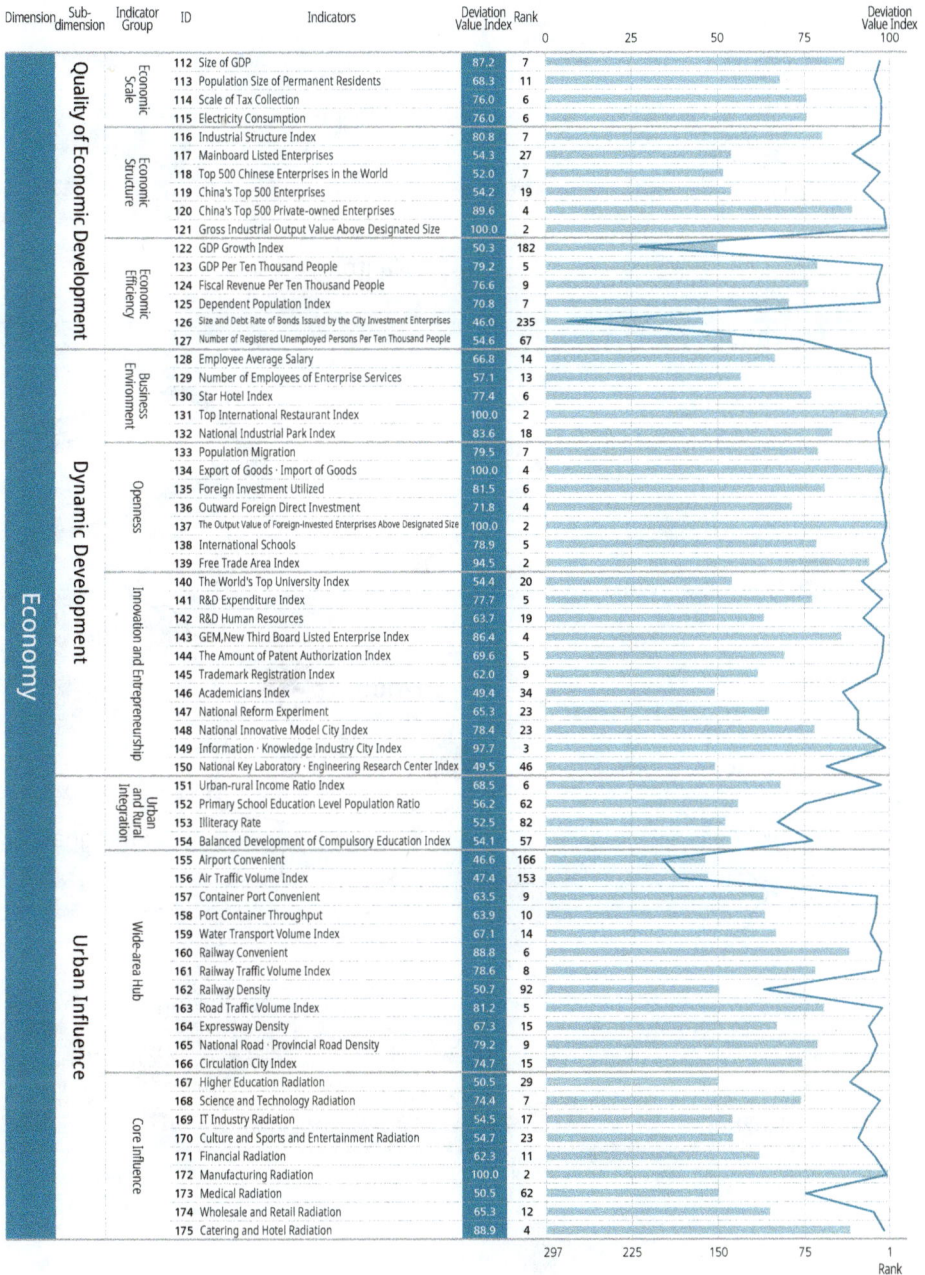

Dimension	Sub-dimension	Indicator Group	ID	Indicators	Deviation Value Index	Rank
Economy	Quality of Economic Development	Economic Scale	112	Size of GDP	87.2	7
			113	Population Size of Permanent Residents	68.3	11
			114	Scale of Tax Collection	76.0	6
			115	Electricity Consumption	76.0	6
		Economic Structure	116	Industrial Structure Index	80.8	7
			117	Mainboard Listed Enterprises	54.3	27
			118	Top 500 Chinese Enterprises in the World	52.0	7
			119	China's Top 500 Enterprises	54.2	19
			120	China's Top 500 Private-owned Enterprises	89.6	4
			121	Gross Industrial Output Value Above Designated Size	100.0	2
		Economic Efficiency	122	GDP Growth Index	50.3	182
			123	GDP Per Ten Thousand People	79.2	5
			124	Fiscal Revenue Per Ten Thousand People	76.6	9
			125	Dependent Population Index	70.8	7
			126	Size and Debt Rate of Bonds Issued by the City Investment Enterprises	46.0	235
			127	Number of Registered Unemployed Persons Per Ten Thousand People	54.6	67
	Dynamic Development	Business Environment	128	Employee Average Salary	66.8	14
			129	Number of Employees of Enterprise Services	57.1	13
			130	Star Hotel Index	77.4	6
			131	Top International Restaurant Index	100.0	2
			132	National Industrial Park Index	83.6	18
		Openness	133	Population Migration	79.5	7
			134	Export of Goods · Import of Goods	100.0	4
			135	Foreign Investment Utilized	81.5	6
			136	Outward Foreign Direct Investment	71.8	4
			137	The Output Value of Foreign-Invested Enterprises Above Designated Size	100.0	2
			138	International Schools	78.9	5
			139	Free Trade Area Index	94.5	2
		Innovation and Entrepreneurship	140	The World's Top University Index	54.4	20
			141	R&D Expenditure Index	77.7	13
			142	R&D Human Resources	63.7	19
			143	GEM,New Third Board Listed Enterprise Index	86.4	4
			144	The Amount of Patent Authorization Index	69.6	5
			145	Trademark Registration Index	62.0	9
			146	Academicians Index	49.4	34
			147	National Reform Experiment	65.3	23
			148	National Innovative Model City Index	78.4	23
			149	Information · Knowledge Industry City Index	97.7	3
			150	National Key Laboratory · Engineering Research Center Index	49.5	46
	Urban Influence	Urban and Rural Integration	151	Urban-rural Income Ratio Index	68.5	6
			152	Primary School Education Level Population Ratio	56.2	62
			153	Illiteracy Rate	52.5	82
			154	Balanced Development of Compulsory Education Index	54.1	57
		Wide-area Hub	155	Airport Convenient	46.6	166
			156	Air Traffic Volume Index	47.4	153
			157	Container Port Convenient	63.5	9
			158	Port Container Throughput	63.9	10
			159	Water Transport Volume Index	67.1	14
			160	Railway Convenient	88.8	6
			161	Railway Traffic Volume Index	78.6	8
			162	Railway Density	50.7	92
			163	Road Traffic Volume Index	81.2	5
			164	Expressway Density	67.3	15
			165	National Road · Provincial Road Density	79.2	9
			166	Circulation City Index	74.7	15
		Core Influence	167	Higher Education Radiation	50.5	29
			168	Science and Technology Radiation	74.4	7
			169	IT Industry Radiation	54.5	17
			170	Culture and Sports and Entertainment Radiation	54.7	23
			171	Financial Radiation	62.3	11
			172	Manufacturing Radiation	100.0	2
			173	Medical Radiation	50.5	62
			174	Wholesale and Retail Radiation	65.3	12
			175	Catering and Hotel Radiation	88.9	4

Figure 3-78 Index Ranking: Economy

Suzhou

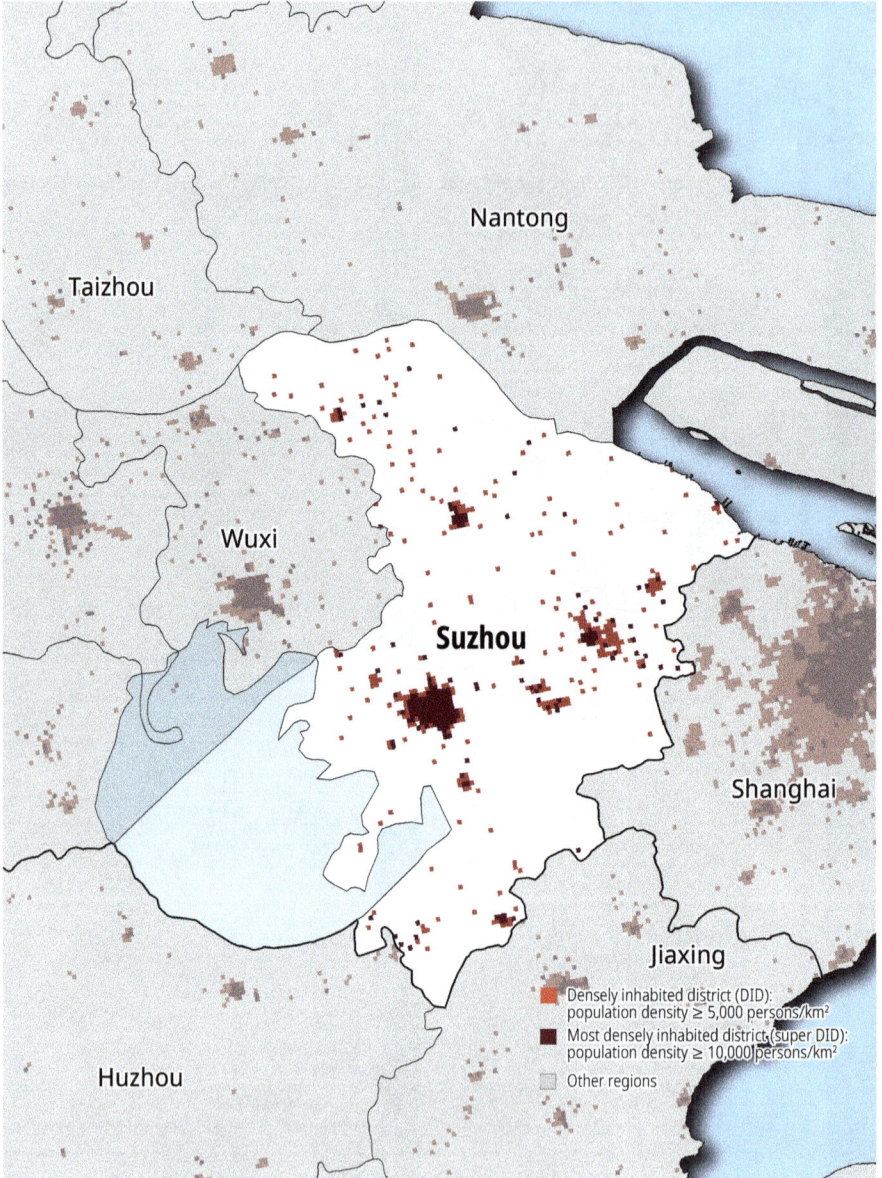

Figure 3-79 DID Analysis

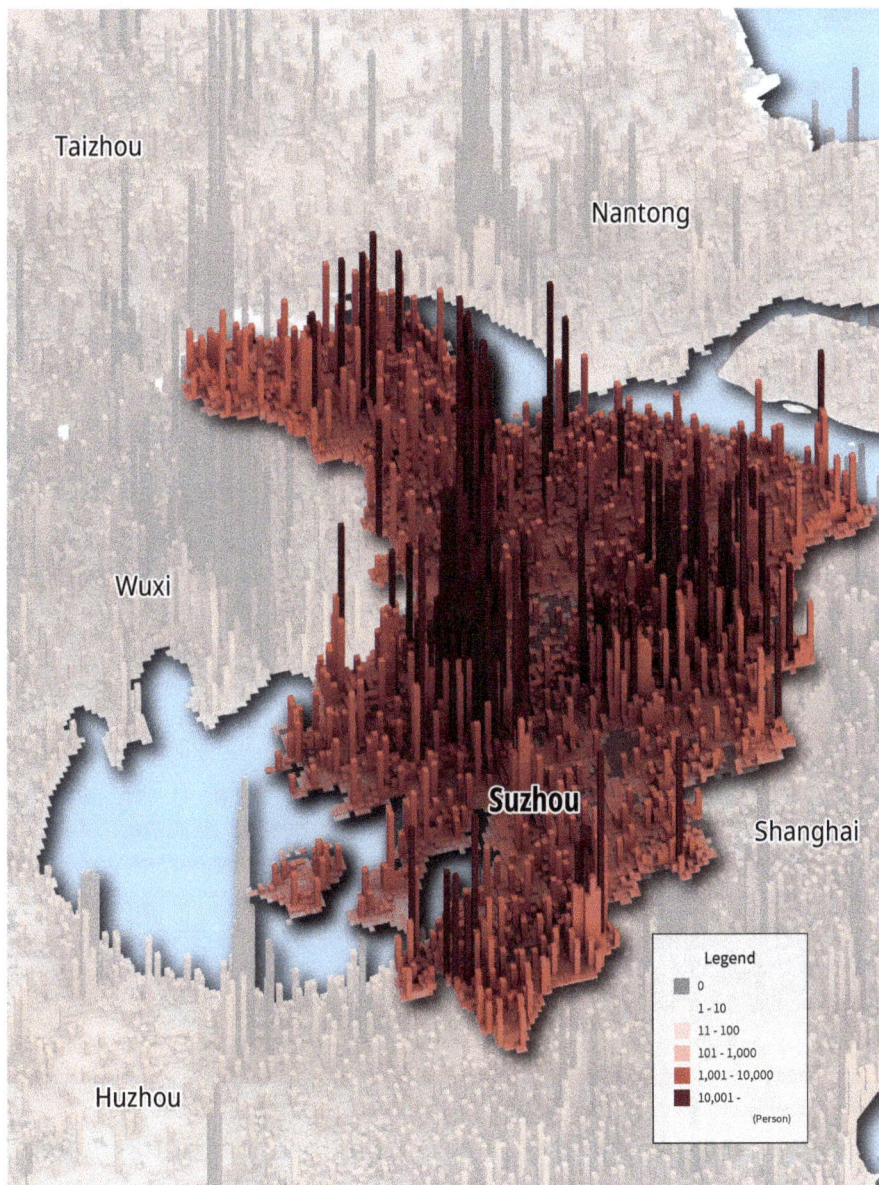

Figure 3-80 Population Size and Density Analysis

9th Nanjing

Nanjing, as it did in 2016, ranked 9th in the comprehensive ranking.

Nanjing did well and ranked 8th within the social dimension. Known as the "ancient capital of six dynasties," Nanjing has been the center of politics, culture, and the commercial economy in the Yangtze River South Region since ancient times. As the capital of Jiangsu Province and one of the central cities of the Yangtze River Delta Megalopolis, Nanjing has become an important cultural, educational, and technological center. In terms of three sub-dimension indicators of the social dimension, Nanjing ranked 6th for status and governance with an outstanding performance, as well as 10th and 7th, respectively, for inheritance and exchange and for quality of life.

Within the economic dimension, Nanjing ranked 10th. Regarding her performance in three sub-dimension indicators of the economic dimension, Nanjing was relatively good and balanced, ranking 11th, 9th and 7th for quality of economic development, dynamic development, and urban influence, respectively.

Nanjing ranked 23rd within the environmental dimension. In terms of three sub-dimension indicators of the environmental dimension, Nanjing did well in and ranked 8th for spatical structure because of a relatively compact urban area and a high-density urban transportation system. However, due to her serious air pollution among other reasons, Nanjing—where mountains, rivers, woods and the city are blended as one—ranked 121st and 83rd for natural ecology and environmental quality, respectively.

Table 3-9 Key Index

Environment

Number of permanent residents:	8,240,000
Land area of administrative region:	6,587 km²
Ranking of available land area per capita:	279
Ranking of forest coverage:	217
Ranking of water resources per capita:	189
Ranking of climate comfort index:	80
Ranking of PM$_{2.5}$ Index:	171
Ranking of densely inhabited district (DID) population :	13
Ranking of rail transit route mileage :	6

Society

Ranking of average house prices :	5
Ranking of cinemas and theater numbers :	8
Ranking of museum and art gallery numbers :	13
Number of domestic tourists:	99,930,000
Number of inbound tourists:	590,000
Ranking of world heritage number :	14
Ranking of international conference number :	10

Economy

Size of GDP:	RMB 972.1 billion
Per-capita GDP:	RMB 118,029 / person
GDP growth rate:	9.3 %
Ranking of per capita revenue in :	15
Ranking of average salaries :	8
Ranking of mainboard listed enterprises :	4
Ranking of goods export in China:	17
Ranking of airport convenience in China:	12
Ranking of container port convenience :	15
Ranking of financial radiation :	12
Ranking of manufacturing radiation :	21
Ranking of IT industry radiation :	5
Ranking of higher education radiation :	3
Ranking of science and technology radiation :	10
Ranking of medical radiation :	12
Ranking of culture and sports and entertainment radiation :	7
Ranking of catering and hotel radiation :	11
Ranking of wholesale and retail radiation :	9

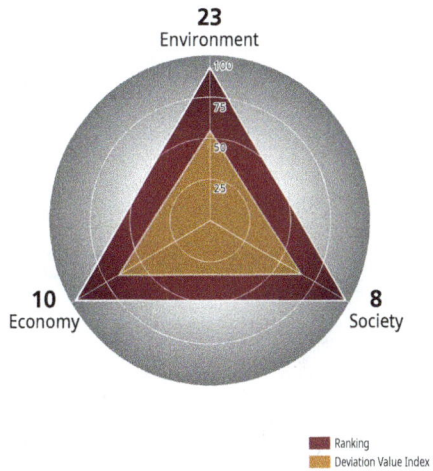

Figure 3-81 Scores of Dimension

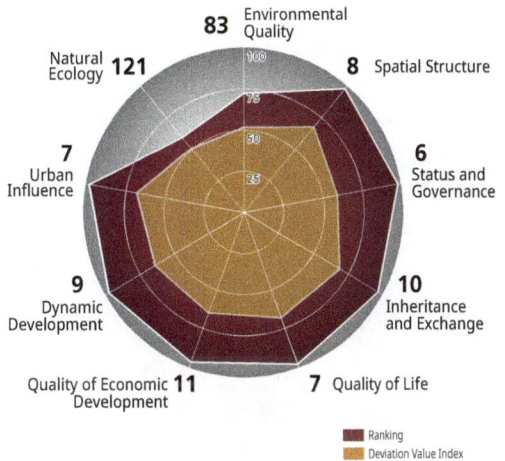

Figure 3-82 Scores of Sub-Dimension

Nanjing

Dimension	Sub-Dimension	Indicator Group	Value
Environment	Natural Ecology	Soil and Water Condition	49.4
		Climate Condition	54.4
		Natural Disaster	49.0
	Environmental Quality	Pollution Load	50.0
		Environmental Protection Efforts	67.5
		Resource Efficiency	52.2
	Spatial Structure	Compact City	69.1
		Transportation Network	67.9
		Urban Facilities	63.1
Society	Status and Governance	City Status	56.6
		Quality of Residents	65.6
		Social Management	57.4
	Inheritance and Exchange	Historical Relics	81.3
		Culture & Entertainment	72.2
		Exchange	60.7
	Quality of Life	Residential Environment	59.8
		Level of Consumption	72.7
		Life Service	67.6
Economy	Quality of Economic Development	Economic Aggregate	66.2
		Economic Structure	66.5
		Economic Efficiency	59.7
	Dynamic Development	Business Environment	67.2
		Openness	58.6
		Innovation and Entrepreneurship	73.1
	Urban Influence	Urban and Rural Integration	58.1
		Wide-area Hub	69.9
		Core Influence	68.1

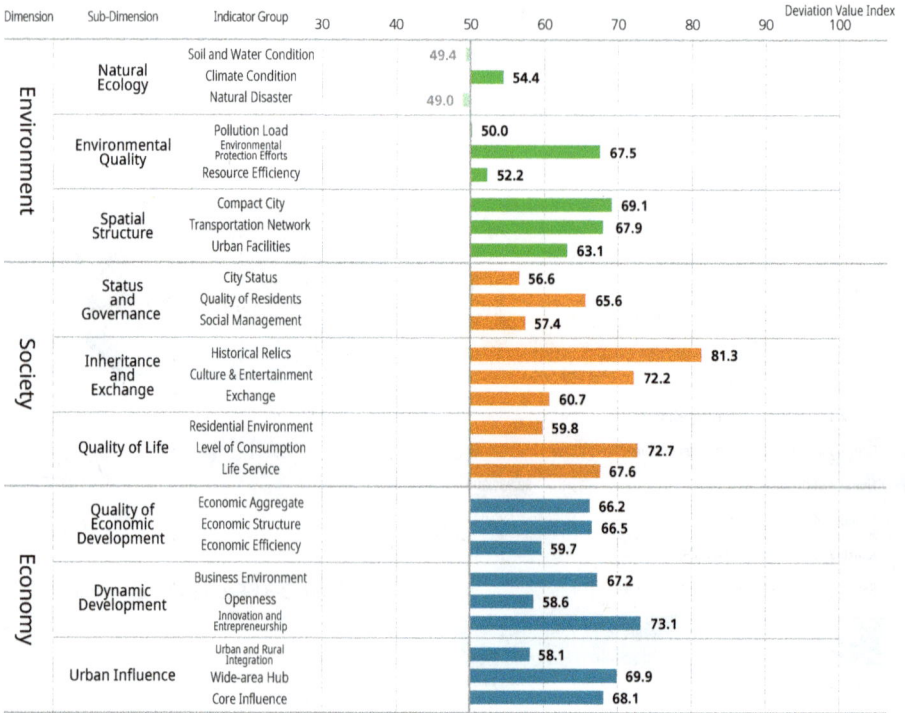

Figure 3-83 Deviation Value of Indicator Group

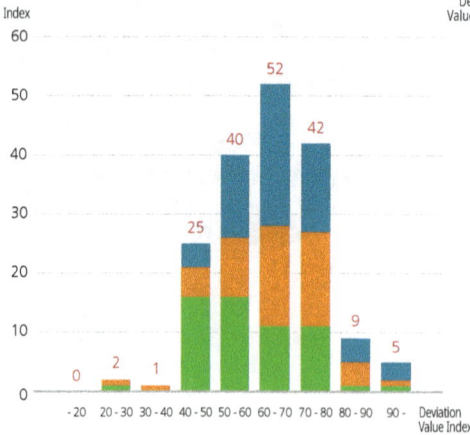

Figure 3-84 Deviation Value Distribution of Indicators

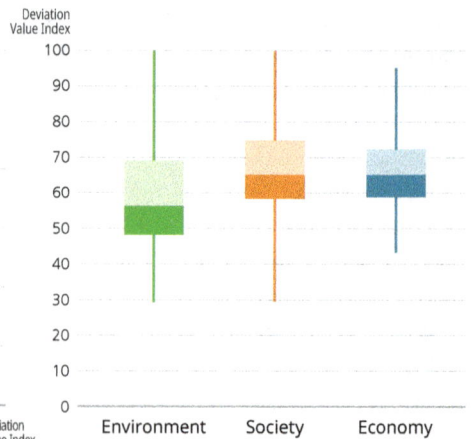

Figure 3-85 Box Plot Distribution of Indicators

Dimension	Sub-dimension	Indicator Group	ID	Indicators	Deviation Value Index	Rank
Environment	Natural Ecology	Soil and Water Condition	1	Available Land Area Per Ten Thousand People	47.8	279
			2	Forest Area	44.9	217
			3	Farmland Area	48.9	130
			4	Pasture Area	48.2	117
			5	Water Area	56.7	26
			6	Water Resources Per Ten Thousand People	49.1	189
			7	National Park · Conservation Area · Scenic Area Index	54.3	51
		Climate Condition	8	Climate Comfort Index	56.2	80
			9	Rainfall	52.6	110
		Natural Disaster	10	Natural Disaster-caused Direct Economic Loss Index	47.1	197
			11	Geological Disaster-caused Direct Economic Loss Index	53.1	1
			12	Disaster Warning	47.9	80
	Environmental Quality	Pollution Load	13	Air Quality Index (AQI)	46.0	184
			14	PM2.5 Index	46.8	171
			15	CO2 Emissions Per Unit of GDP	41.3	236
			16	Volume of Sulphur Dioxide Emission	48.1	265
			17	Volume of Industrial Soot(dust) Emission	45.6	262
			18	Proportion of National and Provincial Water Sections in Category III and Above Meeting the Quality Standard	63.8	1
			19	Areas Environmental Average Noise Value	56.4	53
			20	Radiation Environmental Air Absorption Dose Rate	80.6	2
		Environmental Protection Efforts	21	Environmental Effort Index	61.7	9
			22	Water-saving Effort Index	50.8	107
			23	Social Organizations for Ecological Environment	55.8	20
			24	National Environmental Protection City Index	73.5	12
			25	National Ecological Environment Evaluation Index	100.0	1
		Resource Efficiency	26	Land Productivity in Built District	51.6	77
			27	Land Productivity in Agriculture, Forestry, Animal Husbandry and Fisheries	57.8	56
			28	Energy Consumption Per Unit of GDP	41.3	236
			29	Projects Labeled with Green Building Design and Evaluation	75.3	6
			30	Comprehensive Utilization Rate of Industrial Solid Waste	53.8	154
			31	Circular Economical City Index	44.6	98
	Spatial Structure	Compact City	32	Population of Densely Inhabited Districts (DIDs)	69.4	13
			33	Area of Densely Inhabited Districts (DIDs)	62.1	18
			34	Proportion of the Population of Densely Inhabited Districts (DIDs)	69.5	20
			35	Proportion of Densely Inhabited Districts (DIDs) in Built District	59.9	18
			36	Population of Super Densely Inhabited Districts (DIDs)	77.5	10
			37	Area of Super Densely Inhabited Districts (DIDs)	72.8	11
			38	Proportion of the Population of Super Densely Inhabited Districts (DIDs)	76.2	8
			39	Proportion of Densely Super Densely Inhabited Districts (DIDs) in Built District	68.0	9
		Transportation Network	40	Urban Rail Transit Density Index	75.6	6
			41	Urban Arterial Road Density Index	64.0	19
			42	Urban Life Road Density Index	64.8	17
			43	Urban Sidewalk • Bicycle Lane Density Index	64.6	21
			44	Urban Rail Transit Distance	73.7	6
			45	Public Bus Passenger Volume Per Ten Thousand People	67.7	21
			46	Public Bus Ownership Per Ten Thousand People	74.0	10
			47	Private Vehicle Ownership Per Ten Thousand People	48.4	265
			48	Taxis Ownership Per Ten Thousand People	63.5	30
			49	Rush Hour Traffic Jam Delay Index	29.4	269
		Urban Facilities	50	Fixed Assets Investment Scale Index	73.2	12
			51	Area of Park Green Land	73.0	7
			52	Green Coverage Rate in Built District	57.3	45
			53	Density of Water Supply Pipelines in Built District	53.3	81
			54	Density of Sewers in Built District	53.5	84
			55	Gas Coverage Rate	55.2	98
			56	Urban Underground Facilities Index	45.5	54

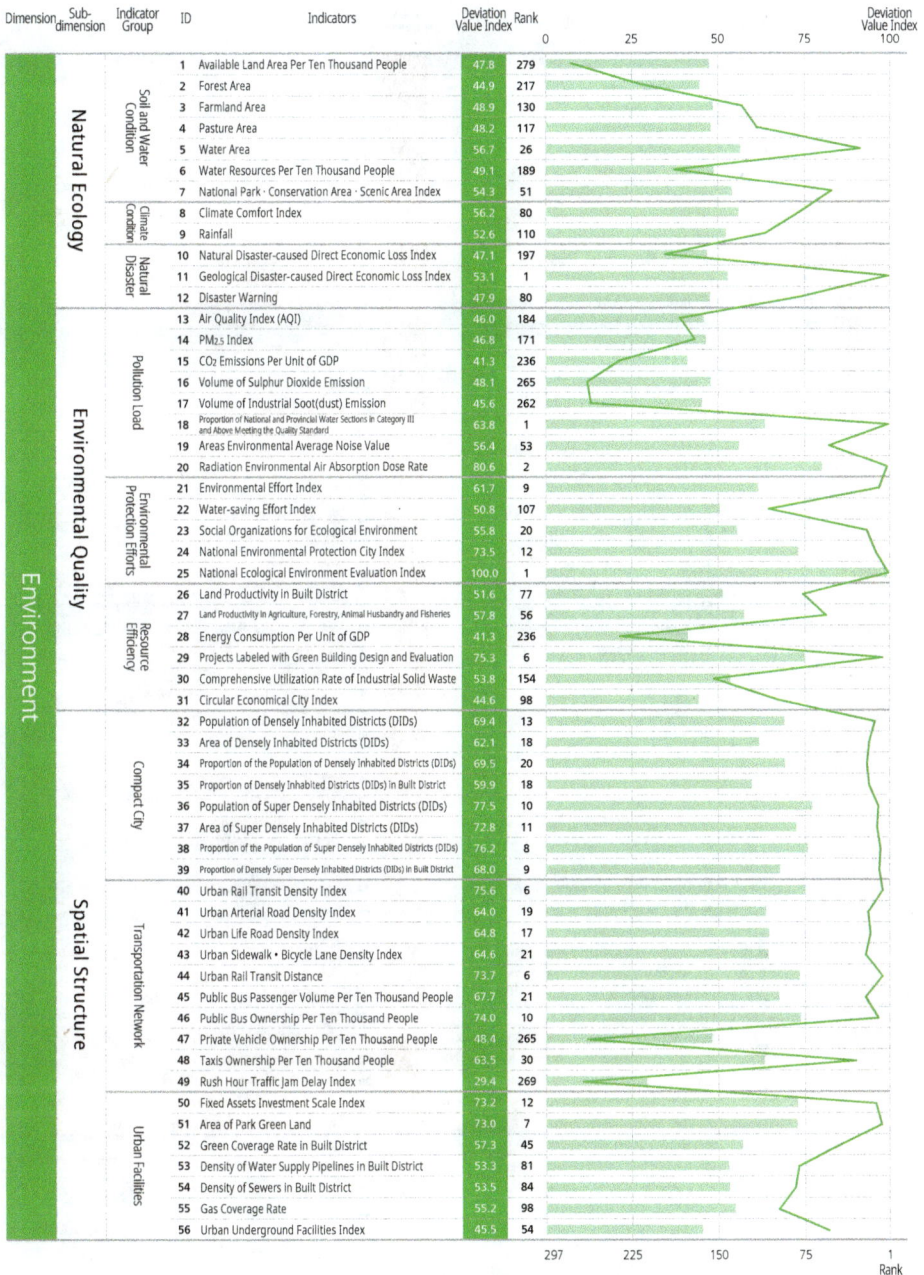

Figure 3-86 Index Ranking: Environment

Nanjing

Dimension	Sub-dimension	Indicator Group	ID	Indicators	Deviation Value Index	Rank
Society	Status and Governance	City Status	57	Administrative Levels	55.8	5
			58	Megalopolis Levels	68.8	1
			59	Core City Levels	59.3	4
			60	Embassies · Consulates	48.9	17
			61	International Organizations	49.4	3
			62	Belt and Road Index	59.7	17
		Quality of Residents	63	Population Natural Growth Rate Index	44.4	206
			64	Population Social Growth Rate Index	54.2	31
			65	Population Structure Index	58.1	21
			66	Population Education Structure Index	77.8	2
			67	Higher Education Index	85.3	8
			68	Outstanding Talent Cultivation Index	77.8	4
			69	Public Finance Expenditure for Education Index	61.2	14
		Social Management	70	Social Services Index	64.2	12
			71	Safe and Reliable City Index	70.8	14
			72	Traffic Safety Index	42.2	289
			73	Social Security Index	35.8	273
			74	Social Organizations	72.6	14
			75	Health and Civilized City Index	56.7	28
			76	Government Website Performance	65.4	12
	Inheritance and Exchange	Historical Relics	77	Historical Status	100.0	3
			78	World Heritage	60.6	14
			79	Famous Historical and Cultural Cities	61.7	7
			80	Intangible Cultural Heritage	66.5	11
			81	Key Cultural Relics Sites Under the Protection	76.6	10
		Culture and Entertainment	82	Theater Consumer Index	72.4	9
			83	Museums · Art Galleries	69.8	13
			84	Sports Venues Index	79.7	6
			85	Zoos · Botanical Gardens · Aquariums	74.3	10
			86	Public Library Collection	70.4	9
			87	Cultural Master Index	60.8	5
			88	Olympic Champion Index	75.0	10
			89	National Culturally Advanced Unit Index	74.9	6
		Personal Exchange	90	Inbound Tourists	51.8	38
			91	Domestic Tourists	66.6	12
			92	Foreign Exchange Earnings from International Tourism	55.8	24
			93	Earnings from Domestic Tourism	77.1	10
			94	International Conferences	60.8	7
			95	Exhibition Industry Development Index	64.5	13
			96	World Tourism City Index	50.6	66
	Quality of Life	Residential Environment	97	Average Life Expectancy	56.4	5
			98	Medicare · Endowment Insurance Coverage Index	67.0	19
			99	Ratio of Average House Prices to Income	29.7	286
			100	Habitat City Index	80.9	4
			101	China's Happiness City Index	87.1	6
		Level of Consumption	102	Retail Sales of Consumer Goods Per Ten Thousand People	83.2	3
			103	Revenue of Hotels and Catering Services Per Ten Thousand People	65.3	10
			104	Telecom Consumption Per Ten Thousand People	60.5	29
			105	Water Consumption for Residential Use Per Ten Thousand People	79.2	8
			106	Top International Brand Index	72.4	7
		Life Service	107	Number of Children in Kindergartens Per Ten Thousand People	45.0	206
			108	Year-end Number of Beds in Nursing Homes	79.4	4
			109	Number of Practicing (Assistant) Physicians	63.0	23
			110	Number of Beds in Health Institutions	61.4	26
			111	First-class Hospitals	74.8	8

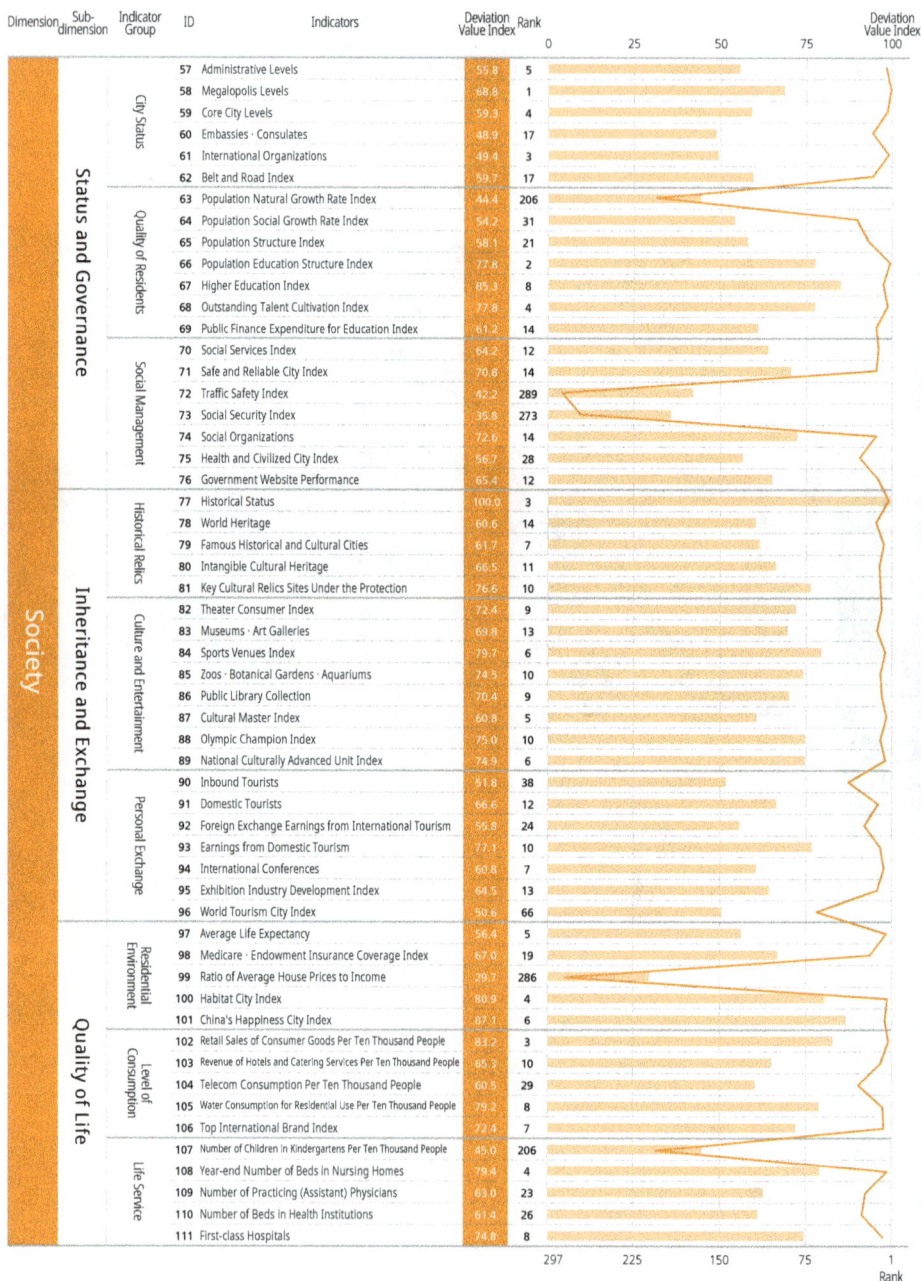

Figure 3-87 Index Ranking: Society

Dimension	Sub-dimension	Indicator Group	ID	Indicators	Deviation Value Index	Rank
Economy	Quality of Economic Development	Economic Scale	112	Size of GDP	72.5	11
			113	Population Size of Permanent Residents	61.3	30
			114	Scale of Tax Collection	64.7	11
			115	Electricity Consumption	64.7	11
		Economic Structure	116	Industrial Structure Index	68.8	12
			117	Mainboard Listed Enterprises	69.9	4
			118	Top 500 Chinese Enterprises in the World	52.0	7
			119	China's Top 500 Enterprises	62.1	6
			120	China's Top 500 Private-owned Enterprises	70.2	12
			121	Gross Industrial Output Value Above Designated Size	69.0	16
		Economic Efficiency	122	GDP Growth Index	58.6	25
			123	GDP Per Ten Thousand People	72.9	10
			124	Fiscal Revenue Per Ten Thousand People	70.6	15
			125	Dependent Population Index	67.0	12
			126	Size and Debt Rate of Bonds Issued by the City Investment Enterprises	45.6	262
			127	Number of Registered Unemployed Persons Per Ten Thousand People	43.4	219
	Dynamic Development	Business Environment	128	Employee Average Salary	73.5	8
			129	Number of Employees of Enterprise Services	61.0	10
			130	Star Hotel Index	69.6	11
			131	Top International Restaurant Index	53.5	14
			132	National Industrial Park Index	72.3	17
		Openness	133	Population Migration	62.8	15
			134	Export of Goods · Import of Goods	57.9	18
			135	Foreign Investment Utilized	62.8	18
			136	Outward Foreign Direct Investment	52.0	31
			137	The Output Value of Foreign-Invested Enterprises Above Designated Size	75.9	7
			138	International Schools	58.6	16
			139	Free Trade Area Index	56.2	25
		Innovation and Entrepreneurship	140	The World's Top University Index	93.2	3
			141	R&D Expenditure Index	67.1	9
			142	R&D Human Resources	82.6	6
			143	GEM,New Third Board Listed Enterprise Index	62.9	10
			144	The Amount of Patent Authorization Index	57.5	15
			145	Trademark Registration Index	61.0	15
			146	Academicians Index	76.9	3
			147	National Reform Experiment	72.0	10
			148	National Innovative Model City Index	72.4	10
			149	Information · Knowledge Industry City Index	73.2	13
			150	National Key Laboratory · Engineering Research Center Index	83.2	3
		Urban and Rural Integration	151	Urban-rural Income Ratio Index	60.9	24
			152	Primary School Education Level Population Ratio	70.7	11
			153	Illiteracy Rate	51.0	94
			154	Balanced Development of Compulsory Education Index	44.5	179
	Urban Influence	Wide-area Hub	155	Airport Convenient	66.3	12
			156	Air Traffic Volume Index	64.2	11
			157	Container Port Convenient	60.7	15
			158	Port Container Throughput	57.1	15
			159	Water Transport Volume Index	54.8	39
			160	Railway Convenient	95.3	3
			161	Railway Traffic Volume Index	64.2	17
			162	Railway Density	83.5	5
			163	Road Traffic Volume Index	53.7	49
			164	Expressway Density	78.3	8
			165	National Road · Provincial Road Density	74.8	11
			166	Circulation City Index	94.9	1
		Core Influence	167	Higher Education Radiation	87.0	3
			168	Science and Technology Radiation	67.9	10
			169	IT Industry Radiation	74.7	5
			170	Culture and Sports and Entertainment Radiation	66.0	7
			171	Financial Radiation	61.5	12
			172	Manufacturing Radiation	59.0	21
			173	Medical Radiation	67.2	12
			174	Wholesale and Retail Radiation	70.2	9
			175	Catering and Hotel Radiation	59.7	11

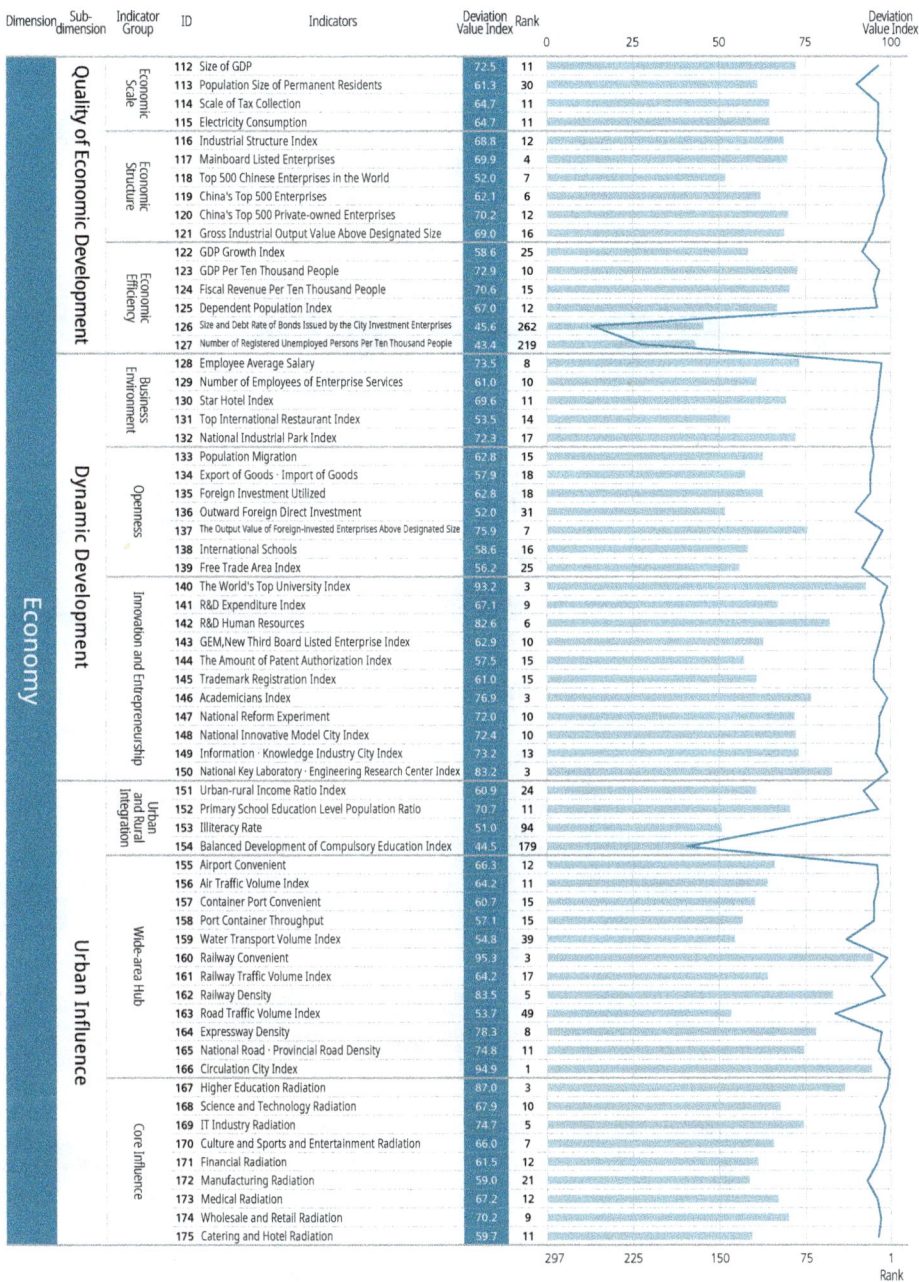

Figure 3-88 Index Ranking: Economy

Nanjing

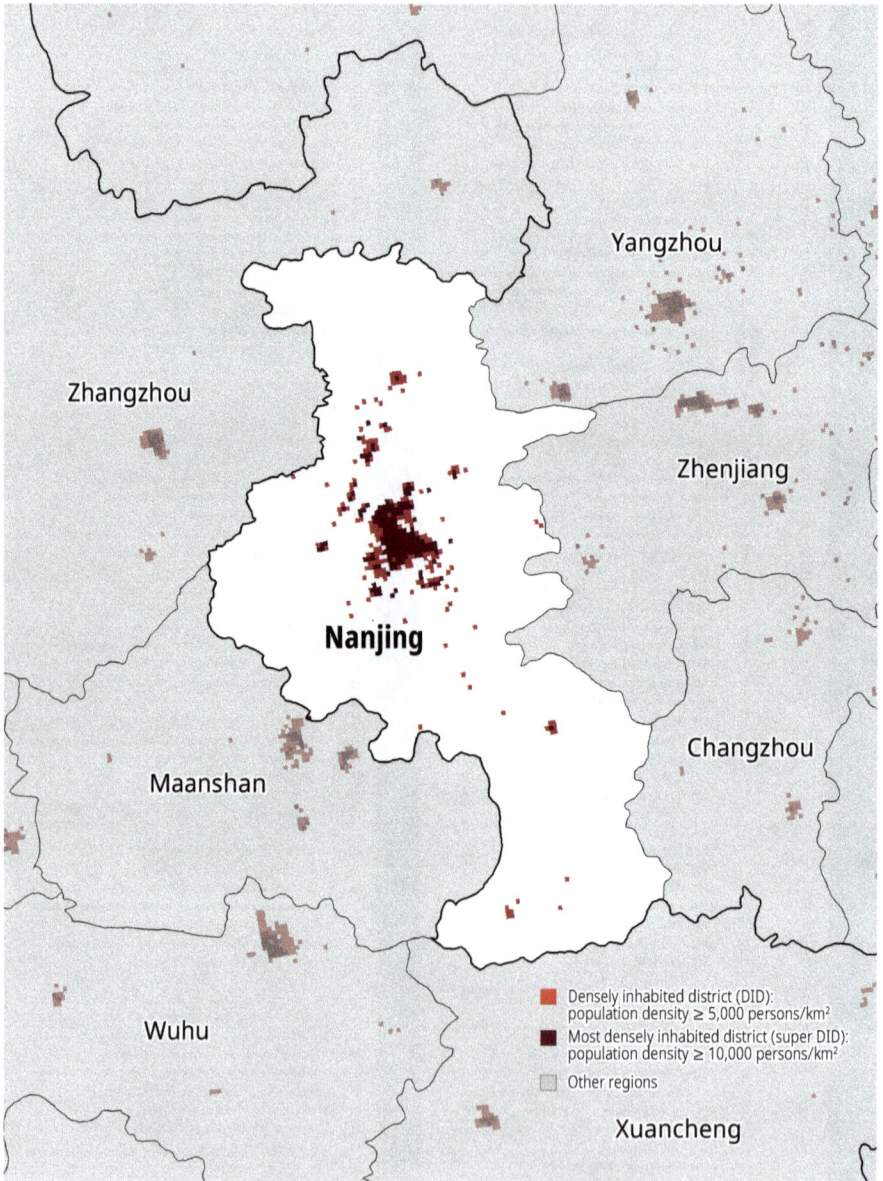

Figure 3-89 DID Analysis

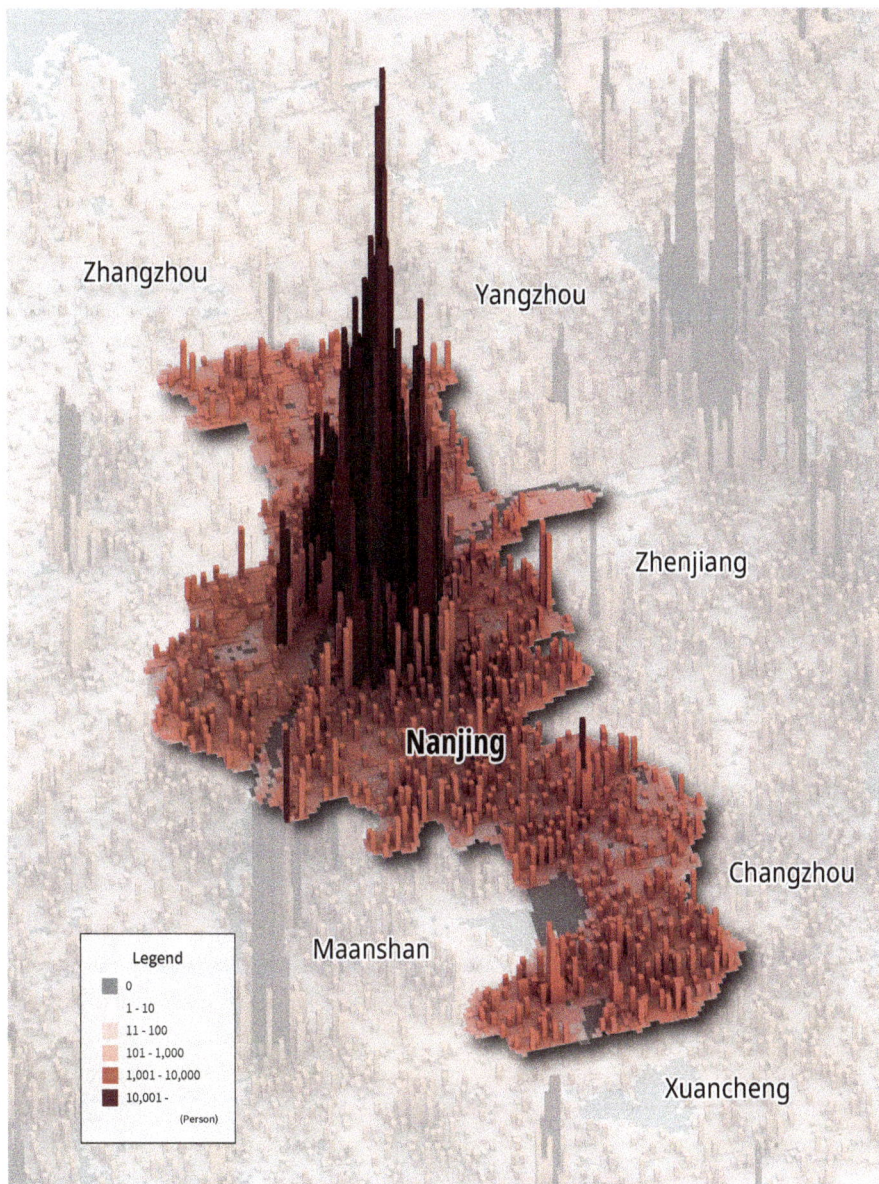

Figure 3-90 Population Size and Density Analysis

10th Chengdu

Chengdu ranked 10th in the comprehensive ranking.

Chengdu ranked 8th within the economic dimension for her excellent performance. As the capital of Sichuan Province and the only city with a net influx of population in the Chengdu-Chongqing Urban Agglomeration, Chengdu has received a large number of migrants. In the southwestern region, Chengdu is the top city not only for the number of foreign consulates, but also for the number of foreign banks and foreign insurance institutions, as well as FORTUNE 500 firms. As a central city, Chengdu provides a plat-form for the region to communicate with the rest of the world. In recent years, Chengdu has developed rapidly in the IT industry, forming a huge IT industrial cluster centered on laptops. In terms of three sub-dimension indicators of the economic dimension, Chengdu ranked 5th for urban influence with her strong capability of radiation, and ranked 7th and 10th for dynamic development and for quality of economic development, respectively.

Chengdu ranked 9th within the social dimension. Since ancient times, Chengdu has been a political, economic, and military center in the southwestern region of China. She also enjoys the reputation of "the Land of Abundance," as a famous historical and cultural city as well as an important central city for tourism. Regarding three sub-dimension indicators of the social dimension, Chengdu performed in a balanced and sound manner and ranked 9th, 11th, and 8th for status and governance, inheritance and exchange, as well as quality of life, respectively.

Chengdu ranked 49th within the environmental dimension. In terms of three sub-dimension indicators of the environmental dimension, Chengdu did best in and ranked 12th for spatial structure. However, due to serious air pollution among other reasons, she ranked 145th and 130th respectively for natural ecology and environmental quality

Table 3-10 Key Index

Environment

Number of permanent residents:	14,430,000
Land area of administrative region:	12,121 km²
Ranking of available land area per capita:	276
Ranking of forest coverage:	135
Ranking of water resources per capita:	183
Ranking of climate comfort index:	66
Ranking of PM$_{2.5}$ Index:	234
Ranking of densely inhabited district (DID) population :	7
Ranking of rail transit route mileage :	15

Society

Ranking of average house prices :	36
Ranking of cinemas and theater numbers :	155
Ranking of museum and art gallery numbers :	4
Number of domestic tourists:	188,700,000
Number of inbound tourists:	2,300,000
Ranking of world heritage number :	14
Ranking of international conference number :	14

Economy

Size of GDP:	RMB 1080.1 billion
Per-capita GDP:	RMB 74,863 / person
GDP growth rate:	6.9 %
Ranking of per capita revenue in :	39
Ranking of average salaries :	20
Ranking of mainboard listed enterprises :	9
Ranking of goods export in China:	24
Ranking of airport convenience in China:	5
Ranking of container port convenience :	255
Ranking of financial radiation :	9
Ranking of manufacturing radiation :	15
Ranking of IT industry radiation :	6
Ranking of higher education radiation :	7
Ranking of science and technology radiation :	5
Ranking of medical radiation :	4
Ranking of culture and sports and entertainment radiation :	4
Ranking of catering and hotel radiation :	7
Ranking of wholesale and retail radiation :	3

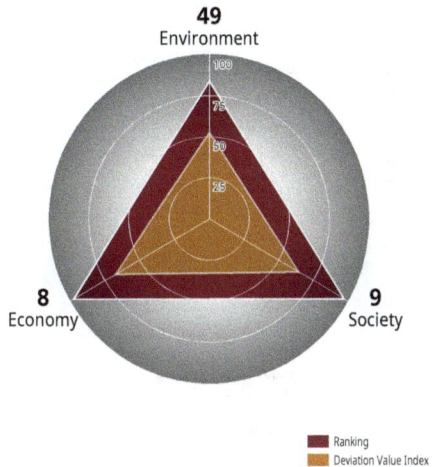

Figure 3-91 Scores of Dimension

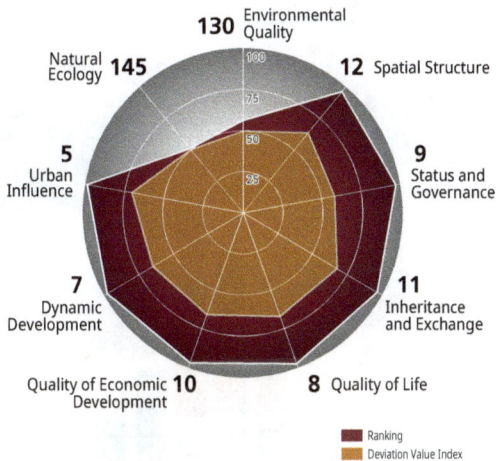

Figure 3-92 Scores of Sub-Dimension

Chengdu

Dimension	Sub-Dimension	Indicator Group	Deviation Value Index
Environment	Natural Ecology	Soil and Water Condition	48.9
		Climate Condition	53.4
		Natural Disaster	48.9
	Environmental Quality	Pollution Load	46.7
		Environmental Protection Efforts	65.8
		Resource Efficiency	52.7
	Spatial Structure	Compact City	71.3
		Transportation Network	58.7
		Urban Facilities	68.0
Society	Status and Governance	City Status	54.7
		Quality of Residents	61.4
		Social Management	62.0
	Inheritance and Exchange	Historical Relics	56.1
		Culture & Entertainment	72.5
		Exchange	71.2
	Quality of Life	Residential Environment	59.8
		Level of Consumption	68.5
		Life Service	71.8
Economy	Quality of Economic Development	Economic Aggregate	73.1
		Economic Structure	65.3
		Economic Efficiency	53.5
	Dynamic Development	Business Environment	68.7
		Openness	61.3
		Innovation and Entrepreneurship	68.6
	Urban Influence	Urban and Rural Integration	57.9
		Wide-area Hub	66.0
		Core Influence	76.8

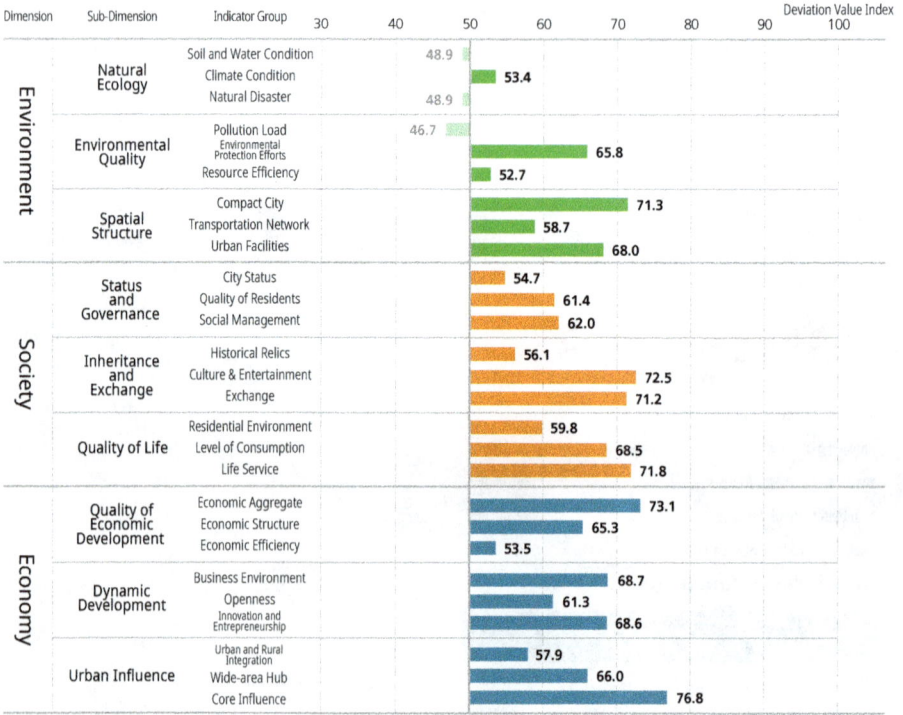

Figure 3-93 Deviation Value of Indicator Group

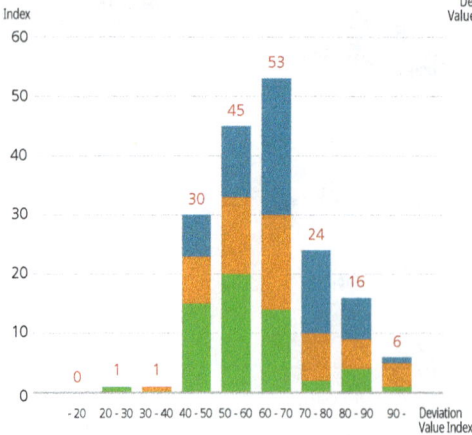

Figure 3-94 Deviation Value Distribution of Indicators

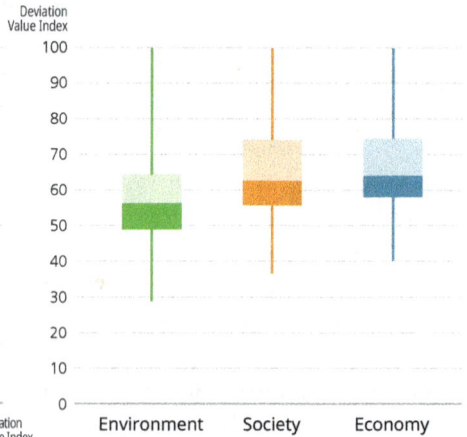

Figure 3-95 Box Plot Distribution of Indicators

118

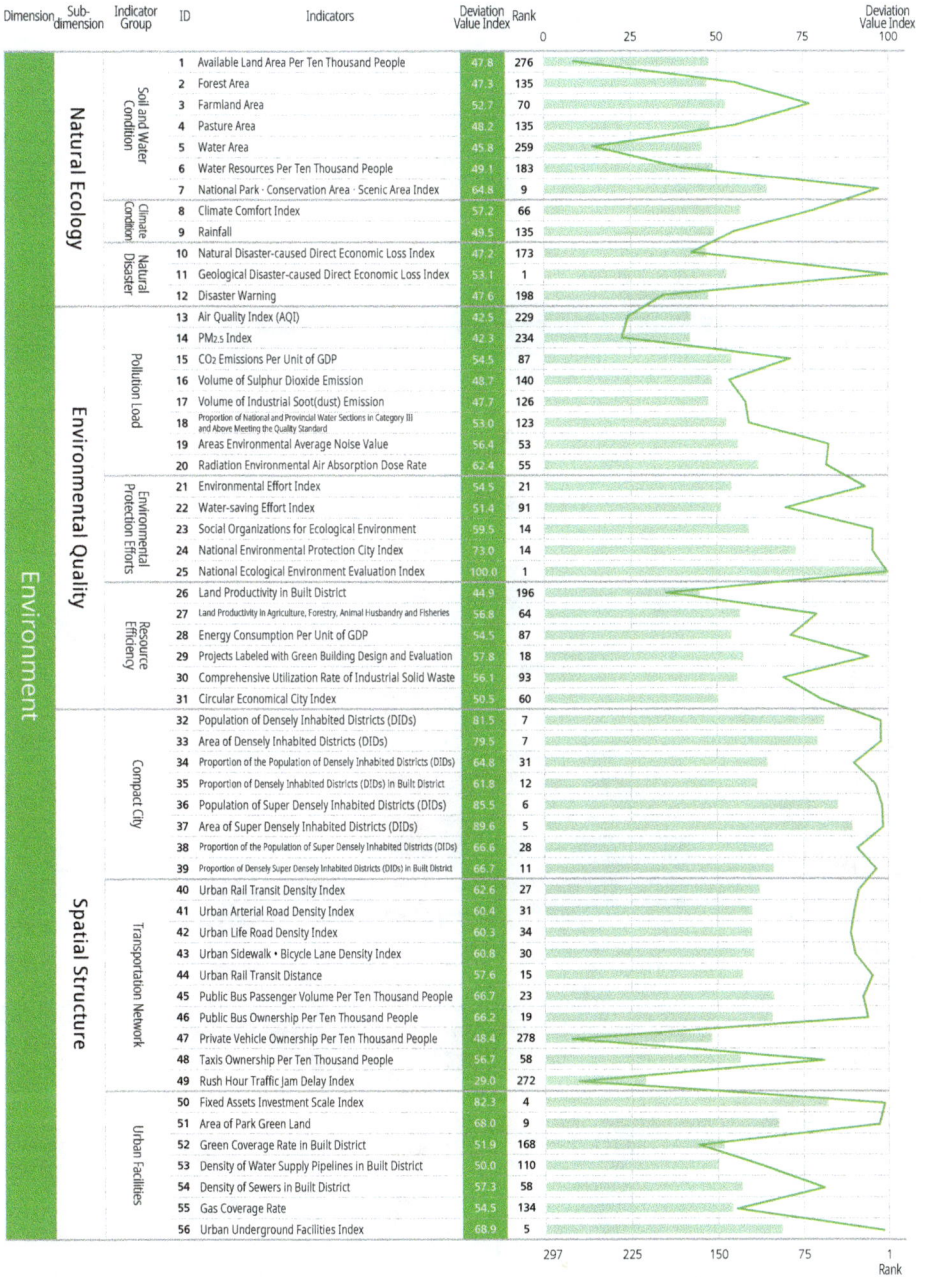

Dimension	Sub-dimension	Indicator Group	ID	Indicators	Deviation Value Index	Rank
Environment	Natural Ecology	Soil and Water Condition	1	Available Land Area Per Ten Thousand People	47.8	276
			2	Forest Area	47.3	135
			3	Farmland Area	52.7	70
			4	Pasture Area	48.2	135
			5	Water Area	45.8	259
			6	Water Resources Per Ten Thousand People	49.1	183
			7	National Park · Conservation Area · Scenic Area Index	64.8	9
		Climate Condition	8	Climate Comfort Index	57.2	66
			9	Rainfall	49.5	135
		Natural Disaster	10	Natural Disaster-caused Direct Economic Loss Index	47.2	173
			11	Geological Disaster-caused Direct Economic Loss Index	53.1	1
			12	Disaster Warning	47.6	198
	Environmental Quality	Pollution Load	13	Air Quality Index (AQI)	42.5	229
			14	PM2.5 Index	42.3	234
			15	CO_2 Emissions Per Unit of GDP	54.5	87
			16	Volume of Sulphur Dioxide Emission	48.7	140
			17	Volume of Industrial Soot(dust) Emission	47.7	126
			18	Proportion of National and Provincial Water Sections in Category III and Above Meeting the Quality Standard	53.0	123
			19	Areas Environmental Average Noise Value	56.4	53
			20	Radiation Environmental Air Absorption Dose Rate	62.4	55
		Environmental Protection Efforts	21	Environmental Effort Index	54.5	21
			22	Water-saving Effort Index	51.4	91
			23	Social Organizations for Ecological Environment	59.5	14
			24	National Environmental Protection City Index	73.0	14
			25	National Ecological Environment Evaluation Index	100.0	1
		Resource Efficiency	26	Land Productivity in Built District	44.9	196
			27	Land Productivity in Agriculture, Forestry, Animal Husbandry and Fisheries	56.8	64
			28	Energy Consumption Per Unit of GDP	54.5	87
			29	Projects Labeled with Green Building Design and Evaluation	57.8	18
			30	Comprehensive Utilization Rate of Industrial Solid Waste	56.1	93
			31	Circular Economical City Index	50.5	60
	Spatial Structure	Compact City	32	Population of Densely Inhabited Districts (DIDs)	81.5	7
			33	Area of Densely Inhabited Districts (DIDs)	79.5	7
			34	Proportion of the Population of Densely Inhabited Districts (DIDs)	64.8	31
			35	Proportion of Densely Inhabited Districts (DIDs) in Built District	61.8	12
			36	Population of Super Densely Inhabited Districts (DIDs)	85.5	6
			37	Area of Super Densely Inhabited Districts (DIDs)	89.6	5
			38	Proportion of the Population of Super Densely Inhabited Districts (DIDs)	66.6	28
			39	Proportion of Densely Super Densely Inhabited Districts (DIDs) in Built District	66.7	11
		Transportation Network	40	Urban Rail Transit Density Index	62.6	27
			41	Urban Arterial Road Density Index	60.4	31
			42	Urban Life Road Density Index	60.3	34
			43	Urban Sidewalk · Bicycle Lane Density Index	60.8	30
			44	Urban Rail Transit Distance	57.6	15
			45	Public Bus Passenger Volume Per Ten Thousand People	66.7	23
			46	Public Bus Ownership Per Ten Thousand People	66.2	19
			47	Private Vehicle Ownership Per Ten Thousand People	48.4	278
			48	Taxis Ownership Per Ten Thousand People	56.7	58
			49	Rush Hour Traffic Jam Delay Index	29.0	272
		Urban Facilities	50	Fixed Assets Investment Scale Index	82.3	4
			51	Area of Park Green Land	68.0	9
			52	Green Coverage Rate in Built District	51.9	168
			53	Density of Water Supply Pipelines in Built District	50.0	110
			54	Density of Sewers in Built District	57.3	58
			55	Gas Coverage Rate	54.5	134
			56	Urban Underground Facilities Index	68.9	5

Figure 3-96 Index Ranking: Environment

Chengdu

Dimension	Sub-dimension	Indicator Group	ID	Indicators	Deviation Value Index	Rank
Society	Status and Governance	City Status	57	Administrative Levels	55.8	5
			58	Megalopolis Levels	49.8	46
			59	Core City Levels	44.1	10
			60	Embassies · Consulates	63.0	4
			61	International Organizations	49.4	3
			62	Belt and Road Index	63.3	9
		Quality of Residents	63	Population Natural Growth Rate Index	42.8	221
			64	Population Social Growth Rate Index	57.4	15
			65	Population Structure Index	55.2	47
			66	Population Education Structure Index	63.0	26
			67	Higher Education Index	90.5	5
			68	Outstanding Talent Cultivation Index	67.0	8
			69	Public Finance Expenditure for Education Index	59.9	17
		Social Management	70	Social Services Index	51.0	96
			71	Safe and Reliable City Index	86.6	3
			72	Traffic Safety Index	42.3	286
			73	Social Security Index	36.7	268
			74	Social Organizations	73.8	11
			75	Health and Civilized City Index	72.3	6
			76	Government Website Performance	66.6	5
	Inheritance and Exchange	Historical Relics	77	Historical Status	47.9	64
			78	World Heritage	60.6	14
			79	Famous Historical and Cultural Cities	61.7	7
			80	Intangible Cultural Heritage	60.7	23
			81	Key Cultural Relics Sites Under the Protection	60.8	24
		Culture and Entertainment	82	Theater Consumer Index	76.5	7
			83	Museums · Art Galleries	87.6	4
			84	Sports Venues Index	55.8	48
			85	Zoos · Botanical Gardens · Aquariums	73.4	13
			86	Public Library Collection	79.2	4
			87	Cultural Master Index	59.4	8
			88	Olympic Champion Index	65.2	14
			89	National Culturally Advanced Unit Index	74.9	6
		Personal Exchange	90	Inbound Tourists	67.2	11
			91	Domestic Tourists	88.8	5
			92	Foreign Exchange Earnings from International Tourism	57.2	23
			93	Earnings from Domestic Tourism	77.2	9
			94	International Conferences	54.6	14
			95	Exhibition Industry Development Index	68.7	8
			96	World Tourism City Index	76.7	7
	Quality of Life	Residential Environment	97	Average Life Expectancy	49.4	19
			98	Medicare · Endowment Insurance Coverage Index	59.0	42
			99	Ratio of Average House Prices to Income	43.2	236
			100	Habitat City Index	67.3	17
			101	China's Happiness City Index	100.0	1
		Level of Consumption	102	Retail Sales of Consumer Goods Per Ten Thousand People	63.6	32
			103	Revenue of Hotels and Catering Services Per Ten Thousand People	56.9	25
			104	Telecom Consumption Per Ten Thousand People	81.9	6
			105	Water Consumption for Residential Use Per Ten Thousand People	67.7	17
			106	Top International Brand Index	88.8	3
		Life Service	107	Number of Children in Kindergartens Per Ten Thousand People	51.8	128
			108	Year-end Number of Beds in Nursing Homes	57.6	35
			109	Number of Practicing (Assistant) Physicians	92.0	4
			110	Number of Beds in Health Institutions	97.4	3
			111	First-class Hospitals	68.0	16

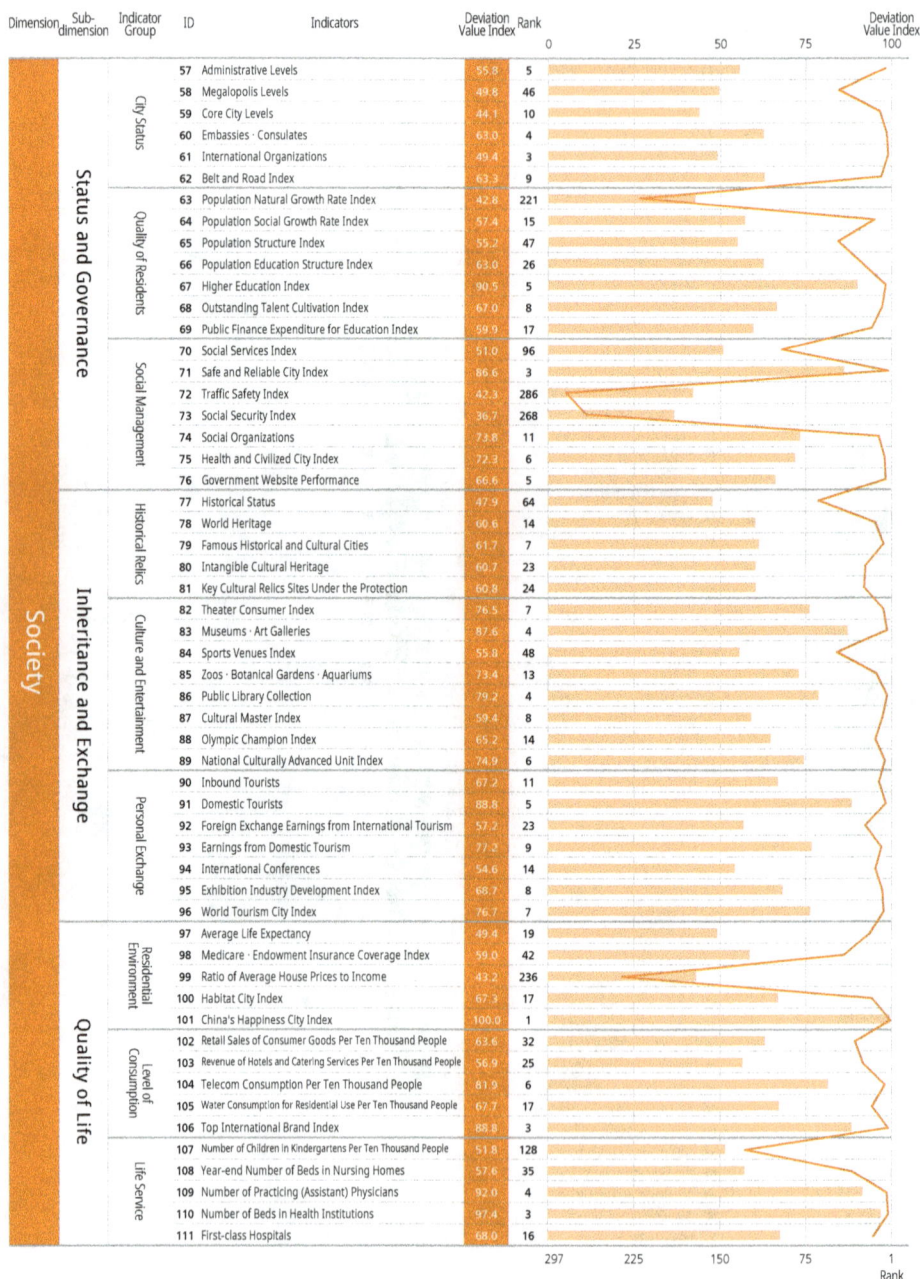

Figure 3-97 Index Ranking: Society

Figure 3-98 Index Ranking: Economy

Dimension	Sub-dimension	Indicator Group	ID	Indicators	Deviation Value Index	Rank
Economy	Quality of Economic Development	Economic Scale	112	Size of GDP	75.8	9
			113	Population Size of Permanent Residents	79.5	5
			114	Scale of Tax Collection	63.9	12
			115	Electricity Consumption	63.9	12
		Economic Structure	116	Industrial Structure Index	73.0	9
			117	Mainboard Listed Enterprises	63.7	9
			118	Top 500 Chinese Enterprises in the World	49.0	25
			119	China's Top 500 Enterprises	55.7	12
			120	China's Top 500 Private-owned Enterprises	61.5	21
			121	Gross Industrial Output Value Above Designated Size	65.5	23
		Economic Efficiency	122	GDP Growth Index	56.6	47
			123	GDP Per Ten Thousand People	58.3	50
			124	Fiscal Revenue Per Ten Thousand People	59.2	39
			125	Dependent Population Index	60.5	35
			126	Size and Debt Rate of Bonds Issued by the City Investment Enterprises	46.3	209
			127	Number of Registered Unemployed Persons Per Ten Thousand People	40.3	262
	Dynamic Development	Business Environment	128	Employee Average Salary	62.6	20
			129	Number of Employees of Enterprise Services	83.1	5
			130	Star Hotel Index	68.1	12
			131	Top International Restaurant Index	57.9	6
			132	National Industrial Park Index	69.8	22
		Openness	133	Population Migration	66.1	10
			134	Export of Goods · Import of Goods	55.2	22
			135	Foreign Investment Utilized	84.1	5
			136	Outward Foreign Direct Investment	53.1	26
			137	The Output Value of Foreign-invested Enterprises Above Designated Size	62.6	16
			138	International Schools	69.7	8
			139	Free Trade Area Index	83.3	12
		Innovation and Entrepreneurship	140	The World's Top University Index	75.4	7
			141	R&D Expenditure Index	63.1	12
			142	R&D Human Resources	71.1	11
			143	GEM,New Third Board Listed Enterprise Index	69.4	7
			144	The Amount of Patent Authorization Index	62.5	9
			145	Trademark Registration Index	70.4	6
			146	Academicians Index	57.4	8
			147	National Reform Experiment	84.4	5
			148	National Innovative Model City Index	78.4	5
			149	Information · Knowledge Industry City Index	73.7	12
			150	National Key Laboratory · Engineering Research Center Index	61.1	12
	Urban Influence	Urban and Rural Integration	151	Urban-rural Income Ratio Index	55.6	44
			152	Primary School Education Level Population Ratio	51.8	103
			153	Illiteracy Rate	52.0	87
			154	Balanced Development of Compulsory Education Index	76.8	6
		Wide-area Hub	155	Airport Convenient	84.9	5
			156	Air Traffic Volume Index	82.9	5
			157	Container Port Convenient	46.8	255
			158	Port Container Throughput	48.0	24
			159	Water Transport Volume Index	46.0	201
			160	Railway Convenient	71.5	12
			161	Railway Traffic Volume Index	66.8	11
			162	Railway Density	59.8	31
			163	Road Traffic Volume Index	60.4	18
			164	Expressway Density	64.1	22
			165	National Road · Provincial Road Density	64.0	22
			166	Circulation City Index	79.6	8
		Core Influence	167	Higher Education Radiation	76.6	7
			168	Science and Technology Radiation	81.3	5
			169	IT Industry Radiation	74.3	6
			170	Culture and Sports and Entertainment Radiation	76.0	4
			171	Financial Radiation	65.7	9
			172	Manufacturing Radiation	64.1	15
			173	Medical Radiation	87.3	4
			174	Wholesale and Retail Radiation	100.0	3
			175	Catering and Hotel Radiation	64.8	7

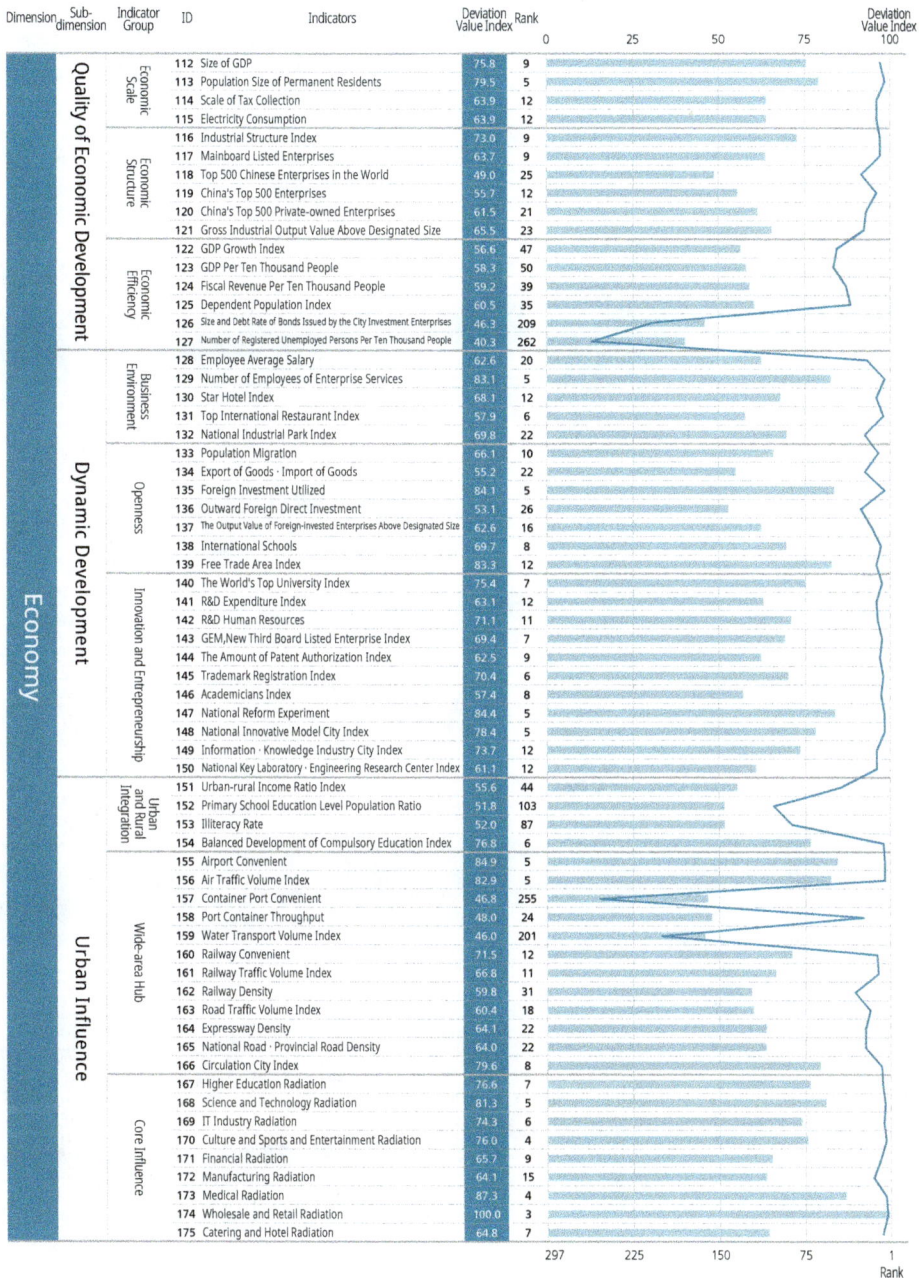

Figure 3-98 Index Ranking: Economy

Chengdu

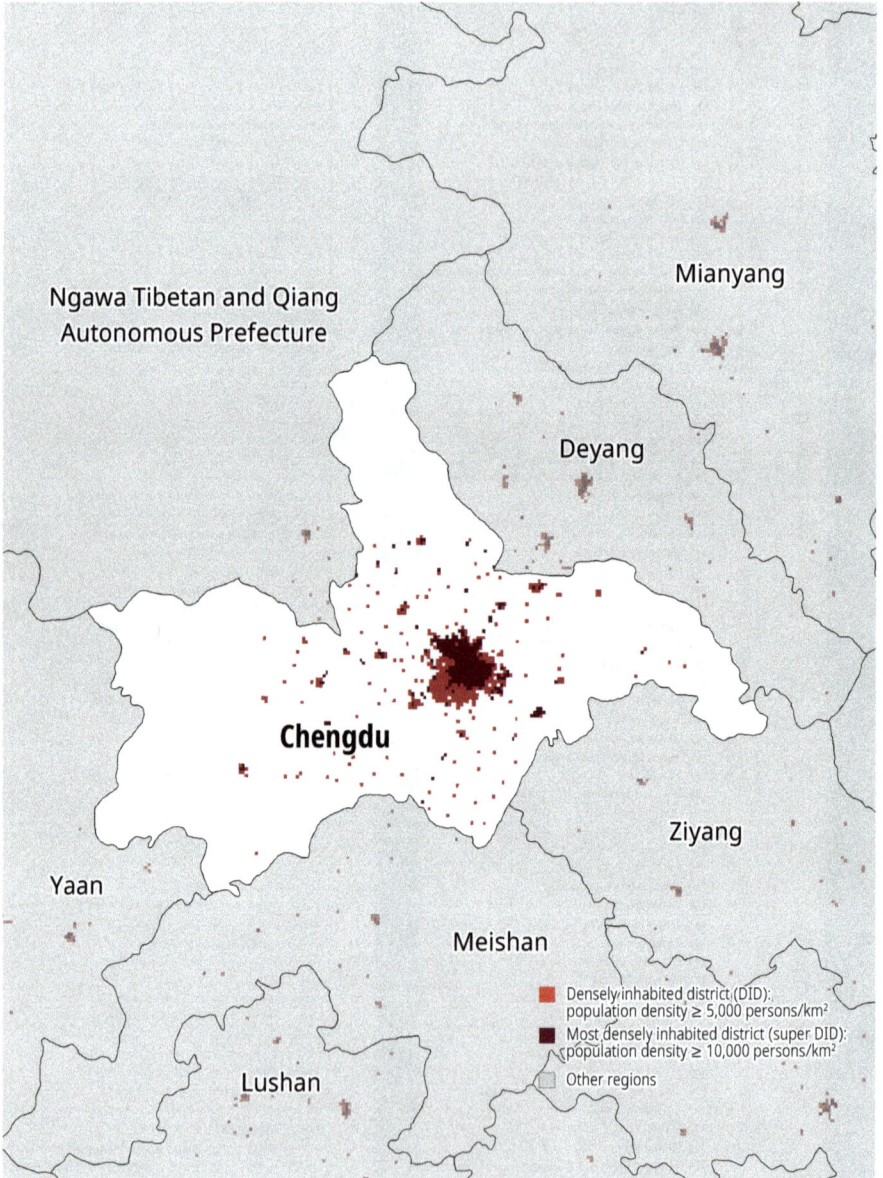

Ngawa Tibetan and Qiang
Autonomous Prefecture

Mianyang

Deyang

Chengdu

Ziyang

Yaan

Meishan

Lushan

■ Densely inhabited district (DID):
  population density ≥ 5,000 persons/km²
■ Most densely inhabited district (super DID):
  population density ≥ 10,000 persons/km²
■ Other regions

Figure 3-99 DID Analysis

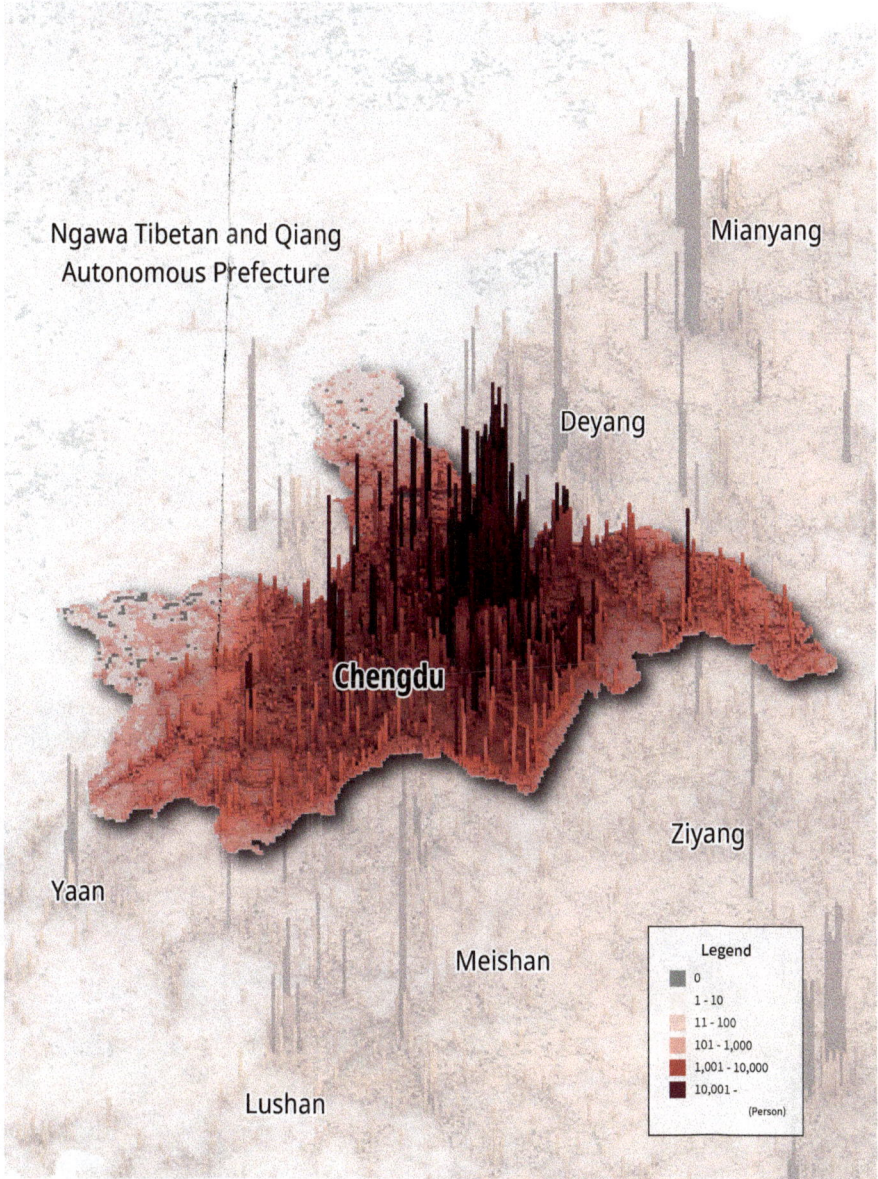

Ngawa Tibetan and Qiang
Autonomous Prefecture

Mianyang

Deyang

Chengdu

Ziyang

Yaan

Meishan

Lushan

Legend

0
1 - 10
11 - 100
101 - 1,000
1,001 - 10,000
10,001 -
(Person)

Figure 3-100 Population Size and Density Analysis

Chapter IV
Graphic Analysis of China's Urbanization

1. Size of GDP

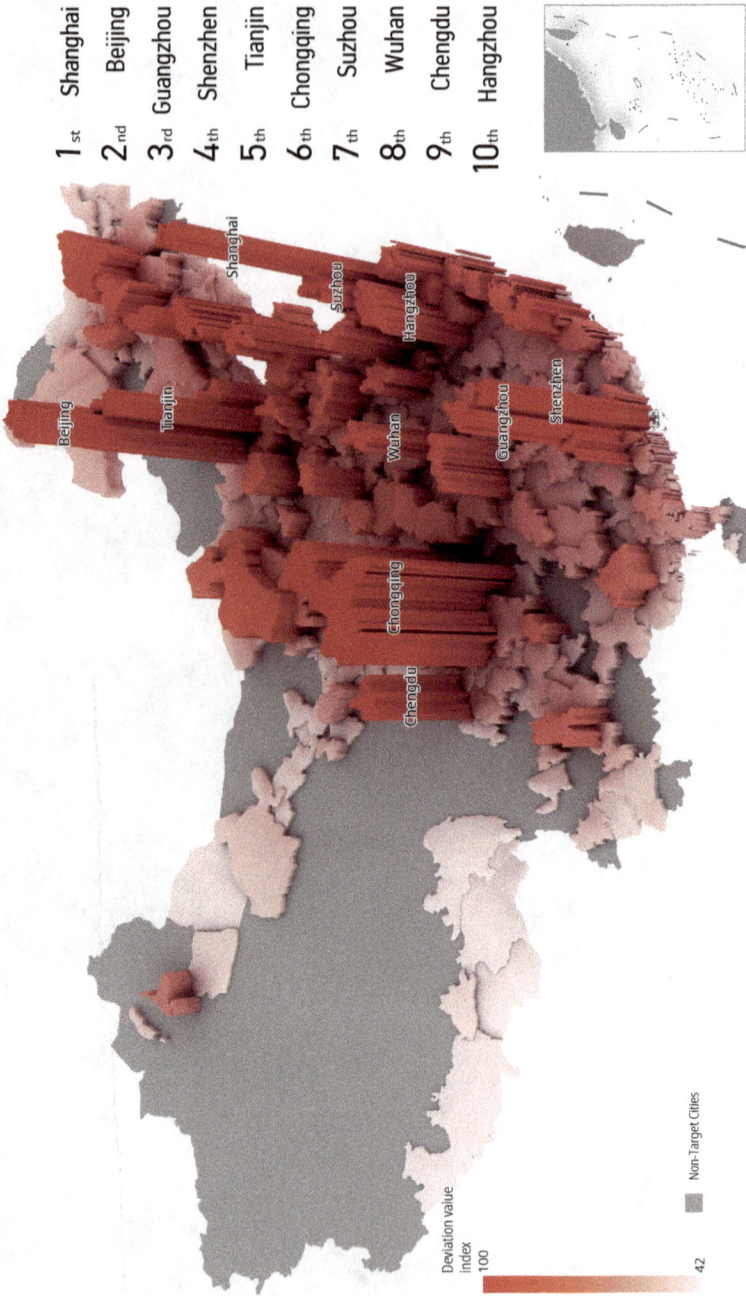

Deviation value
index
100

42

Non-Target Cities

1st Shanghai
2nd Beijing
3rd Guangzhou
4th Shenzhen
5th Tianjin
6th Chongqing
7th Suzhou
8th Wuhan
9th Chengdu
10th Hangzhou

Figure 4-1 Wide-Area Analysis Diagram of GDP Size

2. DID Population

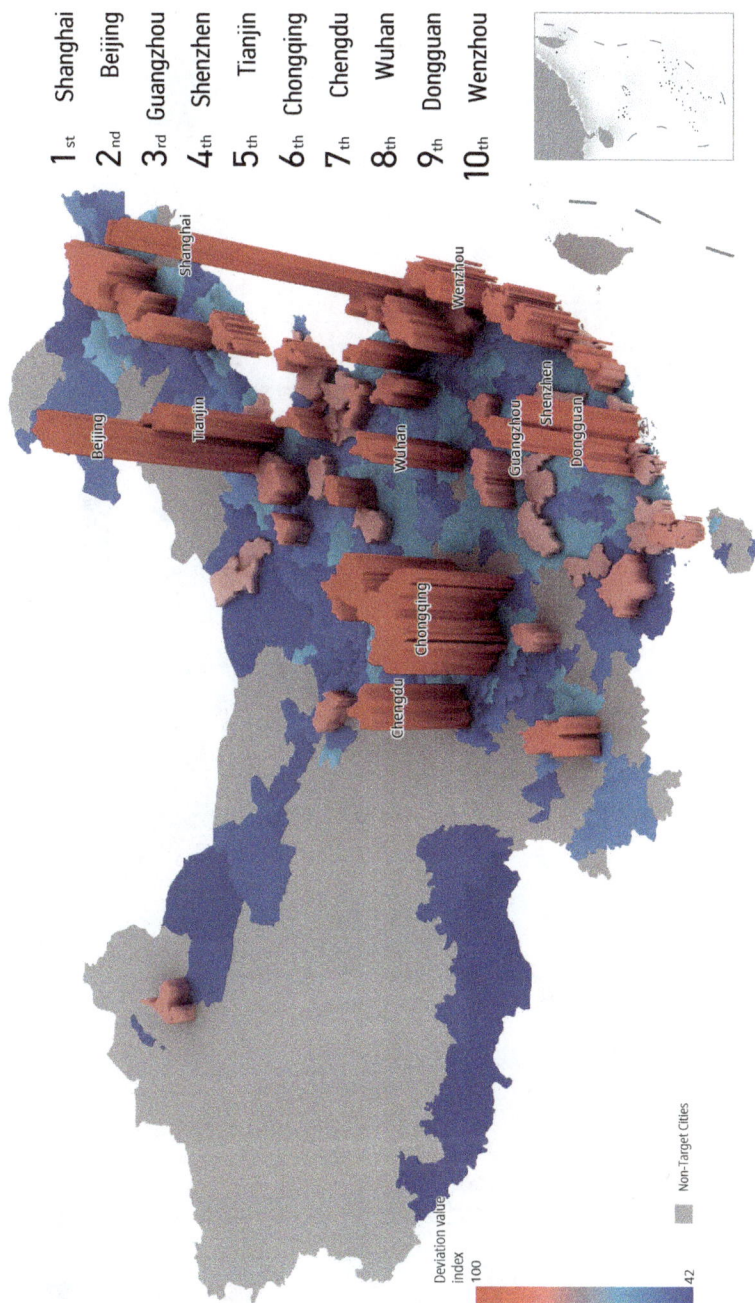

Figure 4-2 Wide-Area Analysis Diagram of DID Population

Deviation value index
100
42

Non-Target Cities

1st Shanghai
2nd Beijing
3rd Guangzhou
4th Shenzhen
5th Tianjin
6th Chongqing
7th Chengdu
8th Wuhan
9th Dongguan
10th Wenzhou

3. Population Migration: Influx

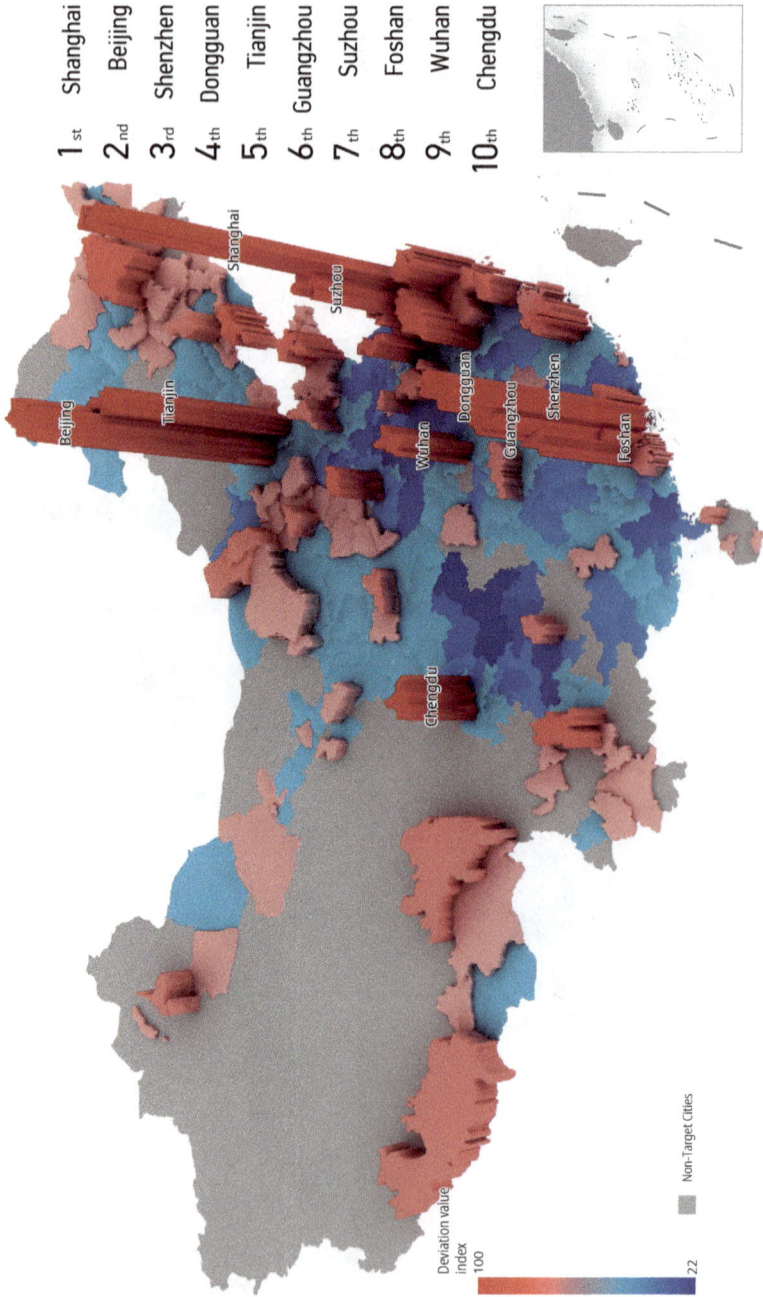

1st	Shanghai
2nd	Beijing
3rd	Shenzhen
4th	Dongguan
5th	Tianjin
6th	Guangzhou
7th	Suzhou
8th	Foshan
9th	Wuhan
10th	Chengdu

Deviation value index
100
22

Non-Target Cities

Figure 4-3 Wide-Area Analysis Diagram of Population Migration: Influx

Note: Cities with permanent population exceeding registered population are classified into influx cities.

4. Population Migration: Outflow

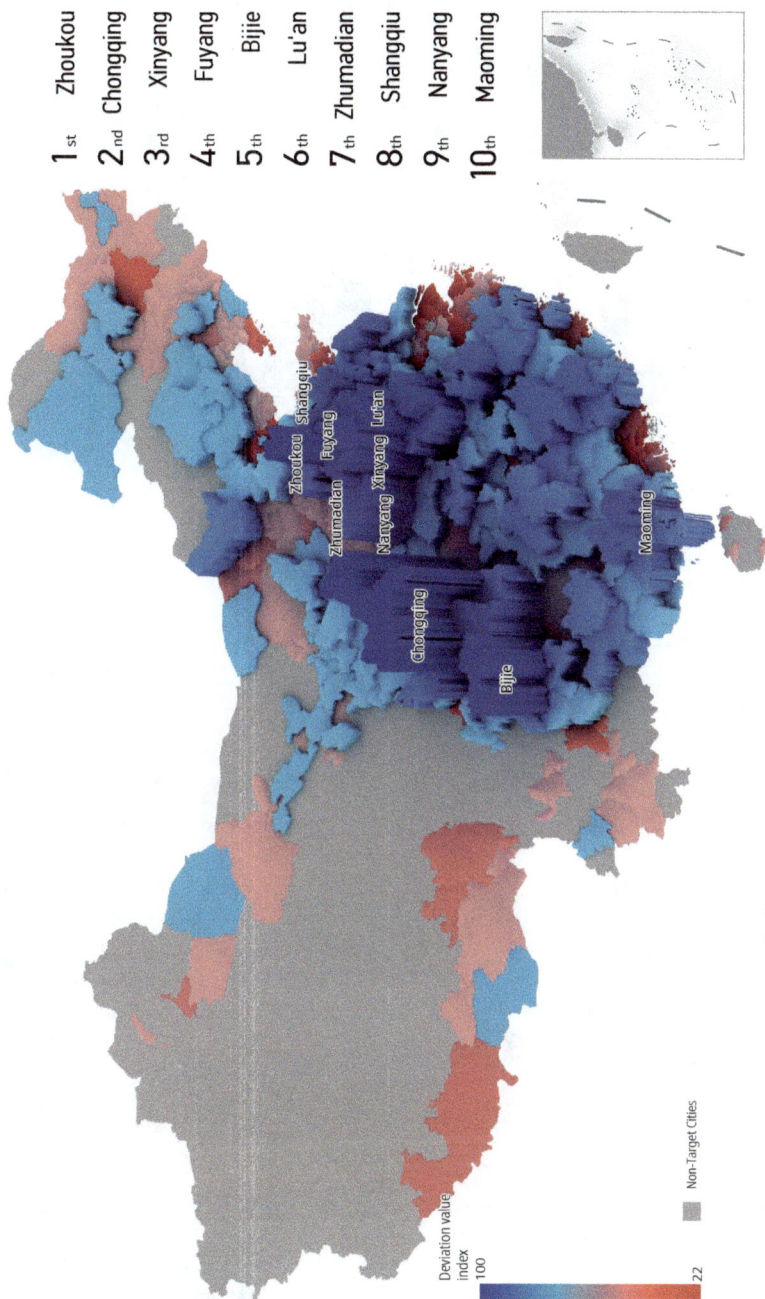

1st	Zhoukou
2nd	Chongqing
3rd	Xinyang
4th	Fuyang
5th	Bijie
6th	Lu'an
7th	Zhumadian
8th	Shangqiu
9th	Nanyang
10th	Maoming

Deviation value index

100

22

Non-Target Cities

Figure 4-4 Wide-Area Analysis Diagram of Population Migration: Outflow

Note: Cities with registered population exceeding permanent population are classified into outflow cities.

5. Gross Industrial Output Value above Designated Size

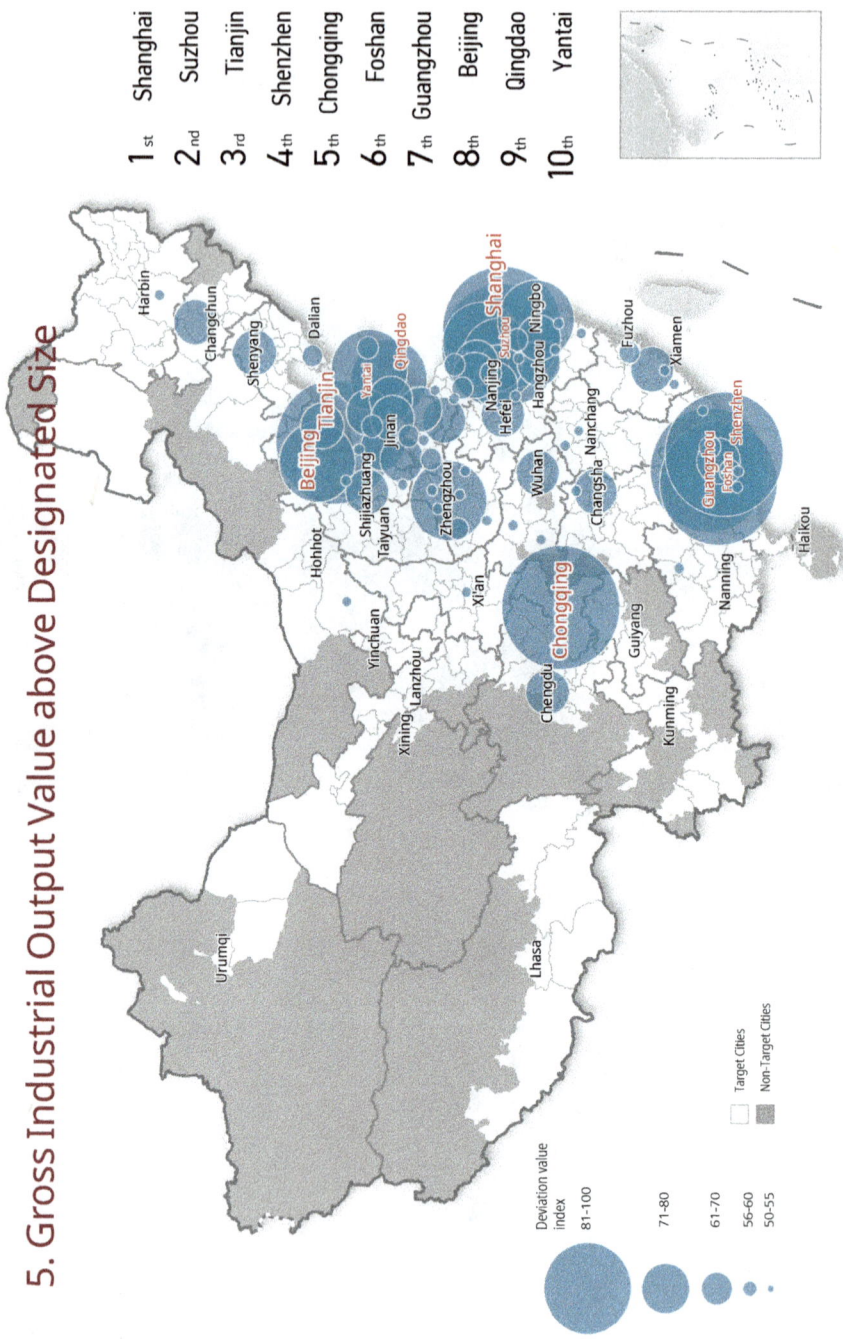

1st	Shanghai
2nd	Suzhou
3rd	Tianjin
4th	Shenzhen
5th	Chongqing
6th	Foshan
7th	Guangzhou
8th	Beijing
9th	Qingdao
10th	Yantai

Deviation value index

81-100
71-80
61-70
56-60
50-55

Target Cities
Non-Target Cities

Figure 4-5 Wide-Area Analysis Diagram of Gross Industrial Output Value above Designated Size

6. Export of Goods

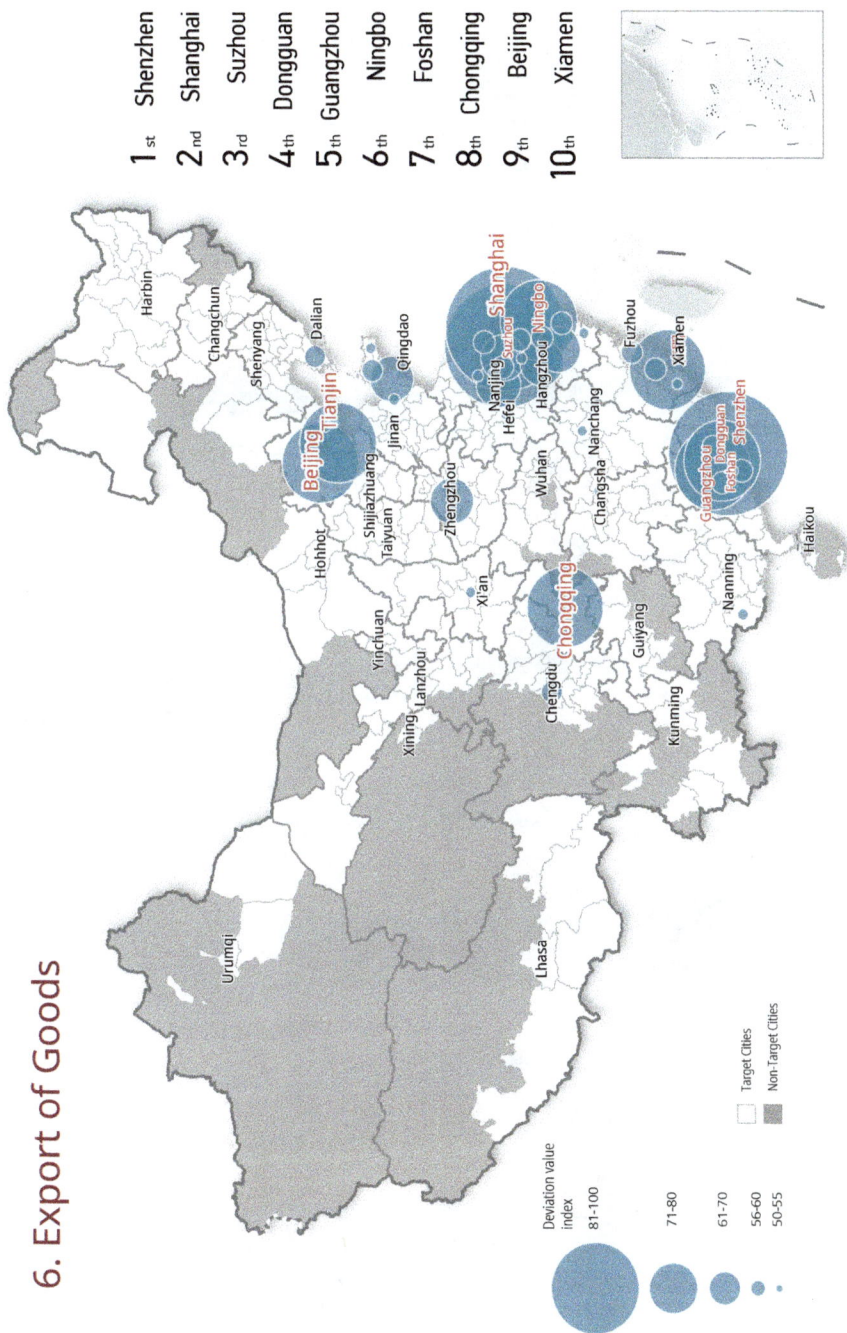

1st	Shenzhen
2nd	Shanghai
3rd	Suzhou
4th	Dongguan
5th	Guangzhou
6th	Ningbo
7th	Foshan
8th	Chongqing
9th	Beijing
10th	Xiamen

Deviation value index
81-100
71-80
61-70
56-60
50-55

Target Cities
Non-Target Cities

Figure 4-6 Wide-Area Analysis Diagram of Export of Goods

7. Container Port Convenience

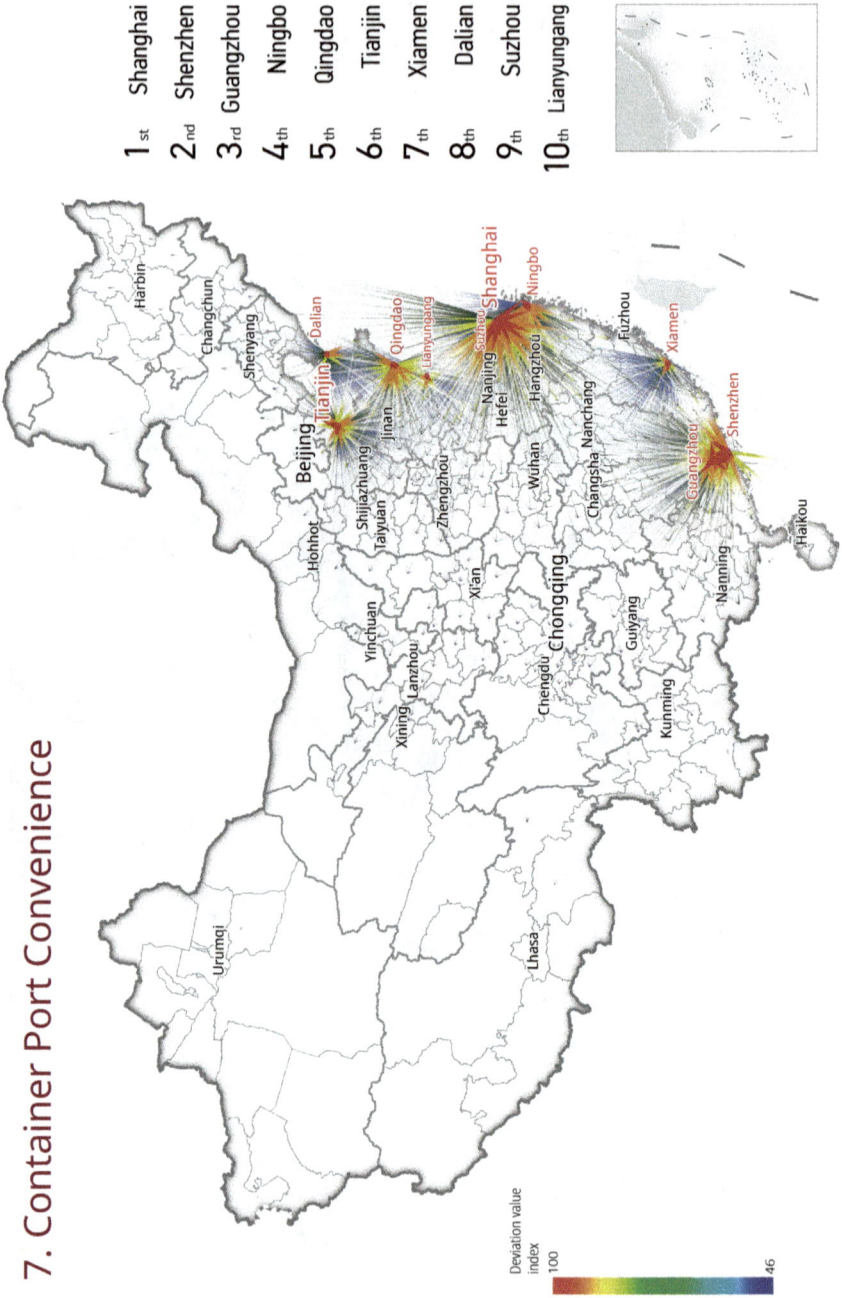

1st Shanghai
2nd Shenzhen
3rd Guangzhou
4th Ningbo
5th Qingdao
6th Tianjin
7th Xiamen
8th Dalian
9th Suzhou
10th Lianyungang

Deviation value index
100
46

Figure 4-7 Wide-Area Analysis Diagram of Container Port Convenience

Note: Container port convenience is an index to define whether a city's container port is convenient to access. It is calculated based on the distance between the city and the container port, and the throughput and the route of the container port.

8. Airport Convenience

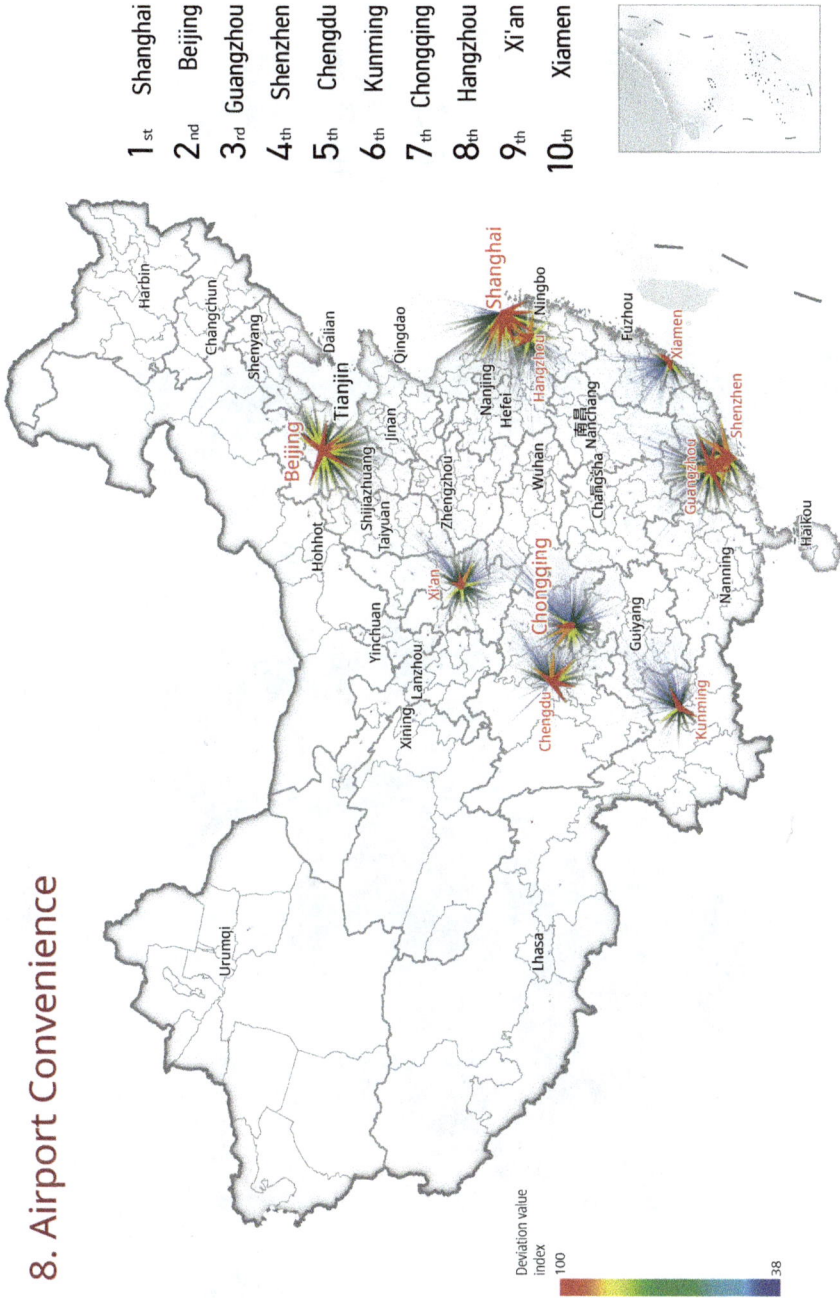

1st Shanghai
2nd Beijing
3rd Guangzhou
4th Shenzhen
5th Chengdu
6th Kunming
7th Chongqing
8th Hangzhou
9th Xi'an
10th Xiamen

Deviation value index
100
38

Figure 4-8 Wide-Area Analysis Diagram of Airport Convenience

Note: Airport convenience is an index to define whether a city's airport is convenient to access. It is calculated based on the distance between the city and the container port, and the throughput and the route of the airport.

9. Air Quality Index

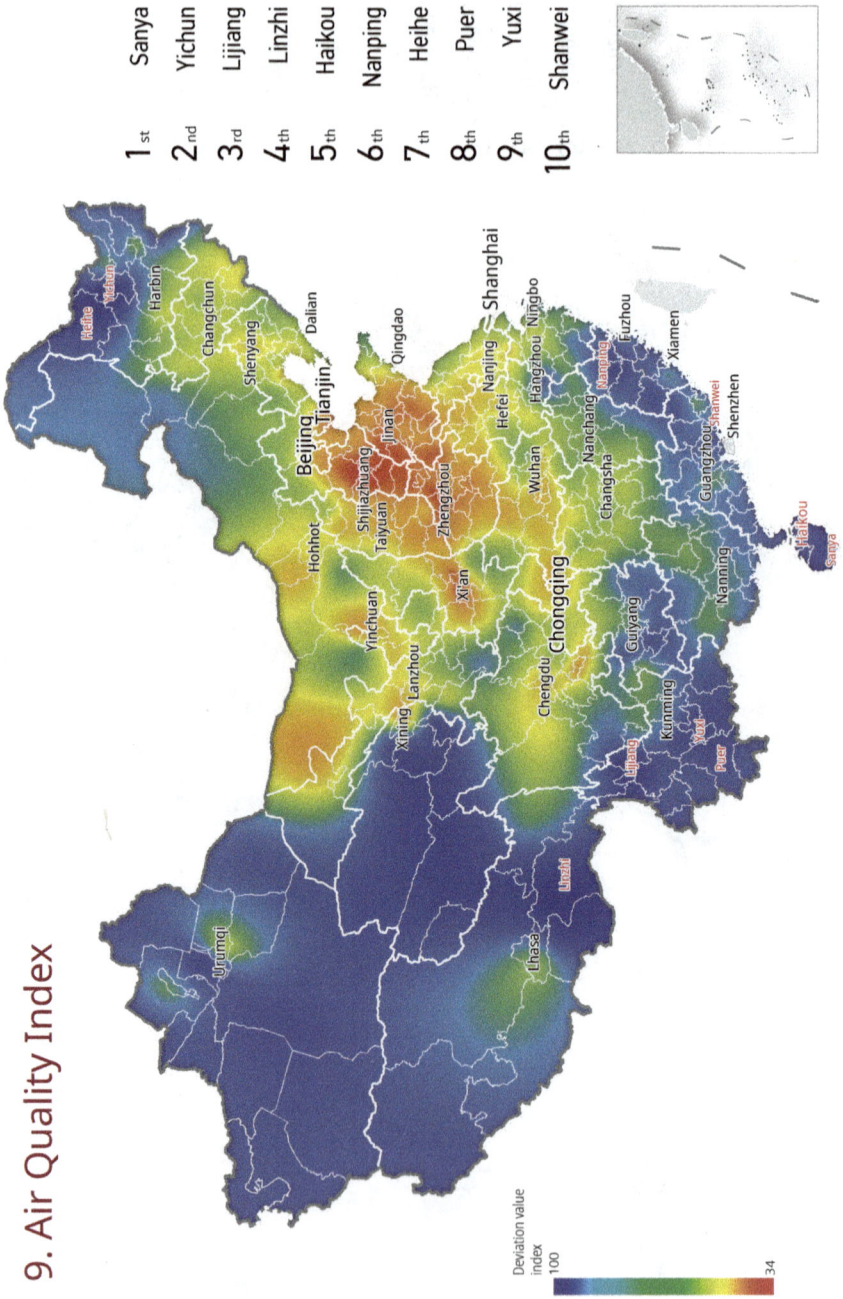

1st	Sanya
2nd	Yichun
3rd	Lijiang
4th	Linzhi
5th	Haikou
6th	Nanping
7th	Heihe
8th	Puer
9th	Yuxi
10th	Shanwei

Deviation value index
100
34

Figure 4-9 Wide-Area Analysis Diagram of Air Quality Index

10. PM2.5 Index

1st	Linzhi
2nd	Sanya
3rd	Lijiang
4th	Yichun
5th	Haikou
6th	Baoshan
7th	Heihe
8th	Nanping
9th	Changdu
10th	Erdos

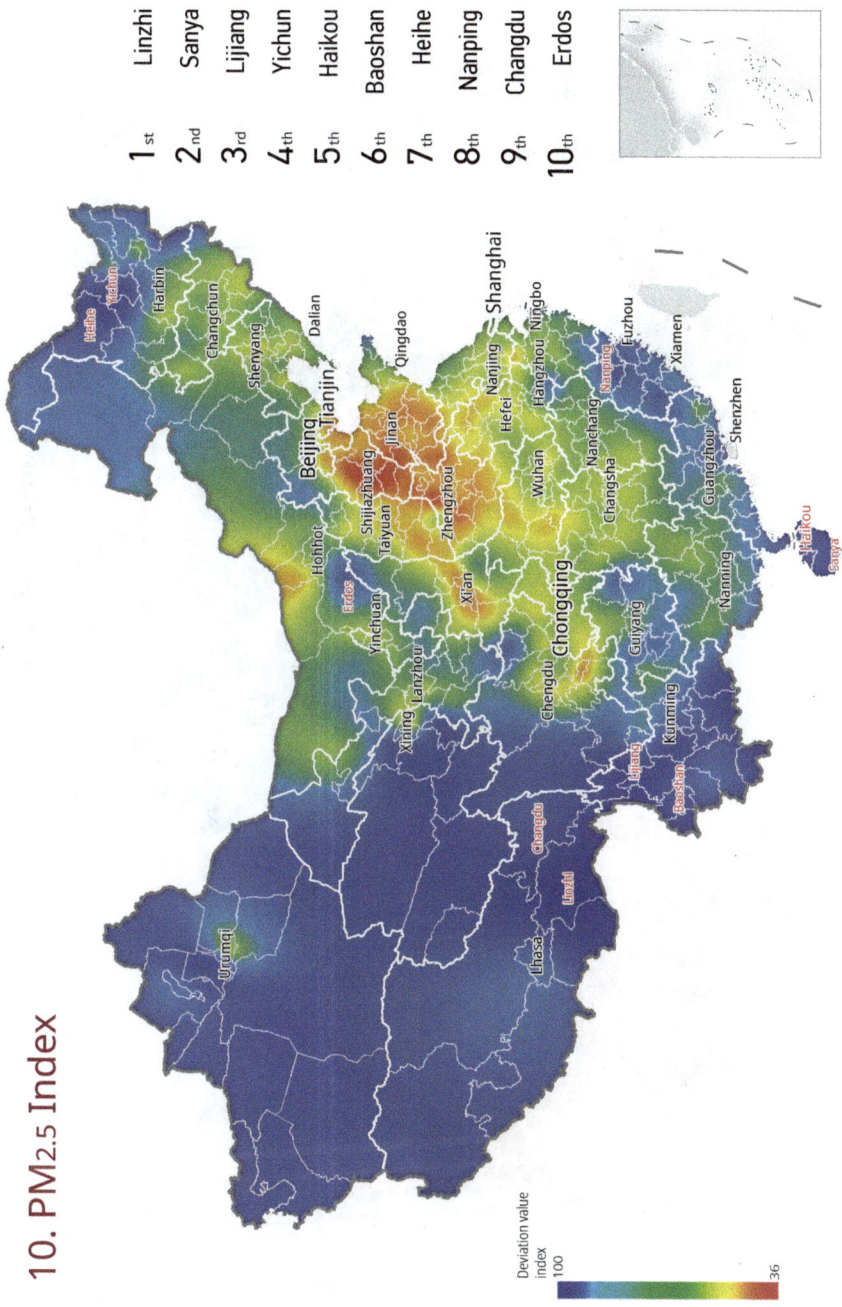

Figure 4-10 Wide-Area Analysis Diagram of PM2.5 Index

Deviation value index
100
36

11. Rainfall

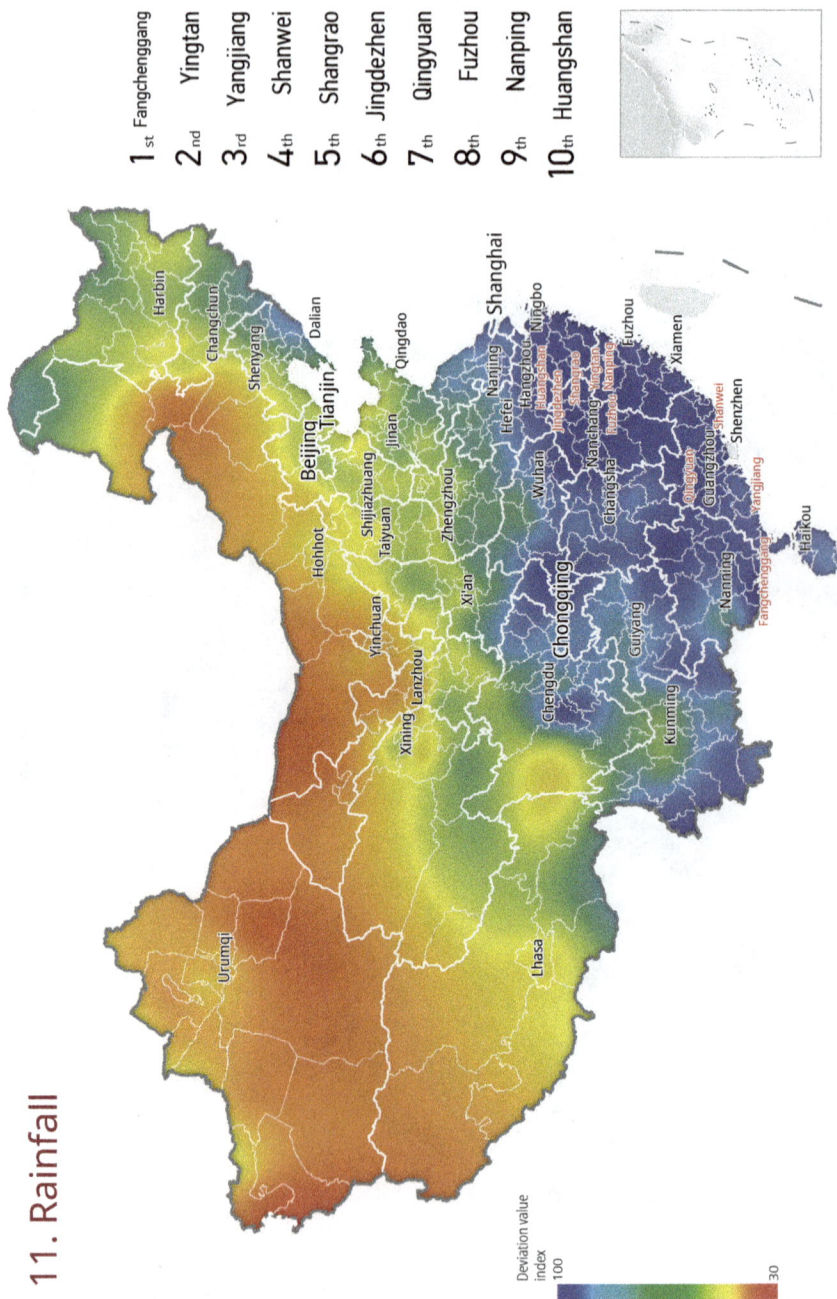

Figure 4-11 Wide-Area Analysis Diagram of Rainfall

1st	Fangchenggang
2nd	Yingtan
3rd	Yangjiang
4th	Shanwei
5th	Shangrao
6th	Jingdezhen
7th	Qingyuan
8th	Fuzhou
9th	Nanping
10th	Huangshan

Deviation value index
100
30

12. Per Capita Water Resources

1st	Linzhi
2nd	Changdu
3rd	Shigatse
4th	Lhasa
5th	Hulun Buir
6th	Ya'an
7th	Nanping
8th	Lishui
9th	Puer
10th	Guilin

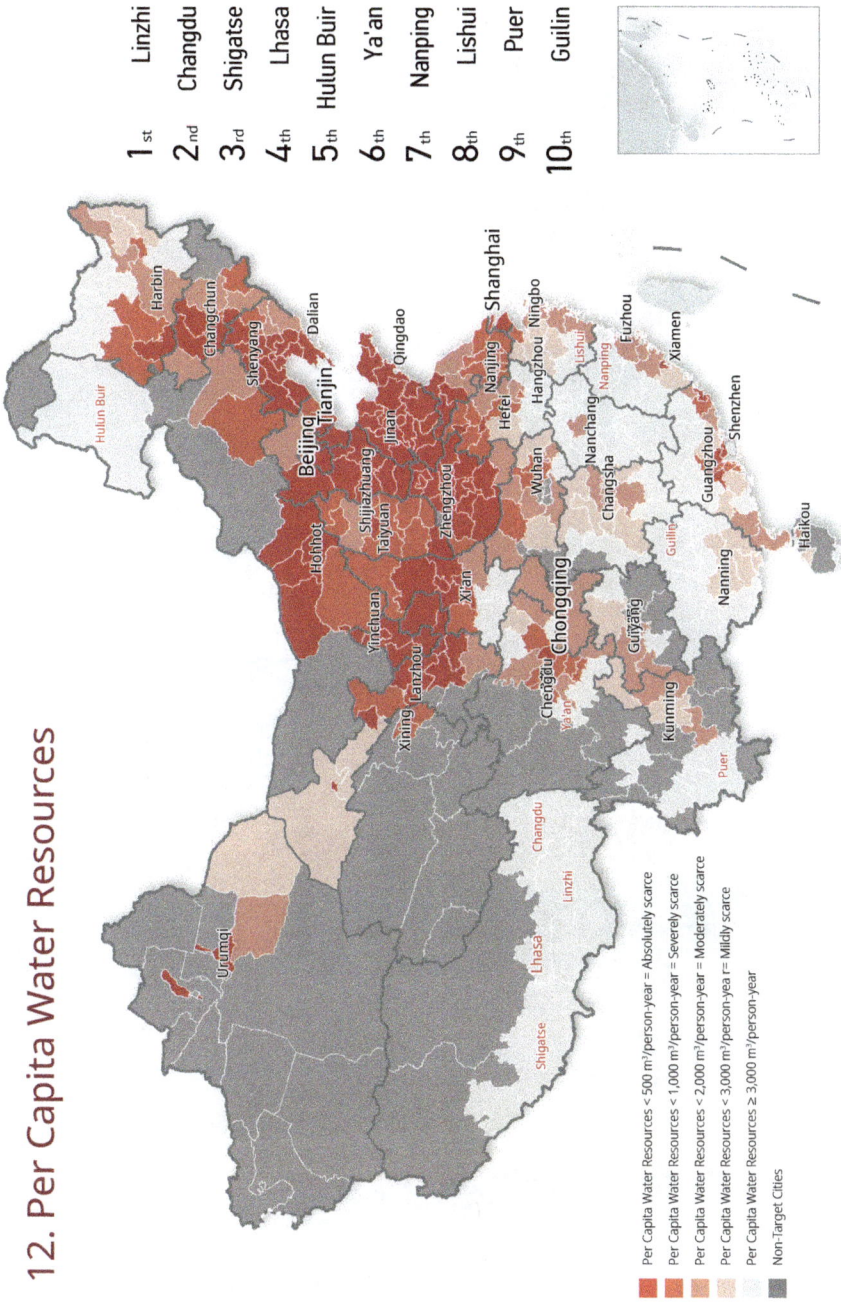

Per Capita Water Resources < 500 m³/person-year = Absolutely scarce
Per Capita Water Resources < 1,000 m³/person-year = Severely scarce
Per Capita Water Resources < 2,000 m³/person-year = Moderately scarce
Per Capita Water Resources < 3,000 m³/person-yea r= Mildly scarce
Per Capita Water Resources ≥ 3,000 m³/person-year
Non-Target Cities

Figure 4-12 Wide-Area Analysis Diagram of Per Capita Water Resources

13. Forest Coverage Rate

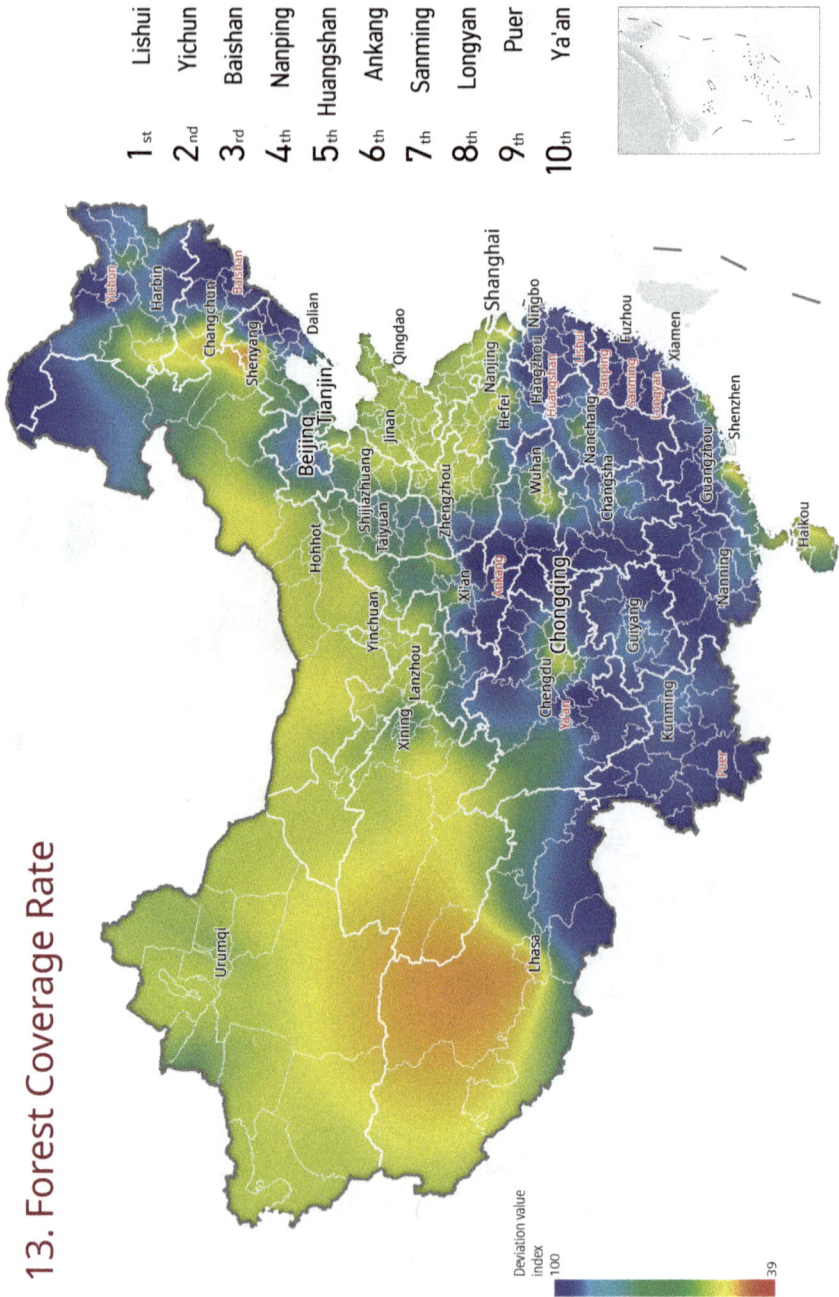

1st	Lishui
2nd	Yichun
3rd	Baishan
4th	Nanping
5th	Huangshan
6th	Ankang
7th	Sanming
8th	Longyan
9th	Puer
10th	Ya'an

Deviation value index
100
39

Figure 4-13 Wide-Area Analysis Diagram of Forest Coverage Rate

14. Proportion of Farmland

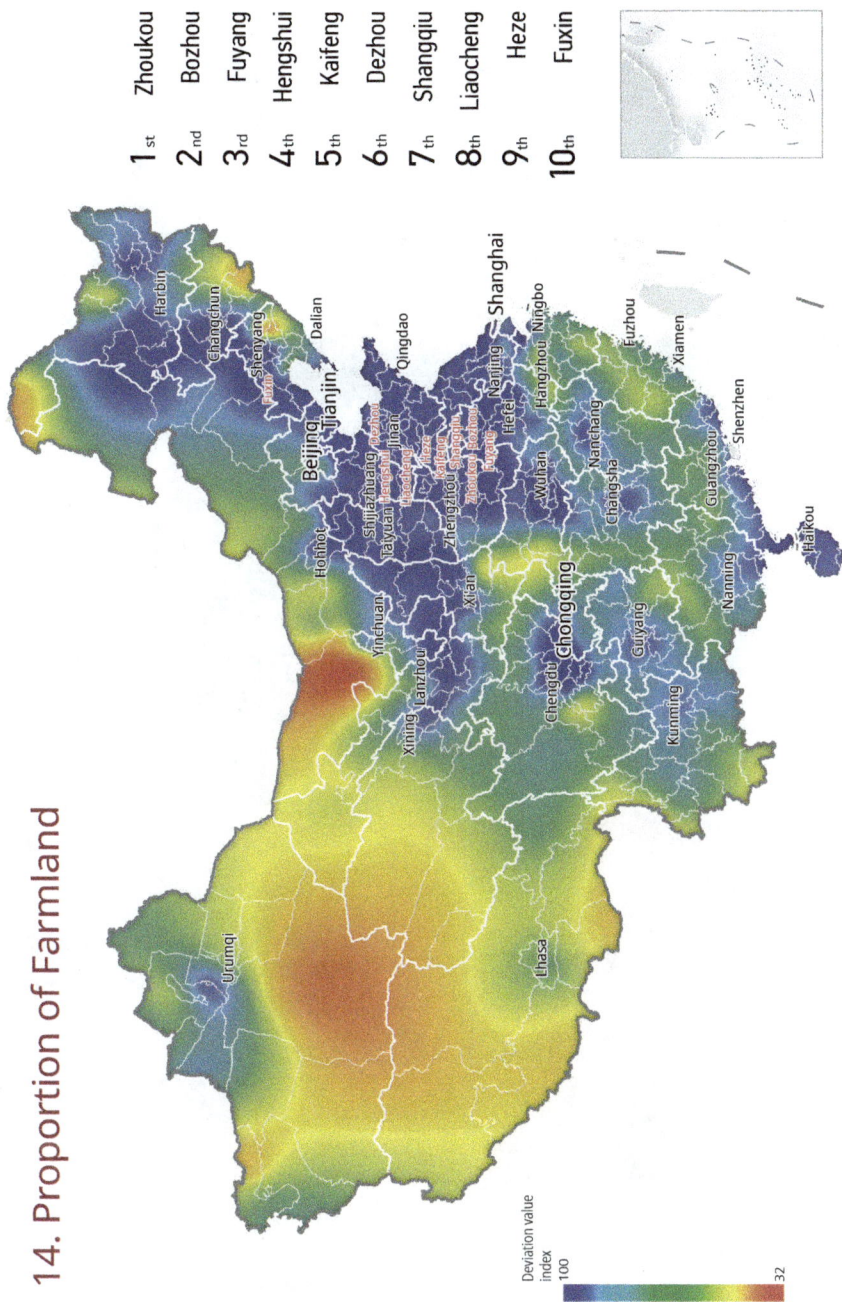

1st	Zhoukou
2nd	Bozhou
3rd	Fuyang
4th	Hengshui
5th	Kaifeng
6th	Dezhou
7th	Shangqiu
8th	Liaocheng
9th	Heze
10th	Fuxin

Deviation value
index
100
32

Figure 4-14 Wide-Area Analysis Diagram of Proportion of Farmland

15. Climate Comfort Index

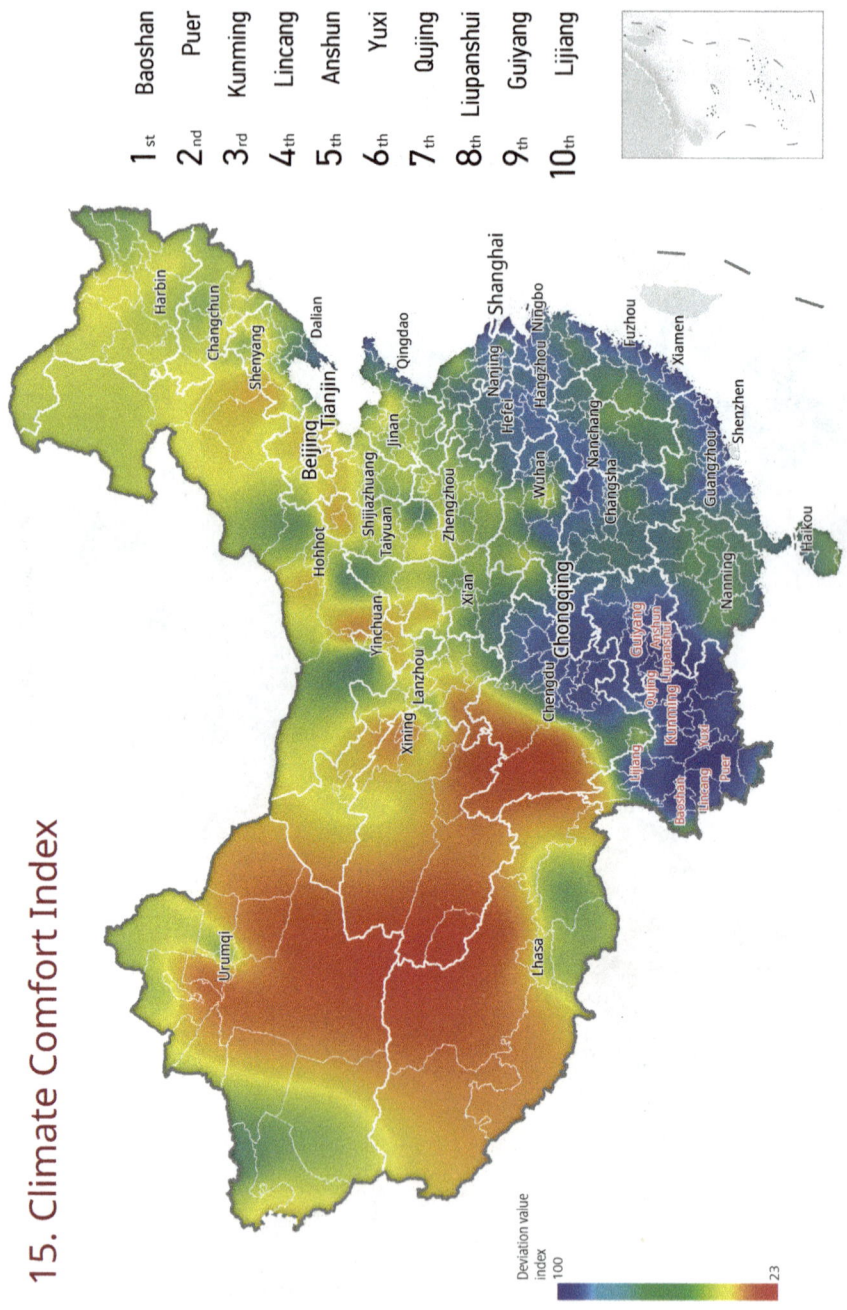

Rank	City
1st	Baoshan
2nd	Puer
3rd	Kunming
4th	Lincang
5th	Anshun
6th	Yuxi
7th	Qujing
8th	Liupanshui
9th	Guiyang
10th	Lijiang

Deviation value index
100
23

Figure 4-15 Wide-Area Analysis Diagram of Climate Comfort Index

16. Historical Relics

1st	Beijing
2nd	Xi'an
3rd	Nanjing
4th	Luoyang
5th	Hangzhou
6th	Chongqing
7th	Suzhou
8th	Shanghai
9th	Zhengzhou
10th	Huangshan

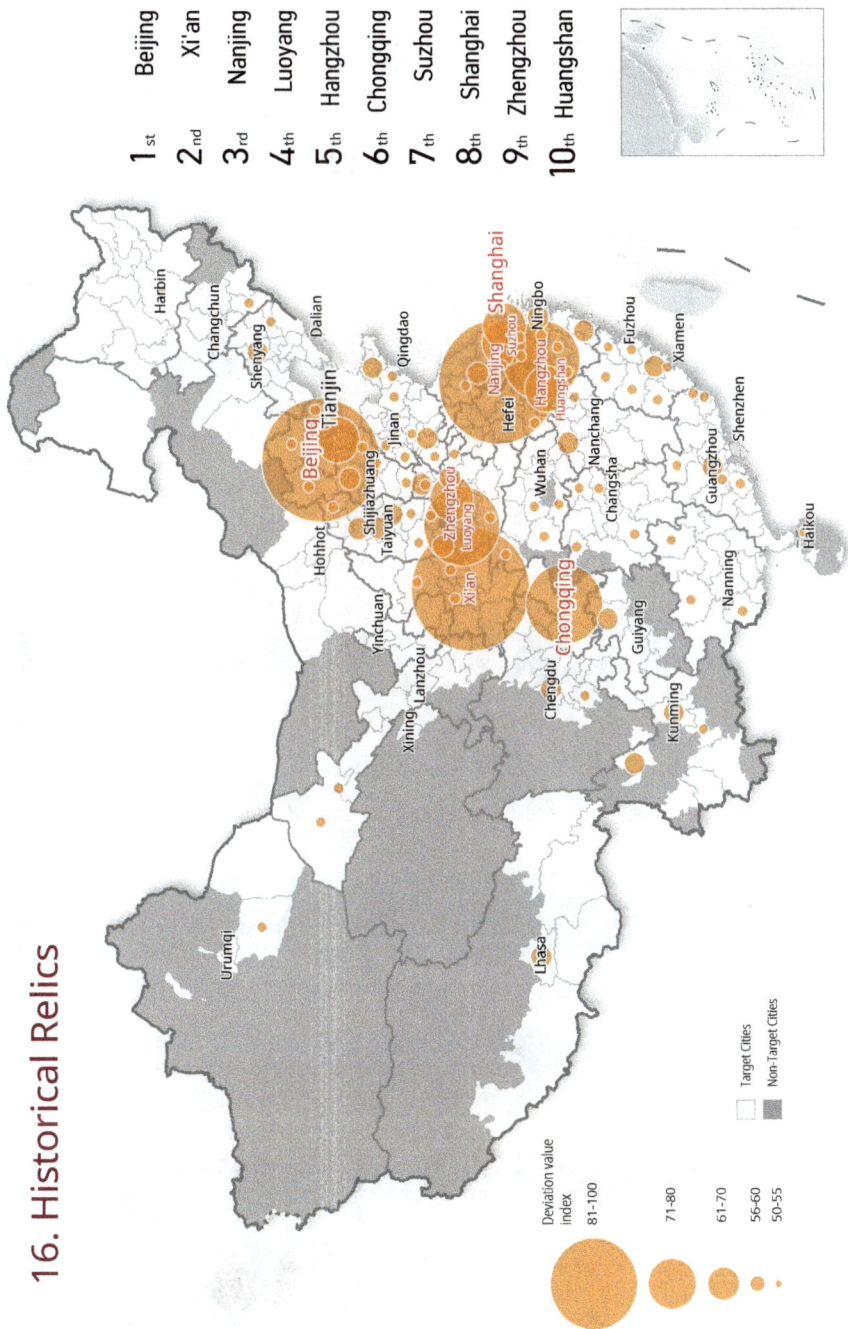

Figure 4-16 Wide-Area Analysis Diagram of Historical Relics

Deviation value index
81-100
71-80
61-70
56-60
50-55

Target Cities
Non-Target Cities

17. Domestic Tourists

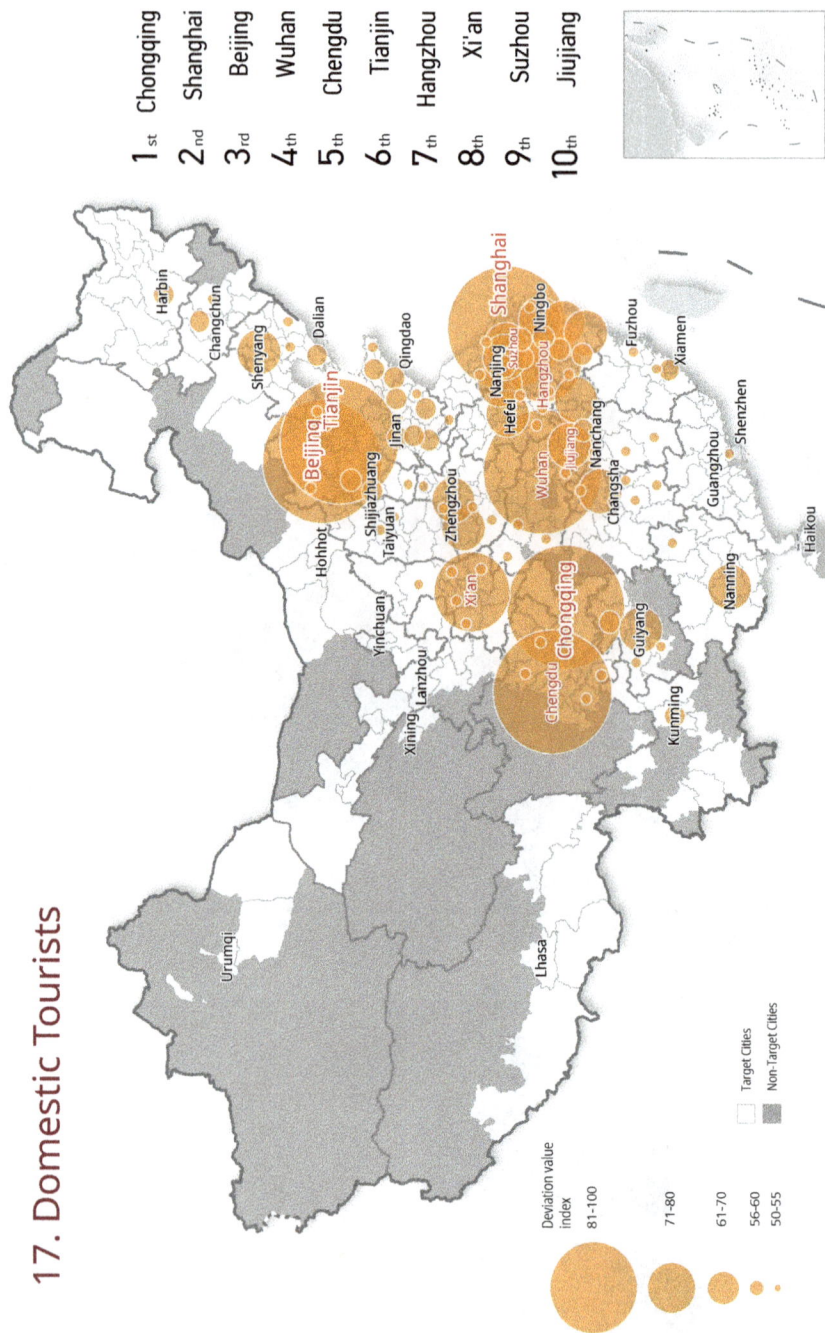

Figure 4-17 Wide-Area Analysis Diagram of Domestic Tourists

1st	Chongqing
2nd	Shanghai
3rd	Beijing
4th	Wuhan
5th	Chengdu
6th	Tianjin
7th	Hangzhou
8th	Xi'an
9th	Suzhou
10th	Jiujiang

Deviation value index
81-100
71-80
61-70
56-60
50-55

Target Cities
Non-Target Cities

18. Inbound Tourists

Rank	City
1st	Shenzhen
2nd	Guangzhou
3rd	Shanghai
4th	Beijing
5th	Hangzhou
6th	Tianjin
7th	Zhuhai
8th	Chongqing
9th	Xiamen
10th	Dongguan

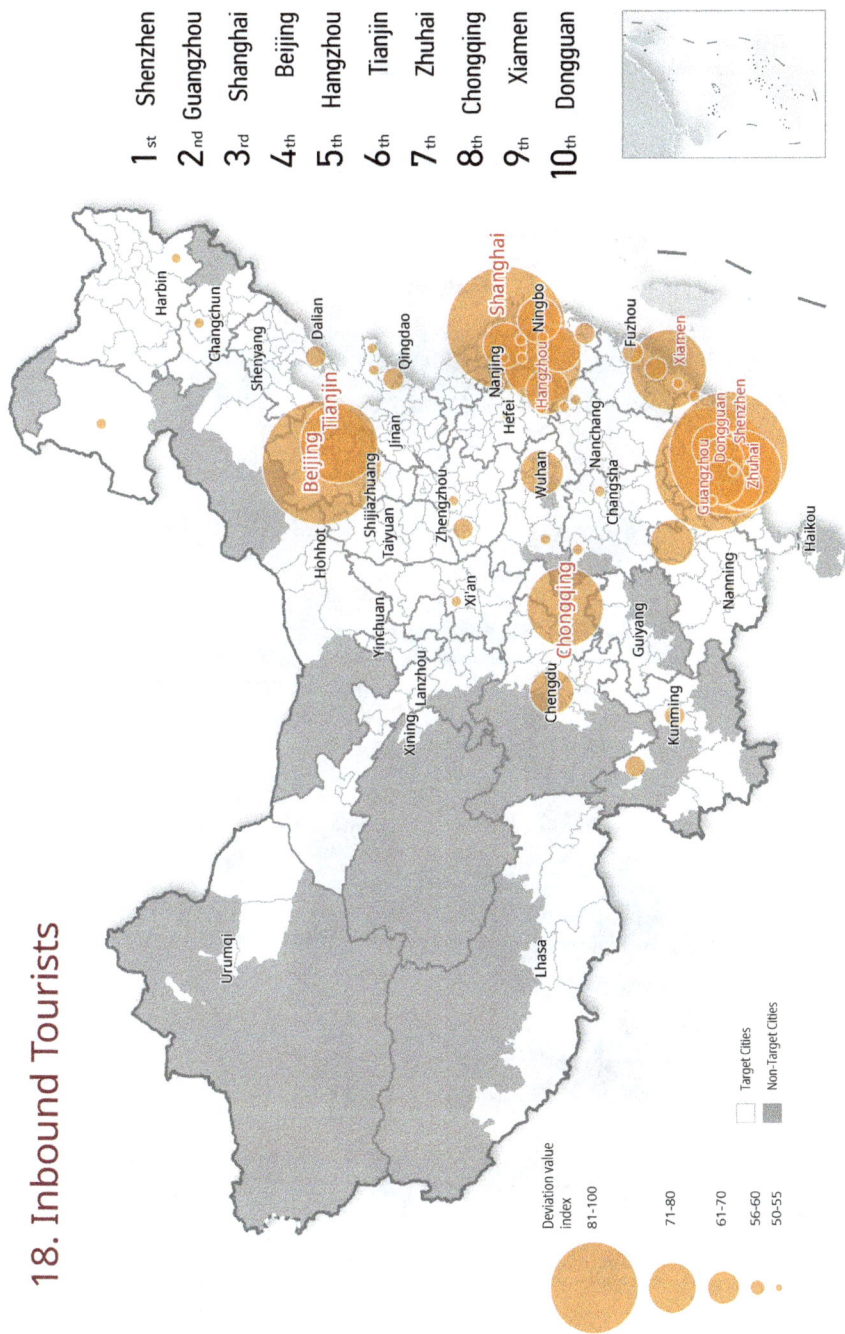

Figure 4-18 Wide-Area Analysis Diagram of Inbound Tourists

Deviation value index
- 81-100
- 71-80
- 61-70
- 56-60
- 50-55

Target Cities
Non-Target Cities

19. Mainboard Listed Enterprises

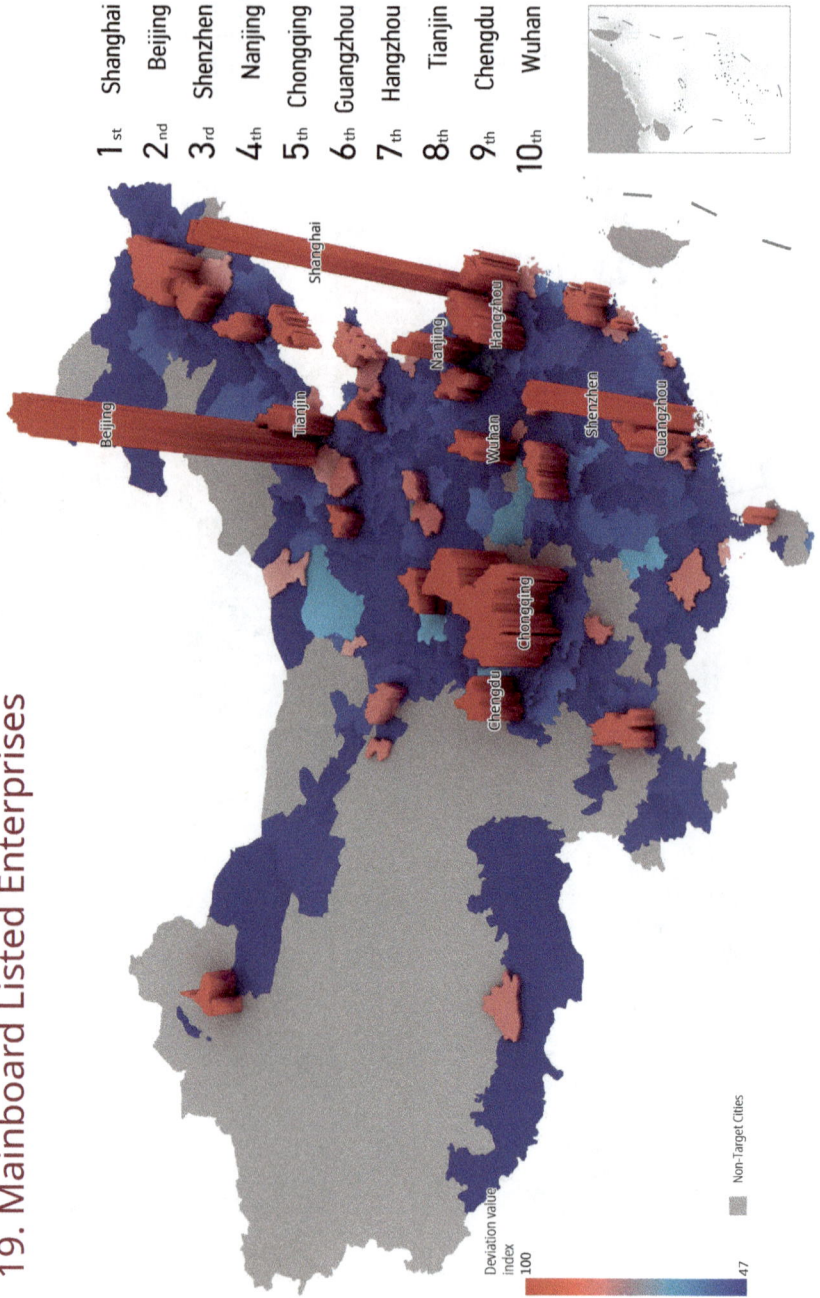

1st	Shanghai
2nd	Beijing
3rd	Shenzhen
4th	Nanjing
5th	Chongqing
6th	Guangzhou
7th	Hangzhou
8th	Tianjin
9th	Chengdu
10th	Wuhan

Deviation value index
100

47

Non-Target Cities

Figure 4-19 Wide-Area Analysis Diagram of Mainboard Listed Enterprises

144

20. Financial Radiation

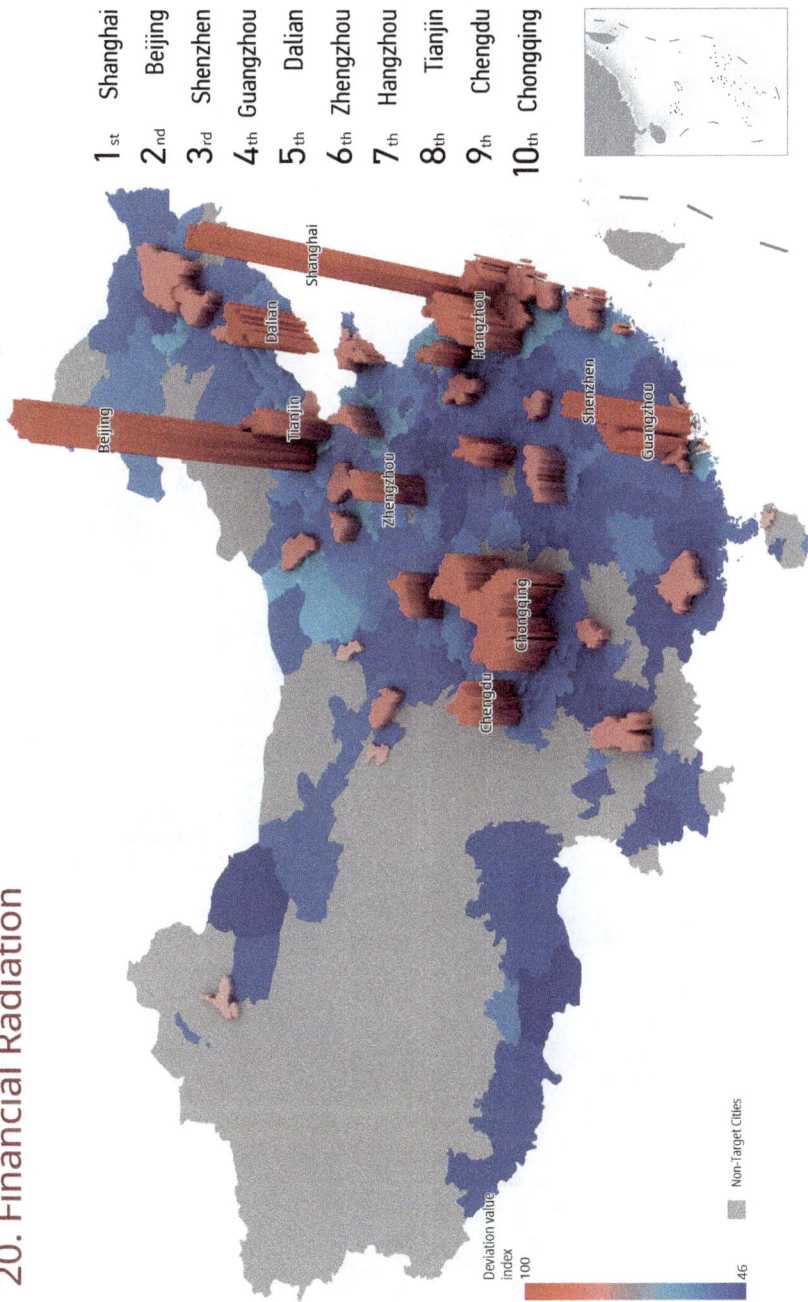

1st	Shanghai
2nd	Beijing
3rd	Shenzhen
4th	Guangzhou
5th	Dalian
6th	Zhengzhou
7th	Hangzhou
8th	Tianjin
9th	Chengdu
10th	Chongqing

Deviation value index
100
46

Non-Target Cities

Figure 4-20 Wide-Area Analysis Diagram of Financial Radiation

Note: Radiation is an index that defines the extent to which a certain function of a city can be utilized externally. It is comprehensively calculated based on the relationship between the number of employees in a certain field in the city and the number of their counterparts nationwide, as well as other related parameters.

21. Manufacturing Radiation

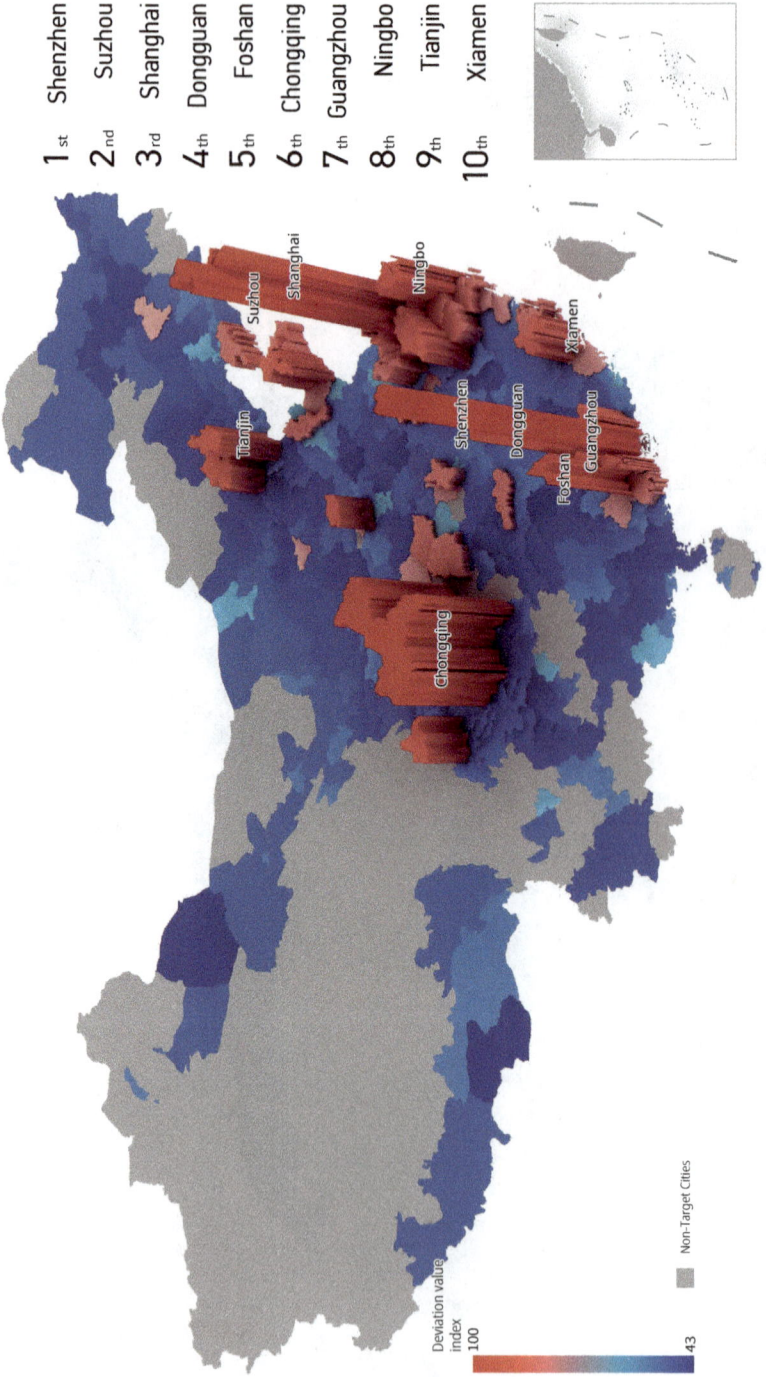

1st	Shenzhen
2nd	Suzhou
3rd	Shanghai
4th	Dongguan
5th	Foshan
6th	Chongqing
7th	Guangzhou
8th	Ningbo
9th	Tianjin
10th	Xiamen

Deviation value index
100
43

Non-Target Cities

Figure 4-21 Wide-Area Analysis Diagram of Manufacturing Radiation

22. IT Industry Radiation

1st	Beijing
2nd	Shanghai
3rd	Shenzhen
4th	Hangzhou
5th	Nanjing
6th	Chengdu
7th	Guangzhou
8th	Chongqing
9th	Xi'an
10th	Fuzhou

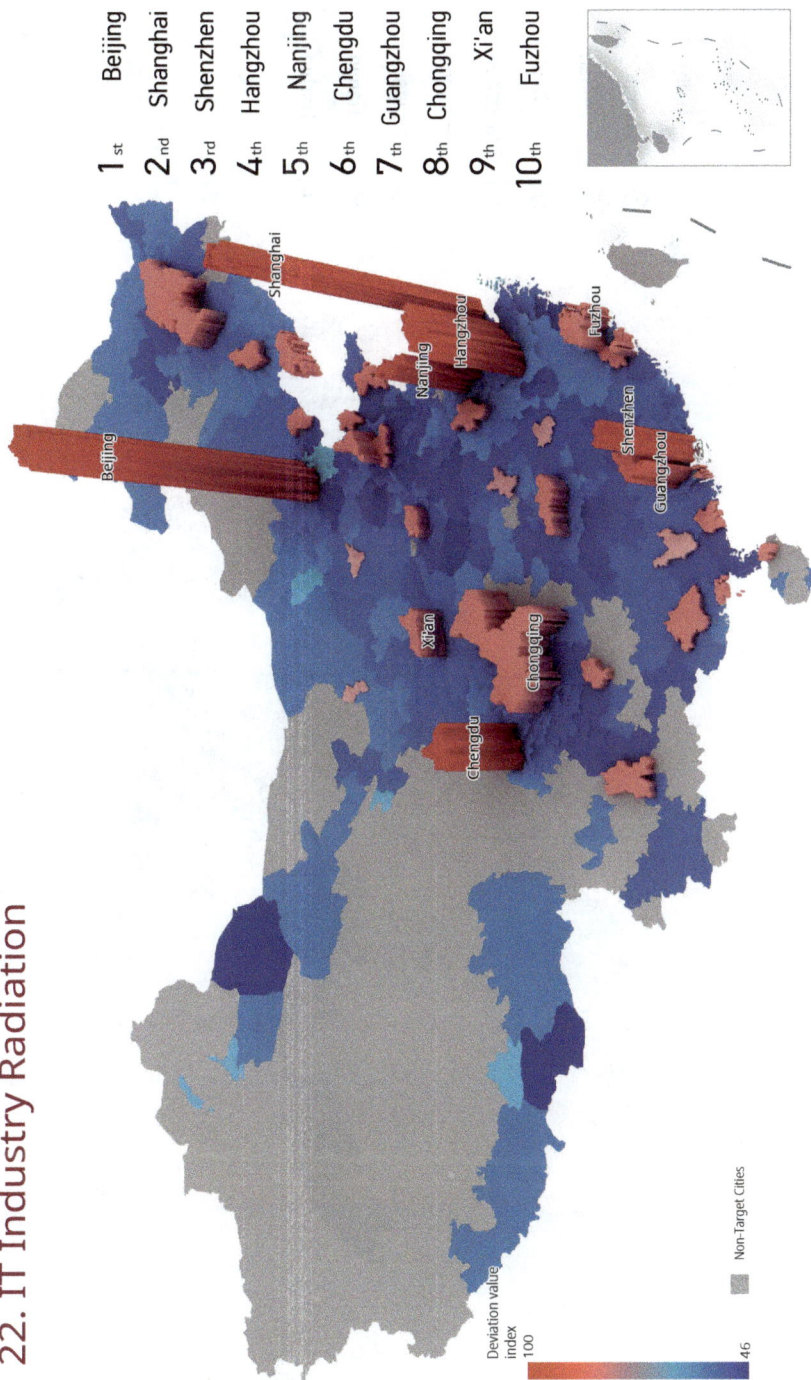

Deviation value index
100
46

Non-Target Cities

Figure 4-22 Wide-Area Analysis Diagram of IT Industry Radiation

23. Higher Education Radiation

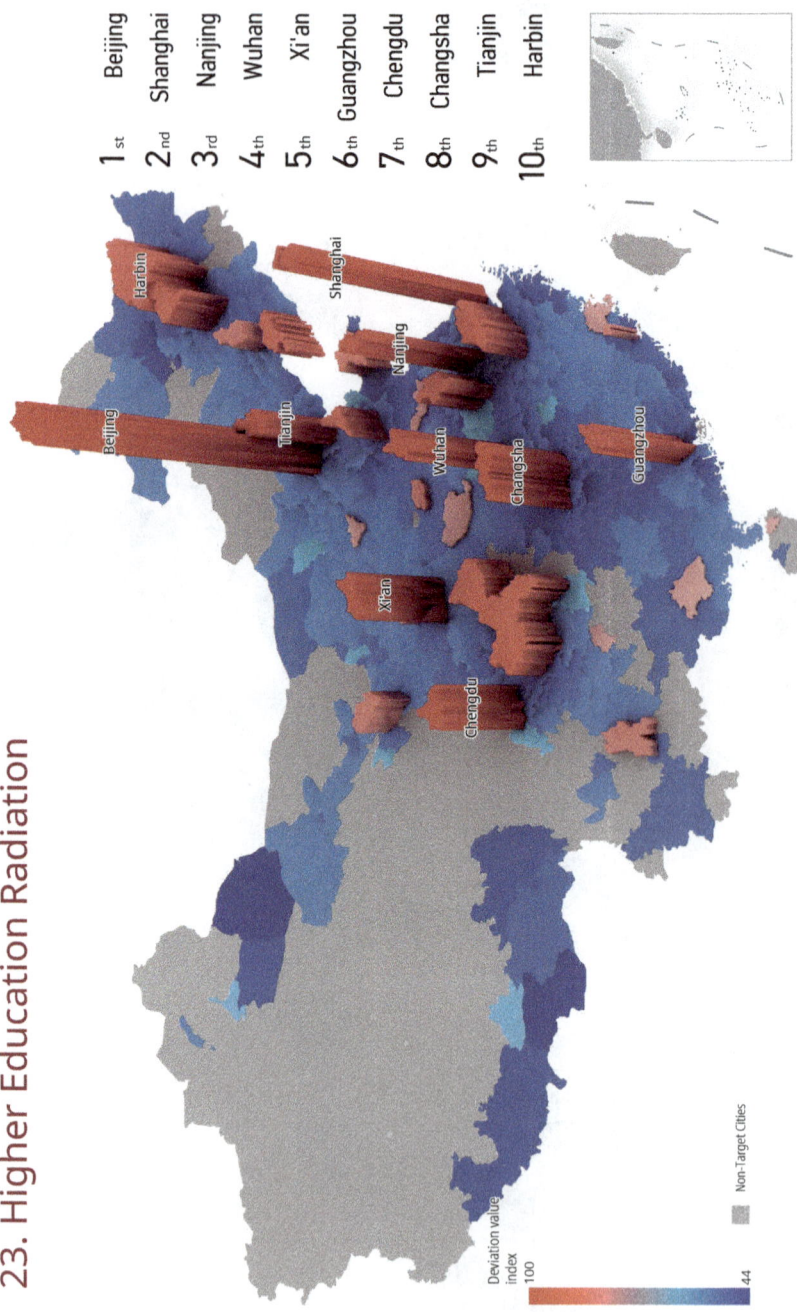

Deviation value index
100
44

Non-Target Cities

1st Beijing
2nd Shanghai
3rd Nanjing
4th Wuhan
5th Xi'an
6th Guangzhou
7th Chengdu
8th Changsha
9th Tianjin
10th Harbin

Figure 4-23 Wide-Area Analysis Diagram of Higher Education Radiation

24. Science and Technology Radiation

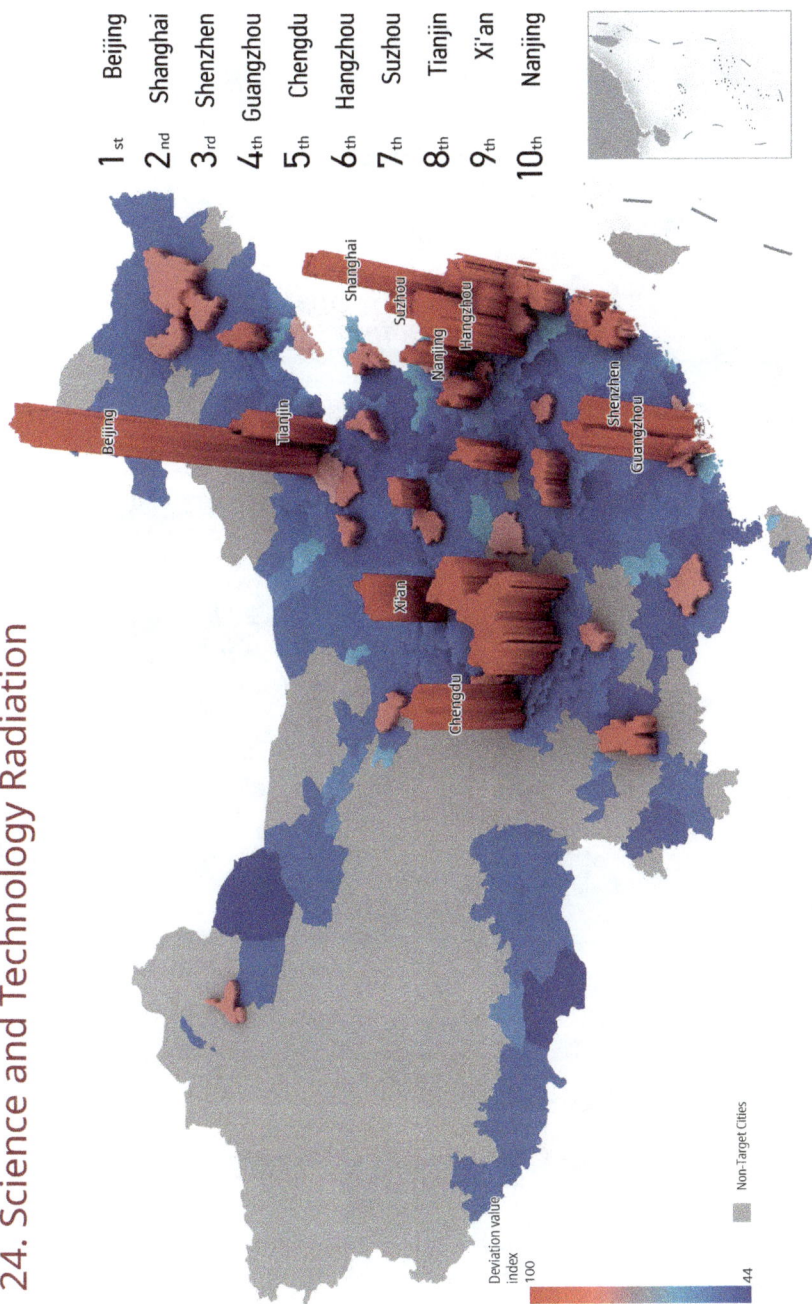

1st	Beijing
2nd	Shanghai
3rd	Shenzhen
4th	Guangzhou
5th	Chengdu
6th	Hangzhou
7th	Suzhou
8th	Tianjin
9th	Xi'an
10th	Nanjing

Deviation value index
100
44

Non-Target Cities

Figure 4-24 Wide-Area Analysis Diagram of Science and Technology Radiation

25. Medical Radiation

Figure 4-25 Wide-Area Analysis Diagram of Medical Radiation

1st Beijing
2nd Shanghai
3rd Guangzhou
4th Chengdu
5th Hangzhou
6th Shenyang
7th Tianjin
8th Xi'an
9th Wuhan
10th Chongqing

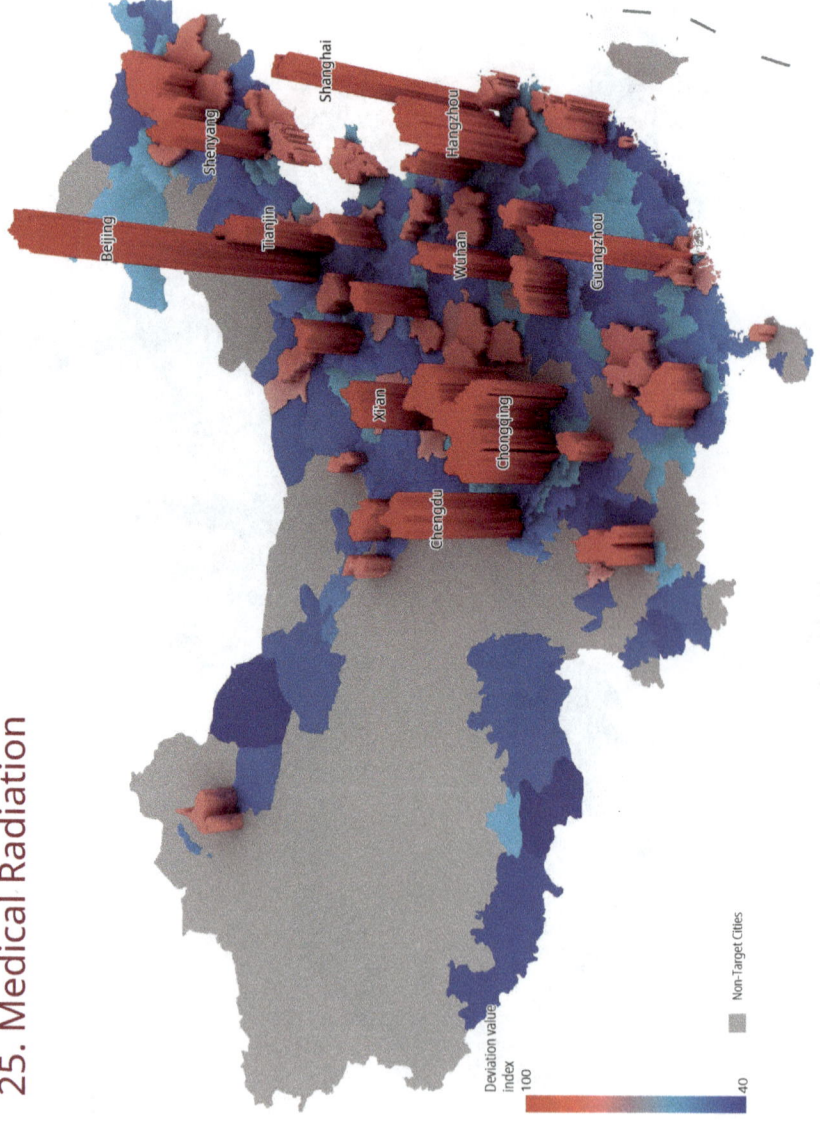

Deviation value index
100
40

Non-Target Cities

26. Culture, Sports and Entertainment Radiation

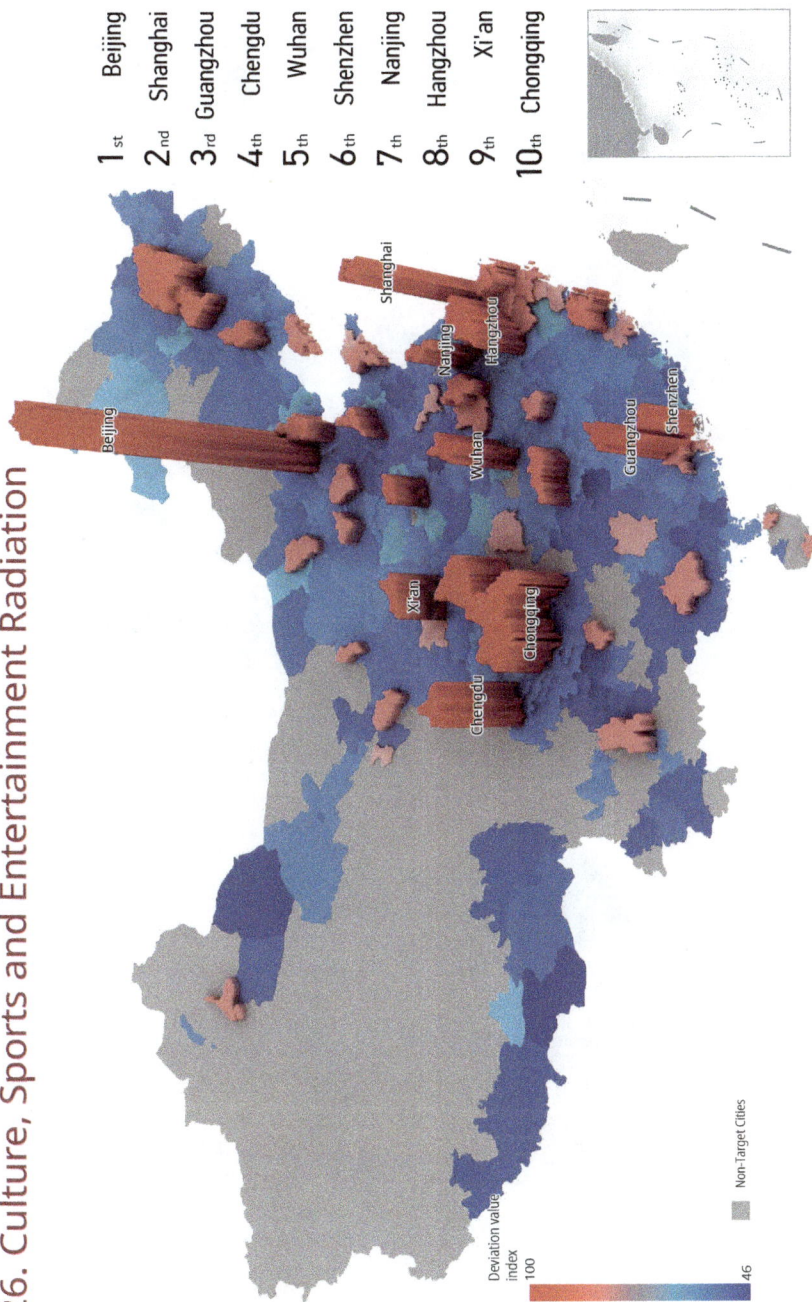

1st	Beijing
2nd	Shanghai
3rd	Guangzhou
4th	Chengdu
5th	Wuhan
6th	Shenzhen
7th	Nanjing
8th	Hangzhou
9th	Xi'an
10th	Chongqing

Deviation value index
100
46

Non-Target Cities

Figure 4-26 Wide-Area Analysis Diagram of Culture and Sports and Entertainment Radiation

27. Catering and Hotel Radiation

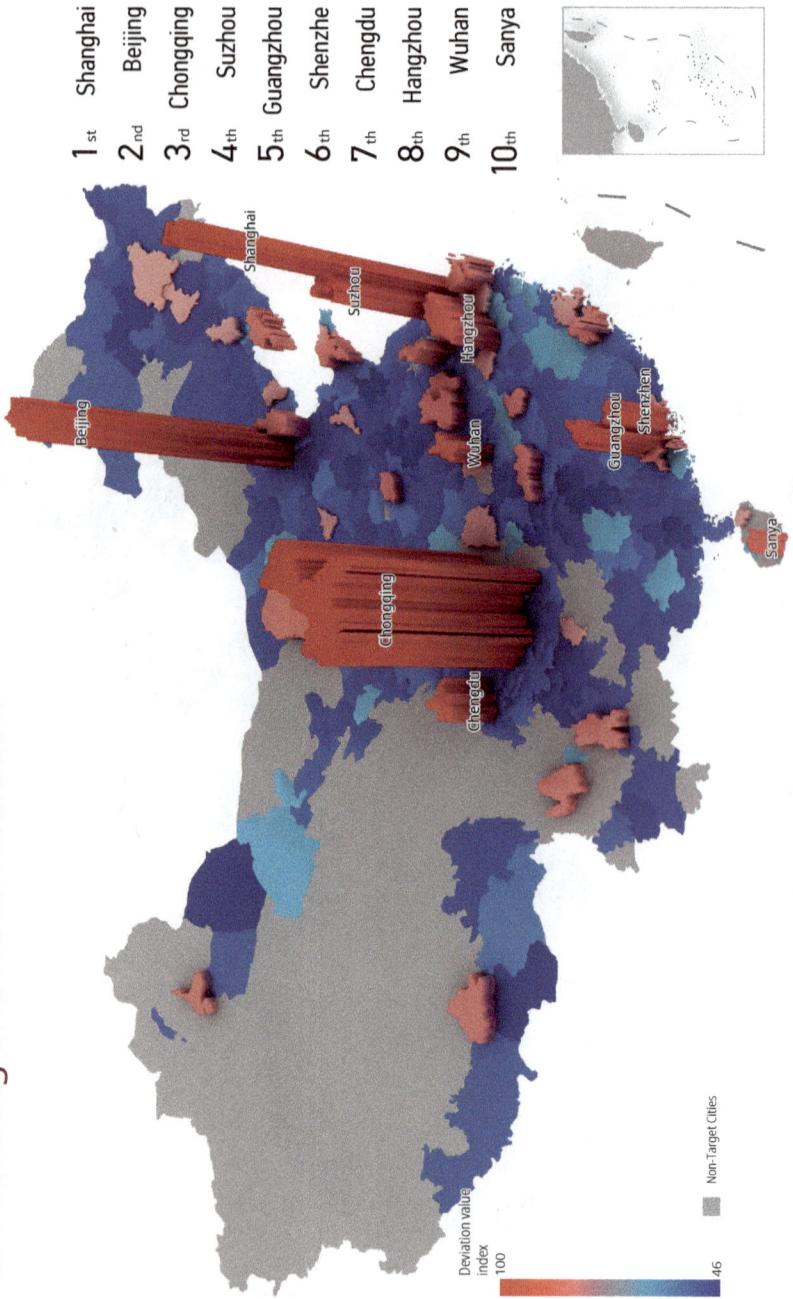

1st	Shanghai
2nd	Beijing
3rd	Chongqing
4th	Suzhou
5th	Guangzhou
6th	Shenzhe
7th	Chengdu
8th	Hangzhou
9th	Wuhan
10th	Sanya

Deviation value index
100
46

Non-Target Cities

Figure 4-27 Wide-Area Analysis Diagram of Catering and Hotel Radiation

152

28. Wholesale and Retail Radiation

Figure 4-28 Wide-Area Analysis Diagram of Wholesale and Retail Radiation

1st Shanghai
2nd Beijing
3rd Chengdu
4th Chongqing
5th Guangzhou
6th Hangzhou
7th Tianjin
8th Shenzhen
9th Nanjing
10th Wuhan

Deviation value index
100
45
Non-Target Cities

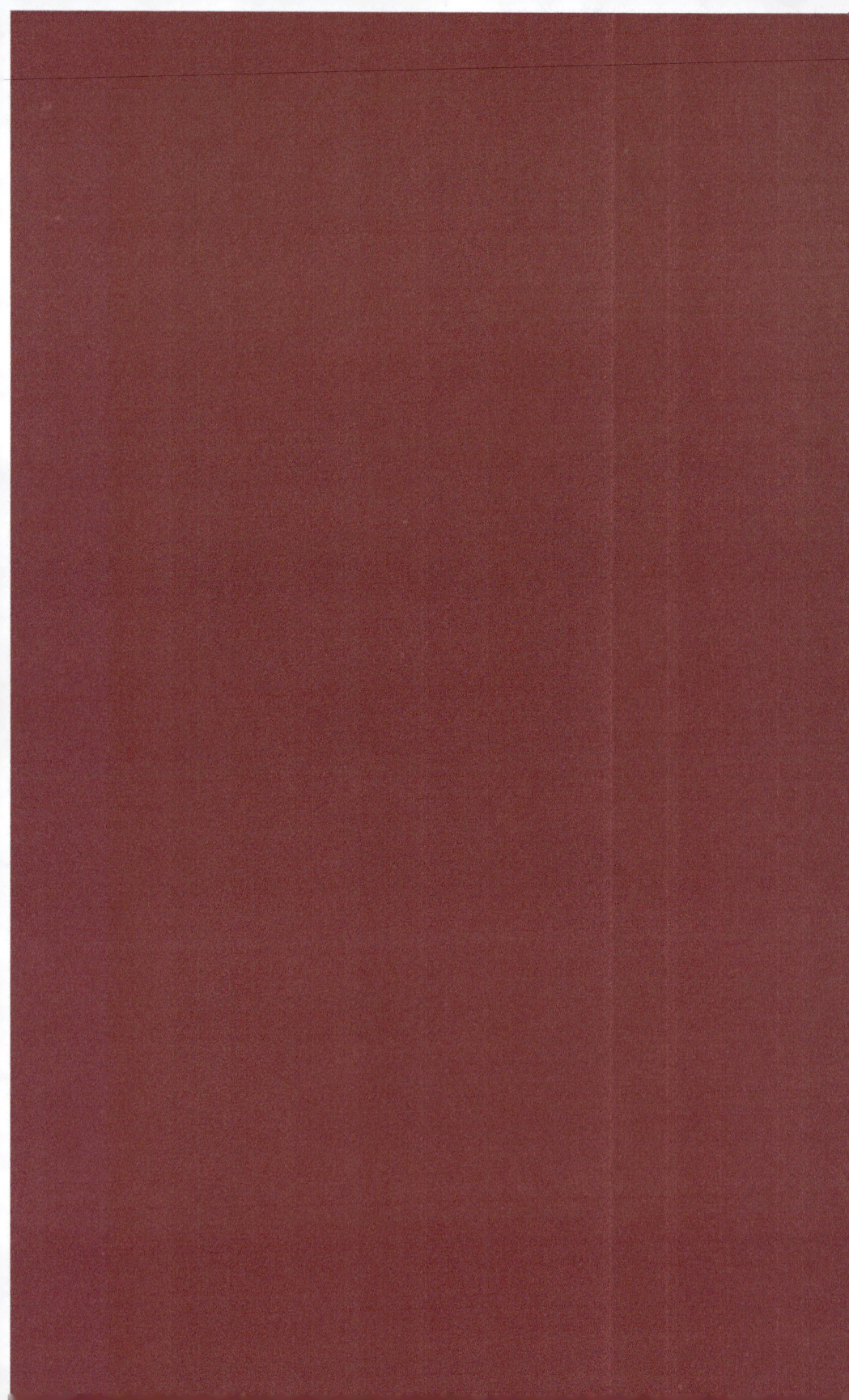

Chapter V

Megalopolis Development Strategy

Zhou Muzhi

1. Current Status and Issues

The Time of Megalopolises

(1) A Century of Cities

The 21st Century is a "century of cities." Data published by the United Nations[1] show that the urban population around the world was no more than 740 million by 1950, accounting for 29.6% of the total population. By 1970, the urban population had risen almost twice to 1.35 billion, accounting for 36.6% of the world's total population. By 2008, the urban population had reached 3.34 billion—4.5 times that of 1950—and thus sent the earth, where more than 50% of its population were living in the cities, into the real "century of cities."

The year 2015 saw a rise in the global urbanization rate to 54%, with an urban population of 3.96 billion as well as an increasingly aggressive urbanization. The urbanization rate is expected to climb to 60% by 2030, meaning approximately 5.1 billion people will be living in the cities. In other words, during the 80 years from 1950 to 2030, the global urban population will expand almost 7 times. It is anticipated that by 2050, the urbanization rate will reach a high level of 85.4% in developed countries and 63.4% in developing countries. Although the concentration of population and the formation of cities may vary in different countries, urbanization will undoubtedly remain the major task for the world in the 21st Century, the century of cities.

Today, developing countries in Asia and Africa are undergoing an urbanization of unprecedented scale. This trend is particularly obvious in the East Asia Region including China. In 1950, the urbanization rate of East Asia was only 17.9%, even lower than the average 19% of developing countries around the world. Subsequent urbanization rate in this region relentlessly soared and went beyond the world average around 2010 and is expected to reach a high level of 77.9% by 2050. This means this region will bridge its gap with developed countries in terms of urbanization rate from 36.7 percentage points in 1950 to 7.5 percentage points in 2050.[2]

In the early days of the foundation of New China, the urbanization rate was only 11.2% in 1950, and due to the long-time policy against urbanization, this rate was still only 17.9% in 1978, the first year of China's reform and opening-up. Later on, the urbanization rate of China gradually sped up and started to show a sharply increased momentum especially in the late 1990s. By 2011, more than half of the Chinese people had become urban residents, and by 2015, 56.1% of the country's population had been urbanized, making China enter the real era of urbanization.[3]

---

[1] Data from the *World Urbanization Prospects* (The 2014 Revision) and *World Population Prospects* (The 2015 Revision) of Department for Economic and Social Affairs of the United Nations.

[2] Refer to Figure 5-1.

[3] Refer to Figures 5-2 and 5-3.

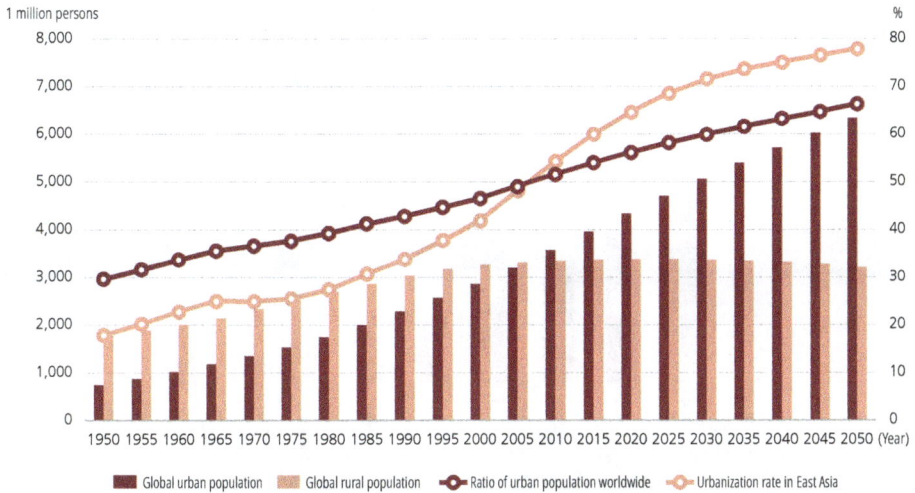

1 million persons   %

Legend: Global urban population | Global rural population | Ratio of urban population worldwide | Urbanization rate in East Asia

Figure 5-1 Changes of Urban and Rural Population and Urbanization Rate in East Asia and the World

Source: Per the *World Urbanization Prospects* (The 2014 Revision) and *World Population Prospects* (2015 Revision) issued by United Nations Department of Economic and Social Affairs (UN DESA).

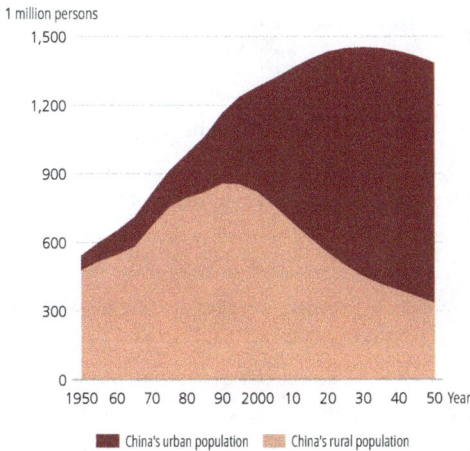

1 million persons

China's urban population | China's rural population

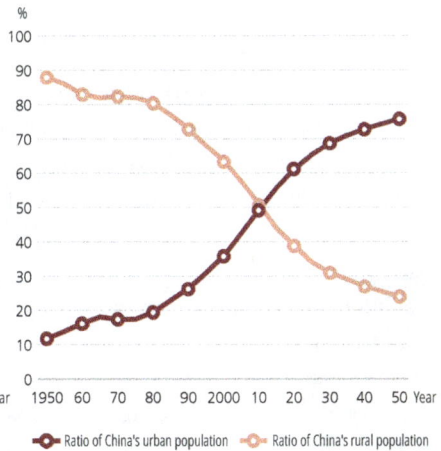

%

Ratio of China's urban population | Ratio of China's rural population

Figure 5-2 Changes of China's Urban and Rural Population

Figure 5-3 Changes of the Ratio of China's Urban Population to Rural Population

Source: It is prepared as per the *World Urbanization Prospects* (The 2014 Revision) and *World Population Prospects* (2015 Revision) issued by United Nations Department of Economic and Social Affairs (UN DESA).

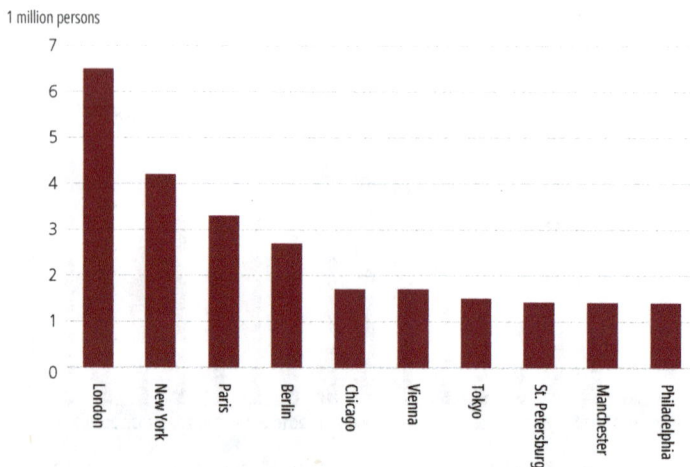

1 million persons

Figure 5-4 Population Ranking: Top 10 Cities in the World (1900)

Source: It is prepared as per the *World Urbanization Prospects* (The 2014 Revision) and *World Population Prospects* (2015 Revision) issued by United Nations Department of Economic and Social Affairs (UN DESA).

The 21st Century is not only about cities, but also large cities and megalopolises. In 1900, the top 10 of the world's largest cities included London in the U.K., New York in the U.S., Paris of France, Berlin of Germany, Chicago of the U.S., Vienna of Austria, Tokyo of Japan, St. Petersburg of Russia, Manchester of the U.K., and Philadelphia of the U.S., among which the biggest, London, had a population of no more than 6.5 million, and from the 6th place of Chicago onward, none of their populations were bigger than 2 million.[4]

After half a century, two megacities with tens of millions population emerged in 1950, respectively being New York of the U.S. and Tokyo of Japan (The Greater Tokyo Metropolitan Area). By 1970, the num-ber of such megacities had slowly increased to three, to further include Osaka (The Kinki Metropolitan Area).[5] Later on, the formation of large cities suddenly sped up, resulting in an increase of megacities to 10 by 1990, with a total population of 150 million and accounting for 2.9% of the then global population.[6] Such an aggressive increase continued and by 2015, there were 29 members in the club of megacities, with

---

[4] Refer to Figure 5-4.

[5] Refer to Figure 5-5.

[6] Refer to Figure 5-6.

a total population of 470 million, accounting for 6.4% of the global population. Among these megacities, 17 are located in Asia, four in South America, three in Africa, three in Europe, and two in North America.[7] The trend of large-city-oriented urbanization is still accelerating and the number of megacities is expected to reach 41 globally in 2050.

One important feature of this trend is the oversized urban population. Tokyo (The Greater Tokyo Metropolitan Area), ranking 1st amongst global megacities in 2015, was incredibly home to 38 million people. This list continued with Delhi of India at the 2nd place, with a population of 25.7 million; Shanghai of China, 3rd place, 23.74 million; São Paulo of Brazil, 4th place, 21.07 million; Mumbai of India, 21.04 million; New Mexico City of Mexico, 6th place, 20.3 million; Beijing of China, 7th place, 20.38 million; Osaka (the Kinki Metropolitan Area) of Japan, 8th place, 20.24 million; Cairo of Egypt, 9th place, 18.77 million; New York, U.S., 10th place, 18.59 million. From the first megacity with a population of tens of millions to the largest city (metropolitan area) where nearly 40 million people lived, the evolution only took more than half a century. This is evidence of the ever intensifying large-city-oriented urbanization.[8]

Another feature of this trend is the rapid development of megacities in the developing world. In 1900, all the top ten largest cities came from developed countries. In 1950 and in 1970, all of the world's megacities also belonged to developed countries. By 2015, however, seven megacities from developing countries had risen to the global top 10. As expected, by 2030, Tokyo (The Greater Tokyo Metropolitan Area) will be the only representative of the developed world in the top 10 list of megacities and remain first, with the rest of the list filled up by cities of developing countries—Delhi of India, Shanghai of China, Mumbai of India, Beijing of China, Dhaka of Bangladesh, Karachi of Pakistan, Cairo of Egypt, Lagos of Nigeria, and New Mexico City of Mexico, respectively. Developing countries will experience a significant trend in large-city-oriented urbanization.

(2) Major Development of Coastal Cities
In 2015, the OECD (Organization for Economic Co-operation and Development) countries owned six megacities with a population more than 10 million, namely, Tokyo (the Greater Tokyo Metropolitan Area), Osaka (The Kinki Metropolitan Area), New York, Los Angeles, Paris, and London. Except Paris, all of these megacities are coastal "port cities." Among the global top 10 megacities, Tokyo (the Greater Tokyo Metropolitan Area), Osaka (the Kinki Metropolitan Area), and New York were the only OECD countries, and all of them are situated on the coast.

This book divides the world's 29 megacities with tens of millions of people into three categories: 1) "waterfront" cities enjoying the advantages of being a port, 2) inland "capital" cities thriving as the

---

[7] Refer to Figure 5-7.
[8] Refer to Figure 5-8.

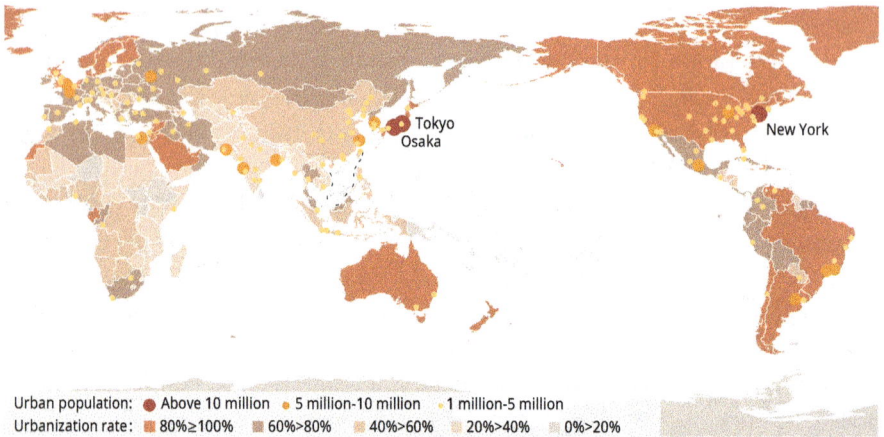

Urban population: ● Above 10 million • 5 million-10 million ∙ 1 million-5 million
Urbanization rate: ■ 80%≥100% ■ 60%>80% ■ 40%>60% ■ 20%>40% ■ 0%>20%

Figure 5-5 Distribution of the World's Megacities and the Urbanization Rate in Various Regions (1970)

Source: It is prepared as per the *World Urbanization Prospects* (The 2014 Revision) and *World Population Prospects* (2015 Revision) issued by United Nations Department of Economic and Social Affairs (UN DESA).

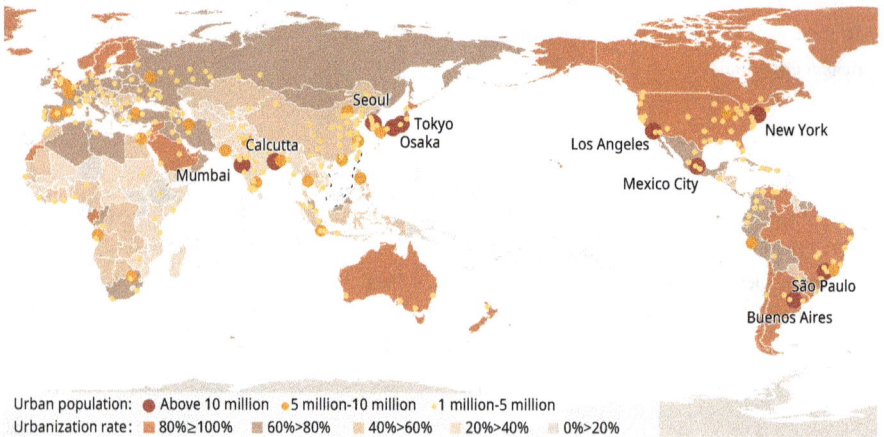

Urban population: ● Above 10 million • 5 million-10 million ∙ 1 million-5 million
Urbanization rate: ■ 80%≥100% ■ 60%>80% ■ 40%>60% ■ 20%>40% ■ 0%>20%

Figure 5-6 Distribution of the World's Megacities and the Urbanization Rate in Various Regions (1990)

Source: It is prepared as per the *World Urbanization Prospects* (The 2014 Revision) and *World Population Prospects* (2015 Revision) issued by United Nations Department of Economic and Social Affairs (UN DESA).

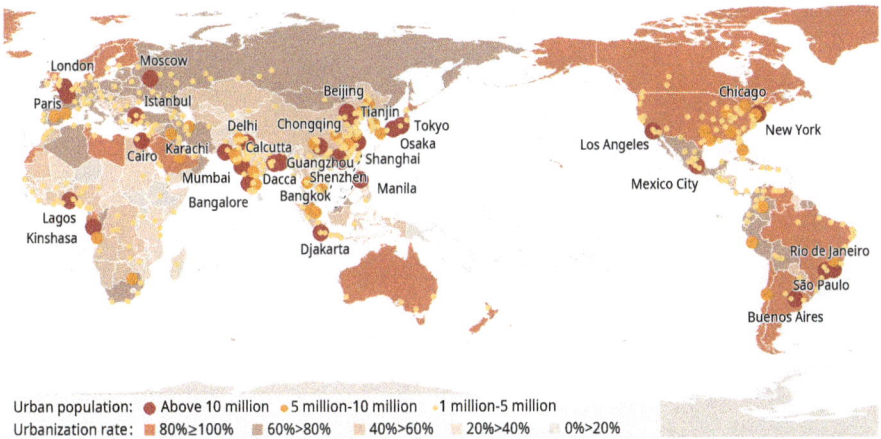

Urban population: ● Above 10 million ● 5 million-10 million · 1 million-5 million
Urbanization rate: ■ 80%≥100% ■ 60%>80% ■ 40%>60% ■ 20%>40% ■ 0%>20%

Figure 5-7 Distribution of the World's Megacities and the Urbanization Rate in Various Regions (2015)

Source: It is prepared as per the *World Urbanization Prospects* (The 2014 Revision) and *World Population Prospects* (2015 Revision) issued by United Nations Department of Economic and Social Affairs (UN DESA).

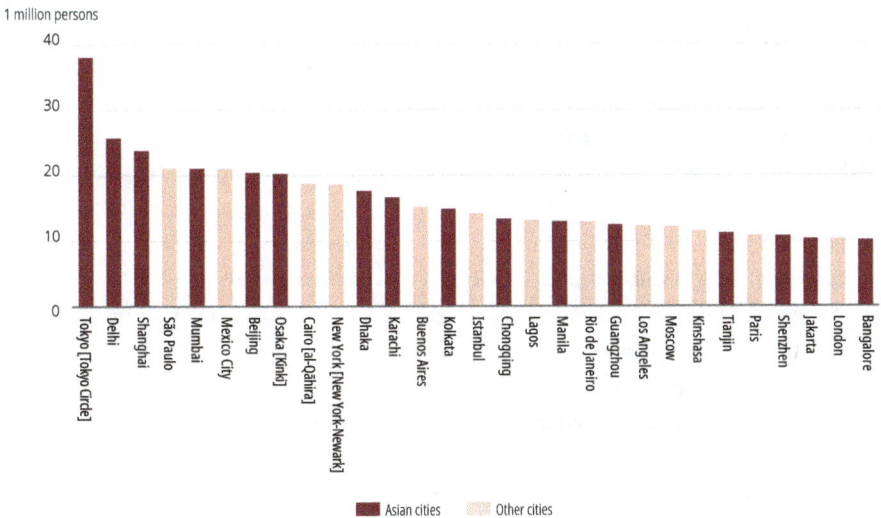

Figure 5-8 Population Ranking: Top 30 Cities in the World (2015)

Source: It is prepared as per the *World Urbanization Prospects* (The 2014 Revision) and *World Population Prospects* (2015 Revision) issued by United Nations Department of Economic and Social Affairs (UN DESA).

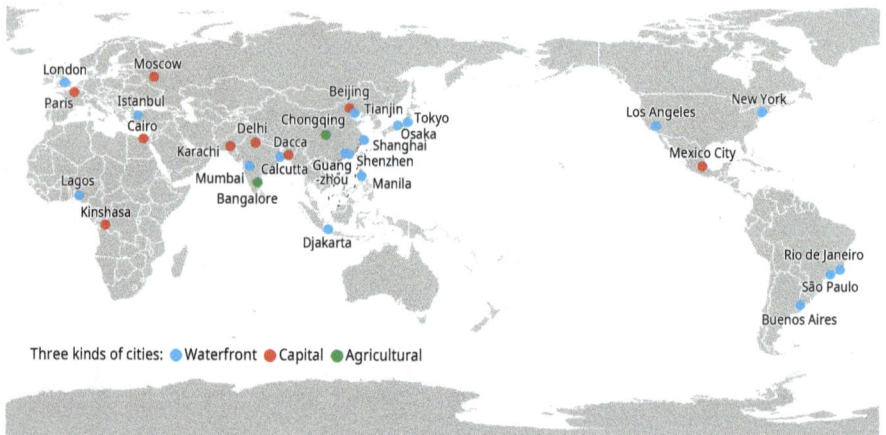

Figure 5-9 Categorical Distribution of the World's Megacities

political and cultural center of a country, and 3) "agricultural" cities starting off as inland central cities with a concentrated agricultural population. 19 of these megacities are on the coast, representing nearly 70%, the overwhelming majority of all the megacities across the world; eight of them are capital cities; and the smallest group, which consists of only two members, both of which are located in developing countries, is agricultural cities.[9]

It is the Age of Discovery that triggered the major development of coastal cities. Particularly, after the industrial revolution, the global allocation and sales of energy resources, raw materials and industrial products based on maritime transport subverted the dominance of continental economy, resulting in the agglomeration of industries and population in coastal port cities. The expanding and accelerating maritime transport as well as the development of globalization further sped up the agglomeration process of talents, industries, funds, and information towards port cities. As a result, a large number of large coastal cities emerged.

Since ancient times, the development of many cities has been closely associated with ports. Compared with land transport, waterway transport costs less and carries greater volume, and thus it is easier for regions with developed waterway transport to become trading hubs and finally evolve into cities. After the Age of Discovery, the development of maritime transport technology has changed the principal vehicle for bulk logistics from waterway transport dominated by river channels to maritime transport, and in the meanwhile, the unfolding globalization has further rapidly enhanced the advantages of port economy, allowing a great number of trading-port-based and industrial-port-based cities, typically represented by New York, Tokyo and Osaka, to achieve a fast development.

---

[9] Refer to Figure 5-9.

Capital megacities, represented by Beijing, Paris and Moscow, are located inland, but most of them are blessed with sound conditions for waterway transport through canal or river channels. Taking Beijing as an example; waterway transport through the Beijing-Hangzhou Grand Canal played an extremely important role in the development history of Beijing. Most of these cities thrived during the age of empires witnessing the prosperity of continental economy. By replacing continental economy, marine economy had become the engine for the development of world economy, and thus heavily impacted and constrained the viability of inland capital cities. Today, the development of inland capital megacities mainly relies on their administrative functions as political and cultural centers and also relies on their geopolitical positions. Of course, many inland capital megacities are supported by adjacent good ports, although they are not facing the ocean directly. For example, there are a few major ports, such as Tianjin and Tangshan, close to Beijing.

There are only two megacities located in agricultural areas, namely, Chongqing of China and Bangalore of India, both of which are central cities in developing countries and were formed in major agricultural regions with good climate conditions and high-density agricultural populations.

As political and cultural centers, capital cities thrive on the basis of their geopolitical significance, and agricultural cities thrive on the basis of sizable high-density agricultural populations, while coastal cities are products of marine economy. The era of great development for port cities was forged by the ocean-based large logistics, large transactions and large-scale exchanges. Today, of their course, the "ports" of coastal megacities are no longer seaports in the narrow sense. Starting by means of their port economy, coastal cities have been evolving their economic entities, generally rendering a continuous drop in the share of their seaports. For example, coastal megacities in developed countries, such as London of the U.K. and San Francisco of the U.S., have even lost half of their functions as ports. Relying on their openness and inclusivity as port cities, however, these cities have successfully shaped themselves into "ports of exchanges" based on information, technology, culture and art in the era of globalization and thus brought up new models for exchange-based economy and urban development.

With the evolution of economy and urban function in complexity, diversity, and scale, port cities and their hinterlands have gradually expanded into unified metropolitan areas in terms of function and space. Metropolitan areas and many surrounding small and medium-sized cities, by way of agglomeration and interactions, have further evolved into "megalopolises," a chain of urban areas covering a large region. Such megalopolises are best represented by the one situated along the Atlantic Ocean in the Northeastern U.S., centered on New York, Washington, and Boston; and the Pacific Coast Megalopolis of Japan, centered on Tokyo, Osaka, and Nagoya. In China, the Yangtze River Delta Megalopolis centered on Shanghai, Jiangsu, and Zhejiang, the Pearl River Delta Megalopolis centered on Hong Kong, Guangzhou, and Shenzhen, and the Beijing-Tianjin-Hebei Megalopolis are also taking shape and becoming three major engines driving the economic development of China.

(3) Formation of Megalopolises

A megalopolis means a chain of metropolitan areas centered on megacities, where a plurality of cities are connected through a high-speed transportation network. A megalopolis has a huge population and a wide range of unique industrial agglomerations. It is an important platform for international transactions and exchanges, leading the country and even the world in political, economic, cultural, information, techno-logical, and financial functions.

1) Northeast Megalopolis of the U.S.

The Northeast Megalopolis of the U.S. (also known as BosWash corridor), is a 970 km chain of metropoli-tan areas consisting of five big cities, Boston, New York, Philadelphia, Baltimore, and Washington, D.C., as well as 40 small and medium-sized cities with a population larger than 100,000.[10] This megalopolis has become an organic urban body through connections by the developed expressway and railway networks, accommodating 44 million people or roughly 16% of the country's population.

Almost every big city in BosWash faces a seaport, particularly the advantageous ports of Boston, New York, and Baltimore, which also provided the earliest gateways for European immigrants to the North America.

Although only accounting for 2% of the country's land area, BosWash holds about one-sixth of the working population in the U.S. The large and high-dense population has made it possible for the develop-ment of industries, commerce as well as culture and entertainment, which enriched and improved the urban functions of this region.

BosWash contributes 30% and 20% to the manufacturing output and GDP of the US, respectively. It is not only the political center, the largest manufacturing base, as well as the commerce and cultural center of the country, but also a financial center for the whole world.

As the oldest city in the U.S., Boston transformed itself from a light-industry-based city to a world-class center of knowledge economy with help of the development of universities and R&D institutions. As the world's financial center and information hub, New York is the largest exchange-based economy that attracts and brings together talents, capital and information. It is also a capital of culture and entertainment with a developed tourism economy. Philadelphia and Baltimore started off by developing ports and indus-tries, and with help of strong industrial capital, they have now achieved a high level of agglomeration in higher education, R&D, culture, entertainment and healthcare. Washington, D.C., which was newly founded in 1790, became the political center of the U.S. in 1800, and the entire city is like a well-organized giant park, a classical representation of capital planning.

---

[10] Refer to Figure 5-10.

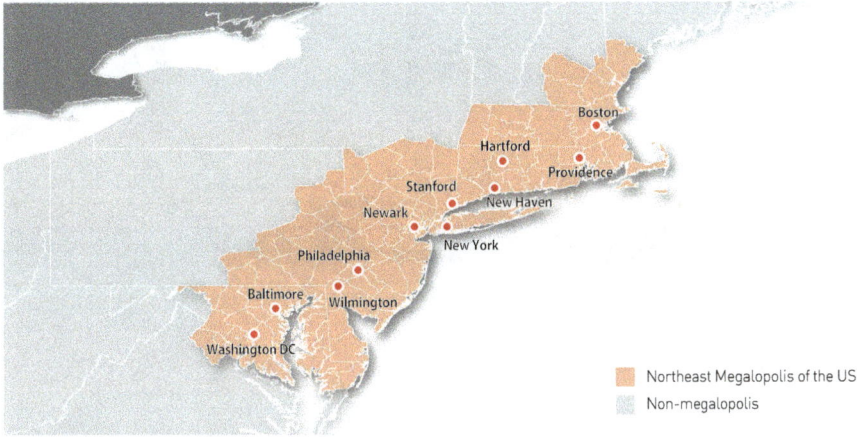

Figure 5-10 Northeast Megalopolis of the US ｜BosWash

This region is not just the origin place of the U.S., but also the political, economic and cultural hub of the country, plus an exchange center between the U.S. and the rest of the world.

The concept of megalopolis was first advocated by the French geographer Jean Gottmann, and he attributed the formation of such a megalopolis to its superior natural and traffic location, which attracts a large number of migrants and further leads to the large-scale agglomeration of industries, consumer markets, as well as business and financial functions.[11]

2) Pacific Coast Megalopolis of Japan

The Pacific Coast Megalopolis of Japan (also known as the Tokaido Megalopolis) means a chain of metropolitan areas primarily consisting of the Greater Tokyo Metropolitan Area, Nagoya Metropolitan Area, and Kinki Metropolitan Area. Densely distributed in this 500 kilometers strip are eight big cities with a population of more than one million (i.e., Tokyo, Yokohama, Kawasaki, Saitama, Nagoya, Kyoto, Osaka, and Kobe) as well as many small and medium-sized cities.[12] This megalopolis has a population of 75.58 million, accounting for 60% of the national total, and contributes 66% of the GDP as well as 62.4% of the manufac-turing value added of Japan with 21.4% of the country's land area. It has further attracted political agencies, cultural facilities and financial institutions, and thus is truly the political, economic, and cultural center of Japan.

---

[11] Gottmann, J., 1961, Megalopolis: The Urbanized Northeastern Seaboard of the United States, New York: K.I.P.
[12] Refer to Figure 5-11.

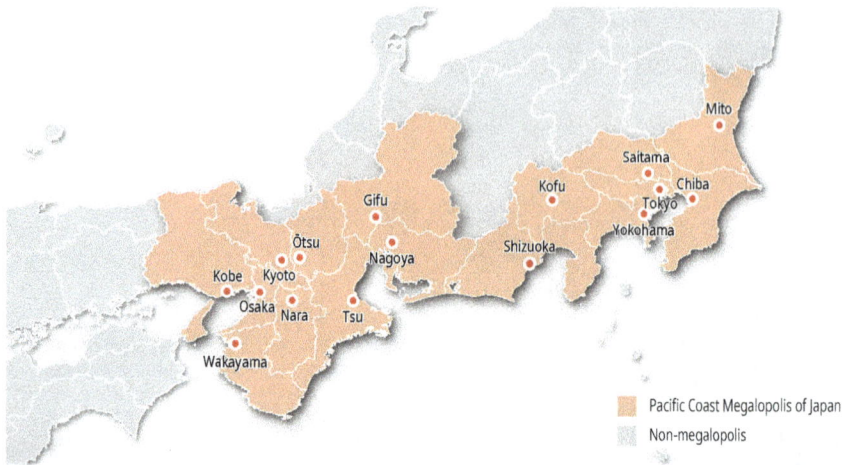

Figure 5-11 The Paci ic-Coast-in-Japan Megalopolis

The Tokyo Bay, Osaka Bay, and Ise Bay, blessed with excellent port conditions, have provided an important basis for the development of this megalopolis. After the WWII, Japan took advantage of the peaceful international environment and utilized the international resources and markets to establish three major coastal industrial zones, namely, Keihin-Keiyo,[13] Hanshin, and Chukyo around these three bay areas.

Relying on the low-cost and high-quality world resources as well as the international markets emerging from free trade, these three major coastal industrial zones have given full play to their advantages in sea transport and completely transformed themselves into the world's largest and most technologically advanced engine for industrial export, which drives the post-war economic recovery and rapid economic growth of Japan and placed this country as the world's second largest economy. At the same time, industrial development has initiated a rapid urbanization process, where the urban population expanded very quickly in three major bay areas and their central regions, forming the Greater Tokyo Metropolitan Area, Nagoya Metropolitan Area, and Kinki Metropolitan Area, in addition to a large number of small and medium-sized cities.

It is noteworthy that the group of ports in the Tokyo, Osaka, and Ise Bay areas have not only supported the development of three major coastal industrial zones, but also the demands for high-standard living from the large population in three major metropolitan areas, through importing a large amount of energy, food

---

[13] Strictly speaking, Keihin and Keiyo are two coastal industrial zones located on the two wings of the Tokyo Bay. For the purposes of convenience, in this report, they are collectively referred to as the Keihin-Keiyo Coastal Industrial Zone affiliated to the Tokyo Bay.

and materials from around the globe and in a highly efficient way. It is precisely the advantage of such a layout of large-scale agglomeration of urban population in port cities that has enabled Japan to enjoy the optimal allocation of global resources and to achieve the efficient development of the urban economy. Today, 94% of Japan's primary energy and 61% of her foods (by Kcal) come from imports.

By way of large-scale land reclamation, the Tokyo, Osaka, and Ise Bays have not only evolved into three major coastal industrial zones, but also provided large-scale transportation hubs such as ports and airports for three metropolitan areas. Also, space has been reserved for the development of large-scale urban constructions, such as central business districts (CBD), international conference centers, waterfront parks, large commercial facilities, and waterfront residential buildings, ensuring the multi-core development of these three metropolitan areas in their transformation from industrial economy to knowledge economy and services economy. Taking the Tokyo Bay as an example—since 1868, a total of 252.9 km² land has been reclaimed, and most of such reclamation was done after the WWII. Most of the facilities related to the 2020 Tokyo Olympics have also been built on the reclaimed land of the Tokyo Bay.

In 1964 and 1969, the sequential operations of the Tokaido Shinkansen and Tomei Expressway, which run through three major metropolitan areas, brought the small and big cities of these major metropolitan areas into close connection and formed a pattern of megalopolis that allowed for the interactive development of major metropolitan areas.

Now Japan is building her Central Shinkansen Maglev Line to connect the Tokyo, Nagoya and Kinki metropolitan areas, in an attempt to shape the Pacific Coast Megalopolis into a more charming metropolitan space for global talents, funds and information. Such a super high-speed traffic artery (500km/h) can be seen as a respond to the ever-intensifying global intercity competition in the context of globalization and knowledge economy.

Megalopolises Leading China's Economy

The rapid development of China's economy is the product of changes in the pattern of economic development of the world combined with the tremendous energy released by China's reform and opening-up. With the development of the information revolution, intercompany transactions and information exchanges have gradually gone electronic. This trend has greatly reduced the cost of international transactions as well as the part of hidden information in intercompany transactions, and thus rapidly expanded the once regionally confined supply chains into the globe. The maturity of high-speed, big-volume transit systems such as avia-tion and maritime transport and the reduction of tariffs on global industrial products have provided favor-able conditions for the global expansion of supply chains.

In this circumstance, for the purpose of winning the increasingly fierce competition in terms of both price and time, companies in the developed countries have begun to abandon the traditional business model covering development, production and sales, concentrate their operating resources on the most competitive core divisions, and optimize their global resource allocation through supply chains to seek greater benefits.

Fortunately, as the business model of global supply chain was gaining ground, China embarked on her reform and opening-up. China introduced the policies for opening-up in her coastal areas, especially in the Pearl River Delta, Yangtze River Delta, and Beijing-Tianjin-Hebei regions, and created a new world for global supply chain through a variety of measures, such as commencing the development of ports, airports, expressways, high-speed railways, and other large infrastructures, opening a large area of industrial land, and providing a sizable low-cost and high-quality labor force. The huge space of opening-up has attracted a large number of foreign companies to invest and set up factories, and in the meantime, has also brought the development opportunities to domestic enterprises and provided the stage for dream pursuers. The enormous energy that was once suppressed in the planned economy era has been released through the large-scale migration and clustering of population in the opening-up regions.

The influx of foreign capital and the growth of domestic enterprises have led to the large-scale industrial agglomeration and the formation of a huge urban space, i.e., megalopolis, which spans across several big cities, in the abovementioned regions.

Today, the three major megalopolises have grown into giant powerhouses for China's economic development. One can say that it is China's open space for global supply chain that has brought the energy for megalopolises and made China the new world factory with sustained high-speed economic growth.

In 2015, the Pearl River Delta Megalopolis (9 cities),[14] Yangtze River Delta Megalopolis (26 cities),[15] and Beijing-Tianjin-Hebei Megalopolis (10 cities)[16] together created 38% of the country's GDP. Compared with economic scale, a higher level of concentration of export and foreign investment became more obvi-ous. The three major megalopolises accounted for 71.6% and 48.5% respectively in the national export of goods and actual use of foreign funds.

---

[14] The Pearl River Delta Megalopolis should include Hong Kong and Macao. Due to data limitations, this report is based on the relevant planning and definitions of the National Development and Reform Commission, and has included only 9 cities, being Guangzhou, Shenzhen, Zhuhai, Foshan, Jiangmen, Zhaoqing, Huizhou, Dongguan and Zhongshan into the Pearl River Delta Megalopolis for analysis.

[15] According to the relevant planning and definitions of the National Development and Reform Commission, the Yangtze River Delta Megalopolis includes Shanghai, Nanjing, Wuxi, Changzhou, Suzhou, Nantong, Yancheng, Yangzhou, Zhenjiang, Taizhou, Hangzhou, Ningbo, Jiaxing, Huzhou, Shaoxing, Jinhua, Zhoushan, Taizhou, Hefei, Wuhu, Ma'anshan, Tongling, Anqing, Chuzhou, Chizhou and Xuancheng (26 cities).

[16] According to the relevant planning and definitions of the National Development and Reform Commission, the Beijing-Tianjin-Hebei Megalopolis includes Beijing, Tianjin, Shijiazhuang, Tangshan, Qinhuangdao, Baoding, Zhangjiakou, Chengde, Cangzhou and Langfang (10 cities).

(1) Locations with Particularly Favorable Natural Conditions

Compared to the inland areas, the three megalopolises are located with particularly favorable natural conditions under the development pattern of globalization. The global supply chain not only seeks to lower the cost of production, but also the cost of logistics, inventory and time. Therefore, all aspects of the global supply chain require a high level of professionalism and a flexible, responsive and swift mechanism, wherein ports and airports have become the crucial factors.

It is the uniquely favorable geographical locations that have helped the three major megalopolises build ports, airports, expressways and high-speed railways in a very short period of time and thus provided good transportation conditions for the high-efficiency operation of global supply chain in China.

1) Port Construction

China has achieved amazing results in the interactive development between industrialization and container ports. In 2016, 7 out of the top 10 container ports in the world were located in China. With the exception of Qingdao, which ranked 8th, all of the other Chinese ports were located in the three megalopolises, including Shanghai which came in 1st, Shenzhen at 3rd, Ningbo-Zhoushan at 4th, Hong Kong at 6th, Guangzhou at 7th, and Tianjin at 10th.

According to the analysis in the *China Integrated City Index 2017*, among the top 30 of the 297 cities at the prefecture level or above in terms of "container port convenience," 22 have been located in the three megalopolises, including the cities listed above. The three megalopolises have been undoubtedly the most convenient areas for container transport in China.[17] With respect to container transport, the Pearl River Delta Megalopolis, the Yangtze River Delta Megalopolis, and the Beijing-Tianjin-Hebei Megalopolis respectively accounted for 25.7%, 35.3%, and 8.3%, adding up to 69.3%, of the national total. The fact that container throughput and cargo exports were highly concentrated in the three megalopolises shows that superior port conditions have been supporting the large-scale operation of global supply chain in the three megalopolises.

2) Airport Construction

The three megalopolises have also achieved amazing results in airport construction. The Pearl River Delta Megalopolis has now developed an aviation system of seven airports, including the Hong Kong International Airport, Macau International Airport, Guangzhou Baiyun International Airport, Shenzhen Bao'an International Airport, Zhuhai Jinwan International Airport, Huizhou Pingtan Airport, and Foshan Shadi Airport. Specifically, the Guangzhou Baiyun International Airport has been not only listed nationally as

---

[17] Refer to Figure 4-7.

3rd in terms of passenger, cargo, and mail throughput,[18] but is also listed 5th across Asia as an international hub airport in terms of the number of flights. As an international hub airport as well, the Hong Kong International Airport has ranked 4th across Asia in terms of the number of flights.

In the Yangtze River Delta Megalopolis, an aviation system has been established to include 16 airports, namely, Shanghai Pudong International Airport, Shanghai Hongqiao International Airport, Hangzhou Xiaoshan International Airport, Nanjing Lukou International Airport, Ningbo Lishe International Airport, Hefei Xinqiao International Airport, Sunan Shuofang International Airport, Changzhou Benniu International Airport, Yangzhou Taizhou International Airport, Jinhua Yiwu Airport, Nantong Xingdong Airport, Yancheng Nanyang Airport, Zhoushan Putuoshan Airport, Taizhou Luqiao Airport, Chizhou Jiuhuashan Airport, and Anqing Tianzhushan Airport. Among these airports, the Shanghai Pudong International Airport has been listed as 1st and 2nd in terms of passenger throughput and cargo and mail throughput, respectively, but also listed as 2nd across Asia as an international hub airport in terms of the number of flights.

In the Beijing-Tianjin-Hebei Megalopolis, an aviation system has been established to include seven airports, namely, Beijing Capital International Airport, Beijing Nanyuan Airport, Tianjin Binhai International Airport, Shijiazhuang Zhengding Airport, Tangshan Sannvhe Airport, Zhangjiakou Ningyuan Airport, and Qinhuangdao Shanhaiguan Airport. Among these airports, the Beijing Capital International Airport has been listed as national 1st and 2nd in terms of passenger throughput and cargo and mail throughput, respectively, but also listed as 1st across Asia as an international hub airport in terms of the number of flights.

According to the analysis of the *China Integrated City Index 2017*, among the top 30 of the 297 cities at the prefecture level or above in terms of "airport convenience," 12 have been located in the three megalopolises, including Shanghai, Beijing, and Guangzhou as the top three. It can be said that the three megalopolises have provided the highest level of convenience for air transportation in China.[19]

The three megalopolises have accounted for 43.6% of the national passenger throughput, with the Pearl River Delta Megalopolis, the Yangtze River Delta Megalopolis, and the Beijing-Tianjin-Hebei Megalopolis accounting for 11.2%, 19.3%, and 13%, respectively. They have also contributed a considerable share of 67.8% in the national cargo and mail throughput, with the Pearl River Delta Megalopolis, the Yangtze River Delta Megalopolis, and the Beijing-Tianjin-Hebei Megalopolis accounting for 18.4%, 33.8%, and 15.6%, respectively. Superior air transport conditions have not only supported the high-speed operation of global supply chain in the three megalopolises, but also greatly promoted the development of their exchange-based economy.

---

[18] For the purposes of this report, the airports in China do not include the international airports in Hong Kong and Macao.
[19] Refer to Figure 4-8

3) Expressways and High-speed Railways

Since the operation of China's first expressway[20] in 1988, 130,000 kilometers of expressways had been completed till the end of 2016. The Pearl River Delta Megalopolis, the Yangtze River Delta Megalopolis, and the Beijing-Tianjin-Hebei Megalopolis have been covered by the most dense expressway system across the nation, and they respectively owned an expressway network of 3,646 kilometers, 9,132 kilometers, and 6,722 kilometers, together accounting for 17.6% of the entire national network in terms of length.[21]

By the end of 2016, a railway network of 124,000 kilometers had been completed in China. The Pearl River Delta, the Yangtze River Delta, and the Beijing-Tianjin-Hebei Megalopolises have three railway transportation networks of 3,053 kilometers, 10,017 kilometers, and 11,790 kilometers, respectively. The railways of the three megalopolises accounted for 17.1% of the national total in terms of length, representing the highest railway density in the country.[22]

According to the analysis of *China Integrated City Index 2017*, among the top 30 of the 297 cities at the prefecture level or above in terms of "the number of high-speed rail services," 19 have been located in the three megalopolises, including Guangzhou, Shanghai, Beijing, Shenzhen, Tianjin, and Nanjing as the top six. It is clear that the three megalopolises have provided the highest level of convenience for high-speed rail transportation in China.

These expressway and railway transport networks have not only significantly shortened the temporal and economic distance between the three megalopolises and the rest of China, but also closely connected the three megalopolises into an organic body with rapid interactions within itself.

(2) Large-scale Utilization of Global Resources

The industrial revolution was initiated in the United Kingdom, which transported the cotton grown in the West Indies to Manchester for processing, and this means the development of modern industry has been based on the utilization of world resources from the very beginning. From a global perspective, because industrial development requires the large-scale and efficient use of world resources, almost all of the industrial activities have been concentrated in coastal areas or around the cities endowed with better inland water transportation since the start of industrial revolution. In contrast, most of the regions without a port have continued to struggle with developing large-scale modern industries.

The era of heavy chemical industries from 1949 to 1978 found China in a pressing international

---

[20] On October 31 1988, the Shanghai-Jiading expressway was put into operation as the first expressway in China. In July 1989, the Ministry of Communications issued the first policy on expressway building.

[21] Due to data limitations, the data of the three megalopolises used in the analysis of expressways are prepared by the municipality directly under the Central Government and by the province.

[22] Due to data limitations, the data of the three megalopolises used in the analysis of railway are prepared by the municipality directly under the Central Government and by the province.

situation where a war might have been waged between China and the then superpowers—the U.S. and the Soviet Union—at any time. China was not positioned to utilize the world resources, and thus the government adopted a policy of industrial distribution mainly based on domestic resources, which resulted in the then heavy industries being deployed in either resource-rich areas or "3rd-tier" inland areas.

The opportunity to change this distribution policy came with the construction of Baoshan Steel Works on the basis of importing raw materials. However, even after the reform and opening-up of China, there were heated debates about whether the Baoshan Steel Works should be built. The central questions were why the steel works based on iron ore import should be built, and why the country should spend a huge amount of money in building the steel works at the estuary of the Yangtze River, where the ground foundation is weak. Due to a lack of understanding for the importance of economic development with imported resources, the construction of Baoshan Steel Works was interrupted.

Today, Baoshan Steel Works has grown into the largest iron and steel group in China, which is a successful demonstration to the Chinese people of the superiority of a coastal development model that utilizes global resources. The rapid increase of the demand for resources such as oil and ores has made China a major resource importer.

Taking the iron ore, as an example, China commenced her import of iron ores in 1981, and the import volume exceeded 100 million tons in 2001. In 2003, China outpaced Japan to become the world's largest importer of iron ores. In 2015, China's iron ore imports reached 952.72 million tons, accounting for 40.8% of the iron ores consumed.[23]

By continuously improving an understanding of transportation costs and environmental costs, coastal iron and steel production bases capable of efficiently using premium imported iron ores are enjoying increasingly apparent advantages. Nowadays, the still widely distributed, scattered, and inefficient Chinese iron and steel businesses based in inland areas will move towards the coast, especially to the three megalopolises and their surrounding areas with strong demands.

The skyrocketing economic growth and the motorization of China have led to a speedy rise in crude oil consumption. In 1993, China changed from a pure exporter of crude oil to a pure importer. Crude oil imports have been climbing ever since. In 2009, imports exceeded domestic production. In 2015, China's crude oil imports reached 328 million tons, accounting for 60.4% of the crude oil consumed.[24]

With deep-water ports, the capability of the three megalopolises in utilizing premium overseas-sourced oil and natural gas in a large-scale and high-efficiency manner gives prominence to their advantages in terms of energy efficiency. The increase in imported energy has not only improved the economic efficiency of the three megalopolises, but also widened the gap between them and the inland areas in terms

---

[23] Refer to Figure 5-12.

[24] Refer to Figure 5-13.

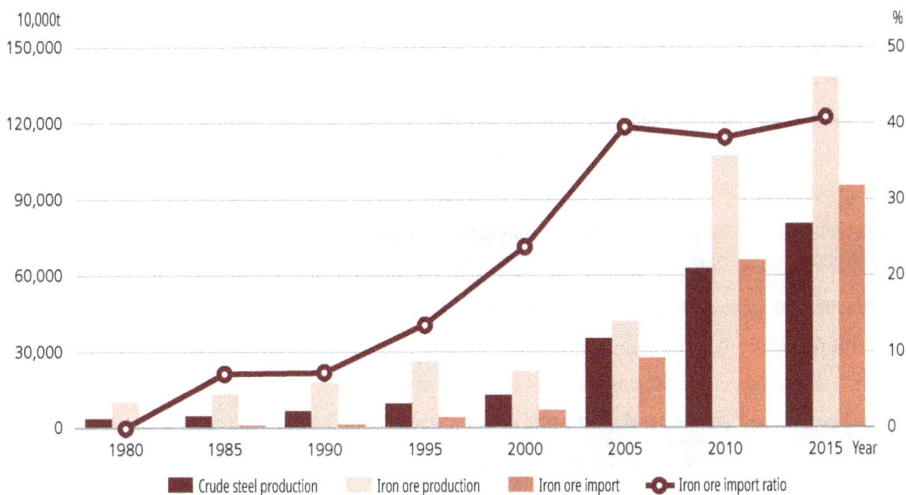

Figure 5-12 Changes of China's Crude Steel Production, Iron Ore Production and Import (1980–2015)

Source: It is prepared as per the *China Statistical Yearbook* issued by the National Bureau of Statistics and the data published by the Ministry of Land and Resources of PRC.

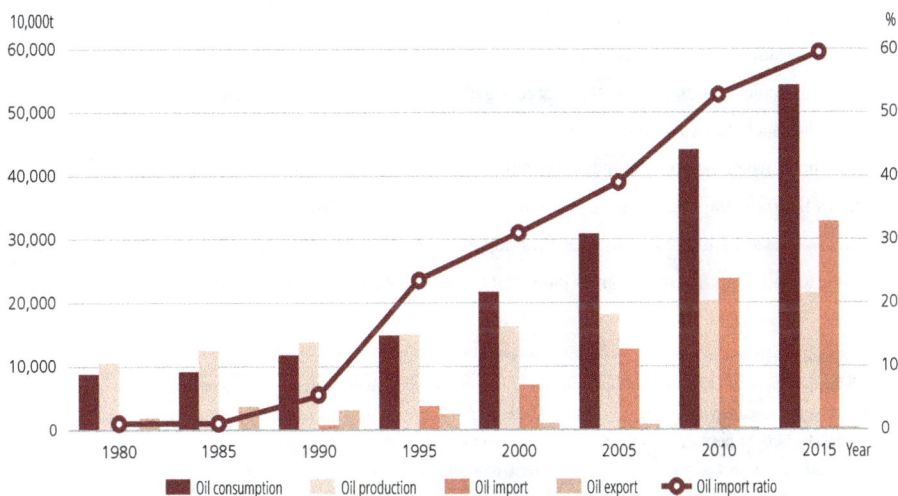

Figure 5-13 Changes of China's Crude Oil Consumption and Import (1980–2015)

Source: It is prepared as per the *China Statistical Yearbook* issued by the National Bureau of Statistics and the data published by the Ministry of Land and Resources of PRC.

of general benefits. This trend will accelerate the concentration of the economy in the three megalopolises and bring fundamental changes to China's land use structure.

(3) Magnified Agglomeration of Emerging Industries

The development of information technology enables the information about technology and skills to be held by intelligent machinery, and such information is required by production activities. This change in industrial technology has enabled the developing countries to compensate for their lack of technical skills and skilled worker reserves by introducing the state-of-the-art intelligent equipment. Thus the threshold of industrialization has been dramatically lowered for the developing countries.[25]

The revolutionary changes in industrial technology have reduced the limit on the space of industrial activities. Given that the developing countries can easily carry out industrial production activities, supply chains have reached into the developing world across national borders. In order to win the competition on efficiency, companies have overcome the irrationality inherent in any full-scale industrial agglomeration protected by national economic barriers and sought an optimal global production and support through building the global supply chain.[26]

Industrial agglomeration based on the global supply chain has therefore come into being at the right moment. Industrial agglomerations in the Silicon Valley of the U.S., and Bangalore of India, as well as in the Yangtze River Delta, the Pearl River Delta, and the Beijing-Tianjin-Hebei regions are typical cases of an emerging industrial agglomeration based on the global supply chain. Specifically, the global supply chain has brought enormous industrial investment to the Yangtze River Delta, Pearl River Delta, and Beijing-Tianjin-Hebei regions in China, endowed with the advantage of traffic locations. Today these three regions have become the world's largest gathering place for the electronics industry, automobile industry, and machinery industry.

In China, where nationwide industrialization is promoted, almost all the cities take industrial development as the most important means of revitalizing the economy. However, China's export industry has been highly clustered in the three major megalopolises. Among the 297 cities at the prefecture level or above, the top 30 cities in terms of gross industrial output value contributed 42.3% of the national total, and

---

[25] With the development of information and communication technology, predominately the semiconductor technology, information and communication technology is combined with mechanical technology to generate a new technology system of Mechatronics. The birth of mechatronics is a revolution comparable to the first industrial revolution aroused by the explosive advancement of mechanical technology. The mechatronics revolution enables industrial products to process and memorize information, while enabling intelligent machinery to replace technology and skills in production. For details of the mechatronics revolution, please refer to the *Mechatronics Revolution and New International Specialization: Asian Industrialization in the Modern World Economy* (Minerva Publishing Company, 1997).

[26] For a theoretical explanation of the global industrial chain, please refer to the Chapter 1 of *The Chinese Economy: Mechanism of its Rapid Growth* by Zhou Muzhi (People's Publishing House, 2008).

the three megalopolises contributed 40.1%.[27] However, with respect to national export of goods, the top 30 cities contributed 76.8% of the national total, and the three megalopolises contributed 71.6%.[28] The fact that a higher-level convergence was found in export of goods for the three megalopolises and the top 30 cities shows that the three megalopolises far outperform other regions of China in terms of the quality of industrial economy. It is foreseeable that the high-quality industrial economy represented by the export industry will increasingly converge to superior cities of the industrial economy, predominantly those in the three megalopolises.

China has been widely regarded as the "world factory," but in China, the three megalopolises are worthy of the name "world factory" indeed.

(4) Increasingly Prominent Position as Centers for Culture, Science & Technology, and High-end Services Industry

In terms of culture, science & technology, and services industry, especially in the high-end services industry, the three major megalopolises are also leading the country. The *China Integrated City Index 2017* defines the concept of radiation to measure the extent for a city function to be used externally, and then performs an evaluation for the radiation of different cities in wholesale & retail, medical care, culture & sports, finance, higher education, science & technology, manufacturing, the IT industry, and catering & hotels. The results show the three megalopolises have a strong radiation in the above areas with which the other cities cannot compete. That is to say, the three megalopolises play a central role in providing high-end functions to the whole country in these areas.

Based on the analysis of the deviation values in wholesale and retail radiation for all the 297 cities at the prefecture level or above, seven out of the top 10 have been located in the three megalopolises, including Shanghai in the 1st, Beijing in the 2nd, Guangzhou in the 5th, Hangzhou in the 6th, Tianjin in the 7th, Shenzhen in the 8th, and Nanjing in the 9th, respectively. The large-scale and high-density gathering of population in the three megalopolises has led to the flourishing development of their wholesale and retail industry, making them the largest, highest-grade, and most content-rich shopping centers in the country.[29]

The top three cities ranked by the deviation values in medical radiation have been Beijing, Shanghai, and Guangzhou, each in one of the three megalopolises. The gathering of large-scale and high-end medical institutions has caused the largest number of patients (nationwide) to be concentrated in these three cities for medical attention.[30]

---

[27] Refer to Figure 4-5.
[28] Refer to Figure 4-6.
[29] Refer to Figure 4-28.

Six of the top eight cities ranked by the deviation values in the culture, sports and entertainment radia-tion have been located in the three megalopolises, with the 1st, 2nd, and 3rd places being taken by Beijing, Shanghai, and Guangzhou, which stood out as cultural and sports centers. Being the capital of China, Beijing has been in a particularly advantageous position as the national cultural center.[31]

The top three cities ranked by the deviation values in the higher education radiation have been Beijing, Shanghai, and Nanjing, and the central cities of the three megalopolises have all been national leaders in higher education, wherein Beijing's position as the national center of higher education has been prominent.[32]

Among the top 30 cities ranked by the deviation values in the science and technology radiation, 19 have been located in the three megalopolises, with the top four being Beijing, Shanghai, Shenzhen, and Guangzhou, all of which are located in the three megalopolises. Beijing's position as the national center of science and technology has again been especially prominent.[33]

Six of the top 10 cities ranked by the deviation values in financial radiation have been located in the three megalopolises. Among them, Shanghai, Beijing, and Shenzhen have been prominent as the three major financial centers.[34]

Among the top 30 cities ranked by the deviation values in manufacturing radiation, 20 have been located in the three megalopolises, and the top five are Shenzhen, Suzhou, Shanghai, Dongguan, and Foshan, all of which are in the three megalopolises.[35]

Among the top 10 cities ranked by the deviation values in IT industry radiation, six are located in the three megalopolises, and the top five are Beijing, Shanghai, Shenzhen, Hangzhou, and Nanjing. This shows the strong advantages of the three megalopolises in the IT industry.[36]

Among the top 30 cities ranked by the deviation values in catering and hotel radiation, 13 have been located in the three megalopolises, where Shanghai and Beijing ranked the 1st and 2nd respectively. The top 10 also included Suzhou, Guangzhou, Shenzhen and Hangzhou.[37]

The era of the city is also an era of urban competition. The mechanism by which a city attracts external talents, funds, and information through her "core power" is known as the "sucker effect."[38]

---

[30] Refer to Figure 4-25.
[31] Refer to Figure 4-26.
[32] Refer to Figure 4-23.
[33] Refer to Figure 4-24.
[34] Refer to Figure 4-20.
[35] Refer to Figure 4-21.
[36] Refer to Figure 4-22.
[37] Refer to Figure 4-27.

The core power of a city is composed of such important elements as wholesale and retail, medical care, culture, sports and entertainment, higher education, science and technology, finance, as well as manufacturing, the IT industry, and catering and hotels. The three megalopolises have developed strong advantages in these areas, which will further bring together talents, funds, and information from the rest of the country and even the world, to continuously fuel growth.

Challenges and Issues in the Era of Megalopolises

In China, there are indeed many people advocating that China's urbanization should follow the model based on small and medium-sized cities. Numerous scholars and officials strongly recommend the development model centering around small and medium-sized cities that Germany, Austria, Switzerland, and even Czechoslovakia and Hungary have experienced. Most of these countries initiated their industrialization process at a rather early stage, and most of their labor transfer from the rural to urban areas came from their surrounding regions. It was a long process for the labor force to transfer from the agriculture to textile industry, to machinery industry, to services industry, and to today's information industry.

In contrast, the latecomers of industrialized countries tended to follow the development model based on big cities during the process of urbanization. Especially in the 20th century, the clustering of industries and population in big cities became the trend of urbanization in different places around the world, where it was apparent that people were inclined to swarm into big cities at one stroke from other parts of the country. As the main body of urban economy, modern industries have developed a stronger and stronger capability of clustering, which contributes most to the change of urbanization process.

The modern urbanization over the past 200 years has been a process from urbanization to big-city-oriented urbanization and to megalopolis-oriented urbanization, where the scale of urban agglomeration keeps growing. The clustering capability of modern industries becomes stronger and stronger, and in the meantime, the scale of cities has a bigger and bigger impact on the efficiency of economy. In particular, with the improvement of urban infrastructure as well as urban management and organization, the benefits of agglomeration are increasingly evident for the enhancement of economic efficiency and the enrichment of urban life. Of course, as the negative effects of agglomeration, there is not only the likelihood of causing big city problems, but the over-concentration of industries and population will also cause macro-level problems such as the uneven development of the country represented by regional disparities.

After the founding of the People's Republic of China, none of the policies pertaining to the

---

38 Also known as the siphonic effect.

decentralization of heavy industries, rural industrialization, and small towns pursued by the Chinese government showed any understanding of the inevitability of population and industries to cluster together in large cities. Therefore, the freedom of distribution of industrial investment and the movement of population were limited and inhibited the development of big cities.

In furtherance of the reform and opening-up policies, liberty has been given to enterprises in their investment and selection of locations, and the tendency of industries to cluster together in areas with high economic efficiency is becoming apparent, which has prompted a large amount of people to migrate towards megalopolises. However, the dual social structure caused by the household registration system has severely prevented our policies from addressing the reality of industries and population gathering in large cities and megalopolises.

In September 2001, the National Development and Reform Commission, the China Daily, the China Association of Mayors, and the Japan International Cooperation Agency jointly organized the "China Urbanization Forum – the Megalopolis Strategy," where the first systematic proposal was tabled in China on policies for megalopolises,[39] initiating discussions on megalopolis-related policies.[40]

In 2006, the Chinese government clearly put forward in her 11th Five-year Plan policies that attached importance to the development of megalopolises. This means that China abandoned the policy of inhibiting the development of large cities, which had been in place for half a century, and began to pay attention to the development of large cities and megalopolises.

The concept of megalopolis was first used by the French geographer Jean Gottmann in his book *Megalopolis* published in 1961, where an area consisting of five major cities on the east coast of the U.S. accommodating 30 million people was called a megalopolis.

Compared with the description by Gottmann, the megalopolises described in this report have undergone profound changes in terms of their inherent productivity and development patterns. The economic subjects of megalopolises have evolved from full-scale industrial structures to components of the global division of labor, giving a more prominent status to the services economy and knowledge economy. It is

---

[39] Refer to Figure 5-14.

[40] From 1999 to 2002, the previous Japan International Cooperation Agency (JICA) worked with the National Development and Reform Commission to implement a three-year large joint research on China's urbanization policies. As a part of the research, a "China Urbanization Forum – the Megalopolis Strategy" was held in September 2001, initiating discussions on megalopolis-related policies. As a result of this policy research, the investigation team proposed social development goals for China's urbanization, including intensive society, mobile society, civil society and sustainable society. In order to achieve the above four social development goals, the investigation team tabled a specific range of policy advice including administrative zoning reform, land use policy reform, local fiscal reform, population migration policy reform, social security system reform, development zone system reform and transportation system construction for metropolitan areas. For details, please refer to the final report of this policy research, *Urbanization: Theme of China's Modernization* (Hunan People's Publishing House, 2001). As head of the investigation, the author presided over the research and writing of the report.

particularly noteworthy that the Northeast Megalopolis of the U.S. is nowhere near any Chinese mega-lopolis today in terms of population size, population density, or intercity division of labor and interaction. More comparable to the Chinese megalopolises is the Pacific Coast Megalopolis of Japan.

The basic concept of megalopolis can be defined as a continuous and closely linked high-density urban space resulting from the agglomeration of multiple metropolitan areas. There are many large, medium, and small cities in this space, and the functions of cities at different levels are organically interlinked in a dense space. The temporal distance and economic distance between these cities are shortened by high-density and high-speed transportation networks, and the vitality generated by the exchanges and transac-tions between these cities is the benefit produced by such a megalopolis.

Accordingly, the metropolitan area can be defined as a commuting circle, but a megalopolis is not the grander version of a daily life circle. Rather, it is a working circle that one can travel to and return from a place within a day, and its central function of exchanging and transacting with the rest of the world is the key to bringing great energy to the cities within.

China's three megalopolises are products of the interactions between the expansion of the global sup-ply chain and the reform and opening-up in the context of the information revolution. In the future, a grow-ing portion of China's economy and population will cluster in the three megalopolises, which will grow to influence the world economy.

Of course, the rise of the three megalopolises has also triggered a major change in China's social and economic structures. It is a serious and urgent challenge facing China as to how to build a large-scale and high-density urban society.

(1) Grand Population Migration

Through 30 years of the planned economy, the People's Republic of China developed a tremendous capac-ity of industrial production to cope with the then severe international environment. However, the household registration system formed in that era which restricted the migration of population, and especially restricted the employment and residence of farmers in cities, has since hindered the healthy development of China's urbanization.

The biggest issue facing China's megalopolises is, above all, how to deal with the large number of migrants. According to the comparative analysis of permanent populations and registered populations in the *China Integrated City Index 2017*, 17 of the top 30 cities where permanent population outnumbered registered population, among all the 297 ones at the prefecture level or above, have been located in the three megalopolises. The top eight cities, namely Shanghai, Beijing, Shenzhen, Dongguan, Tianjin, Guangzhou, Suzhou, and Foshan, have also been located in the three megalopolises.

The Pearl River Delta Megalopolis, the Yangtze River Delta Megalopolis, and the Beijing-Tianjin-Hebei Megalopolis have respectively accepted 26,232,000, 21,903,000 and 12,855,000 permanent

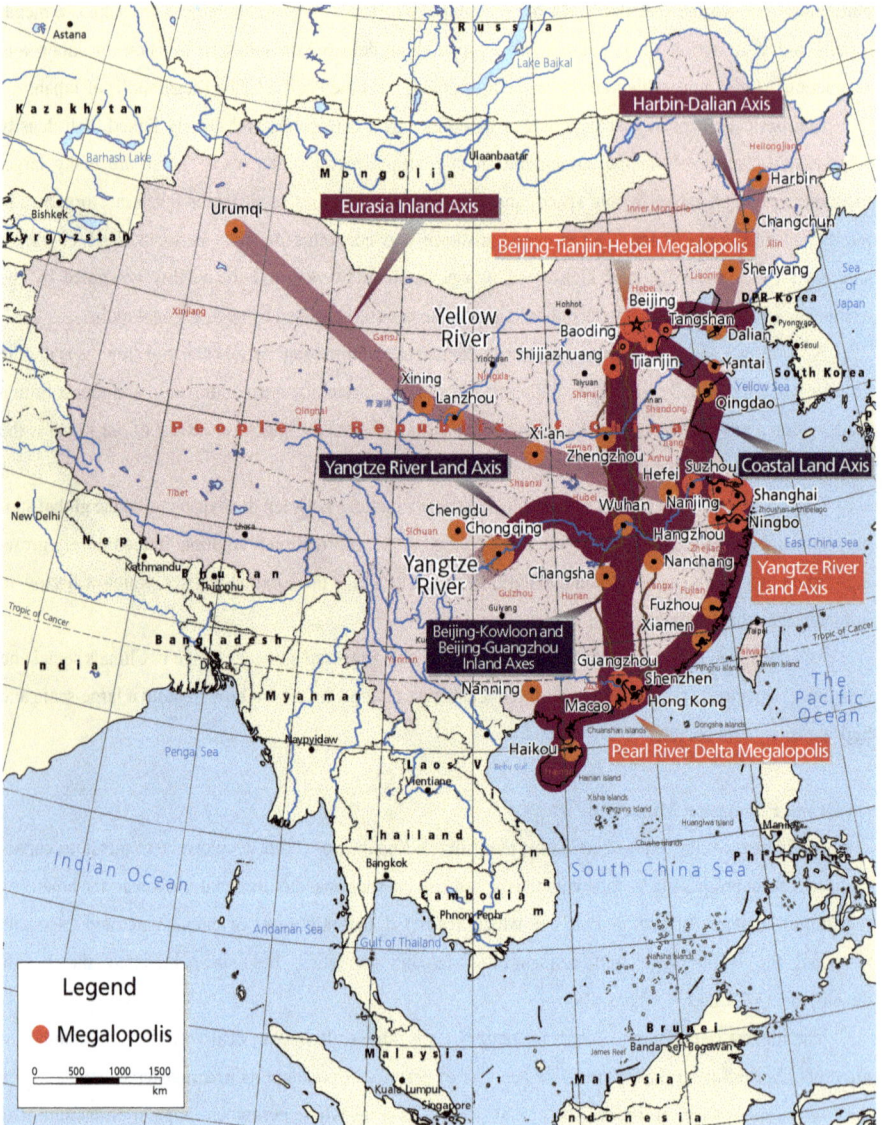

Figure 5-14 Sketch Map of the Strategy of Chinese Megalopolis

Source: Zhou Muzhi. (2001). *Urbanization: Theme of China's Modernization.* Hunan People's Publishing House.

residents without household registration, meaning that the three megalopolises together have already accepted a net influx of more than 60 million people. The top three cities, Shanghai, Beijing, and Shenzhen, have received a net influx of 9,723,000, 8,253,000 and 7,829,000 people, respectively.[41]

The above data show that a large number of migrants have relocated to the three megalopolises. However, the restrictions of an institutionalized dual society have not allowed tens of millions of migrant workers to become urban residents, despite their long stays in the megalopolises. They remain under various restrictions and endure discriminations in work and life space, and most of them are kept outside of the social security and public service system of the cities. A divided social structure has not only reinforced and expanded the income and social welfare disparities between social groups, but also the disparities between two groups with different identities living in the same urban space, which further highlights the resulting social contradictions and unfairness.

China needs to build a tolerant and open urban society that transforms the large-scale migration of people into the energy for economic and social development. To this end, China urgently needs to fundamentally reform her dual social structure, change the household registration system, and establish a universal security system with compulsory education, medical care, and elderly care at its core as well as a fair system of basic public service, for the purpose of alleviating institutional impacts adverse to migration and promoting the healthy and stable development of her urban society.

It is an urgent and serious challenge for China to build a harmonious urban society.

(2) Densification and De-densification of Cities

Since the 1990s, the fanatically hot development zones and real estate boom have driven the rapid urbanization in China, resulting in the dramatic expansion of urban construction areas. The sudden arrival of an automobile society has brought profound harms such as space fragmentation, traffic congestion, environmental pollution, and normalized lengthy commuting among others, to the unprepared Chinese cities. At the same time, it has also spread the phenomena of chaotic development and low development, which accelerate the low-density development of cities.

A city is a space where a population of certain density clusters. On the one hand, High density that does not conform to the level of infrastructure and management is an important cause of urban problems. On the other hand, however, an over-sparse urban population is an important contributor to the hindrance of the industrial economy, especially the development of the services economy, and prevents of the quality of life of urban residents from being improved. China's urban population is defined by urban administrative zoning. Due to a lack of measurement of population density, urban population cannot accurately reflect the actual state of urbanization. The lack of analytical focus is responsible for the long-term misunderstanding in China on the

---

[41] Refer to Figure 4-3 and Figure 4-4.

issue of urban density, from both the perception of and the policies for urban construction and urbanization.

The *China Integrated City Index 2017*, with reference to the definitions of urban population in the developed countries, introduces a concept of Densely Inhabited District (DID hereafter) and attempts to provide a more accurate analysis of Chinese cities and urbanization. Specifically, the Index defines a chain of areas with more than 5,000 people per square kilometer as a densely inhabited district, or DID.[42]

In Japan, the so-called urbanization rate is another word for the DID population ratio. The definition of urban population in the Population Census implemented by the Japanese government refers to the DID population. The DID population ratio of Tokyo has now reached 88.7%, that of the Greater Tokyo Metropolitan Area (Tokyo, Saitama, Chiba and Kanagawa) has reached 67.1%, that of the Pacific Coast Megalopolis (Greater Tokyo Metropolitan Area, Nagoya Metropolitan Area and Kinki Metropolitan Area) has reached 49.3%, and that of the entirety of Japan has also reached 33.9%.[43]

In contrast, the current DID population ratio of China is only 29.9%, 4 percentage points below that of Japan. The DID population ratio of Shenzhen is 88.7% and ranks first in the country. Regarding other megacities in the three megalopolises, namely, Shanghai, Guangzhou, Beijing, and Tianjin, their DID population ratios are 79.3%, 74.2%, 66.8% and 62.0%, respectively. In Japan, the 12 big cities each with more than 1 million people achieve a total DID population ratio of 80.5%—although the megacities in China still fall behind regarding this ratio, though the gap is narrowing. Among the three megalopolises with the largest urban population at the highest density, the DID population ratio of the Pearl River Delta Megalopolis is 65.2%,[44] but for the Yangtze River Delta Megalopolis and the Beijing-Tianjin-Hebei Megalopolis, this ratio is only 46.5%[45] and 35.9%,[46] respectively. Despite being the highest of the three, the DID population ratio of the Pearl River Delta Megalopolis still falls behind the Pacific Coast Megalopolis, but the gap has been gradu-ally narrowed. Further, from the Pearl River Delta Megalopolis to the Yangtze River Delta Megalopolis and to the Beijing-Tianjin-Hebei Megalopolis, the DID population ratio appears to be stepping down, and this indicates a clear difference in the urbanization process of the three megalopolises.

At the same time, however, it is noteworthy that the DID population density of China, where the urban management and infrastructure still fall behind Japan, is higher than the DID population density of Japan. More specifically, China's DID average population density is 14,162 people/km², which exceeds

---

[42] In the *China Integrated City Index 2016*, the DID definition was borrowed from Japan, whereby a chain of areas with a population over 4,000 people/km² was defined as a DID. On the basis of this definition, a DID comparative analysis was conducted between China and Japan. In the *China Integrated City Index 2017*, the OECD definition was used to define a chain of areas with a population over 5,000 people/km² as a DID. This book provides a DID analysis of China, Japan and other parts of the world with this new definition.

[43] Refer to Figure 5-15.

[44] Refer to Figure 5-20.

[45] Refer to Figure 5-25.

[46] Refer to Figure 5-30.

Japan's equivalent by 2,926 people/km.[2]

Based on the above two sets of data—the DID population density of China is nearly 3,000 people/km[2] higher than Japan, but the DID population ratio of China is 4% lower than Japan—it is concluded that the "partial over-density" caused by the excessive DID population density is commonplace in Chinese cities. So are issues such as the low DID population ratio and the backward structure of urbanization. It is particularly noteworthy Chinese cities face the issue of low-density development in a considerable proportion of the built-up areas, and this issue is especially serious for cities heavily relying on factory economy. On the other hand, a large number of DIDs are scattered outside the built-up areas. These structural contradictions are the source of many problems such as urban traffic problems, environmental problems, inconvenient living, and underdeveloped services economy in China.

The density of the urban population is related to industries and, in particular, is clearly related to the productivity of the services industry. An over-sparse population is an important reason for the decline of an industry, especially the productivity of the services industry. Over-sparsity is also responsible for the increase of infrastructure and public service cost, financial burden, and energy consumption. At the same time, relative to a city's organizing capacity and infrastructure level, an over-dense population is an important factor in the occurrence of many urban problems.

Emphasis on the negative effects brought by the clustering of a high-density population has dominated the urban policies and public opinions in the developed countries. However, with the improve-ment of urban infrastructure and management, the awareness is gradually growing for the positive effects of urban density in improving productivity, convenience, and diversity. This trend has accelerated the big-city-oriented and megalopolis-oriented urbanization worldwide.

Therefore, China's urban policies need to improve urban organizing capacity and infrastructure level to maximize the positive effects of urban density in improving productivity, conve-nience, and diversity. It is also necessary to give relief to cities with partially over-dense populations and to seek the alignment between population density and urban management and infrastructure. Attention is thus required in the next step of China's urbanization for the improvement of a city's cohesiveness, vitality, and charm by raising the overall density and relieving partial over-density of the city.

China's large-scale migration of population still continues. The next few decades will not only see an ongoing influx of the rural labor force into the city, but further accelerated population migration between cities, as well. The megalopolis will still be the largest urban space for accepting the influx of population. The agglomeration effect is the source of power behind the development of megalopolis—to meet the big chal-lenge of building a high-density urban society, China's megalopolises need to promote the positive effects and prevent the negative effects of agglomeration through improving the level of urban construction and management.

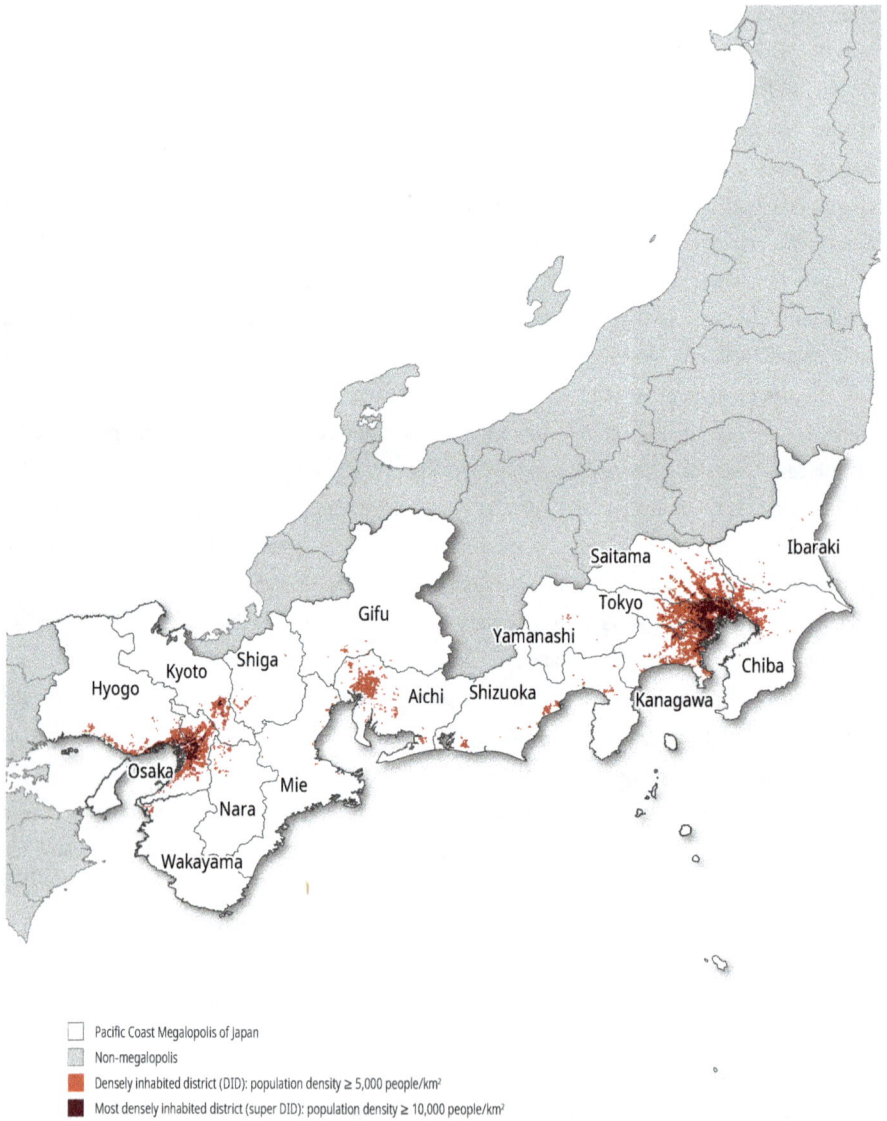

Legend:
- Pacific Coast Megalopolis of Japan
- Non-megalopolis
- Densely inhabited district (DID): population density ≥ 5,000 people/km²
- Most densely inhabited district (super DID): population density ≥ 10,000 people/km²

Figure 5-15 Analysis Diagram of DIDs in the Japan Pacific Coast Megalopolis

Source: It is prepared as per the satellite remote sensing and analysis data published by the Cloud River Urban Research Institute.

(3) Development of the Knowledge Economy

The development of China's megalopolises is a product of the dramatic changes of world pattern and, to be precise, a product of China's alignment with the requirements of the re-integration of global manufacturing under the trend of information revolution. However, just after achieving a tremendous power of industrial production, China is now facing the continuous global depreciation of industrial products and the soaring value of knowledge products, as well as the challenge that the distribution criteria of global wealth is transitioning from the industry economy to knowledge economy.

1) Depreciation of Industrial Products

The division of work across the global supply chain is based on the division of interests among all the segments. Although advantages for international competition have been achieved in such segments as assembly by using cheap labor, the interests obtainable from the supply chain are still limited for China. Most of the profits are carved up by overseas enterprises engaged in the segments of research and development, core components and parts production, software development, brand management, logistics, and sales, among others.

Due to such a division of interests in the global supply chain and China's current role in the supply chain, the country still has a long way to go to become an economic power in spite of her rapid economic growth over the past 30 years.

The depreciation of industrial products is the result of the information revolution that changes the wealth distribution mechanism. Industrial productivity has been the underlying mechanism of global wealth since the industrial revolution, and thus compared to industrial products, the terms of trade for primary products have been deteriorating. By establishing an international trading system advantageous to indus-trial products, the industrialized countries have captured enormous wealth from the rest of the world after the industrial revolution.

However, the global expansion of the supply chain has allowed industrialization to rapidly progress in the developing countries, especially those in East Asia. The production and exports of industrial products are no longer a privilege of the developed countries. The extensive participation of the developing countries in industrial production, headed by China, has lowered the value of industrial products and dramatically worsened their terms of trade but, at the same time, drastically improved the terms of trade for knowledge products including intellectual property, copyrights, patents, brands and trademarks, and business models. The creativity of knowledge has replaced industrial productivity as the underlying criteria for the creation and distribution of global wealth.

2) Increasingly Aggressive Agglomeration and Concentration

The global supply chain has caused profound changes of industrial structure in developed countries. Industrial companies are now more focused on technology development, brand management, and the production of software as well as core components and parts. Services such as finance, transportation, communication, wholesale, and retail have grown into the leading industries supporting economic development. Film and television, publishing, and other copyright businesses, that symbolize the knowledge economy are enjoying increased popularity. The services economy and the knowledge economy have become the mainstays of urban economies in the developed countries.

Industrial economy comes with a strong agglomeration effect. Such effect causes the industrial economy to be highly concentrated in specific regions of a particular country. Such a characteristic is not only responsible for the unbalanced regional development in all modern countries, but also the North-South issues between the developing and developed countries.

The agglomeration of the industrial economy has caused industries and population to be concentrated in cities, especially big cities. The agglomeration effect of big cities has not only greatly improved the productivity of modern society, but also provided people with a colorful urban living environment. Nevertheless, people living in cities have also paid a huge price for air pollution, small living space, traffic congestion, and long-distance commuting, to name but a few. Therefore, modern people, in their pursuit of high economic efficiency and the richness of urban life, also yearn for an idyllic lifestyle.

Upon the arrival of the information revolution in the 1980s, many futurists, such as Alvin Toffler (author of *The Third Wave*), predicted that the use of information technology would allow people to enjoy an idyllic lifestyle while conducting economic activities at high efficiency, with the result that the economic role of cities would be greatly reduced. Upset with big city problems and unbalanced development, the people then placed great expectations on such propositions.

The reality tells us an opposite story, however. We have seen the role of big cities, instead of being weakened, ever strengthening in our information society. Compared with the industrial economy, the knowledge economy has magnified the power for the agglomeration of population and industries in big cities, as illustrated by the evolution of urban development in Japan. The era of the industrial economy has found the concentration of industries of Japan in four metropolitan areas, namely, Tokyo, Osaka, Nagoya, and Kitakyushu. When transitioning to the knowledge economy, however, Japan was unable to decentralize her population and industries, but rather experienced a unipolar centralization towards the Greater Tokyo Metropolitan Area. Such a unipolar centralization is the result of the knowledge economy, which is strongly oriented towards urban areas. It can be said that the era of the industrial economy required Japan to have four metropolitan areas as the economic hubs for her industries, but after stepping into the knowledge economy, the Greater Tokyo Metropolitan Area has been the only one qualified thus far to be an international hub for the agglomeration of the knowledge economy. The case of Japan shows that the information revolution, rather than reducing the role of big cities, has made them ever more important.

3) Benefits of Access Economy

The orientation of the knowledge economy towards big cities comes from the nature of this economy.

Underlying the knowledge economy are humans themselves as the carriers of information. Knowledge economy essentially works in the way that people make judgments about information and produce knowledge through communications. In this sense, the efficiency of information exchange and creation determines the productivity of the knowledge economy.

There are two types of information held by people—one is the information that can be digitized, formalized, and turned into texts, and the other is the information that cannot be digitized, formalized, turned into texts, or arbitrarily disclosed—the latter is more important than the former. In this sense, information exchange solely relying on information technology is just part of the story, as the information held by people includes both the externally transmissible one (through information technology) and the intransmissible one. The externally transmissible information can travel around the earth at 300,000 kilometers per second, prompting people to engage with each other and exchange information that cannot be separated from people. The development of information technology does not reduce but rather increases the contacts and communications between people.

Similar to the fact that the "effect of economies of scale" determines the benefits of industrial economy, the "effect of access economy"[47] determines the benefits of the knowledge economy. Specifically, the efficiency of contacts and communications between people is the determinant for the productivity of the knowledge economy.

The diversity, convenience, and innovation of access are crucial to the productivity of knowledge economy. Difference in knowledge backgrounds is extremely important to the knowledge economy as compared to the information homogeneity that is valued by the industrial economy. Communications between people with different intellectual and cultural background are more valuable than that between people with the same background of information.

The diversity of information carriers as well as the convenience and innovation of their access determine the productivity of the knowledge economy. The knowledge economy is the real exchange-based economy, while megalopolises are the best platform to provide the knowledge economy the space for communications. Megalopolises will play an ever-growing role in an information society and further aggregate more economy and population.

4) Three Megalopolises as Leaders of the Knowledge Economy in China

In 2012, China outnumbered the U.S. in terms of invention and patent applications and ranked first in the

---

[47] For a theoretical explanation of the economic effect of access in knowledge economy, please refer to Chapter 6 of *The Chinese Economy: Mechanism of its Rapid Growth* by Zhou Muzhi (People's Publishing House, 2008).

world for the first time. As the origin of the greatest number of patent applications today, China sources 58.5% of her patents granted from the three megalopolises, with the Pearl River Delta Metropolis, the Yangtze River Delta Megalopolis, and the Beijing-Tianjin-Hebei Metropolis respectively accounting for 13.3%, 35.1%, and 10.1% of the national total. A very clear type of megalopolis-oriented knowledge economy can also be found in China. With 51.7% of the country's scientific researchers, the three megalopolises are leaders of China's knowledge economy, and worthy of the name.

The best way to improve access to knowledge economy is to bring people with various intellectual and cultural background into the same space for convenient and swift interactions as well as knowledge innovation. With a large population and a strong platform for interaction with the rest of the world, a megalopolis is exactly an ideal space to realize the diversified, novel, and convenient access to knowledge. To this end, a megalopolis, as a platform for an exchange-based economy in the era of the knowledge economy, should be inclusive enough to embrace people from all over the country and even around the world. Therefore, a megalopolis requires not only the development of physical functions supporting the exchange-based economy and trading economy, but also the inclusivity and diversity to accommodate people from all over the country and around the world.

Given the depreciation of industrial products and the appreciation of knowledge products, China needs her megalopolises to undertake the great task of developing the knowledge economy. The issue of how to realize the evolution of megalopolises, which began with the factory economy,[48] into spaces for the knowledge economy does not only concerns the development of these megalopolises themselves, but also decides the future of China. In the 21st century, China's megalopolises must go beyond the world factory and become a great platform for knowledge creation.

(4) Highly Advanced Services Economy

In the developed countries, the services economy has replaced the industrial economy as the mainstay of the urban economy, and such a change is taking place in China as well.

As the world factory, China has excess capacity in many fields such as iron and steel, automobiles, and electronics. At the same time, however, there is a serious supply shortage in higher education, medical care, elderly care, culture, entertainment, and other service sectors.

The services economy is not only the key to improving and enriching the life of urban residents, but it is also an important contributor to improving the efficiency of the industrial economy.

Therefore, the development of the services economy has become a crucial factor to China's economic transformation and development. As the national leaders of services economy, the three

---

[48] The so-called factory economy refers to an industrial structure in which the functions of the factory are excessively relied upon, but there is a lack of the functions of headquarters, R&D, brand management, sales and after-sales services.

megalopolises need to densify urban spaces, loosen control, improve openness, and make great efforts for the development of the services economy.

(5) Challenges from the Eco-environment

Rapid industrialization and urbanization have brought China a profound environmental crisis. Pollution (of air, water quality and soil), the loss of biodiversity, garbage siege, and severe water shortage, which were brought by industry, daily living, and travel, have caused serious damages to the ecological environment of cities and their surrounding areas. As the leaders of industrialization and urbanization, three major megalopolises are facing particularly acute issues of ecological environment.

Based on the definition of per capita water resources by the United Nations,[49] the analysis in the *China Integrated City Index 2017* shows today 99 cities in China have been under extreme shortage of water, and 49 are under serious shortage of water. Specifically, eight out of the 10 cities in the Beijing-Tianjin-Hebei Megalopolis have been under extreme water shortage, and one city is under serious water shortage; one out of the 26 cities in the Yangtze River Delta Megalopolis has been under extreme water shortage, and 10 face serious water shortage; three out of the nine cities in the Pearl River Delta Megalopolis have also been under extreme water shortage , and three have serious water shortage.[50] It is apparent that water resources have been a major constraint upon the development of China's megalopolises. More seriously, the severe water pollution caused by industrialization and urbanization has made this issue even worse.

Air pollution is also a serious problem besetting Chinese cities today. Taking $PM_{2.5}$ as an example, *China Integrated City Index 2017* conducted an analysis for the deviations from the average value of the annual dynamic data of $PM_{2.5}$ in 297 cities across China, and the results show: for the 10 cities in the Beijing-Tianjin-Hebei Megalopolis, the average deviation value has been 61.1, wherein Beijing's deviation value has been 64.9, much higher than the national average (50.0), indicating far worse air quality in this region than the national average; for the 26 cities in the Yangtze River Delta Megalopolis, the average deviation value has been 50.7, almost equal to the national average; and for the nine cities in the Pearl River Delta Megalopolis, the average deviation value has been 41.2, much better than the national average.[51]

Based on the above analyses, it is apparent that the issue of water resources is extremely serious in the Beijing-Tianjin-Hebei Megalopolis, with air pollution being far worse than the Yangtze River Delta Megalopolis or the Pearl River Delta Megalopolis. Besides the climatic and geographical factors, it is also evidence that the quality of industrialization and urbanization in the Beijing-Tianjin-Hebei Megalopolis falls behind the other two megalopolises.

---

[49] According to the Unite Nations' definition of water resources, the areas where the annual per capita water resource are less than 500 cubic meters are under extreme shortage; the areas where the annual per capita water resources are less than 1,000 cubic meters and more than 500 cubic meters are under serious water shortage.

[50] Refer to Figure 4-12.

[51] Refer to Figure 4-10.

The first and foremost task in China's urbanization is to find a way for the three megalopolises to take a lead on achieving the low-carbon and water-saving development friendly to the eco-environment.

(6) Development of Inland Urban Agglomerations

Compared with inland areas, the most prominent advantages of the three megalopolises are their geographic locations characterized by deep-water port resources, their functions as hubs for large transactions and large-scale exchanges with the rest of the world, as well as their inclusive and open cultures. Although some city clusters are emerging in inland China, such as the Chengdu-Chongqing, Middle Yangtze River, and Guanzhong Plain Urban Agglomerations, these are not comparable to the three megalopolises in terms of their pattern of exchanges and transactions with the rest of the world.

Nevertheless, the development of urban agglomerations in inland areas is an inevitable trend. Centered on the municipality directly below the Central Government and provincial capitals, inland big cities have been developing very rapidly, showing an increasingly clear trend for economies and populations to be clustered and concentrated towards big cities. With the improvement of the transportation infrastructure, as well as the furtherance of work division and collaboration, a plurality of big, medium-sized, and small cities located in areas with better development conditions are gradually shaping a clustering space in the form of urban agglomeration. Urban agglomerations have become the cores of supporting the development of inland areas.

Being far away from deep-water ports is a hindrance to the economic development of inland areas. Therefore, inland urban agglomerations need to choose industries with less impact in terms of transportation cost as the engine for their economic development.

The inland areas have a smaller environmental capacity than the coastal areas and also have a bigger environmental impact on the downstream rivers. Their environmental issues should be addressed with greater care in the development of cities and industries. In addition, the serious water shortage in the north has made it an unavoidable challenge as to how to build up the water-saving models of economic development and living.

Thus, sectors of the knowledge economy and services economy appear to be particularly important because they are less sensitive to transportation costs and are environment-friendly. Especially as a development center of the region, an inland urban agglomeration will have an immediate impact on the regional development through functioning as a transportation hub, as well as the center for commerce, finance, education, science and technology, culture, entertainment, and medical care. The inland urban agglomerations should be committed to driving the development of the entire region by way of improving these functions.

In short, social and economic development of inland China depends on the development of big cities and urban agglomerations.

Megalopolises Reshaped by Great Changes

According to the analysis in the *China Integrated City Index 2017*, it can be confirmed that in the national ranking for deviation values under the "business environment" indicator group[52], all the top 10 cities were located in the three megalopolises, except Chongqing ranking 7th and Chengdu ranking 8th. Beijing and Tianjin from the Beijing-Tianjin-Hebei Megalopolis respectively ranked 1st and 6th; Shanghai, Suzhou, Hangzhou and Nanjing from the Yangtze River Delta Megalopolis respectively ranked 2nd, 5th, 9th and 10th; Shenzhen and Guangzhou from the Pearl River Delta Megalopolis respectively ranked 3rd and 4th. These three megalopolises possess clear advantages in their business environment.

According to the analysis in the *China Integrated City Index 2017*, it can be confirmed that in the ranking for deviation values under the "openness" indicator group[53], 13 out of the top 20 cities were located in the three megalopolises: six cities headed by Shanghai as 1st came from the Yangtze River Delta Megalopolis; two cities headed by Beijing as 2nd came from the Beijing-Tianjin-Hebei Megalopolis; and five cities headed by Shenzhen as 3rd came from the Pearl River Delta Megalopolis. These three megalopolises lead the way for China's open economy. According to the analysis in the *China Integrated City Index 2017*, it can also be confirmed that in the ranking for deviation values under the "exchange" indicator group,[54] 10 out of the top 20 cities were located in the three megalopolises: five cities headed by Shanghai as 1st came from the Yangtze River Delta Megalopolis; two cities headed by Beijing as 2nd came from the Beijing-Tianjin-Hebei Megalopolis; and three cities headed by Shenzhen as 3rd, came from the Pearl River Delta Megalopolis. These three megalopolises lead the way for China's exchange-based economy.

Facing the challenges of economic slowdown, severe environmental problems, and excess capacity in traditional industries, China today is once again standing at a historic moment of change, just like standing at the crossroad of reform and opening up more than 30 years ago. The megalopolises, as the flag-bearers of China's reform and opening-up, should take on the great tasks of changing social mechanisms, building up a power-house for knowledge economy, and leading the transformation and upgrading of China's economy.

---

[52] The indicator group of business environment consists of data such as average wage, number of employees in the service industry, high-star-level hotel index, number of unemployed people registered per 10,000 persons, and ratio of tax revenue to fiscal revenue.

[53] The indicator group of openness consists of data such as population migration index, exports of goods, imports of goods, amount of actual foreign capital used, proportion of foreign-funded industrial enterprises and number of consulates and embassies.

[54] The indicator group of exchange consists of data such as the number of inbound tourists, number of domestic tourists, number of international conferences, exhibition industry development index and tourism city index.

To do so, megalopolises need to cultivate, care, and induce the social vitality, they need to enhance the endogenous mechanism of development, they need to build up the engine for knowledge economy, they need to improve the quality of urban life, and they also need to construct an open urban space full of intellectuality and charm.

The megalopolises are essential to reshaping China's society and economy in the midst of great changes.

2. The Pearl River Delta Megalopolis

The Pearl River Delta area consists of a part of the Guangdong Province and the two special administrative regions, Hong Kong and Macao. In the early days when China implementing her policy for reform and opening-up, Hong Kong and Macao were still under the rule of the United Kingdom and Portugal, respec-tively. In 1997 and 1999, Hong Kong and Macao were returned to China consecutively as special adminis-trative regions. The Pearl River Delta Megalopolis should include Hong Kong and Macao, but due to data restrictions, this report refers to the definition for the relevant planning given by the National Development and Reform Commission (NDRC) and mainly includes Guangzhou, Shenzhen, Zhuhai, Foshan, Jiangmen, Zhaoqing, Huizhou, Dongguan and Zhongshan as the members of the Pearl River Delta Megalopolis for analysis.

Experimental Zones under the Reform and Opening-up Policy

In 1980, Shenzhen, Zhuhai, and Shantou of the Guangdong Province and four cities of the Fujian Province including Xiamen were designated as the "special economic zones," which marked the opening of China to the outside world.

It is the roll-out of the global supply chain that has ignited the economic development of Guangdong. In the early 1980s, Guangdong Province took the lead in the country by launching a processing trade policy that rewarded the use of imported raw materials and parts for processing and export. A large number of overseas companies were attracted by such preferential policies to invest and set up factories in Guangdong. At that time, the business model of the global supply chain that was implemented in the developing countries had matured in South Korea, Taiwan, Singapore, and Hong Kong, collectively known as the "Four Asian Tigers," after their transformation towards NIEs.[1] As the labor cost rose in the Four Tigers, the opening of Guangdong, which is adjacent to Hong Kong, provided a new space for the global supply chain. By 1993, more than 80% of Hong Kong's manufacturing companies had shifted their production to South China, predominately to Guangdong Province, and built more than 30,000 factories in this region. Three million mainland Chinese employees were then working in these Hong Kong-funded enterprises, almost five times the labor force in the manufacturing industry of Hong Kong. By accepting the large-scale transfer of Hong Kong's manufacturing industry, Guangdong laid a solid industrial foundation for her great development later on.

Hong Kong's well-established position as a financial, trading, and shipping center has also played an

---

[1] The OECD published a report in 1979 entitled *The Impact of Newly Industrializing Countries on Production and Trade in Manufactures*, which named Brazil, Mexico, Spain, Portugal, Greece, Yugoslavia, South Korea, Taiwan China, Hong Kong China and Singapore as Newly Industrializing Countries (NICs). However, in the 1980s, only the NICs in Asia, such as South Korea, Taiwan China, Singapore and Hong Kong China continued to grow economically, and those in Latin America and Europe fell into economic stagnation. Therefore, in the 1988 Toronto Summit, the Asian NICs were renamed as Newly Industrial-izing Economies (NIEs).

important role in the industrial development of Guangdong. In return, Guangdong's economic develop-ment has also brought Hong Kong the businesses from Mainland China and tremendous opportunities for development. Thanks to the high demand of the people and goods flows from the Mainland, the airport and port of Hong Kong have both become one of the most important hubs in Asia. Hong Kong's financial market has also benefited from the large number of listed Chinese companies and thus shown exuberant vitality.

Guangdong, which started off processing trade in clothing, electronics, and toys, has grown into one of the world's biggest agglomerated industrial complexes that cover substantially all the industrial sectors, such as electronics, machinery, automobile, iron and steel, petroleum and chemical, after more than 30 years of development.

The rapid growth of local enterprises in Guangdong has been particularly noteworthy. Represented by Huawei, ZTE, TCL, Gree, and Midea, a large number of local enterprises have grown into powerful, internationally renowned companies.

Large Number of Migrants

Guangdong, which first implemented the reform and opening-up policy, attracted tens of millions of people from all over the country to seek opportunities. The vitality that had been long constrained by the planned economy was erupting across the country in the form of pursuing dreams in Guangdong, and thus triggered an unprecedented migration.

As a steady source of cheap labor, migrant workers enabled Guangdong to satisfy the rapidly increasing demand for labor in the process of industrialization. A large number of professionals, as goes the then catch-phrase "Peacocks Flying to the Southeast," relocated from inland areas to Guangdong for opportunities.

According to the analysis in the *China Integrated City Index 2017*, six out of the nine cities in the Pearl River Delta Megalopolis, namely, Shenzhen, Dongguan, Guangzhou, Foshan, Zhongshan, and Huizhou, have respectively received 7.829 million, 6.304 million, 4.959 million. 3.541 million, 1.623 million, and 1.185 million permanent residents without household registration. Migrant intakes by Jiangmen and Zhuhai have been relatively small—605,000 and 510,000, respectively. Zhaoqing has been the only city with a net outflow of population amounting to 323,000. Until now, a total number of 26,232,000 permanent residents without household registration have been received by the Pearl River Delta Megalopolis—the region with the largest number of migrant workers in China.[2]

---

[2] Refer to Figure 4-3 and 4-4.

The sizable agglomeration of industries and population in the Pearl River Delta region has shaped a chain of densely populated urban areas, that is, the Pearl River Delta Megalopolis.

The formation of new industrial agglomerations requires abundant human resources. The Pearl River Delta Megalopolis has attracted a large number of migrant talents and labor by providing an inclusive environment and thus overcome the constraints of human resource reserve as well as achieved the rapid development of both its society and economy.

Infrastructure Development

The agglomeration of industries in the global supply chain requires not only an open system, but also a connection of the infrastructure network to the rest of the world.

First and foremost, the global supply chain requires a large port with enough capacity to support its significant trade volume. Blessed with a long deep-water shoreline, the Pearl River Delta Megalopolis comes with particularly favorable natural conditions in this regard. In addition, at the time when Guangdong first introduced her processing trade policy, Hong Kong had become one of the few modern ports in the world and its well-developed maritime transport industry guaranteed the rapid development of global supply chain in Guangdong.

As beneficiaries of the volume maritime transport resulting from the global supply chain, Shenzhen Port and Guangzhou Port have both made a leap to the world's third and eighth largest container ports.

According to the analysis in the *China Integrated City Index 2017*, Shenzhen ranked 2nd nationwide in terms of the convenience of container port. In addition, another eight cities from the Pearl River Delta Megalopolis ranked among the top 30 in terms of such convenience. This megalopolis, which has accounted for 25.7% of the national container port throughput, becomes the most convenient region for maritime transport in China.[3]

The roll-out of the global supply chain in the Pearl River Delta has been promoting the personnel exchanges and the air transport of goods across regions and borders. Today, an aviation system has been formed in this region to include the Hong Kong International Airport, Macau International Airport, Guangzhou Baiyun International Airport, Shenzhen Bao'an International Airport, Zhuhai Jinwan International Airport, Huizhou Pingtan Airport, and Foshan Shadi Airport. The passenger throughput as well as cargo and mail throughput from the airports of this megalopolis contributed 11.2% and 18.4% of the national total, respectively.

According to the analysis in the *China Integrated City Index 2017*, Guangzhou and Shenzhen respectively ranked 3rd and 4rd nationwide in terms of airport convenience. In addition, another four cities from this

---

[3] Refer to Figure 4-7.

megalopolis, Foshan, Zhongshan, Dongguan, and Zhuhai, ranked among the top 30 in terms of such conve-nience. This megalopolis has become a very convenient region for exchanges with the rest of the world.[4]

A dense network of expressways, high-speed railways, and inland waterways has shaped the Pearl River Delta Megalopolis into a large-scale organism for industrial agglomeration with a high level of division of work.

Substantial investment in the Pearl River Delta Megalopolis for ports, airports, expressways, high-speed railways, waterways, electricity, and other features has greatly improved the level of infrastructure in this region. It is these efforts that guaranteed the efficient operation of the global supply chain.

Characteristics of Spatial Structure

Industrial development has driven the Pearl River Delta Megalopolis to take in a large influx of migrants and aggregate a major urban population. Guangzhou and Shenzhen have become megacities with a perma-nent population of 13.501 million and 11.379 million, respectively. Two big cities, Dongguan and Foshan, follow with 8.254 million and 7.431 million permanent residents. Next are Huizhou, Jiangmen, Zhaoqing and Zhongshan, each with a population between 3 and 4 million. Even Zhuhai accommodates 1.634 million people, the smallest population among all the cities in this region.

The sizable agglomeration of industries and population in the Pearl River Delta Megalopolis has led to the formation of a densely populated area that covers 2,584.2 km² in total, a high-density urbanized region calculated by the DID area. Through a DID analysis, this report finds the following three character-istics of the spatial structure in this megalopolis.

First of all, the Pearl River Delta Megalopolis has the highest urbanization rate of population in China. Compared to her permanent population of 58.743 million, the Pearl River Delta Megalopolis had a DID population of 38.282 million, accounting for 65.2% of the total. In particular, population was more highly concentrated in the urban area of Shenzhen, where the DID population represented 88.7% of the total, ranking No. 1 in China. Also, 74.2% of Guangzhou's population fell under the DID category, slightly lower than Shenzhen. In Dongguan and Zhongshan, the DID population ratios reached 74.7% and 65.4%, respectively; in Zhuhai and Foshan, 64.7% and 63.9%; and in Huizhou and Jiangmen, 46% and 42.3%. The lowest ratio, 30%, has been found in Zhaoqing.

Second, this megalopolis is characterized by her layout of "three large, two medium and three small." The "three large," Shenzhen, Guangzhou, and Dongguan, contained a DID area of 594.4 km², 570.3 km², and 485.9 km², respectively. Foshan had a DID area of 335.1 km², the majority of which has been adjacent

---

[4] Refer to Figure 4-8.

to the DID area of Guangzhou, and is therefore counted as part of the Greater Guangzhou. Jiangmen, Huizhou, Zhongshan, Zhaoqing, and Zhuhai had smaller and scattered DIDs.

The DID of Greater Guangzhou formed by Guangzhou and Foshan had a population of 9.63 million, constituting the largest urban segment of this megalopolis. Shenzhen had a DID population of 9.211 million, second to the Greater Guangzhou area. Dongguan and Foshan had a DID population of 6.308 million and 4.725 million, respectively. Huizhou and Zhongshan, as the "two medium", had a DID population of 2.143 million and 2.106 million, respectively. As the "three small", Jiangmen, Zhuhai and Zhaoqing all had a DID population below 2 million.[5]

Last but not least, the Pearl River Delta Megalopolis also formed "one long and one short" chains of urban areas. "One long" means the dense urban area formed by Guangzhou, Dongguan, Shenzhen, and Hong Kong. "One short" means the shorter chain of urban areas gradually forming from the densely populated area of Greater Guangzhou, which consists of Guangzhou and eastern Foshan, to the north corner of Zhongshan and the northeast corner of Jiangmen.[6]

The spatial structure of "three large, two medium, and three small" has also been confirmed by economic indicators: the size of GDP, volume of export goods, and the total value of regional production of the tertiary industry generated by Guangzhou (plus Foshan), Shenzhen, and Dongguan, the "three large" members, have contributed 78%, 85%, and 82% of the total in the Pearl River Delta Megalopolis, respectively.

Features of Industrial Structure

Powerful industrial agglomeration has been shaped in the Pearl River Delta Megalopolis, which contributed 8% of China's GDP in the secondary industry and even 22.7% of the country's volume of export goods. As a region thriving from the interactions with the global supply chain, this megalopolis has been strongly export-oriented in her industrial development.

In the early days of reform and opening-up, by using Hong Kong as a center for international aviation and shipping, trade, and finance among others, Guangdong managed to grow her factory economy at a high speed—the "store in front, factory in back" model, where Hong Kong and Guangdong respectively functioned as a center and a factory, earned considerable fame among their contemporaries. Today, with her industrial and population agglomeration, the Pearl River Delta Megalopolis has also established a series of centers for international aviation and shipping, trade, finance, technological innovation, culture and sports, and tourism and exhibitions. The type of economy in this megalopolis has

---

[5] "Large", "medium" and "small" are relative terms for descriptive purposes.
[6] Refer to Figure 5-20.

also transformed from a pure factory type to an industrial one that incorporates headquarters, scientific research, and sales.

If analyzing the effects of Pearl River Delta Megalopolis on the following areas with the concept of radiation in the *China Integrated City Index 2017*, we find that: In the wholesale and retail area, Guangzhou and Shenzhen were prominently advantaged by their radiation and ranked 5th and 8th respectively in the country, highlighting both cities as the shopping centers. Compared to the agglomeration of large-volume, high-quality, and content-rich wholesale and retail industry in these two cities, other cities were weak in this respect and failed to make it into the top 30 in the country. In other words, Guangzhou and Shenzhen have served other cities as their shopping centers.[7]

In the area of science and technology, both Shenzhen and Guangzhou had a strong radiation and respectively ranked 3rd and 4th nationwide. The top 30 in the ranking of science and technology radiation also included Dongguan and Zhongshan as 18th and 24th, respectively. With respect to the size of R&D personnel, Shenzhen and Guangzhou ranked 3rd and 4th respectively in the country, and the entire Pearl River Delta Megalopolis accounted for 11% of the national total. These two cities also scored 2nd and 4th respectively in the national ranking of patent applications granted, and the megalopolis accounted for 13.3% of the national total in this respect. By having Shenzhen and Guangzhou as the cores, this region has grown into one of the most important R&D centers[8] in China.

In terms of the radiation of higher education, Guangzhou ranked 6th in the country, standing out in the Pearl River Delta Megalopolis as the only one from this region that qualified for the top 30. Shenzhen and Dongguan came with a negative radiation, which indicated higher education in these emerging cities still fell behind their strong demand for talents. The university students in this megalopolis accounted for 6.1% of the national total, which was a sign of relative weakness in the higher education area[9], compared to the Beijing-Tianjin-Hebei Megalopolis and the Yangtze River Delta Megalopolis.

Shenzhen, whose securities trading market was launched in 1991, has become one of the three major financial centers in the country and ranked 3rd in terms of the financial radiation. Among the top 30 club of this ranking, Guangzhou scored 4th[10] nationwide.

In the area of culture and sports, Guangzhou and Shenzhen respectively ranked 3rd and 6th for their radiation in the national top 30, but still significantly fell behind Beijing and Shanghai. At the same time, Shenzhen as an emerging city still appeared to be weaker than the provincial capital of Guangzhou in this area. In the Pearl River Delta Megalopolis, it is apparent that cultural and sports facilities and

---

[7] Refer to Figure 4-28.

[8] Refer to Figure 4-24.

[9] Refer to Figure 4-23.

[10] Refer to Figure 4-20.

activities have been relatively concentrated in Guangzhou.[11]

As for the medical radiation, Guangzhou and Foshan were the only members of the Pearl River Delta Megalopolis listed among the national top 30, taking the 3rd and 29th places, respectively. Many cities had a negative radiation, which was a sign that the medical services in these emerging cities were not self-sufficient. Compared to the Beijing-Tianjin-Hebei and Yangtze River Delta Megalopolises, the Pearl River Delta is still relatively weak in the medical area, with the number and level of medical institutions and personnel falling behind her economic development.[12]

In the manufacturing area, the Pearl River Delta Megalopolis appeared to be strongly advantaged. All the other seven cities except Jiangmen and Zhaoqing have ranked among the national top 30 for their manufacturing radiation. Shenzhen had the most obvious advantage and ranked first in the country. Dongguan, Foshan, Guangzhou, Huizhou, Zhongshan, and Zhuhai took the 4th, 5th, 7th, 13th, 16th and 20th places,[13] respectively.

In view of the IT radiation, Shenzhen, Guangzhou and Zhuhai were the only members of the Pearl River Delta Megalopolis listed among the national top 30, taking the 3rd, 7th and 21st places,[14] respectively.

In terms of catering and hotel radiation, Guangzhou and Shenzhen from the Pearl River Delta Megalopolis ranked 5th and 6th in the country, respectively. Dongguan and Zhuhai have also become members of the top 30 club, respectively ranking 17th and 25th.[15] Neighboring Hong Kong, Shenzhen has received the largest number of inbound tourists in the country, with Guangzhou at the 2nd place. The Pearl River Delta Megalopolis, which had welcomed 29.1% of the country's inbound tourists, was already one of the largest exhibition centers in the country. This megalopolis has a great potential in developing an exchange-based economy and tourism economy.[16]

In short, although the Pearl River Delta Megalopolis lacks a city like Beijing or Shanghai that is capable of functioning as a national center, Guangzhou and Shenzhen have grown into megacities with a population over 10 million, and these two cities have become the dual core leading the development of this megalopolis. In the areas of manufacturing, export, finance, and R&D, Shenzhen has even outperformed Guangzhou to become the leader of this region. However, as a provincial capital, Guangzhou still maintains strong advantages in such areas as culture, sports, medical services and higher education. The manufacturing industry is developing very fast in other cities. Dongguan, Foshan, Huizhou, Zhuhai, and Zhongshan have also ranked among the national top 30 in terms of cargo exports, respectively at 4th,

---

[11] Refer to Figure 4-26.
[12] Refer to Figure 4-25.
[13] Refer to Figure 4-21.
[14] Refer to Figure 4-22.
[15] Refer to Figure 4-27.
[16] Refer to Figure 4-18.

7th, 16th, 19th and 21st places,[17] respectively. However, these cities have remained relatively weak in the development of the service industry, and thus it is urgent for them to transform and upgrade their factory-based economy into a genuine urban economy by developing their services economy and enriching their urban functions.

Evaluation and Analysis of Megalopolis

Among the three megalopolises, the Pearl River Delta Megalopolis has apparent advantages of "water and soil endowment" and "climate conditions."[18] As one of the most developed industrial areas in the country, this megalopolis has serious environmental problems such as water and soil pollution. However, her air pollution, compared to the poor air quality besetting the Beijing-Tianjin-Hebei Megalopolis, is relatively moderate. Among the 30 cities with the least $PM_{2.5}$ pollution in the country, Zhuhai, Huizhou and Shenzhen ranked 22nd, 24th, and 26th, respectively. For indicator groups including "resource efficiency," "environmental protection efforts," "compact city," "transportation network," and "urban facilities,"[19] this megalopolis also ranked relatively high nationwide. As a result, Shenzhen won the championship in the *China Integrated City Index 2017* under the Environmental Dimension, with Guangzhou ranking 4th; Zhuhai, 7th; Zhongshan, 11th; and Dongguan 15th.[20]

According to the analysis for the deviation values of nine cities in the Pearl River Delta Megalopolis under the Environmental Dimension, Shenzhen stood at the top of the list with obvious advantages, followed by Guangzhou, Zhuhai, Zhongshan, Dongguan and Foshan, which were set apart by small differ-ences and ranked 2nd, 3rd, 4th, 5th and 6th, respectively. Huizhou and Jiangmen fell under the third tier, and Zhaoqing came at the bottom.[21]

Among the top 20 cities in the *China Integrated City Index 2017* under the Social Dimension, Guangzhou and Shenzhen respectively ranked 3rd and 7th.[22]

According to the analysis for the deviation values within this megalopolis under the Social Dimension, we can find that Guangzhou had prominent advantages as the provincial capital, followed by Shenzhen

---

[17] Refer to Figure 4-6.
[18] "Water and soil condition" and "climate condition" are indicator groups under the environmental dimension in the *China Integrated City Index 2017.*
[19] "Resource efficiency", "environmental protection efforts", "compact city", "transportation network" and "urban facilities" are also indicator groups under the environmental dimension in the *China Integrated City Index 2017.*
[20] Refer to Figure 2-6.
[21] Refer to Figure 5-17.
[22] Refer to Figure 2-10.

ranking 2nd. The other cities significantly fell behind the former two. Zhuhai, Foshan, Dongguan and Zhongshan belonged to the second tier, ranking 3rd, 4th, 5th and 6th, respectively. Huizhou and Jiangmen were in the third tier, with Zhaoqing at the bottom.[23]

The Pearl River Delta Megalopolis, which first implemented the reform and opening-up policy in the country and thrived through interactions with the global supply chain, has gained in economic strength. Among the top 20 cities in the *China Integrated City Index 2017* under the Economic Dimension, there were four cities coming from this megalopolis, Shenzhen, Guangzhou, Dongguan and Foshan, ranking 3rd, 4th, 14th and 17th, respectively. This is evidence for the collective strength of this megalopolis under the Economic Dimension.[24]

From the *Index's* analysis for the deviation values within this megalopolis under the Economic Dimension, it can be observed that Shenzhen and Guangzhou had outstanding advantages; Dongguan and Foshan were second-tier cities, ranking 2nd and 3rd, respectively; Zhongshan, Zhuhai and Huizhou were in the third-tier, ranking 5th, 6th, and 7th, respectively; and Jiangmen and Zhaoqing as the second last and the last.[25]

Shenzhen and Guangzhou did very well and took the 3rd and 4th places in the overall ranking of the *China Integrated City Index 2017*, which highlights their strength as the two core cities of the Pearl River Delta Megalopolis. Dongguan, Foshan and Zhuhai were also among the national top 30 and ranked 18th, 21st and 22nd,[26] respectively.

From the comprehensive analysis for the deviation values within this megalopolis, it can be confirmed that Shenzhen and Guangzhou ranked top two with obvious advantages. Ranking from the 3rd to the 8th place were Dongguan, Foshan, Zhuhai, Zhongshan, Huizhou, and Jiangmen, respectively, with Zhaoqing at the bottom.[27]

Challenges in the Next Stage

According to the analysis in the *China Integrated City Index 2017*, the Pearl River Delta Megalopolis, a forerunner in the urbanization of China that has also progressed the furthest, has reached a DID population ratio of 65.2%, the highest in the country. This number was 15.9 percentage points higher than the 49.3% of the Pacific Coast Megalopolis of Japan. It is also noteworthy that the density of DID population in the Pearl River Delta Megalopolis was higher than that in the Pacific Coast Megalopolis

---

[23] Refer to Figure 5-18.
[24] Refer to Figure 2-14.
[25] Refer to Figure 5-19.
[26] Refer to Figure 2-2.
[27] Refer to Figure 5-16.

of Japan by 3,245 persons/km².

The above data shows that from the perspective of spatial structure, the first challenge for the Pearl River Delta Megalopolis lies in the inadequate concentration of its population in the DIDs. There were still 20.46 million people, or 34.8% of the total, living in the non-DID areas. It still has a long way to go towards urbanization.

Second, the density of DID population has relatively exceeded the urban organization capacity and infrastructure level in the Pearl River Delta Megalopolis. This is the second challenge facing the spatial structure of this megalopolis.

The third challenge includes two aspects: on the one hand, a considerable amount of low-density development has taken place in the built-up urban areas of this region, especially in the industrial development zones and new districts; on the other hand, a large number of DIDs were scattered outside the built-up areas, resulting in the problem that these areas fell relatively behind in infrastructure support, public service support and social management.

In sum, the Pearl River Delta Megalopolis urgently needs to further her urbanization and change its land development model based on a factory economy in order to accelerate the evolution from factory to industrial economy and urban economy. To this end, it is necessary to develop the services economy in order to improve the quality of urban life and the efficiency of economic activities. Meanwhile, it is also necessary to enhance the level of urban management and infrastructure to create a high-density, large-scale urban society. As the forerunner in reform and opening-up, as well as urbanization, the Pearl River Delta Megalopolis has the responsibility to pioneer new models and acquire new experience for the success of China's urbanization in the next stage.

Hunan Province

Jiangxi Province

Guangxi
Zhuang
Autonomous
Region

Guangdong Province

Zhaoqing
9th

Guangzhou
2nd

Huizhou
7th

Foshan
4rd

Dongguan
3th

Shenzhen
1st

Zhongshan
6th

Hong Kong

Jiangmen
8th

Zhuhai
5th

Macao

Deviation value
index
214

146

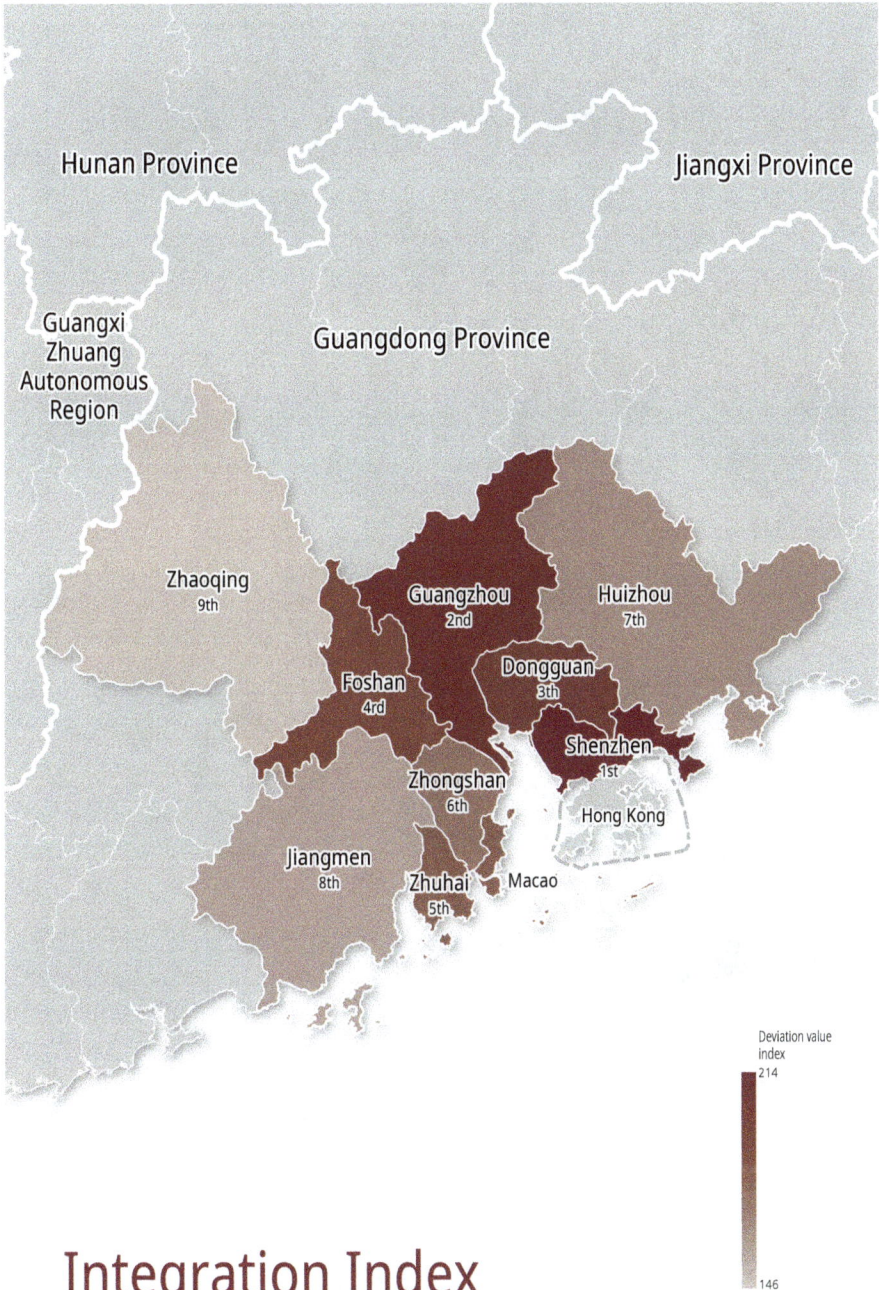

Integration Index

Figure 5-16 Analysis Diagram of Integrated Index of the Pearl River Delta Megalopolis (9 Cities)

Note: Rankings from Figure 5-16 to Figure 5-19 refer to those of 9 cities within the Pearl River Delta Megalopolis.

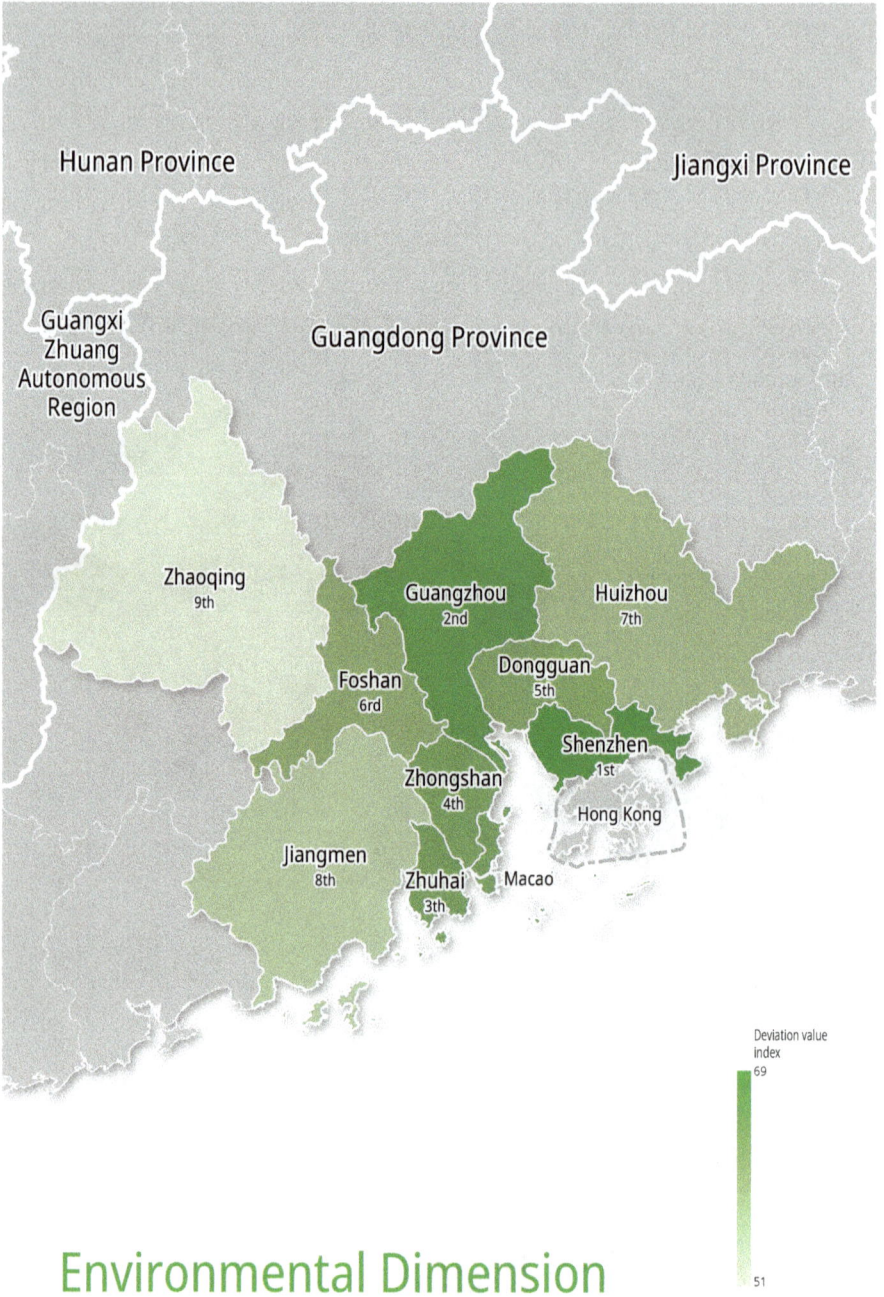

Hunan Province

Jiangxi Province

Guangxi Zhuang Autonomous Region

Guangdong Province

Zhaoqing
9th

Guangzhou
2nd

Huizhou
7th

Foshan
6rd

Dongguan
5th

Shenzhen
1st

Zhongshan
4th

Hong Kong

Jiangmen
8th

Zhuhai
3th

Macao

Deviation value index
69

51

Environmental Dimension

Figure 5-17 Analysis Diagram of Environmental Dimension of the Pearl River Delta Megalopolis (9 Cities)

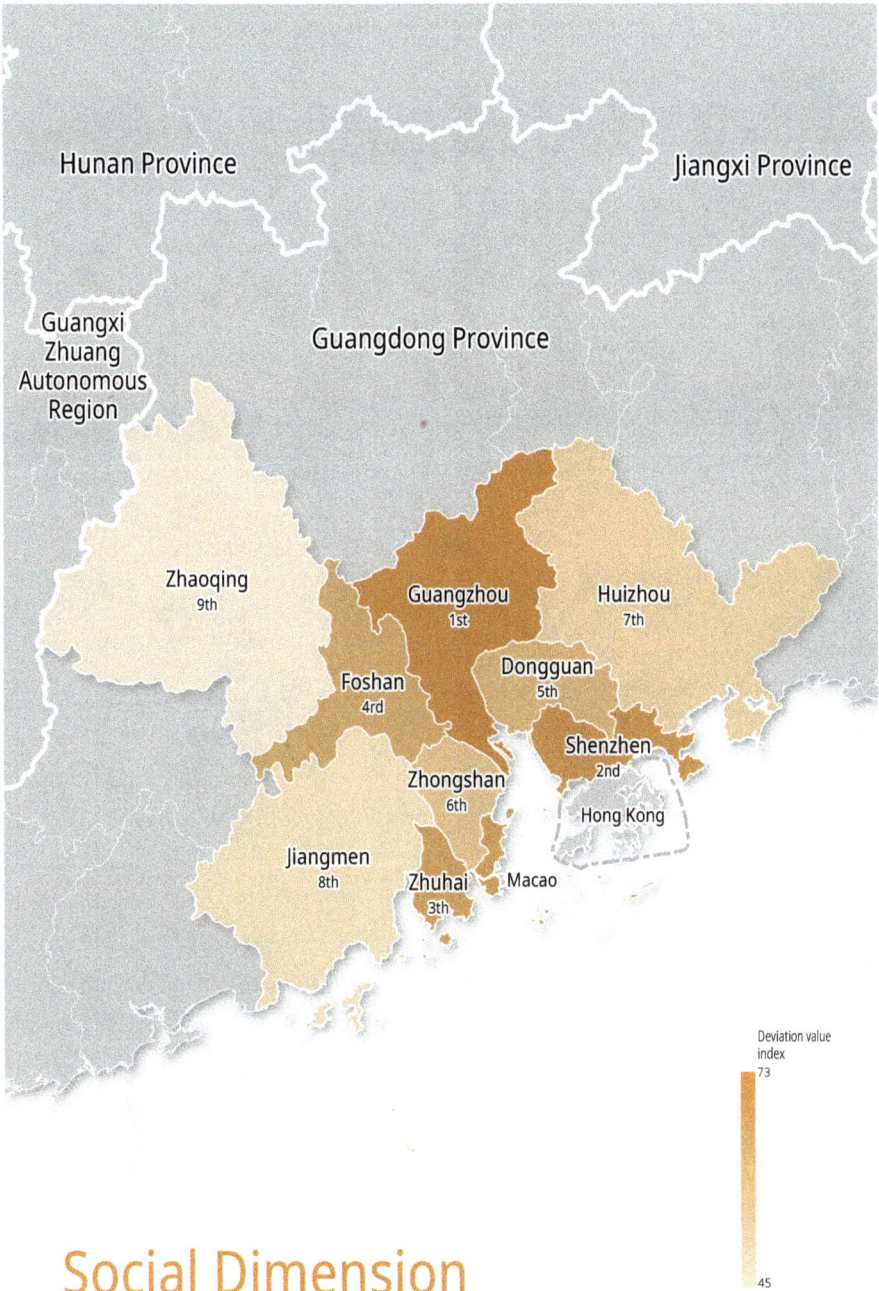

Figure 5-18 Analysis Diagram of Social Dimension of the Pearl River Delta Megalopolis (9 Cities)

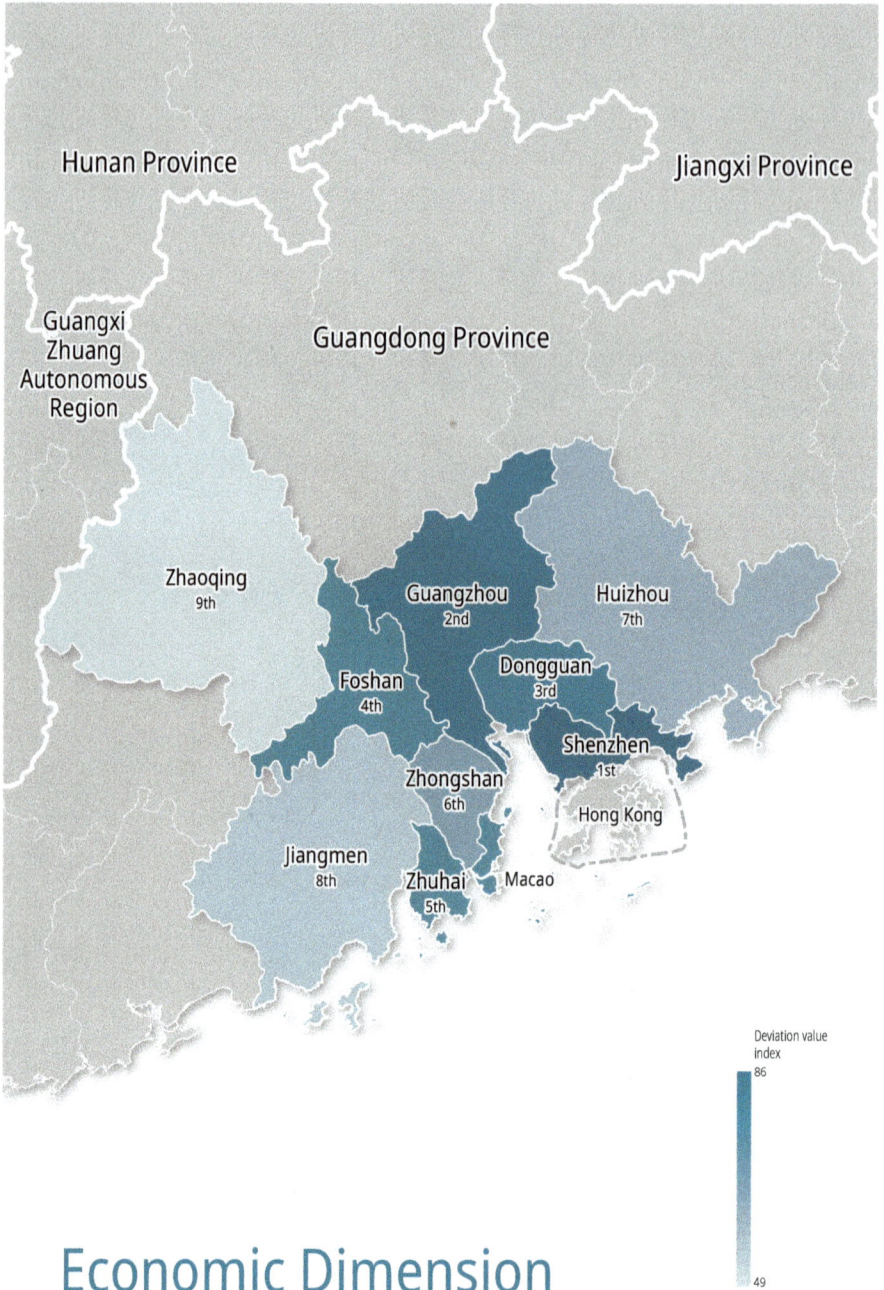

Hunan Province

Jiangxi Province

Guangxi Zhuang Autonomous Region

Guangdong Province

Zhaoqing
9th

Guangzhou
2nd

Huizhou
7th

Foshan
4th

Dongguan
3rd

Zhongshan
6th

Shenzhen
1st

Hong Kong

Jiangmen
8th

Zhuhai
5th

Macao

Deviation value index
86

49

Economic Dimension

Figure 5-19 Analysis Diagram of Economic Dimension of the Pearl River Delta Megalopolis (9 Cities)

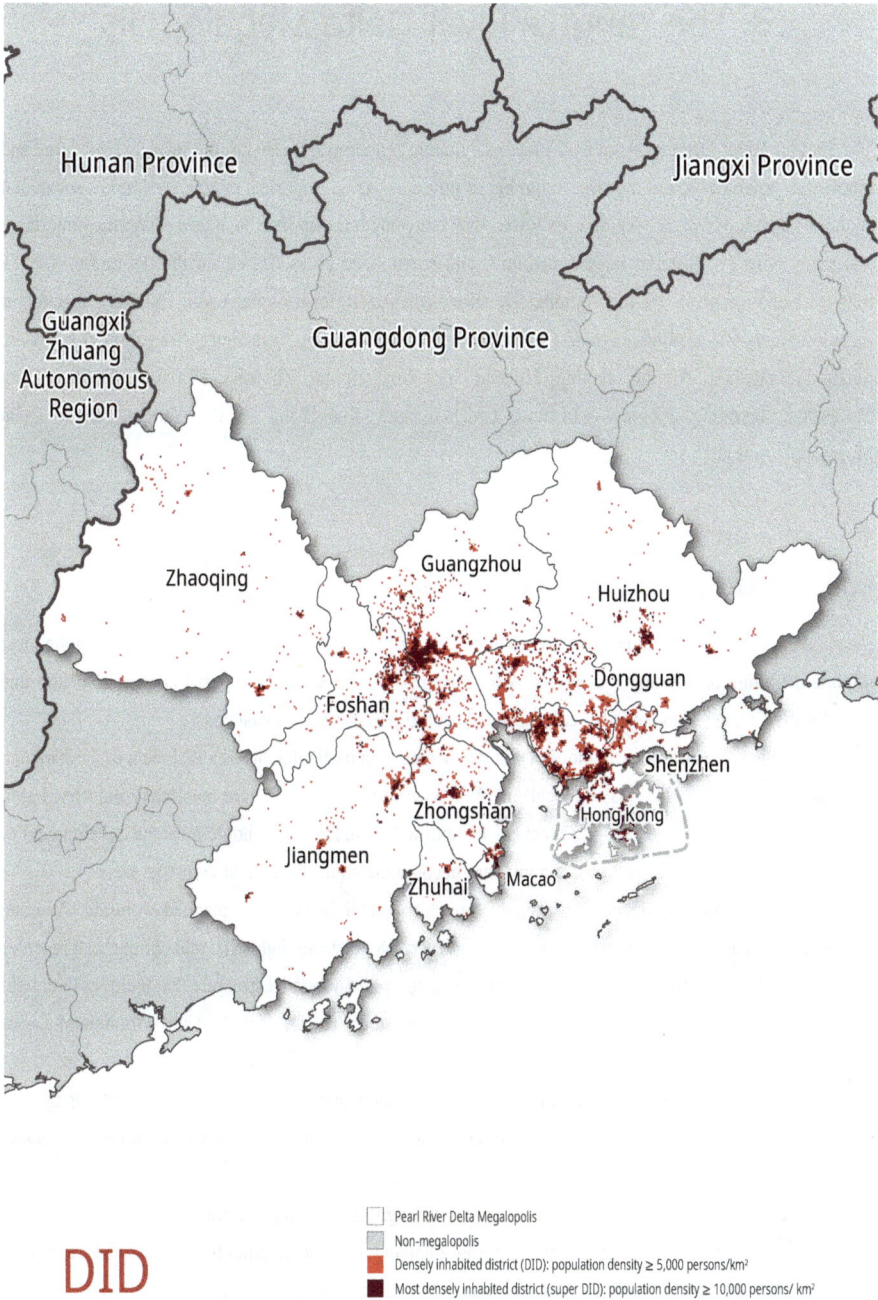

Hunan Province

Jiangxi Province

Guangxi
Zhuang
Autonomous
Region

Guangdong Province

Zhaoqing

Guangzhou

Huizhou

Foshan

Dongguan

Shenzhen

Zhongshan

Hong Kong

Jiangmen

Zhuhai

Macao

DID

☐ Pearl River Delta Megalopolis
◻ Non-megalopolis
■ Densely inhabited district (DID): population density ≥ 5,000 persons/km²
■ Most densely inhabited district (super DID): population density ≥ 10,000 persons/ km²

Figure 5-20 Analysis Diagram of DIDs in the Pearl River Delta Megalopolis

Source: It is prepared as per the satellite remote sensing and analysis data published by the Cloud River Urban Research Institute.

3. The Yangtze River Delta Megalopolis

The Yangtze River Delta is one of China's most dynamic economies. It also has the strongest industrial and innovative capabilities, and the largest number of migrants. As an important engine for China's social and economic development, the region is endowed with convenient transportation, a vast economic hinterland, and many densely clustered large-, medium-, and small-sized cities. Based on the definitions for the relevant planning given by the National Development and Reform Commission (NDRC), this report includes Shanghai, Nanjing, Wuxi, Changzhou, Suzhou, Nantong, Yancheng, Yangzhou, Zhenjiang, Taizhou, Hangzhou, Ningbo, Jiaxing, Huzhou, Shaoxing, Jinhua, Zhoushan, Taizhou, Hefei, Wuhu, Ma'anshan, Tongling, Anqing, Chuzhou, Chizhou, and Xuancheng in the Yangtze River Delta Megalopolis for analysis.

Pudong's Development Initiating Great Growth

Since its opening as a port due to the First Opium War in 1843, Shanghai has grown to become the most important trading and financial center of Asia. Shanghai is also China's largest transportation hub due to its location on the Yangtze River estuary in the central part of China's east coast.

Shanghai is the birthplace of modern industry in China. In particular, the establishment of the Jiangnan Manufacturing Bureau (Jiangnan Arsenal) in 1865 ushered in China's modern machinery industry. Later, in 1890, the creation of the Shanghai Mechanical Textile Bureau lay the foundation for the development of China's textile industry. Since then, Shanghai has become the country's largest industrial base.

After the founding of the People's Republic of China, under the system of planned economy, Shanghai lost its function as a trade and financial center. However, due to strong industrial and commercial reserves and its prime location, Shanghai was able to build up a complete industrial structure that includes both light industry and heavy industry, and has therefore been consistently the top industrial and commercial city of China.

Nonetheless, in the 1980s, compared with Guangdong that achieved rapid development by first implementing the reform and opening-up policy, Shanghai's economy, which was dominated by state-owned enterprises, stagnated.

While state-owned enterprises were struggling through the hardships of the 1980s, township and village enterprises emerged, which, in Jiangsu and Zhejiang Provinces, quickly accumulated capital by utilizing talent, equipment, technologies, and brands from state-owned enterprises in Shanghai.

The resources of Shanghai and the vitality of Jiangsu and Zhejiang have contributed to the rapid rise of township and village enterprises, laying a solid industrial foundation for the Yangtze River Delta, as well as fostering a strong entrepreneurial spirit. This has provided the underpinning of the region's rapid development.

The year 1990 saw the launch of the Shanghai Pudong New District by the Chinese government, ushering in a historic period of major development for the region.

Taking the development of Pudong as an opportunity, Shanghai was able to reverse the downturn and was permitted to implement an aggressive investment invitation policy, while the central government reformed state-owned enterprises. Private enterprises also grew and became a dynamic force driving Shanghai to move forward.

During the 1980s to 1990s, when township and village enterprises were flourishing, small towns played the main role in the urbanization of the Yangtze River Delta due to the state's control over the development of cities. A large number of fast-growing small towns emerged around the stagnant larger cities. Such a phenomenon of small towns surrounding large and medium-sized cities caught worldwide attention and became known as the "Southern Jiangsu Model."

Pudong's development not only provided great opportunities to Shanghai, but also to the entire Yangtze River Delta region. The government expected that the development of Pudong New District would promote the economic development of the entire region by invigorating the Shanghai economy and transforming it into a financial and trading center. In 1992, the government launched a policy for developing cities across the region and positioned Shanghai as "the flagship to realize the coordinated development of the Yangtze River region." It also invested in a broad range of infrastructure including ports, airports, and expressways to turn Shanghai into a national financial and shipping center.

As a result of Pudong's development, governments at all levels across the Yangtze River Delta raced to set up development zones, launched various preferential policies, and took the initiative to promote investment. What is more important, since the late 1990s, the state has gradually relaxed its control over large and medium-sized cities, resulting in a rapid expansion of urban construction, and the rapid agglomeration of industries and population.

The Yangtze River Delta has grown into the largest agglomerated industrial complex in the world covering all major industrial sectors: electronics, machinery, automobiles, iron and steel, petroleum, and chemicals. The rapid development of these industries has driven the growth of cities in the region. The cities, each with their own characteristics, have constituted a system where work is highly divided, by way of a high-density transportation network, thereby forming a large-scale clustered urban space: a megalopolis. The Yangtze River Delta Megalopolis, comprised of 26 cities, has today grown into a major engine for China's economic development.

Large Number of Migrants

Following the 1990s, large numbers of migrants began to flood into the Yangtze River Delta region. At the same time, large-scale population migration has also taken place from rural to urban areas and from local cities to large cities within the region.

According to the *China Integrated City Index 2017*, Shanghai has the largest migrant population in China with 9.723 million permanent residents without household registration. Many other cities in the region have large numbers of permanent residents without household registrations: Suzhou, 3.946 million; Ningbo, 1.959 million; Hangzhou, 1.783 million; Wuxi, 1.702 million; Nanjing, 1.702 million; Jiaxing, 1.09 million; Changzhou, 993,000; and Tonglong, 854,000. The migrant populations for Jinhua, Hefei, Shaoxing, Zhenjiang, Huzhou, and Zhoushan were between 670,000 and 170,000, and for Taizhou was 74,000. Net population outflows took place in Ma'anshan, Yangzhou, Chizhou, Wuhu, Xuancheng, Nantong, Taizhou, Chuzhou, Yancheng, and Anqing. The number of outflows in Yancheng and Anqing exceeded one million.[1]

The sizable agglomeration of industries and population in the Yangtze River Delta has formed a chain of densely populated urban areas. The megalopolis now has a total of 21.9 million permanent residents without household registration, second only to the Pearl River Delta Megalopolis.

The Yangtze River Delta Megalopolis has realized the rapid development of its society and economy by providing a space for the incubation of domestic and foreign enterprises, allowing talent to flourish and embracing the energy of the new era.

Extensive Infrastructure Construction

In 2004, Shanghai was designated as the international shipping center of China. In 2016, the Shanghai Port had developed into the largest container port of the world. According to the *China Integrated City Index 2017*, the Ningbo-Zhoushan Port ranked as the 3rd largest container port in China and fourth largest in the world. Suzhou Port and Nanjing Port respectively came in 10th and 15th in the national container throughput ranking; and Shanghai possessed the nation's most convenient container port. In addition, 12 cities in the Yangtze River Delta Megalopolis ranking among the national top 30 in terms of convenience. The megalopolis, accounting for 35.3% of the national container port throughput, is the largest shipping center in China[2].

Designed as East Asia's aviation hub, Shanghai Pudong International Airport now serves the

---

[1] Refer to Figure 4-3 and 4-4.

[2] Refer to Figure 4-7.

second highest number of passengers in China. In addition, another three international airports in the Yangtze River Delta Megalopolis, namely Shanghai Hongqiao, Hangzhou Xiaoshan, and Nanjing Lukou, are in the top 30 for passenger traffic. Other airports in the region include: Ningbo Lishe International Airport, Hefei Xinqiao International Airport, Sunan Shuofang International Airport, Changzhou Benniu International Airport, Yangzhou Taizhou International Airport, Jinhua Yiwu Airport, Nantong Xingdong Airport, Yancheng Nanyang Airport, Zhoushan Putuoshan Airport, Taizhou Luqiao Airport, Chizhou Jiuhuashan Airport, and Anqing Tianzhushan Airport. Altogether, the region now benefits from a huge aviation system formed of 16 airports.

According to the *China Integrated City Index 2017*, Shanghai ranked 1st in the national airport convenience ranking. The Yangtze River Delta Megalopolis accounted for 19.3% of national airport passenger traffic and 33.8% of the national airport cargo and mail traffic, making it the largest air transport center of China.[3]

Large airports and ports have enhanced the business environment for exchanges and transactions between the Yangtze River Delta Megalopolis and the rest of the world. The megalopolis is also connected by a densely-distributed network of expressways, high-speed railways, and inland waterways. When combined, this infrastructure enables a huge organic industrial agglomeration with a high level of division of work. Large-scale infrastructure investment has laid a good foundation for the social and economic development of this megalopolis.

Characteristics of Spatial Structure

Having gone through the development of township and village enterprises and small towns in the 1980s, and the large-scale industrialization and urban development commencing from the mid-to-late 1990s, the Yangtze River Delta has received a large influx of people, forming a large agglomeration of the urban population. Shanghai, with a permanent population of 24.15 million, is the largest megacity in China. Suzhou has also grown into a megacity with a permanent population of over 10 million. The two provincial capitals, Hangzhou and Nanjing, follow closely behind, and they are expected to become megacities with over 10 million people in the near future. Seven other cities in the region have populations between 5 million and 7.8 million: Ningbo, Hefei, Nantong, Yancheng, Wuxi, Taizhou, and Jinhua. Fifteen other cities have between 1 million and 5 million residents: Shaoxing, Changzhou, Taizhou, Anqing, Jiaxing, Yangzhou, Chuzhou, Wuhu, Zhenjiang, Huzhou, Xuancheng, Ma'anshan, Chizhou, Tongling, and Zhoushan. The region has a total of 150 million permanent residents, accounting for 11.7% of the national population.

---

[3] Refer to Figure 4-8.

According to the *China Integrated City Index 2017*, the total DID population in the Yangtze River Delta Megalopolis reached 70.172 million, accounting for 17.2% of the national total and making this population the largest urban population group in China. However, its ratio of DID population was only 46.5%, 14.6 percentage points lower than that of the Pearl River Delta Megalopolis.

The sizable agglomeration of industries and population in the Yangtze River Delta has led to the for-mation of a densely populated area that covers 4,792.4 km² in total, a high-density urbanized area calculated by DID area. This report provides an analysis of the spatial structure of this megalopolis by using DID, with the following three findings.

One important feature of this megalopolis is that the 26 cities within vary substantially in terms of development level. Although the DID population ratio of Shanghai has reached 79.3%, there were 19 cities with DID population ratios below 50%. with Chizhou was at the bottom with a ratio of only 5.6%.

Again, in space terms, this megalopolis is also characterized by the "one large, eleven medium and fourteen small" layout. "One large" refers to Shanghai, which has a DID population of 18.709 million. "Eleven medium" refers to 11 cities with a DID population of between 2 and 6 million: Suzhou, Nanjing, Hangzhou, Ningbo, Hefei, Wuxi, Taizhou, Jinhua, Changzhou, Shaoxing, and Nantong. "Fourteen small" refers to the 14 cities with a DID population of less than 2 million: Jiaxing, Yangzhou, Yancheng, Zhenjiang, Wuhu and Taizhou. Anqing, Huzhou, Ma'anshan, Chuzhou, Zhoushan, Xuancheng, Tongling, and Chizhou have a DID population of less than 1 million.

The megalopolis is further characterized in spatial structure by two chains of urban areas known as "one dense and one sparse." "One dense" refers to the relatively dense chain of urban areas formed along the south bank of the Yangtze River, including Shanghai, Nanjing and Wuzhou. "One sparse" refers to the chain of urban areas along Hangzhou Bay including Shanghai, Hangzhou and Ningbo. Compared to the former, this urban chain is relatively loose.[4]

The GDP, population size, DID population size and DID area of the 12 cities in both chains of urban areas account for 69.2%, 56.3%, 70.9%, and 66.6% of the total volume of the Yangtze River Delta Megalopolis.

Features of Industrial Structure

The Yangtze River Delta Megalopolis possesses the strongest industrial strength in China, accounting for 18.6% of the country's regional gross production in the secondary sector, and 35.1% of the country's total cargo exports. It is the largest industrial center and export base of China. The Yangtze River Delta Megalopolis is now also a center for finance, trade, technological innovation, culture and sports, and tourism.

---

[4] Refer to Figure 5-25.

If we analyze the 26 cities in the Yangtze River Delta Megalopolis for deviation values in the following fields using the *China Integrated City Index 2017*, we find that: in the wholesale and retail area, Shanghai is the largest shopping center in China. Hangzhou ranked 6th, Nanjing ranked 9th, Suzhou ranked 12th, and Wuxi ranked 21st in wholesale and retail sector. However, they were at most regional shopping centers compared to agglomeration in Shanghai of large-magnitude, high-quality, and content-rich wholesale and retail businesses.[5]

In the science and technology sector, Shanghai ranks second place nationally. In addition, 12 cities including Hangzhou, Suzhou, Nanjing, Ningbo, Wuxi, Shaoxing, Nantong, Hefei, Changzhou, Jiaxing, Taizhou, and Huzhou, also ranked among the national top 30.[6] The Yangtze River Delta Megalopolis enjoys 26% of the whole country's R&D manpower and holds 35.1% of patents granted in China, making it the largest R&D center in the country.

Regarding the higher education sector, Shanghai ranked second only to Beijing. Nanjing ranked 3rd, Hefei ranked 11th, and Hangzhou ranked 13th. All of them have been higher education bases that export talent across the whole country.[7] The proportion of college students in the Yangtze River Delta is 14.2%, making it the largest higher education center in China.

The Shanghai Stock Market opened in 1990, and the Shanghai Futures Exchange Market opened in 1999, making Shanghai the largest financial center of China. Hangzhou ranked 7th, Suzhou ranked 11th, Nanjing ranked 12th, Ningbo ranked 15th, Wuxi ranked 23rd, and Hefei ranked 27th in the financial sector.

In the culture, sports and entertainment sector, Shanghai ranked 2nd in the whole country and was the national cultural and sports center immediately after Beijing. Nanjing, Hangzhou, Ningbo, Hefei, Suzhou, and Wuxi, respectively ranked 7th, 8th, 16th, 20th, 23rd, and 26th.[8]

In the medical sector, Shanghai ranked national 2nd and was the national medical center immediately after Beijing. Hangzhou and Nanjing ranked respectively national 5th and 12th, each with certain regional medical radiation.[9]

In the manufacturing sector, Suzhou overtook Shanghai to rank 2nd, and the latter ranked 3rd. Nine cities including Ningbo, Wuxi, Hangzhou, Nanjing, Jiaxing, Shaoxing, Nantong, Jinhua, and Changzhou respectively ranked 8th, 11th, 12th, 21st, 22nd, 24th, 26th, 27th, and 28th. A total of 11 cities in the Yangtze River Delta Megalopolis ranked among top 30 in the country, accounting for more than

---

[5] Refer to Figure 4-28.
[6] Refer to Figure 4-24.
[7] Refer to Figure 4-23.
[8] Refer to Figure 4-26.
[9] Refer to Figure 4-25.

one-third of the list. They demonstrate the strong advantages of the megalopolis in manufacturing.[10]

As for the IT sector, Shanghai ranked only below Beijing. Hangzhou, Nanjing, Suzhou, Hefei, and Wuxi ranked 4th, 5th, 17th, 24th, and 27th respectively.[11]

In the catering and hotel sector, Shanghai was incomparably advantaged over other cities, ranking first in the country. Suzhou, Hangzhou, Nanjing, Ningbo, Wuxi and Hefei respectively ranked 4th, 8th, 11th, 14th, 26th and 30th.[12]

Shanghai ranked 3rd in the country in terms of inbound tourist traffic. Hangzhou, Jinhua, Ningbo, and Suzhou ranked respectively 5th, 18th, 19th, and 20th. The Yangtze River Delta Megalopolis contributed 19.9% to the number of inbound tourists across the country,[13] making it one of the largest tourist destinations in the country, with great potential to develop an exchange-based and tourism economy.

In sum, in the Yangtze River Delta Megalopolis, plays a national central role in various functions. Provincial capitals such as Nanjing, Hangzhou, and Hefei also play an important regional role. Suzhou, Ningbo, Wuxi, and Changzhou are developing rapidly, and possess strong industrial functions in the manufacturing and service sectors.

Evaluation and Analysis of Megalopolis

Only four of the 26 cities in the Yangtze River Delta rank among the top 20 in the environmental dimension of the *China Integrated City Index 2017*. Shanghai, Suzhou, and Hangzhou ranked 6th, 10th, and 14th places respectively. According to the U.N. standard on per capita water resources, 11 cities in the region suffer from extreme water shortage. Large-scale industrialization and urbanization have placed a huge burden on the ecological environment of the region.[14]

According to the analysis of this megalopolis in the index for its internal deviation values under the environmental dimension, we can see that Shanghai was prominently advantaged. Although Suzhou fell behind Shanghai, it managed to secure the second place. Suzhou, Hangzhou, Nanjing, Zhoushan, Hefei, and Ningbo had similar deviation values and fell under the second tier, respectively ranking 2nd, 3rd, 4th, 5th, 6th, and 7th. Taizhou, Wuxi, Zhenjiang, Changzhou, Wuhu, Yangzhou, Shaoxing, Anqing, Nantong, Jinhua, and Tongling constituted the third tier. Yancheng, Jiaxing, Huzhou, Taizhou, Ma'anshan, Chizhou, Chuzhou, and Xuancheng fell under the 4 tier, with Xuancheng at the bottom.[15]

---

[10] Refer to Figure 4-21.
[11] Refer to Figure 4-22.
[12] Refer to Figure 4-27.
[13] Refer to Figure 4-18.
[14] Refer to Figure 2-6.

Shanghai ranked 1st under the economic dimension in the *China Integrated City Index 2017*. Also in the top 20 were Suzhou which ranked 6th, Hangzhou at 9th, Nanjing at 10th, Ningbo at 13th, and Wuxi at 15th. The fact that these six cities have ranked among the national top 20 under the Economic Dimension fully demonstrates the economic strength of the Yangtze River Delta Megalopolis.[16]

According to the analysis in the Index of this megalopolis for its internal deviation values under the economic dimension, we find that Shanghai had outstanding advantages, and the five cities (Suzhou, Hangzhou, Nanjing, Ningbo, and Wuxi) fell under the second tier. Fourteen cities (Hefei, Changzhou, Nantong, Shaoxing, Jiaxing, Zhenjiang, Jinhua, Taizhou, Yangzhou, Yancheng, Taizhou, Huzhou, Zhoushan, and Wuhu) were in third 3rd tier. Six cities (Tongling, Ma'anshan, Xuancheng, Chuzhou, Anqing, and Chizhou) were classified into the fourth tier.[17]

Under the social dimension in the *China Integrated City Index 2017*, five cities in the Yangtze River Delta Megalopolis ranked among the top 20. They were: Shanghai, 2nd; Hangzhou, 5th; Nanjing, 8th; Suzhou, 13th; and Ningbo, 16th. Economic strength has been a strong support for the social development of the region.[18]

According to the analysis of this megalopolis in the Index for its internal deviation values under the Social Dimension, we find that Shanghai had outstanding advantages, and Hangzhou, Nanjing, and Suzhou had excellent scores, falling under the second tier.[19] Twelve cities (Ningbo, Wuxi, Hefei, Changzhou, Jinhua, Jiaxing, Shaoxing, Nantong, Yangzhou, Huzhou, Zhenjiang, and Taizhou) were classified into the third tier. Ten cities (Zhoushan, Yancheng, Taizhou, Wuhu, Ma'anshan, Anqing, Xuancheng, Tongling, Chizhou, and Chuzhou) were members of the fourth tier. Tongling, Chizhou, and Chuzhou ranked 3rd, 2nd, and 1st from the bottom of the list respectively.

Based on the overall ranking, Shanghai earned an outstanding grade, ranking 2nd. In addition, another five cities, Hangzhou, Suzhou, Nanjing, Ningbo, and Wuxi, were also in the top 20, ranking 7th, 8th, 9th, 12th, and 20th respectively. They were an example of the strong power of the Yangtze River Delta Megalopolis as a group.[20]

According to this comprehensive, we find that Shanghai stood out among all others. Hangzhou, Suzhou, and Nanjing were similar in their comprehensive deviation values, falling into the second tier with clear advantages. Ningbo and Wuxi were close behind.[21]

---

[15] Refer to Figure 5-22.
[16] Refer to Figure 2-14.
[17] Refer to Figure 5-24.
[18] Refer to Figure 2-10.
[19] Refer to Figure 5-23.
[20] Refer to Figure 2-2.

Challenges in the Next Stage

According to the *China Integrated City Index 2017*, the ratio of DID population in the Yangtze River Delta Megalopolis was 18.7 percentage points lower than that of the Pearl River Delta Megalopolis, and 80.8 million people were still living in non-DID areas. Urbanization has remained a rather tough task.

However, the density of DID population in the Yangtze River Delta Megalopolis is slightly higher than the Pearl River Delta Megalopolis, rising to 14,642 persons/km², which is higher than the Pacific Coast Megalopolis of Japan by 3,073 persons/km². Such high density unmatched by the level of urban manage-ment and infrastructure has given rise to partial over-density in this region.

It is noteworthy that considerable low-density development has taken place in the urban built-up areas of this megalopolis, but at the same time, a large number of DIDs have been scattered outside the built-up areas, resulting in the relative falling behind of infrastructure support, public service support, and social management.

In sum, there is an urgent need for the Yangtze River Delta Megalopolis to further its urbanization and change its land development model based on its factory economy in order to accelerate the evolution from a factory economy to an industrial and urban economy. To this end, it is necessary to make great efforts to develop the service economy in order to improve the quality of urban life and the efficiency of economic activities. Improvement is also required in urban management and infrastructure to create a high-density, large-scale urban society and to provide new development models for the next-stage of urbanization in China.

---

[21] Refer to Figure 5-21.

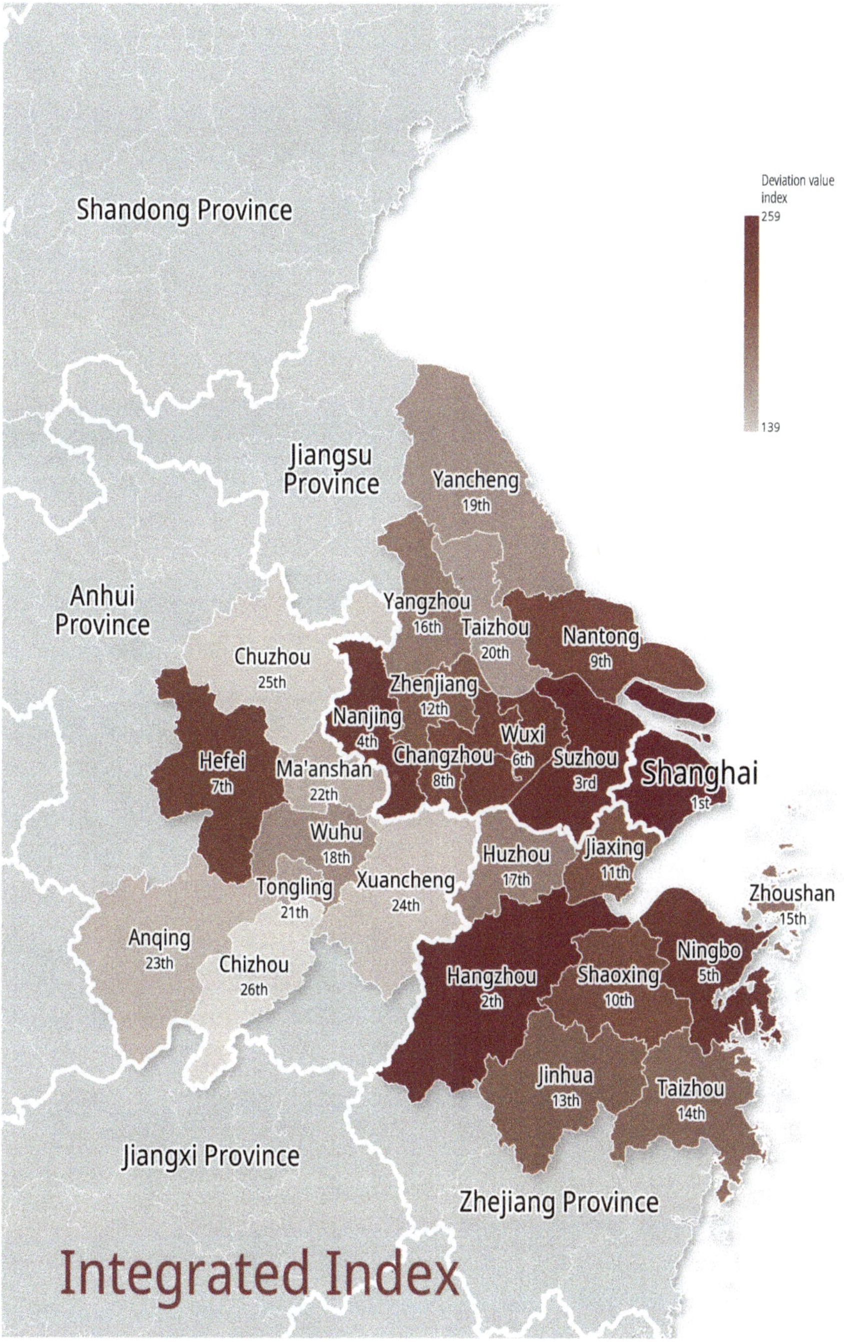

Deviation value
index
259

139

Shandong Province

Jiangsu
Province

Yancheng
19th

Anhui
Province

Chuzhou
25th

Yangzhou
16th
Taizhou
20th

Nantong
9th

Zhenjiang
12th

Nanjing
4th

Wuxi
6th

Hefei
7th

Ma'anshan
22th

Changzhou
8th

Suzhou
3rd

Shanghai
1st

Wuhu
18th

Jiaxing
11th

Tongling
21th

Xuancheng
24th

Huzhou
17th

Zhoushan
15th

Anqing
23th

Chizhou
26th

Hangzhou
2th

Shaoxing
10th

Ningbo
5th

Jiangxi Province

Jinhua
13th

Taizhou
14th

Zhejiang Province

Integrated Index

Figure 5-21 Analysis Diagram of Integrated Index of the Yangtze River Delta Megalopolis (26 Cities)

Note: Rankings from Figure 5-21 to Figure 5-24 refer to those of 26 cities within the Yangtze River Delta Megalopolis.

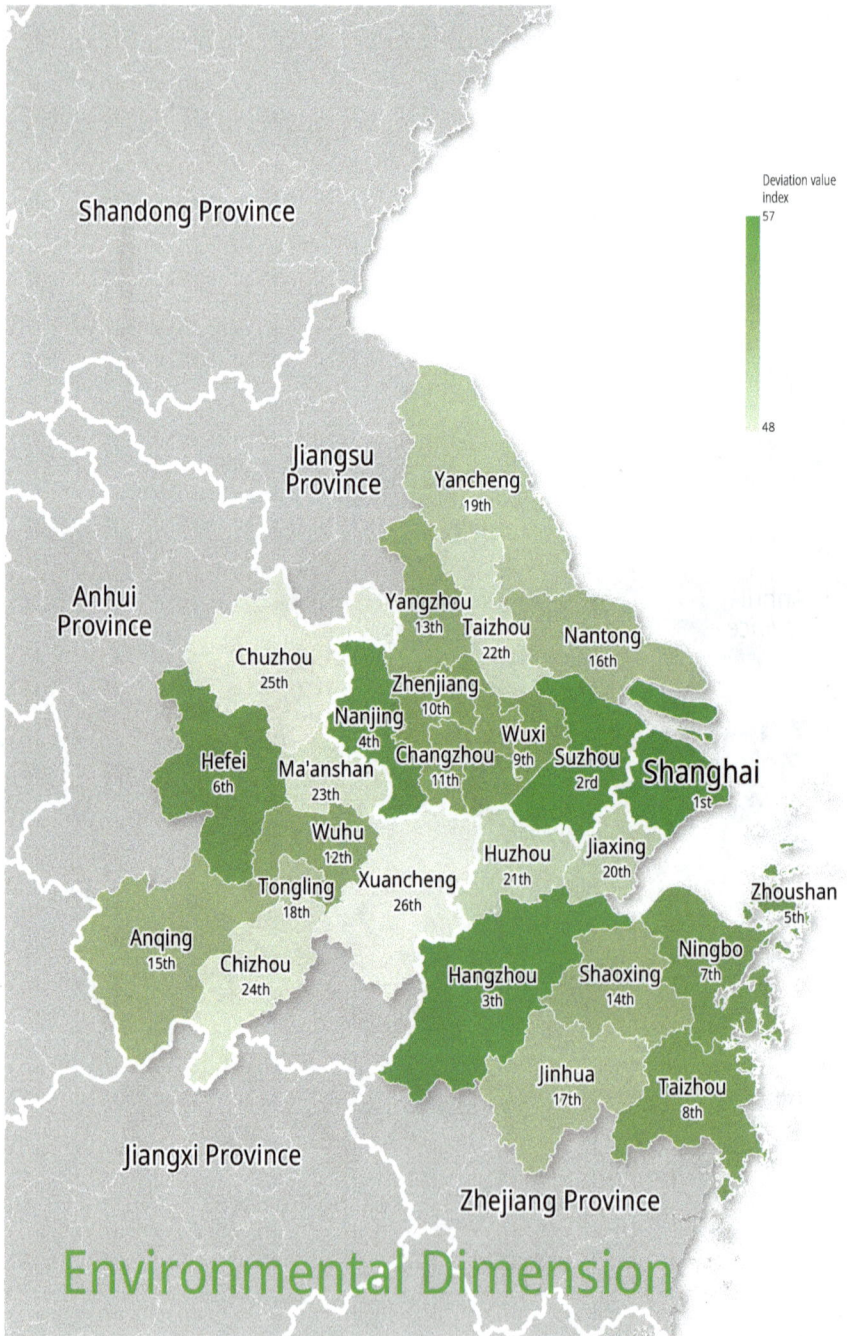

Legend:
Deviation value index
57
48

Map labels:

Shandong Province

Jiangsu Province

Anhui Province

Yancheng 19th

Chuzhou 25th

Yangzhou 13th Taizhou 22th

Nantong 16th

Zhenjiang 10th

Nanjing 4th

Wuxi 9th

Hefei 6th

Ma'anshan 23rd

Changzhou 11th

Suzhou 2rd

Shanghai 1st

Wuhu 12th

Tongling 18th

Xuancheng 26th

Huzhou 21th

Jiaxing 20th

Zhoushan 5th

Anqing 15th

Chizhou 24th

Ningbo 7th

Hangzhou 3rd

Shaoxing 14th

Jiangxi Province

Jinhua 17th

Taizhou 8th

Zhejiang Province

Environmental Dimension

Figure 5-22 Analysis Diagram of Environmental Dimension of the Yangtze River Delta Megalopolis (26 Cities)

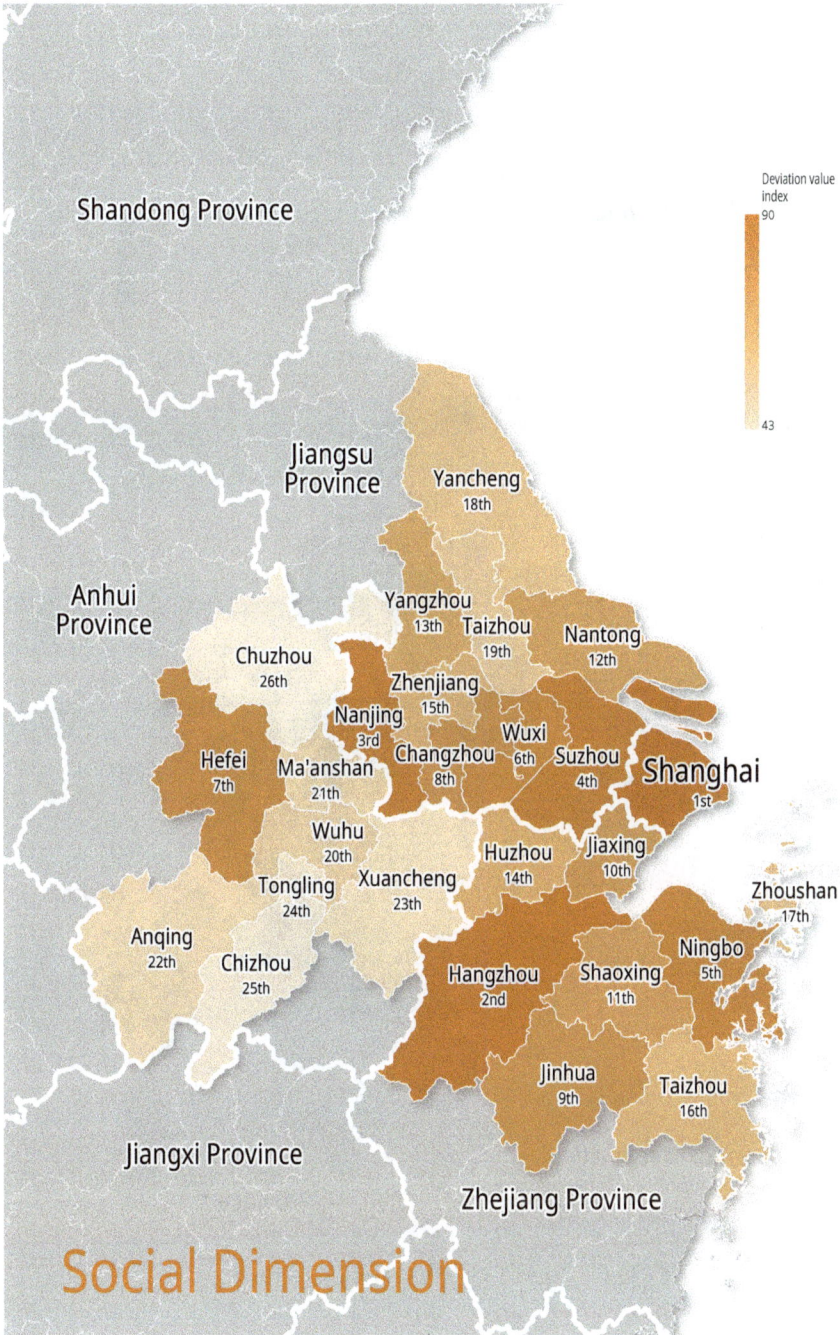

Deviation value
index
90

43

Shandong Province

Jiangsu
Province

Yancheng
18th

Anhui
Province

Chuzhou
26th

Yangzhou
13th

Taizhou
19th

Nantong
12th

Zhenjiang
15th

Nanjing
3rd

Changzhou
8th

Wuxi
6th

Suzhou
4th

Shanghai
1st

Hefei
7th

Ma'anshan
21th

Wuhu
20th

Xuancheng
23th

Huzhou
14th

Jiaxing
10th

Zhoushan
17th

Tongling
24th

Ningbo
5th

Anqing
22th

Chizhou
25th

Hangzhou
2nd

Shaoxing
11th

Jinhua
9th

Taizhou
16th

Jiangxi Province

Zhejiang Province

Social Dimension

Figure 5-23 Analysis Diagram of Social Dimension of the Yangtze River Delta Megalopolis (26 Cities)

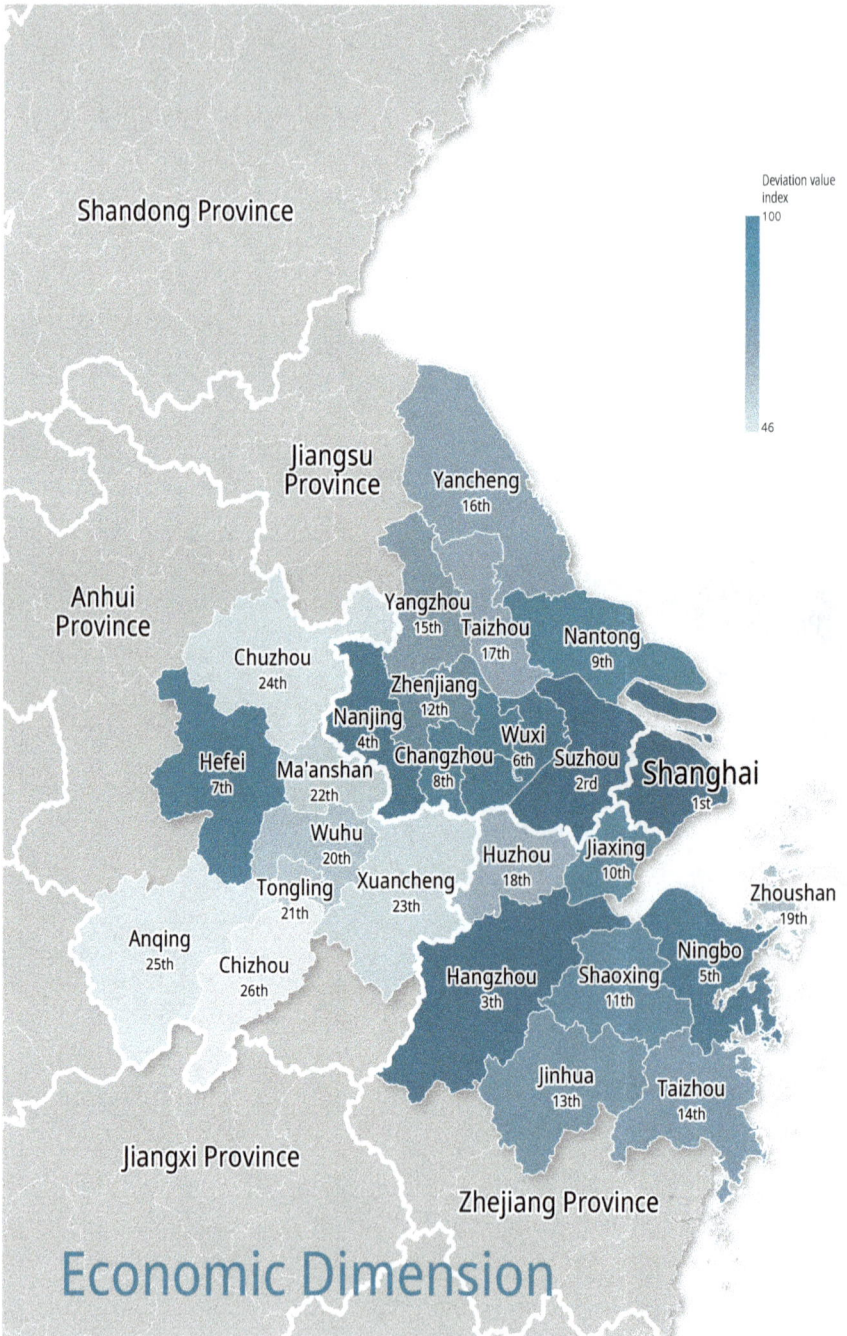

Deviation value
index
100

46

Shandong Province

Jiangsu
Province

Yancheng
16th

Anhui
Province

Chuzhou
24th

Yangzhou
15th

Taizhou
17th

Nantong
9th

Zhenjiang
12th

Nanjing
4th

Wuxi
6th

Hefei
7th

Ma'anshan
22th

Changzhou
8th

Suzhou
2rd

Shanghai
1st

Wuhu
20th

Huzhou
18th

Jiaxing
10th

Tongling
21th

Xuancheng
23th

Zhoushan
19th

Anqing
25th

Chizhou
26th

Hangzhou
3th

Shaoxing
11th

Ningbo
5th

Jinhua
13th

Taizhou
14th

Jiangxi Province

Zhejiang Province

Economic Dimension

Figure 5-24 Analysis Diagram of Economic Dimension of the Yangtze River Delta Megalopolis
(26 Cities)

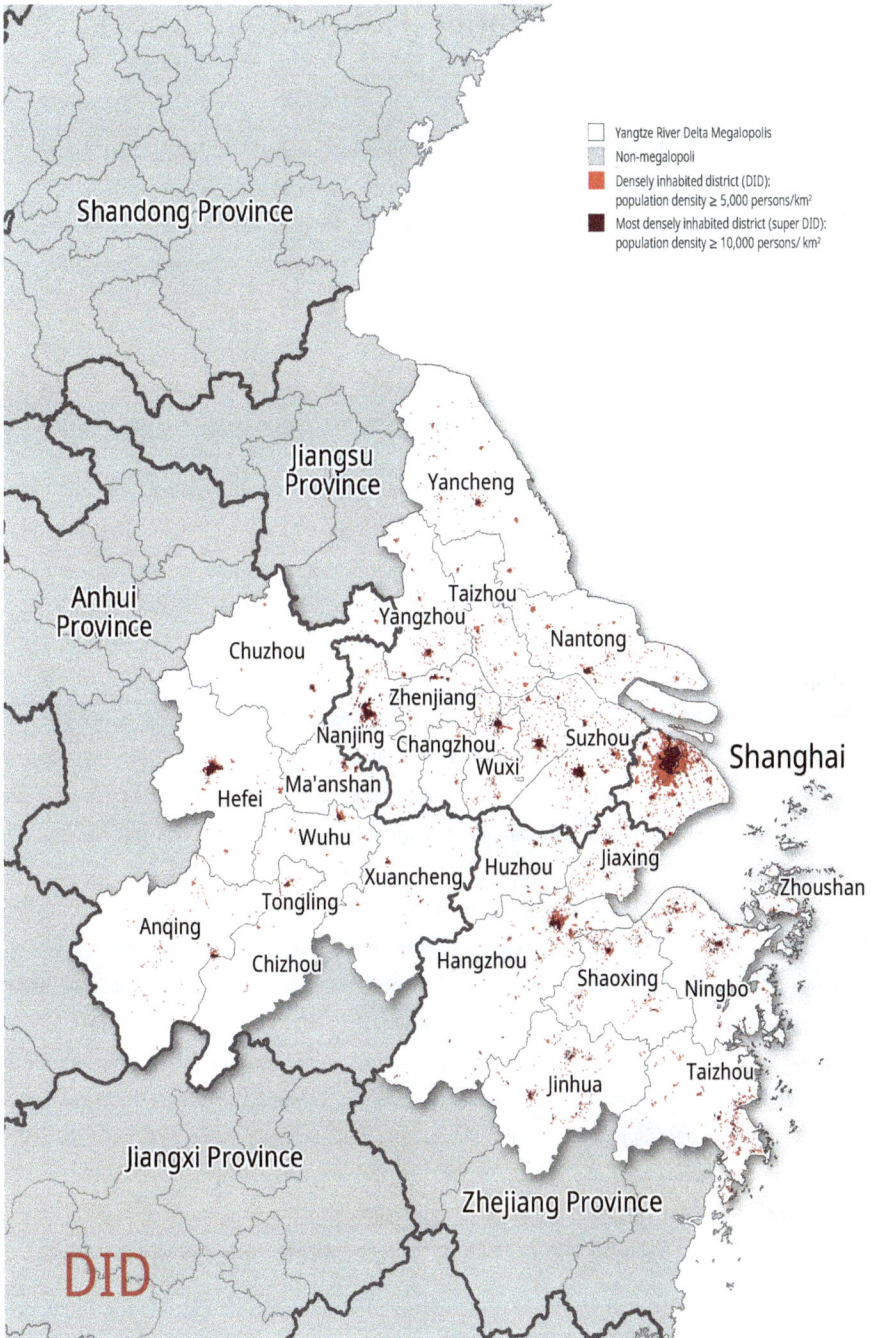

Figure 5-25 Analysis Diagram of DIDs in the Yangtze River Delta Megalopolis

Source: It is prepared as per the satellite remote sensing and analysis data published by the Cloud River Urban Research Institute.

4. The Beijing-Tianjin-Hebei Megalopolis

As a new engine for China's economic development, the Beijing-Tianjin-Hebei Megalopolis centered on Beijing and Tianjin is entering a period of great development. According to the definitions of the National Development and Reform Commission in the relevant planning, this report includes Beijing, Tianjin, Shijiazhuang, Tangshan, Qinhuangdao, Baoding, Zhangjiakou, Chengde, Cangzhou, and Langfang as part of the Beijing-Tianjin-Hebei Megalopolis for analysis.

Beijing and Tianjin as Dual Cores

The Beijing-Tianjin-Hebei region, which consists of the national capital and its environs, faces the Bohai Sea and is backed by Taiyue Mountain, making it a very important strategic position. Although the region encompasses two municipalities directly administered by the central government, Beijing and Tianjin, its surrounding urban development lags behind, manifesting the remarkable issue of "dual structure."

(1) Beijing

Beijing, the capital of China, is the core of the Beijing-Tianjin-Hebei Megalopolis. It has been a key strategic stronghold and local center in the north since the unification of China by Qin Shi Huang, the First Emperor of the Qin dynasty in 221 BC. Since 1272, it has successively been the capital for the Yuan, Ming and Qing dynasties. On October 1,1949, Beijing was officially designated as the capital of the People's Republic of China.

Beijing had originally been a consumer city before the founding of the People's Republic of China (PRC), but was after positioned as a political, cultural, and educational center, as well as an industrial base and sci-tech hub. During 30 years' development of heavy industry, Beijing has established an economic structure based on production and even once stood atop of all of the heavy industry cities in Northern China.

A knowledge-economy oriented transformation centered on new technology was proposed for the economy of Beijing following reform and opening-up. The Beijing Olympic Games gave the city an opportunity to successfully transform from an industrial base to a service-economy-based municipality by establishing the development concept of a "The People's, High-Tech and Green Beijing."

Today holding together the political and economic management functions of China, Beijing is a center of education, science and technology, culture and media, health care, and international exchanges.

(2) Tianjin

Tianjin is the second largest city in the Beijing-Tianjin-Hebei Megalopolis.

Tianjin began its history at the opening of the Grand Canal in the Sui Dynasty as a port for transporting grain from the south into Northern China. The gateway to Beijing since the Yuan Dynasty, Tianjin has always been a place of military significance and a pivotal point for the water transport of food supplies.

The modern industry of Tianjin began with the establishment of the Tianjin Machine Manufacturing Bureau by the Qing Government during the Self-Strengthening Movement. The introduction of technical equipment from the West and the engagement of foreign technicians have opened the door to Tianjin's modernization. During the Self-Strengthening Movement, Tianjin's achievements in railways, telegraph, telephone, postal service, mining, modern education, and justice stood out across the country. Tianjin was then the second largest industrial and commercial city in China and the largest financial and trade center in Northern China.

After the founding of the PRC, Tianjin, Beijing and Shanghai became municipalities directly administered by the central government, which further enhanced Tianjin's position as an industrial base.

The year 1984 saw the establishment of the Tianjin Economic and Technological Development Zone, for which active investment promotion policies were introduced. In 2005, the Chinese government set up the "Tianjin Binhai New District" and launched a strategy to develop the Beijing-Tianjin-Hebei Region into a new pole of growth after the Pearl River Delta and the Yangtze River Delta through the construction of new districts. Tianjin has now attracted many domestic and foreign companies such as Airbus, Shell, FAW Toyota, and Samsung Electronics. It has also become a large industrial agglomeration dominated by eight major sectors: aerospace, electronic information, oil exploitation and processing, marine chemical engineering, modern metallurgy, automobile and equipment manufacturing, food processing, and bio-pharmaceutics.

Large Number of Migrants

According to the analysis in the *China Integrated City Index 2017*, Beijing received 8.253 million permanent residents without household registration, ranking second to Shanghai in terms of migrant intake across China. Tianjin, has received 5.201 million permanent residents without household registration. Net popula-tion influxes to Shijiazhuang, Tangshan, and Qinhuangdao respectively amounted to 413,000, 252,000, and 117,000. In contrast, net outflows have taken place in Langfang, Zhangjiakou, Chengde, Cangzhou, and Baoding, with Baoding losing over 500,000 of its population.

Centered on Beijing and Tianjin, a chain of relatively densely populated urban areas, has gradually formed the Beijing-Tianjin-Hebei Megalopolis. At present, the megalopolis has received as many as 12.855 million permanent residents without household registration, close to half of the number received by the Pearl River Delta Megalopolis.[1]

---

[1] Refer to Figure 4-3 and 4-4.

Extensive Infrastructure Construction

As the maritime gateway to Beijing, Tianjin Port has ranked 6th in the nation and 10th in the globe for container throughput. According to the *China Integrated City Index 2017*, Tianjin has ranked 6th in the nation for container port convenience and is the only one among the Beijing-Tianjin-Hebei Megalopolis to have made the top 30 for such convenience. The megalopolis has accounted for 7.3% of the national container port throughput and is the largest marine transport center[2] in Northern China.

Compared to marine transport, the Beijing-Tianjin-Hebei Megalopolis is more evidently advantaged in air transport. The Beijing Capital International Airport has not only attained the largest passenger traffic in China, but has also ranked first in Asia for the number of flights. Tianjin Binhai International Airport has also ranked 20th in the country for passenger throughput. Together with Beijing Nanyuan Airport, Shijiazhuang Zhengding Airport, Tangshan Sannuhe Airport, Zhangjiakou Ningyuan Airport, and Qinhuangdao Shanhaiguan Airport, a broad aviation system of seven airports has been formed in the megalopolis.

As one of the largest air transport centers in China, the Beijing-Tianjin-Hebei Megalopolis accounts for 13% of national passenger traffic and 15.6% of national cargo and mail throughput via its airports.

Beijing has taken 2nd place in the national ranking for airport convenience. In addition, another two cities from this megalopolis, Tianjin and Langfang, have made the top 30 in the same ranking.[3]

Large airports and ports have improved the business environment for the Beijing-Tianjin-Hebei Megalopolis and enabled much trade and interaction with the rest of the world. Expressways and high-speed railways further connect the cities within the region. Large-scale infrastructure investment has laid a sound foundation for the social and economic development of the Beijing-Tianjin-Hebei Megalopolis.

Characteristics of Spatial Structure

The Beijing-Tianjin-Hebei Megalopolis includes four megacities with more than 10 million permanent residents. Beijing, Tianjin, Baoding, and Shijiazhuang, have respectively ranked as the 3rd, 4th, 7th, and 10th most populous cities in China. Beijing accommodates a permanent population of more than 20 million. Tangshan and Cangzhou both have a permanent population of 7 million; Langfang and Zhangjiakou have 4 million permanent residents each; while Chengde and Qinhuangdao each have 3 million people. Permanent residents in this megalopolis add up to 90.26 million, accounting for 7% of the national total.

According to the *China Integrated City Index 2017*, a total of 32.381 million residents lived in the

---

[2] Refer to Figure 4-7.

[3] Refer to Figure 4-8.

DIDs of the Beijing-Tianjin-Hebei Megalopolis, accounting for 7.9% of the national total DID population. Those residents constitute the largest urban population group in China. However, the region's DID population ratio was only 35.9%, which was 29.3% lower than that of the Pearl River Delta Megalopolis, and the lowest in China's three megalopolises.

The total size of the densely populated areas in the Beijing-Tianjin-Hebei region has reached 2,230.7 km². Large and high-density urbanized areas have formed in this megalopolis. This report analyzes the spatial structure of the Beijing-Tianjin-Hebei Megalopolis by applying DID and generates the following characteristic findings.

One important feature of the Beijing-Tianjin-Hebei Megalopolis is the significant gap among the development levels of the 10 cities within. For example, Beijing and Tianjin have a DID population ratio of 66.8% and 62%, while the other eight cities have less than 30% (with the exception of Shijiazhuang at 31.1%), and Langfang ranks at the bottom with only 9.3%.

The megalopolis is also characterized by the "two large, three medium, and five small" pattern. Beijing, capital of China, accounts for one of the "two large" cities. With 13.441 million residents living in the DIDs, the city has far outperformed the other cities in the region with its size and functions. The other is Tianjin, which has a DID population of 8.226 million. As a municipality directly administered by the central government and the maritime gateway to Northern China, Tianjin has become a large regional central city. The "three medium" cities are Shijiazhuang, Baoding, and Tangshan, with DID populations of more than 1.5 million and under 3.5 million. The "five small" cities are Cangzhou, Qinhuangdao, Zhangjiakou, Chengde, and Langfang, with DID populations of less than 1 million.

The Beijing-Tianjin-Hebei Megalopolis is further characterized by "one horizontal and one vertical" urban axes. The "horizontal" axis extends linearly through the area between Beijing and Tianjin. The "vertical" axis extends through the area along Beijing-Guangzhou Line, from Beijing to Baoding and then to Shijiazhuang. The two axes are expected to form a chain of urban areas in the future, but at present the degree of urban continuity is still relatively sparse. That is to say, this megalopolis has not yet become an urban area chain consisting of DID areas with a sufficiently developed size in spatial structure.[4]

Features of Industrial Structure

As one of the largest industrial bases in China, the Beijing-Tianjin-Hebei Megalopolis has strong industrial strength, accounting for 7.3% of the country's regional gross production in the secondary sector, and 5.8% of the country's total cargo exports.

---

[4] Refer to Figure 5-30.

Centered on Beijing, the Beijing-Tianjin-Hebei Megalopolis has functioned as a powerful headquarters, and as a center for technological innovation, culture and sports, health care, finance, tourism, and more.

When we analyzed the 10 cities of the Beijing-Tianjin-Hebei Megalopolis for deviation values in the following areas using the radiation concept in the *China Integrated City Index 2017*, we find that: In the wholesale and retail area, Beijing was the 2nd largest shopping center in China. Although Tianjin ranked 7th in wholesale and retail radiation, it was at most a regional shopping center compared to the agglomera-tion in Beijing of large-size, high-quality, and content-rich wholesale and retail businesses.[5]

In the category of science and technology, Beijing ranked national 1st with its strong radiation, while Tianjin also made the top 30 and ranked 8th. The Beijing-Tianjin-Hebei Megalopolis accounted for 13.4% of the whole country's R&D manpower and held 10.1% of the total patents granted in China, making it one of the largest R&D centers in the country.[6]

In the field of higher education, Beijing's powerful radiation effect is unmatched by other cities and shoulders the heavy responsibility of cultivating talent for the whole country. Tianjin also ranked national 9th in the higher education radiation. The Beijing-Tianjin-Hebei Megalopolis accommodated for 8.4% of the total country's college students and remains an important center for higher education in China.[7]

In the field of culture and sports, Beijing also enjoyed influential power unmatched by other cities. Although Tianjin and Shijiazhuang respectively ranked national 12th and 28th in this aspect of radiation, they were at most regional cultural and sports centers.[8]

Beijing is also home to a large number of top-class medical institutions and received patients seeking medical consultation from all over the country, making it the national center for medical care. Tianjin and Shijiazhuang ranked national 7th and 27th, respectively, in medical radiation, so each had a certain regional medical radiation.[9]

In the ranking of financial radiation, Beijing ranked 2nd in the country, and the financial industry was an important part of the city's economy. Tianjin also ranked 8th in this respect.[10]

In the manufacturing space, both Tianjin and Beijing ranked among the national top 30, coming in respectively at 9th and 19th in terms of their radiation.[11]

In the IT field, Beijing has been incomparably advantaged over other cities. As one of the four

---

[5] Refer to Figure 4-28.

[6] Refer to Figure 4-24.

[7] Refer to Figure 4-23.

[8] Refer to Figure 4-26.

[9] Refer to Figure 4-25.

[10] Refer to Figure 4-20.

[11] Refer to Figure 4-21.

municipalities directly under the control of the central government, Tianjin was not in the national top 30. Instead, Qinhuangdao managed to rank 29th in the country.[12]

Concerning the catering and hotel radiation, Beijing was slightly inferior to Shanghai, ranking national 2nd nationally, while Tianjin ranked 15th.[13]

Beijing and Tianjin ranked 4th and 6th respectively across China in terms of the number of inbound tourists. The Beijing-Tianjin-Hebei Megalopolis represented 7.7%[14] of the national total. Beijing and Tianjin even ranked 3rd and 6th in terms of the number of domestic tourists across China, for which the whole megalopolis accounted for 7.6% of the national total.[15]

In addition to being a center for politics, science, technology, culture, arts, and international exchanges, Beijing is the largest provider of convention and exhibition services in the country. The Beijing-Tianjin-Hebei region is endowed with historical significance and Chinese heritage and perhaps has the greatest potential for developing an exchange-based economy and tourism economy.

In sum, Beijing, as China's political, cultural, and technological hub, is leading the development of the Beijing-Tianjin-Hebei Megalopolis by functioning as the national center. Tianjin serves not only as the maritime gateway to the region, but also as an important industrial base in Northern China, manifesting considerable technological, cultural, educational and medical radiation. Industry also plays an important role in the economies of Shijiazhuang, Tangshan, and Baoding. All members of the Beijing-Tianjin-Hebei Megalopolis, except Beijing and Tianjin, are relatively under-developed in culture, education and services, despite the fact that Shijiazhuang, as a provincial capital, functions to a certain extent as a regional center.

Evaluation and Analysis of Megalopolis

There is a serious shortage of water resources in the Beijing-Tianjin-Hebei Region. If viewed against the U.N. standard on per capita water resources, eight out of the 10 cities in the megalopolis are dealing with extreme water shortage.[16] The extended period of lacking water has not only become a constraint to the development of the Beijing-Tianjin-Hebei Megalopolis, but has also led to serious over-exploitation of groundwater. The problem of environmental pollution is also very prominent in the region. Of the top 30 cities with the most serious $PM_{2.5}$ pollution in China, four were part of the

---

[12] Refer to Figure 4-22.

[13] Refer to Figure 4-27.

[14] Refer to Figure 4-18.

[15] Refer to Figure 4-17.

[16] Refer to Figure 4-12.

Beijing-Tianjin-Hebei Megalopolis.[17] In the *China Integrated City Index 2017* under the environmental dimension, Beijing (17th) was the only one from the Beijing-Tianjin-Hebei Megalopolis that ranked among the top 20.[18]

According to the analysis of this megalopolis in the Index for its internal deviation values under the environmental dimension, we determine that Beijing was in the first place. Tianjin, Shijiazhuang, Chengde, Qinhuangdao, Zhangjiakou, and Tangshan fell under the 2nd tier, ranking 2nd, 3rd, 4th, 5th, 6th, and 7th respectively. Cangzhou and Langfang fell under the 3rd tier. Baoding was at the bottom with the lowest deviation value.[19]

Under the economic dimension in the *China Integrated City Index 2017*, Beijing ranked 2nd and Tianjin 5th, which was a full manifestation of the economic strength of the two municipalities directly administered by the central government.[20]

According to the analysis of this megalopolis in the Index for its internal deviation values under the economic dimension, we find that Beijing made a powerful showing at 1st place. Tianjin ranked 2nd but fell behind Beijing to a relatively large extent. In comparison, the other cities still had a long way to go to catch up with Beijing and Tianjin.[21]

The ranking under social dimension in the *China Integrated City Index 2017* greatly demonstrates Beijing's advantages as the capital. Beijing achieved the best score and holds a safe lead. Tianjin ranked 6th and also had apparent social advantages as a municipality directly administered by the central government.[22]

According to the analysis of this megalopolis in the Index for its internal deviation values under the social dimension, we find that Beijing was far ahead of other cities, ranking 1st. Tianjing still fell behind Beijing to a relatively large extent, though it ranked 2nd. In comparison, there was even a larger gap between the other cities and Beijing and Tianjin.[23]

Under the overall ranking in the *China Integrated City Index 2017*, Beijing is the champion with its strength as the capital, while Tianjin ranked 5th.[24]

According to the comprehensive analysis of this megalopolis for its internal deviation values in the Index, we find that Beijing had obvious overall advantages, while Tianjin largely fell behind, ranking 2nd. Shijiazhuang, Tangshan, Qinhuangdao, Baoding, Langfang, and Chengde ranked 3rd, 4th, 5th, 6th,

---

[17] Refer to Figure 4-10.
[18] Refer to Figure 2-6.
[19] Refer to Figure 5-27.
[20] Refer to Figure 2-14.
[21] Refer to Figure 5-29.
[22] Refer to Figure 2-10.
[23] Refer to Figure 5-28.
[24] Refer to Figure 2-2.

and 7th, respectively. Due to severe environmental problems, Cangzhou ranked 2nd from the bottom of the overall ranking within the Beijing-Tianjin-Hebei Megalopolis, while Zhangjiakou was at the bottom.[25]

In conclusion, Beijing has unmatched advantages and plays an irreplaceable role when compared to other cities in terms of social, cultural, technological, and headquarter metrics. As a municipality directly administered by the central government, Tianjin is also endowed with obvious advantages in these areas. In the economic sphere, both cities are powerful. However, Tianjin, Shijiazhuang, Tangshan, and Baoding are structured to have a larger proportion of industry, but at uneven levels. Environmental sacrifices for low-quality industrialization have put severe pressure on the environment. In addition, shortage of water resources, backward urban construction, and climate and geographical concerns have led to the outbreak of a profound ecological crisis in the Beijing-Tianjin-Hebei Megalopolis. It is a serious challenge for the development of the region.

Challenges in the Next Stage

According to the analysis in the *China Integrated City Index 2017*, the ratio of DID population in the Beijing-Tianjin-Hebei Megalopolis was 29.3 percentage points lower than that of the Pearl River Delta Megalopolis, with 57.88 million people living in non-DID areas. The urbanization mission has been rather arduous for this megalopolis.

On the other hand, the density of its DID population was at a high point of 14,516 persons/km[2], which was higher than that of the Pacific Coast Megalopolis of Japan by 2,947 persons/km[2]. Such high density unmatched by the level of urban management and infrastructure has given rise to partial over-density in this region.

It is noteworthy that considerable low-density development has taken place in the urban built-up areas of this megalopolis, but at the same time, a large number of DIDs have been scattered outside the built-up areas, resulting in the relative falling behind of infrastructure support, public service support, and social management in these areas.

In conclusion, there is an urgent need for the Beijing-Tianjin-Hebei Megalopolis to further its urbanization and make great efforts to develop the service economy in order to improve the quality of urban life and the efficiency of its economic activities. It also needs to improve its urban management and infrastructure to create a high-density, large-scale urban society and to pioneer a model for the next stage of urbanization in China.

---

[25] Refer to Figure 5-26.

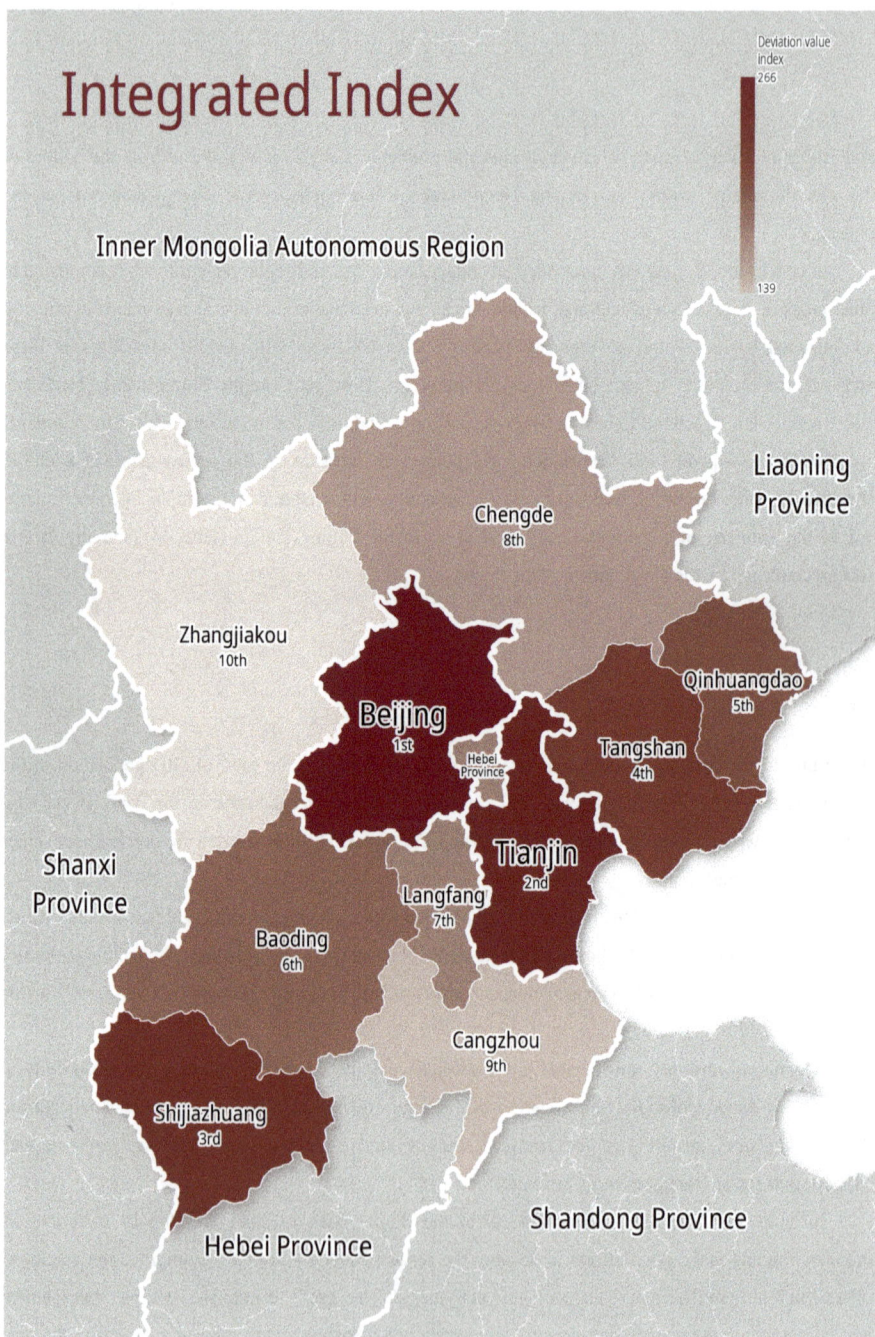

Integrated Index

Deviation value index
266

139

Inner Mongolia Autonomous Region

Liaoning Province

Chengde
8th

Zhangjiakou
10th

Beijing
1st

Hebei
Province

Qinhuangdao
5th

Tangshan
4th

Shanxi
Province

Tianjin
2nd

Langfang
7th

Baoding
6th

Cangzhou
9th

Shijiazhuang
3rd

Shandong Province

Hebei Province

Figure 5-26 Analysis Diagram of Integrated Index of the Beijing-Tianjin-Hebei Megalopolis (10 Cities)

Note: Rankings from Figure 5-26 to Figure 5-29 refer to those of 10 cities within the Beijing-Tianjin-Hebei Megalopolis.

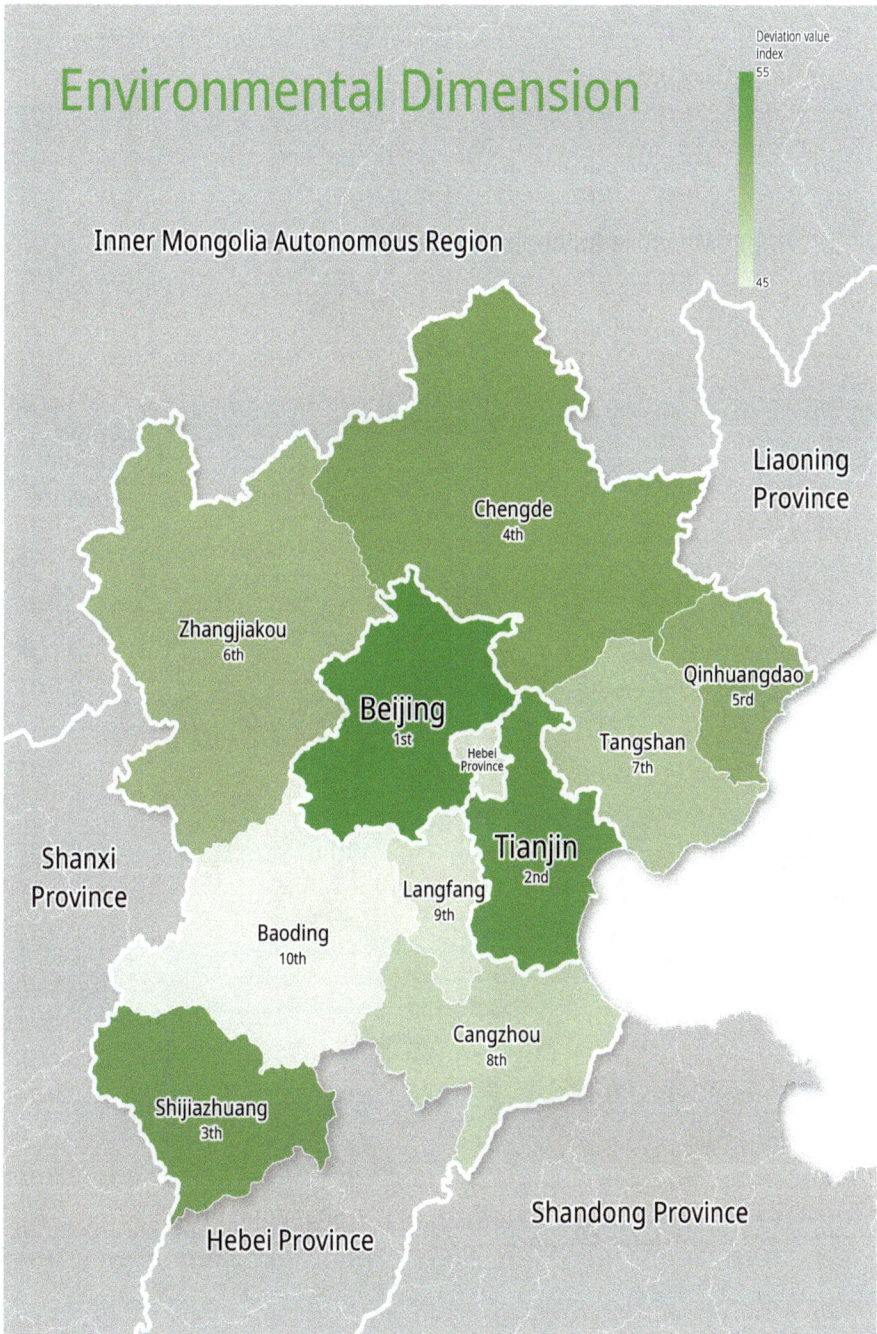

Environmental Dimension

Deviation value index
55
45

Inner Mongolia Autonomous Region

Liaoning Province

Chengde
4th

Zhangjiakou
6th

Qinhuangdao
5rd

Beijing
1st

Hebei Province

Tangshan
7th

Shanxi Province

Tianjin
2nd

Langfang
9th

Baoding
10th

Cangzhou
8th

Shijiazhuang
3th

Shandong Province

Hebei Province

Figure 5-27 Analysis Diagram of Environmental Dimension of the Beijing-Tianjin-Hebei Megalopolis (10 Cities)

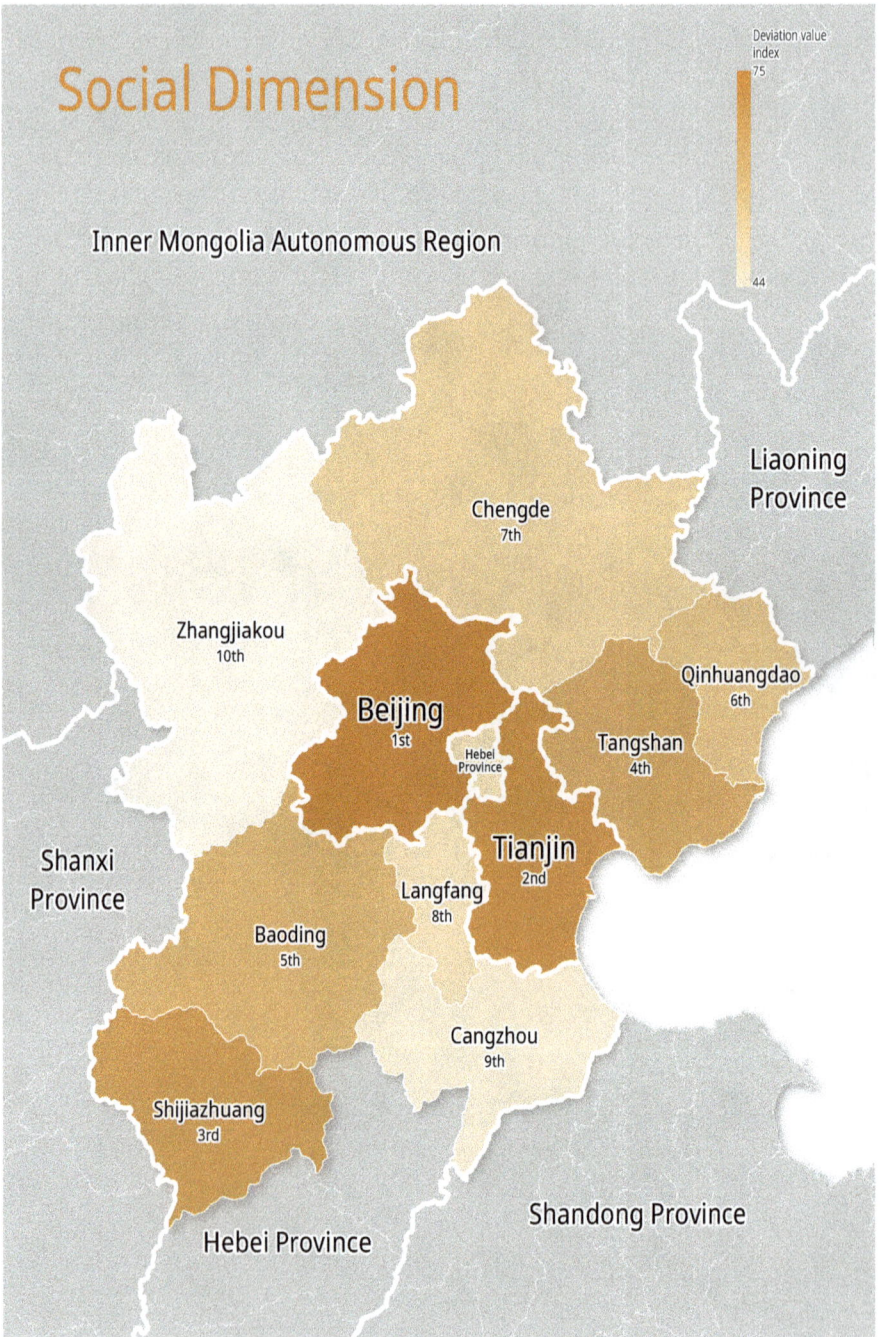

Figure 5-28 Analysis Diagram of Social Dimension of the Beijing-Tianjin-Hebei Megalopolis (10 Cities)

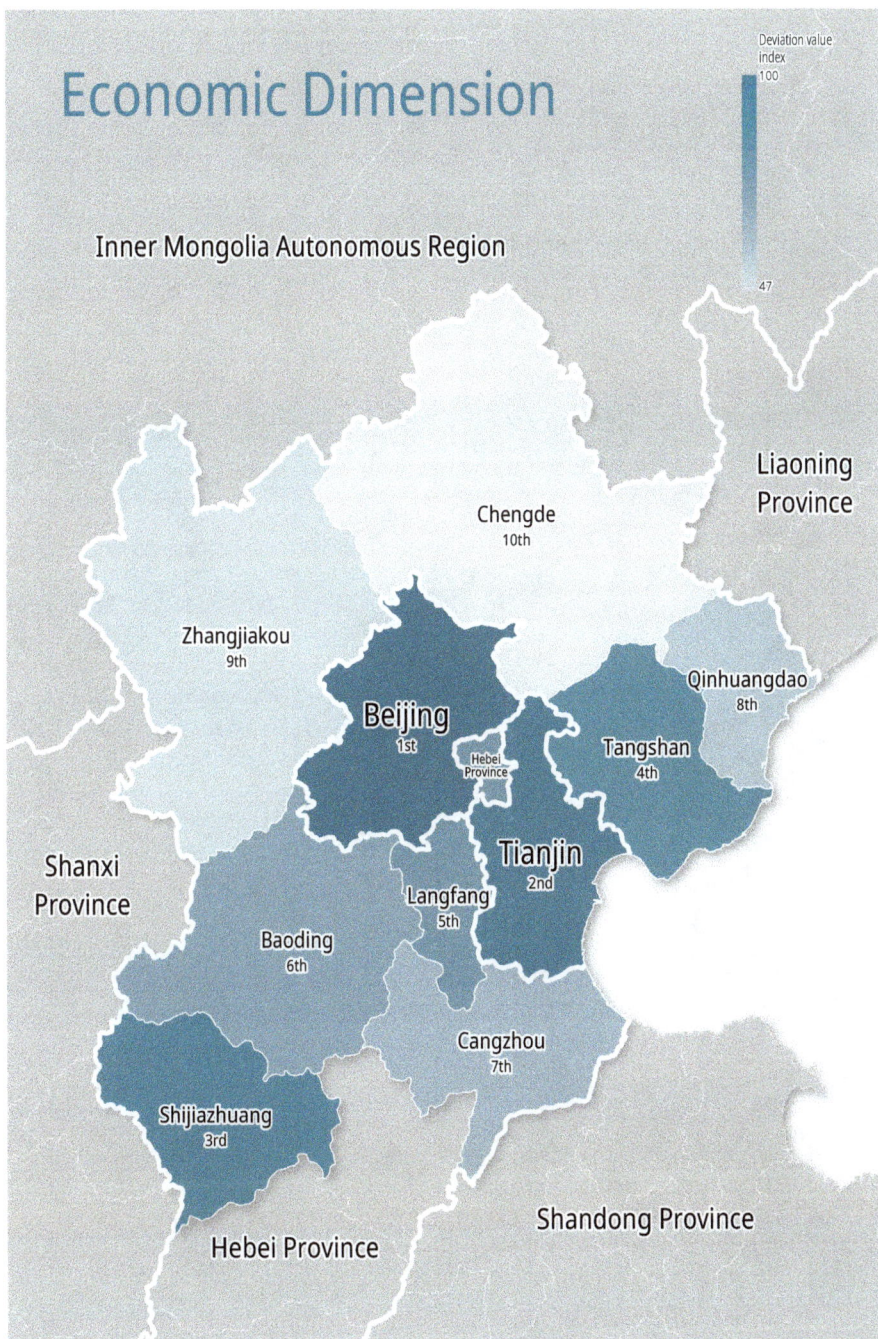

Figure 5-29 Analysis Diagram of Economic Dimension of the Beijing-Tianjin-Hebei Megalopolis (10 Cities)

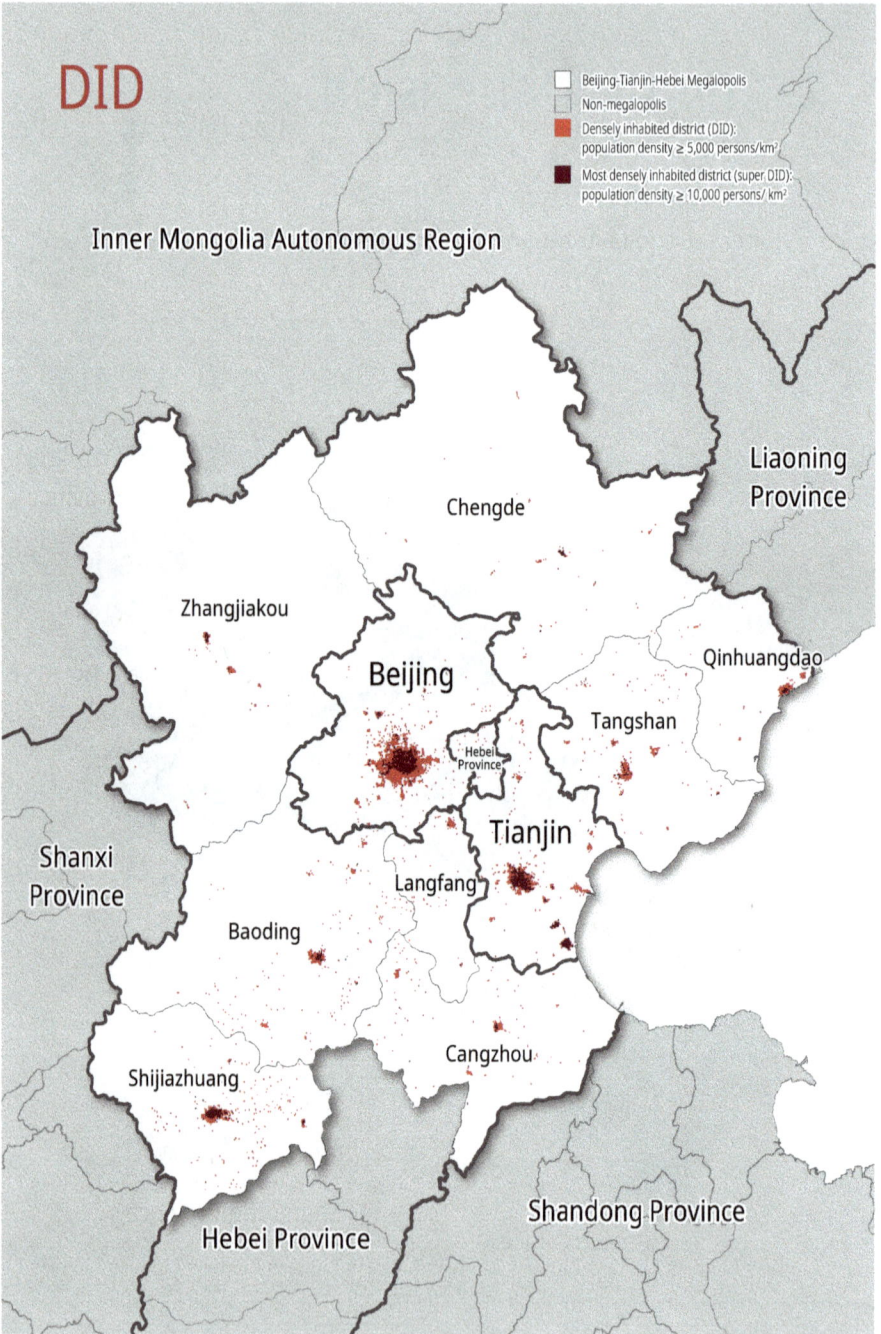

DID

Beijing-Tianjin-Hebei Megalopolis
Non-megalopolis
Densely inhabited district (DID):
population density ≥ 5,000 persons/km²
Most densely inhabited district (super DID):
population density ≥ 10,000 persons/ km²

Inner Mongolia Autonomous Region

Liaoning
Province

Chengde

Zhangjiakou

Beijing

Qinhuangdao

Tangshan

Hebei
Province

Tianjin

Shanxi
Province

Langfang

Baoding

Cangzhou

Shijiazhuang

Shandong Province

Hebei Province

Figure 5-30 Analysis Diagram of DIDs in the Beijing-Tianjin-Hebei Megalopolis

Source: It is prepared as per the satellite remote sensing and analysis data published by the Cloud River Urban Research Institute.

5. The Chengdu-Chongqing Urban Agglomeration

The Chengdu-Chongqing urban agglomeration spans the Sichuan Province and Chongqing City. It is located in the upper reaches of the Yangtze River; neighboring Hunan and Hubei in the east; Yunnan and Guizhou in the south; Qinghai and Tibet in the west; and Shaanxi and Gansu in the north. It functions as the strategic key point linking east to west, and north to south. Chongqing and Chengdu are typical "agricultural" megacities developed from densely populated agricultural areas, and now both function as core cities in this megalopolis. According to the definitions of the National Development and Reform Commission (NDRC) in the relevant planning, this report includes Chongqing (Yuzhong, Wanzhou, Qianjiang, Fuling, Dadukou, Jiangbei, Shapingba, Jiulongpo, Nan'an, Beibei, Qijiang, Dazu, Yubei, Banan, Changshou, Jiangjin, Hechuan, Yongchuan, Nanchuan, Tongnan, Tongliang, Rongchang, Bishan, Liangping, Fengdu, Dianjiang, Zhongxian, and parts of Kaixian and Yunyang), Chengdu, Ya'an (except Tianquan and Baoxing), Mianyang (except Beichuan and Pingwu), Ziyang, Leshan, Luzhou, Nanchong, Deyang, Yibin, Guang'an, Suining, Dazhou (except Wanyuan), Zigong, Meishan, and Neijiang in the Chengdu-Chongqing Urban Agglomeration for analysis.

Chengdu and Chongqing as Two Cores

The Chengdu-Chongqing urban agglomeration accounts for 6.4% of the national GDP and 8% of the total permanent population. Leading the development of this urban agglomeration are the two megacities, Chongqing and Chengdu.

(1) Chongqing

Located in the upper reaches of the Yangtze River, Chongqing is an important port on the Yangtze River waterway, and it has historically been a political, economic, and military center of strategic significance.

Recent history has witnessed Chongqing go through three critical turning points: namely, the opening of Chongqing as a commercial port, Chongqing as the wartime capital, and "The Third-Front Movement."

In 1890, China and the United Kingdom signed the Supplementary Treaty to the Chefoo Convention, which opened Chongqing to the world as a commercial port with customs set up. Then foreign countries began not only to set up consulates and concessions in Chongqing, but also established a large number of foreign companies and factories. Chinese national capital also emerged with a number of mod-ern industrial enterprises formed. This trend brought opportunities for the development of modern industry in Chongqing, making it the first industrial city in Western China.

In 1937, the government of the Republic of China promulgated the Declaration on Moving Nationalist Government to Chongqing, which designated Chongqing as the wartime capital. Chongqing served as the national political and military center during the War of Resistance Against Japan, and absorbed a large number of personnel and industries being moved inland, laying the foundation for its modern industry. Its historic status as the provisional capital lifted Chongqing from a dock city located in the secluded west to a world landmark equally famous as London, Washington, D.C., and Moscow. The fierce collision and integration between exotic elements brought by the wave of wartime migration and local culture quickly sent Chongqing to the forefront of Chinese urban culture.

Since the founding of the People's Republic of China and especially since the Third-Front Movement in 1964, Chongqing, as the core municipality of the movement, has continued to receive a large number of industrial and mining enterprises, scientific research organizations, and related personnel being moved inland, and it has become a strong industrial base in inland China.

Since the policy of reform and opening-up, and particularly since its upgrade to a municipality directly administered by the central government in 1997, Chongqing has experienced rapid development and led the social and economic growth of the southwestern region. It is worth mentioning that its electronics industry has been developing rapidly in recent years, bringing together a great number of internationally and nationally famous enterprises, such as Foxconn, Asus, Acer, and Hewlett-Packard. As a result, Chongqing has become a major gathering place for electronics businesses.

As a leader of the southwest, Chongqing has a strong position in commerce, finance, culture, science and technology, education, and medical care; functioning as an important center for the development of the region.

(2) Chengdu

Chengdu, capital of the Sichuan Province, is located in the hinterland of the Chengdu Plain. Blessed with a flat terrain and abundant natural resources, Chengdu has traditionally been reputed as a "land of abundance," and has consistently been the political, economic, and military center of the southwest.

In 1877, the Governor of Sichuan, Ding Baozhen, founded the Sichuan Machinery Bureau in Chengdu, which was an important achievement of the Self-Strengthening Movement. It was the first example of the development of modern national industry and military industry in Sichuan.

Subsequent to the founding of the PRC, railway construction opened the door to the once isolated Sichuan Basin. In 1952, the Chengdu-Chongqing railway was completed and put into operation. In 1956, the Baoji-Chengdu railway was completed in Huangshahe, Gansu. In 1970, the Chengdu-Kunming railway was put into operation. The opening of these railway lines provided new resources for the development of Chengdu.

The "Third-Front Movement" has had a profound impact on Chengdu. With much construction underway, Chengdu has received a large number of industrial and mining enterprises, scientific research organizations, and related personnel from all around the country. As a result, the city's scientific research and industrial strength has been improved. Thanks to the Third-Front Movement, Chengdu has formed a modern industrial system encompassing machinery, electronics, aviation, metallurgy, and chemistry, and has become an industrial hub with strategic significance in China.

Chengdu has experienced rapid development since the reform and opening-up policy. Built-up areas have grown from 18 km^2 at the beginning of the PRC to over 400 km^2, with the arrival of more than 2.3 million permanent residents without household registration. Chengdu is the only city in the Chengdu-Chongqing urban agglomeration with a net influx of population.

In the central and western regions, Chengdu ranked 1st in the number of foreign consulates, as well as in the number of foreign banks, foreign insurance organizations, and Fortune Global 500 enterprises setting up businesses there. Chengdu provides a platform for the southwestern region to interact with the rest of the world.

The IT industry has experienced rapid growth in Chengdu in the recent years, exemplified by Cisco, GM, Siemens, Philips, Wistron, Foxconn, Dell, Lenovo and other Chinese and foreign companies establishing their presence in the city. The city has created a large industrial agglomeration centered on laptops, which leads the export industries in the region.

As a central city in the southwest, Chengdu possesses strong radiation in commerce, finance, culture, science and technology, education, and medical care, functioning as an important center for the develop-ment of the region.

Large Population Out lows

Since the Chengdu-Chongqing region is relatively under-urbanized and quite densely populated, its two core cities do not have enough ability to absorb all the population, resulting in a large outflow of people.

According to the *China Integrated City Index 2017*, among the 16 cities in the Chengdu-Chongqing urban agglomeration, Chengdu was the only one that received 2.377 million permanent residents without household registration. Other cities suffered from net population outflows, and Chongqing had a net outflow of 3.553 million people. A total of 11.499 million people have moved out of this urban agglomeration, making it one of the regions in China with the largest population outflow.[1]

Infrastructure Development

The inland Chengdu-Chongqing urban agglomeration does not have the advantage of a beachfront region.

---

[1] Refer to Figure 4-3 and 4-4.

It must rely on the time-consuming and costly Yangtze River shipping highways and railways for bulk material transport. Logistical costs are the biggest constraint to the development of this region. In this sense, Chongqing, endowed with the Yangtze River waterway, is apparently advantaged for logistics due to her location in the region.[2]

Air transport is well-developed in the Chengdu-Chongqing urban agglomeration. According to the *China Integrated City Index 2017*, Chengdu and Chongqing respectively ranked 4th and 14th in the country in terms of airport convenience. Today, an aviation system of seven airports (Chongqing Jiangbei International Airport, Chengdu Shuangliu International Airport, Luzhou Lantian Airport, Mianyang Nanjiao Airport, Nanchong Gaoping Airport, Yibin Laiba Airport, and Dazhou Heshi Airport) has been established in the region. Together these airports account for 8.9% of national passenger traffic and 6.4% of cargo and mail throughput nationally. This represents the highest level of development in air transport in inland China.[3]

In 1995, the Chengdu-Chongqing Expressway, that connects the two core cities, was put into operation. Twenty years later, in 2015, the Chengdu-Chongqing High-speed Railway was put into operation, further shortening the time and economic distance between the two core cities.

The large-scale investment by the Chengdu-Chongqing urban agglomeration in transportation facilities such as airports, expressways, and high-speed railways has not only greatly improved its transportation to the outside world, but also put the different divisions of the urban agglomeration into closer collaboration.

Characteristics of Spatial Structure

Chongqing and Chengdu have become megacities with 30.166 million and 14.658 million permanent residents, respectively; followed by Nanchong and Dazhou with permanent populations of 6.364 million and 5.568 million, respectively. Mianyang, Yibin, and Luzhou each have populations of around 4 million; Neijiang, Ziyang, Deyang, Suining, Leshan, Guang'an, and Meishan each have 3 million or so; Zigong, with 2 million; and Ya'an, with 1.547 million or so.

The Chengdu-Chongqing urban agglomeration has developed into a densely populated area covering a total of 3,770.2 km², a high-density urbanized area when measured by DID area. This report provides an analysis of the spatial structure of this megalopolis by using DID and presents the following three findings.

The Chengdu-Chongqing urban agglomeration is characterized in spatial terms by its large

---

[2] Refer to Figure 4-7.

[3] Refer to Figure 4-8.

population and low urbanization rate. In comparison to its permanent population of 98.239 million, this region only had a DID population of 24.192 million (24.6%). This figure was 40.6 percentage points lower than that of the Pearl River Delta Megalopolis.

This Urban Agglomeration is also characterized by its "two large and many small" pattern. The "two large" cities, Chongqing and Chengdu, respectively covered 542.2 km² and 475.2 km² areas. The remaining "many small" cities had relatively small and dispersed DIDs.

Regarding the size of DID population, Chongqing and Chengdu had 7.619 million and 7.523 million respectively; while Nanchong and Dazhou had between 1 million and under 1.5 million. The other 12 cities all had less than 1 million; with Meishan at the bottom with only 186,000.

The Chengdu-Chongqing urban agglomeration is further characterized by its spatial structure by the fact that although the core cities, Chongqing and Chengdu, have been connected by expressways and high-speed railways, a chain of urban areas has not yet been formed along the lines due to geographical features and urbanization levels.[4]

The "two large" cities' spatial structure can also be ascertained by economic indicators. The size of GDP, cargo exports and regional gross production from the tertiary sector in Chongqing and Chengdu have respectively accounted for 60.4%, 89.9% and 72.2% of the Chengdu-Chongqing urban agglomeration's total.

Features of Industrial Structure

The Chengdu-Chongqing urban agglomeration has formed a certain level of industrial agglomeration, which is particularly manifested in IT industry since IT has been developing rapidly in recent years in Chongqing and Chengdu. The urban agglomeration has accounted for 6.5% of the regional gross produc-tion from the secondary sector across China, and 3.9% of the country's cargo exports.

When we analyzed the 16 cities in the Chengdu-Chongqing urban agglomeration for the following areas using the radiation concept in the *China Integrated City Index 2017*, we found the following. In the wholesale and retail area, Chengdu and Chongqing have both been prominently advantaged by their radiation, ranking 3rd and 4th respectively in the country. It has highlighted both cities as regional shopping centers.[5]

In the science and technology radiation, Chengdu ranked 5th and Chongqing 12th. The size of R&D manpower and the number of patents granted in the Chengdu-Chongqing urban agglomeration respectively accounted for 5.6% and 6.7% of the national total, making it an important R&D and technological center in inland China.[6]

---

4 Refer to Figure 5-35.
5 Refer to Figure 4-28.

As for higher education radiation, Chengdu and Chongqing respectively ranked 7th and 16th in the country. Of China's university students, 7.6% were educated in the Chengdu-Chongqing urban agglomeration, which therefore makes it an important center for higher education in China.[7]

In terms of financial radiation, Chengdu and Chongqing ranked among the top 30 in the nation, respectively coming in at 9th and 10th place.[8]

In the medical field, Chengdu and Chongqing respectively ranked national 4th and 10th with their radiation and were therefore important regional medical centers.[9]

In the fields of culture, sports, and entertainment, Chengdu and Chongqing were also members of the national top 30[10] with their radiation, respectively taking the 4th and 10th places.

In manufacturing, Chongqing and Chengdu ranked among the national top 30, respectively at 6th and 15th.[11]

On the IT front, Chengdu and Chongqing ranked 5th and 12th, respectively, with their radiation, which was a manifestation of the rapid development the IT industry in the two cities.[12]

Regarding catering and hotels, both Chongqing and Chengdu have done a good job, ranking among national top 10 with their radiation, respectively coming in at the 3rd and 7th places.[13]

Chongqing and Chengdu ranked national 8th and 11th respectively in the number of inbound tourists[14] received. The Chengdu-Chongqing urban agglomeration accounted for 4.7% of the national total of inbound tourists. Chongqing and Chengdu respectively ranked 1st and 5th for the number of domestic tourists, with the Chengdu-Chongqing urban agglomeration accounting for 10.1% of the national total.[15] With rich natural endowments and long-standing historical and cultural resources, this urban agglomeration possesses a great potential to develop its tourism economy and an exchange-based economy.

In sum, Chongqing and Chengdu are prominently advantaged in the manufacturing and service sectors of the Chengdu-Chongqing urban agglomeration, with strong radiation compared to their surrounding areas. In comparison, the remaining cities largely fall behind the core cities, and the pattern of "two large and many small" is distinct.

---

[6] Refer to Figure 4-24.

[7] Refer to Figure 4-23.

[8] Refer to Figure 4-20.

[9] Refer to Figure 4-25.

[10] Refer to Figure 4-26.

[11] Refer to Figure 4-21.

[12] Refer to Figure 4-22.

[13] Refer to Figure 4-27.

[14] Refer to Figure 4-18.

[15] Refer to Figure 4-17.

Evaluation and Analysis of Megalopolis

Under environmental dimension of the *China Integrated City Index 2017*, Chongqing (9th) was the only one from the Chengdu-Chongqing urban agglomeration that ranked among the top 20[16] in the country.

According to the analysis of this urban agglomeration in the *Index* for its internal deviation values under the environmental dimension, we see that Chongqing was the best performer ranking 1st. Chengdu and Ya'an ranked respectively 2nd and 3rd.

Suining and Nanchong were similar in their deviation values, ranking 4th and 5th respectively.[17]

Chongqing and Chengdu were among the top 20 cities under the social dimension in the *China Integrated City Index 2017*, having respectively ranked 4th and 9th.[18]

According to the analysis of this urban agglomeration in the Index for its internal deviation values under the under the social dimension, we find that Chongqing and Chengdu had prominent advantages. They were far ahead of the other cities by a significant difference in deviation values.[19]

Chongqing and Chengdu respectively ranked 7th and 8th among the top 20 cities under the economic dimension in the *China Integrated City Index 2017*.[20]

According to the analysis of this urban agglomeration for its internal deviation values under the economic dimension, we find that Chongqing and Chengdu had prominent advantages. They were far ahead of the other cities by a significant difference in deviation values.[21]

Under the overall ranking in the *China Integrated City Index 2017*, Chongqing and Chengdu ranked 6th and 10th respectively, manifesting the strength of the two core cities in the Chengdu-Chongqing urban agglomeration.[22]

According to the comprehensive analysis in the Index of this urban agglomeration for its internal deviation values, we find that Chongqing and Chengdu were far ahead of other cities. In this region, there was a distinct "two large and many small" pattern.[23]

---

[16] Refer to Figure 2-6.
[17] Refer to Figure 5-32.
[18] Refer to Figure 2-10.
[19] Refer to Figure 5-33.
[20] Refer to Figure 2-14.
[21] Refer to Figure 5-34.
[22] Refer to Figure 2-2.
[23] Refer to Figure 5-31.

Challenges in the Next Stage

According to the analysis in the *China Integrated City Index 2017*, the ratio of DID population in the less urbanized Chengdu-Chongqing urban agglomeration was no more than 24.6% (40.6 percentage points lower than that of the Pearl River Delta Megalopolis) and 63.95 million people were still living in non-DID areas. One big challenge for this urban agglomeration in terms of spatial structure is how to significantly improve its urbanization.

Next, the density of DID population in the Chengdu-Chongqing urban agglomeration was 7,376.4 persons/km², lower than that of the Pacific Coast Metropolis of Japan by 4,192.6 persons/km². It is a challenge as how to improve the region's density of DID population and urban intelligence.

The third challenge is that considerable low-density development has taken place in the built-up areas of this urban agglomeration, but at the same time, a large number of DIDs were scattered outside the built-up areas, resulting in their seriously falling behind of infrastructure support, public service support, and social management in these areas.

In conclusion, there is an urgent need for the Chengdu-Chongqing urban agglomeration to further its urbanization and make great efforts to develop the service economy in order to improve the quality of urban life and the efficiency of its economic activities. It also needs to improve urban management and infrastructure to create a high-density, large-scale urban society and to pioneer a model for the next stage of urbanization in inland China.

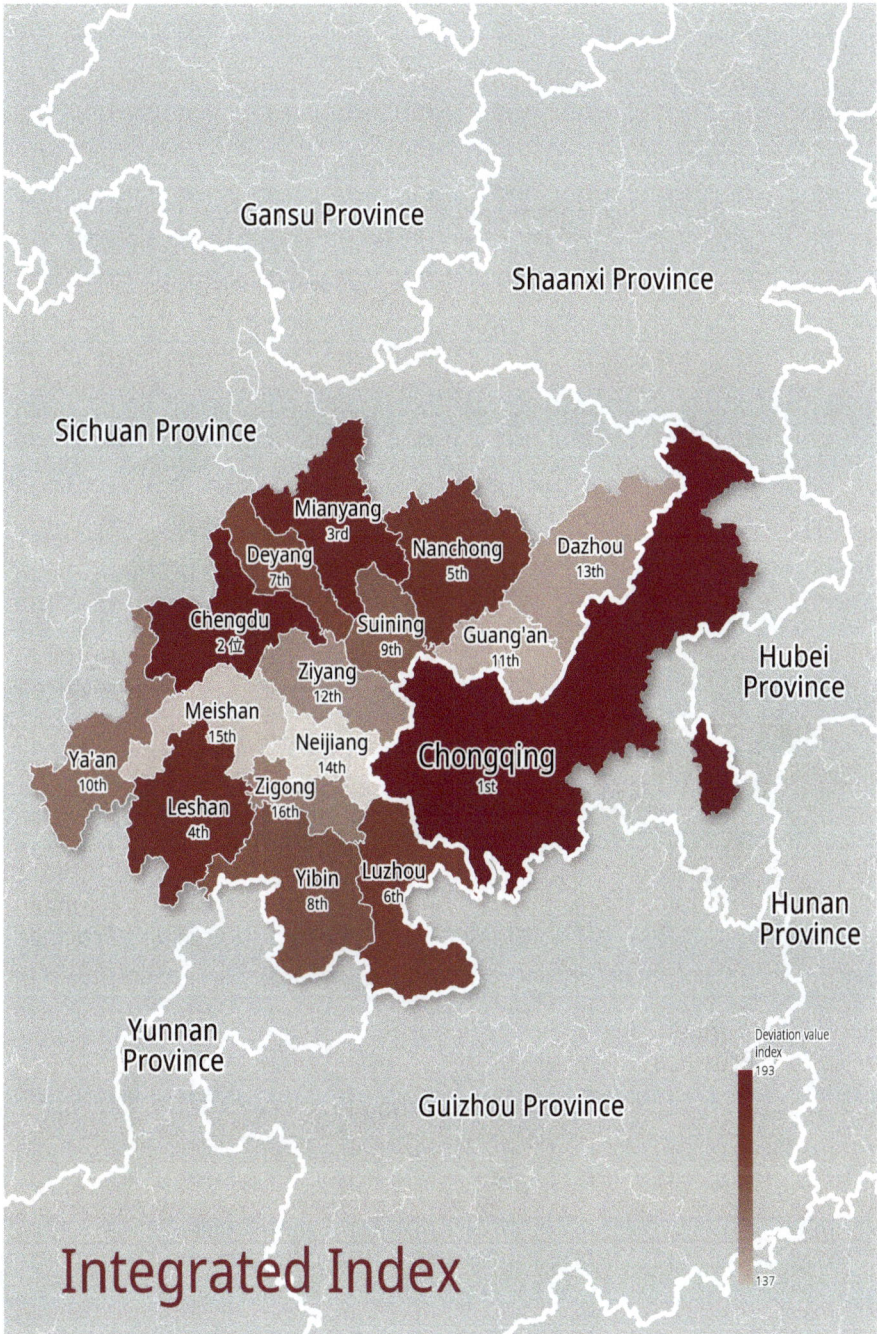

Gansu Province

Shaanxi Province

Sichuan Province

Mianyang
3rd

Deyang
7th

Nanchong
5th

Dazhou
13th

Chengdu
2位

Suining
9th

Guang'an
11th

Hubei
Province

Ziyang
12th

Meishan
15th

Neijiang
14th

Chongqing
1st

Ya'an
10th

Zigong
16th

Leshan
4th

Hunan
Province

Yibin
8th

Luzhou
6th

Yunnan
Province

Deviation value
index
193

Guizhou Province

Integrated Index

137

Figure 5-31 Analysis Diagram of Integrated Index of the Chengdu-Chongqing Urban Agglomeration
(16 Cities)

Note: Rankings from Figure 5-31 to Figure 5-34 refer to those of 16 cities within the Chengdu-Chongqing Urban Agglomeration.

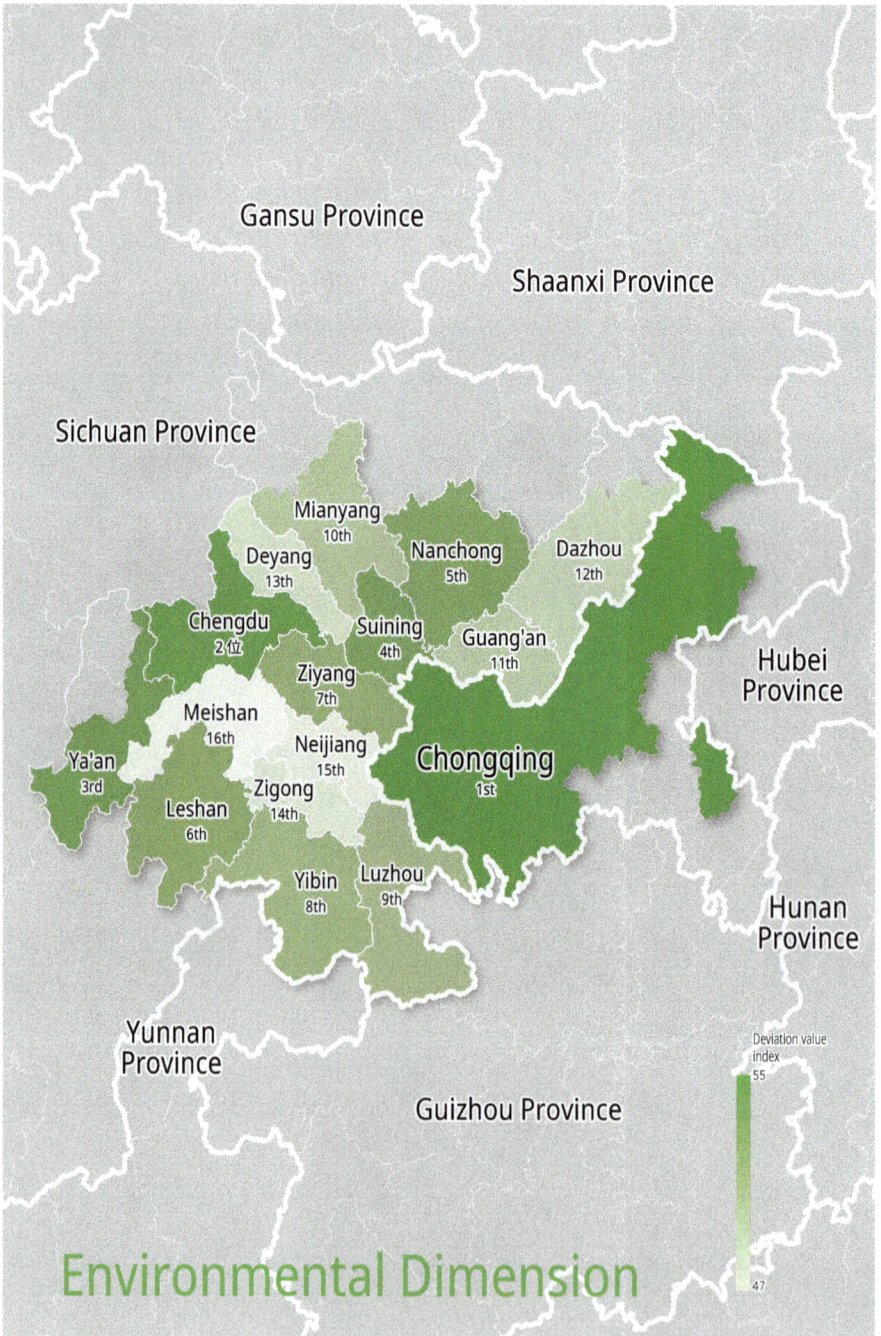

Gansu Province

Shaanxi Province

Sichuan Province

Mianyang
10th

Deyang
13th

Nanchong
5th

Dazhou
12th

Chengdu
2位

Suining
4th

Guang'an
11th

Hubei
Province

Ziyang
7th

Meishan
16th

Neijiang
15th

Chongqing
1st

Ya'an
3rd

Zigong
14th

Leshan
6th

Yibin
8th

Luzhou
9th

Hunan
Province

Yunnan
Province

Guizhou Province

Deviation value
index
55

Environmental Dimension

47

Figure 5-32 Analysis Diagram of Environmental Dimension of the Chengdu-Chongqing Urban Agglomeration (16 Cities)

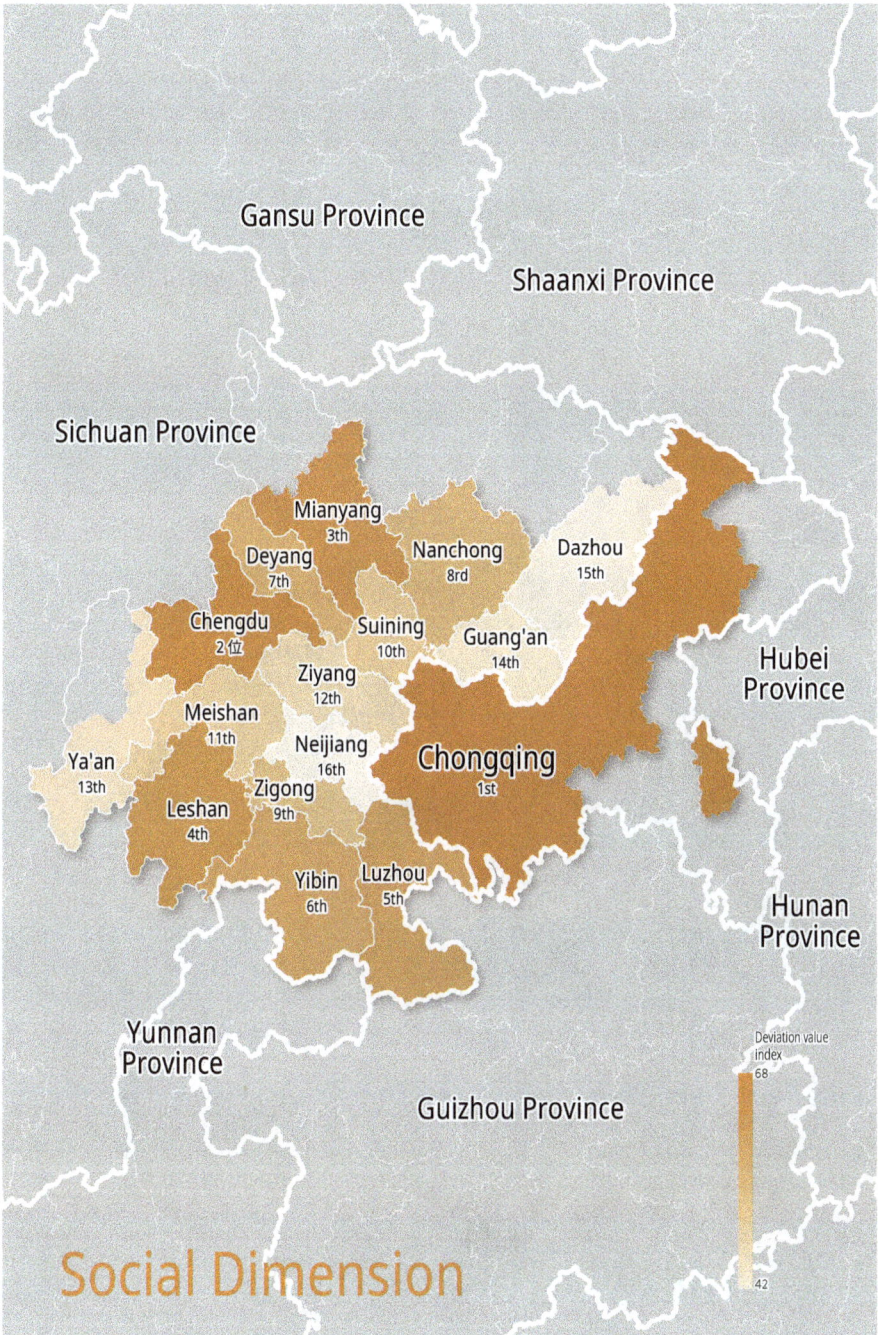

Gansu Province

Shaanxi Province

Sichuan Province

Mianyang
3th

Deyang
7th

Nanchong
8rd

Dazhou
15th

Chengdu
2位

Suining
10th

Guang'an
14th

Ziyang
12th

Hubei
Province

Meishan
11th

Neijiang
16th

Chongqing
1st

Ya'an
13th

Zigong
9th

Leshan
4th

Yibin
6th

Luzhou
5th

Hunan
Province

Yunnan
Province

Guizhou Province

Deviation value
index
68

42

Social Dimension

Figure 5-33 Analysis Diagram of Social Dimension of the Chengdu-Chongqing Urban Agglomeration
(16 Cities)

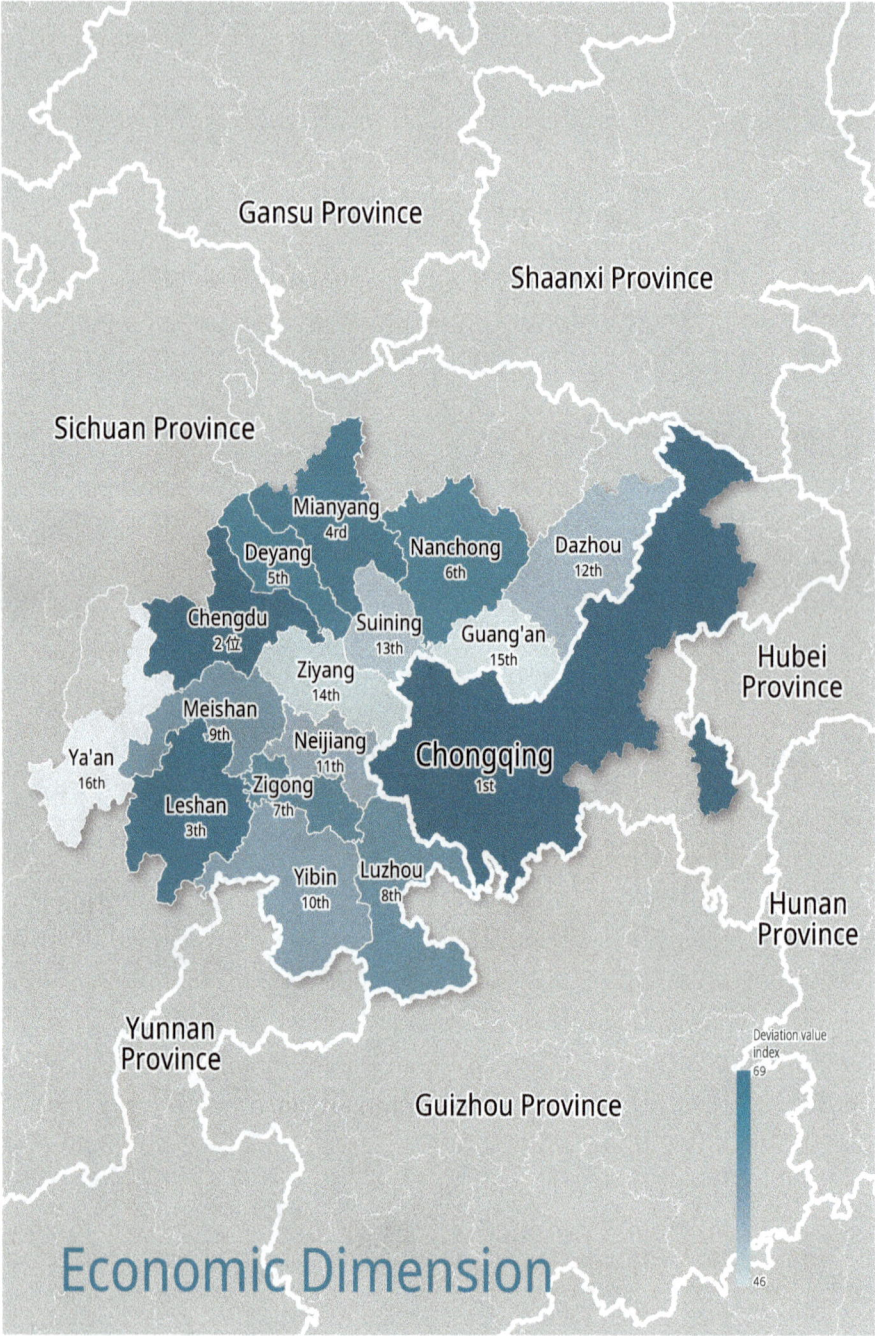

Gansu Province

Shaanxi Province

Sichuan Province

Mianyang
4rd

Deyang
5th

Nanchong
6th

Dazhou
12th

Chengdu
2位

Suining
13th

Guang'an
15th

Ziyang
14th

Hubei
Province

Meishan
9th

Neijiang
11th

Ya'an
16th

Chongqing
1st

Leshan
3th

Zigong
7th

Yibin
10th

Luzhou
8th

Hunan
Province

Yunnan
Province

Guizhou Province

Deviation value
index
69

Economic Dimension

46

Figure 5-34 Analysis Diagram of Economic Dimension of the Chengdu-Chongqing Urban
Agglomeration (16 Cities)

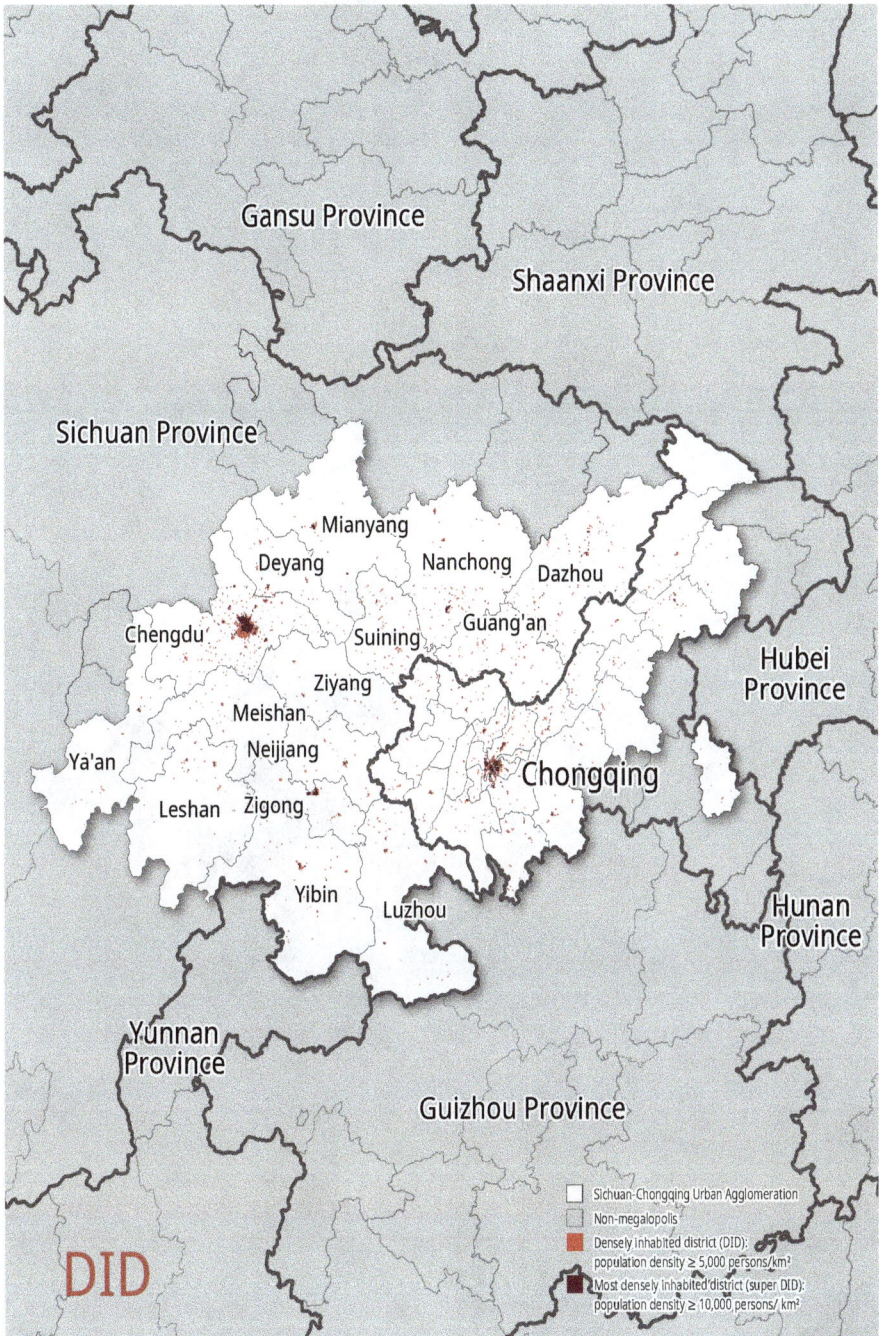

Figure 5-35 Analysis Diagram of DIDs in the Chengdu-Chongqing Urban Agglomeration (16 Cities)

Source: It is prepared as per the satellite remote sensing and analysis data published by the Cloud River Urban Research Institute.

Chapter VI

Development Strategy of Core City

Zhou Muzhi

1. Mega-city Era

If we call the 20th century a "Century of Urbanization," then the 21st century is technically the "Century of Cities," or even the "Century of Big Cities."

The 20th century witnessed the surge of global urban population by a factor of more than 10, growing from 250 million to 2.8 billion, so it deserves to be called a century of explosive growth of global urbanization. The world was aggressively urbanized in an ever-accelerating manner, technically making itself an "Urban Planet." For the first time in 2008, the global urban population outnumbered the rural population, meaning that more than half of the people on this planet lived in cities. According to the forecast by the United Nations, the world population will have reached 9 billion by 2050, and 6 billion of them will be urban residents.

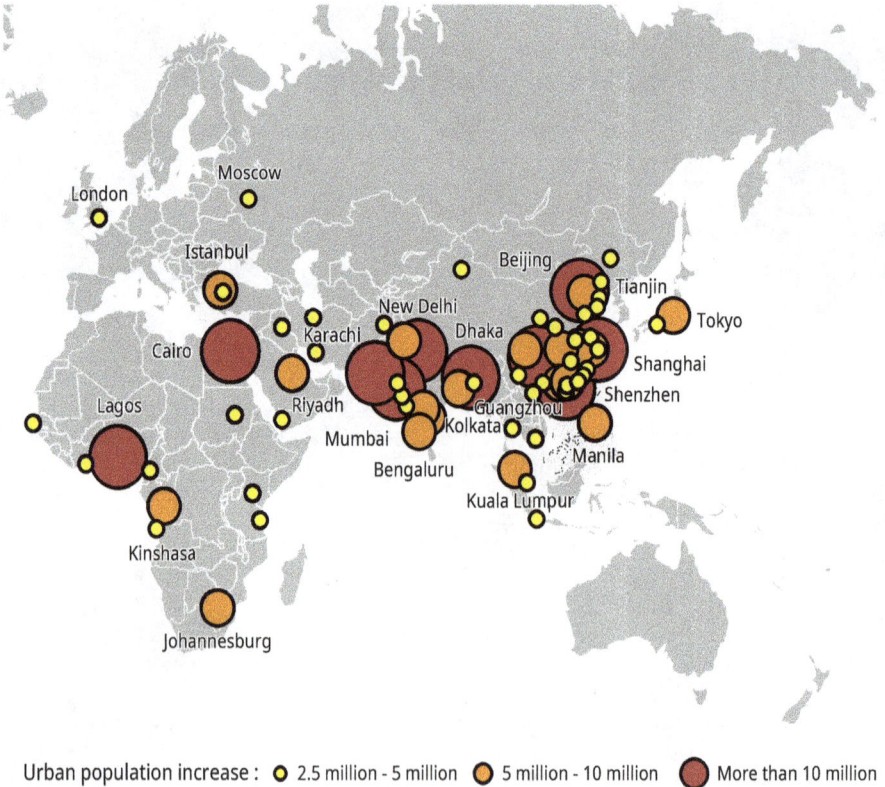

Urban population increase : ○ 2.5 million - 5 million ◐ 5 million - 10 million ⬤ More than 10 million

Figure 6-1 Distribution of Cities Worldwide with an Urban Population Increase of More than 2.5 Million (1980-2015)

Source: *World Urbanization Prospects* (2014 Revision) and *World Population Prospects* (2015 Revision) issued by the United Nations Department of Economic and Social Affairs (UN DESA).

It is particularly noteworthy that the population of large cities has experienced an explosive growth worldwide since 1980. During the 35 years from 1980 to 2015, the global urban population increased by 1.27 billion people, almost equal to the population of the whole China. In this time span, a growth of urban residents by 2.5 million took place in 92 cities around the world (See Figure 6-1); 35 cities underwent an urban population growth of larger than 5 million; and 11 cities, beyond 10 million. It is especially notable that the combined growth of the urban population in these 92 cities amounted to 500 million, nearly 40% of the total growth of urban population over the same period in the whole world. Concurrently with this fierce level of global urbanization, people have entered the era of large-city-oriented urbanization and megacity-oriented urbanization.

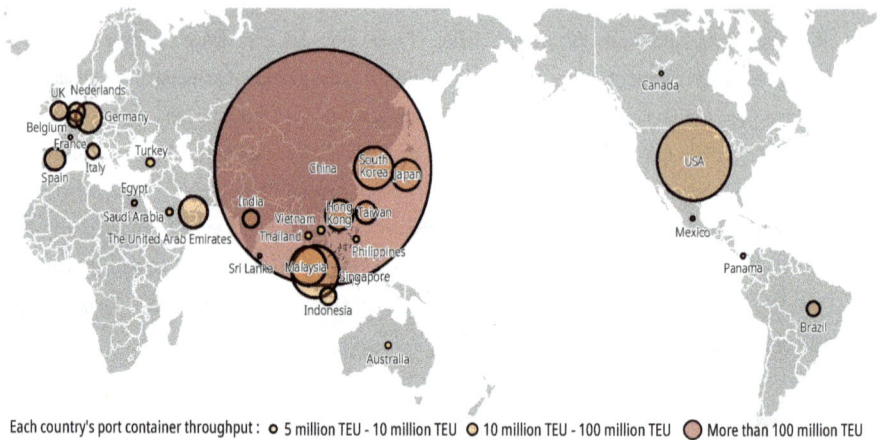

Each country's port container throughput： ○ 5 million TEU - 10 million TEU ○ 10 million TEU - 100 million TEU ⬤ More than 100 million TEU

Figure 6-2 Port Container Throughputs of Major Countries and Regions (2016)

Source: World Bank Open Data, the *Containerization International Yearbook* of International Association of Ports and Harbors (IAPH), the *Review of Maritime Transport* of United Nations Conference on Trade and Development (UNCTAD), and the CI-Online data.

Today, 29 megacities in the world have more than 10 million urban residents. Among these megacities, 19 are situated on the coastline and eight are inland capital cities. Being coastal or administrative centers has become the key to the great economic development of cities.

The furious information revolution and globalization have led us to embarked on large-city-oriented urbanization and mega-city-oriented urbanization. By attracting talents, enterprises and funds from around the world, large cities are expanding so rapidly that they have become leaders in the development and transformation of regional, national, and even global economies.

Since the 1980s, the information revolution and globalization have acted in an interdependent manner to facilitate the great integration of different technologies, industries, areas, and regions, as well as the great integration between countries and cities, and between cities and rural villages. Great integrations bring great change, and great change bring great developments. Integrations and changes based on exchanges and transactions have deduced the rapid development of large cities. The national economy was broken up to be reborn under such great integrations and restructurings. In contrast, large cities have risen amongst the tide of globalization and become the new mainstay dominating the world economy. Coastal cities and administrative centers, in particular, have provided a big stage for the great integrations, change, and restructurings with their openness, convenient transportation, and centralized functions.

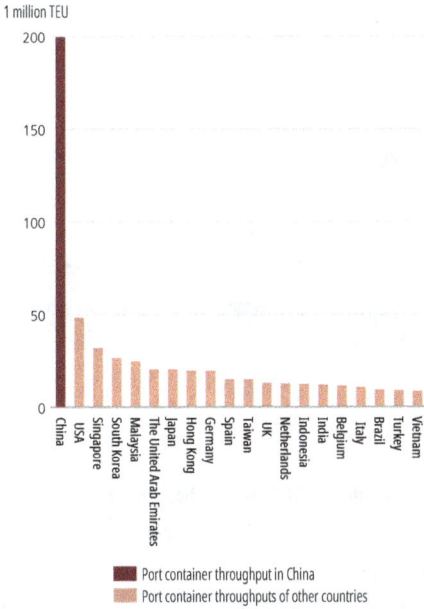

Figure 6-3 Top 20 Countries and Regions with Most Port Container Throughputs (2016)

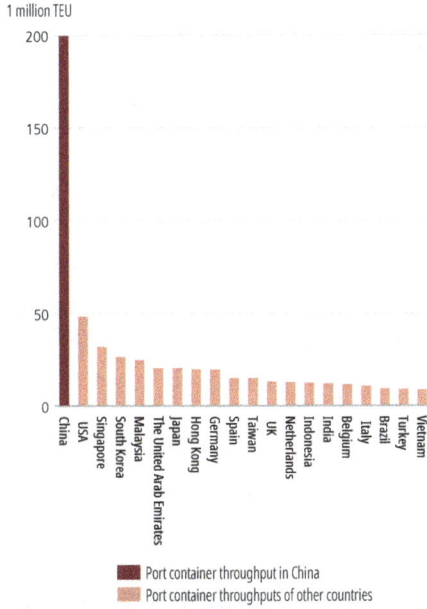

Figure 6-4 Throughputs Net Increase of Top 20 Countries and Regions with Most Port Container Throughputs (1980-2016)

Source: World Bank Open Data, the *Containerization International Yearbook* of International Association of Ports and Harbors (IAPH), the *Review of Maritime Transport* of United Nations Conference on Trade and Development (UNCTAD), and the CI-Online data.

The explosive development of large cities results from the changes in the pattern of global development.

If established under an economic structure that has been pretty much a closed loop, the traditional system of national economy will generally encompass a relatively complete capital chain, industrial chain, and technology chain. However, globalization driven by the information revolution has broken this pattern, and the transportation revolution is backing such globalization.

The transportation revolution means the development and improvement of a high-speed aviation system represented by jumbo jets and a large-scale maritime transport system represented by container shipping. This revolution has facilitated and accelerated beyond our expectations the international flow of people and goods, and greatly reduced the cost of such exchanges. It also presents globalization as the most powerful driving force for the world's economic development.

From 1980 to 2016, the global actual GDP increased by 6.8 times. Over the same period, the global container throughput via ports[1] increased by 18.9 times.[2] International passengers have also increased by 4.4 times[3] worldwide in the same period. The development of the world economy is interdependent with the increase in the international flow of people and goods.

Another major driving force behind globalization is the information revolution. The information revolution means the development of the knowledge economy as triggered by semiconductor technology and Internet technology. In the 15 years between 2000 and 2015, revenue from the global communication and information service industry increased by 5.9 times.[4] During the 24 years between 1990 and 2014, value added to the global knowledge-intensive business services, including education, medical care, health, business, finance, and communication services, increased by 4.3 times.[5]

The relatively stable international environment after the Cold War has been beneficial to the transpor-tation revolution and the information revolution in promoting the aggressive globalization process and changing the pattern of global economic development.

With the development of information technology, the IT industry has been in the dominating position of the world's economic development, and its penetration into other fields has even triggered the cross-infiltration between academic fields, as well as the cross-integration of different areas of industrial technol-ogy. This has further caused the intersection and restructuring of the technology chain, industrial chain and capital chain at the international level. Integration and restructuring have become the theme of innovation and entrepreneurship. The integration that goes beyond academic or professional expertise and industry or national borders has ignited the exchange-and-trading-based economy, stoking the economic development of the world. Emerging industries and companies have sprung up. The national economy was melted down to be reborn under such great integration and restructuring. As a big stage for this integration and restructuring, large cities are on the rising wave of globalization and have become the new mainstay of the world's economy.

Of course, the establishment and change of relevant institutional systems is also an important driver of the globalization process. If the international trading system preceding the World Trade Organization (WTO) that was established in 1995 can be referred to as "Globalization 1.0," the WTO can be called "Globalization 2.0." The WTO has greatly promoted the globalization process and further

---

[1] Calculated based on the international standard container specifications (ISO specifications), where a 20ft container = 1TEU, and a 40ft container = 2 TEU.

[2] Calculated based on the *Containerization International Yearbook* by the IAPH, the *Review of Maritime Transport* by the UNCTAD and the CI-Online data.

[3] Calculated based on the data from the *UNWTO Tourism Highlights*.

[4] Calculated based on the data from the *Information Economy Report* by the UNCTAD.

[5] Calculated based on *Science and Engineering Indicators 2014* by the NSF.

benefited the development of China. China's accession to the WTO and the Globalization 2.0 system has made her the "World Factory" and the world's largest trading country. Her coastal cities have hence achieved an explosive development.

The Trans-Pacific Partnership Agreement (TPP) launched by the U.S. during the Obama Administration can be described as an attempt to explore and structure a framework for Globalization 2.1. The TPP, which has huge differences from the WTO, aimed at further enhancing intellectual property rights, opening services and finance, and strengthening the corporate rights and interests by using the ISDS provisions. The Obama Administration was attempting to reinforce the advantages of the U.S. in the areas of intel-lectual property, services industry, as well as investment and finance by launching the 2.1 version of Globalization.

Japan has also been transforming herself from a major exporter for industrial products to an export power for investments and intellectual properties, from which two areas she has already made great profits. Thus Japan felt an urgent need to establish a new international mechanism to secure and expand her interests in the areas of international investment, intellectual property, the service industry, and international trade. On this count, the U.S. and Japan shared the same interests, and so they advocated for the establishment of the TPP.

According to the calculations of Japan's Ministry of Agriculture, Forestry and Fisheries, after her accession to the TPP, Japan's food self-sufficiency rate would be reduced from the current 39% (by Kcal) to 13%, which is one of the major reasons why the TPP was strongly opposed in Japan. However, the Abe Administration has changed the past national policies that protected agriculture, medical care and financial services, in pursuit of the benefits from the Globalization 2.1 by sacrificing some of the domestic interests that the country had made every effort to protect after the WWII.

In the era of Globalization 2.0, especially since China joined the WTO, a global shakeout has taken place in the mechanism and distribution of industrial production. Industrial capital from the U.S. has achieved greater benefits and gains in this process, but the traditional industrial zones in the U.S. have suffered from such catastrophes as factory bankruptcy and the unemployment of workers. So to speak, Globalization 2.0 has divided the U.S. into two major interest groups, the beneficiaries and the victims—from the perspective of cities, the former concentrated in big coastal cities, and the latter is mostly distributed in the inland old industrial zones as well as small and medium-sized cities.

In the U.S. presidential election of 2016, the Democratic candidate Hillary Clinton was supported by almost all the large coastal cities in the U.S. In contrast, the Republican candidate Donald Trump was predominantly supported by the inland's old industrial zones and small and medium-sized cities. A clear line was drawn between these two candidates. In this sense, that U.S. election was a contest of social awareness and a fight for political and economic interests between the beneficiaries and victims—in other words, between large coastal cities and the inland small and medium-sized cities under the Globalization 2.0. That is why any and all scandals and indiscreet remarks disclosed of Donald Trump during the campaign failed to shake his support groups. In the face of the globalization shakeout and the siphon effect of large cities, the inland old industrial zones, small and medium-sized cities and rural areas had long been unhappy, and the outbreak of such unhappiness sent Trump to victory.

Coincidentally, the same sort of unhappiness triggered the UK's Brexit Vote this year, which also represented a standoff between Greater London, a megacity, and small and medium-sized cities. As a result, the Greater London Area, which insisted on "Bremain," lost to the great number of small and medium-sized cities and rural areas that sought to vent their dissatisfaction via "Brexit."

The increasingly intensive unipolar centralization in Tokyo has also caused a "political" standoff between megacities and small and medium-sized cities in Japan. Relying on the small constituency-based election system to the advantage of the vast rural areas and small and medium-sized cities, the Liberal Democratic Party of Japan (LDP), as the ruling party, still won the election for the House of Representatives in October 2017, but the intensifying impulse among metropolitan voters to opt for new political representation has posed a huge threat to the LDP.

On January 23, 2017, Trump signed an executive order on the first day of his presidency to officially announce the withdrawal of the U.S. from the TPP. This was because Trump was no longer satisfied with the impact of Globalization 2.1 on customs tariffs and trade barriers, but instead took such an intensive measure as reducing the corporate tax rate from 35% to 20%, upgrading the Globalization game to Version 3.0. This was an attempt to instantly make the U.S. a sought-after destination of global industrial capital and to induce the return of industries. After several twists and turns, the U.S. Congress passed the tax reform bill at the end of 2017, making Trump's strategy of Globalization 3.0 into reality.

After the withdrawal of the U.S. from TPP, the remaining 11 Asia-Pacific states[6] negotiating TPP issued a joint statement on November 11, 2017, announcing that they have "reached an agreement on a number of fundamental parts" and decided to rename the TPP as CPTPP (Comprehensive Progressive Trans-Pacific Partnership). Notwithstanding the withdrawal of the U.S., Japan still pushed forward Globalization 2.1 in the form of CPTPP and attempted to make the game rules of Globalization 2.1 to maximize her own national interest.

Abe and Trump were each playing a big game of globalization—one wanted to become the rule maker of Globalization 2.1, and the other was looking to upgrade the game straight to Version 3.0. The introduction of Versions 2.1 and 3.0 will undoubtedly further the meaning of globalization and accelerate its progress. This state of affairs will have profound impact on the global political and economic patterns, as well as the political, economic, and even social structures of the U.S. and Japan, and further have a

---

[6] The 11 states to the CPTPP are Japan, Australia, Canada, Chile, New Zealand, Mexico, Peru, Singapore, Malaysia, Brunei and Vietnam.

far-reaching effects on the world's city landscape. It will certainly lead to major changes in China's society and economy too.

The rapid development of the exchange-and-trading-based economy under the globalization has promoted large-city-oriented urbanization and mega-city-oriented urbanization. The considerable siphonic effect of large cities in attracting people, enterprises, and capital from all over the world is also inducing profound socio-economic contradictions and changes within each country. The traditional national economy that was pretty fairly a closed loop is evolving into a globalized economy dominated by large cities. Major profound changes have taken place to the economic structures of human society.

Specifically, there are a few reasons for the continuous growth of large cities that play a leading role in the above major changes:

(1) Changes of Location Advantages of the Exchange-and-trading-based Economy

Thanks to the ongoing acceleration, expansion, and enhancement of global networks of population flow, logistics, information, and finance, which encompasses aviation, maritime transport, and the Internet, the global expansion of the supply chain and the value chain from production to service and to sales has become increasingly easier. The global wave of elements integration dominated by the exchange-and-trading-based economy has reshaped the location advantages of different regions. Coastal cities with an advantage of ports and administrative centers have been the first to grab opportunities in this round of dramatic changes.

In fact, the first trigger for the major development of coastal cities was the Great Navigation. Particularly, based on the maritime transport after the industrial revolution, the global deployment and sales of raw materials and industrial products subverted the dominant position of continental economy, leading to the agglomeration of industries and population in coastal port cities. Relying on the economic advantages of their ports, a large number of trade-port-based and industrial-port-based cities have experienced a rapid development—New York, Tokyo and Osaka are typical examples of such cities. Since the 1980s, globalization has further intensified the gathering of talents, enterprises, information, and funds in port cities, leading to the rise of a large number of sizable coastal cities.

Of course, the "port" of a coastal city today is more than just a narrowly defined port for maritime transport. For example, coastal megacities in developed countries, such as London of the U.K. and San Francisco of the U.S., have even lost half of their functions as ports. However, by relying on their openness and inclusivity as port cities, these cities have successfully built an "exchange port" for economy, informa-tion, technology, culture, and art in the era of globalization, and have shaped a new model for cities of an exchange-and-trading-based economy. In this sense, openness and inclusivity have become the most fundamental conditions for developing an exchange-and-trading-based economies.

Similar to coastal cities, the continuous expansion of administrative centers represented by the capitals have also contributed to the unique characteristics of openness and inclusivity. Another reason for such expansion is that the functions of these administrative cities in politics, economy, culture, transportation and information have been manifested and magnified in the new round of development.

From the distribution of today's 29 megacities around the world with a population of over 10 million, it is observed that 19 are coastal cities, eight are capitals, and only two of them are non-capital inland cities, which, however, though they are both regional centers.

(2) Amplification of the Siphonic Effect

The so-called siphonic effect refers to the ability demonstrated by a city of a certain scale to attract people, enterprise, and capital and the phenomenon of such ability being given play.

The amplification of the siphon effect is firstly attributed to the continuous acceleration and expansion of the population flow network, logistics network, information network and financial network, resulting in the increasing coverage of the network hub city. The enhanced hub function further magnifies the central function of the city and strengthens the siphon effect of the city.

The amplification of the siphon effect is also due to the essential need of developing the knowledge economy and services economy. Even though the knowledge economy that is represented by the IT and information content industries and has been developed rapidly since the 1980s, and though the service economy is continuously upgrading itself, it is still necessary to provide a relaxed, tolerant, and diversified social environment, as well as a population of certain size and density as the soil for the incubation and development of the knowledge and services economies. This is also why central cities and coastal cities that provide a relatively relaxed, tolerant, and diversified social environment dominate the development of the knowledge and services economies.

The knowledge economy and the service economy are the most powerful driving forces for the growth of today's world. The interdependent relationships between both economies and the size and density of a population is what promotes the rapid large-city-oriented and megacity-oriented urbanization.

(3) Improvement of Cities' Carrying Capacity

By way of improving the urban infrastructure and urban management, cities are able to significantly increase their capacity for the density and size of population. Taking the Greater Tokyo Metropolitan Area as an example When this area accommodated more than 10 million people around 1950, it had been seriously plagued by environmental pollution, traffic congestion, housing shortage, and inadequate infrastructure among other large-city problems, and thus was considered "too big" and "too dense." As such, the Japanese government undertook a series of policy measures to prevent people and industries from being concentrated and gathered in Tokyo, and it was even prepared to relocate their capital. However, due to the improvement of urban infrastructure and urban management, as well as the result-ing significant increase of capacity, the past "large-city problems" have been no longer a major social issue in such cities, in spite of the current population of this area already being close to 40 million.

It is precisely the improvement in the city's carrying capacity that makes possible the increasing size and density of today's cities.

2. Enlightenment and Reference from Greater Tokyo Metropolitan Area

The Greater Tokyo Metropolitan Area consists of the Tokyo Metropolis as well as the Kanagawa, Chiba, and Saitama Prefectures. Tokyo, Yokohama, Kawasaki, and Saitama—each with more than one million people—and a great number of small and medium-sized cities are densely distributed on this 13,562 square-kilometer territory. This metropolitan area, where the total population already exceeded 10 million in 1950, is one of the very first megacities in the world. Today, the population of this area has even reached 38 million, making it the largest "city" of the whole world. The Greater Tokyo Metropolitan Area contributes 32.3% of Japan's GDP with only 3.6% of the country's land, and also brings together government agencies, cultural facilities as well as financial institutions—this area really deserves the title of Japan's political, economic, and cultural center.[1] Moreover, Tokyo is also a world-renowned international metropolis, ranking third in the Global Power City Index, immediately after London and New York.[2]

According to the study of *Asia Integrated City Index 2017* conducted by the Cloud River Urban Research Institute, the success of the Greater Tokyo Metropolitan Area mainly relies on the following four factors:

(1) Diversified Central Functions Complementing Each Other
The Greater Tokyo Metropolitan Area is a "city" with the most diversified central functions around in the world.

From the political perspective, this area accommodates the imperial palace, the Diet of Japan, as well as the highly centralized administrative ministries and commissions of the central government. A large number of headquarters of Japanese companies cluster around such places as Ōtemachi and Marunouchi, and 58.2% of Japan's listed companies are headquartered in the Greater Tokyo Metropolitan Area.

Keihin and Keiyo are representatives of the world's largest and most advanced coastal industrial zones, and mass groups of supporting companies agglomerate around the Greater Tokyo Metropolitan Area. In terms of cargo exports (see Figure 6-6), the Kanagawa Prefecture, where the Keihin Industrial Zone is located, ranks 4th in the country; the Chiba Prefecture, where the Keiyo Industrial Zone is located, is 5th; and the Tokyo Metropolis, 16th. Manufacturing exports from the Greater Tokyo Metropolitan Area accounts for 29.5%—close to one-third—of the total amount of Japan.

As a financial center, Tokyo is not only home to Japan's largest stock exchange, but also to the headquarters of Japanese financial institutions. An analysis of financial radiation (see Figure 6-7) shows the Tokyo Metropolis is the only one standing out from the 47 prefectures[3] across Japan with her powerful

---

[1] Unless otherwise specifically noted, the data of Japan cited in this report came from the *Asia Integrated City Index 2017* by the Cloud River Urban Research Institute.

[2] *Global Power City Index Yearbook 2017* by the Mori Memorial Foundation Institute for Urban Strategies.

[3] The Government of Japan consists of 3 levels, the Central Government and those at the levels of prefecture and municipality. Japan has one "metropolis", one "territory", two "urban prefectures" and 43 prefectures, namely 47 prefectures in total.

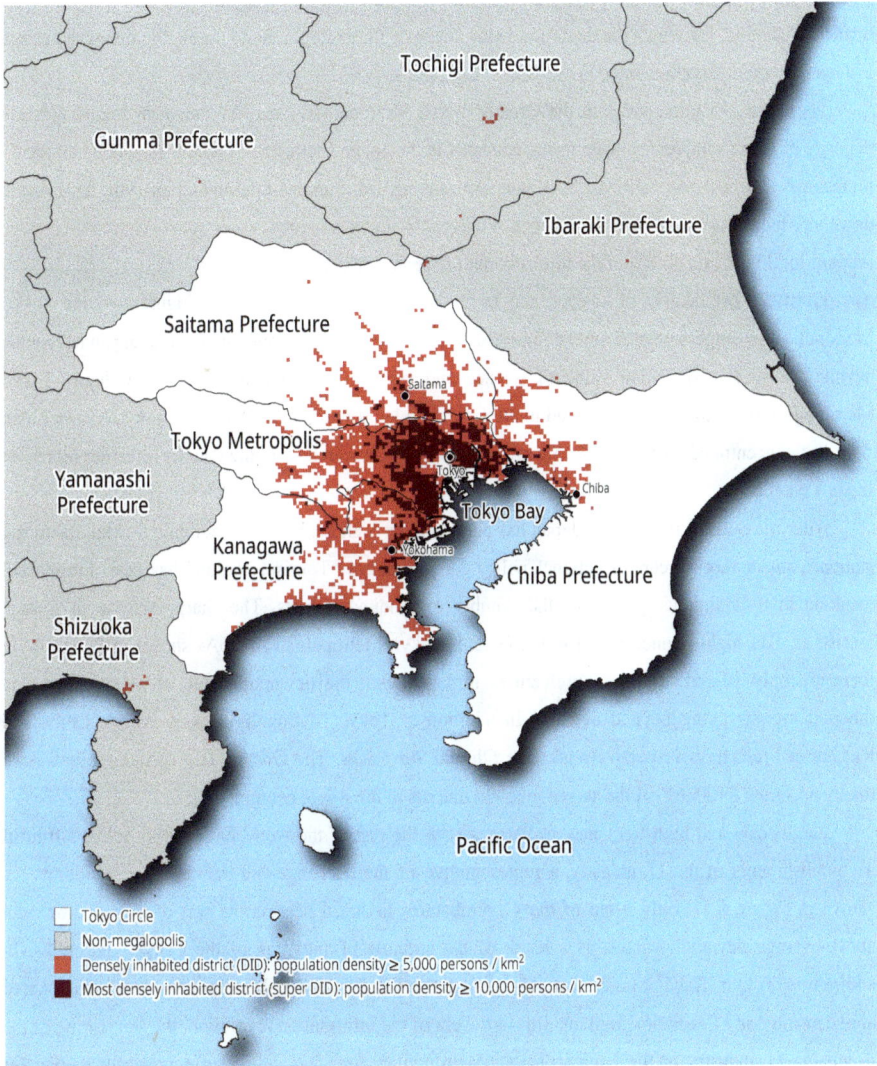

Figure 6-5 Analysis Diagram of Tokyo Metropolitan Area DID

Source: It is prepared as per the *Asia Integrated City Index 2017* by the Cloud River Urban Research Institute.

Note: In the *China Integrated City Index 2016*, we draw on the Japanese DID standard, namely taking the clustered area with a population density of more than 4,000 per square kilometer as the norm for comparative analysis of the DIDs in China and Japan. In the *China Integrated City Index 2017*, we use the OECD standard to define the area with a population density of more than 5,000 per square kilometer as the DID. This report uses this new norm to analyze the DIDS in China, Japan and other cities of the world.

financial radiation, for which the deviation value is above 50 (average). So to speak, the financial centers of Japan are highly agglomerated in the Tokyo Metropolis.

There are 225 universities in the Greater Tokyo Metropolitan Area. As shown in Figure 6-8, the majority of Japan's university students are educated in the Tokyo Metropolis, ranking 1st among all the 47 prefectures across Japan, followed by Kanagawa ranking 3rd; Saitama 6th; and Chiba, 9th. As a result, university faculty resources and the number of university students in the Greater Tokyo Metropolitan Area account for 35.2% and 40.8% of the total amount of Japan, respectively.

From the perspective of science and technology radiation, as shown in Figure 6-9, the Tokyo Metropolis also outperforms all other counterparts. Only five of the 47 prefectures across Japan have gone beyond the median deviation value of science and technology radiation, and two of them—Tokyo Metropolis and Kanagawa—are located in the Greater Tokyo Metropolitan Area, i.e., Tokyo Metropolitan Area has concentrated 59.8% of R&D funds and 68.7% of researchers in the country, creating 60.6% of Japan's patents.

After the Second World War, Japan has been holding high the banner of building a "Manufacturing Nation", but in recent years, a national policy for building a "Tourism Nation" has been introduced, resulting in a continuous growth of the number of inbound tourists. The sharp increase in foreign tourists is also highly concentrated in the Greater Tokyo Metropolitan Area. As shown in Figure 6-10, there are only 10 out of the 47 prefectures in Japan with the deviation value of overnight-staying inbound tourists going beyond average. In addition to Tokyo Metropolis ranking No. 1, Chiba and Kanagawa Prefectures respectively take the 6th and 9th places. The Greater Tokyo Metropolitan Area totally accounts for 35.6% of the stayed inbound tourists in the whole country.

Large-scale and high-frequency exchanges with the rest of the world have led to Tokyo's fruitful accomplishments in the IT industry, a representative of the exchange-and-trading-based economy. As shown in Figure 6-11, only 3 out of the 47 prefectures in Japan possess the sort of IT radiation with above-average deviation values, as a result of the stronger IT radiation of the Tokyo Metropolis. In addition to Tokyo, Kanagawa Prefecture—part of the Greater Tokyo Metropolitan Area—has scored above average in IT radiation, ranking 3rd. In the era of the information revolution, the flourishing of the promising IT industry in the Greater Tokyo Metropolitan Area has cultivated a powerful engine for the development of this region.

The multimodal transportation hub, diversified central functions, and powerful development engine has made the Greater Tokyo Metropolitan Area into the development center for Japan. As shown in Figure 6-12, there are 12 out of the 47 prefectures in Japan with their GDP deviations going beyond average. It is not only the Tokyo Metropolis scoring a deviation value far higher than other regions—Kanagawa, Saitama, and Chiba Prefectures also rank 4th, 5th, and 6th respectively. Again, the Greater Tokyo Metropolitan Area contributes nearly one-third of Japan's GDP.

(2) Advantages of Tokyo Bay Area Being Fully Demonstrated

Blessed with a prime port, the Tokyo Bay has played a huge role in the post-war development of the Greater Tokyo Metropolitan Area.

After the Second World War, Japan fully utilized a peaceful international environment to promote the development of coastal industries on the basis of global resources and markets. In particular, she took an initiative to construct the two wings of the Tokyo Bay, that is, the "Keihin" and "Keiyo" coastal industrial zones. By making use of the cheap but high-quality resources from around the world such as crude oil and grain and the global markets provided by free trade, the Keihin and Keiyo industrial zones have given best play to maritime transport, and become the world's largest and most technologically advanced power-houses for the export industry. Further, these two coastal industrial zones have driven the post-war recovery and high-speed growth of Japan's economy, and once established Japan as the world's second largest economy. Today, although the economic mainstay of the Greater Tokyo Metropolitan Area has already shifted to the services industry and the knowledge industry, cargo exports[4] from the Tokyo Bay still account for nearly 30% of Japan's total.

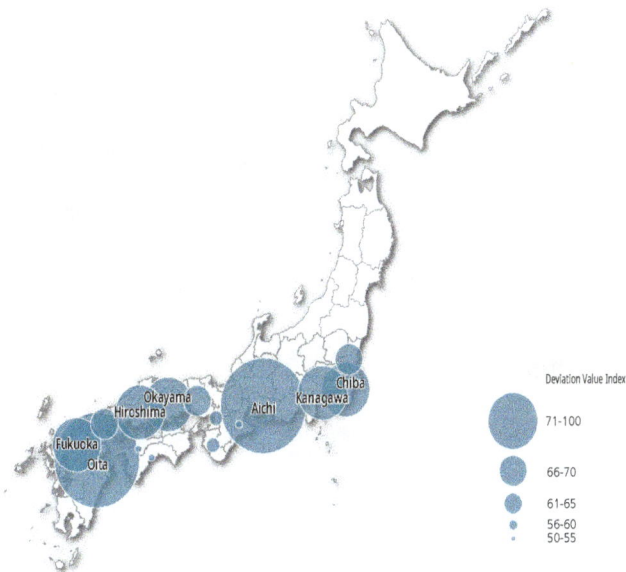

Figure 6-6 Wide-Area Analysis Diagram of Japan Export

Source: It is prepared as per the *Asia Integrated City Index 2017* by the Cloud River Urban Research Institute.
[4] Refers to cargo exports by value.

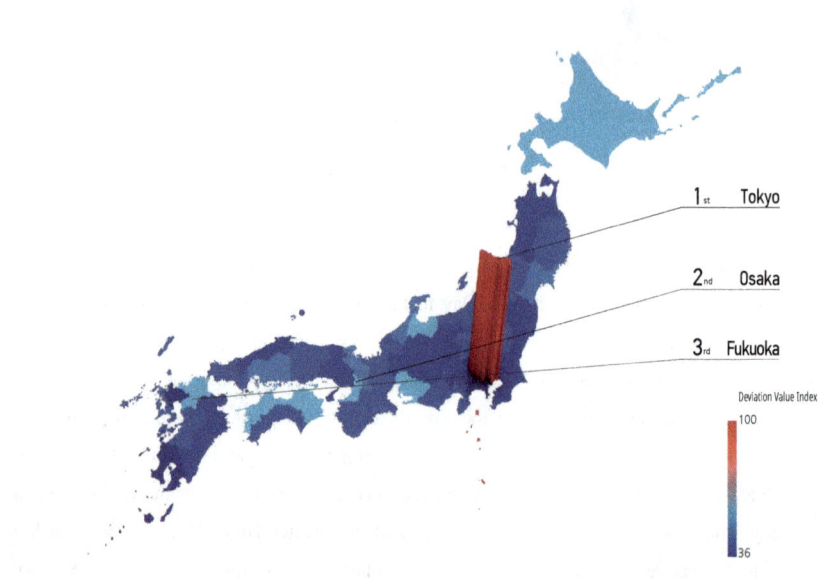

Figure 6-7 Wide-Area Analysis Diagram of Japan Financial Radiation

Source: It is prepared as per the *Asia Integrated City Index 2017* by the Cloud River Urban Research Institute.

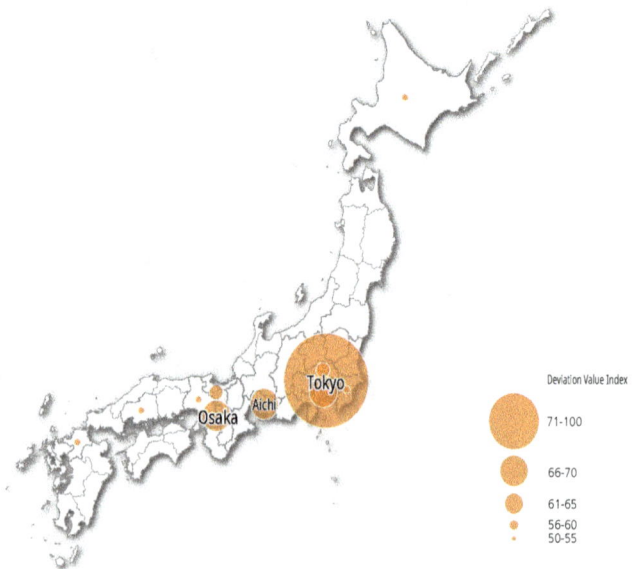

Figure 6-8 Wide-Area Analysis Diagram of the Number of Current Japanese College Students

Source: It is prepared as per the *Asia Integrated City Index 2017* by the Cloud River Urban Research Institute.

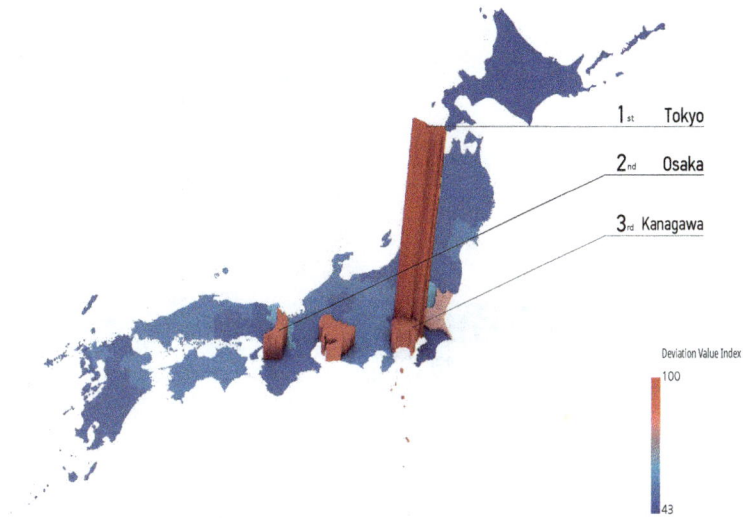

Figure 6-9 Wide-Area Analysis Diagram of Japan Science and Technology Radiation

Source: It is prepared as per the *Asia Integrated City Index 2017* by the Cloud River Urban Research Institute.

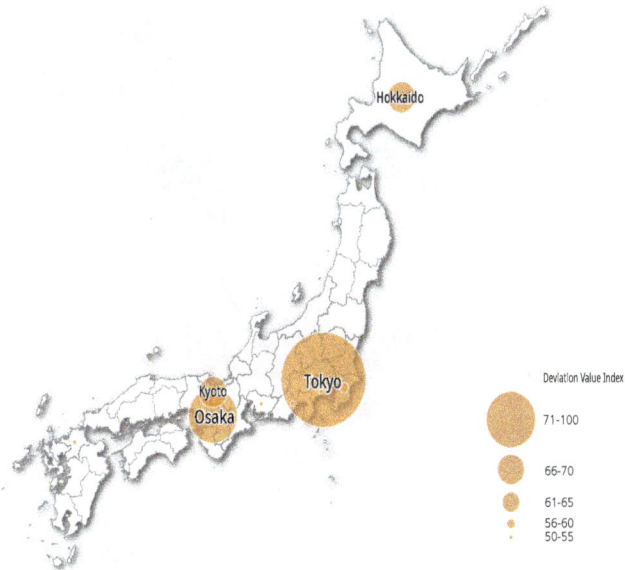

Figure 6-10 Wide-Area Analysis Diagram of Japan Inbound Tourists Stay Times

Source: It is prepared as per the *Asia Integrated City Index 2017* by the Cloud River Urban Research Institute.

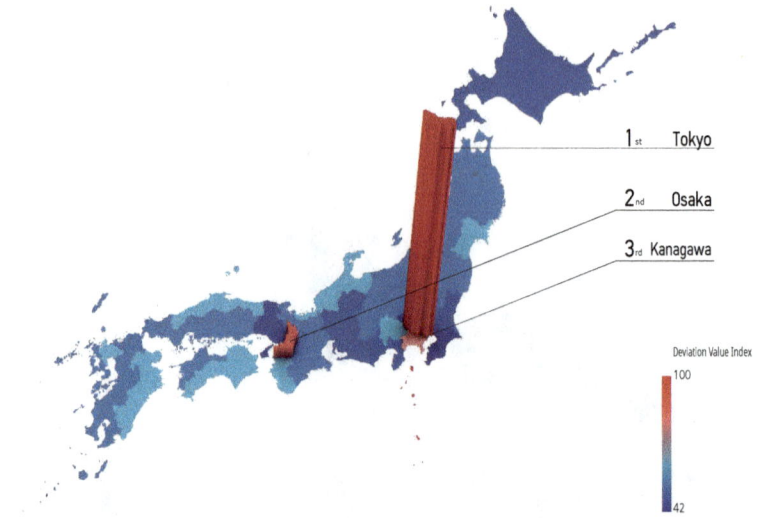

Figure 6-11 Wide-Area Analysis Diagram of Japan IT Industry Radiation

Source: It is prepared as per the *Asia Integrated City Index 2017* by the Cloud River Urban Research Institute.

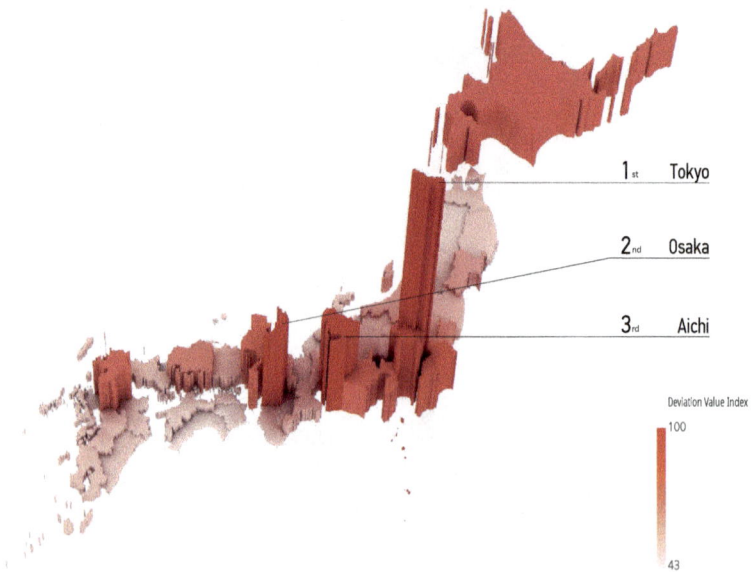

Figure 6-12 Wide-Area Analysis Diagram of Japan GDP

Source: It is prepared as per the *Asia Integrated City Index 2017* by the Cloud River Urban Research Institute.

The rapid development of the export industry has triggered the urbanization process, and the expansion of population around Tokyo Bay and its hinterland cities has created larger cities of over one million people, such as Tokyo, Yokohama, Kawasaki, and Saitama, promoting the formation of the Greater Tokyo Metropolitan Area.

It is worth noting that the group of ports in the Tokyo Bay Area has not only supported the development of the coastal industrial zones, but also sustained the ongoing growth of population in the metropolitan area and their high demand for a quality life by efficiently importing a large amount of energy, foods, and materials from all over the world.

Nowadays, the cargo imports[5] via the Tokyo Bay account for nearly 40% of the national total. It is fair to say the large-scale agglomeration of urban population near the ports in the bay area has enabled Japan to enjoy the optimized allocation of global resources and achieve the highly efficient development of her cities. This has rendered the current status that Japan has to rely on imports for 94% of her primary energy and 61% of her foods (by Kcal).

The spatial development of the Greater Tokyo Metropolitan Area is characterized by land reclamation. Since 1868, a total of 252.9 square kilometers of land has been reclaimed, most of which was implemented after the Second World War. For example, the majority of the related facilities for the 2020 Tokyo Olympic Games are also built on the land reclaimed for the Tokyo Bay.

More than just the large coastal industrial zones that have been created by the large-scale land reclamation. Vast space has also been provided by such reclamation for the development of large transportation hubs including ports and airports in the metropolitan area, and for large-scale urban developments such as the central business districts (CBDs), international conference centers, waterfront parks, large commercial facilities, and waterfront houses. With the new city core constructed so, the Greater Tokyo Metropolitan Area has managed to transition from an industrial economy to a knowledge economy and services economy and has also achieved a pattern of multi-core spatial development.

(3) Wide-area Infrastructure Amplifying Central Functions

The development of wide-area infrastructure, including airports, ports, Shinkansen, and expressways that provide connections to other cities and even the rest of the world, has amplified the central functions of Tokyo.

Japan successfully realized an economic leap by promoting the development of wide-area infrastructure after the Second World War. To welcome the 1964 Tokyo Olympic Games, Japan launched and accelerated the wide-area infrastructure development in the early 1960s. By 1965, Japan had only built 190 km of expressways, 515 km of Shinkansen and 5 airports with runways longer than two kilometers.

---

[5] Refers to cargo imports by value.

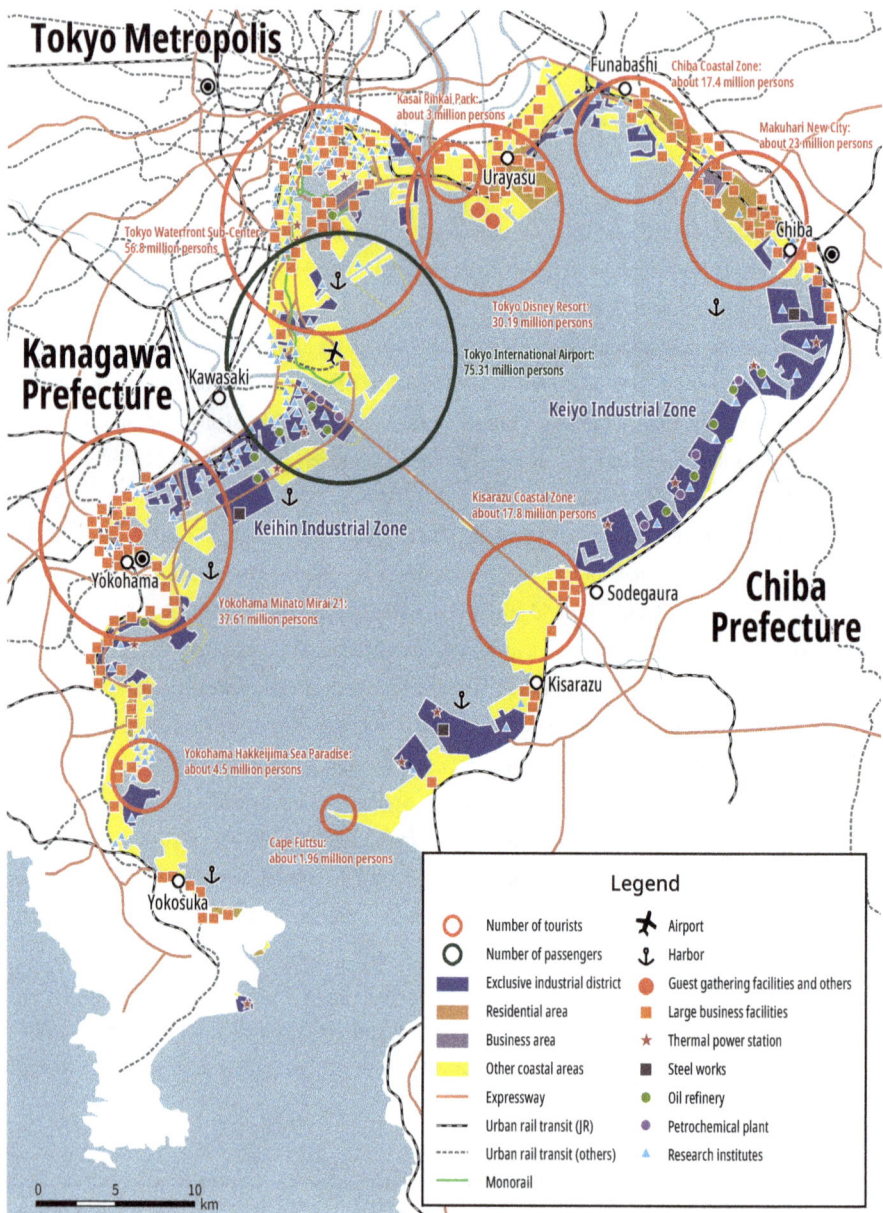

Figure 6-13 Tokyo Bay Coastal Zone's Distribution of Land Use and the Guest Gathering Status of Large Facilities

Source: It is prepared as per the research results of the Research Institute for Urban & Environmental Development (JAPAN) and Cloud River Urban Research Institute.

After an extended period of large-scale infrastructure development, however, Japan is now supported by 10,492 km of expressways, 2,624 km of Shinkansen and 66 airports with runways longer than two kilometers.

Such a development of wide-area infrastructure has turned the entire territory of Japan into a high-speed and convenient network, and as a result, this network enhanced and amplified the central functions of Tokyo. This report takes the high-speed railways as an example to further analyze the effect of wide-area infrastructure development on promoting economic growth and amplifying central functions.

Japan created the concept of high-speed railways and named it Shinkansen. In the past, railways in every country around the world were running on a mixed network for both passengers and freights, and thus the on-time rate and speed-per-hour of passenger lines were significantly limited. In 1964 and just before the Tokyo Olympics, Japan launched the world's first dedicated high-speed passenger line—Shinkansen. This line enabled the intercity express passenger transportation through the Tokyo, Nagoya, and Kinki metropolitan areas, where cities of all sizes became closely connected. The pattern of a mega-lopolis was then created for the interactive development of three metropolitan areas.

It is noteworthy that the fast traffic arteries connecting the three metropolitan areas of the Pacific Coast Megalopolis of Japan included—first and foremost—the high-speed railways, and the expressways running through the three metropolitan areas came as second. These expressways were not put into operation until 5 years later in 1969. In contrast, other megalopolises around the world, such as the Northeast Megalopolis of the U.S., were connected by expressways.

The construction of a rapid transportation system connecting different cities has promoted the development of core cities. Today, the Tokyo Station, the Shinkansen stations in Tokyo, and the Shinkansen stations in the Greater Tokyo Metropolitan Area are respectively serving 24.2%, 30.5%, and 39% of the national total of passengers on the Shinkansen lines. In other words, almost 80% of the Shinkansen passengers travel between the Greater Tokyo Metropolitan Area and other cities. This indicates the most important role of the Shinkansen is to connect the Greater Tokyo Metropolitan Area with other cities.

The Shinkansen best differentiates itself from the air transport by providing direct connections to the central area of each city, and this characteristic is worth great attention. Taking the Tokyo Station as an example: with five Shinkansen lines intersecting there, this station receives an average of 175,000 passengers every day; at the same time, this station provides interchanges to 15 urban rail lines, with an average pas-senger flow of 832,000 per day. The high-speed intercity transportation is thus seamlessly connected to the urban transportation extending in all directions. This achievement greatly enhances the convenience for people to travel between cities and further strengthens the interactive development pattern of cities.

The primary role of the Shinkansen lies in significantly shortening the temporal and spatial distance between the Greater Tokyo Metropolitan Area and other cities, which further supports and promotes the high-speed exchange of personnel in between. As a result, the central functions of Tokyo have been strengthened in a continuous way, leading to further concentration of the population and economy. Therefore, the Shinkansen is also a major driver for strengthening the central role of megacities.

In 1965, the Greater Tokyo Metropolitan Area had a population of 21.02 million. Back then, this metropolitan area contributed 21.2% and 28% to the national population and GDP, respectively. Half a century later in 2015, the Greater Tokyo Metropolitan Area had a population of 38 million, almost double the size of 1965, and in the meantime, this metropolitan area increased its share in the population and GDP of Japan to 29.9% and 32.3%, respectively. As proposed by Tanaka Kakuei in 1972 in his representative work, *Plan for Remodeling the Japanese Archipelago*, the Japanese government has for decades mightily supported the economic development outside of the three metropolitan areas. The government also tried to prevent population and economy from being concentrated towards Tokyo. However, the unipolar centralization in Tokyo tended to progress more aggressively, and in such a progression, one cannot ignore the role of the Shinkansen as an important driver.

Following the Shinkansen, Japan has now begun the construction of a Maglev Chuo Shinkansen that connects the Tokyo, Nagoya, and Kinki megalopolitan areas. As planned, the Maglev Chuo Shinkansen will be a 500 km/h super-high-speed traffic artery to connect the three metropolitan areas into an even more close-knit megalopolis, in both temporal and spatial terms. By doing so, Japan will create a huge urban space that is more attractive to global talent, capital, and information, in response to the intensifying competition between world cities in the face of globalization and knowledge economy.[6] Such a super-high-speed traffic artery will further change the spatial pattern of Japan, while magnifying and mani-festing the enormous central functions of the Greater Tokyo Metropolitan Area.

(4) Successful High-density Development

Density is a crucial key to any discussions of urban issues. This report defines an area with more than 5,000 people per square kilometer as a Densely Inhabited District (DID), and then uses this concept to conducts an accurate and valid analysis of population density.

According to the analysis by the Cloud River Urban Research Institute, the ratio of DID population in Tokyo is as high as 87.3%, and in the Greater Tokyo Metropolitan Area, this ratio is 58.8%. Most of the residents of the Greater Tokyo Metropolitan Area have already lived in densely populated areas. The Greater Tokyo Metropolitan Area, where 29.9% of Japan's population resides, contributes 55.2% to the national DID population. The difference is 25.3%. With a higher urbanization rate than the national aver-age, this metropolitan area has 23.36 millions of its urban population living in the DIDs. It is exactly such

---

[6] The Tokyo-Nagoya Section of the Maglev Chuo Shinkansen is expected to be put into operation in 2027, and the Nagoya-Osaka Section in 2037. By then the Tokyo, Nagoya and Kinki metropolitan areas will have been brought together into the more closely connected megalopolis.

a large DID population that supports the booming of the knowledge economy and services industry in the Greater Tokyo Metropolitan Area.

This report analyzes the correlations between the size of DID population in various prefectures around Japan, the gross regional production of the tertiary sector, and the R&D internal expenditures.[7] The results show a high correlation coefficient of 0.92 between the DID population size and the gross regional production of the tertiary sector, indicating an extremely strong correlation between the DID population size and the service economy. The correlation coefficient between the DID population size and the R&D internal expenditure is also as high as 0.8, showing a high level of correlation between the DID population size and the knowledge economy.

It is exactly the large and highly-dense urban population concentrated in the Greater Tokyo Metropolitan Area that has laid the foundation for the development of the service and knowledge economies in this megalopolis, and fostered the efficient society and economy development. As a result, this metropolitan area has been home to 58.2% of the listed companies in Japan and also contrib-uted 60.6% of the total amount of Japan's patent authorization.

High-quality DIDs are essential to the development of modern urban economy. As shown in Figure 6-14, the DIDs in Japan are highly concentrated in the Greater Tokyo Metropolitan Area, Nagoya Metropolitan Area, and Kinki Metropolitan Area. The three metropolitan areas constitute the Pacific Coast Megalopolis of Japan (also known as the Tokaido Megalopolis, accommodates 86.3% of the country's total DID population and 83.8% of her DID areas as well as creates 63.7% of Japan's national GDP.

Today, the DIDs in Japan have reached 3,761 square kilometers, accounting for 10% of Japan's land area; the DID population has reached 42.29 million, accounting for 33.3% of the national total, wherein the Greater Tokyo Metropolitan Area accommodates more than half of Japan's national DID population.

The above analysis shows that the high-quality urbanization of one-third of the population is precisely what has supported Japan's development and efficiency. More than half of this high-density and high-quality population is concentrated in the Greater Tokyo Metropolitan Area, which has combined a variety of the central functions of Japan.

In China, there has always been a misconception about urban population density. Many people believe that population density is the cause of such urban problems as traffic congestion, environmental pollution, and inconvenient living. It seems like the lack of urban organizational capability should be held accountable for these urban problems. Instead, high-density population provides the essential soil for the

---

[7] The correlation analysis is used to analyze the strength of correlation between two given factors. A "positive" correlation coefficient ranges between 0 and 1. The closer the coefficient is to "1", the stronger the correlation is between the two factors. The range of 0.9-1 is considered to be "full correlation". Although the so-called full correlation does not clarify the causal relationship between the two factors, it shows that there is a strong correlation between them. The range of 0.8-0.9 is considered to be "extremely strong correlation" and that of 0.6-0.8 is considered to be "strong correlation".

development of high-end service and knowledge economies. Without a certain density and size of population, many industries cannot survive or develop. The Greater Tokyo Metropolitan Area provides good soil for the development of the knowledge and service economies precisely by continuously improving its capability of managing large-scale, high-density urban population and the level of relevant infrastructure. This provision has not only promoted the ongoing growth of the urban economy through transformations and upgrading, but it has also secured the continuous improvement of the life quality of urban residents.

Hokkaido

Tokyo

Aichi

Osaka

Fukuoka

■ Densely inhabited district (DID): population density ≥ 5,000 persons / km^2
■ Most densely inhabited district (super DID): population density ≥ 10,000 persons / km^2

Figure 6-14 Analysis Diagram of DIDs in Whole Japan

Source: It is prepared as per the *Asia Integrated City Index 2017* by the Cloud River Urban Research Institute.

3. Meaning and Structure of Core City Index

The world embarking on the era of large cities and megacities was highly coincident with China's reform and opening-up. During this period, China evolved her policy from de-urbanization to the development of small towns, and then to new urbanization based on urban agglomerations. China has also begun large-city-oriented and megacity-oriented urbanization.

Among the 92 world cities with a population growth of more than 2.5 million between 1980 and 2015, 30 were Chinese cities, accounting for nearly one third; among the 35 world cities with a population growth of more than 5 million, 12 were Chinese cities, accounting for over one third; and among the 11 world cities with a population growth of more than 10 million, five were Chinese cities, representing nearly one half.

During that period, China's urban population increased by 380 million, accounting for 30% of the total growth of urban population around the world for the same time span. In China, there were 30 cities enjoying a population increase of more than 2.5 million, and in aggregate, the urban population of these 30 Chinese cities increased by 170 million, accounting for 33.4% of the total growth of urban population in the above-mentioned 92 world cities.

Based on the above data and analysis, it is evident that China's rapid urbanization, as well as large-city-oriented and megacity-oriented urbanization, are highly resonant with the global trend at the same frequency.

It is even more noteworthy that the 30 Chinese cities with an urban population growth of more than 2.5 million[1] are predominantly administrative centers such as the capital, municipalities directly under the Central Government and provincial capitals, or coastal cities. This finding corresponds to the above analysis and infer the relationship between large-city-oriented urbanization and core cit-ies as well as coastal cities.

Today, for the above 30 Chinese cities, the total residents with household registration fall behind the total permanent residents by 70.22 million. In other words, there are more than 70 million migrants living in those 30 cities. The 30 cities that have attracted a large number of people contribute 39.2% of the total GDP, 67.0% of the total exports of goods, 58.1% of the total number of inbound tourists, and 56.4% of the total amount of valid patent authorization in China. Moreover, 66.3% of the country's mainboard listed enterprises are also concentrated in these 30 cities. It can be said that these cities have exactly led the devel-opment of China's society and economy since the reform and opening-up.

Innovation and entrepreneurship are the most important means to pursue prosperity in the era of integration and transformation into an exchange-and-trading-based economy. The number of listed

---

[1] The 30 cities are: Shanghai, Beijing, Shenzhen, Guangzhou, Chongqing, Tianjin, Dongguan, Foshan, Nanjing, Chengdu, Wuhan, Hangzhou, Suzhou, Xi'an, Xiamen, Zhengzhou, Shantou, Qingdao, Harbin, Zhongshan, Kunming, Dalian. Changsha, Shenyang, Jinan, Ningbo, Urumqi, Nanning, Hefei, Fuzhou.

companies can be used as a key index to measure the results of innovation and entrepreneurship. By using the *China Integrated City Index 2017* and targeting the 297 cities at the prefecture level or above, the author has performed a correlation analysis for the relationships between the listed companies (on the main boards of Shanghai, Shenzhen, and Hong Kong stock exchanges) and relevant indicators such as transportation hub, opening and communications, and radiation (i.e., the extent to which a city function is used externally).

The correlation analysis is a technique used to analyze the strength of correlation between two given factors. A "positive" correlation coefficient ranges between 0 and 1—the closer the coefficient is to "1," the stronger the correlation is between two factors. Specifically, for the coefficient, the range of 0.9-1 is considered as "complete correlation," 0.8-0.9 is considered as "extremely strong correlation," and 0.6-0.8 is considered as "strong correlation."

The above-mentioned analysis finds the following: The correlation coefficients between the listed companies and airport convenience, container port convenience, and railway convenience are respectively, 0.79, 0.70, and 0.66, confirming a "strong correlation" between the number of listed companies and the elements of a city's transportation hub; the correlation coefficients between the listed companies and import and export of goods, foreign investment utilized, and inbound tourists received are, respectively, 0.83, 0.74, and 0.71, confirming a "strong correlation" and "extremely strong correlation" between the number of listed companies and the elements of a city's communications with the outside world; the correlation coefficients between the listed companies and financial radiation, IT radiation, wholesale and retail radiation, catering and hotel radiation, science and technology radiation, cultural and sports radiation and higher education radiation were respectively 0.97, 0.93, 0.89, 0.88, 0.88, 0.86, and 0.84, confirming an "extremely strong correlation" or even "complete correlation" between the number of listed companies and the various types of radiation of a city.

Evidently a strong correlation is existed between the listed companies and a variety of elements, such as transportation hub, communications, and radiation effect. This means that the richness and strength of urban contents play a key role in determining the number of listed companies. In other words, the integration of various elements forms the basis for creating a new era of prosperity.

Of course, the richness and strength of urban contents imply that there will be a large urban population. The correlation analysis further shows that the correlation coefficient between the number of listed companies and the size of DID population (population in densely inhabited districts) is as high as 0.85, which represents an "extremely strong correlation."

However, the expansion of the size of an urban population is a test of the capacity of the city. By improving the level of infrastructure and urban management, cities are able to significantly increase their capacity to align governance with the density and size of population. Taking the Greater Tokyo Metropolitan Area as an example: with a population of more than 10 million around 1950, this metropolitan area was once seriously plagued by "big city diseases" such as environmental pollution, traffic congestion, housing shortage, and inadequate infrastructure, and it was considered "too big" and "too dense." To solve these problems, the Japanese government adopted a series of policies and measures to prevent population and industries from being concentrated and clustered in Tokyo and was even once prepared to relocate their capital. However, through improving the level of infrastructure and urban management, the functioning capacity of Tokyo has been greatly increased. This metropolitan area, where the population is now nearly 40 million, has become one of the most influential cities around the world, without any trace of "big city diseases."

At the same time, however, many megacities in the world, such as São Paulo of Brazil, Mumbai of India, and Lagos of Nigeria, are still facing severe slum issues.

The development and governance of cities need urban intelligence—it is the different levels of urban intelligence that has led to the sharply different outcomes in cities with an equally large population.

Large-city-oriented urbanization and megacity-oriented urbanization are essentially about competition between core cities. Key to this competition is to improve the city's siphoning capability of attracting and clustering people, funds, and materials, as well as their related capacity to develop and strengthen their central functions at the regional, national, and global levels. Therefore, the way to appropriately evaluate, cultivate, and enhance the central functions of cities should become an important national strategy for the purpose of wining in the global trend of large-city-oriented urbanization and megacity-oriented urbanization. As such, on the basis of the *China Integrated City Index*, this report develops and compiles the *China Core City Index* to classify and evaluate the primary central functions of Chinese cities as well as to provide an analysis for the ranking of central functions of 297 cities at the pre-fecture level or above in China.

The *China Core City Index* restructured the data in the *China Integrated City Index* that are strongly correlated to the evaluation of the central functions of cities and regrouped them into 10 dimensions, including "city status, city power, radiation ability, wide-area hub, opening and communications, business environment, innovation and entrepreneurship, ecological resources and environment, quality of life, and culture and education." Under each dimension, three sub-dimensions are set up, and each such sub-dimension is sup-ported by several indicator groups, for the construction of a value system indicative of core cities and an indicator system for evaluating the central functions of cities.

China Core City Index is intended to interpret changes in the pattern of the world and mechanisms in urban development via the application of big data indicators, to improve urban intelligence, and make contributions to help Chinese cities win the competition of large-city-oriented urbanization and megacity-oriented urbanization.

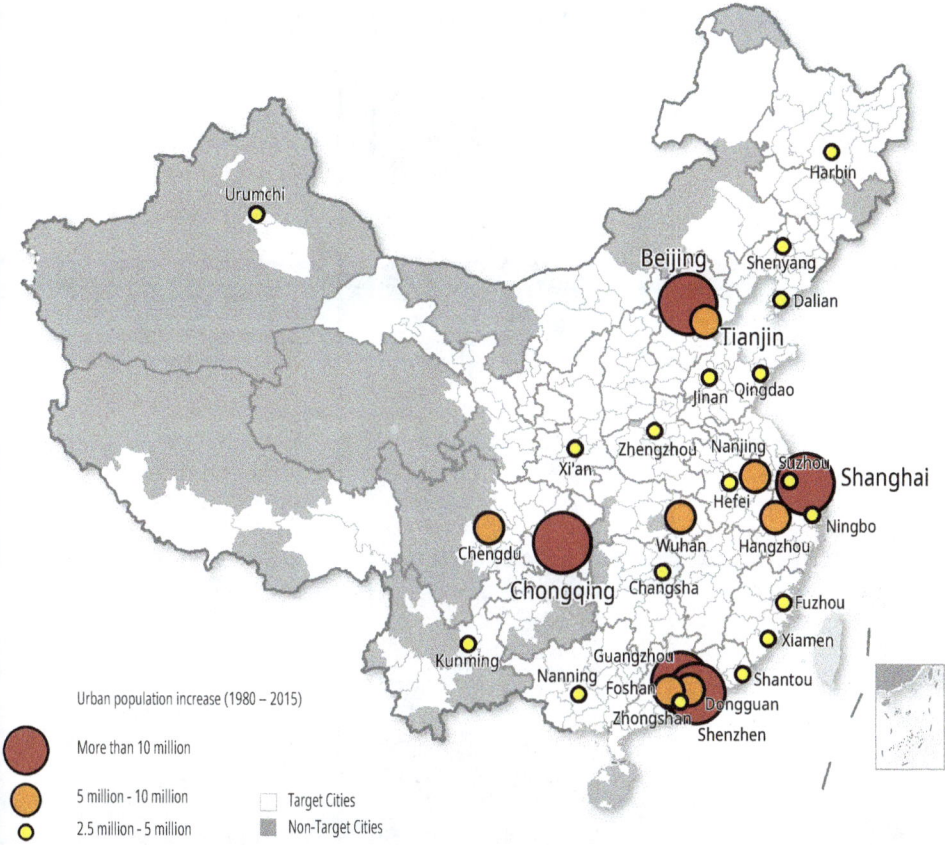

Figure 6-15 Distribution of Chinese Cities with Urban Population Increase of More than 2.5 Million (1980-2015)

Source: It is prepared as per the *World Urbanization Prospects* (The 2014 Revision) and *World Population Prospects* (2015 Revision) issued by United Nations Department of Economic and Social Affairs (UN DESA).

City Status	Opening and Communications	Business Environment
Administrative Function	International Trade	Industrial Park Support
Megalopolis	International Investment	Business Support
Belt and Road	Communications Performance	Urban Transportation

City Power		Innovation and Entrepreneurship
Economic Scale		R&D Agglomeration
Population Size		Innovation and Entrepreneurship Vitality
Enterprise Agglomeration	China Core City Index	Policy Support

Radiation Ability		Ecological Resources and Environment
Industry Radiation		Resource and Environment Qualities
Science and Technology, Higher Education Radiation		Environmental Efforts
Life Services Radiation		Resource Efficiency

Wide-Area Hub	Culture and Education	Life Quality
Waterway Transportation	Culture and Entertainment	Safety and Livability
Air Transportation	Culture and Humanity	Living Consumption
Road Transportation	Talent Training	Medical and Welfare

Figure 6-16 Structure Diagram of China Core City Index

4. Comprehensive Ranking of Core City Index

As illustrated in Figure 6-17 and 6-18, the top 37 cities in the comprehensive ranking of *China Core City Index* include all the municipalities directly under the Central Government, provincial capitals, and cities under independent planning, plus Suzhou.

It goes without saying that as the capital, Beijing is the champion in the comprehensive ranking of *China Core City Index*. Specifically, Beijing ranks 1st in seven out of the 10 dimensions, i.e., city status, city power, radiation ability, business environment, innovation and entrepreneurship, quality of life, and culture and education. Under the dimension of opening and communications, Beijing slightly falls behind Shanghai and ranks 2nd. Due to its inland location without any ports, Beijing ranks 3rd under the dimension of wide-area hub. As a result of such issues as air quality and water shortage, Beijing also ranks 3rd under the dimension of ecological resources and environment. All in all, Beijing is not only the most important core city in China and the core of the Beijing-Tianjin-Hebei Megalopolis, but also a cosmopolitan metropolis with great influence in the world.

As the primary core city in the Yangtze River Delta Megalopolis, Shanghai ranks 2nd in the comprehensive ranking of *China Core City Index*, which is truly deserved. Among the 10 dimensions, Shanghai ranks 1st under wide-area hub, opening and communications, and ecological resources and environment; it is 2nd under city status, city power, radiation ability, business environment, innovation and entrepreneurship, quality of life, and culture and education. It can be said that Shanghai is representative of the core cities in China and also a cosmopolitan metropolis that plays a decisive role in the global economy.

As the primary core city in the Pearl River Delta Megalopolis, Guangzhou ranks 3rd in the comprehensive ranking of *China Core City Index*. Among the 10 dimensions, Guangzhou ranks 2nd under wide-area hub; and 3rd under city status, business environment, quality of life, and culture and education. As a provincial capital, Guangzhou is advantaged and privileged in these dimensions. However, except radiation ability, Guangzhou has underperformed Shenzhen in all other dimensions. Guangzhou ranks 4th under city power and ecological resources and environment, 5th under radiation ability and innovation and entre-preneurship, and 6th under opening and communications.

Also a part of the Pearl River Delta Megalopolis, Shenzhen, neither a municipality directly under the Central Government nor a provincial capital, has taken advantage of its privileged position as a special economic zone and successfully leaped to the 4th place in the comprehensive ranking of *China Core City Index*. She is a typical new-born coastal megacity. Among the 10 dimensions, Shenzhen has done best in ecological resources and environment, securing the 2nd place. She ranks 3rd under city power, opening and communications, and innovation and entrepreneurship, 4th under wide-area hub and business environment, and 8th under the quality of life. It can be said that both Guangzhou and Shenzhen, as twin stars of the Pearl River Delta Megalopolis, are representative core cities in China and also cosmopolitan metropolises gaining significant attention for global economic development.

From 5th to 10th in the comprehensive ranking are Tianjin, Chongqing, Hangzhou, Chengdu, Wuhan,

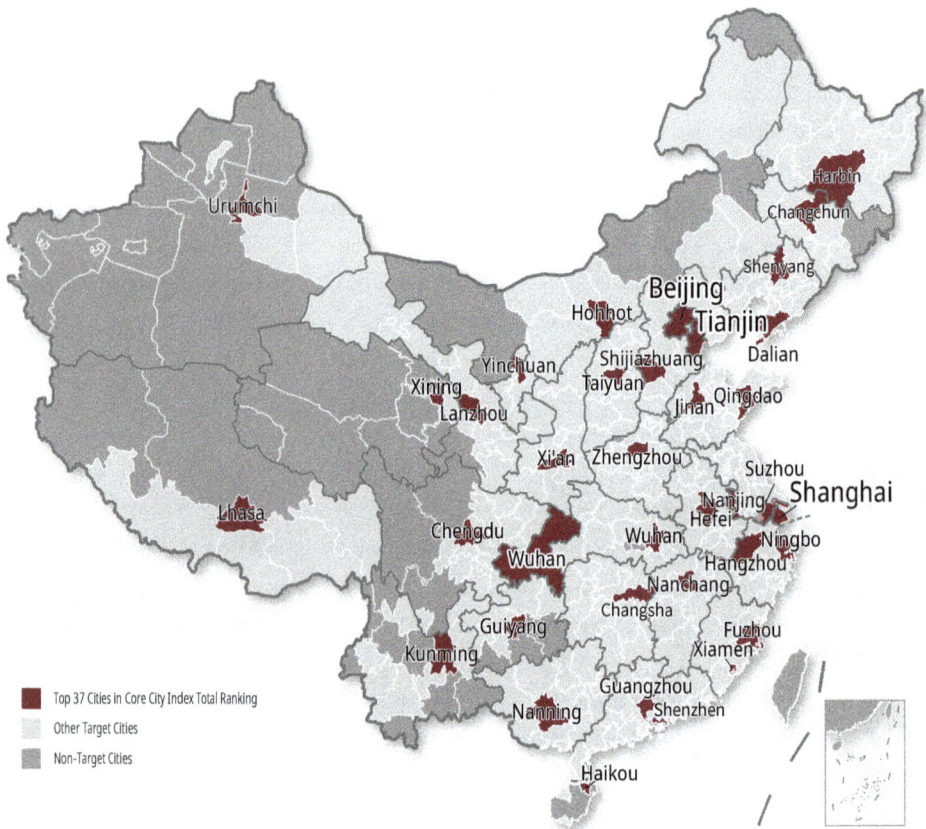

Figure 6-17 Diagram of China Core City Index Total Ranking Top 37 Cities

and Nanjing. These cities are quite remarkable for their ranking scores and have their respective edges. They are representative of the regional core cities in China.

Suzhou, 13th in the comprehensive ranking, is the only one among the top 37 core cities that is neither a provincial capital nor a city under independent planning. Without the support of (high) administrative level, Suzhou ranks 4th under opening and communications as well as innovation and entrepreneurship, 5th under business environment, and 7th under city power and ecological resources and environment. These excellent results are truly worth attention.

Also noteworthy is that Kunming and Urumqi have joined the top 20 in the comprehensive ranking, mainly due to the geopolitical importance of their locations as border cities.

The top 37 core cities have contributed 40.7% of China's GDP as well as 54.4% of patent authoriza-tion, 59.9% of goods exports, and 55.3% of inbound tourists in the country. As the most attractive centers

Rank	City	Deviation Value Index

Rank	City		Deviation Value Index
1	Beijing		100.0
2	Shanghai		100.0
3	Guangzhou		76.2
4	Shenzhen		73.6
5	Tianjin		68.3
6	Chongqing		66.0
7	Hangzhou		63.9
8	Chengdu		62.9
9	Wuhan		62.7
10	Nanjing		62.4
11	Xi'an		58.5
12	Shenyang		56.4
13	Suzhou		55.2
14	Changsha		55.2
15	Zhengzhou		54.8
16	Jinan		54.8
17	Ningbo		54.6
18	Harbin		54.4
19	Kunming		54.4
20	Urumqi		54.4
21	Hefei		54.4
22	Changchun		54.2
23	Qingdao		54.1
24	Fuzhou		53.8
25	Xiamen		53.0
26	Dalian		52.7
27	Shijiazhuang		51.7
28	Nanchang		51.4
29	Guiyang		51.2
30	Nanning		51.1
31	Taiyuan		51.1
32	Haikou		50.7
33	Lanzhou		50.4
34	Hohhot		49.7
35	Yinchuan		49.1
36	Xining		48.7
37	Lhasa		48.5

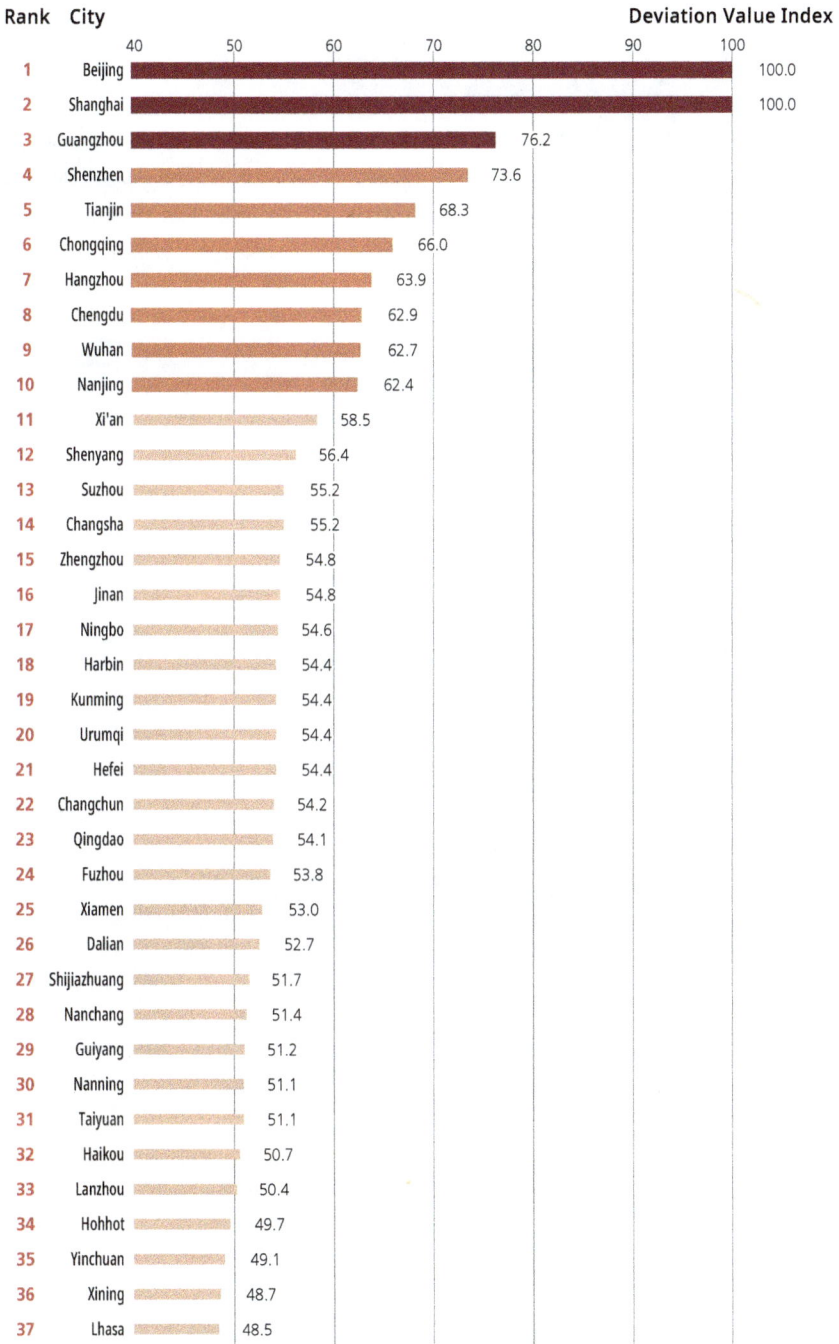

Figure 6-18 China Core City Index Total Ranking Top 37 Cities

for migrants in the process of urbanization, these core cities today have accommodated 63.38 million residents without household registration. These cities have not only accounted for 25.4% of China's population, but also 42.7% of the DID population in the country. The high-density population and strong central functions have cultivated enormous creativity—the top 37 core cities have been responsible for incubating 72.4% of China's mainboard listed enterprises, which are in turn leading the social and economic development of China.

5. Indicators to Annotate Core Cities

This report provides a further analysis of the top 20 cities in the comprehensive ranking using the *China Core City Index*.

(1) City Status

In the *China Core City Index*, city status is the first dimension. The most important central function of a core city is the function level of her political administration. Under this dimension, our focus is not only on the administrative level of a city, but also on her position in international affairs.

In furtherance of "taking urban agglomeration as the major form to promote urbanization,"[1] the Core City Index pays particular attention to the evaluation of cities as the urban agglomeration centers, and also lays stress on their role and performance in three major national strategies, namely, the Belt and Road Initiative, the Yangtze River Economic Belt, and the Coordinated Development of Beijing-Tianjin-Hebei Region.

Therefore, under this dimension, three sub-dimensions have been determined as the administrative function, megalopolis conditions, and the Belt and Road Index, which further constitutes of seven indicator groups: administrative levels, Embassies and Consulates, international organizations, megalopolis levels, core city levels, Belt and Road Index, and historical status.

The top 10 members in terms of city status are Beijing, Shanghai, Guangzhou, Tianjin, Chongqing, Nanjing, Hangzhou, Wuhan, Chengdu, and Xi'an, respectively.

1) Administrative Function

Under this sub-dimension, Beijing, Shanghai, and Guangzhou rank as the top three, respectively. The advantageous positions are taken by administrative centers (i.e., the capital, municipalities directly under the Central Government and principal capitals) and the cities with a concentration of embassies, consulates, and international organizations.

2) Megalopolis Conditions

Under this sub-dimension, Beijing, Shanghai and Guangzhou have shared 1st place, and Shenzhen, Tianjin, Nanjing, and Hangzhou have shared 4th place. The core cities of the Pearl River Delta, the Yangtze River Delta, and Beijing-Tianjin-Hebei Megalopolises are all in the leading positions.

3) Belt and Road Index

Under this sub-dimension, Beijing, Shanghai, Shenzhen, Guangzhou, Nanjing, Tianjin, Xi'an, Urumqi,

---

[1] The National Plan for Development Priority Zones promulgated and implemented by the State Council in 2010.

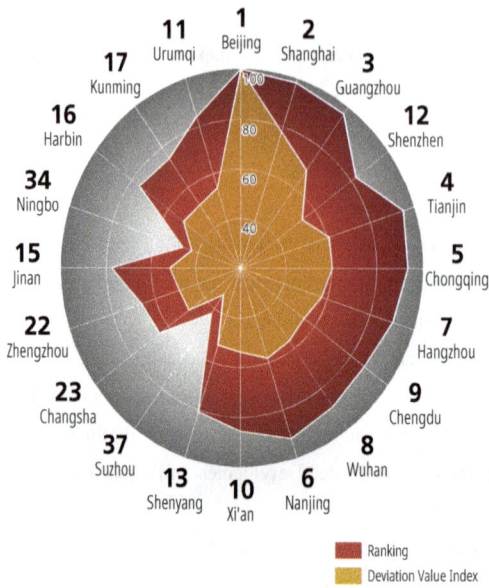

Figure 6-19 Dimension Indicator of City Status

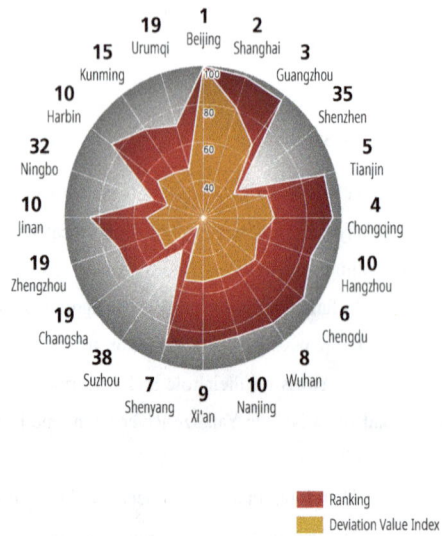

Figure 6-20 Sub-Dimension Indicator of Administrative Functions

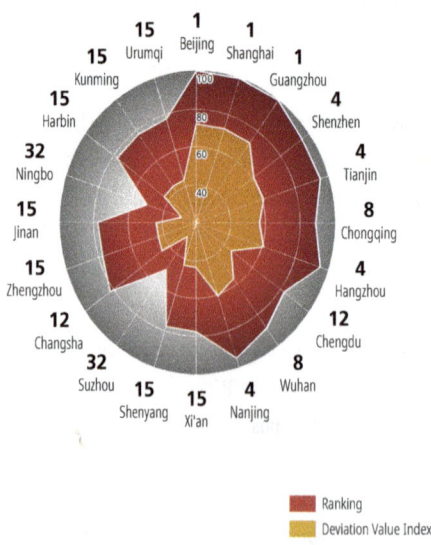

Figure 6-21 Dimension Indicator of Megalopolis

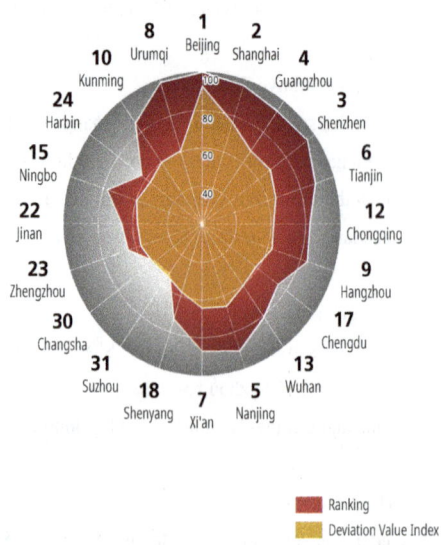

Figure 6-22 Sub-Dimension Indicator of Belt and Road

Figure 6-23 Important Indicators of Top Six Core Cities in City Status Ranking

Hangzhou, and Kunming rank as the top 10, respectively. This sub-dimension consists of two indicator groups, namely, historical status and Belt and Road Index. The latter is a comprehensive indicator for the geopolitical importance of a city's location and for the performance of her trade and investment as well as personnel exchange.

Figure 6-23 shows the important indicators of the top six core cities in the ranking of city status. From the perspective of administrative level, it is apparent that the four municipalities directly under the Central Government are completely advantaged. From the perspective of megalopolis level, all the top five cities belong to the Beijing-Tianjin-Hebei, Yangtze River Delta and Pearl River Delta Megalopolises. From the perspective of international affairs, Beijing as the capital has gathered all of the embassies, while Shanghai and Guangzhou have clustered a majority of the consulates. From the perspective of Belt and Road Index, Beijing and Shanghai enjoy the most outstanding positions; Guangzhou, Tianjin and Chongqing respectively take the 4th, 5th, and 6th places, relying on their extensive trade and investment and considerable personnel exchanges; Nanjing ranks relatively behind as 17th.

(2) City Power

City power is one of the underlying conditions for measuring core cities. This dimension not only focuses on evaluating a city's economic and population scale, but also on its ability to serve as an economic hub. Therefore, three sub-dimensions are set up under this dimension: economic scale, population size, and enterprise agglomeration. These are further comprised of 11 indicator groups: size of GDP, scale of tax

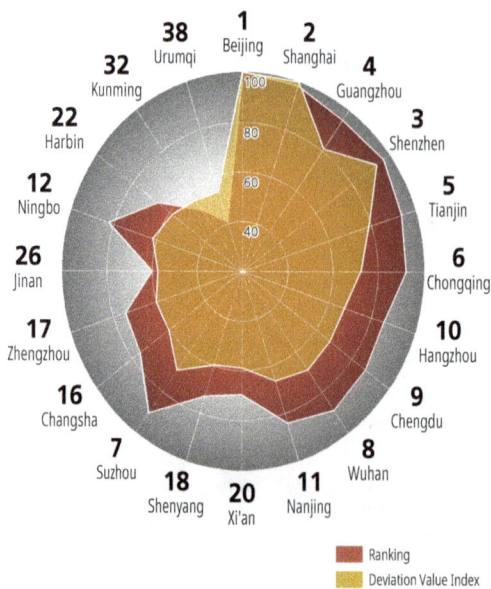

Figure 6-24 Dimension Indicator of City Power

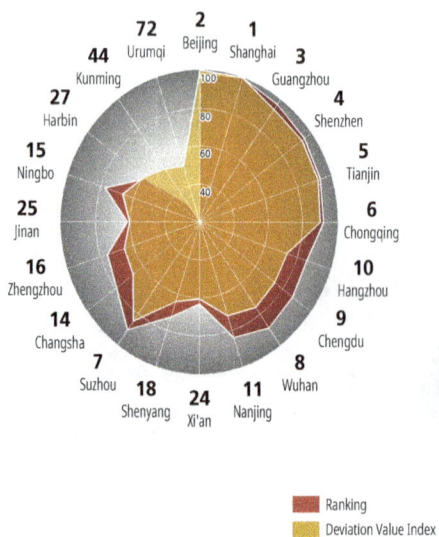

Figure 6-25 Sub-Dimension Indicator of Economic Scale

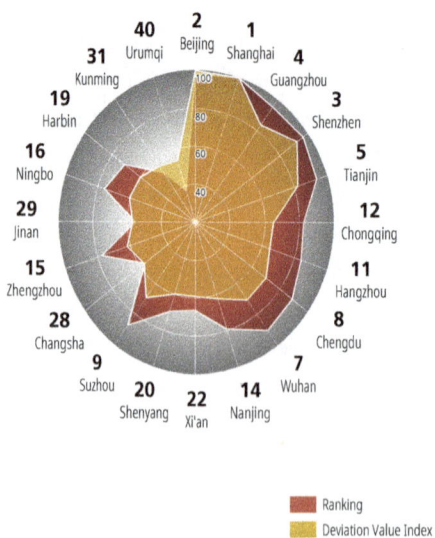

Figure 6-26 Sub-Dimension Indicator of Population Size

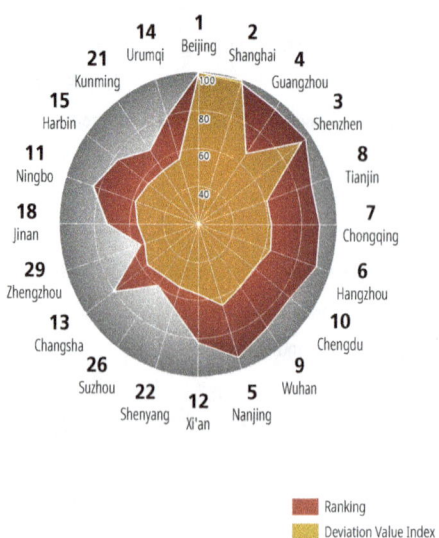

Figure 6-27 Sub-Dimension Indicator of Enterprise Agglomeration

Figure 6-28 Important Indicators of Top Six Core Cities in City Power Ranking

collection, fixed assets investment scale index, electricity consumption, permanent residents, DID population, permanent resident growth rate index, population migration, Top 500 Chinese Enterprises in the World, China's Top 500 Enterprises, and mainboard listed enterprises index.

The top 10 cities in city power ranking are Beijing, Shanghai, Shenzhen, Guangzhou, Tianjin, Chongqing, Suzhou, Wuhan, Chengdu, and Hangzhou.

1) Economic Scale

Under the sub-dimension of economic scale, the top 10 cities are Shanghai, Beijing, Guangzhou, Shenzhen, Tianjin, Chongqing, Suzhou, Wuhan, Chengdu, and Hangzhou. Suzhou, neither a provincial capital nor a city under independent planning, ranks 7th. Kunming and Urumqi fall relatively behind, ranking 44th and 72nd, respectively. The four municipalities directly under the Central Government have the best advantage under this dimension. At the same time, cities such as Guangzhou, Shenzhen, and Suzhou have also been able to compete against the municipalities directly under the Central Government in economic size.

2) Population Size

Under the sub-dimension of population size, the top three cities are, respectively, Shanghai, Beijing, and Shenzhen, and these three cities also received the largest number of migrants in the country. In terms of the size of the DID population, the top four cities in the country are Shanghai, Beijing, Guangzhou, and Shenzhen.

Only Chongqing and Nanning out of the top 37 cities in the Core City Index have a net outflow of population. In particular, Chongqing's population outflow is second only to Zhoukou in China. Therefore, although Chongqing tops all others in the country in population size of permanent residents, it ranks no higher than 12th in population size.

3) Enterprise Agglomeration

Under the sub-dimension of enterprise agglomeration, Beijing, Shanghai, and Shenzhen rank as the top three respectively, with particularly apparent advantages in their deviation values. This indicates the considerable scale of agglomeration of corporate headquarters in the three cities.

In terms of the mainboard listed enterprises of Shanghai, Shenzhen and Hong Kong, Shanghai, Beijing and Shenzhen ranked in the top three. However, in terms of the Fortune Global 500 and China's Top 500 Enterprises, the top three are Beijing, Shanghai, and Shenzhen. This shows that Beijing is home to more headquarters of Fortune Global 500 corporations and China's Top 500 enterprises than Shanghai.

Figure 6-28 shows the important indicators of the top six core cities in city power ranking. In GDP size, Shanghai, Beijing, Guangzhou, Shenzhen, Tianjin, and Chongqing are the top six. Being part of the top six, Guangzhou and Shenzhen manifested their economic strength to compete against the four municipalities directly under the Central Government.

The four municipalities directly under the Central Government, Chongqing, Shanghai, Beijing and Tianjin, ranked top four in terms of permanent residents. Although Chongqing is in the 1st place in this ranking, it only ranked 6th in DID population. This means that the urbanization of Chongqing is relatively far behind. On the contrary, Guangzhou and Shenzhen, which ranked 6th and 8th in permanent residents, leaped to the 3rd and 4th place respectively in DID population ranking, which is a manifestation of the level and quality of urbanization in these two cities.

Beijing, Shanghai, Shenzhen and Guangzhou were the top four cities in the ranking of China's Top 500 Enterprises; the headquarters of which are predominately located in these four cities. Tianjin ranked 7th, while Chongqing fell behind at 12th place.

(3) Radiation Ability

For a city to be defined as a "core city" it must function as a hub influencing the surrounding areas and even the rest of the country. Therefore, the measurement of a city's radiation ability was key to the evaluation of core cities.

The radiation ability in this report is an indicator to measure the range of a core city's functions of affecting the rest of the country and its surrounding areas. This dimension not only takes consideration of a city's radiation ability in industries, science and technology, higher education, etc., but also attaches importance to the radiation ability in life service.

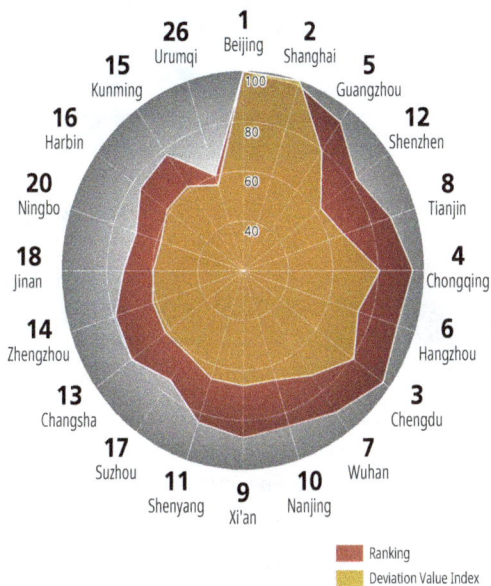

Figure 6-29 Dimension Indicator of
Radiation Ability

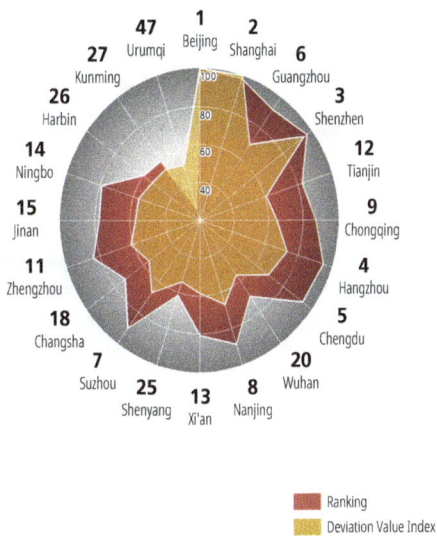

Figure 6-30 Sub-Dimension Indicator of
Industry Radiation

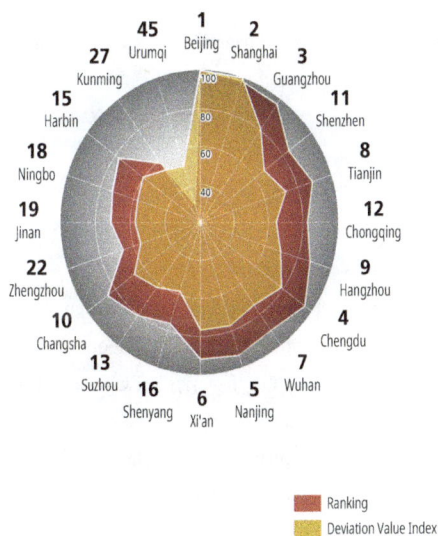

Figure 6-31 Sub-Dimension Indicator of Science
and Technology·Higher Education Radiation

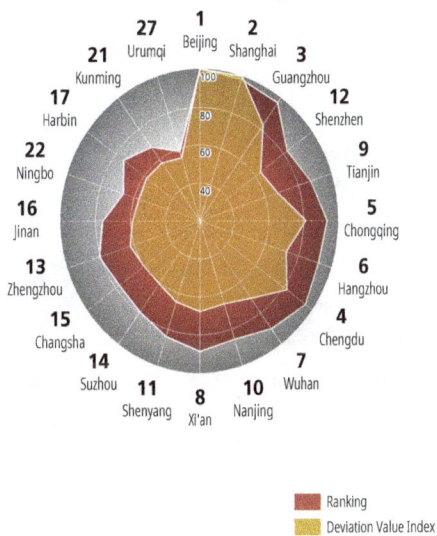

Figure 6-32 Sub-Dimension Indicator of
Life Services Radiation

Radiation Ability	Manufacturing Radiation	IT Industry Radiation	Science and Technology Radiation	Culture and Sports and Entertainment Radiation
Beijing 1	Shanghai 3	Beijing 1	Beijing 1	Beijing 1
Shanghai 2	Chongqing 6	Shanghai 2	Shanghai 2	Shanghai 2
Chengdu 3	Guangzhou 7	Hangzhou 4	Guangzhou 4	Guangzhou 3
Chongqing 4	Hangzhou 12	Chengdu 6	Chengdu 5	Chengdu 4
Guangzhou 5	Chengdu 15	Guangzhou 7	Hangzhou 6	Hangzhou 8
Hangzhou 6	Beijing 19	Chongqing 8	Chongqing 12	Chongqing 10

Figure 6-33 Important Indicators of Top 6 Core Cities in Radiation Ability Ranking

Therefore, this dimension is composed of three sub-dimensions, namely, industry radiation, science and technology/higher education radiation, and life services radiation; which further consists of manufacturing radiation, IT industry radiation, financial radiation, science and technology radiation, higher education radiation, culture, sports and entertainment radiation, medical radiation, wholesale and retail radiation, and catering and hotel radiation indicator groups.

The top 10 cities in the radiation ability ranking are Beijing, Shanghai, Chengdu, Chongqing, Guangzhou, Hangzhou, Wuhan, Tianjin, Xi'an, and Nanjing.

1) Industry Radiation

The top 10 cities in industry radiation are Beijing, Shanghai, Shenzhen, Hangzhou, Chengdu, Guangzhou, Suzhou, Nanjing, Chongqing, and Dalian. From the perspective of deviation values, Beijing, Shanghai and Shenzhen are significantly advantaged in such radiation as compared to other cities.

From the specific data, the top 10 cities in the manufacturing radiation are Shenzhen, Suzhou, Shanghai, Dongguan, Foshan, Chongqing, Guangzhou, Ningbo, Tianjin, and Xiamen. Exports from these cities accounted for 49.4% of the entire country. They are technically the "factories" of China. It is worth noting that these manufacturing power-houses are all located on the coast, except for Chongqing.

The top 10 cities in the IT industry radiation are Beijing, Shanghai, Shenzhen, Hangzhou, Nanjing, Chengdu, Guangzhou, Chongqing, Xi'an, and Fuzhou. These cities are leaders of the development of the IT economy in China today.

The top 10 cities in the financial radiation are Shanghai, Beijing, Shenzhen, Guangzhou, Dalian, Zhengzhou, Hangzhou, Tianjin, Chengdu, and Chongqing.

2) Science and Technology · Higher Education Radiation

The top 10 cities in the higher education radiation are Beijing, Shanghai, Guangzhou, Chengdu, Nanjing, Xi'an, Wuhan, Tianjin, Hangzhou, and Changsha. From the perspective of deviation values, Beijing and Shanghai are extremely powerful in this radiation.

From the specific data, the top 10 cities in science and technology radiation are Beijing, Shanghai, Shenzhen, Guangzhou, Chengdu, Hangzhou, Suzhou, Tianjin, Xi'an, and Nanjing.

The top 10 cities in higher education radiation are Beijing, Shanghai, Nanjing, Wuhan, Xi'an, Guangzhou, Changsha, Chengdu, Tianjin, and Harbin.

3) Life Services Radiation

The top 10 cities in the life services radiation are Beijing, Shanghai, Guangzhou, Chengdu, Chongqing, Hangzhou, Wuhan, Xi'an, Tianjin, and Nanjing. From the perspective of deviation values, the radiation power of Beijing and Shanghai is significantly superior to that of other cities.

From the specific data, the top 10 cities in culture, sports and entertainment radiation are Beijing, Shanghai, Guangzhou, Chengdu, Wuhan, Shenzhen, Nanjing, Hangzhou, Xi'an, and Chongqing.

The top 10 cities in medical radiation are Beijing, Shanghai, Guangzhou, Chengdu, Hangzhou, Shenyang, Tianjin, Xi'an, Wuhan, and Chongqing.

The top 10 cities in wholesale and retail radiation are Shanghai, Beijing, Chengdu, Chongqing, Guangzhou, Hangzhou, Tianjin, Shenzhen, Nanjing, and Wuhan.

The top 10 cities in catering and hotel radiation are Shanghai, Beijing, Chongqing, Suzhou, Guangzhou, Shenzhen, Chengdu, Hangzhou, Wuhan, and Sanya.

Figure 6-33 shows the important indicators of the top six core cities in radiation ability ranking. Beijing ranked 19th in the country in the manufacturing radiation, but 1st in the radiation of IT industry, science and technology, as well as culture, sports and entertainment, where it secured an advantaged and unbeatable prime position.

Shanghai ranked 3rd in the country in the manufacturing radiation, and 2nd in IT industry radiation, science and technology, as well as culture, sports and entertainment, where it shows strong radiation abilities.

Guangzhou has ranked 3rd in the country in culture, sports and entertainment radiation, 4th in the science and technology radiation, and 7th in manufacturing and IT industry radiation. Although Guangzhou underperforms compared to Shenzhen in the radiation of manufacturing, IT, finance and science and technology, it is stronger than the latter in the radiation of higher education, culture, sports and entertainment, medical, wholesale and retail, as well as catering and hotel.

Although Chengdu underperforms Chongqing in manufacturing and the catering and hotel radiation, it is stronger than the latter in IT, financial, science and technology, higher education, culture and sports and entertainment, medical, and wholesale and retail radiation.

(4) Wide-area Hub

Being a transportation hub is an extremely important function of a core city and is the basis to enhance and magnify other central functions.

The dimension of wide-area hub is used to measure the conditions and capacity of the land, waterway, and air transportation facilities of a city. This dimension is composed of three sub-dimensions, namely, waterway transportation, air transportation, and land transportation; and further consists of 11 indicator groups, namely, container port convenience, port container throughput, water transport volume index, airport convenience, air traffic volume index, railway convenience, railway traffic volume index, railway density index, expressway density index, national road/provincial road density index, and road traffic volume index.

The top 10 cities in the wide-area hub ranking are Shanghai, Guangzhou, Beijing, Shenzhen, Tianjin, Qingdao, Ningbo, Wuhan, Xiamen, and Chengdu. Blessed with sea, air, and land advantages, Shanghai and Guangzhou are the prominent cities among wide-area hubs.

1) Waterway Transportation

In the sub-dimension of waterway transportation, which includes sea and river transport, coastal cities such as Shanghai, Shenzhen, Ningbo, Guangzhou, Qingdao, Tianjin, Xiamen, and Dalian are endowed with prominently advantaged container ports. In contrast, inland cities are under significant limitations. However, relying on the Yangtze River or the tributary fairways, Suzhou, Nanjing, Hefei, Chongqing, Wuhan and other cities have also made great achievements in waterway transportation.

2) Air Transportation

In the sub-dimension of air transportation, Shanghai, Beijing, and Guangzhou are the top three and are the largest air transportation hubs in China. In view of the dependence of southwestern and northwestern cities on air transportation, Chengdu, Kunming, Chongqing, Xi'an, and Urumqi rank relatively high, respectively at the 5th, 6th, 7th, 8th, and 15th places.

3) Land Transportation

For the sub-dimension of land transportation via roads and railways (including high-speed railways), Guangzhou, Beijing, Wuhan, Shanghai, Suzhou, and Shenzhen ranked in the top six. It is apparent from the deviation values that Guangzhou, Beijing, and Wuhan are outstanding land transportation hubs. On the

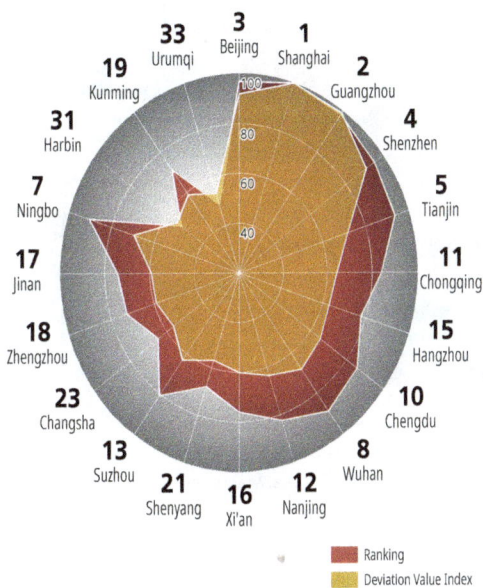

Figure 6-34 Dimension Indicator of Wide-Area Hub

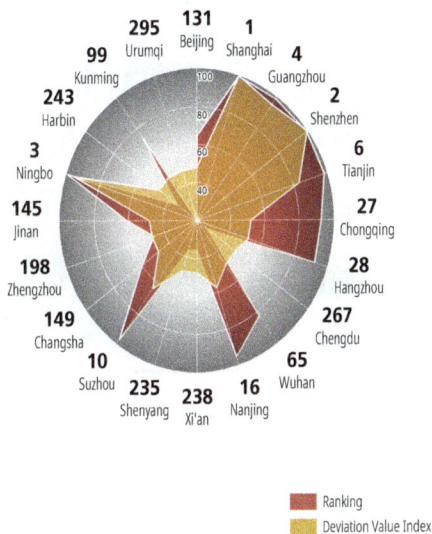

Figure 6-35 Sub-Dimension Indicator of Waterway Transportation

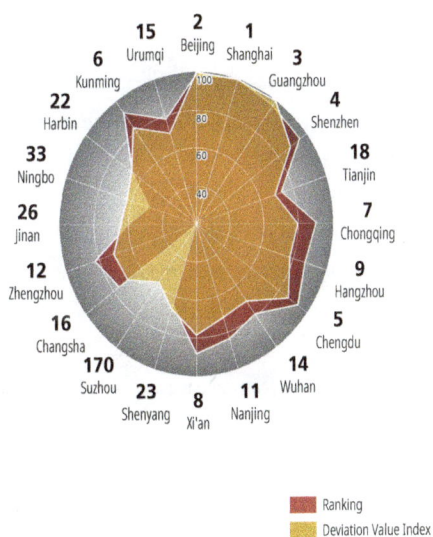

Figure 6-36 Sub-Dimension Indicator of Air Transportation

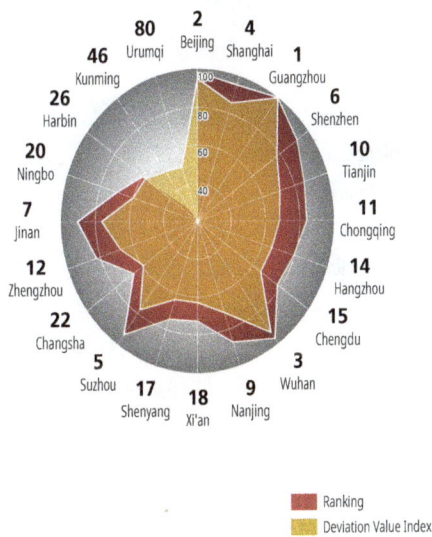

Figure 6-37 Sub-Dimension Indicator of Road Transportation

Wide-Area Hub	Container Port Convenience	Airport Convenience	Railway Convenience	Expressway Density Index
Shanghai 1	Shanghai 1	Shanghai 1	Guangzhou 1	Shenzhen 1
Guangzhou 2	Shenzhen 2	Beijing 2	Shanghai 2	Shanghai 2
Beijing 3	Guangzhou 3	Guangzhou 3	Beijing 4	Guangzhou 4
Shenzhen 4	Qingdao 5	Shenzhen 4	Shenzhen 5	Tianjin 6
Tianjin 5	Tianjin 6	Tianjin 13	Tianjin 10	Qingdao 18
Qingdao 6	Beijing 62	Qingdao 14	Qingdao 57	Beijing 20

Figure 6-38 Important Indicators of Top Six Core Cities in Wide-Area Hub Ranking

contrary, border cities such as Kunming and Urumqi rank relatively low.

Specific indicator data shows that the top 10 convenient cities for rail travel (high-speed rail trains, EMUs, and common passenger trains) were Guangzhou, Shanghai, Nanjing, Beijing, Shenzhen, Suzhou, Wuhan, Hangzhou, Zhengzhou, and Tianjin, which have become hubs for passenger transport via high-speed railways.

Figure 6-38 shows the important indicators of top six core cities in wide-area hub ranking. As the 1st city in the wide-area hub ranking, Shanghai ranks 1st in terms of container port convenience and airport convenience, and 2nd in terms of railway convenience and expressway density index. Put simply, Shanghai is a wide-area hub core city with a full set of sea, air, and land facilities.

Similar to Shanghai, Guangzhou is also a wide-area hub core city with a full set of sea, air, and land facilities. It ranks 1st for railway convenience, 3rd for container port and airport convenience, and 4th in the expressway density index.

Beijing comes without a seaport and therefore ranks 3rd in the wide-area hub ranking. As one of the largest aviation hubs in the country, Beijing ranks 2nd for airport convenience and 4th for railway convenience.

(5) Opening and Communications

Opening and communications is an important indicator to measure the level of personnel, financial and material exchanges, as well as globalized trading.

This dimension is composed of three sub-dimensions of international trade, international investment and exchange performance; which further consists of 11 indicator groups: export of goods, import of goods, foreign investment utilized, outward foreign direct investment, inbound tourists, domestic tourists, foreign exchange earnings from international tourism, earnings from domestic tourism, world tourism city index, international conferences, and exhibition industry development index.

The top 10 cities in the opening and communications ranking are Shanghai, Beijing, Shenzhen, Suzhou, Tianjin, Guangzhou, Chongqing, Dongguan, Hangzhou, and Chengdu.

1) International Trade

The top 10 cities in the international trade ranking are Shanghai, Shenzhen, Beijing, Suzhou, Dongguan, Guangzhou, Tianjin, Ningbo, Foshan, and Xiamen.

The top 10 cities in terms of export of goods are Shenzhen, Shanghai, Suzhou, Dongguan, Guangzhou, Ningbo, Foshan, Chongqing, Beijing, and Xiamen.

The top 10 cities in terms of import of goods are Beijing, Shanghai, Shenzhen, Suzhou, Dongguan, Tianjin, Guangzhou, Xiamen, Dalian, and Ningbo. The huge imports have, on the one hand, provided the raw materials and components and parts needed for the industries of these cities, reflecting the essential pattern of China's industrial development, which involves large volumes of import and export. On the other hand, imports have been supporting the city dwellers' increasingly strong and high-end demands. From cereals to high-end consumer goods, Chinese urban residents are globalizing their buying options.

2) International Investment

The top 10 cities in the international investment ranking are Shanghai, Beijing, Tianjin, Shenzhen, Chongqing, Suzhou, Chengdu, Dalian, Dongguan, and Hangzhou.

The top 10 cities in the ranking of foreign investment utilized are Tianjin, Shanghai, Beijing, Chongqing, Chengdu, Suzhou, Dalian, Hangzhou, Wuhan, and Shenzhen. Due to the impact of large investment cases, some fluctuations have taken place, but these high-ranking cities still remain the most attractive destinations for foreign investment in China.

The top 10 cities in terms of outward foreign direct investment are Shanghai, Beijing, Shenzhen, Suzhou, Dongguan, Tianjin, Ningbo, Guangzhou, Foshan, and Hangzhou. In just a few decades, China has grown from an economy extremely short of capital, needing to attract foreign investment at any cost, to a country with tremendous overseas investment capabilities. It is these high-ranking cities that have clusters of pioneering Chinese enterprises which are making outbound investment.

3) Exchange Performance

The top 10 cities in the ranking of exchange performance are Shanghai, Beijing, Guangzhou, Shenzhen,

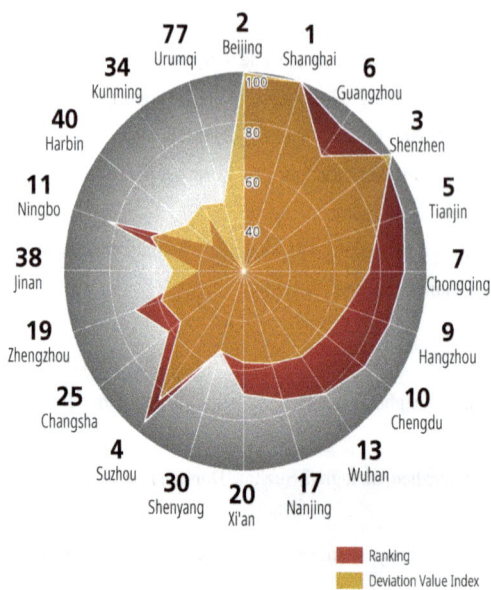

Figure 6-39 Dimension Indicator of
Opening and Communications

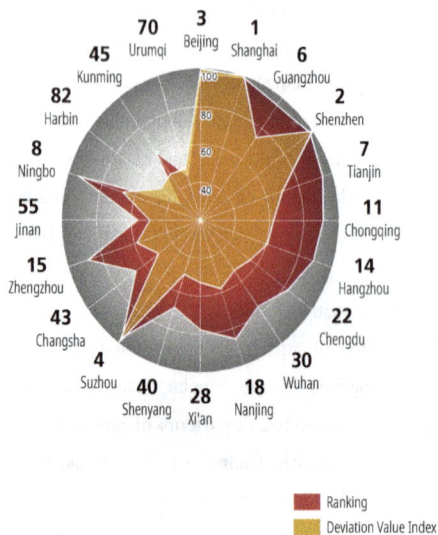

Figure 6-40 Sub-Dimension Indicator of
International Trade

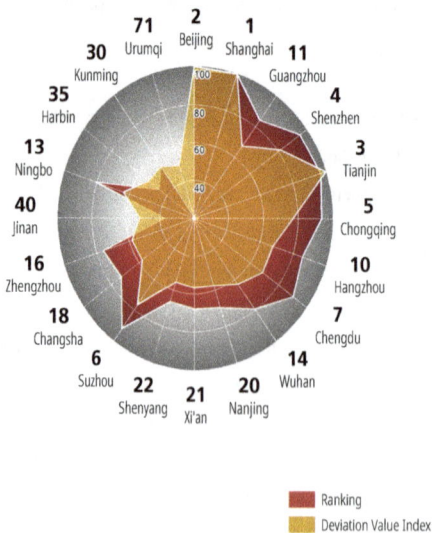

Figure 6-41 Sub-Dimension Indicator of
International Investment

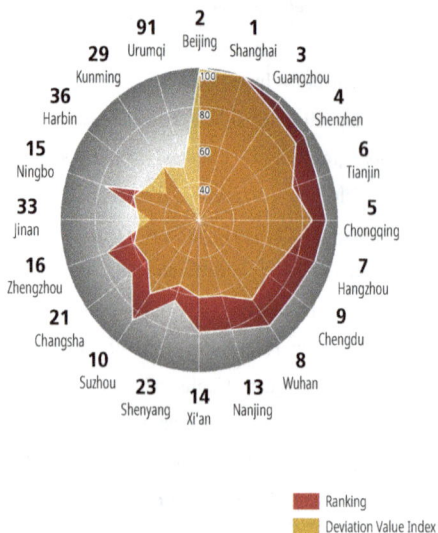

Figure 6-42 Sub-Dimension Indicator of
Communication Performance

Chongqing, Tianjin, Hangzhou, Wuhan, Chengdu, and Suzhou.

Specifically, the top 10 cities in receiving inbound tourists are Shenzhen, Guangzhou, Shanghai, Beijing, Hangzhou, Tianjin, Zhuhai, Chongqing, Xiamen, and Dongguan. However, Shanghai leaps to 1st place in terms of foreign exchange earnings from international tourism. The top 10 cities in this regard are Shanghai, Guangzhou, Shenzhen, Beijing, Tianjin, Hangzhou, Xiamen, Suzhou, Dongguan, and Chongqing. Compared to the number of tourists, the cities that have more to offer tend to earn more in foreign exchange from international tourists.

The top 10 cities in receiving domestic tourists are Chongqing, Shanghai, Beijing, Wuhan, Chengdu, Tianjin, Hangzhou, Xi'an, Suzhou, and Jiujiang. However, when it comes to earnings from domestic tour-ism, the ranking is instead: Beijing, Shanghai, Tianjin, Guangzhou, Wuhan, Chongqing, Hangzhou, Suzhou, Chengdu, and Nanjing. It is also apparent that compared to the number of tourists, the cities that have more to offer tend to earn more from domestic tourists. This is evidence of the direct relationship between tourism earnings and richness of content in cities.

The top three cities in hosting international conferences are Shanghai, Beijing, and Shenzhen. The top three cities in the ranking exhibition industry development index are Shanghai, Guangzhou, and Beijing. It is not unreasonable to say that Shanghai, Beijing, Guangzhou, and Shenzhen are the best developed exhibition centers in China.

Figure 6-43 shows the important indicators of the top six core cities in opening and communications rank-ing. As the 1st city in this dimension, Shanghai ranks 2nd in terms of export of goods, import of goods, and foreign investment utilized; 1st in outward foreign direct investment; 2nd in receiving domestic tourists; 3rd in receiving inbound tourists; and 1st in terms of international conferences and the exhibition industry development index.

Beijing ranks 9th in terms of export of goods, but 1st in terms of the import of goods, so it manages to secure the 3rd place in the sub-dimension of international trade. Similarly, though ranking 3rd in foreign investment utilized, Beijing is 2nd in making outward foreign direct investment, winning 2nd place in the sub-dimension of international investment. At the same time, Beijing not only ranks 3rd in the number of domestic tourists received and 4th for the number of inbound tourists, but is also one of the most active exhibition centers in China. That is why Beijing ranks 2nd in the dimension of opening and communications.

Taking the 3rd place in the opening and communications, Shenzhen ranks first in terms of goods export and third in terms of goods import in the country; 10th in the foreign investment utilized and 3rd in outward foreign direct investment; and 1st in receiving inbound tourists. As for international conferences and exhibition industry development index, it also ranks 3rd and 5th.

It is particularly noteworthy that Suzhou, which is neither a provincial capital nor a city under

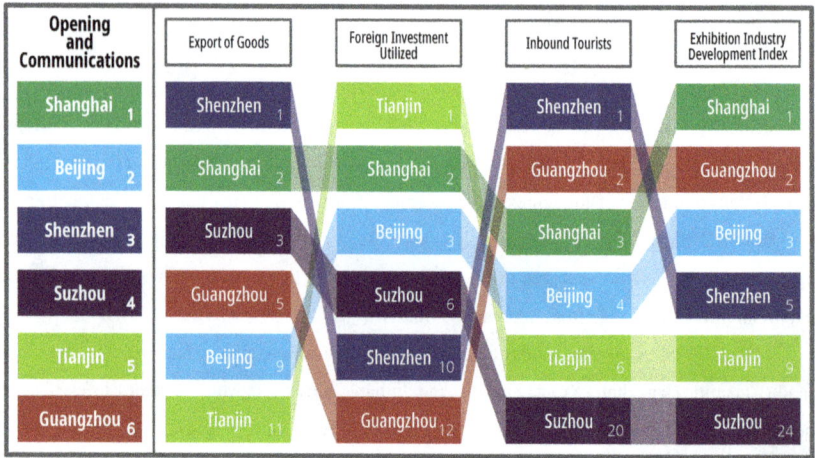

Figure 6-43 Important Indicators of Top Six Core Cities in Opening and Communication Ranking

independent planning, has managed to secure the 4th place in the opening and communications dimension. This is attributable to its capability around international trade (ranking 3rd in the export of goods and 4th in the import of goods) and international investment (ranking 6th in foreign investment utilized and 4th in out-ward foreign direct investment).

(6) Business Environment

A corresponding business environment must support the blooming of an exchange-and-trade-based economy.

This business environment dimension is an indicator to evaluate the ability of a city to support an exchange-and-trading-based economy. This indicator not only considers the level of pure business support, but also evaluates the city's policy support level. It is worth mentioning that this indicator also takes traffic standards into consideration when judging a city's business environment.

Therefore, this dimension is composed of three sub-dimensions: industrial park support, business support, and urban transport. It further consists of nine indicator groups: national industrial park index, free trade area index, employee average salary index, number of employees of enterprise services, star hotel index, top international restaurant index, bus capacity per ten thousand people, urban rail transit distance, and urban sidewalk/bicycle lane density index.

The top 10 cities for business environment are Beijing, Shanghai, Guangzhou, Shenzhen, Suzhou, Tianjin, Nanjing, Chongqing, Xiamen, and Wuhan.

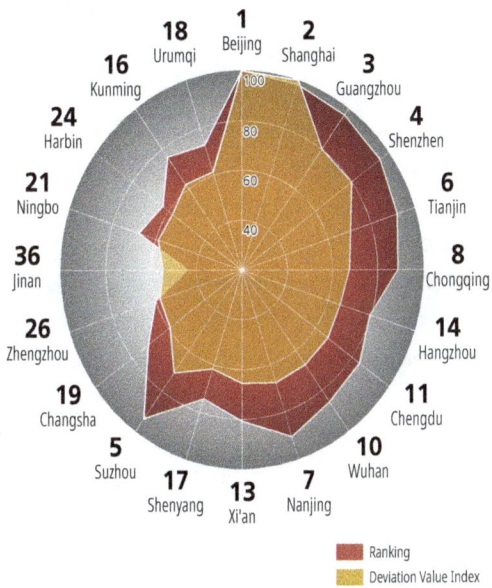

Figure 6-44 Dimension Indicator of Business Environment

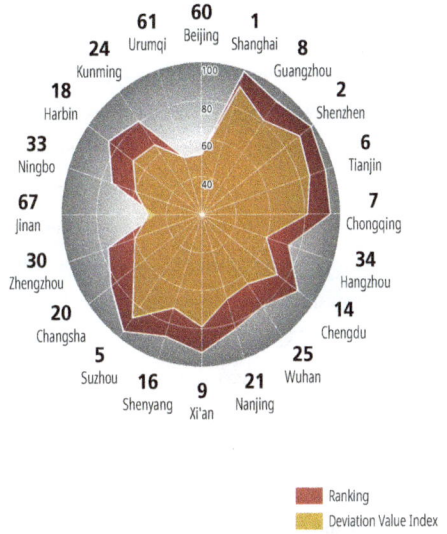

Figure 6-45 Sub-Dimension Indicator of Industrial Park Support

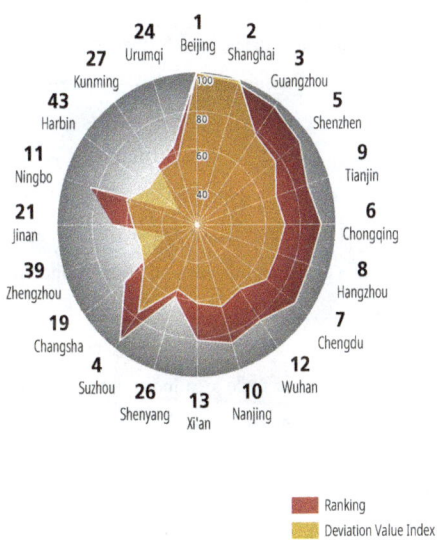

Figure 6-46 Sub-Dimension Indicator of Business Support

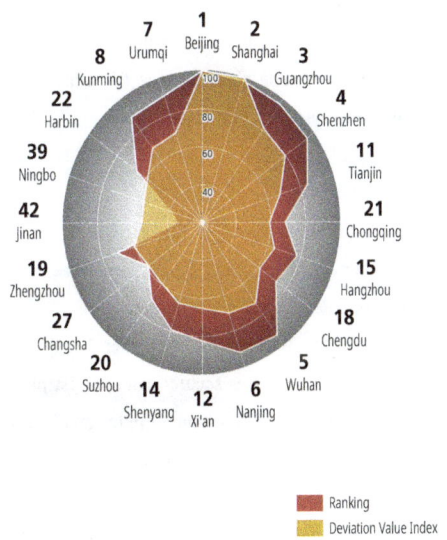

Figure 6-47 Sub-Dimension Indicator of Urban Transportation

1) Industrial Park Support

Industrial park support is a type of reform and opening-up measure with Chinese characteristics. China has set up many national special zones and new zones and parks, including special economic zones, national new zones, national economic and technological development zones, and national high-tech industrial parks. It also set up a series of "free trade parks" that encourage international trade and investment; including national free trade areas, national comprehensive bonded zones, national bonded zones, national bonded port areas, national bonded logistics centers, and export processing zones. The top 10 cities with the best industrial park support are Shanghai, Shenzhen, Xiamen, Zhuhai, Suzhou, Tianjin, Chongqing, Guangzhou, Xi'an, and Dalian. It is noteworthy that these cities, except Xi'an, are situated all along the coast and the Yangtze River.

2) Business Support

The top 10 cities in terms of business support are Beijing, Shanghai, Guangzhou, Suzhou, Shenzhen, Chongqing, Chengdu, Hangzhou, Tianjin, and Nanjing. All of these cities are situated within China's three Megalopolises (the Yangtze River Delta, the Pearl River Delta and the Beijing-Tianjin-Hebei) and the Chengdu-Chongqing Urban Agglomeration.

3) Urban Transport

The top six cities in terms of urban transport are Beijing, Shanghai, Guangzhou, Shenzhen, Wuhan, and Nanjing. The six top cities for urban rail transit distance are Beijing, Shanghai, Guangzhou, Wuhan, Shenzhen, and Nanjing.

Figure 6-48 shows the important indicators of the top six core cities in business environment ranking. As the highest-ranking city in this dimension, Beijing is 1st in both the employee average salary index and the number of employees of enterprise services around China. It is also 2nd in the star hotel index and 3rd in the top international restaurant index.

As the 2nd ranking city under this dimension, Shanghai has performed well in all indicators. For example, the city has secured national 1st place nationally in the free trade area index, star hotel index, and top international restaurant index and 2nd place for urban rail transit distance.

Taking the 3rd place under this dimension, Guangzhou ranks 3rd for both business support and urban transport, as well as 8th for industrial park support.

Ranking 4th, Shenzhen performs relatively well in all related indicators under the business environment dimension. Among all the sub-dimensions, it ranks 2nd for industrial park support, 4th for urban transport, and 5th for business support.

Figure 6-48 Important Indicators of Top Six Core Cities in Business Environment Ranking

(7) Innovation and Entrepreneurship

Innovation and entrepreneurship support the integration, reorganization, and explosion of an exchange-and-trading-based economy and provide the primary driving force for the development of core cities.

Therefore, the dimension of innovation and entrepreneurship is not only focused upon the resources and investment for research and development, but also upon the results of such research and development. This dimension even lays greater stress on the achievements of entrepreneurship and provides an evaluation of the policy support in this area.

To this end, this dimension is composed of three sub-dimensions: R&D agglomeration, innovation and entrepreneurship vitality, and policy support; which further consist of 10 indicator groups: R&D internal expenditures, local public finance expenditure for science and technology index, R&D personnel, academicians index, new third board listed enterprise index (GEM), amount of patent authorization index, national reform experiment, national innovative model city index, information· knowledge industry city index, and national key laboratory/engineering research center index.

The top 10 cities under the dimension are Beijing, Shanghai, Shenzhen, Suzhou, Guangzhou, Hangzhou, Tianjin, Nanjing, Chengdu, and Wuhan.

1) R&D Agglomeration

The top 10 cities in the R&D agglomeration ranking are Beijing, Shanghai, Shenzhen, Tianjin, Nanjing,

Guangzhou, Hangzhou, Xi'an, Suzhou, and Wuhan. In terms of deviation values, Beijing, Shanghai, and Shenzhen far outperform other cities; an indication that these three cities are significantly ahead of other cities in respect to R&D expenditures and R&D personnel reserves.

From the specific data, the top 10 cities in R&D internal expenditures are Beijing, Shanghai, Shenzhen, Tianjin, Suzhou, Guangzhou, Xi'an, Hangzhou, Nanjing, and Wuhan. The top 10 cities in terms of local public finance expenditure for the science and technology index are Beijing, Shanghai, Shenzhen, Tianjin, Suzhou, Guangzhou, Zhuhai, Hangzhou, Wuhan, and Nanjing.

The top 10 cities in the R&D personnel ranking are Beijing, Shanghai, Shenzhen, Tianjin, Xi'an, Nanjing, Changzhou, Hangzhou, Guangzhou, and Chongqing. The top 10 cities in the academicians index ranking are Beijing, Shanghai, Nanjing, Xi'an, Wuhan, Tianjin, Changchun, Hangzhou, Chengdu, and Shenyang.

2) Innovation and Entrepreneurship Vitality

The top six ranking cities for innovation and entrepreneurship vitality are Beijing, Shenzhen, Shanghai, Suzhou, Guangzhou, and Hangzhou.

From the specific data, the top six ranking cities on the new third board listed enterprise index (GEM) are Beijing, Shenzhen, Shanghai, Suzhou, Hangzhou, and Guangzhou.

The top six cities in terms of the amount of patent authorization index are Beijing, Shenzhen, Shanghai, Guangzhou, Suzhou, and Dongguan.

3) Policy Support

The top 10 cities under the sub-dimension of policy support are Shanghai, Beijing, Chongqing, Tianjin, Hefei, Changsha, Chengdu, Nanjing, Suzhou, and Wuhan.

Figure 6-53 shows the important indicators defining the top six core cities for innovation and entrepreneurship. As the prime city under this dimension, Beijing ranks 1st in the country in terms of R&D agglomeration and innovation and entrepreneurship vitality. On the specific indicators, it has ranked 1st for R&D internal expenditures, the local public finance expenditure for science and technology index, R&D personnel, the academicians index, the amount of patent authorization index, and the new third board listed enterprise index (GEM). This is an indication that Beijing not only benefits from strong scientific and technological resources and significant investment, but is also able to transform the results of research into sound industrial technologies.

Ranking 2nd and 3rd under the dimension of innovation and entrepreneurship are Shanghai and Shenzhen respectively. Among the specific indicators, Shenzhen has ranked 3rd in R&D agglomeration, 2nd in innovation and entrepreneurship vitality; and Shanghai has respectively secured the second and third

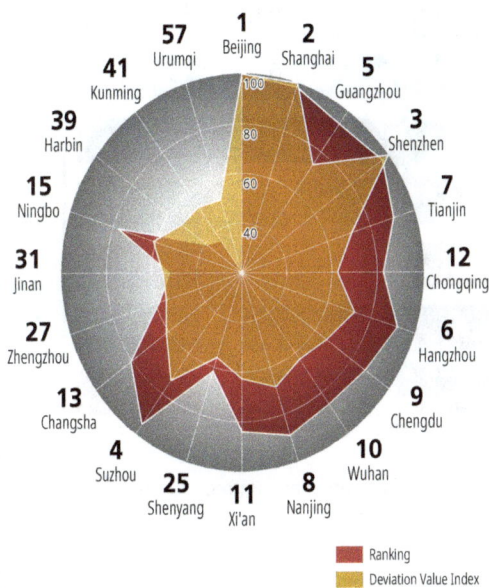

Figure 6-49 Dimension Indicator of
Innovation and Entrepreneurship

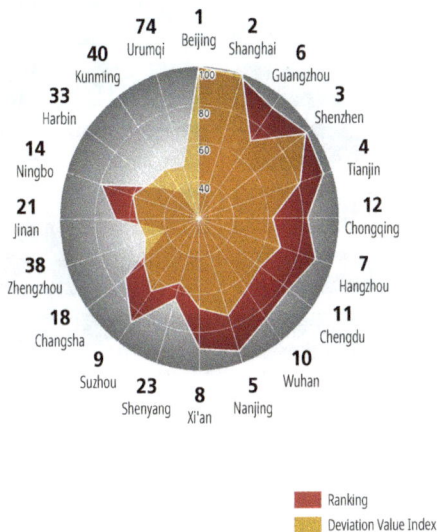

Figure 6-50 Sub-Dimension Indicator of
R&D Agglomeration

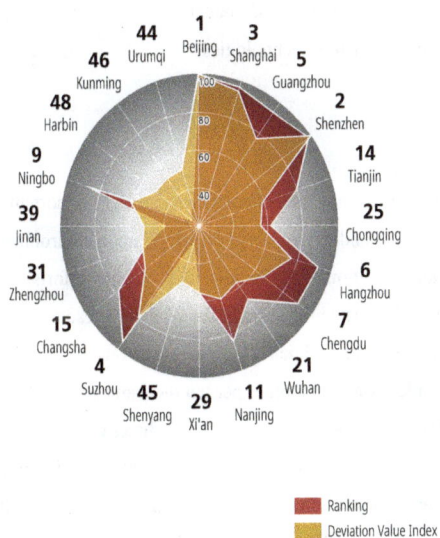

Figure 6-51 Sub-Dimension Indicator of
Innovation and Entrepreneurship Vitality

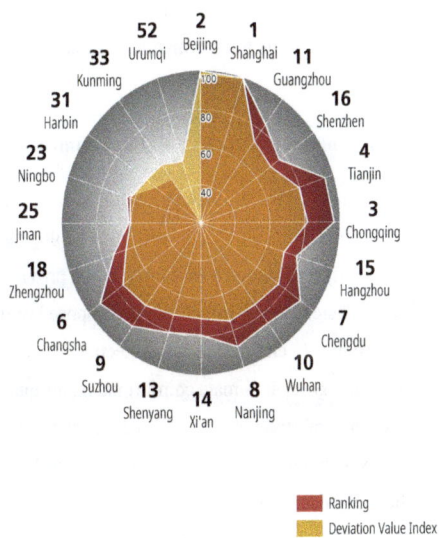

Figure 6-52 Sub-Dimension Indicator of
Policy Support

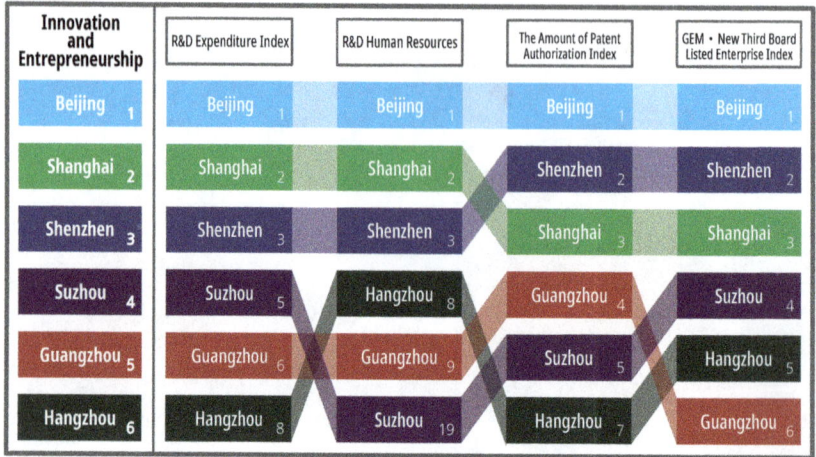

Innovation and Entrepreneurship	R&D Expenditure Index	R&D Human Resources	The Amount of Patent Authorization Index	GEM · New Third Board Listed Enterprise Index
Beijing 1	Beijing 1	Beijing 1	Beijing 1	Beijing 1
Shanghai 2	Shanghai 2	Shanghai 2	Shenzhen 2	Shenzhen 2
Shenzhen 3	Shenzhen 3	Shenzhen 3	Shanghai 3	Shanghai 3
Suzhou 4	Suzhou 5	Hangzhou 8	Guangzhou 4	Suzhou 4
Guangzhou 5	Guangzhou 6	Guangzhou 9	Suzhou 5	Hangzhou 5
Hangzhou 6	Hangzhou 8	Suzhou 19	Hangzhou 7	Guangzhou 6

Figure 6-53 Important Indicators of Top Six Core Cities in Innovation and Entrepreneurship Ranking

places. From the specific indicator data, Shanghai ranks 2nd in terms of R&D internal expenditures, the local public finance expenditure for science and technology index, and R&D personnel, while Shenzhen ranks 3rd. In terms of the amount of patent authorization index and new third board listed enterprise index (GEM), Shenzhen has ranked 2nd and Shanghai 3rd. This shows that Shenzhen slightly underperforms Shanghai in terms of R&D resources and investment, but Shenzhen does better than Shanghai in R&D efficiency and the transformation of research results into industrial technologies.

(8) Ecological Resources and Environment

The quality of the ecological environment and resource efficiency are becoming increasingly important to urban development. This dimension of ecological resources and environment is focused upon environmental quality and resource efficiency, while providing an evaluation of environmental protection efforts.

Therefore, this dimension is composed of three sub-dimensions, namely the quality of resources and environment, environmental protection efforts, and resource efficiency. These further consists of 15 indicator groups: climate comfort index, air quality index, water resources per ten thousand people, forest area, natural disaster-caused direct economic loss index, geological disaster-caused direct economic loss index, disaster warning, area of park green land, environmental effort index, projects labeled with green building design and evaluation, national environmental protection city index, circular economical city index, DID population index, energy consumption per unit of GDP, and urban land output rate.

The top 10 cities under the dimension of ecological resources and environment are Shanghai, Shenzhen, Beijing, Guangzhou, Chongqing, Tianjin, Dongguan, Suzhou, Hangzhou, and Sanya.

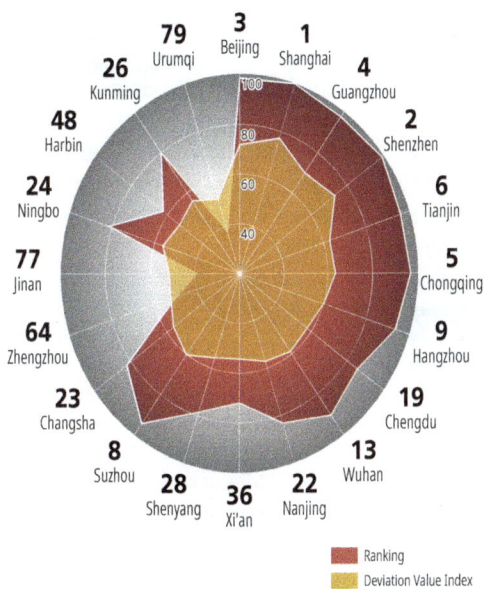

Figure 6-54 Dimension Indicator of Ecological Resources and Environment

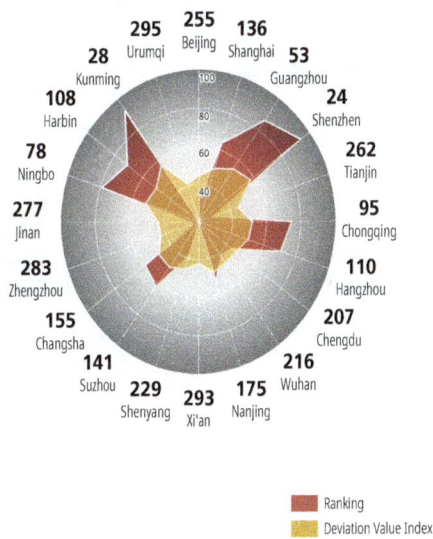

Figure 6-55 Sub-Dimension Indicator of Resource and Environment Quality

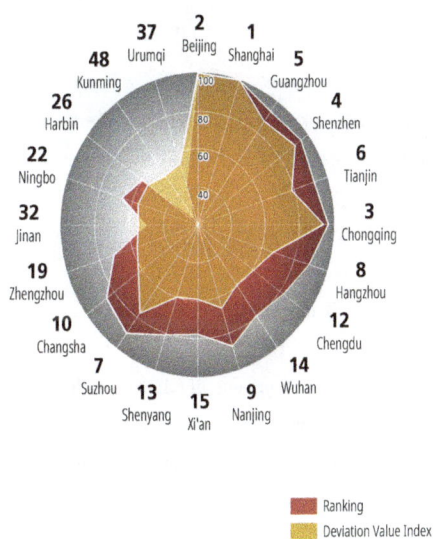

Figure 6-56 Sub-Dimension Indicator of Environmental Efforts

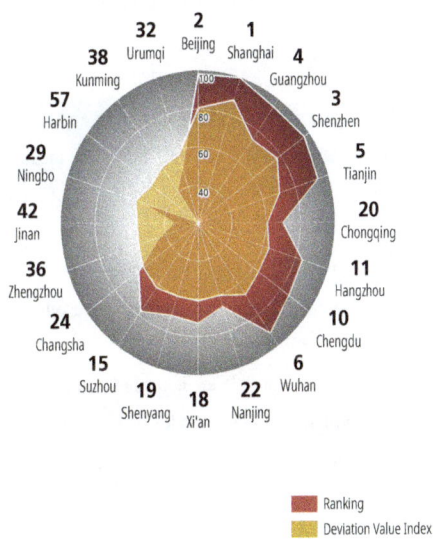

Figure 6-57 Sub-Dimension Indicator of Resource Efficiency

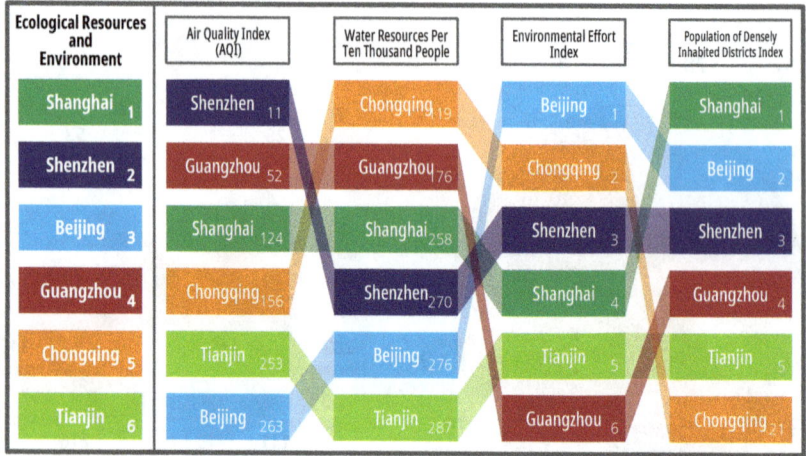

Ecological Resources and Environment	Air Quality Index (AQI)	Water Resources Per Ten Thousand People	Environmental Effort Index	Population of Densely Inhabited Districts Index
Shanghai 1	Shenzhen 11	Chongqing 19	Beijing 1	Shanghai 1
Shenzhen 2	Guangzhou 52	Guangzhou 76	Chongqing 2	Beijing 2
Beijing 3	Shanghai 124	Shanghai 258	Shenzhen 3	Shenzhen 3
Guangzhou 4	Chongqing 156	Shenzhen 270	Shanghai 4	Guangzhou 4
Chongqing 5	Tianjin 253	Beijing 276	Tianjin 5	Tianjin 5
Tianjin 6	Beijing 263	Tianjin 287	Guangzhou 6	Chongqing 21

Figure 6-58 Important Indicators of Top Six Core Cities in Ecological Resources and Environment Ranking

1) Quality of Resources and Environment

Most of the core cities fail to meet expectations in regards to the quality of resources and the environment. The six relatively high-ranking core cities are Haikou (9th), Shenzhen (24th), Kunming (28th), Fuzhou (37th), Xiamen (39th), and Guangzhou (53rd).

2) Environmental Protection Efforts

Relying on strong financial resources and relatively advanced thinking, core cities perform better in environmental protection efforts. The top 10 cities are Shanghai, Beijing, Chongqing, Shenzhen, Guangzhou, Tianjin, Suzhou, Hangzhou, Nanjing, and Changsha.

3) Resource Efficiency

The top six cities in the ranking of resource efficiency are Shanghai, Beijing, Shenzhen, Guangzhou, Tianjin, and Wuhan.

Resource efficiency is further composed of energy consumption per unit of GDP, urban land output rate and DID population index. It is particularly worth mentioning that if properly planned, organized and managed, a city with a higher proportion of DID population does better in infrastructure efficiency, traffic efficiency, energy efficiency, services industry efficiency, and convenience of life.

Figure 6-58 shows the important indicators of the top six core cities in ecological resources and environment ranking. Shanghai ranks 1st in terms of environmental protection efforts and resource efficiency. However, it falls behind in the air quality and water resources per 10,000 people categories. Shanghai has only ranked national 136th nationally under the sub-dimension of the quality of resources and environment.

Although Shenzhen, which ranks 2nd under this dimension, falls behind in terms of water resources per 10,000 people, it has performed relatively well in all other sub-dimensions.

Beijing seriously falls behind under the quality of resources and environment, but it has won the 2nd place in both environmental protection efforts and resource efficiency, which helps to lift its ranking under this dimension into 3rd place.

(9) Quality of Life

Quality of life is one of the important factors to high-end groups. Also, a high quality of life relies on the services industry making it an essential pillar of urban development. Safety and livability are the first and foremost concerns when a city is evaluated in the quality of life dimension. At the same time, this dimension is focused upon the evaluation of the level of living consumption, and also particularly upon the access to medical care and welfare of the city.

Therefore, quality of life is composed of three sub-dimensions: safety and livability, living consumption, and medical care and welfare. These further consists of 15 indicator groups: the habitat city index; health and civilized city index; safe and reliable city index; China's Happiness City Index; traffic safety index; social security index; retail sales of consumer goods per 10,000 people; top international brand index; revenue of hotels and catering services per 10,000 people; telecom consumption per 10,000 people; water consumption for residential use per 10,000 people; average life expectancy; number of practicing (assistant) physicians; first-class hospitals; and year-end number of beds in nursing homes.

The top 10 cities in terms of quality of life are Beijing, Shanghai, Guangzhou, Tianjin, Hangzhou, Chengdu, Nanjing, Shenzhen, Chongqing. and Wuhan.

1) Safety and Livability

The top 10 cities under this sub-dimension are Shanghai, Suzhou, Chengdu, Hangzhou, Beijing, Nanjing, Tianjin, Ningbo, Wuxi, and Changsha.

Regarding the specific data, the top 10 cities in the ranking of China's Happiness City Index are Chengdu, Hangzhou, Changsha, Changchun, Ningbo, Beijing, Nanjing, Shanghai, Xi'an, and Tianjin.

The top 10 ranking cities in the health and civilized city index are Shanghai, Beijing, Tianjin, Chongqing, Hangzhou, Chengdu, Suzhou, Wuxi, Kunming, and Xi'an.

2) Living Consumption

The top three cities under this sub-dimension are Beijing, Shanghai, and Guangzhou, with Shenzhen,

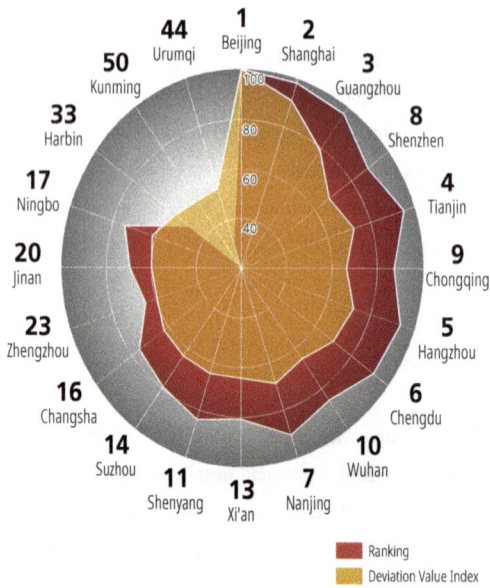

Figure 6-59 Dimension Indicator of Life Quality

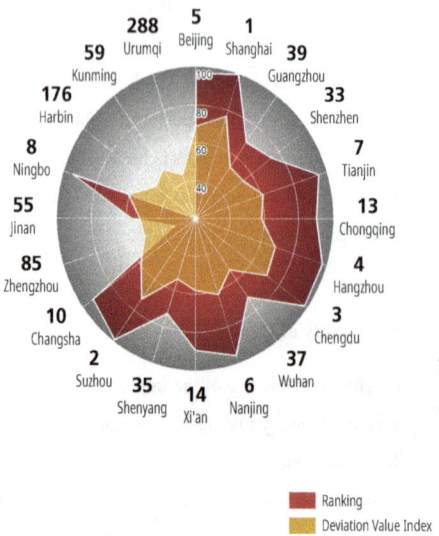

Figure 6-60 Sub-Dimension Indicator of Safety and Livability

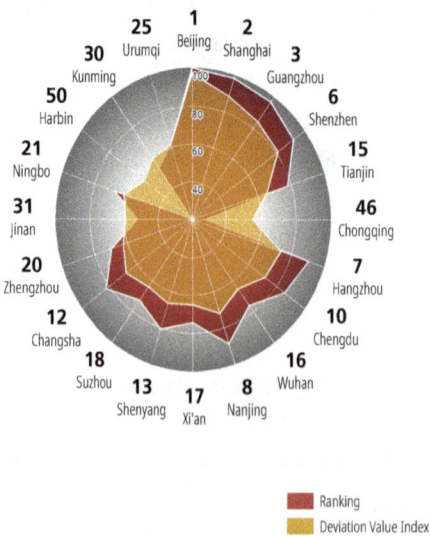

Figure 6-61 Sub-Dimension Indicator of Living Consumption

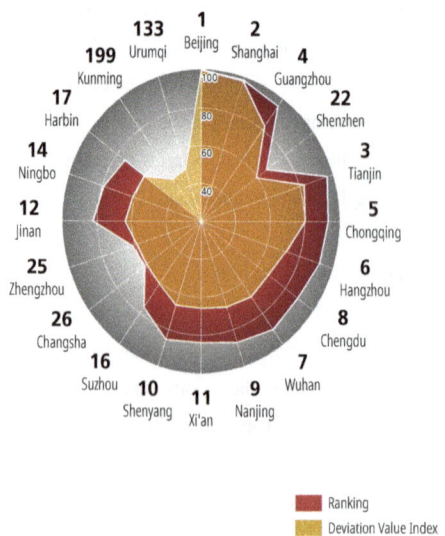

Figure 6-62 Sub-Dimension Indicator of Medical and Welfare

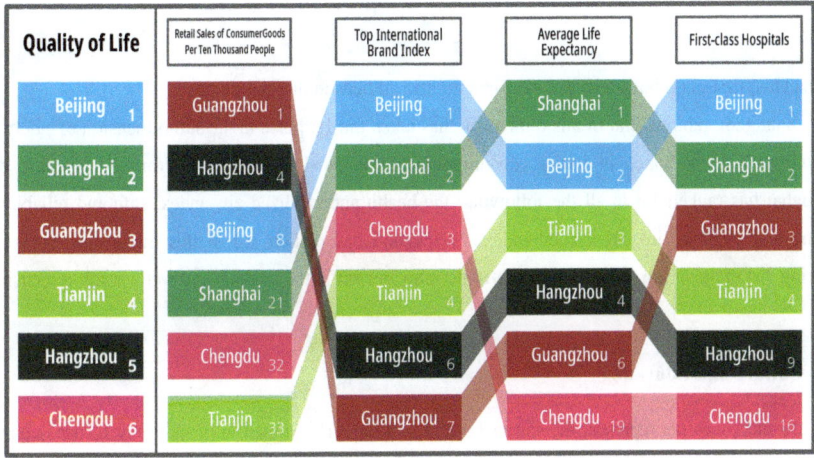

Figure 6-63 Important Indicators of Top Six Core Cities in Life Quality Ranking

Hangzhou, and Nanjing ranking 6th, 7th, and 8th respectively.

The specific data shows that the top six ranking cities in terms of retail sales of consumer goods per 10,000 people are Guangzhou, Zhuhai, Nanjing, Hangzhou, Changsha, and Wuhan. The top six cities in terms of revenue from hotels and catering services per 10,000 people are respectively Sanya, Zhuhai, Beijing, Shenzhen, Guangzhou, and Shanghai. These two indicators not only reflect the level of living consumption in the city, but are also beneficial to cities with a larger amount of migrant consumption. That is why cities like Sanya and Zhuhai can move up in their ranking.

The top six cities in the top international brand index are Beijing, Shanghai, Chengdu, Tianjin, Shenyang, and Hangzhou.

3) Medical and Welfare

The top 10 cities under this sub-dimension are Beijing, Shanghai, Tianjin, Guangzhou, Chongqing, Hangzhou, Wuhan, Chengdu, Nanjing, and Shenyang.

The specific data shows that the top six ranking cities for average life expectancy ranking are Shanghai, Beijing, Tianjin, Hangzhou, Nanjing, and Guangzhou. The top six cities in the ranking of first-class hospitals are Beijing, Shanghai, Guangzhou, Tianjin, Xi'an, and Wuhan.

Figure 6-63 shows the important indicators of the top six core cities in quality of life ranking. Beijing ranks 1st under this dimension, backed by its top scores in two of the sub-dimensions: living consumption, and medical and welfare. From the specific data, Beijing has ranked national 1st in the rankings of top international brand index, telecom consumption per 10,000 people, number of practicing (assistant) physicians, first-class hospitals, and year-end number of beds in nursing homes.

Shanghai, ranking 2nd in this dimension, has taken the 1st place in the sub-dimension of safety and livability, and 2nd place in living consumption and medical and welfare. From the specific data, Shanghai has ranked 1st in all the following: the health and civilized city index, safe and reliable city index, and average life expectancy index. Guangzhou has ranked 3rd in this dimension, backed by ranking 3rd in the living consumption sub-dimension and 4th in the medical and welfare sub-dimension.

(10) Culture and Education

Culture and education represent the spiritual world of a city. This dimension is not only focused upon the venues and related consumption of culture and entertainment in a city, but also provides an evaluation of its global culture, national culture and humanity. It lays even greater stress on investment in education and the training of outstanding talents.

Therefore, this culture and education dimension is composed of the three sub-dimensions: culture and entertainment, culture and humanity, and talent training. These further consists of 13 indicator groups: the theater consumer index; museums/art galleries; sports venues index; zoos/botanical gardens/aquariums, public library collections, the world's top university index, cultural master index, Olympic champion index, local public finance expenditure for education index, number of children in kindergartens per 10,000 people, international schools, higher education index, and outstanding talent cultivation index.

The top 10 cities for culture and education are Beijing, Shanghai, Guangzhou, Wuhan, Nanjing, Tianjin, Chengdu, Xi'an, Hangzhou, and Chongqing.

1) Culture and Entertainment

The top 10 cities under this sub-dimension are Beijing, Shanghai, Guangzhou, Chongqing, Shenzhen, Wuhan, Chengdu, Hangzhou, Nanjing, and Tianjin. Among them, Beijing and Shanghai far outperform other cities in deviation values, showing the leading roles of the two cities in the culture and entertainment.

From the specific data, the top six cities under the theater consumer index are Beijing, Shanghai, Shenzhen, Wuhan, Guangzhou, and Hangzhou.

The top six cities in the museums and art galleries ranking are Beijing, Shanghai, Xi'an, Chengdu, Wuhan, and Chongqing. The top six ranking cities for sports venues are Beijing, Shanghai, Chongqing, Tianjin, Guangzhou, and Nanjing. The top six ranking cities for zoos/botanical gardens and aquariums are Beijing, Shanghai, Chongqing, Guangzhou, Shenyang, and Tianjin. The top six cities in the public library collections ranking are Shanghai, Beijing, Shenzhen, Chengdu, Guangzhou, and Hangzhou.

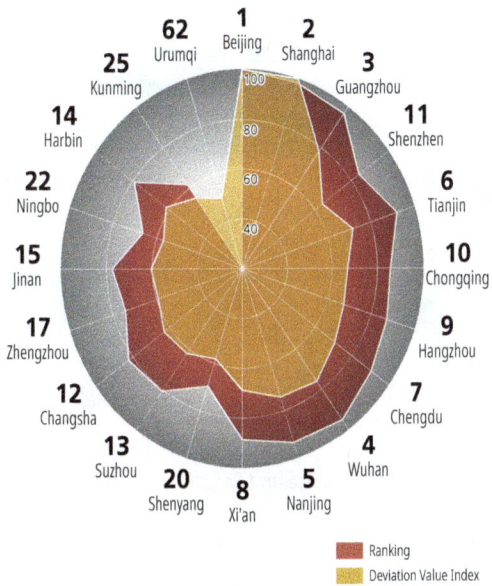

Figure 6-64 Dimension Indicator of Culture and Education

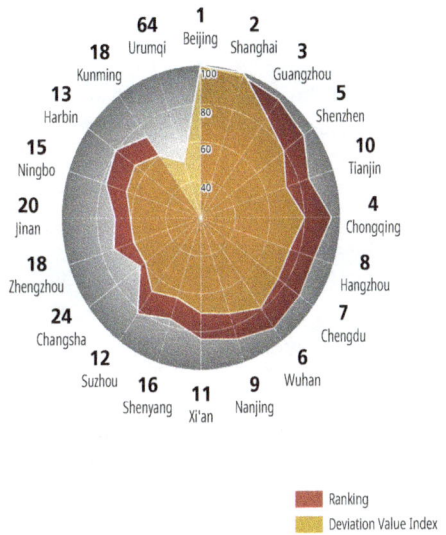

Figure 6-65 Sub-Dimension Indicator of Culture and Entertainment

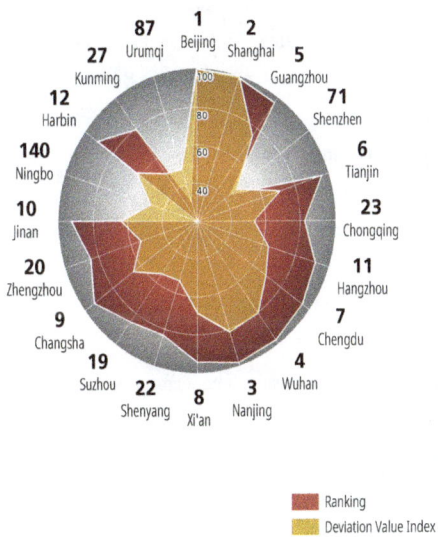

Figure 6-66 Sub-Dimension Indicator of Culture and Humanity

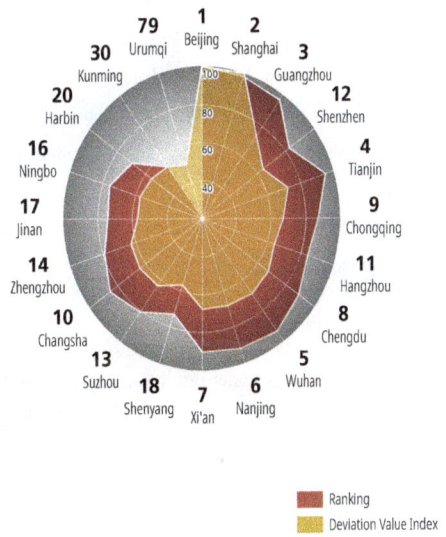

Figure 6-67 Sub-Dimension Indicator of Talent Training

Culture and Education	Theater Consume Index	Museums Art Galleries	The World's Top University Index	Cultural Master Index
Beijing 1	Beijing 1	Beijing 1	Beijing 1	Beijing 1
Shanghai 2	Shanghai 2	Shanghai 2	Shanghai 2	Shanghai 2
Guangzhou 3	Wuhan 4	Wuhan 5	Nanjing 3	Guangzhou 3
Wuhan 4	Guangzhou 5	Guangzhou 8	Wuhan 4	Nanjing 5
Nanjing 5	Nanjing 9	Tianjin 11	Guangzhou 5	Tianjin 7
Tianjin 6	Tianjin 18	Nanjing 13	Tianjin 7	Wuhan 10

Figure 6-68 Important Indicators of Top Six Core Cities in Culture and Education Ranking

2) Culture and Humanity

The top 10 cities under this sub-dimension are Beijing, Shanghai, Nanjing, Wuhan, Guangzhou, Tianjin, Chengdu, Xi'an, Changsha, and Jinan. Among them, Beijing and Shanghai far outperform other cities in deviation values, manifesting the extraordinary status of the two cities in the areas of culture and humanity. On the contrary, cities such as Shenzhen, Urumqi, and Ningbo fall relatively behind in this dimension.

The specific data shows that the top six cities in the world's top university index are Beijing, Shanghai, Nanjing, Wuhan, Guangzhou, and Xi'an.

The top six cities under the cultural master index are Beijing, Shanghai, Guangzhou, Xi'an, Nanjing, and Zhengzhou.

The top six cities under the Olympic champion index are Beijing, Shanghai, Wuhan, Guangzhou, Hangzhou, and Shenyang.

3) Talent Training

The top 10 cities under this sub-dimension are Beijing, Shanghai, Guangzhou, Tianjin, Wuhan, Nanjing, Xi'an, Chengdu, Chongqing, and Changsha. Beijing and Shanghai far outperform other cities in deviation values, which is a result of China's educational resources being concentrated in the two cities.

The top six cities in terms of international schools are Shanghai, Beijing, Shenzhen, Guangzhou, Suzhou, and Zhengzhou.

The top six cities in the outstanding talent cultivation index are Beijing, Shanghai, Tianjin, Nanjing, Hangzhou, and Xi'an.

Figure 6-68 shows the important indicators of the top six core cities in the culture and education ranking. Beijing secures the top spot in all sub-dimensions: culture and entertainment, and culture, entertainment and talent training. It is also 1st in the following indicator groups: theater consumer index, museums and art galleries, zoos, botanical gardens and aquariums, the world's top university index, higher education index, cultural master index, Olympic champion index, outstanding talent cultivation index, and local public finance expenditure for education index. It is clearly China's prime city in regards to culture and education.

Shanghai has ranked 2nd in the same sub-dimensions, including in culture and education. Shanghai additionally ranks 1st for its public library collection and international schools.

Guangzhou, ranking 3rd in this dimension, takes the 3rd place under the sub-dimensions of culture and entertainment and talent training, as well as 5th in the culture and humanity sub-dimension.

Chapter VII

Expert Reviews

"Baton" for New Urbanization

Zhou Qiren

Langrun Chair Professor, National School of Development at Peking University, Ph.D. in Economics

For more than 20 years, the rapid progress of urbanization in China has relocated a sizable population towards cities and towns, along with large-scale infrastructure investment and construction, resulting in the growth and expansion of cities in physical size. The urbanization that had long fallen behind was finally accelerated.

Common sense tells us the reason why a city becomes a city lies in her capability of conducting large, diverse, complex, and more colorful economic and cultural activities in a very limited space. That said, it is inevitable to define a city by density. As to why the population and resources should be held together in a high-density form in space, the answer is that clustering improves the division of labor, and the refined division of labor improves productivity, which will thereby greatly increase the income of people in the city.

However, the reality is that in China's urbanization to date, the expansion of built-up areas still proceeds faster than the growth of urban population, i.e., "the urbanization of land outpaces that of the population." It is very interesting that the economic aggregate of China is impressive, but when it comes down to per capita figures, it is still falling behind. The same is true for cities, which are enormous by the aggregate, but tiny by the density. Such analogy makes some sense, doesn't it?

One reason is that in our definition, "city" is a broad administrative zone that includes both urban areas and suburbs, and even large rural areas. The fact that for many years cities have been governing counties with counties transformed into cities, and the vaguely defined "urban-rural integration," have created our concept of the "city" that is different from and not much comparable to its universal definition. Where urban and rural areas are merged, the boundary is blurred, but due to dominance of administrative power, a "city" will rise once a big circle is drawn on the map with roads and properties built.

However, "Rome was not built in one day." Any rush to get it done will make it difficult even just to manage the physical look, let alone the environment, financial sustainability, management and civil culture, the development of which takes time.

Then there comes the issue of "the next step of urbanization." To make it clear, China's urbanization has reached a turning point. The large-scale dismantling and construction and even forced requisition and dismantling for the sole purpose of expansion, is hardly sustainable in whatever way. There has to be a turn in the next step of urbanization, but where should we turn to? This is worth considering for decision mak-ers, managers, and constructors of the city.

One piece of experience from China's economic development in the past few years is to emphasize planning and direction. On March 16, 2014, the Central Committee of the Communist Party of China and the State Council issued the *National New-type Urbanization Plan (2014-2020)*, which provides clearly directed principles, guidelines, and key tasks for the nationwide development of urbanization in the future. The key to the implementation of this Plan is to follow the law of urbanization and truly follow the path of new urbanization with Chinese characteristics, which is people-oriented with synchronized development [of industrialization, information technology, urbanization, and agricultural modernization], optimized lay-out, ecological civilization, and cultural heritage.

Having had the strategic direction in place, we still need a workable "baton." This is also part of the Chinese experience. A set of appropriate indicators for evaluation will work as competitive opportunities and match points that direct decision makers, managers, and constructors of the cities to act in the direc-tion specified in major policies in the process of collaboration and competition. From this point of view, Prof. Zhou Muzhi and his team, with the support and participation of the Department of Development Planning, NDRC, have provided a scientific indicator system for any transformation in the next step of urbanization by presenting this *China Integrated City Index*, which was the fruit of their painstaking and meticulous investigation, analysis and comparison. This also provides solid academic support for the shap-ing of a "baton" to promote new urbanization on the basis of ongoing improvement.

I especially agree with the core understanding obtained from this research that many of the prob-lems and challenges presently faced by Chinese cities, including megacities, can be resolved by seeking "moderate densification." Past discussions of urban issues have limited our basic options to "developing big cities or developing small and medium cities." We hardly realized that a city should not only be measured by a dimension of size, but also the density of multiple variables. We have many megacities in China now, but that does not mean we have "ultra-dense cities." A large part of the space in many megacities is of gravely low density, rendering failures to produce high comprehensive benefits in ecology, economy and culture. Therefore, regardless of whether we are dealing with large, medium, or small cities, or even rural towns, the task to update our understanding of them from the perspective of density. We advise the reader to bear especially this in mind.

Profile

Zhou Qiren

Born in 1950, Prof. Zhou has been engaged in the investigation and research on reform and development issues at the Chinese

Academy of Social Sciences and the Research Centre for Rural Development of the State Council. In the 1990s, he studied successively in the United Kingdom and the U.S., and later obtained his PhD degree from UCLA. At the end of 1995, he returned to China to teach at the China Center for Economic Research at Beijing University, as well as at the School of Economics of Zhejiang University, School of Economics of Fudan University, China Europe International Business School, Graduate School of the People's Bank of China and the Cheung Kong Graduate School of Business. From 2008 to 2012, he served as Director of the China Center for Economic Research at Beijing University and Dean of the National School of Development at Beijing University. From 2010 to 2012, he served as a member of the Monetary Policy Committee of the People's Bank of China.

Prof. Zhou's research is focused on such areas as property rights and contracts, economic system evolution, corporate and market organizations, monopoly and regulation, land system reform and urbanization as well as monetary and financial aspects.

Major works: *The Theme of Development: Transformation of the National Economic Structure of China* (1987, Sichuan People's Publishing House); *Rural Change and Development in China 1978-1989* (1994, Oxford University Press); *Survey on Different Regional Development in China 1978-1989* (1994, Oxford University Press); *Competition Among .Coms: Openness and Competition in the Telecommunication Industry of China* (2001, Joint Publishing Hong Kong); *Property Rights and Institutional Changes* (2004, Beijing University Press); *Observing the Great Economic Era* (2006, Beijing University Press); *The Economics of the Real World* (2006, Beijing University Press); *Income is a Series of Events* (2006, Beijing University Press); *Things Wins Chess Game* (2007, Beijing University Press); *Essays of Medical Care Reforms in China* (2008, Beijingg University Press); *What did China Do Right?* (2010, Beijing University Press); *The Lessons of Currency* (2012, Beijing University Press); *Competition and Prosperity* (2013, CITIC Press); *The Logic of Reform* (2013, CITIC Press); *Urban and Rural China* (I) (2013, CITIC Press); *Urban and Rural China* (II) (2014, CITIC Press).

Genuine Reflection of an Unflat China

Zhang Zhongliang

Director, Department of Social, Science and Technology and Cultural Statistics of National Bureau of Statistics, PRC and Ph. D. in Economics

(I)

In June 2006, Prof. Zhou Muzhi returned to Beijing from MIT and brought me a book, *The World Is Flat*.

Muzhi said that this book was very popular in the U.S., and its insight was also very interest-ing: the world has "flattened," with individuals replacing the states and the corporations' role to drive globalization. If you are capable and imaginative enough, all the resources in the world will be at your service. The world is also getting smaller, given that the rapid advancement of technology and communica-tions has brought people around the world close.

Shortly afterwards, the Chinese translation of The World Is Flat became available.

Then there was a very popular American movie, depicting an American going to India and training a group of Indians, who ended up competing with him for jobs. The theme of the movie seems to evolve around cultural difference and cultural shock, but its background is globalization, where more and more American companies will outsource their operations in order to capitalize on the cheap labor in India and China. The world is flattening. The U.S. is slowly going down and India and China are rising rapidly.

Again, the name of the movie is *"The World is Flat."*

(II)

More than a decade has passed, and the configuration of the world has changed significantly.

The rise of China is the most noted change among all.

One piece of data vividly illustrates this: China's GDP has grown from 10 trillion CNY in 2000 to 82.7 trillion CNY in 2017, and China's world ranking in economy has leaped from the 6th to the 2nd.

This rise of China is highlighted by such a phenomenon: These years in New York, Paris and Tokyo, groups and groups of Chinese visitors have been the most distinguishable in tourist attractions and luxury stores. Statistics tells us that in 2017, 130 million Chinese citizens traveled overseas, and their overseas tax rebates on shopping accounted for more than one-third of the global total.

If we focus our view on the U.S., China, and India, Friedman's prediction seems to be right — the world is flattening.

(III)

However, this world is not just about the U.S., China and India.

Ten years ago, the BRIC states provided exciting opportunities for investors; now, however, Brazil and Russia are trapped in economic recession. The aura of the "BRIC" seems to have become past tense.

The ten years have witnessed one after another "failed" country. These countries have been hit by both economic stagnation and social unrest. Their road ahead is not smooth, but rather checkered or even perilous.

There is a list of 30 most failed countries within the U.S. media. This list is available online. If you have read it, you may have the feeling that these 30 countries are indeed failed countries, but there are worse-off countries that haven't been included.

In fact, many empirical studies find that only a few countries, such as China, have reaped benefits from globalization in the past decade. By contrast, a considerable number of countries have paid a huge price. The world is not becoming flat. The world is becoming uneven.

(IV)

It was June again. Prof. Zhou Muzhi returned to Beijing from Tokyo, and we chatted in a cafe.

Prof. Zhou said that in the past 10 years, only one city in Japan experienced a large population growth. That is the metropolitan area of Tokyo.

He continued that similar phenomena have happened in many economies. Over the past decade, most of the population growth and economic activities have peaked at a few dazzling spots, where the world's best talents, the largest portion of economic resources and the greatest companies concentrated.

Prof. Zhou concluded that the world has never been flat, and neither has China been flat.

(V)

China is not flat. This was my first impression of the *China Integrated City Index*, an achievement of Prof. Zhou Muzhi and his team.

Prof. Zhou introduced deviation values into his *China Integrated City Index*, as the criteria against which all aspects of a city's "performance" are evaluated.

The deviation value means a value that deviates from the relative average value, reflecting the place of a city among all of her counterparts.

He showed me some of the deviation values:

In respect of the medical radiation, there are 22 cities whose deviation values are higher than 60. And Beijing and Shanghai have even gone beyond 100. As opposed to these, there are 27 cities whose deviation values are below 45. This clearly demonstrates a high level of unevenness.

In respect of population movement, there are 16 cities whose deviation values go beyond 60, representing a considerable population increase. Three of them, in particular, come with deviation values of more than 100. By contrast, there are as many as 47 cities whose deviation values are lower than 45, representing a considerable population drop. Again, this demonstrates a high level of unevenness.

He also showed me some plane "3D charts." In these "charts," there are outstanding peaks and depressed rock bottoms. In addition, it is likely that the dazzling peaks may become more outstanding, and the depressed rock-bottoms keep sinking.

(VI)

We talked about the rise and fall of home prices.

Prof. Zhou Muzhi said that the real estate market is a good example of the comparative status of Chinese cities.

Ten years ago, home prices in almost all cities were on the rise, although such rise was sharp in some cities and moderate in some others. Now, however, the prices continue to rise in some cities, while having stagnated or even dropped in some others.

The differentiation among cities is, to some extent, responsible for the rise and fall of home prices, but it is the differentiation in resource allocation, population movement, and economic growth that drives the home prices fundamentally. In the past, we were all on the same track. Some were running and some others walking. Now, however, some are still running, some are still walking, and some have stopped.

(VII)

The day after my meeting with Muzhi, I was invited to give a speech at a meeting. The title of the speech was "When is the spring of China's economy?"

After the speech, the audience initiated chats with me. An audience from Southern China told me, "Dr. Zhang, our town is different from what you described. We never saw winter. We've only been in the spring."

Yet an audience from the north argued, "our situation is different as well. We have been stuck in win-ters all these years, and we could only dream about the spring."

I was rather embarrassed. I had forgotten about differentiation, which was the hallmark of China's economy. So, I defended my position, "I was talking about the general matters, a national average, which evens out the ups and downs."

I was reminded of *China Integrated City Index* by Muzhi. With a framework for evaluation, Muzhi was ahead of me, exemplifying the differentiation and fluctuations with deviation.

While a framework gives us a stronger sense of direction, differentiation makes us distanced and detached.

(VIII)

In *The World is Flat*, Friedman recalls that his parents often told him when he was a child: "Tom, finish off your meal, and don't forget that the Chinese are starving."

Prof. Zhou Muzhi's *China Integrated City Index* seems to be delivering the same message.

This is an era of ongoing differentiation. Some cities are full of promise and potential, and some others are in deep trouble and have lost its directions. Although economic growth and social development are bringing China to the next level, the uneven pattern has not changed in essence. In a way, it is not becoming flat, but rather increasingly unbalanced.

(VIIII)

We need benchmarks and references on this rugged road.

Prof. Zhou Muzhi's *China Integrated City Index* proposes a new set of benchmarks and references.

Profile
Zhang Zhongliang

Born in 1962, he worked as: Associate Researcher, Chinese Academy of Management Science; Researcher, National Institute of Science and Technology Policy (Japan); Executive Director, CAST Center for Economic Evaluation; Director, China Economic Monitoring and Analysis Center; Director, Statistical Education Center of the National Bureau of Statistics; Director, Department of Finance of the National Bureau of Statistics.

Part-time positions: Vice President, China Association of Market Information and Research. Past part-time positions: member of the All-China Youth Federation; Secretary General, the PECC Financial Market Development Committee (China); President, periodical office for China Monthly Economic Indicators; President, periodical office for China National Conditions and Strength.

A Brand New Universal Indicator System for Cities

Yokoyama Yoshinori

Social systems architect, director of EMP (Executive Management Program) of the University of Tokyo; dean of HBMS (Hiroshima Business and Management), and former head of Tokyo office, McKinsey & Company

It is critical that city performance indicators are understood and recognized by wide variety of different interest groups. Therefore, these indicators must be clear, concise, easy to understand and remember.

To that end, the *China Integrated City Index* establishes a three-tier structure consisting of "Governing thought," "Mission," and "Performance indicators" from abstraction to concreteness.

The Governing thought is not only targeted at Chinese cities, but also focused on the future direction of global urban development. The Mission refers to the important issues sorted out under the Governing thought, in accordance with the national conditions and the stages of urban development of China. The Performance indicators are the digital manifestation of the Governing thought and the Mission, divided into dimension, sub-dimension, and indicator group categories.

There are only three dimensions in the *China Integrated City Index*, and each dimension consists three sub-dimensions, each of which further consists of three indicator groups. Such a 3x3x3 structure is concise and clear as well as easy to remember and discuss.

A city is a complex of many "social systems" with intangibles as well as tangibles in visible forms such as roads, buildings, and green plants. A social system is "a system that creates and provides value for the consumers and residents," by enabling horizontal connection among different sectors and industries. For example, the social system for medical care is not only related to the hospitals and pharmacies and pharmaceutical and device companies in the medical industry, but also creates and provides value via col-laboration and interaction with many other related industries such as IT, construction, finance, and insur-ance. The city is defined by the collection of many interacting social systems. Therefore, the establishment of city performance indicators requires a comprehensive and systematic thinking.

At the same time, the city is not an isolated being. It is also very important how to evaluate her rela-tionship with other regions and cities and even with the rest of the world.

Every city has her own characteristics in natural conditions. The establishment of indicators should not only encompass considerations for the natural conditions that humans are unable to manage, such as climate, water, and soil, but also be focused on the evaluation of the city's adaptability to the environment and the diversity, flexibility, and sustainability of the time.

The city as an entity consumes materials and energy and gets rid of solid, liquid, and gaseous waste on an ongoing basis. It is in itself a damage to nature. It is also noteworthy that the city seems to be an organism, capable of certain degree of self-adjustment. The ideal city for the future will include an established and effective circulation system with an emphasis on her self-repair capability, doing little harm to the process of consumption, discharge, and destruction.

Based on the above considerations, the governing thought of the *China Integrated City Index* is to pursue a city that encourages "harmony among urban residents" and "diversified development patterns" and "works around circular economy activities." Its mission can be concisely described as encompassing "the coexistence of a reasonable urban structure and economic development," "the mechanism of bridging the economic gap" and "the emphasis of importance to the relevance with the rest of the world and the surrounding areas." In terms of indicator selection, special attention is paid to "economy, environment and quality of life," "sustainability beyond the changing times" and "contribution to the vicinity."

For a city, different times will see different pursuits and issues. The *China Integrated City Index* needs to keep abreast of the times and readjust and improve the selection of indicators on an ongoing basis, so that it will remain relevant and progressive in providing guidance for and evaluation of urban development.

Profile

Yokoyama Yoshinori

Born in 1942, Prof. Yokoyama graduated from the Department of Architecture, School of Engineering, the University of Tokyo, and holds Master of Architecture in Urban Design from Harvard University and an MBA from MIT Sloan School. He used to work for Mayekawa Kunio Architects and Associates. In 1975, he joined McKinsey & Company and served as head of its Tokyo office. He has served as Senior Researcher at the METI's Research Institute of Economy, Trade and Industry, Auditor at the Industrial Revitalization Corporation of Japan, and member of the National Diet of Japan Fukushima Nuclear Accident Investigation Commission. Prof. Yokoyama has established and managing EMP for 10 years. He served program professor in charge of EMP at the University of Tokyo between 2014 and 2017.

Construction of an Ecological City and the Integrated City Index

Takeuchi Kazuhiko

Project Professor, The University of Tokyo; Chair, Central Environment Council, Government of Japan; Former Senior Vice-Rector, United Nations University; Ph. D., Agrobiology

In China, where urbanization is in rapid progress, it is a major issue as to how to realize the low carbon development of a city and the sustainable development of her economy. In China, which has become the world's 1st state in carbon dioxide emission, problems such as air pollution, water pollution, and traffic congestion are significant. The expanding cities also have adverse effects on the ecosystem, leading to increasingly severe issues including a reduction in biodiversity and the degradation of natural capital.

Under such high-speed urban development in China, there is an urgent need to explore a new mechanism capable of comprehensively addressing global environmental problems and reducing environmental pollution. The author advocates that "3E," i.e., energy (low carbon), environment (improvement of water, air, etc.) and ecosystem (symbiosis between the city and nature), should be used to benchmark the construction of eco-cities.

The *China Integrated City Index* co-compiled by the National Development and Reform Commission of China and Cloud River Urban Research Institute, which highly accords with the "3E" benchmarks integrating a global vision and regional perspectives, is a comprehensive city indicator with great influence on international society.

In order to achieve a sustainable urban development, three major goals of social development need to be set against the 3E benchmarks.

The first goal is to realize a low carbon society. Regional water quality and atmospheric environment should be improved while efforts are paid to promote low-carbon energy and mitigate climate change. Especially in the developing Asian cities, energy consumption is still on the rise. If we do not work hard to advance the replacement with renewable energy and improve the efficiency of energy use, it will be difficult to ensure the sustainable development of the city.

The second goal is to realize a circular economy. Sustainable development should be realized by minimizing the use of natural resources and waste emissions, and by recycling resources in compliance with the 3R principles, namely, to reduce raw materials, recycle, and reuse. In China, special attention also needs to be paid to the recycling of resources in promoting upgrades to buildings and infrastructure.

The third goal is to realize a symbiotic society between humans and nature. A society allowing for symbiosis and interactions between humans and nature should be created to produce synergistic effects. Special attention should be paid to the maintenance of the forests, agricultural lands, and waters around the city, so that the city can, on the one hand, enjoy the ecological services provided by the rural areas; and on the other, provide various support and feedback to the rural areas. In doing so, a naturally symbiotic society will be built, allowing for coordinated development between them.

With the Pearl River Delta and the Yangtze River Delta as the representatives, many big Chinese cities that have witnessed high-speed development are concentrated in delta and coastal areas. Extreme weather conditions such as sea level rise, heavy rain, and floods caused by climate change are disasters of great harm to cities. Therefore, it is necessary to recognize that "3E" is not only a benchmark for a sustain-able society, but also an important measure to mitigate the risks of climate change. A consensus should be reached between the government and the public for practical measures to be taken and for supervision over the results of implementation.

The *China Integrated City Index* seeks sustainable development from the environmental, social, and economic dimensions and, with nine sub-dimensions including natural ecology, living standard, and dynamic development, as well as with 27 indicator groups including environmental load, life service, and economic structure, to name a few, it seeks to establish up a complete integrated system for evaluation of urban development. It should be used not only for comprehensive diagnosis of development conditions of Chinese cities, but also for indicating the direction of her development.

Another major feature of the *China Integrated City Index* is the use of a large number of expressive charts to present vast amounts of information in a very concise and understandable way. It is very important to both the government and the public to explore how to think about and grasp the complex urban system in an all-round and integrated manner. This kind of "visualized index" not only largely enhances our under-standing of the status quo of China's urbanization, but also provides all stakeholders of the city with clear insight into the characteristics and problems of the city, in order to make important contributions to the sustainable development of the city.

Profile

Takeuchi Kazuhiko

Born in 1951, he served as: Lecturer, Tokyo Metropolitan University; Associate Professor in the Faculty of Agriculture, Professor in the Asian Natural Environmental Science Center, and Professor in the Graduate School of Agricultural and Life Sciences at the University of Tokyo; Director, Integrated Research System for Sustainability Science (IR3S) at the University of Tokyo; Acting Chair for the Council of Food, Agriculture and Rural Area Policies. He took up his current post in 2017. He also serves as Editor-in-Chief of the journal Sustainability Science published by Springer-Nature.

The Next Stage of Urbanization: Centralization or Decentralization?

Zhang Zhongliang

Director, Department of Social, Science and Technology and Cultural Statistics of National Bureau of Statistics, PRC and Ph. D. in Economics

(I)

In 1898, Ebenezer Howard, founder of the garden city movement, made a prediction that in time, London, a city of 6.6 million residents, would see her population drop to 20%, and the other 80% would move to the "new towns" scattered around London.

Prediction are speculative by nature, and in reality, London's population did not evolve in the manner predicted by Howard. but has grown with the same momentum as before, and by 1939, reached a record high of 8.6 million.

As the population continued to grow, the "urban diseases" became increasingly serious. In response, in 1940, the Barlow Royal Commission, a branch of the British Government in charge of the population issues of London, published the Barlow Report, which advocated the decentralization of industries and population from central London. In 1946, the British Government promulgated The New Town Act to initiate a new town movement, which established eight satellite towns around London. In 1988, after a 50-year net outflow of population, the London eventually created a new record of 6.37 million people.

Just as every coin has two sides, the drawbacks existed alongside the benefits. The New Town Movement mitigated the urban diseases, but exacerbated the recession of London, as opposed to people's expectations. Accordingly, the New Town Movement was ended, and a revival movement was launched. Contrary to the decentralization of urban population in the New Town Movement, the revival movement was oriented to promote the return of the population and reinvigorate the city. One piece of data demonstrates the effect: by the end of 2015, the population of London had exceeded the peak of 1939, reaching 8.54 million, while the population commuting to London for work was as high as 10.31 million.

(II)

All roads lead to Rome.

We saw similar patterns in New York.

The past 100 years saw New York's population undergo changes at three stages. The first stage was marked by the steady growth of population, when the population and economic activities continued to increase, and peaked at 7.89 million in 1950. Then came the second stage, where the population stopped growing. The worsening of "urban diseases" and the implementation of the urban function decentralization plan relocated people to the surrounding towns. The population dropped to a 7.07 million low in 1980. Eventually, the 1980s marked the start of the third stage. Driven by the optimized urban planning and upgraded industries, the population rebounded to 8.55 million in 2015. The population of the New York Metropolitan Area has already exceeded 10 million since 1950, and reached 18.59 million today.

A similar scene can be found in Tokyo.

After the Second World War, Japan entered a period of rapid urbanization. Rural population relocated to large cities, especially in Tokyo.

In the 1960s, in response to the pervasive urban diseases, the capital area governance plan intended to decentralize the urban functions of Tokyo was created, and new cities including the Tama Garden City, Tama New Town, Kohoku New Town, Chiba New Town, and Tsukuba Science City emerged in the vicinity of Tokyo. The outward relocation of the manufacturing industry and the suburbanization of population inflows worked in the same direction. By 1995, the population of Special wards of Tokyo had fallen to a 7.97 million low.

In the mid-to-late 1990s, the population movement in Tokyo was reversed, putting an end to the sub-urbanization of the population, and signaling a "return to the heart of the capital." In 2002, the implementa-tion of the urban regeneration plan effectively alleviated traffic congestion in the city and resulted in the resumption of population growth in the Special wards of Tokyo where, by 2014, the population had exceeded 13 million, and in the Tokyo Metropolitan Area it had reached as high as 38 million.

(III)

Now let's take another look at Howard's prediction.

From the perspective of a metropolitan area, if the concentration of population and economic activi-ties in big cities is referred to as centralization, and movement to the surrounding areas as decentralization, then Howard was right in his prediction on decentralization.

However, the history of the world's urban evolution shows that centralization and decentralization are actually two sides of the same coin in urban evolution, alternating cyclically. Sometimes, centralization overpowers decentralization. Sometimes, decentralization overpowers centralization. Other times, the two trends are equally powerful and break even. However, relatively speaking, centralization is the stronger trend.

In fact, almost all major cities, including London, New York, and Tokyo, have gone through a process from centralization to decentralization and then to re-centralization.

A city develops as a result of the agglomeration effect and appears as centralized. However, when the population and economic activities reach an extreme value, where the "scale does not produce economic effects," decentralization will dominate, inevitably resulting in the stagnation of urban expansion, and the relocation of population and economic activities to the surrounding areas.

However, when the power of decentralization comes into play, centralization dwindles. After a period of time, centralization will once again overpower decentralization and take the lead in a new round of agglomeration and expansion.

Behind centralization and decentralization is the efficiency of resources utilization, which is determined by the transportation infrastructure, technology level, and urban intelligence.

Accordingly, the upgrade in transportation infrastructure and improvement in technology and urban intelligence will magnify the force of agglomeration. The reason why big cities have urban diseases is less attributable to the excessive functions of the cities, than to the insufficiency in transportation infrastructure, technology and urban intelligence to take on their huge responsibilities.

Fifty years ago, when the Special wards of Tokyo had a population of 8.89 million, there was city-wide anxiety about urban diseases. Now, however, the population there has exceeded 13 million, and there are fewer complaints about the population being too excessive or the density being too high.

Why?

Because the current transportation infrastructure, technology and urban intelligence have far exceeded the previous standards, and so has the city's carrying capacity.

The carrying capacity of a city is not fixed, but rather a variable that changes with the time and space. Different cities may be largely different in their carrying capacity at the same point in time, and the same city may have different carrying capacity at different times. In general, a city will experience growth in her carrying capacity over time, and such capacity will become stronger as her transportation infrastructure, technology, and intelligence improve.

(IV)

From a national perspective, we found that urbanization in most countries is also a process from centralization to decentralization and then to re-centralization.

Looking at the population migration, the urbanization process in the major countries of world generally consists of four stages:

The first stage is the urbanization of small towns. The population moves from rural to urban areas, and the subjects of such urbanization are small cities and small towns.

The second stage is the urbanization of large cities. After the urbanization rate has reached 50%, the population migration is mainly in the form of relocation from small cities and towns to big cities, and relocation of rural population either to small cities and small towns to fill the vacancies left by their population out-flow, or directly to big cities.

The third stage is the suburbanization of large cities. After the urbanization rate has reached 70%, the big cities will become the subjects of urbanization, and the predominant population migration will be the movement of urban population in big cities to their suburbs.

The fourth stage involves metropolitan areas and megalopolises. The suburbs evolve into small and medium cities, and form a synergistically enhanced metropolitan area within areas of big cities. A few metropolitan areas located in a specific area rely on their developed transportation infrastructure or space to organize a compact and economically connected megalopolis.

Accordingly, the first and second stages involve centralization, the third stage is decentralization; and the fourth stage is about re-centralization.

The S-curve theory of urban evolution and the inverted U-shape theory of economic development have interpreted the above process from different perspectives.

Let us take another look at what is happening in China.

One argument is that since the reform and opening up, China has achieved the development that has taken the developed countries one or two hundred years to achieve in just 30 years or so.

Disregarding other fields, the argument is valid with respect to urbanization.

In 1978, less than 17.92% of China's population was urbanized. By 2016, however, this figure has risen to 57.35%.

As part of this process, initially in the 1980s, the rapid development of township-or-village-based enterprises led to the blossoming of small towns across China, driving the rapid urbanization in the country.

The 1980s was the time for small towns, and the 1990s set the stage for big cities, when a large number of working people flowed from rural villages or small towns to big cities. At the policy level, just as in the 1980s, there had been voices to "put the size of big cities under control" due to anxiety about urban diseases. Yet the acceleration of the marketization process and the sudden outburst of energy from the agglom-eration effect of big cities made it a goal for almost every Chinese city of variable scale to follow the path of urbanization. Visibly, the downtown areas expanded rapidly, and almost every big or medium-sized city became a construction site.

In the 21st century, our urbanization rate started from the 36.22% baseline in 2000. In the "official vocabulary," the big city is no longer a derogatory term, and policy orientation has also changed from "putting the size of large cities under control" to "coordinating the development of large, medium and small cities and small towns."

It was also during this period that megacities like Shanghai and Beijing initiated their suburbanization actions to decentralize the pressure on the central urban areas. Take Shanghai as an example. Five major new cities were established, including Jiading, Songjiang, Qingpu, Nanqiao, and Lingang, which absorbed a large number of new population but did not become destinations for population agglomeration. They are even less attractive to transplants than urban-rural fringe zones.

Looking back on the past 40 years, we note that China's urbanization process is not different from that of the major countries of the world. However, due to the huge regional differences in China, some regions, such as those in the west, are still at the second stage of urbanization; and some others, such as the Pearl River Delta and the Yangtze River Delta, are already at the third or even fourth stage.

As the Nobel-Prize-winning economist Joseph E. Stiglitz said, the urbanization in China and the high-tech development in the U.S. will be the two major events affecting the development of human societ-ies in the 21st century. In the past 40 years, the accelerated urbanization has transformed the Yangtze River Delta, the Pearl River Delta, and the Beijing-Tianjin-Hebei megalopolises, leading population and eco-nomic activities to further gather in large cities. In this process, despite the decentralizing tendencies, the real control remains with the centralizing power.

(V)

Nevertheless, China's urbanization has always been characterized by two kinds of ideas, i.e., the decentral-ized urbanization dominated by small and medium cities, and the centralized urbanization dominated by large cities. In other words, we have two options, decentralization and centralization.

Then, in the new era, what is China's choice, to be urbanized by centralization or decentralization?

At the macro level, or from the national perspective, centralization may be the most appropriate option.

There are at least four reasons.

First, the larger the city is, the stronger the carrying capacity becomes for population and industries. There will be more employment opportunities and higher income, with lower production and transaction costs, and the cost of infrastructure and public services will be diluted due to the large scale. By contrast, the smaller the city is, the more difficult it will be to have economies of scale. Due to poor returns, it is also difficult for smaller cities to secure capital support for infrastructure and pollution control.

In fact, research conducted by the World Bank show that cities with a population of less than 150,000 can hardly produce net returns to scale.

Perhaps some will argue that in China, many small cities and even small towns are quite prosperous.

The issue is that these well-developed small cities or small towns are generally located around big cities or within the reach of metropolitan areas. Statistics show that 90% of the "Top 100 Towns" are located in the core areas of the Yangtze River Delta and the Pearl River Delta. In a sense, the prosperity of these small cities and small towns, in turn, verifies the advantage of centralization.

This is the principle, which we cannot go against.

Second, international experience shows that at the second stage of urbanization, when the urbaniza-tion rate rises from 50% to 70%, the general trend of migration is embodied by the gathering of people in big cities. In the U.S, large cities with a population of more than 5 million contributed 12.2% to the national population in 1950, and 24.6% in 2010. In Japan, the population of three major metropolitan areas, namely Tokyo, Osaka, and Nagoya, accounted for 23.9% of the national population in 1884, and 47.3% in 1973.

Some studies have pointed out that cities with the fastest growing number of permanent residents in China from 2011 to 2015 were Beijing, Shanghai, Guangzhou, Shenzhen and Tianjin, with an average annual growth rate of 1.9%; followed by nine up-and-coming second-tier cities with an average annual growth rate of 1.2%; next were 19 additional second-tier cities, with an average annual growth rate of 0.9%; while 43 third-and-fourth-tier cities had only achieved an average annual growth rate of 0.4%. In consideration of the national natural population growth rate of 0.5% from 2011 to 2015, could we assert that in general, third-and-fourth-tier cities have entered the stage of net population outflow?

This is the overwhelming trend, which we cannot go against.

Third, there is an opinion that the development of small towns should be placed at the top of the list, because big cities are already overcrowded and overwhelmed, unable to benefit from positive externality.

This point of view is quite debatable. Data shows that compared to most of the big cities in the world, the population is not of high density in big Chinese cities. For example, Shanghai is the largest city in China, with a population that accounts for less than 3% of the country. In contrast, half of the Italians vol-untarily "pack themselves" on 8% of their land; there are over 3,000 counties in the U.S., but the top 244 by population density have clustered half of the Americans; the Tokyo Metropolis takes up only 0.6% of Japan's land area but accommodates 10% of Japan's population.

In fact, the issue with our big cities is not concerning in and of itself. Yet when compared to other countries, our transportation infrastructure, technology, and urban intelligence still falls behind to certain extent, or in other words, our urban governance does not appear to be in line with our transportation infra-structure, technology, and urban intelligence.

There is another argument that our big cities are unable to afford more migrants with their infrastruc-ture and government financial resources, and it costs much less to do the same through small towns.

Is there any problem with the financial resources of big city governments? The contrary is the case. In statistical terms, in China, the bigger the city, the stronger her financial resources; and the smaller the city, the more financial constraints it faces. For a bigger city, the fiscal question is about whether a financial investment should be made and whether it is effectively made, rather than whether it is fiscally possible to execute a plan. Besides, the bigger the city, the better the infrastructure develops to attract social capital.

In contrast, a smaller city or town is more likely to rely on the state for financial support. Without large investment, it is difficult to develop industrial agglomeration and the corresponding logistics, finan-cial, and technical service facilities, and difficult to create jobs. Even if jobs could be created, the cost of an individual job would be far greater than its counterpart in big cities. The past few years have seen much preference for the development of specialized towns in some areas, with tens even hundreds of millions of RMB invested. Some studies have, however, indicated that the jobs created and the potential economic impact are actually quite disappointing.

Moreover, for a country like China with such population density and land scarcity, any decision to opt for an urbanization path that favors small cities and small towns, it will absolutely occupy more land. If so, how do we ensure that "the Chinese people hold the rice bowls in their own hands"?

This is common sense, which we cannot go against.

Fourth, big cities are probably the best at retaining the incoming population. Before 2015, there had been talks about "escaping from Beijing, Shanghai, and Guangzhou," but the reality is that the native population of Beijing, Shanghai and Beijing "escaped" to New York, London, and Tokyo, rather than "escaping" from big cities. It is an indisputable fact that the Chinese population has been flowing to big cities.

People also flow to big cities for better job prospects, higher wages, more entertainment options, and even better food choices. The opportunities are not the same for small and medium cities or small towns. People like to draw on the advantages and avoid the disadvantages. People go wherever there are more opportunities, higher income and more comfortable and exciting life; provided, of course, that they can make independent choices.

If you do a survey on whether people are willing to live in a big city or a small town given they can make their own independent choices. I believe that most of them would prefer a big city to a small town.

This is public opinion, which we cannot go against.

(VI)

The Chinese Government has made it clear that the urbanization in China should be aimed at the urban pattern dominated by megalopolises with coordinated development of large, medium and small cities.

It is correct and realistic to opt to be "dominated by megalopolises."

It is correct because in one sense, today's international economic competition has evolved into something between megalopolises, and domestic economic development has been upgraded to the development of megalopolises. This is most strongly evidenced by the face that the Greater New York, Greater Los Angeles, and the Great Lakes regions contribute 67% to the U.S. GDP; and the Pacific Coast Megalopolis of Japan, consist-ing of Tokyo, Hanshin, and Nagoya, contributes 70% to Japan's GDP.

The reality is that China's traditional province-based or administrative-region-based economy has begun to transform into megalopolis-based economy. The megalopolis has become the main platform for China's economy to move towards high quality and sustainability and to participate in international economic competition. In 2015, the Beijing-Tianjin-Hebei, Yangtze River Delta, and Pearl River Delta Megalopolises created 40% of the country's GDP with 5.2% of the country's land area, which is an impor-tant signal.

Then, who are the subjects of a megalopolis?

The answer is central cities.

In fact, an important experience from the urbanization in the world is to build up "megalopolises" of different levels by relying on the radiation and driving forces of central cities, including international metropolises, national central cities, regional central cities, and local small and medium cities. In this process, big cities, as central cities, are not only the "engine" for metropolis development, but also the "engine" for national economic development.

Agglomeration still defines central cities and provides guarantee for their functions to be brought into play and values to be realized. In fact, almost all central cities expand by absorbing talents, capital, resources and experience from the surrounding areas, from the rest of the country and the rest of the world, although over time, agglomeration will change to include highly technology-intensive and value-adding industries or economic factors.

Only through agglomeration will a central city create and continue to strengthen her economies of scale and economic efficiency.

Also, only through agglomeration will a central city create and continue to strengthen its potential economic energy and "polarization effect" beyond other cities.

Cities like Beijing and Shanghai have to, for the moment, put their total permanent population under control, but this does not mean they no longer need to be agglomerated. In fact, Beijing and Shanghai need to be both decentralized and agglomerated. They also need to take advantage of the opportunities arising from such decentralization to gather resource elements that contribute to improving the core urban functions, urban values and urban intelligence, to provide support for them to improve carrying capacity and achieve sustainable growth.

(VII)

In nature, there is a phenomenon of "no grass growing at the root of a big tree." Why? Because the big tree has strong roots that seize all the surrounding water and nutrients, and absorbs and blocks the sunlight, eliminating any conditions for the growth of weeds.

If a city does something similar to her surroundings in agglomeration, then she no longer qualifies as a central city.

Why?

Because, as a center, she should have companions around her, rather than standing alone, lonely and cold.

Therefore, a central city should think and act like a central city, produce effects of diffusion and radiation, help cities within the megalopolis to stand out and promote the economic growth of the outskirts and even the whole country. In fact, almost all the big cities grow up and strong in their radiation and services to the surrounding areas, to the rest of the country and even to the rest of the world.

A central city should be a towering tree that provides a good shade for people to "enjoy the cool," rather than a big tree with "no grass growing" at its root.

However, to "enjoy the cool" does not mean that all the cities develop at the same pace. Resources are limited after all. Imbalance is a prerequisite and an inevitable flipside to development.

Any blind pursuit of moving at the same pace may end up falling back at the same pace.

Paul Graham, father of Silicon Valley entrepreneurship, said in *Cities and Ambition*:

"There is always one or two cities in a country that catch the attention of the young people in that country, just as what London is to the U.K., New York to the U.S., and Paris to France, where you can feel the pace of and the heartbeat of that country" (n.p.). [Translator's note: This sentence cannot be found in the book Cities and Ambition]

In China, Beijing, Shanghai, Guangzhou and Shenzhen are cities of this kind. However, they are not enough. What China needs should not be just one or two such cities, but 10 or even dozens of such cities.

Centralization and Choice of Development Path of Megalopolises

Li Xin

Deputy Secretary General of Beijing Municipal People's Political Consultative Conference; Professor, Chinese Academy of Sciences; Doctor of Science

It was not until more than 10 years ago when I returned to China from Canada and was officially trans-ferred to Beijing Municipal Environmental Protection Bureau that I initially touched upon the issue on urban planning and development. I was involved in a project headed by Wang Guangtao, former Minister of Construction, entitled *Research on the Relationship between Beijing Urban Planning and Meteorological Conditions as well as Air Pollution.* Later I was again involved when being focused on the research around the development mechanism for regional air pollution and the process of pollutant transport, due to my role as leader and organizer of the project *Research on Air Quality Assurance Measures for Beijing and the Surrounding Five Provinces and Cities during the 2008 Olympic Games.*

With rapid industrialization and urbanization, the surge in resident population has resulted in many obvious "urban diseases" such as traffic congestion, water shortage, insufficient supply of public services, and difficulties in public security. Since 2013, people's daily life has greatly suffered from frequent occurrence of regional haze caused by fine particulate matter ($PM_{2.5}$) pollution. Some folks have to migrate overseas. Already serving in the district government then, I began to study urban air pollution issues from a broader and more systematic perspective, based on my experience in general urban administration, and was once again focused on urban planning and development issues. On the basis of some international cases of green city development, and by taking the Mentougou District of Beijing as an example, I developed a comprehensive evaluation system based on 6 dimensions including economic support, social prog-ress, quality of life, resources carrying and environmental protection, and 34 indicators for annual development evaluation, in an attempt to lead the transformation of the regional economy giving priority to ecology. At the end of 2014, during my study visit to Germany, when I exchanged my ideas with experts on urban planning and sustainable development, I was deeply impressed by the concept and practice of the German "decentralized" megalopolis development they presented. It was clearly different from the current megalopolis development model of China where the population and economic activities were concentrated in a few "prominent mountain peak" cities.

By chance in 2016, I was fortunate to participate in the *China Integrated City Index 2016* book release conference, and met with the main authors, Prof. Zhou Muzhi, Director Xu Lin, and some senior members of the project team. For more than a year, I have been learning from them, who have been good teachers and friends rather than seniors to me.

Prof. Zhou believes that in the process of urbanization, post-industrialization countries tend to follow large city development models of the "prominent mountain peak" style, which, especially after the Second World War, has become the trend of urbanization development around the world. The economies of scale of urban agglomeration have an increasingly obvious effect on improving the efficiency of economic development and enriching urban life. Especially for the development of knowledge economy and service economy, the cluster of high-density population in megalopolises has greatly facilitated the direct interactions between people of different knowledge and cultural backgrounds. This is precisely the determinant for the productivity of knowledge economy and may be well exemplified by my acquaintance of and get-together with the seniors. He also said that many urban diseases are caused by the so-called "overcrowding." What is "overcrowding"? It is simply the partial clustering of population in high density in urban areas, which overruns the capacity of urban infrastructure and management. He explained to me the devel-opment process of Tokyo (the metropolitan area), which is the most comparable to Beijing, from the dis-tress of urban problems caused by "overcrowding," to the functional decentralization under strong administrative power, then to the gathering of a larger population, and to the realization of a high-density modern international urban society, which allows me to follow the development process of the era and have a fuller understanding of urbanization development models.

Prof. Zhou said that in more than five years, Chinese and foreign experts from various fields have consid-ered and sorted the experiences and lessons of urbanization development both inside and outside China, as well as the latest philosophy of megalopolis development by digitization and indexation of the same, and established a comprehensive evaluation system on the sustainable urbanization from economic, environmental, and social dimensions after repeated discussions, giving priority to the ecology, pursuing quality of economic develop-ment and improving social services. In addition, the indicator system is open and constantly re-adjusted and improved as required by the era. The number of indicators increased from 133 in 2016 to 176 in 2017.

By using practical statistical data, satellite data and geographic and spatial data that are available, all 297 cities at the prefecture level or above were analyzed with introduction of deviation values (values deviating from the relative average values), to reflect the various indicator scores of the cities evaluated as compared to the average of all cities. This was to some extent a comprehensive assessment, a "physical examination" of the development states of the cities at or above the prefecture level. The analysis for 2016 and 2017 presents to us the extremely uneven urbanization development in the eastern and western regions of China, and it also discloses the imbalance and inadequacy of spatial development in the same region or city. In addition, the *Index* is also focused on the development characteristics and existing challenges of the major megalopolises such as the Pearl River Delta, the Yangtze River Delta, the Beijing-Tianjin-Hebei region, and the Chengdu-Chongqing region, as well as foresight on future reforms.

Beijing ranked first in the overall ranking of cities due to her nature as the capital. The region she is located in has developed into a megalopolis with both Beijing and Tianjin as cores and a relatively dense population. However, due to the existing capacity of infrastructure, public services and management of the Beijing-Tianjin-Hebei that is seriously unaligned to the high-density population cluster, Beijing has been deeply mired in urban disease such as water shortage, air pollution and traffic congestion. It is desirable that the progressing of the construction of Beijing Sub-center should enhance the spatial agglomeration of Tongzhou and its surrounding areas, to mitigate the "overcrowding" issue that part of Beijing urban area cannot afford the needs of management and infrastructure. Is the establishment of Xiong'an New District similar to the German development philosophy that I mentioned earlier of "decentralizing" megalopolises? It is intended to weaken Beijing's "central" status and form a well-connected, collaborated and mutually enhanced symbiotic urban agglomeration, in order to effectively re-adjust the connectivity between spatial structures of individual cities and regions, and alleviate the developmental imbalance between cities in the Beijing- Tianjin-Hebei region. Of course, I do not know the original intention and basis of this strategic concept, but was just providing a rough speculation based on my understanding and analysis of its location, resource endowment and related planning. If such philosophy and concept are indeed adopted, the districts of Beijing will be required to play a better role in radiation and driving the process, based on the *Beijing Urban Master Plan (2016-2035)* approved by the Central Government. In particular, the districts of Beijing bordering Tianjin and Hebei need to be more open-minded and, on the basis of clear functional positioning of the Master Plan, consideration should be given to the collaboration with Tianjin and Hebei with a focus on the general landscape of coordinated development in the region, to break through administrative barri-ers, and formulate a synergistic development plan for the districts of Beijing bordering Tianjin and Hebei, to realize coordinated uniformity of planning in such areas as land use, general transportation, industrial layout and eco-environment protection.

Any promotion of balanced development of inter-regional urbanization is also a process of redistribu-tion and re-engineering of the complicated interest pattern of regional economy and society. This process requires not only scientifically quantified indicators to guide the formulation of corresponding policies and urban plans, but also sufficient considerations of the accumulated social contradictions and issues due to the earlier rapid development of urbanization, to formulate and improve public hearing procedures that all stakeholders have the right to participate in, so that the stakeholders can be mutually coordinated. Although such coordination will bring some loss of efficiency, adequate communication and coordination will largely ensure the operability of policies and plans and their acceptability to urban residents and may minimize the fair damage caused by policy mistakes. This was often overlooked in past urban construction and manage-ment. As Prof. Zhou said, any imperfections in the urban planning system also have a series of negative impacts on urban construction and development.

Regional development indeed requires the establishment of philosophy and principle of comprehensive spatial development, to achieve relative alignment and coordination between population, resources and environment and economic and social development within a certain scale of space. The *China Integrated City Index* precisely reflects this philosophy and principle, not only providing a comprehensive evaluation standard for urban construction and development, but also operational guidance for urban planning. In accordance with the requirements of the *Beijing Urban Master Plan (2013-2035)*, the government should establish a normalized mechanism for one "physical examination" to be performed per year and one assessment every 5 years against urban construction and development, to provide an evalu-ation system of 42 indicators. The Beijing Municipal Government plans to introduce a third party to carry out annual assessment of urban construction in 2018. Perhaps the *China Integrated City Index* may provide helpful and scientific references and guidance for that purpose.

There would be different pursuits and impressions for different times in urban development, and different groups of people would have different expectations and ideals. Whether it is the "decentralized" small town group development model represented by Germany, or the "centralized" super-large city devel-opment model by Tokyo, New York, and Paris after the Second World War, they all have their own advan-tages and disadvantages. The "centralization" development model seems to utilize resources more efficiently; and "decentralization" seems to be better in concurrently managing the balance of regional development. If we look at it from a broader perspective, should megalopolis development go after both the "centralized" and the "decentralized" development approaches?

The seniors said that this is an era of constant differentiation, some areas are full of vitality and tension, and some others in deep trouble and cannot get themselves out. Perhaps this is the reason why people are inexhaustibly motivated to keep summarizing on their experiences and lessons to explore urban development models. In any case, it is our goal to achieve a dynamic balance between the human social and economic development and the carrying capacity of natural resources and environment, as referred to as ecological civilization.

Profile

Li Xin

Born in 1968, Mrs. Li successively served as Associate Professor and then Professor at the Institute of Atmospheric Physics, the Chinese Academy of Sciences, primarily engaged in the research fields of atmospheric turbulence and atmospheric environ-ment. In 2004, she was transferred to the Beijing Municipal Environmental Protection Bureau, serving as Deputy Chief Engineer and Director of the Department of Science and Technology and International Cooperation, Director of the Department of Environmental Monitoring, and Director of the Department of Atmospheric Environment Management. she was mainly responsible for the security work related to air quality of the Beijing 2008 Olympic Games. In 2010, she was transferred to the Mentougou District of Beijing as Deputy Mayor of the District, mainly in charge of environmental protection, education, medi-cal care and health, culture and sports, subdistricts and labor security, among others. Since the beginning of 2017, she has been serving as Deputy Secretary-General of the Beijing Municipal People's Political Consultative Conference and Vice Chairman of the Beijing Municipal Committee of the China Association for Promoting Democracy. Part-time positions: Professor and Doctoral Adviser at the Institute of Atmospheric Physics, the Chinese Academy of Sciences; Professor at the College of Environmental Sciences and Engineering, Beijing University.

Research areas: chaotic characteristics of atmospheric turbulence, coherent structure and complexity research; characteristics of air pollution and research on its development mechanism; research on the pollutant transport and transformation mechanism between Beijing and surrounding areas; numerical forecast, projection and research on regional air quality.

Research achievements: Published more than 60 Chinese and English language academic papers on Chinese core academic journals and international SCI journals. Authored the *Analytical Research on the Concentration and Source of Inhalable Particles in Beijing, Beijing Air Quality Assurance for the 29th Olympic Games - Research on the Measures of Five Provinces and Cities in North China, Evaluation Report on the Effect of Measures for Beijing Air Quality Assurance for the 29th Olympic Games, Recommendations on Sustainable Urbanization, Recommendations on Regional Smog Management* and other scientific reports. Chief Editor and Translator for: *USEPA Air Quality Criteria for Particulate Matter* (China Environmental Science Press, 2008 edition).

Core Cities' "Mobility" Strategy

Yokoyama Yoshinori

Social systems architect, director of EMP (Executive Management Program) of the University of Tokyo, dean of HBMS (Hiroshima Business and Management), and former head of Tokyo office, McKinsey & Company

Vladimir Putin, President of Russia, first visited Japan when he was Deputy Mayor of St. Petersburg. When Japanese newspaper reporters asked about his impression of Japan, he replied, "There is no discontinuity between cities." This answer was very fresh. It might be what he felt while looking at the scenery through the windows on the Tokaido Shinkansen.

Indeed, it is mostly vast forests between cities in Russia. Though Japan's Tokaido Megalopolis (also known as the Pacific Coast Megalopolis of Japan) accounts for less than 22% of the country's land area, it is home to 60% of the Japanese people. From the satellite night shots of the Japanese archipelago, a chain of shining and dazzling areas can be found along the Tokyo-Nagoya-Osaka region.

The Greater Tokyo Metropolitan Area (GTMA) defined by the commuting circle accounts for one-third of Japan's population and GDP, and 40% of Personal Financial Assets (PFA). Although the fact that urbanization as a global phenomenon has been around for a long time, the emergence of such a huge metropolitan area is a great undertaking unimaginable in the past.

The transportation system deserves credits in promoting the formation of the Tokaido Megalopolis and the GTMA. At the beginning of the 20th century, urban designers started advocating "functionalism" as a counter-argument for "eclecticism," its credo was "form follows function." At that time, the functions of a city were considered "to live," "to work," and "to play." However, the experience of the Australian capital Canberra tells the world that it is impossible to design a charming city only by these three points.

The question of what kind of function is required of a city has always been one for exploration. By the middle of the 20th century, people had believed that a city should have more functions. Japanese archi-tect Arata Isozaki proposed "to encounter," and another architect, Kisho Kurokawa, proposed that "to move" should become a new function of the city. However, the design of "Festival Plaza" of Expo '70 in Osaka based on the concept of "to encounter," of which Arata Isozaki was a member of design team, show the failure of this concept. Hurrying through the diagonal of the Festival Plaza, people swarming from one exhibition hall to another did not effectively "encounter" here.

However, "to move" advocated by Kisho Kurokawa is indeed an important function of the city. The Tokaido Shinkansen for the purposes of the Tokaido Megalopolis, and the JR Yamanote sen a circular commuter line for the purposes of the Greater Tokyo Metropolitan Area, both bear the important function of "mobility."

The Tokaido Shinkansen not only incorporated the new technology for all the carriages are equipped with a motor instead of a locomotive pulling carriages like the case of France's TGV which came to operation 17 years after the Tokaido Shinkansen. In this sense it is the world's first high-speed electric train system dedicated to passenger transport. Opened on the eve of the Tokyo Olympics in 1964, the Tokaido Shinkansen runs through the three metropolitan areas of Tokyo, Nagoya, and Kinki, bringing their large and small cities into close connection, and realizing a megalopolis pattern allowing for the interactive development of the three metropolitan areas.

Although without special new technology, the JR Yamanote Line is the result of a philosophically innovative thinking, expanding the core of a city, the Central Business District (CBD), from a "point" to a "circle," with many modal change points improving the diversity and density of urban activities in Tokyo and creating a successful case in the history of urban design in the world.

The central business district of Tokyo has been mainly composed of the Marunouchi area between Tokyo Station and the Imperial Palace since Meiji. In the era of private railroad expansion connecting the suburbs to the urban areas, almost all private railways wanted access to the Tokyo Station. In response, the German engineers hired by the Japanese Government (the Ministry of Railways) had proposed to build a loop-shaped Yamanote Line, to connect existing stations including the Tokyo Station near the Imperial Palace, the Ueno Station on the Tohoku Main Line, the Shinjuku Station on the Chuo Main Line, and the Shinagawa Station on the Tokaido Main Line; the ministry used this idea and the private railway companies were required not to connect their railways to the Tokyo Station, but to the loop-shaped Yamanote Line for transfer. For that purpose, new stations such as Ikebukuro, Shibuya and Osaki have been added as transfer stations (modal change points) to private railways in addition to the existing stations. With the massive inflows of transferring passengers, high-density economic activity bases were gradually developed around these stations, resulting in Tokyo having several central business districts. A city usually has only one central business district.

It takes an hour to travel one round on the Yamanote Line. That means, it is within the psychologically acceptable range for the passengers to reach their destination station within 30 minutes. Another advantage of having a loop without an end-point is the easiness to ensure the number of passengers at each station. At the beginning of the 20th century, in Boston, the U.S., the world's most advanced subway network was built, but it shrunk until the middle of the 1960s. It was forced out of service mainly because it was difficult for the branch line to ensure enough passengers, resulting in a decrease in passenger number on the main line connected to the branch line, and entering a vicious circle. It was recovered to some extent later. Among the four lines that crossed over in the grid in the central business district, like the four lines crossing the well-shaped cross, the red line ending at Harvard Square was also extended into a loop, which was a rare example in American cities built based on cars. However, the Boston loop is different from the Tokyo loop, and there is no transfer function. The resulting pattern of urban development is completely different.

The urban air pollution caused by "to move" has almost become a big problem of every big city today. But, Tokyo, as the largest city in the world, is less troubled by this problem. This is due to the exhaust emission restrictions introduced in 1970, but the larger contributor is the urban public rail transit system with a developed transfer function. Of course, this system lacks the door-to-door convenience, and it is difficult to thoroughly relieve the pain caused by the overcrowded carriages during peak commuting hours. Viewed from the scale of the Greater Tokyo Metropolitan Area today of 38 million people, the circle by the Yamanote Line is becoming closer and closer to a size of point.

The electric vehicles that China is developing vigorously today will become an important countermeasure to reduce urban air pollution. However, for the transportation in central cities with large populations, it is more important to focus on the development of an "Electric Personnel Mover System" (EPMS) where electric vehicles and urban rail transit are highly connected. By focusing on the development of a transfer system between electric vehicles and urban rail transit, EPMS can not only achieve urban traffic with zero emissions, but also door-to-door convenience and efficiency of urban public rail transit, thereby meeting the complexity of urban activities. Of course, to achieve this, we need to depend on innovations of urban design.

A society on the wheels has once led to the decline of the central business districts in the U.S. and the "Doughnut Effect". In the future, the EPMS to be rolled out in the central cities should not only support the development of the CBD as the city core, but also realize the linkage of multiple CBDs through the transportation network, expand the scope of urban economic activities, and seek for the pattern of multi-core development of central cities.

How to consider "mobility" is indeed an important strategy for determination of the development pattern for central cities.

Chapter VIII

Data Interpretation of Indicators

1. Environment

Table 8-1 Interpretation of Indicators : Environment

Dimen-sion	Sub-dimen-sion	Indicator Group	ID	Indicators	Use Data Name	Data Sources
Environment	Natural Ecology	Soil and Water Condition	1	Available Land Area Per Ten Thousand People	Available Land Area (km²) and Population Size of Permanent Residents (10,000 People)	Satellite Remote Sensing Data
			2	Forest Area	Forest Area (km²)	Satellite Remote Sensing Data
			3	Farmland Area	Farmland Area (km²)	Satellite Remote Sensing Data
			4	Pasture Area	Pasture Area (km²)	Satellite Remote Sensing Data
			5	Water Area	Water Area (km²)	Satellite Remote Sensing Data
			6	Water Resources Per Ten Thousand People	Total Water Resources (10,000 m³) and Population Size of Permanent Residents (10,000 People)	Statistical Yearbooks of Various Provinces, Statistical Yearbooks of Various Cities and Statistical Communiques on National Economy and Social Development of Various Cities
			7	National Park · Conservation Area · Scenic Area Index	National Forest Parks (Nr.), National Geological Parks (Nr.), National Wetland Parks (Nr.), Pilot Programs for National Park System (Nr.), National Nature Reserves (Nr.), National Wetland Reserves (Nr.), National Marine Sanctuaries (Nr.), National A-level Tourist Scenic Spots (Nr.), National Scenic Areas (Nr.), National Garden Cities (Nr.), and National Forest Cities (Nr.)	Data published by the State Council of the People's Republic of China, the Ministry of Natural Resources of the People's Republic of China, the Ministry of Ecology and Environment of the People's Republic of China, the Ministry of Culture and Tourism of the People's Republic of China and the State Forestry and Grassland Administration of China
		Climate Condition	8	Climate Comfort Index	10°C-28°C (Days)	Internet big data
			9	Rainfall	Precipitation (mm)	Statistical Yearbooks of Various Provinces, Statistical Yearbooks of Various Cities and Statistical Communiques on National Economy and Social Development of Various Cities
		Natural Disaster	10	Natural Disaster-caused Direct Economic Loss Index	Natural Disaster-caused Direct Economic Loss (10,000 CNY)	Data published by the Ministry of Civil Affairs of the People's Republic of China
			11	Geological Disaster-caused Direct Economic Loss Index	Geological Disaster-caused Direct Economic Loss (10,000 CNY)	Data published by the Ministry of Civil Affairs of the People's Republic of China
			12	Disaster Warning	Disaster Warning (Times)	Internet big data
	Environmental Quality	Pollution Load	13	Air Quality Index (AQI)	AQI Average	Internet big data
			14	PM₂.₅ Index	PM₂.₅ Average	Internet big data
			15	CO_2 Emissions Per Unit of GDP	CO2 Emissions Per Ten Thousand Yuan GDP (Tons of Carbon Dioxide/10,000 CNY)	Statistical Yearbooks of Various Provinces, Statistical Yearbooks of Various Cities and Statistical Communiques on National Economy and Social Development of Various Cities
			16	Volume of Sulphur Dioxide Emission	Volume of Industrial Sulfur Dioxide Emission (Tons)	China Urban Statistical Yearbooks
			17	Volume of Industrial Soot(dust) Emission	Volume of Industrial Soot (Dust) Emission (Tons)	China Urban Statistical Yearbooks
			18	Proportion of National and Provincial Water Sections in Category III and Above Meeting the Quality Standard	Water Quality Level	Data published by the Ministry of Ecology and Environment of the People's Republic of China

Table 8-2 Interpretation of Indicators : Environment

Dimension	Sub-dimension	Indicator Group	ID	Indicators	Use Data Name	Data Sources
Environment	Environmental Quality	Environmental Protection Efforts	19	Areas Environmental Average Noise Value	Areas Environmental Average Noise Value (dB(A))	Statistical Yearbooks of China
			20	Radiation Environmental Air Absorption Dose Rate	Radiation Environmental Air Absorption Dose Rate (nGy/h)	Data published by the Ministry of Ecology and Environment of the People's Republic of China
			21	Environmental Effort Index	Environmental Protection Investment (10,000 CNY), Local Public Finance Income (10,000 CNY)	China Urban Statistical Yearbooks, Statistical Yearbooks of Various Provinces, Statistical Yearbooks of Various Cities and Statistical Communiques on National Economy and Social Development of Various Cities
			22	Water-saving Effort Index	Total Water Supply (10,000 Tons), Total Water Resources (10,000 Cubic Meters) and Population Size of Permanent Residents (10,000 People)	China Urban Statistical Yearbooks, Statistical Yearbooks of Various Provinces, Statistical Yearbooks of Various Cities and Statistical Communiques on National Economy and Social Development of Various Cities
			23	Social Organizations for Ecological Environment	Number of Social Organizations for Ecological Environment (Nr.)	China Civil Affairs' Statistical Yearbooks
			24	National Environmental Protection City Index	National Ecological Demonstration Areas (Nr.), National Environmental Protection Model Cities (Nr.), National Ecological Civilization Construction Demonstration Area (Nr.), National Greening Model Cities (Nr.), National Excellent Cities on Comprehensive Improvement of Urban Environment (Nr.), and Pilot Cities of City Betterment and Ecological Restoration Programs (Nr.)	Data published by the Ministry of Ecology and Environment of the People's Republic of China
			25	National Ecological Environment Evaluation Index	National Ecological Cities (Districts and Counties) and National Ecological Towns (Nr.)	Data published by the Ministry of Ecology and Environment of the People's Republic of China
		Resource Efficiency	26	Land Productivity in Built District	Regional Gross Production from the Secondary Sector (10,000 CNY), Regional Gross Production from the Tertiary Sector (10,000 CNY) and Area of Built Districts (Square Kilometer)	Satellite Remote Sensing Data and China Urban Statistical Yearbooks
			27	Land Productivity in Agriculture, Forestry, Animal Husbandry and Fisheries	Regional Gross Production from the Primary Sector (10,000 CNY) and Land Areas in Agriculture, Forestry, Animal Husbandry and Fisheries (Square Kilometer)	Satellite Remote Sensing Data and China Urban Statistical Yearbooks
			28	Energy Consumption Per Unit of GDP	Energy Consumption Per Ten Thousand Yuan GDP (Tons of Standard Coal/10,000 CNY)	Statistical Yearbooks of Various Provinces, Statistical Yearbooks of Various Cities and Statistical Communiques on National Economy and Social Development of Various Cities
			29	Projects Labeled with Green Building Design and Evaluation	Star-level Projects Labeled with Green Building Design and Evaluation (Nr.)	Data published by the Ministry of Housing and Urban-Rural Development of the People's Republic of China
			30	Comprehensive Utilization Rate of Industrial Solid Waste	Comprehensive Utilization Rate of General Industrial Solid Waste (%)	China Urban Statistical Yearbooks
			31	Circular Economical City Index	National Circular Economy Pilot Cities (Nr.) and National Comprehensive Demonstration Cities of Energy Saving and Emission Reduction Fiscal Policy (Nr.)	Data published by the National Development and Reform Commission of the People's Republic of China
		Compact City	32	Population of Densely Inhabited Districts (DIDs)	DID Population (10,000 People)	Satellite Remote Sensing Data
			33	Area of Densely Inhabited Districts (DIDs)	DID Area (km²)	Satellite Remote Sensing Data

Table 8-3 Interpretation of Indicators : Environment

Dimension	Sub-dimension	Indicator Group	ID	Indicators	Use Data Name	Data Sources
Environment	Environmental Quality	Compact City	34	Proportion of the Population of Densely Inhabited Districts (DIDs)	DID Population (10,000 People) and Population Size of Permanent Residents (10,000 People)	Satellite Remote Sensing Data, Statistical Yearbooks of Various Provinces, Statistical Yearbooks of Various Cities and Statistical Communiques on National Economy and Social Development of Various Cities
			35	Proportion of Densely Inhabited Districts (DIDs) in Built District	DID Area (km²) and Area of Built Districts (km²)	Satellite Remote Sensing Data
			36	Population of Super Densely Inhabited Districts (DIDs)	Population of Super Densely Inhabited Districts (DIDs) (10,000 People)	Satellite Remote Sensing Data
			37	Area of Super Densely Inhabited Districts (DIDs)	Area of Super DIDs (km²)	Satellite Remote Sensing Data
			38	Proportion of the Population of Super Densely Inhabited Districts (DIDs)	Population of Super DIDs (10,000 People) and Population Size of Permanent Residents (10,000 People)	Satellite Remote Sensing Data, Statistical Yearbooks of Various Provinces, Statistical Yearbooks of Various Cities and Statistical Communiques on National Economy and Social Development of Various Cities
		Environmental Protection Efforts	39	Proportion of Densely Super Densely Inhabited Districts (DIDs) in Built District	Area of Super DIDs (km²) and Area of Built Districts (km²)	Satellite Remote Sensing Data
			40	Urban Rail Transit Density Index	Mileage of Urban Rail Transit Lines (km), Land Area of Administrative Regions (km²) and Proportion of the Population of DIDs (%)	Satellite Remote Sensing Data, Statistical Yearbooks of Various Provinces, Statistical Yearbooks of Various Cities and Statistical Communiques on National Economy and Social Development of Various Cities
			41	Urban Arterial Road Density Index	Mileage of Urban Arterial Roads (km), Land Area of Administrative Regions (km²) and Proportion of the Population of DIDs (%)	Satellite Remote Sensing Data, Statistical Yearbooks of Various Provinces, Statistical Yearbooks of Various Cities and Statistical Communiques on National Economy and Social Development of Various Cities
			42	Urban Life Road Density Index	Mileage of Urban Life Roads (km), Land Area of Administrative Regions (km²) and Proportion of the Population of DIDs (%)	Satellite Remote Sensing Data, Statistical Yearbooks of Various Provinces, Statistical Yearbooks of Various Cities and Statistical Communiques on National Economy and Social Development of Various Cities
			43	Urban Sidewalk • Bicycle Lane Density Index	Mileage of Urban Sidewalks and Bicycle Lanes (km), Land Area of Administrative Regions (km²) and Proportion of the Population of DIDs (%)	Satellite Remote Sensing Data, Statistical Yearbooks of Various Provinces, Statistical Yearbooks of Various Cities and Statistical Communiques on National Economy and Social Development of Various Cities
			44	Urban Rail Transit Distance	Mileage of Rail Transit Lines (km)	Satellite Remote Sensing Data
			45	Public Bus Passenger volume Per Ten Thousand People	Annual Total Public Bus Passenger Volume (10,000 People) and Population Size of Permanent Residents (10,000 People)	China Urban Statistical Yearbooks, Statistical Yearbooks of Various Provinces, Statistical Yearbooks of Various Cities and Statistical Communiques on National Economy and Social Development of Various Cities
			46	Public Bus Ownership Per Ten Thousand People	Actual Ownership of Operating Public Buses at the Year-end (Nr.) and Population Size of Permanent Residents (10,000 People)	China Urban Statistical Yearbooks, Statistical Yearbooks of Various Provinces, Statistical Yearbooks of Various Cities and Statistical Communiques on National Economy and Social Development of Various Cities
			47	Private Vehicle Ownership Per Ten Thousand People	Private Vehicle Ownership (Nr.) and Population Size of Permanent Residents (10,000 People)	Statistical Yearbooks of Various Provinces, Statistical Yearbooks of Various Cities and Statistical Communiques on National Economy and Social Development of Various Cities

Table 8-4 Interpretation of Indicators : Environment

Dimen-sion	Sub-dimen-sion	Indicator Group	ID	Indicators	Use Data Name	Data Sources
Environment	Spatial Structure	Urban Facilities	48	Taxis Ownership Per Ten Thousand People	Taxi Ownership (Nr.) and Population Size of Permanent Residents (10,000 People)	China Urban Statistical Yearbooks, Statistical Yearbooks of Various Provinces, Statistical Yearbooks of Various Cities and Statistical Communiques on National Economy and Social Development of Various Cities
			49	Rush Hour Traffic Jam Delay Index	Rush Hour Traffic Jam Delay Index	Internet big data
			50	Fixed Assets Investment Scale Index	Fixed Assets Investment (10,000 CNY)	China Urban Statistical Yearbooks
			51	Area of Park Green Land	Area of Park Green Land (Hectare)	China Urban Statistical Yearbooks
			52	Green Coverage Rate in Built District	Green Coverage Rate in Built Districts (%)	China Urban Construction Statistical Yearbooks
			53	Density of Water Supply Pipelines in Built District	Density of Water Supply Pipelines in Built Districts (km/km²)	China Urban Statistical Yearbooks
			54	Density of Sewers in Built District	Density of Sewers in Built Districts (km/km²)	China Urban Statistical Yearbooks
			55	Gas Coverage Rate	Gas Coverage Rate (%)	China Urban Statistical Yearbooks
			56	Urban Underground Facilities Index	Pilot Cities of Underground Pipe Gallery Construction (Nr.) and Pilot Cities of Sponge City Program (Nr.)	Data published by the Ministry of Finance of the People's Republic of China and the Ministry of Housing and Urban-Rural Development of the People's Republic of China

2. Society

Table 8-5 Interpretation of Indicators : Society

Dimen-sion	Sub-dimen-sion	Indicator Group	ID	Indicators	Use Data Name	Data Sources
Society	Status and Governance	City Status	57	Administrative Levels	Assessment at the administrative levels of municipality directly under the central government, provincial capital, city under independent planning and prefecture-level city	China Urban Statistical Yearbooks
			58	Megalopolis Levels	Assessment at the Megalopolis Levels	China Urban Statistical Yearbooks
			59	Core City Levels	Assessment at the Core City Levels	China Urban Statistical Yearbooks
			60	Embassies · Consulates	Embassies and Consulates (Nr.)	Data published by the Ministry of Foreign Affairs of the People's Republic of China
			61	International Organizations	International Organizations (Nr.)	Internet big data
			62	Belt and Road Index	Location Assessment for the Belt and Road	Data published by the National Development and Reform Commission of the People's Republic of China and Internet big data
		Quality of Residents	63	Population Natural Growth Rate Index	Population Natural Growth Rate (‰)	China Urban Statistical Yearbooks
			64	Population Social Growth Rate Index	Population Natural Growth Rate (‰) and Population Size of Permanent Residents (10,000 People) Population Aged 0-14 Years (10,000 People),	China Urban Statistical Yearbooks, Statistical Yearbooks of Various Provinces, Statistical Yearbooks of Various Cities and Statistical Communiques on National Economy and Social Development of Various Cities
			65	Population Structure Index	Population Aged 15–64 Years (10,000 People), Population Aged over 65 Years (10,000 People), and Population Size of Permanent Residents (10,000 People)	The Sixth Nationwide Population Census Data, Statistical Yearbooks of Various Provinces, Statistical Yearbooks of Various Cities and Statistical Communiques on National Economy and Social Development of Various Cities
			66	Population Education Structure Index	Population with a University Degree (College Degree and Above) (10,000 People), Population with a High School Degree (including Secondary School Degree) (10,000 People), Population with a Middle School Degree (10,000 People), and Population Size of Permanent Residents (10,000 People)	The Sixth Nationwide Population Census Data, Statistical Yearbooks of Various Provinces, Statistical Yearbooks of Various Cities and Statistical Communiques on National Economy and Social Development of Various Cities
			67	Higher education Index	Number of Ordinary University and College Students (10,000 People), Number of Secondary Vocational Education School Students (10,000 People) and Number of Full-time Teachers of Ordinary Universities and Colleges (10,000 People)	China Urban Statistical Yearbooks
			68	Outstanding Talent Cultivation Index	National First-level Actors/Actresses (Persons), National First-level Artists (Persons), Olympic Champions (Persons), National Masters of Sports (Persons), Academicians of the Chinese Academy of Sciences and Chinese Academy of Engineering (Persons), and the Mao Dun Literary Prize Winners (Persons)	Data published by the General Administration of Sport of China and Internet big data
			69	Public Finance Expenditure for Education Index	Local Public Finance Expenditure for Education (10,000 CNY) and Population Size of Permanent Residents (10,000 People)	China Urban Statistical Yearbooks, Statistical Yearbooks of Various Provinces, Statistical Yearbooks of Various Cities and Statistical Communiques on National Economy and Social Development of Various Cities

Table 8-6 Interpretation of Indicators : Society

Dimension	Sub-dimension	Indicator Group	ID	Indicators	Use Data Name	Data Sources
Society	Status and Governance	Social Management	70	Social Services Index	Volunteer Services in Social Services (Person-time), Volunteer Services for Social Work (Person-time), Year-end Employers for Social Services (10,000 People), Year-end Employers for Social Work (10,000 People), Blood Donation without Repayment Advanced Cities (Nr.) and National Double Support Model City Index (Nr.)	Data published by the Ministry of Civil Affairs of the People's Republic of China, the General Political Department of the Chinese People's Liberation Army and the National Health Commission of the People's Republic of China, and China Civil Affairs' Statistical Yearbooks
			71	Safe and Reliable City Index	National Excellent Cities in All-round Improvement of Social Security (Nr.), National High-quality Demonstration Cities (Nr.), National Advanced Cities for Law Publicity and Education (Nr.), National Demonstration Cities for the Construction of a Social Credit System (Nr.) and National Food Security Model Cities (Nr.)	Data published by the State Council of the People's Republic of China, the Ministry of Human Resources and Social Security of the People's Republic of China, and the CPC Central Committee for the Comprehensive Management of Public Security
			72	Traffic Safety Index	Amount of Traffic Accident-caused Losses (10,000 CNY) and Traffic Accident-caused Deaths (10,000 People)	Statistical Yearbooks of Various Provinces, Statistical Yearbooks of Various Cities and Statistical Communiques on National Economy and Social Development of Various Cities
			73	Social Security Index	Amount of Fire Accident-caused Losses (10,000 CNY) and Fire Accident-caused Deaths (10,000 People)	China Fire Control Statistical Yearbooks
			74	Social Organizations	Number of Social Organizations (Nr.)	China Civil Affairs' Statistical Yearbooks
			75	Health and Civilized City Index	National Health City (Nr.), National Civilized City (Nr.) and National Demonstration Community Health Service Center (Nr.)	Data published by the National Health Commission of the People's Republic of China
			76	Government Website Performance	Evaluation of Chinese Government Website Performance	Data published by the China Software Testing Center
	Inheritance and Exchange	Historical Relics	77	Historical Status	Duration for Central Governance and Serving as a Capital (Years) and Duration for Opening and Commercial Intercourse (Years)	Internet big data
			78	World Heritage	World Heritage (Nr.)	Data published by the UNESCO
			79	Famous Historical and Cultural Cities	Famous Historical and Cultural Cities (Nr.)	Data published by the State Administration of Cultural Heritage of the People's Republic of China
			80	Intangible Cultural Heritage	Intangible Cultural Heritage (Nr.)	Data published by the UNESCO and the State Council of the People's Republic of China
			81	Key Cultural Relics Sites Under the Protection	Key Cultural Relics Sites Under the Protection (Nr.)	Data published by the State Administration of Cultural Heritage of the People's Republic of China
		Culture & Entertainment	82	Theater Consumer Index	Number of Theaters and Cinemas (Nr.), Box Office (10,000 CNY) and Cinema Admissions (Person-time)	Internet big data
			83	Museums · Art Galleries	Museums (Nr.) and Art Galleries (Nr.)	Internet big data
			84	Sports Venues Index	Area of Sports Venues (10,000 Square Meters)	Internet big data
			85	Zoos · Botanical Gardens · Aquariums	Zoos (Nr.), Botanical Gardens (Nr.) and Aquariums (Nr.)	Internet big data
			86	Public Library Collection	Public Library Collection (10,000 Volumes)	China Urban Statistical Yearbooks

Table 8-7 Interpretation of Indicators : Society

Dimension	Sub-dimension	Indicator Group	ID	Indicators	Use Data Name	Data Sources
Society	Inheritance and Exchange	Exchange	87	Cultural Master Index	National First-level Actors/Actresses (Persons), National First-level Artists (Persons), and the Mao Dun Literary Prize Winners (Persons)	Internet big data
			88	Olympic Champion Index	Olympic Champions (Persons) and National Masters of Sports (Persons)	Data published by the General Administration of Sport of China
			89	National Culturally Advanced Unit Index	National Culturally Advanced Unit (Nr.)	Data published by the Ministry of Culture and Tourism of the People's Republic of China
			90	Inbound Tourists	Number of Inbound Tourists (10,000 People)	Statistical Yearbooks of Various Provinces, Statistical Yearbooks of Various Cities and Statistical Communiques on National Economy and Social Development of Various Cities
			91	Domestic Tourists	Number of Domestic Tourists (10,000 People)	Statistical Yearbooks of Various Provinces, Statistical Yearbooks of Various Cities and Statistical Communiques on National Economy and Social Development of Various Cities
			92	Foreign Exchange Earnings from International Tourism	Foreign Exchange Earnings from International Tourism (10,000 USD)	Statistical Yearbooks of Various Provinces, Statistical Yearbooks of Various Cities and Statistical Communiques on National Economy and Social Development of Various Cities
			93	Earnings from Domestic Tourism	Earnings from Domestic Tourism (100,000,000 CNY)	Statistical Yearbooks of Various Provinces, Statistical Yearbooks of Various Cities and Statistical Communiques on National Economy and Social Development of Various Cities
			94	International Conferences	International Conferences (Number)	Internet big data
			95	Exhibition Industry Development Index	Exhibition Industry Development Index	China Exhibition Data Statistics Report
			96	World Tourism City Index	Travel + Leisure's Recommendations (Nr.), Tripadvisor - Top 10 Destinations (Nr.), Mastercard's Recommendations (Nr.), Euromonitor International's Recommendations (Nr.), List of China's Excellent Tourist Cities (Nr.), Global Tourism Demonstration Zones (Nr.), World Excellent Tourism Destination Cities (Nr.) and National Tourism Standardization Demonstration Cities (Nr.)	Internet big data
	Quality of Life	Residential Environment	97	Average Life Expectancy	Average Life Expectancy of Population (Years)	China Population and Employment Statistics Yearbooks
			98	Medicare · Endowment Insurance Coverage Index	Number of People Participating in the Basic Medical Insurance for Urban Workers (10,000 People), Number of People Participating in Basic Old-age Insurance for Urban Workers (10,000 People), and Population Size of Permanent Residents (10,000 People)	China Urban Statistical Yearbooks, Statistical Yearbooks of Various Provinces, Statistical Yearbooks of Various Cities and Statistical Communiques on National Economy and Social Development of Various Cities
			99	Ratio of Average House Prices to Income	Annual Average House Price (CNY), Employee Average Salary (CNY) and Total Family Income (CNY)	Statistical Yearbooks of Various Provinces, Statistical Yearbooks of Various Cities, Statistical Communiques on National Economy and Social Development of Various Cities and Internet big data
			100	Habitat City Index	Cities Winning China Residential Environment Prize (Nr.) and Cities Winning United Nation Habitat Award (Nr.)	Data published by the Ministry of Housing and Urban-Rural Development of the People's Republic of China

Table 8-8 Interpretation of Indicators : Society

Dimension	Sub-dimension	Indicator Group	ID	Indicators	Use Data Name	Data Sources
Society	Quality of Life	Level of Consumption	101	China's Happiness City Index	Happiest City In China (Nr.)	Internet big data
			102	Retail Sales of Consumer Goods Per Ten Thousand People	Total Retail Sales of Consumer Goods (10,000 CNY) and Population Size of Permanent Residents (10,000 People)	China Urban Statistical Yearbooks, Statistical Yearbooks of Various Provinces, Statistical Yearbooks of Various Cities and Statistical Communiques on National Economy and Social Development of Various Cities
			103	Revenue of Hotels and Catering Services Per Ten Thousand People	Revenue of Hotels and Catering Services (10,000 CNY) and Population Size of Permanent Residents (10,000 People)	China Urban Statistical Yearbooks, Statistical Yearbooks of Various Provinces, Statistical Yearbooks of Various Cities and Statistical Communiques on National Economy and Social Development of Various Cities
			104	Telecom Consumption Per Ten Thousand People	Telecom Service Revenue (10,000 CNY) and Population Size of Permanent Residents (10,000 People)	China Urban Statistical Yearbooks, Statistical Yearbooks of Various Provinces, Statistical Yearbooks of Various Cities and Statistical Communiques on National Economy and Social Development of Various Cities
			105	Water Consumption for Residential Use Per Ten Thousand People	Water Consumption for Residential Use (10,000 Tons) and Population Size of Permanent Residents (10,000 People)	China Urban Statistical Yearbooks, Statistical Yearbooks of Various Provinces, Statistical Yearbooks of Various Cities and Statistical Communiques on National Economy and Social Development of Various Cities
			106	Top International Brand Index	Top International Brand Stores (Nr.)	Internet big data
		Life Service	107	Number of Children in Kindergartens Per Ten Thousand People	Number of Children in Kindergartens (Persons) and Population Size of Permanent Residents (10,000 People)	Statistical Yearbooks of Various Provinces, Statistical Yearbooks of Various Cities and Statistical Communiques on National Economy and Social Development of Various Cities
			108	Year-end Number of Beds in Nursing Homes	Year-end Number of Beds in Nursing Homes (Nr.)	China Civil Affairs' Statistical Yearbooks
			109	Number of Practicing (Assistant) Physicians	Number of Practicing (Assistant) Physicians (Persons)	China Urban Statistical Yearbooks
			110	Number of Beds in Health Institutions	Number of Beds in Health Institutions (Nr.)	China Urban Statistical Yearbooks
			111	First-class Hospitals	Number of First-class Hospitals (Nr.)	Data published by the National Health Commission of the People's Republic of China

3. Economy

Table 8-9 Interpretation of Indicators : Economy

Dimension	Sub-dimension	Indicator Group	ID	Indicators	Use Data Name	Data Sources
Economy	Quality of Economic Development	Economic Aggregate	112	Size of GDP	Regional Gross Production (10,000 CNY)	China Urban Statistical Yearbooks
			113	Population Size of Permanent Residents	Population Size of Permanent Residents (10,000 People)	Statistical Yearbooks of Various Provinces, Statistical Yearbooks of Various Cities and Statistical Communiques on National Economy and Social Development of Various Cities
			114	Scale of Tax Collection	Various Tax Revenues (10,000 CNY)	Statistical Yearbooks of Various Provinces, Statistical Yearbooks of Various Cities and Statistical Communiques on National Economy and Social Development of Various Cities
			115	Electricity Consumption	Total Electricity Consumption (10,000 Kilowatt Hours)	China Urban Statistical Yearbooks
		Economic Structure	116	Industrial Structure Index	Regional Gross Production from the Primary Sector (10,000 CNY), Regional Gross Production from the Secondary Sector (10,000 CNY), and Regional Gross Production from the Tertiary Sector (10,000 CNY)	China Urban Statistical Yearbooks
			117	Mainboard Listed Enterprises	Mainboard Listed Enterprises (Nr.)	Data published by the Shanghai Stock Exchange, the Shenzhen Stock Exchange and the Hong Kong Stock Exchange
			118	Top 500 Chinese Enterprises in the World	Top 500 Chinese Enterprises in the World (Nr.)	Internet big data
			119	China's Top 500 Enterprises	China's Top 500 Enterprises (Nr.)	Internet big data
			120	China's Top 500 Private-owned Enterprises	China's Top 500 Private-owned Enterprises (Nr.)	Internet big data
			121	Gross Industrial Output Value Above Designated Size	Gross Industrial Output Value above Designated Size (10,000 CNY)	China Urban Statistical Yearbooks
		Economic Efficiency	122	GDP Growth Index	Regional Gross Production (10,000 CNY)	China Urban Statistical Yearbooks
			123	GDP Per Ten Thousand People	Regional Gross Production (10,000 CNY) and Population Size of Permanent Residents (10,000 People)	China Urban Statistical Yearbooks, Statistical Yearbooks of Various Provinces, Statistical Yearbooks of Various Cities and Statistical Communiques on National Economy and Social Development of Various Cities
			124	Fiscal Revenue Per Ten Thousand People	Local Public Finance Income (10,000 CNY) and Population Size of Permanent Residents (10,000 People)	China Urban Statistical Yearbooks, Statistical Yearbooks of Various Provinces, Statistical Yearbooks of Various Cities and Statistical Communiques on National Economy and Social Development of Various Cities
			125	Dependent population Index	Population Aged 0-14 Years (10,000 People), Population Aged over 65 Years (10,000 People), and Population Size of Permanent Residents (10,000 People)	The Sixth Nationwide Population Census Data, Statistical Yearbooks of Various Provinces, Statistical Yearbooks of Various Cities and Statistical Communiques on National Economy and Social Development of Various Cities
			126	Size and Debt Rate of Bonds Issued by the City Investment Enterprises	Local Public Finance Income (10,000 CNY) and Size of Bonds Issued by the City Investment Enterprises (10,000 CNY)	China Urban Statistical Yearbooks and Internet big data
			127	Number of Registered Unemployed Persons Per Ten Thousand People	Number of Registered Unemployed Persons in Cities and Towns at the Year-end (10,000 People) and Population Size of Permanent Residents (10,000 People)	China Urban Statistical Yearbooks, Statistical Yearbooks of Various Provinces, Statistical Yearbooks of Various Cities and Statistical Communiques on National Economy and Social Development of Various Cities

Table 8-10 Interpretation of Indicators : Economy

Dimension	Sub-dimension	Indicator Group	ID	Indicators	Use Data Name	Data Sources
Economy	Dynamic Development	Business Environment	128	Employee Average Salary	Employee Average Salary (CNY)	Statistical Yearbooks of Various Provinces, Statistical Yearbooks of Various Cities and Statistical Communiques on National Economy and Social Development of Various Cities
			129	Number of Employees of Enterprise Services	Number of Employees of Enterprise Services (Finance, Real Estate, Leasing, Business Services and Scientific Research) (10,000 People)	China Urban Statistical Yearbooks
			130	Star Hotel Index	One-star Hotels (Nr.), Two-star Hotels (Nr.), Three-star Hotels (Nr.), Four-star Hotels (Nr.) and Five-star Hotels (Nr.)	Data published by the Ministry of Culture and Tourism of the People's Republic of China and the Tourism and Governmental Affairs Websites of Various Provinces
			131	Top International Restaurant Index	Top International Restaurants by The Asias 50 Best (Nr.) and Top International Restaurants by Tripadvisor (Nr.)	Internet big data
			132	National Industrial Park Index	Special Economic Zones (Nr.), National New Zones (Nr.), National Economic and Technological Development Zones (Nr.) and National High-tech Industrial Development Zones (Nr.) and National Border Economic Cooperation Zones (Nr.)	Data published by the National Development and Reform Commission of the People's Republic of China, the Ministry of Commerce of the People's Republic of China and the Ministry of Science and Technology of the People's Republic of China
		Openness	133	Population Migration	Population Size of Permanent Residents (10,000 People) and Registered Population (10,000 People)	China Urban Statistical Yearbooks, Statistical Yearbooks of Various Provinces, Statistical Yearbooks of Various Cities and Statistical Communiques on National Economy and Social Development of Various Cities
			134	Export of Goods · Import of Goods	Goods Exports (10,000 USD) and Goods Imports (10,000 USD)	Statistical Yearbooks of Various Provinces, Statistical Yearbooks of Various Cities and Statistical Communiques on National Economy and Social Development of Various Cities
			135	Foreign Investment Utilized	Amount of Foreign Investment Utilized in the Current Year (10,000 USD)	China Urban Statistical Yearbooks
			136	Outward Foreign Direct Investment	Amount of Outward Foreign Direct Investment (10,000 USD) and Goods Exports (10,000 USD)	China Urban Statistical Yearbooks, Statistical Yearbooks of Various Provinces, Statistical Yearbooks of Various Cities and Statistical Communiques on National Economy and Social Development of Various Cities
			137	The Output Value of Foreign-invested Enterprises Above Designated Size	Output Value of Foreign-invested Enterprises above Designated Size (10,000 CNY)	China Urban Statistical Yearbooks
			138	International Schools	International Schools (Nr.)	Internet big data
			139	Free Trade Area Index	National Free Trade Areas (Nr.), National Comprehensive Bonded Zones (Nr.), Bonded Zones (Nr.), Export Processing Zones (Nr.), Bonded Logistics Centers (Nr.), National Bonded Port Areas (Nr.), National Key Cities Attaining Gradient Shift of Processing Trade (Nr.), China's Top 100 Foreign Trade Cities (Nr.) and National Pilot Cities for Innovation and Development of Service Trade (Nr.)	Data published by the National Development and Reform Commission of the People's Republic of China, the Ministry of Commerce of the People's Republic of China and the General Administration of Customs of the People's Republic of China
			140	The World's Top University Index	Academic Ranking of World Universities (Nr.), THE World University Rankings (Nr.), QS World University Rankings (Nr.), Ranking Web of World Universities (Nr.), Project 985 Universities (Nr.) and Project 211 Universities (Nr.)	Data published by the Ministry of Education of the People's Republic of China and Internet big data

Table 8-11 Interpretation of Indicators : Economy

Dimension	Sub-dimension	Indicator Group	ID	Indicators	Use Data Name	Data Sources
Economy	Dynamic Development	Innovation and Entrepreneurship	141	R&D Expenditure Index	R&D Internal Expenditure (10,000 CNY)	China Statistical Yearbooks, Statistical Yearbooks of Various Provinces, Statistical Yearbooks of Various Cities and Communiques on Major Data of R&D Resources of Various Provinces and Cities
			142	R&D Human Resources	R&D Personnel (Persons)	China Statistical Yearbooks, Statistical Yearbooks of Various Provinces, Statistical Yearbooks of Various Cities and Communiques on Major Data of R&D Resources of Various Provinces and Cities
			143	GEM · New Third Board Listed Enterprise Index	GEM Listed Enterprises (Nr.) and New Third Board Listed Enterprises (Nr.)	Data published by the Shenzhen Stock Exchange
			144	The Amount of Patent Authorization Index	Amount of PCT Patent Application (pcs.) and Amount of Domestic Patent Authorization (pcs.)	Data published by the Intellectual Property Bureaus and Scientific and Technological Information Offices of Various Provinces and Statistical Communiques on National Economy and Social Development of Various Cities
			145	Trademark Registration Index	Amount of Trademark Registration (pcs.)	Data published by the State Administration for Industry & Commerce of the People's Republic of China
			146	Academicians Index	Academicians of the Chinese Academy of Sciences and Chinese Academy of Engineering (Persons)	Data published by the Chinese Academy of Sciences and the Chinese Academy of Social Sciences
			147	National Reform Experiment	National Experimental Zones for Integrated Reform (Nr.), National Cultural Industry Demonstration (Pilot) Parks (Nr.), State Comprehensive Pilot Projects for the New Urbanization (Nr.), Characteristic Town Index (Nr.), Ocean Economy Innovative Development Demonstration Cities (Nr.), Pilot DemonstrationCities for Made in China 2025 (Nr.), and National Pilot Cities for Public Hospital Reform and Other Related Work (Nr.)	Data published by the National Development and Reform Commission of the People's Republic of China, the Ministry of Industry and Information Technology of the People's Republic of China and the National Health Commission of the People's Republic of China
			148	National Innovative Model City Index	National Advanced Cities of Scientific and Technological Progress (Nr.), National Independent Innovation Demonstration Zones (Nr.), Comprehensive National Science Centers (Nr.), National Innovative Pilot Cities (Nr.) and National High-Tech Industrial Bases (Nr.)	Data published by the National Development and Reform Commission of the People's Republic of China, the Ministry of Science and Technology of the People's Republic of China and the Ministry of Industry and Information Technology of the People's Republic of China
			149	Information · Knowledge Industry City Index	National Intellectual Property Demonstration Cities (Nr.), Internet + Index (Nr.), National Copyright Demonstration Cities (Nr.), Pilot Cities for Cloud Computing Innovation Services (Nr.), Pilot Cities for Digital City Management (Nr.), National Smart City Pilot Projects (Nr.), National Pilot Cities for InformationConsumption (Nr.), National Pilot Cities for Convergence of the Three Network (Nr.), National Experimental Zones for Integration of Informatization and Industrialization (Nr.), National E-Commerce Demonstration Cities (Nr.), and Demonstration Cities of "Broadband China" (Nr.)	Data published by the National Development and Reform Commission of the People's Republic of China, the Ministry of Commerce of the People's Republic of China, the Ministry of Industry and Information Technology of the People's Republic of China and the National Intellectual Property Administration of the People's Republic of China
			150	National Key Laboratory · Engineering Research Center Index	National Key Laboratories (Nr.), National· Engineering Technical Research Centers (Nr.) and National Engineering Research Centers (Nr.)	Data published by the State Council of the People's Republic of China and the Ministry of Science and Technology of the People's Republic of China
			151	Urban-rural Income Ratio Index	Per Capita Disposable Income of Urban Residents (CNY), Per Capita Net Income of Rural Households (CNY) and Total Family Income (CNY)	Data published by the Intellectual Property Bureaus and Scientific and Technological Information Offices of Various Provinces and Statistical Communiques on National Economy and Social Development of Various Cities

Table 8-12 Interpretation of Indicators : Economy

Dimension	Sub-dimension	Indicator Group	ID	Indicators	Use Data Name	Data Sources
Economy	Urban Influence	Urban and Rural Integration	152	Primary School Education Level Population Ratio	Population with a Primary School Education Level (10,000 People) and Population Size of Permanent Residents (10,000 People)	The Sixth Nationwide Population Census Data, Statistical Yearbooks of Various Provinces, Statistical Yearbooks of Various Cities and Statistical Communiques on National Economy and Social Development of Various Cities
			153	Illiteracy Rate	Illiterate Population (10,000 People) and Population Size of Permanent Residents (10,000 People)	The Sixth Nationwide Population Census Data, Statistical Yearbooks of Various Provinces, Statistical Yearbooks of Various Cities and Statistical Communiques on National Economy and Social Development of Various Cities
			154	Balanced Development of Compulsory Education Index	Balanced Development of Compulsory Education Index (Nr.), National Advanced Areas for "Two Basics" Program (Nr.) and National Experimentation Areas for Preschool Education Reform (Nr.)	Data published by the Ministry of Education of the People's Republic of China
		Wide-area Hub	155	Airport Convenient	Passenger Throughput (10,000 People), Cargo and Mail Throughput (10,000 Tons), Executive Flight (Number), Punctuality Rate (%), Total Runway Distance (Meter), Number of Runways (Nr.), and Distance from City Center to Airport (Kilometer)	Satellite Remote Sensing Data, Data published by the Civil Aviation Administration of China and Internet big data
			156	Air Traffic Volume Index	Passenger Throughput (10,000 People) and Cargo and Mail Throughput (10,000 Tons)	Data published by the Civil Aviation Administration of China
			157	Container Port Convenient	Port Throughput (10,000 TEUs) and Distance from City Center to Port (Kilometer)	Data published by the Ministry of Transport of the People's Republic of China and Satellite Remote Sensing Data
			158	Port Container Throughput	Main Port Throughput (10,000 TEUs)	Data published by the Ministry of Transport of the People's Republic of China
			159	Water Transport Volume Index	Waterway Passenger Volume (10,000 People) and Waterway Freight Volume (10,000 Tons)	China Urban Statistical Yearbooks
			160	Railway Convenient	Number of High-speed Rail Services (Times), Number of EMU Services (Times) and Number of Ordinary Train Services (Times)	Data published by the Ministry of Railways of the People's Republic of China and Internet big data
			161	Railway Traffic Volume Index	Railway Passenger Volume (10,000 People) and Railway Freight Volume (10,000 Tons)	China Urban Statistical Yearbooks
			162	Railway Density	Mileage of Urban Railway Lines (Kilometer) and Land Area of Administrative Regions (Square Kilometer)	Satellite Remote Sensing Data and China Urban Statistical Yearbooks
			163	Road Traffic Volume Index	Road Passenger Volume (10,000 People) and Road Freight Volume (10,000 Tons)	China Urban Statistical Yearbooks
			164	Expressway Density	Mileage of Expressways (Kilometer) and Land Area of Administrative Regions (Square Kilometer)	Satellite Remote Sensing Data and China Urban Statistical Yearbooks
			165	National Road · Provincial Road Density	Mileage of National Roads and Provincial Roads (Kilometer) and Land Area of Administrative Regions (Square Kilometer)	Satellite Remote Sensing Data and China Urban Statistical Yearbooks
			166	Circulation City Index	Demonstration Cities for Integrated Transport Services (Nr.), China Logistics Node Cities (Nr.), China Service Outsourcing Demonstration Cities (Nr.), Nationwide Modern Logistics Demonstration Cities in Circulation Areas (Nr.), Urban Joint Distribution Pilot Zones and Comprehensive Pilot Zones of Modern Service Industry (Nr.)	Data published by the Ministry of Commerce of the People's Republic of China and the Ministry of Transport of the People's Republic of China and Internet big data

Table 8-13 Interpretation of Indicators : Economy

Dimen-sion	Sub-dimen-sion	Indicator Group	ID	Indicators	Use Data Name	Data Sources
Economy	Urban Influence	Core Influence	167	Higher Education Radiation	Employees for Higher Education (10,000 People), Total Employees (10,000 People), Academic Ranking of World Universities (Nr.), THE World University Rankings (Nr.), QS World University Rankings (Nr.), Ranking Web of World Universities (Nr.), Project 985 Universities (Nr.) and Project 211 Universities (Nr.)	Data published by the Ministry of Education of the People's Republic of China, China Urban Statistical Yearbooks and Internet big data
			168	Science and Technology Radiation	Scientific and Technical Employees (10,000 People), Total Employees (10,000 People), and Amount of Patent Authorization (pcs.)	Data published by the Intellectual Property Bureaus and Scientific and Technological Information Offices of Various Provinces, China Urban Statistical Yearbooks and Statistical Communiques on National Economy and Social Development of Various Cities
			169	IT Industry Radiation	Employees for Information Transmission, Computer Services and Software (10,000 People), Total Employees (10,000 People), and Number of IT Enterprises and Listed Companies (Nr.)	China Urban Statistical Yearbooks and Internet big data
			170	Culture and Sports and Entertainment Radiation	Employees for Culture and Sports and Entertainment (10,000 People), Total Employees (10,000 People), Number of Theaters and Cinemas (Nr.), Box Office (10,000 CNY), Cinema Admissions (Person-time), National First-level Actors/Actresses (Persons), National First-level Artists (Persons), and the Mao Dun Literary Prize Winners (Persons)	China Urban Statistical Yearbooks and Internet big data
			171	Financial Radiation	Financial Industry Employees (10,000 People), Total Employees (10,000 People), Stock and Futures Exchan-ges (Nr.), Year-end Deposit Balance of RMB of Financial Institutions (10,000 CNY) and Year-end Loan Balance of RMB of Financial Institutions (10,000 CNY)	China Urban Statistical Yearbooks and Internet big data
			172	Manufacturing Radiation	Manufacturing Industry Employees (10,000 People), Total Employees (10,000 People), and Goods Exports (10,000 USD)	China Urban Statistical Yearbooks, Statistical Yearbooks of Various Provinces, Statistical Yearbooks of Various Cities and Statistical Communiques on National Economy and Social Development of Various Cities
			173	Medical Radiation	Medical Industry Employees (10,000 People), Total Employees (10,000 People), and Number of First-class Hospitals (Nr.)	Data published by the National Health Commission of the People's Republic of China and China Urban Statistical Yearbooks
			174	Wholesale and Retail Radiation	Employees for Wholesale and Retail Industry (10,000 People), Total Employees (10,000 People), Total Retail Sales of Consumer Goods (10,000 CNY) and Top International Brand Stores (Nr.)	China Urban Statistical Yearbooks and Internet big data
			175	Catering and Hotel Radiation	Employees for Hotels and Catering Services (10,000 People), Total Employees (10,000 People), One-star Hotels (Nr.), Two-star Hotels (Nr.), Three-star Hotels (Nr.), Four-star Hotels (Nr.), Five-star Hotels (Nr.), Top International Restaurants by The Asias 50 Best (Nr.) and Top International Restaurants by Tripadvisor (Nr.)	China Urban Statistical Yearbooks and Internet big data

Chief Editor

Zhou Muzhi

President of Cloud River Urban Research Institute, Professor of Tokyo Keizai University, Ph.D. in Economics

Born in 1963. Experience: The former Ministry of Machine-Building Industry of PRC; Researcher, Research Institute for Urban & Environmental Development, Japan; Senior Researcher, International Development Center of Japan; Visiting Researcher, Policy Research Institute, Ministry of Finance, Japan; Overseas Non-voting Representative, the Chinese People's Political Consultative Conference; Visiting Researcher, Harvard University; Visiting Professor, Massachusetts Institute of Technology; Research Fellow, the Chinese Academy of Sciences. Concurrent posts: Visiting Professor, the University of International Business and Economics; Visiting Researcher, the Japan Environmental Sanitation Center; and Independent Director, MTI Corporation.

Major works: *Entering the Cloud Computing Era* (2010, People's Publishing House), *The Chinese Economy: Mechanism of its Rapid Growth* (2008, People's Publishing House), *The Chinese Economy: Mechanism of its Rapid Economic Growth* (2007, Nihon Keizai Hyouronsha), *Megalopolis in China* (2004, World Affairs Press), *A Mechanical Electronic Revolution and the New International Division of Labor: Asian Industrialization in the Modern World Economy* (1997, MINERVA Shobo, 13th Japan Electro-Communications & Social Sciences Award).

Editor-in-Chief for: *China City Ranking - China Integrated City Index 2017* (2018, NTT Publishing Co., Ltd, co-edited by Chen Yajun, Xu Lin), *China City Ranking - China Integrated City Index 2016* (2018, NTT Publishing Co., Ltd, co-edited by Xu Lin), *China Integrated City Index 2017* (2017, People's Publishing House, co-edited by Chen Yajun, Xu Lin), *China Integrated City Index 2016* (2016, People's Publishing House, co-edited by Xu Lin), *China 30 Years from Now* (2011, Joint Publishing HK, co-edited by Yang Weimin), *The Third Thirty Years: A New Direction for China* (2010, People's Publishing House, co-edited by Yang Weimin), *The Transformation of Economic Development Model in China* (2005, World Affairs Press), *Urbanization: Theme of China's Modernization* (2001, Hunan People's Publishing House).

Chen Yajun

Director, Department of Development Planning, NDRC, Ph.D. in Management

Born in 1965, Mr. Chen has long been engaged in the development of national industrial poli-cies and medium-to-long-term plans. He participated in the formulation of the "9th Five-year Plan" for China, and was a major member of the drafting panel for the "10th Five-year Plan", "11th Five-year Plan" and the "12th Five-year Plan", as well as the principal drafter of mega-lopolis development plans such as the *Chengdu-Chongqing Urban Agglomeration Plan*.

Editor-in-Chief for: the *China City Ranking - China Integrated City Index 2017* (2018, NTT Publishing Co., Ltd, co-edited by Zhou Muzhi, Xu Lin), *China Integrated City Index 2017* (2017, People's Publishing House, co-edited by Zhou Muzhi, Xu Lin)

Xu Lin

Director, China Center for Urban Development, M.S. in Economics, M.S. in Public Administration

Born in 1962, Mr. Xu was sent to work in the countryside in 1977 after graduation from high school,and joined the Department of Long-Term Planning of the State Planning Commission following his graduation from Nankai University in 1989 with a Master's degree. He was awarded the Humphrey Fellowship by the U.S. Government to study at the American University. He was awarded the Lee Kuan Yew Scholarship by the Singapore Government to study at the Lee Kuan Yew School of Public Policy under the National University of Singapore. He also obtained a Master's degree in Public Administration after his study at the Harvard Kennedy School. He has served as the Director of both the Department of Fiscal and Financial Affairs and the Department of Development Planning, NDRC. He took up his current post in 2017.

Mr. Xu has participated in the preparation of a number of five-year plans for the economic and social development of China, the regional development planning and national new urbanization planning of China, and the formulation of national industrial policies; and took part in the formulation of major reform schemes for the fiscal and financial areas, and in the development of and supervision over capital markets, especially the bond market and private equity investment, having served three terms on the SIEVC of the CSRC as a member. Mr. Xu was also involved in China's negotiations to join the World Trade Organization, especially responsible for the negotiations of industrial policies and industrial subsidies.

Editor-in-Chief for: the *China City Ranking - China Integrated City Index 2017* (2018, NTT Publishing Co., Ltd, co-edited by Zhou Muzhi, Chen Yajun), *China City Ranking - China Integrated City Index 2016* (2018, NTT Publishing Co., Ltd, co-edited by Zhou Muzhi), *China Integrated City Index 2017* (2017, People's Publishing House, co-edited by Zhou Muzhi, Chen Yajun), *China Integrated City Index 2016* (2016, People's Publishing House, co-edited by Zhou Muzhi)